To J. N.

IRELAND IN THE AGE OF IMPERIALISM AND REVOLUTION 1760-1801

BY

R. B. McDOWELL

CLARENDON PRESS · OXFORD
1979

Oxford University Press, Walton Street, Oxford OX2 6DP

OXFORD LONDON GLASGOW
NEW YORK TORONTO MELBOURNE WELLINGTON
KUALA LUMPUR SINGAPORE JAKARTA HONG KONG TOKYO
DELHI BOMBAY CALCUTTA MADRAS KARACHI
NAIROBI DAR ES SALLAAM CAPE TOWN

Published in the United States by Oxford University Press, New York

© R. B. McDowell 1979

British Library Cataloguing in Publication Data

McDowell, Robert Brendan
    Ireland in the age of imperialism and revolution,
1760–1801.
    1. Ireland – History – 1760–1820
    I. Title
941.507   DA947   79–40413

ISBN 0–19–822480–X

Printed in Great Britain by
Western Printing Services Ltd, Bristol

Contents

List of Abbreviations

Acknowledgements

Transcripts of crown copyright records in the Public Record Office appear by permission of the Controller of Her Majesty's Stationery Office. I am grateful for permission to use material under their control to the Most Revd Dr Dermot Ryan, archbishop of Dublin, the duke of Abercorn, the trustees of the duke of Portland, the marquess of Camden, the marquess of Downshire, the Earl Fitzwilliam and the trustees of the Fitzwilliam settled estates, the trustees of the National Library of Scotland, the Kent county council, the Misses Duffin, Mr D. H. W. Neilson and Mrs J. G. C. Spencer Bernard.

I am very much indebted to Dr T. W. Moody and to Dr D. E. W. Wormell for advice and to Dr C. J. Woods for many helpful criticisms and suggestions. I have greatly appreciated the assistance of the staff of the Oxford University Press and am grateful to the staff of the libraries and record repositories in which I have worked, for their assiduous and kindly help, and my thanks are due to Miss K. O'Sullivan for secretarial assistance.

I

THE BACKGROUND

I

The Economic and Social Structure

The eighteenth century, so far as western Europe was concerned, possessed a distinctive flavour, preserved for posterity in its architecture and in its prose. It was a self-assured era, balanced, energetic and elegant, precise and restrained, confident that its standards of reference were soundly selected and consciously civilized. These qualities strike an observer with such force and clarity that for a moment other aspects of the age may be obscured. Outward assurance could mask uncertainties and doubts; and beneath the polished surface of a well-mannered and ordered life there was discontent and ugly violence. An Irish magazine could in the same issue print neatly turned verses about nymphs and swains and grim reports of assaults and affrays. During the last decade of the century revolution starkly revealed many of the tensions in European society and brought home to the established world how frail were the foundations on which its civilization rested.

In Ireland a contrast of attitudes was strongly marked. Satisfaction with the existing order and optimism were often tempered by the belief that in some respects it was faulty and inequitable. Irish institutions were often found to be defective in detail when tested by the new popular concept, efficiency. Non-conformists, catholics and protestants, even when they accepted the social and political standards of the established world, bitterly resented the disabilities imposed on the dissenter. Irishmen were proud of their constitution, a replica of the British, but their complacency was disturbed by an awareness that until 1782 at least, the Irish constitution lacked many of the distinctive features of its revered prototype. Moreover, many Irishmen, though they respected property and regarded land as the most respectable form of property, nevertheless were determined to end the landed interest's near monopoly of parliamentary power.

There was another sphere in which criticism was rife.

Though the social framework and the economic order were taken for granted it was widely felt that there was in Ireland too much poverty and too little prosperity. A continuous theme of public discussion was that something must be done to develop Ireland's considerable economic potentialities. One great cause of Ireland's backwardness was easily grasped by the plain man—the restraints on Irish industry and trade imposed by Great Britain during the first three-quarters of the century. Irishmen were always acutely conscious of British predominance and of the proximity of the larger island (an awareness which contrasts with the intermittent British interest in Ireland). At a time when Great Britain was distinguished for intellectual vigour, economic advance and imperial expansion, Irishmen were proud to be able to participate in the British heritage. At the same time however they were eager to assert Ireland's distinctive character. It was a painful if stimulating task to reconcile these two tendencies and if some Irishmen readily accepted British supremacy others, irked by the restraints which partnership imposed, demanded separation. But it would be a mistake to dwell emphatically on dissatis-faction, implying that it was the prevalent note in Irish life. Public-spirited, articulate men were convinced that they were living in a developing country with excellent prospects. Past conflicts and ill-conceived imperial economic planning had retarded Ireland's advance, but from the middle of the century population and productivity were both rapidly increasing. At the close of the century it was authoritatively estimated that Ireland had a growing population of over 4,000,000—in fact it may have been 5,000,000—about one-third of the total population of the British Isles. The propensity of the Irish population to increase at this time is a phenomenon not easily explained. A long period of peace had certainly eliminated one check on growth, and better communications had lessened the impact of local scarcity. Two of the essentials of life, food and fuel, were readily available in the form of the nutritious, easily cultivatable potato and turf. A third, shelter, was scarcely a problem when a cabin could be so quickly erected. Opportuni-ties for employment were, it seems, increasing with the spread of arable, subdivision, developing industry and emigration, seasonable or permanent; and with a strong sense of expansion and future well-being diffusing itself through Irish society, the prudential checks on population growth, which may not in fact have been very influential, were bound to be weakened.[1]

Passing from population to productivity, Ireland in the eighteenth century was renowned as an important source of primary products. About the middle of the eighteenth century the great *Encyclopédie*, in the entry relating to Ireland, informed its readers that there 'Le sol y est très fertile & abondant en excellens pâturages'. At the close of the century a Dublin edition of the *Encyclopaedia Britannica* ('printed in a superb style, suitable to the spirit and taste of the Irish nation'),[2] also referred to Ireland's fertility, emphatically declaring that once Ireland 'felt the happy effects of an unshackled commerce and a general emancipation this country will not be inferior to any on the the globe under the same parallel'. The Irish revenue authorities indicated the nature and range of Ireland's economic activities when they grouped Irish exports under headings. The first five of these were the products of corn, fish, flax-seed, sheep (including woollen goods) and cattle (including tallow, tongues, hams, hogs and bacon), and these five headings covered 99 per cent of the exports—the remainder being classified under miscellaneous.[3] Irish industry was to an overwhelming extent dependent on agriculture. The linen and woollen industries, distilling, brewing, tanning, the manufacture of candles and glue-making, were all based on agricultural products. Geographically too, industrial and agricultural activities were closely interwined. The textile industries, great employers of man and woman power, were still largely domestic and rural industries. The farmer in the north was often a weaver (even sometimes employing journeymen) and the women of a farming household were frequently engaged in spinning. Agricultural improvers might deplore this disregard for specialization—one traveller who noted that Ulster farmers who were weavers, remarked that 'their hands were hurt for the loom by handling implements of husbandry'.[4] But the loss, if

---

[1] For the population of Ireland see K. H. Connell, *The population of Ireland 1750–1845* (1950).
[2] See prospectus for the 1791 Dublin edition bound in vol. 1 in T.C.D. library.
[3] CUST 1/15.
[4] C. Abbot, Journal of a tour in Ireland, 1792 (P.R.O./30/9/23).

any, in efficiency may have been balanced by the cheerful confidence bred by having two sources of income. Corn mills, bolt mills, and the new cotton mills were often situated in rural surroundings where water power was available and where, it was hoped, the hands would be removed from the temptations of urban life, including incipient trade unionism.[5]

With agriculture looming so large in the economy, its standards and development were bound to be subjects of intense national concern. This was especially so in the later eighteenth century when agricultural improvement was regarded as fashionable, patriotic and profitable. It combined the enjoyment of rural pursuits with the contemporary enthusiasm for applied science and technology. 'The gentleman and the farmer', a public-spirited landlord wrote about 1800, 'are no longer incongruous terms; the necessary appendages of agriculture, botany, chemistry and mineralogy, are become fashionable studies and have superseded the unprofitable levity which too often bore sway in our moments of pleasure, so derogatory to the wisdom and dignity of an enlightened nation.' Those who thought agriculture beneath them, were reminded by a clergyman that it was 'the theme of Cicero's praise and afforded to Virgil subjects for the most polished and finished poems of antiquity'.[6]

Enthusiastic agricultural improvers applied severe standards. Arthur Young, always crusading against agricultural inertia, after his Irish tour pronounced that Ireland was five centuries behind England in the management of arable ground and a century behind in the use of turnips and clover. However, he admitted that in breeding sheep and cattle Ireland was only a few degrees behind, and when it came to lime manuring, Irish gentlemen understood it 'very well and practiced it with uncommon spirit'.[7] Mr Justice Willes, a shrewd, well-informed contemporary of Young, writing about 1760, thought that Ireland was fifty years behind England 'in the cultivation and improvement of the land', but added, that 'a man has a figure

---

[5] The employees of a cotton works in Queen's Country made an unsuccessful attempt to form a union (C. Coote, *Statistical survey of the Queen's County* (1801), p. 105).

[6] C. Coote, *Statistical survey of the King's County* (1801), p. viii; H. Townsend, *A general and statistical survey of the County of Cork* (1810), i, p. 189.

[7] A. Young, *Tour of Ireland* (1892), pp. 22, 93, 104.

in his county in proportion to the improvements he makes'.[8] It should also be remembered that when Young visited areas in England and Wales at a distance from the great zone of advanced agriculture in the south-east, he found them backward and was constrained occasionally to make 'a retrograde digression'. Shortly before Young toured Ireland, Sir John Parnell, an Irish country gentleman who was a keen improver, visiting England, was struck by the conservatism he encountered. Near Hertford when he inquired about Young he was told 'he writes very well but . . . he does not manage himself as well as he would have others.' Parnell concluded that 'prejudice against anything whatever out of the old road is equally strong all the world over'. He also felt after travelling through the Midlands that 'the English gentry should improve their own desert heaths . . . before they abuse the Irish too freely about their want of spirit in improving.' Englishmen, Parnell complained, 'if conversation turned on improvement . . . pretty soon express their amazement at the stupidity and laziness of the Irish in not improving more than they do—but as I was pretty well master of what tracts of country capable of improvement lay untouched in their own neighbourhood, I never failed to repay them in their own coin.'[9]

Parnell himself, when travelling in England, paid particular attention to fencing, gates and 'instruments of husbandry', making careful drawings of those which impressed him favourably. His friend Bellingham Boyle, of Glenfield, County Dublin, an M.P., was one of the 'great masters of farming in Ireland'. Two of Boyle's apophthegms which impressed Parnell were—that 'to a gentleman attached to farming as he ought to be the vicinity of the farm buildings to his home was a pleasure' and that a landlord should have some of his ground in tillage, because 'though a gentleman may make a little by corn, the satisfaction of growing according to one's own whim, making little experiments etc. is so pleasing'. Arthur Young, when he toured Ireland in 1776, met a number of spirited improvers who were eager to discuss their methods of farming or estate management. Down in County Cork he visited Lord Shannon (the second earl, a calculating politician), 'a

---

[8] E. Willes, Copies of letters describing the country of Ireland (Add. MS 25252).
[9] J. Parnell, Journal (L.S.E. library).

distinguished improver'. Shannon paid 'extreme attention to composts', gave bounties to labourers, 'but only such as speak English and do something more than fill a cart' and presented one of his large turnips to the Dublin society—'but I am afraid', Young wrote, 'it did not animate as many as it ought'. Up in the north in County Antrim, Young met James Leslie of Leslie Hall, 'a warm admirer of husbandry practising on a scale not often to be met with'. Leslie had a wheat crop equal to any in England, and secured a bull of 'Mr Blackwell's breed'. A few years earlier Edmund Burke arranged that 'one of the finest bull calves . . . of the short-horned Holderness breed', should be sent over to his cousin's farm in County Cork[10] and towards the end of the century several landlords, including Lord Donegall, Lord Bective and Maxwell, bishop of Meath, introduced English breeds of cattle.[11] Maher of Queen's County paid four hundred guineas for the services of a Leicester ram, and the Revd Thomas Percy (nephew of the bishop of Dromore) 'bought the true Berkshire breed' of swine to County Antrim.[12] Irrigation and drainage were skilfully planned by landlords such as C. B. Ponsonby in County Kilkenny, Thomas Poole in County Cork, Keon, who reclaimed 'pouchy and wet' fields in Leitrim, and William Curtis of Annamore, Kings' County, who by 'draining, gravelling and planting changed the face of his county'.[13] Planting was very popular for both utilitarian as well as aesthetic reasons—a plantation, it was pointed out, might 'make provision for a very numerous family besides the advantages of ornamenting and sheltering'.[14] A number of landowners were keenly interested in new and improved agricultural implements. A Mr Christie, in County Down, claimed to have erected the first threshing machine in Ireland in 1796; David La Touche, in County Dublin, constructed a large boiler which could steam seven hundredweight

[10] *Correspondence of Edmund Burke*, ed. T. Copeland, i, p. 329.

[11] R. Thompson, *Statistical survey of the County of Meath* (1802), p. 298; J. Dubourdieu, *Statistical survey of the County of Antrim* (1812), p. 325.

[12] C. Coote, *Statistical survey of the Queen's County* (1801), p. 99; J. Dubourdieu, *Statistical survey of the County of Antrim*, p. 13.

[13] W. Tighe, *Statistical observations relative to the County of Kilkenny* (1802), pp. 368–369; H. Townsend, *A general and statistical survey of the County of Cork*, i, pp. 357–8; J. McParlan, *Statistical survey of the County of Leitrim* (1802), pp. 52–3; C. Coote, *Statistical survey of the King's County* (1801), p. 85.

[14] T. J. Rawson, *Statistical survey of the County of Kildare* (1807), p. 70.

of mash; John Rawson in Kildare devised a hay-lifting machine of timber and rope which cost only £10. Wynne of Hazelbrook, who 'as a farmer stands unrivalled', invented a plough. Amongst those who introduced the Scotch plough into Ireland was John Foster, the speaker, a great practical agriculturalist, who on his lands round Collon used a Midlothian plough. His neighbour, the Revd Daniel Beaufort, the antiquarian, introduced a patent drill on his land and another country clergyman, William Richardson, a sometime fellow of Trinity, a vigorous exponent of the value of applied science, wrote and experimented on the growth of grasses.[15]

At the close of the century the cause of agricultural improvement was being advanced by two societies, the Dublin society, founded in 1731 and chartered in 1750 for 'the promoting of husbandry and other useful arts' and the Farming society of Ireland, founded under the patronage of the Dublin society in 1800. The Dublin society awarded premiums to successful agriculturalists and manufacturers, subsidized for a time an experimental farm, provided scientific lectures and in the last decade of the century promoted the study of mineralogy and laid out a garden on the outskirts of Dublin. The Farming society, which had by 1803 seven hundred life members, aimed at raising standards of breeding and cultivation by educating and encouraging the working farmer. It organized agricultural shows with prizes, and its secretary attended at the society's rooms in Sackville Street 'to give information to even the most ignorant farmer'. These societies brought together enthusiasts for improvement and evinced a determination to raise agricultural standards in Ireland. For success the Farming society required the backing of local societies, and shortly after it was founded at least four county societies were formed—the Midland farming society (for Queen's County, Tipperary and Kilkenny) and the Cork, Down and Wexford societies (in Wexford, recovering from insurrection, the gentry were very anxious 'to turn the attention of the country to improvement').

[15] J. Dubourdieu, *Statistical survey of the County of Down* (1802), p. 52; H. Dutton, *Observations on Mr Archer's statistical survey of the County of Dublin* (1802), pp. 37–40. R. Thompson, *Statistical survey of the County of Meath*, pp. 111–15; J. McEvoy, *Statistical survey of the County of Tyrone* (1802), p. 13; T. J. Rawson, *Statistical survey of the County of Kildare*, pp. 197–9; H. F. Berry, *History of the Royal Dublin Society* (1915), pp. 146, 149–51, 223–4.

But the Cork society was very badly supported and a number of counties, including those in the west where it was acknowledged that there was plenty of scope for improvement, failed to form an agricultural society. Even Kildare, subject one would have expected to metropolitan influences, lacked a farming society in the early years of the nineteenth century. In the late eighteenth century an agricultural society had been started in Athy under the patronage of the duke of Leinster. It raised some money, encouraged the use of clover and its future seemed promising, until there was a discussion on tithe which led to a breach between the clergy and laity and the collapse of the society. It was also ominous that towards the close of the eighteenth century the Dublin society was very seriously concerned about the number of subscriptions in arrears, and efforts to reduce the arrears led to a decline in membership.[16]

Those who were endeavouring to raise the standards of Irish agriculture had a number of obstacles to overcome—the prevalence of small farms on which it might be difficult to apply up-to-date technology and whose owners certainly lacked the requisite capital; the custom of leasing large tracts of land to middlemen who sublet and lacked a long-term interest in the soil; the practice of remunerating labourers by grants of land; the existence of farms in partnership (with consequent disputes) and the conservatism of the Irish farmers, 'averse to everything out of the track of their grandfathers'.[17] Finally, and not least powerful, was the fact that many of those on the higher levels of the agrarian system, landlords, graziers, large- and middle-sized farmers were, towards the close of the century, enjoying incomes which afforded them a margin—in some instances a substantial one—after meeting essential expenses. In addition to making their living they had plenty of other outlets for their energies—social, political and sporting, interests which could easily become all-absorbing. As economic men, Irish landlords and farmers realized that they had a large and expanding market in Great Britain and an ample supply

[16] W. Tighe, *Statistical observations relative to the County of Kilkenny*, pp. 591–7; H. Townsend, *General and statistical survey of the County of Cork*, ii, p. 175; R. Fraser, *Statistical survey of the County of Wexford* (1807), p. 83; J. Dubourdieu, *Statistical survey of the County of Down*, p. 249; T. J. Rawson, *Statistical survey of the County of Kildare*, pp. 58–9.
[17] T. J. Rawson, *Statistical survey of the County of Kildare*, p. 4.

of cheap labour in Ireland. Therefore they could consciously or unconsciously decide not to sacrifice immediate pleasure to maximizing future profits by strenuous self-denial economy and planning. For many landowners estate management consisted simply of 'letting the different farms, receiving the rents and regulating the turf-bogs'.[18]

Understandably then there were in Ireland at the close of the eighteenth century large areas in which agriculture was, by good contemporary standards, backward. In these areas the countryside was studded with badly built farmhouses, the hedges badly kept, methods of cultivation were archaic and slovenly and the implements employed clumsy and old-fashioned. There were of course considerable regional variations. The north-east counties and the country round Dublin were, generally speaking, in advance of the west and south, and in a single county there could be strikingly different zones and a single estate could be outstanding amongst its neighbours. During the century Irish agriculture had managed to reduce greatly the possibility of famine, the spread of the potato ensuring for the bulk of the population a staple food. Again, from the middle of the century the amount of land devoted to tillage had been greatly increased. Tillage, encouraged by bounties and stimulated by the demands of a growing home population and the British market, had been extended not only by breaking up pasture to a limited extent but also by bringing waste land into cultivation. Even the severest critics of Irish agriculture at the turn of the century would have to admit that it was maintaining a growing population, both feeding the inhabitants of Ireland and providing the exports which paid for the imports they required or enjoyed.

Irish industry, largely based on Irish agriculture, was completely overshadowed by it but was a source of great expectations. Taking into account, as contemporaries did, the importance of easily accessible raw materials, well placed harbours, cheap labour and abundant water power, Ireland seemed to have great industrial potential. Two great industries, brewing and distilling, were directly based on Irish agriculture, their raw material being barley, a widely grown crop. There were at the close of the eighteenth century in Ireland 1,700 maltsters,

[18] J. Dubourdieu, *Statistical survey of the County of Down*, p. 29.

800 breweries (261 'strong' brewers, 58 'small' brewers and 484 'retailing' brewers), and over 100 distilleries.[19] Owing to changes in taxation and the revenue laws made in the early eighties, which favoured the larger distilleries, there was a trend towards concentration in the production of whiskey, the number of distilleries falling rapidly while the output of spirits was rising. Both industries, distilling and brewing, had a large home market, but both were subject to severe competition, brewers from imported English beer (which in the seventies they implicitly admitted was better than Irish) and of course from spirits; licensed distillers from illegal distillation. Illegal distillation was so widespread that at the beginning of the nineteenth century it was estimated that one-third of the very large quantity of spirits consumed in Ireland had not paid duty, being produced by what were termed 'private' distillers— sometimes tinkers, who had the technical skill required for making stills out of copper, and sometimes even a 'respectable' farmer, who might employ a 'wretched creature' as his 'working man'.[20]

A well-known journalist probably caught the feelings of many Irishmen when in his poem 'A glass of whiskey' he wrote,

> When cold in the winter it warms you so heartily,
> When hot in the summer it cools you like ice.
> In trouble—false friends without grief I can part you,
> Good whiskey's my friend and I take its advice.

To social reformers spirit drinking was one of the great evils of Irish life. Whiskey, 'more destructive than crocodile of the Nile or the tigers of Africa', was largely responsible for the miseries and vices of the poor.

> The drunkard's tax is self imposed,
> And harder to endure,
> Not all the taxes help so much
> Oppress the labouring poor.[21]

---

[19] *Commons' Jn. Ire.*, xvi, pp. ccccxliii, dxvii; xv, pp. cxci–ii; *Commons' Jn.*, lvii, pp. 1138–9.

[20] *Fifth report of the commission appointed to inquire into fees*, pp. 167, 223–47, H.C. (124) 1806–7; *Report of the committee on the distilleries in Ireland*, p. 11, H.C. (269), 1812–13, vi.

[21] W. P. Carey, in *Masonic magazine*, Dec. 1793; *D.E.P.*, 28 Sept. 1797; *Agricola's letters denouncing the pernicious effects of the cheapness of spirituous liquors* (1791), and sheet

From the seventies the brewers were asking for legislative encouragement—protective tariffs and a change in the incidence of taxation. They made great play with the argument that an increase in beer drinking would lead to a decline in the consumption of spirits and was 'the only means of abridging the numerous vices of the lower orders of the people, and producing industry and due subordination amongst them'. Grattan, a strong advocate of the brewers' cause, was concerned at seeing an increase in the consumption of spirits accompanied by a fall in that of beer, 'this growth of poison and this decline in nutriment'; he urged that heavy duties should be imposed on whiskey, 'to prohibit the lower order of the people from the consumption of spirits', and also suggested that J.P.s should be given 'new and summary powers' to deal with persons selling unlicensed spirits.[22]

Much of the violence of Irish life in the century could probably be traced to spirit drinking. But already a shift in liquor consumption, which was to have an immense influence on Irish life, was under way. During the second half of the century imports of tea increased about fifteenfold; but as it cost four shillings a pound, it seemed to social reformers at the close of the century that the only conceivable substitute for spirits was beer.

In 1791 the house of commons decided that 'it would tend to diminish the consumption of spirits if considerable encouragement were given to the brewery' and in 1795 the beer tax was abolished and the malt tax raised without an abatement for the distiller. During the brewers' campaign the County Clare distillers petitioned against further restrictions on their industry, emphasizing that 'the cause of inebriety of the peasantry proceeds from the great number of whiskey houses which are supplied with a deleterious stuff from the private stills'.[23] The Irish distilling industry as a whole was remarkably silent, perhaps because it realized it was too firmly established in Irish life to be seriously weakened by legislative activity, and

in Haliday collection 588. The vices were said to include forming trade combinations with the object of obtaining higher wages.

[22] *Commons' Jn. Ire.*, vi, p. 204; xiv, p. 69; ix, p. clv; xvi, p. 36; *Parl. Reg. Ire.*, xi, pp. 68–9.

[23] *Commons' Jn. Ire.*, xiv, p. 191.

in fact the consumption of whiskey tended to rise in spite of increased taxation.

The two principal Irish textile industries, linen and wool, were also of course based on agriculture. Linen was undoubtedly Ireland's most successful industry—from 1737 Patrick Ewing (apparently based on Chapelizod) was supplying the royal household with table linen.[24] Throughout the century linen was manufactured not only extensively in Ulster but at many points scattered throughout the south and west, improving landlords sometimes going to considerable trouble to promote the industry in their locality so as to provide employment for their tenantry. Towards the close of the century optimists expected the linen industry would grow in importance in the south and west and in 1798 the Linen board's inspector for Connaught reported that in that province it was 'materially improving', helped by an immigration of weavers driven from County Armagh by sectarian rioting.[25] But the signs of growth were in fact few and far between—even an economic optimist about 1795 felt that the linen manufacture was not 'well fitted to the genius of the people' in the south,[26] and the small isolated linen-manufacturing communities in the southern provinces were bound to be seriously discouraged by the downward fluctuations, inevitable in an industry dependent on an international market. Already the linen industry was strongly concentrated in Ulster, a prospering, protestant province. In the north there were enterprising enterpreneurs directing the industry, there were many yarn and cloth markets, Belfast and Newry having linen halls, and, with spinning and weaving forming a subsidiary employment for many households, there was a very large reserve of skilled, industrious and sometimes ambitious labour. A mid-eighteenth-century traveller noted that from Monaghan to Carrickfergus, with ribbon development along the road, the country seemed to be one great village, with bleach fields resembling patches of unmelted snow.[27] The linen industry made an immense contribution to Ulster's prosperity, and with its British, European and trans-atlantic

[24] *Commons' Jn. Ire.*, vii, p. 25.
[25] *Linen board report* (1798), p. 13.
[26] T. Wallace, *An essay* (1798), p. 114.
[27] E. Willes, Copies of letters. (Add. MS 25252).

markets, kept Ulstermen closely in touch with the outlook of an era marked by economic expansion and technological advance.

The Irish woollen industry may have been somewhat under-rated. It after all clothed most Irishmen. It was a well-worn theme that it had been ruined or seriously damaged by English and English inspired legislation, and it had certainly been a victim of mercantilism. At the close of the seventeenth century an Irish act had imposed heavy export duties on woollen manufactures and in 1699 an English act forbade the export of Irish woollen manufactures, except to England, where they were subject to heavy import duties. This legislation was discouraging and may well have been unnecessary. The English woollen industry, with its immense resources of skill and capital, could have ignored the risk of Irish competition in its own markets and would almost certainly, even in the face of protective duties, have obtained a strong footing in the Irish market by relying on the quality of English cloth and fashion-consciousness. As for the bulk of the Irish population, the farmers and labours, they wore Irish cloth, frieze, often locally manufactured. Only in County Antrim were imported clothes worn by the labourers, 'a great quantity of secondhand clothes, many of them very good' being imported from Scotland and sold in the markets.[28] After the repeal of the restrictions a small quantity of serges from Ireland was exported from Ireland to the colonies and Europe. But in the nineties the growth of this trade ceased, owing, it was asserted, to a temporary cause, the war.[29]

Compared to linen and wool, silk was a weak industry. Established at the close of the seventeenth century, apparently by Huguenot refugees, it was confined to Dublin, dependent on a fashion-conscious market and exposed to severe competition, especially in the second half of the century, from East Indian muslins, which, a silk merchant complained, in 1773, were being 'worn even by the lower ranks of the people'. The fortunes of the industry fluctuated. About 1730 there were said to be 700 silk looms in Dublin. Thirty years later the number had fallen to 53, but in 1785 it was said that there were sometimes 3,000 looms at work. However, in spite of the high reputation of some

[28] J. Dubourdieu, *Statistical survey of the County of Antrim*, pp. 498–9.
[29] T. Wallace, *An essay*, p. 159. W. Tighe, *Statistical observations relative to the County of Kilkenny*, p. 545.

Irish poplins and tabinets, in 1793 the industry was again badly depressed, 'many industrious working hands suffering all the horrors of pinching penury', and this depression seems to have marked the beginning of a long decline.[30]

The fourth Irish textile industry, cotton, had all the signs of a great growth industry, and Irishmen were confident they could share in its success. In 1777 two enterprising Belfast men managed to combine charity with business by suggesting that the children in the poor-house be employed in cotton spinning and later, forming a company, they filled some vacant rooms in the house with their machinery. So, as a Belfast writer later declared, 'a poor house was the cradle of the cotton trade of Ireland .[31] It should be added however that Charles Chadwick claimed in 1780 that he was 'the first person who ever formed a practicable plan for introducing the cotton manufacture to Ireland', by bringing modern machines and 'a number of the best working hands in England' to Newmarket in County Clare.[32] English workmen who emigrated to Ireland, were, it was said, 'in general not of the most sober and steady kind' (though useful enough as instructors),[33] so it is not suprising that many of Chadwick's hands subsequently went off to County Kildare to work for Robert Brooke. Brooke, who had served with distinction in the Bengal army, was eager to establish in Ireland 'a new and great manufacture', cotton. He encouraged a Dublin cabinet-maker to construct new types of machinery and he built on 'a reclaimed bog' in County Kildare, a village with a mill and artisans' dwellings, which he prophetically named Prosperous. Here Brooke took steps 'for the establishment of order and sobriety, and for conquering the indolence into which the lower orders of the people of Ireland have fallen', and he gave employment to weavers throughout the surrounding countryside, affording bread to 6,000 men, women and children, the women and children being as 'busily employed as the men'. Brooke invested £30,000 in his enterprise and secured about the same amount in government grants. But, as a candid friend remarked, Brooke 'suffered great impositions from his

[30] *Commons' Jn. Ire.*, ix, p. ccli; xi, p. 394; xv, p. 209.
[31] *B.N.L.*, 7 May 1805.
[32] *Commons' Jn. Ire.*, xi, p. 59.
[33] Lord Sheffield, *Observations on the manufactures, trade and present state of Ireland* (1785), p. 194.

being ignorant of the business'. He over-invested in buildings, bought defective machines and had trouble in securing adequate supplies of fuel and water. In the end he failed and left Ireland. Trustees, appointed by parliament, tried to salvage his enterprise but in the end it was wound up.[34] Other Irish cotton concerns fared better. For instance Joseph Smith of Lancaster came over about 1780 and erected at Balbriggan 'a complete set of the machinery now in use in Great Britain for spinning by water' cotton twist, his mill five stories high, containing 2,500 spindles.[35] By the end of the century cotton was being manufactured at Cork, Blarney, Limerick, Drogheda, Londonderry and Belfast, which last indeed seemed destined to be a cotton town. As early as 1784 a water-powered spinning mill had been erected in Belfast and by the early nineties a steam engine had been installed in a Belfast cotton-spinning factory. At the time of the union there were at least twelve cotton firms in the town and it was said that the industry gave direct employment to 13,500 workers.[36]

A knowledgeable observer, discussing Ireland's economic prospects at the close of the seventies, pointed out that Ireland had 'little coal, is ill provided with wood and is also without inland navigation'.[37] But, as has been seen, improving landlords were busy making plantations, and the exploitation of Ireland's mineral resources and the construction of inland waterways were arousing considerable interest. Though there was not in Ireland a zone which 'smoaks' like the country round Birmingham,[38] there were coal mines in Ballycastle in County Antrim, in County Tyrone, in Kilkenny and near Lough Allen. The Ballycastle mine, which employed about 200 colliers, was reported in 1790 to be sending 12,000 of coal a year to Dublin (the inhabitants of nearby Londonderry preferred, it was said, to burn English coal).[39] Ballycastle itself had become a small manufacturing town, with a brewery, a glasshouse,

---

[34] A letter from Mr. Brooke (1786); Commons' Jn. Ire., x, p. 229; xi, p. 57; xii, pp. ccxiv, cclvii; 32 Geo. III, c. 41.
[35] Commons' Jn. Ire., xi, pp. 51–2.
[36] B.N.L., 4 Feb. 1800, 7 May. 1805; N.S., 13 Mar. 1794.
[37] W. Eden, Letters to the earl of Carlisle, 3rd ed. (1780), p. 166.
[38] A. Young, Tours in England and Wales (reprinted 1932), p. 142.
[39] G. L. Davies, 'The town and coalfield of Ballycastle', in Irish Geography, iii, pp. 206–15. C. Abbot, A tour.

salt works, a tannery and a nail manufactory. The Tyrone coalfields managed in 1783 to obtain a parliamentary grant for a 'steam engine' for pumping water out of the workings, but at the close of the century only a few pits were being worked at Dungannon and Coalisland, the flooding being 'annoying' and the short canal connecting the coalfields with Lough Neagh 'almost choked up with weeds'.[40] A more successful, if small, coalfield was to be found near Kilkenny at Ferod and Castlecomer, where there were pits with two steam engines.[41] The most promising field was at Arigna, near Lough Allen, where, it was authoritatively stated, there were extensive coal and iron deposits. In the middle eighties Mary Reilly and her sons took over the mines and erected expensive machinery for mining and iron smelting. But royalties were high and transport costs prohibitive, so in 1789 the Reillys applied for parliamentary assistance. A number of witnesses—including Kirwan, the distinguished chemist, and two successful businessmen, later conspicuous in radical politics, Henry Jackson and Thomas Braughall—supported the petition before a house of commons committee, which pronounced in favour of a grant. But the chancellor of the exchequer quashed the proposal when it came before the house. In 1793 the Reillys went bankrupt and their enterprise was taken over by Peter La Touche, the banker, who, before relinquishing the project, lost a considerable sum of money. Years later, pointing to a gate of Arigna iron on his Bellevue estate, he declared it had cost him £80,000.[42]

One of the causes of the Arigna collapse was inadequate transportation. Irishmen during the eighteenth century shared the general conviction that 'one of the chief sources of vigour and wealth to a nation is easy and cheap communication',[43] and a parliamentary committee was impressed 'by the avidity' with which public grants for canal building were sought after. Nevertheless, compared to the contemporary British achievement only a very moderate amount was accomplished. At the

[40] *Commons' Jn. Ire.*, xi, p. 69.

[41] W. Tighe, *Statistical observations relative to the County of Kilkenny*, pp. 43–86.

[42] *Commons' Jn. Ire.*, xi, pp. ccclxii–iii; xiii, pp. 21, ccxvii–viii; *Parl. Reg. Ire.*, xi, pp. 130–1; *Report on the Arigna ironworks* (1801); R. Griffith, *Thoughts and facts relating to inland navigation*, 2nd ed. (1795), p. 21; I. Weld, *Roscommon* (1832), pp. 33–77.

[43] R. Griffith, *Thoughts and facts*, p. 3.

close of the century there were in Ireland seven minor 'navigations'—the Shannon (twelve miles between Banagher and Limerick), the Barrow (thirty-four miles), the Boyne and Strabane canals (attempts to make these rivers navigable), the Tyrone navigation, in a badly neglected state; the Newry canal, which was meeting all its expenses from its own 'rich resources' (toll receipts amounting to £1,200 per annum) and the Lagan canal, connecting Belfast and Lough Neagh, which, on account of the Lagan being 'a mountain river' functioned irregularly.[44] There were also in course of construction two great canals, the Grand and the Royal. Both of these canals, starting at Dublin and running straight across the midlands, were expected to stimulate economic life over very wide areas. By 1800 the Grand canal (begun in 1772) had not quite reached the Shannon, and the Royal (begun in 1789) had only advanced about twenty miles west of Dublin. Its promoters had not allowed for the rapid rise in land values in the Dublin area and there had been miscalculations over water levels. Cautious common sense dictated that the Royal canal should not have been begun until it was clear that the success of the Grand canal justified its construction. In fact at the beginning of the nineteenth century the Grand canal company, though it had received £60,000 from parliament, was in financial difficulties, and the Royal canal company, which had secured £66,000 from parliament, was moving steadily towards bankruptcy.[45]

Spectacular business failure, especially when public money is involved, overshadows humdrum success. But it must be admitted that Prosperous, Arigna and the canals had an ominous significance—suggesting that in Ireland, a country dominated by the landed interest, exuberant economic ambition and optimism could be combined with inexperience and a dangerous lack of business acumen. Moreover, though according to an active member of the Royal Irish Academy, writing in 1789, 'steam is universally allowed to be the greatest moving power we have', by the beginning of the nineteenth century the use of steam engines was spreading only slowly in Ireland.

[44] *Commons' Jn. Ire.*, xix, pp. miv–mxlii; J. McEvoy, *Statistical survey of County Tyrone*, pp. 131–2; J. Dubourdieu, *Statistical survey of the County of Down*, p. 26.
[45] *Report of the committee appointed to inquire into the tolls on the Grand canal of Ireland*, p. 4 H.C. (169), 1805, iv.

However, about the time of the union as the eighteenth century gave place to the nineteenth, intelligent, well-informed economic experts considered that the Irish economy was fundamentally in a healthy condition. The provision trade, broadened to include considerable cereal exports, could count on an expanding market in Great Britain. The prospects for linen and cotton were promising, and there were small industries with growth potential, such as glass and possibly pottery. Ireland at the moment produced little except coarse earthenware, but the presence of abundant supplies of red clay encouraged the belief that Kilkenny might become the Staffordshire of Ireland.[46]

Ireland, largely dependent on agriculture, was, to an overwhelming extent, a rural country. If a concentration of 200 houses is treated as an urban area, then slightly over 10 per cent of the Irish population was urban. But it could be argued that 200 houses constitutes merely a large village, and if a more strict definition of a rural area is taken—1,000 houses or upwards—then only 7 per cent of the population lived in urban surroundings.[47] Another way of expressing the position is to say that, Dublin and Cork excepted, the centre of every Irish town was only about a quarter of an hour's walk from the open country. Nevertheless, the urban areas were of immense importance. As market towns, ports, county and assizes towns, centres of economic, administrative and fashionable activity, they stimulated the whole community. Dublin especially was a great dominating and inspiring national phenomenon. Prominent amongst Irish cities, being about twice the size of Cork and eight times as large as Belfast, Dublin was also undoubtedly the second city in the British Isles, having twice the population of either of its nearest rivals, Edinburgh and Manchester. London was of course much larger, but nevertheless Irishmen were annoyed to hear English visitors to Dublin referring to London as 'town',[48] and an English barrister, to his amusement, was unable to convince 'a professor of Dublin university' that

[46] *Trans. R.I.A.*, iii, p. 113; G. Bowie, 'Waterwheels, windmills, and stationary steam engines in Ireland', in *Irish Economic History*, iii, pp. 80–2; James Watt and Company, Soho: Boulton and Watt catalogue of old engines (Birmingham Reference Library); T. Wallace, *An essay*, p. 245.

[47] *Commons' Jn., Ire.* xix, pp. dccclvii–lxxii.

[48] J. O'Keefe, *Recollections* (1826), i, p. 343.

London was the finer city.[49] In any event in the opinion of an Irish writer, Dublin was 'if not the first . . . the completest city in Europe, if not the world'.[50]

The city had been spreading steadily and by 1800 the built-up area was moving towards the canals and the Circular Road (constructed *c.* 1763–*c.* 1783). To a visitor approaching Dublin by sea, 'the city and the adjacent parts presented a prospect scarcely to be excelled; a wide, expanded semi-circle, ornamented on each side with villages and country houses'. The prospect however was, towards the close of the century, slightly changing, as with land values in the Dublin neighbourhood rising, some suburban landlords, Lords Fitzwilliam of Merrion, Carysfort and Trimleston, were 'parcelling out their parks into small villa estates'.[51] During the eighteenth century two fashionable areas developed, one on each side of the river, both lying to the east. The north-east fashionable quarter, 'which might vie with most in Europe',[52] included Sackville Street and its mall leading northwards to Rutland Square, in which by about 1800 eight peers and two prelates had their residences, and by the close of the century north-eastwards to Mountjoy Square (begun in the early nineties). The southside fashionable zone comprised Saint Stephen's Green, Merrion Square and 'some short streets inhabited by great families'. In 1796 these two fashionable residential areas were at last linked by a new wide street running northwards from College Green and a new bridge (Carlisle bridge), for years the lowest bridge on the river, which had been projected in 1782—the whole scheme having delayed for years by the cost of buying up property near the city centre. To the west of Sackville Street was a business and middle-class residential area with its hub at Smithfield, the great livestock and hay market of Dublin. Between the quays on the south bank and Dame Street lay a district of 'low taverns and bagnios, eating houses and whiskey shops'. The south-west quarter was a 'large manufacturing town', of slaughterhouses, soap manufactories, carrion houses, distilleries, glass houses, lime kilns, dairies', with numerous lanes and courts

[49] G. Cooper, *Letters on the Irish nation* (1800), p. 15.
[50] *Letters addressed to parliament* . . . *on various improvements of the metropolis* (1786), p. 3.
[51] *H.J.*, 11 Sept. 1776; C. Abbot, A tour.
[52] R. Hitchcock, *A historical view of the Irish stage* (1788), i, p. 81.

occupied by 'working manufacturers, the labouring poor and beggars'. All this part of Dublin, a visitor remarked, 'is wretchedness and dirt'.[53] It is scarcely surprising. Sanitary facilities were seriously deficient and, in the absence of a system of poor relief, the large artisan population was bound to be badly hit when trade was depressed.

Dublin was not only by contemporary standards a very large town, but it contained a remarkable range of activities which reacted on one another. It was the seat of the viceregal court, the meeting place of the Irish parliament, and the legal and administrative capital of the country. It was a university city, and the headquarters of the army in Ireland, an important garrison town, with a barracks, built during the war of the Spanish succession, believed to be 'the largest and most complete of any in Europe'.[54] It was also the greatest Irish port and the largest urban industrial centre in Ireland.

Dublin had been founded as a trading place and by the close of the eighteenth century was by far the foremost Irish port. During the century a massive breakwater, the south wall, running about three miles into the sea and sheltering the Poolbeg anchorage, had been built and Dublin had become a terminus of the two great canals, which were destined to traverse the centre of Ireland and link the Shannon to the east coast. Besides being a great shipping and distributing centre, Dublin had also a very wide range of industries—brewing, distilling, sugar-baking, tanning, glue-manufacturing, coach-building, and textiles—silk, wool and cotton. Its place in Ireland's economic life was aptly symbolized by the erection, beside the castle, of the Royal Exchange (opened in 1779), 'perhaps the most elegant structure of its kind in Europe';[55] by the establishment of a stock exchange in 1799 and by the foundation of the bank of Ireland in 1783. Dublin by then had four private banks (increased to five by 1800) and two well-established insurance companies, and all the directors of the new national bank were Dublin bankers or merchants.

Dublin's importance as an economic centre is also illustrated

[53] C. Abbot, A tour; *Letters addressed to parliament*, p. 183; J. Warburton, J. Whitelaw and R. Walsh, *History of the city of Dublin* (1818), i, pp. 443–6.
[54] J. Malton, *A picturesque and descriptive view of the city of Dublin* (1794), p. ii.
[55] R. Pool and J. Cash, *Views of the most remarkable public buildings in the city of Dublin* (1780), p. 43; 39 Geo. III, c. 40.

in another very different way. The concentration of large numbers of artisans in the city led to the formation of combinations and urban labour troubles—unusual phenomena in eighteenth-century Ireland. Early in the reign of George III the *Freeman's Journal*, the organ of Dublin liberalism, was complaining that the Dublin journeymen, 'constantly on the watch to take advantage of their employers', were discouraging capital investment by their 'turnings out'.[56] In the later decades of the century fairly strong combinations seem to have been formed in Dublin amongst the tailors, shoemakers, printers, shipwrights, wool-combers, flax-dressers, broadcloth-weavers, hosiers, rope-makers, lamplighters, masons and carpenters. In the seventies it was said that it was impossible to dismiss one of the Dublin lamplighters 'without discharging the whole'.[57] The masons, Gandon discovered, when supervising the erection of the Custom house, were strongly organized. They insisted that newcomers should 'be subject to the laws of their combination', encouraged the English carpenters and stone-cutters Gandon brought over to insist on higher wages, and, to his great irritation, used the subscriptions they collected not only to form a sickness and funeral fund but to subsidize 'orators' (trade-union leaders). The Dublin carpenters seem to have been particularly aggressive, it being reported in the early nineties that their combination was issuing a membership ticket, inscribed 'Unite or perish', and raising a fund to assist journeymen charged with combining. It was also asserted that by aggressive action over the previous thirty years the carpenters had managed to raise their wages from ten shillings to a guinea a week, and to reduce their hours from thirteen to twelve a day. Some skilled groups tried to limit the number of apprentices taken by their masters, and workers in the textile trades used threats and violence in their efforts to prevent their masters employing or giving out work to country journeymen.[58]

The activities of the organized Dublin journeymen seem to have been largely responsible for the legislation directed against combinations—legislation which had as its avowed

[56] *Free. Jn.*, 3 Dec. 1763.
[57] *Commons' Jn. Ire.*, x, pp. 115, 120; xv, p. 86; *H.J.*, 28 May, 11 July 1792, 2 May 1794; *D.E.P.*, 11 Sept. 1796; *Commons' Jn. Ire.*, ix, p. dclii.
[58] J. Gandon, *Life of James Gandon* (1846), p. 64; *H.J.*, 7 July 1790, 15 June 1792; *D.J.*, 29 Sept. 1792; *D.E.P.*, 11 Sept. 1796.

aims 'to secure to every man the fullest enjoyment of that property he has in his own labour . . . and to extend throughout this kingdom the benefits of free trade'. In 1772 it was enacted that persons in Dublin, who allowed their houses to be used as meeting places for journeymen clubs (bound together by illegal oaths to advance wages), were to be fined. The same measure fixed wages and hours for journeymen tailors, and journeymen shipwrights. Tailors were to be paid 1s. 4d. to 1s. 8d. a day and were to work from 6 a.m. to 8 p.m. (with half an hour for breakfast and an hour for dinner); shipwrights were to be paid 2s. to 2s. 6d. a day and were to work from 6 a.m. to 6 p.m. with similar breaks. The justices at quarter session could vary the wage rates and anyone refusing to work for these wages, or failing to pay them, was to be fined. In 1780 a more comprehensive statute declared all combinations whether of employers or employees to be 'a nuisance', and a long list of activities, which might be regarded as evincing the existence of a combination, were made punishable by fines.[59] More severe penalties were included in a measure which passed the house of commons in 1792. A journeyman changing employers could not take service with a new employer unless he could produce a certificate of good conduct from his former master—with the right of appeal to a justice of the peace if a certificate was refused. An apprentice who left his master could be imprisoned and publicly whipped. When the bill reached the lords, Fitzgibbon, the lord chancellor, with characteristically contemptuous moral vehemence attacked it 'as such a system of oppression and of injustice as should not be countenanced in that house'. It would, he argued, alienate the artisan from society and turn children into criminals. As a result of his intervention the bill was rejected by the lords. But the legislation and proposed legislation against combinations shows that manifestations of working-class power were arousing some apprehension in parliament and in Dublin business circles.[60]

Dublin business life was immensely invigorated by the large political and fashionable world which gathered in the capital.

---

[59] 19 & 20 Geo. III, c. 9. When in 1799 the journeymen tailors asked for an increase of 2s. 6d. a week (on a wage of 3s. a day) the attorney-general, appearing for the employers, advised the journeymen to abandon 'the idle habit of what is vulgarly termed "keeping Saint Monday" ' (H.J., 17 July 1799).

[60] H.J., 23 Mar. 1792.

Its conspicuous expenditure stimulated the luxury trades and the building industry. About 1800, eighty-one secular peers and seventeen prelates and a number of large landowners had town residences in Dublin—in a few instances great urban mansions standing apart with a forecourt, but generally large terraced houses. In addition the Irish administration had to be housed, and during the last quarter of the century about £340,000 was spent in making extensions to the houses of parliament, and in erecting a record office, a new four courts (opened 1796) and a custom house which served both the port of Dublin and was the revenue commissioners' office. The Custom house, one of Gandon's masterpieces, was dismissed by Grattan, thinking in political rather than aesthetic terms, as 'a building which is more a proof of prodigality in the directors than of taste in the architect, a building of the sixth rank in architecture but of first rate in extravagance'. [61]

The citizens of Dublin also urged their own civic requirements on parliament with some success. The Dublin House of industry from 1777 received a large annual grant, the Dublin Paving board and the Dublin Wide street commissioners received financial assistance from parliament and when the Dublin merchants erected an exchange parliament bore a substantial part of the cost.

Dublin law and medicine also benefited substantially from the city being a capital. Land-owning frequently leads to litigation—Sir Murtagh Rackrent had 47 suits, of which 'he never lost one but seventeen; the rest he gained with costs, double costs, treble costs sometimes, but never that did pay'. So it is scarcely surprising that in a city which proved attractive to so many landowners, there were at the close of the century about 1,300 attornies. Dublin medicine was encouraged by plenty of wealthy patients, and the miseries of the sick poor, brought home with vivid force by urban concentration, inspired the benevolent to found and support hospitals and dispensaries—which provided opportunities for clinical study. There were at the end of the century ten hospitals in Dublin and three dispensaries (providing advice and medicine gratis to the poor). Five of the hospitals were general hospitals and five specialist institutions—Saint Patrick's (founded by Jonathan

[61] *Commons' Jn. Ire.*, xiv, p. **ccxxiv**; xv, p. cxciv; *Parl. Reg. Ire.*, x, p. 150.

Swift) for the insane; the hospital for incurables; Simpson's hospital for blind and aged men; the Lying-In hospital, founded in 1745, and the Lock hospital (opened in Townshend Street in 1792) for veneral disease. In the year 1792–3 this hospital treated 2,000 cases, a grim reminder that venereal disease was a serious problem. There were a large number of prostitutes in the city, many of them living in the liberties but soliciting in 'the more opulent parts of the city'. According to the *Dublin Evening Post*, a leading liberal newspaper, prostitutes and street-walkers were the prime cause of much of Dublin crime. The *Evening Post* urged that prostitutes found in the street should be arrested and confined in penitentiaries. It thought that it would be impossible to suppress brothels—many of which were, it asserted, encouraged by wine and spirit merchants—but it suggested they should be licensed and regulated. The keeper should be responsible for the property of visitors, no intoxicating liquors should be sold, and the prostitutes should be medically inspected.[62]

By legislation enacted in 1785 and 1800 the Dublin medical school (controlled by Trinity college and the Royal college of physicians) was placed on an improved and extended basis, with Sir Patrick Dun's hospital as its teaching hospital. In 1784 the surgeons, long dissatisfied with their 'preposterous' corporate connection with the barbers and peruke makers, secured a professional organisation, the Royal college of surgeons being chartered as an examining and licensing body. It soon began to provide medical teaching and the expansion of the forces at the end of the century provided posts for many Irish-trained surgeons. In 1791 'the company of the apothecaries hall' was constituted and empowered to examine and license those wishing to practice as apothecaries.[63] In short, by the close of the century Dublin medical training was by contemporary standards well organized and the foundations for the achievements of the great age of Dublin medical teaching had been firmly laid.

Those whom duty or pleasure called to the capital found that

---

[62] J. Warburton, J. Whitelaw and R. Walsh, *History of the city of Dublin*, i, p. 447; *D.E.P.*, 14 Sept. 1797; *H.J.*, 25 Aug. 1797; *Commons' Jn. Ire.*, xvii, p. 33.

[63] J. Malton, *A picturesque and descriptive view of the city of Dublin*, p. 15; C. A. Cameron, *History of the Royal college of surgeons in Ireland* (1886), p. 111; 31 Geo. III, c. 34.

Dublin afforded a far more varied and entertaining life than could be enjoyed elsewhere in Ireland. There were to be found 'the elegant delights of plays, ridottos, public breakfasts, Castle balls, circular road canters, new garden concerts, and Blackrock casinos'.[64] During much of the century Dublin had two theatres and in 1798 the Theatre Royal, its manager, Frederick Edward Jones, claimed, was 'in point of convenience, elegance and decoration... not exceeded by any theatre in Europe'.[65] A lighter form of entertainment was provided by Astley's circus, at the Amphitheatre Royal, where equestrian displays (including the humours of bad horsemanship), rope walking and pantomime could be seen, and where, by 'a multiplicity of machinery and scenery', spectacles such as the siege of Valenciennes and the landing at Toulon could be staged. A skilful use of painting and light could produce remarkable effects. For instance at the Lyceum an eruption of Mount Vesuvius was shown in which 'the effect of fire is most strikingly and interestingly represented'. Panoramas of London and Westminster, of the Bay of Dublin, and of the taking of Seringpatam, were displayed and at the Shakespeare gallery in Exchequer Street, improved musical classes and a 'philosophical pyrotechina' offered 'a rational and elegant entertainment'.[66]

There were three well-known clubs, the Sackville Street, the Kildare Street and Daly's, the latter, beside the houses of parliament, having a coffee room, a writing room, a hazard room and private dining room.[67] The Dublin Library society in Eustace Street (annual subscription two guineas), which was building up a valuable collection of books and which provided a newspaper and conversation room, felt it had 'an equal claim on the patriotism and taste' of its members.[68]

The public assembly room of Dublin was the Rotunda which Mosse, the founder of the Lying-In hospital, built beside the hospital 'a noble circular room', opened in 1767 as an income-earning asset. After further building in 1785 there were, in addition to the Rotunda, a waiting hall for chairmen, vestibule

[64] J. O'Keefe, *The Wicklow mountains*, Act II, scene i.

[65] *Commons' Jn. Ire.*, xvii, p. 37.

[66] *D.J.*, 7 Jan., 18 Mar. 1794, 12 Mar. 1796; *H.J.*, 30 Mar. 1793, 21 Feb. 1794; Journal kept in Dublin, 21 July 1801 (R.I.A. 24 k 14).

[67] *D.J.*, 28 Sept. 1796; C. Abbot, A tour.

[68] *H.J.*, 15 Aug. 1791.

or bar, and card, tea and ballrooms. Besides being a source of revenue to the hospital the rooms provided constant entertainment. For the perpetual subscribers (a limited group) there were six annual assemblies, with attendance limited to 400 each, at which coffee, lemonade, cards, dancing and a supper of plain meats and wine could be enjoyed.[69] There was also a weekly promenade, concerts and an annual fandango for the benefit of the textile industries. Finally, there was in Dublin a continuous succession of private parties, balls and suppers. 'I can scarcely tell what I wrote', a fashionable young woman told one of her correspondents, 'from the eternal rat-tat on my door'. And Arthur Young indicated the vigour of Dublin social life by noting that at most parties the company was too numerous for the apartments.[70]

Lord Carlisle, a popular viceroy, noted another feature of Dublin social life. 'The whole town of Dublin', he wrote, 'is one large family or company under one roof and everything is known and made the subject of conversation immediately after it happens.'[71] Carlisle, contemplating Dublin society, as a viceroy inevitably would, *de haut en bas*, may, when he spoke of the whole, have meant only a small segment, the great magnates and higher officials, who dined and were dined by the lord lieutenant. But the boundaries of the world of power and fashion were not easily defined and were bound to be to some extent subjectively fixed. The four hundred who attended the annual assemblies at the Rotunda may have felt, reasonably enough, that they constituted the hard core of Dublin society. But the Rotunda promenades were much cheaper than the assemblies, and at these and at concerts, the theatre, charity sermons, and the subscription assemblies at Blackrock and in the public rooms at Leixlip, the respectable middle classes at least rubbed shoulders with the nobility and gentry, and might feel they were enjoying essentially the same mode of life.[72] Bacon, the well-known volunteer and United Irishman, when master of the tailors' guild, gave 'an elegant ball and supper at the tailors hall, to a very numerous and respectable

[69] *A list of the proprietors of licences on private sedan chairs*[1787].

[70] H. Fitzmaurice to Lady Chatham, 2 Feb. 1765 (P.R.O. 30/8/32).

[71] Carlisle to Fitzwilliam, 15 Sept. 1794 (W.W.M. f. 30).

[72] The cost of a promenade was for a gentleman 3s., for a lady 1s. (*D.J.*, 31 Mar. 1798).

company'. When a dancing master gave a ball, open to the public, at the Exhibition rooms, a correspondent, who had been accustomed 'to resort [to] the most fashionable circles', assured the readers of the *Dublin Chronicle* that he was never more agreeably entertained. A Dublin citizen who was not a member of one of the well-known clubs, could, at Hyde's coffee house, retire from the public coffee room to a spacious apartment with newspapers, reserved for subscribers of a guinea a year. When one of the high sheriffs of Dublin gave a dinner, most of his guests, as might be expected, were aldermen and city men, but he managed to secure a brace of peers and a baronet, and 'to a sumptous board succeeded loyal toasts and social happiness'.[73]

Malton, whose prints convey such a powerful, if idiosyncratic, impression of *fin de siècle* Dublin, in his account of a city which, he believed, had attained 'a claim of beauty', emphasized the importance in urban development of well-planned public services—he instanced a supply of fresh water and sewers. He was conscious that Dublin during the century had been struggling with the problems which rapid growth kept thrusting on it in an acute form—problems of police, planning, health and social welfare. The machinery for handling these problems was complex and inadequate and experimental attempts to improve or supplement it were not altogether successful. Dublin had an elaborate civic constitution. The governing body was composed of two houses, the lord mayor and aldermen (twenty-four in number), and the sheriffs and commons—ninety-six representatives of the guilds, together with the sheriffs' peers (citizens who had been chosen to serve as sheriff). Within the city the grand jury of the county of the city of Dublin had partial responsibility for gaols and some bridges, and a substantial part of the urban area lay outside the city's jursidiction, being within the manors of Saint Sepulchre, Thomas Court and Donore, the deanery of Saint Patrick's, Glasnevin and Kilmainham (the first three being known as the Liberties). Within a manor its lord, represented by his seneschal, had a measure of criminal and civil jurisdiction, and was responsible for municipal services. However, it should be added that two statutory bodies set up for Dublin during the

[73] *H.J.*, 25 Aug. 1790; *Dublin Chronicle*, 3 Mar. 1791; D.J., 7 Mar., 1 May 1794.

eighteenth century, the police commissioners and the Paving board, were empowered to act within the whole urban area.

At the beginning of the eighteenth century the government of the city was dominated by a powerful oligarchy, the board of aldermen. The aldermen, elected for life, chose the lord mayor and sheriffs, filled vacancies in their own body by co-option and selected the members of the common council from names proposed by the guilds. Such a plenitude of power was bound to provoke opposition, and from the forties, Charles Lucas, self-righteous, courageous, vehement and vulgar, was conducting a strident campaign against the aldermen, whose privileges, he contended, were gained in the arbitrary Stuart era or usurped.[74] The city liberals seem to have wanted a constitution on the London pattern, with elected aldermen, and in the late fifties three measures regulating municipal elections in Dublin were introduced into the house of commons. The aldermen protested indignantly that 'the popular method of election would be highly prejudicial to the trade and industry of the city', and one of their supporters hinted that leading civic reformers were shopkeepers panting to become lord mayor.[75] In 1760 parliament adopted a complicated compromise solution. It was enacted that the guilds should directly elect their representatives on the common council; that the common council should nominate eight persons for the office of sheriff, out of which the aldermen would select two; that when there was a vacancy on the board of aldermen the commons should nominate four persons, one of which the aldermen should co-opt; and that the alderman who was to serve as lord mayor should be proposed by the board and approved by the commons.[76] The act of 1760 was an undoubted, if not far-reaching, victory for the city liberals. Admittedly it only transferred a measure of power from a small, close-knit group to a number of privileged corporations. But the guilds at least comprised a large segment of the Dublin business world—merchants, manufacturers and shopkeepers, and the alterations in the municipal system made in 1760 demonstrated

[74] C. Lucas, *A letter to the free citizens and freeholders of Dublin* (1748) fourth address, pp. 16–20.

[75] *Commons' Jn. Ire.*, vi, p. 83; *The present constitution of the city of Dublin* (1750), pp. 13–14.

[76] 33 Geo. II, c. 16.

that oligarchy might be forced to concede, and this helps to explain the robust confidence with which the city liberals, such as Lucas and Tandy, conducted themselves in city politics and even on a wider stage.

A considerable amount of the corporation's time was absorbed in working the city constitution, in elections and in the appointment of civic officials, managing the markets and in handling the city revenues and property. The corporation managed to provide Dublin with one essential of urban life—a supply of fresh water. From the Middle Ages the city had obtained its water from the Dodder river. This source was supplemented in 1772 when a committee of the corporation, the Pipe water committee, entered into an agreement with the Grand canal company, the company undertaking to provide 'a full and ample supply of water'; and a few years later, in 1776, it was enacted that every householder in Dublin should construct a branch pipe to convey water from the nearest main pipe to his house. Four other important municipal services were, during the eighteenth century, removed from the corporation's sphere, and entrusted to statutory bodies. The ballast office (reconstructed in 1786 with a very small representation of the corporation) was made responsible for the port and quays; the police commissioners (1786) for the preservation of the peace; the Paving committee (1774) for paving and lighting, and the Wide streets commissioners (1757) for town planning.

Dublin's street pattern was largely determined by a few great landowners (including the city), but in 1757 parliament with the aim of securing a well-planned approach from the river to the Castle, constituted a body of commissioners empowered to buy (if necessary by compulsion) and sell land, and lay out 'a wide and convenient street'. After this operation was completed the Wide streets commissioners (co-opted or nominated by the lord lieutenant), subsidized by special taxes and parliamentary grants, continued to function. They did not plan the city's development on a grand scale but they intervened decisively at a number of strategic points. A commission whose activities were so conspicuous was unlikely to escape criticism, and in the autumn of 1798 a bill granting the commission the proceeds of a new tax on coals landed at Dublin was strongly, though unsuccessfully, opposed in the house of commons. The tax was denounced as bearing hard on the poor—'fire was next to food the greatest comfort of the poor'—and as unnecessary. At a time when the country's resources were being strained by war, the commissioners, it was declared, were spending money with 'lavish profusion' on 'whims and caprices'. They were contemplating, Barrington said, a new street running through the college park, 'to save fashionable personages the trouble of rolling in their carriages through College Green'. In reply the speaker, Foster, emphasized that the commissioners had always been carrying out the intentions of parliament, and Beresford pointed out that improvements to the Custom house quay, which enabled vessels to come up to the new bridge, lessened the cost of inland carriage of coal.[77]

A few years earlier it was widely suspected that the commission was involved in an ugly scandal. In 1791, Henry Ottiwell, a Dublin businessman,[78] obtained from the commissioners, by private treaty, a large block of land between the Custom house and the new bridge as well as some plots west of the bridge on what were alleged to be, remarkably favourable terms. It was also suggested that Ottiwell had a secret partner in this transaction, John Claudius Beresford, a banker, who was the son of John Beresford, who was both a Wide street commissioner and a revenue commissioner. The whole matter was investigated by three house of lords committees and a house of commons committee. It was shown that urban land values fluctuated sharply and suddenly and it was argued that a private sale might secure a better bargain for the public than an auction (which could be influenced by 'a combination' amongst the Dublin builders). John Beresford declared that he had no interest in Ottiwell's bargain and did not know who his partners were, 'good, bad or indifferent', and it should be added that the evidence connecting him with Ottiwell was weak. As for Ottiwell, when asked for the names of his partners, he refused to answer the question, saying if he did so 'it might involve him in litigation and injure his property'. The house of commons committed him to Newgate for a few weeks and resolved that the commissioners for Wide streets had exceeded their powers. However, even opposition speakers declared that

[77] *D.E.P.*, 6, 13, 15 Sep. 1798.
[78] Henry Ottiwell appears in the Dublin directory as 'flour and whiskey factor'.

the commission had not acted dishonourably and a bill was passed confirming the agreement with Ottiwell. John Beresford considered himself an ill-used man. Writing to an intimate friend he explained that, finding the Wide Street commissioners in financial difficulties and that 'nobody gave themselves any trouble but myself', he had negotiated the best bargain he could with Ottiwell. And he repudiated with scorn the insinuation they were in league with one another. In fact Beresford, who enjoyed official work, seems to have been public-spirited and Ottiwell, simply seems to have been successful in a bold speculation—after all, as it was pointed out in the house of lords, Dublin builders, could not be expected to behave as knights-errant.[79] But the episode helps to explain the cynical comment of a Dublin diarist who at the beginning of the nineteenth century noted that 'the eastern or genteel side of the city is daily rising into magnificence under the auspices of the commissioners of wide streets, who, it is rumoured, are merely by the touch of public money also rising in the same manner.'[80]

In the early seventies the Dublin streets were in such an unsatisfactory condition that the house of commons decided that a special commission should be set up to be responsible for their paving. The corporation was determined to keep this important sphere of municipal administration under its own control and when in 1774 it was enacted that a Paving board for Dublin should be constituted, it was provided that a substantial number of its members should be aldermen or common councillors—the remainder being either high officials sitting *ex officio* or persons of status named in the act. The Paving board had a short, unhappy history. It tried to do too much at once, it got into debt. It appointed inexperienced supervisors and the contractors, 'a sad drunken set', used defective materials. Many streets were left unprovided with sewers, and some of the sewers were badly constructed and became blocked. The scavengers, whose carts were expected to clear away street and domestic filth, were ill-organized and negligent. Liaison between the Paving board and the Pipe water commissioners was almost non-existent, with the result

[79] *D.J.*, 15, 31 Mar. 1796; J. Beresford to Auckland, 1 Apr. 1795 (Add. MS 34453).
[80] Journal kept in Dublin (R.I.A. 24 K 14).

that newly laid streets were pulled up so that decayed wooden
water pipes could be replaced. Finally, it was noticed that while
streets in which members of the city corporation lived were
well paved, 'the squares, streets and places where the nobility
and gentlemen of fortune lived were neglected.'[81]

Parliament reacted vigorously. The house of commons
appointed committees of inquiry in 1779 and 1784, each with a
strong chairman, and steps were taken to set up a new paving
commission, completely independent of the city corporation, to
which a wide range of duties was entrusted. The aldermen
and common councilmen protested loudly suggesting that the
new body would be expensive, and appealing to the charter.
But on this issue parliament showed itself contemptuous of
vested interests and traditional rights; after all, the scandalous
state of the streets 'was obvious to every person who passes
through them'—including M.P.s. In 1786 it was enacted that a
new Paving board should be constituted, composed of six
directors and five commissioners, named in the act. The
directors, who were upaid, were empowered to fill vacancies
in their own body by co-option and to dismiss and appoint
commissioners who were to be paid. The board was to manage
the paving, cleansing and lighting of the streets, prevent
nuisances, construct sewers and drains and erect fountains.[82]
About twenty years after its creation, the new Paving board's
activities were to be the subject of a long and searching report,
which reiterated many of the charges made against the board
formed in 1774. Dublin was still

> O in all place and shape and kind
> Beyond all thought and thinking
> The graceful with the gross combined,
> The stately with the stinking.

Cork, the second city of Ireland, had a population of about
half that of Dublin. 'Trade', a visitor to Cork remarked, 'is the
predominant passion here', and the city was both a great port,
the exporting centre of the Munster provision trade and a naval
station of some importance, providing protection for the West

[81] *Commons' Jn. Ire.*, ix, pp. dcxlvi–lxxiv; x, pp. ccclx–lxxii. 13 & 14 Geo. III, c.
22, 26 Geo. III, c. 6.
[82] 26 Geo. III, c. 32.

and East Indian trade routes. The city was not distinguished for its public buildings, and though canals gave the centre of Cork a picturesque appearance, a tourist complained they sometimes smelt offensively. But some of the merchants houses were declared to be 'magnificent', and the general prospect of Cork, with houses covering the hills, was compared to that of Oporto or Lyons.[83]

If Cork was undoubtedly the second city in Ireland, which city or town held the third place is uncertain—Waterford, Limerick, Drogheda and Belfast could all be claimants. The first three were medieval cities (Waterford and Limerick of Norse origin) and important ports, and Drogheda's importance for the local linen industry is indicated by a linen hall, built in 1774. Belfast was chartered only in the seventeenth century, but it grew remarkably fast and was destined to become the only Irish example of a nineteenth-century industrial city, a tremendous concentration of productive power. Even in the eighteenth century it held a distinctive place amongst Irish towns as the commercial centre of the linen industry, in the zone where that industry was best established and most successful, and as the capital of protestant dissent.[84] Standing at the mouth of the fertile and busy Lagan valley, where the river debouched into a large sheltered bay, it was a flourishing port, participating in the cross-channel and transatlantic trade. In March 1791, the year in which the Belfast society of United Irishmen was founded, William Ritchie of Glasgow came over and inspected the harbour. He returned a few months later with some skilled men and started a shipyard—a step which marked an important stage in the development of the great Belfast shipbuilding industry. Belfast's importance as a commercial centre was indicated by its two linen halls—the Brown linen hall (1773) and the White linen hall, a great rectangular building, standing on the south side of the town at the head of of the newly built Donegall Place, a broad street of large houses, one of which was said to be equal to many in Grosvenor

---

[83] *A tour through Ireland by two English gentlemen* (1748), p. 90; T. Smollet, *The present state of all nations* (1769), p. 25; C. Abbot, A tour, 1792; R. Twiss, *A tour of Ireland* (1776), p. 134.

[84] For eighteenth-century Belfast see G. Benn, *History of the town of Belfast*, 2 vols. (1877, 1880); id. *History of the town of Belfast with an account of its former and presen state* (1823); R. W. M. Strain, *Belfast and its charitable society* (1961).

Square. The White linen hall was one of a series of buildings which marked the growing importance of the town, the exchange or assembly room (1769), the new parish church (1774), the poor house (1774), and the new theatre (1778), soon superseded by a larger building (1784). Belfast, a visitor remarked about the close of the eighties, had 'an English look', being, except for a few cabins built of brick, 'full of inhabitants who seem busy and are all wealthy'.[85]

Ecclesiastical building in Belfast clearly suggested the denominational balance. There was a single parish church, a simple catholic church (1783), in an obscure street to the west of the town centre, a methodist meeting house (1800) and four presbyterian churches of which the most striking was the new church (1783) of the First presbyterian congregation. An elliptical building with a graceful front, it aroused the admiration of John Wesley and of the earl-bishop of Derry, who, forwarding a subscription towards its cost, wrote that it did 'equal honour to the taste of the subscribers and the talent of the architect'.[86] A combination of business enterprise, and presbyterianism, predominant amongst the intellectual and business leaders of Belfast, gave a distinctive character to the community. As businessmen, the citizens of Belfast were active and generally successful in a great era of economic expansion; as presbyterians, sharing in the Scottish enlightenment, they were conscious that their opinions were in accord with the progressive thinking of the time. Their religion and their economic activities nourished the spirit of study and creative self-reliance which distinguished the town. The corporation of Belfast, controlled by Lord Donegall, existed mainly to return M.P.s. Admittedly several of the eighteenth-century sovereigns were leading citizens and active magistrates, otherwise the municipal machinery was of little value. The deficiencies were however supplemented by community action. In the mid-eighteenth century a group of citizens founded the charitable society which in the early seventies opened the poor-house, a large, symmetrical, well laid-out building affording accommodation to the aged and infirm poor, and poor children. The charitable society set up a dispensary, raised money by supply-

[85] Beaufort, A tour (T.C.D. MS 4038).
[86] *Historical memorials of the First presbyterian church in Belfast* (1887), p. 21.

ing the town with fresh water and introduced the cotton industry into the north of Ireland by arranging that the poor-house children should be instructed in cotton spinning. In 1783 the Belfast chamber of commerce was founded; in 1785 a Ballast board responsible for improving the harbour was constituted and in 1800, by one of the last acts passed by the Irish parliament, a body of commissioners elected by the rate-payers was, along with the corporation, entrusted with the paving, cleansing and lighting of the town. The community also tackled the question of education. In 1786 a number of citizens founded the Belfast Academy which soon, under James Crombie and William Bruce, successively principals as well as ministers of the First congregation, became established as a successful grammar school, and which also for some years provided public lectures in philosophy and science. In 1788 the Belfast Reading society, which four years later transformed itself into the Belfast Society for promoting knowledge, was founded and was soon busy building up a liberally selected library which was to become an important cultural influence in Belfast.

All this had to be accomplished without financial aid from the state, or even from grand-jury taxation, for Belfast was not a county town. As Dr Alexander Haliday said, when outlining the charitable, economic and cultural activities of his fellow citizens, 'unassisted in public treasure, we have only ourselves to trust to for all this'. With a touch of provincial self-superiority he added that Belfast had no money to spend on ballooning—it had been suggested a balloon ascent might follow a Belfast volunteer review. 'Let these light gaudy machines', Haliday wrote, 'with superb, empty custom houses and hollow police bills remain with other vain and costly luxuries in the metropolis.'[87] Haliday can certainly be taken as reflecting intelligent opinion in Belfast. He was, it was said, for many years 'the real representative of his native town, while the nominal one was scarcely known even by name'. The son of a well-known non-subscribing minister and a graduate of Glasgow, he played a prominent part in the political, cultural, and convivial life of Belfast. An attentive physician, he was a keen whig, 'the judicious advocate of civil and religious liberty', and a poet, though it had to be accepted that his political ardour damaged

[87] *Charlemont MSS HMC*, ii, p. 38.

his poetry: he 'argued in verse and reasoned in rhyme rather more than is suited to poetry'. His fellow townsmen were proud of the fact that visitors to the north 'never failed to find in the physician of a country town, an urbanity of manners, a variety of information, a happy and opportune wit', a trace of which survives in Haliday's painstakingly playful letters to his venerated friend, Lord Charlemont.[88]

The Irish economic system had one undoubted achievement to its credit: it was maintaining in varying degrees of comfort a growing population. Contemporary statistics (the hearth money returns) suggest that in Ireland the social pyramid was broadly based and tapered sharply to a very narrow point. According to these returns there were in Ireland in the early nineties approximately 700,000 houses. Houses with one hearth or exempted on the grounds of poverty amounted to 85·5 per cent of the total, houses with two to four hearths inclusive amounted to 6·7 per cent; houses with five to eight hearths to 2·1 per cent and houses with over eight hearths amounted to less than 1 per cent of the total. There were 1,300 houses with 13 or more hearths, 367 with more than 20 hearths (including two gigantic 114 hearth mansions, both in County Kildare). The thin upper strata were clearly the landed magnates and the wealthier (or more extravagant) gentry. Those with more than one hearth were probably in the lower reaches of that elastic social grouping, the middle class. The bottom layer, the one-hearth category, was by no means homogeneous in composition. Twenty per cent of the houses were exempt from payment on compassionate grounds, the occupants being sick, aged, widowed or unemployed. Some of the families concerned, having lost a small farm, were living in a hut or outhouse, the father looking for work, while the mother, it was said, 'chars with' a farmer, or begged. The one-hearth households must have included labourers, cottiers, small farmers, tradesmen (skilled artisans) and hucksters. According to an inland revenue official, concerned to show that many one-hearth occupants could well afford to pay the tax, they included, in addition to the classes above mentioned, graziers, farmers with moderate-sized holdings, in 'respect to self-comfort and in-

[88] 'Character of Dr Haliday' enclosed in letter of William Drennan to Mrs McTier, Mar. 1802 (Drennan papers 967).

dependence equal to any man', gentlemen's stewards, and dairy keepers. He was probably right up to a point—to limit deliberately the number of hearths in a house was an obvious form of tax avoidance—nevertheless, the statistics show what a very high proportion of the population lived in small houses or cabins and how conspicuous were the bigger houses.[89]

The shape of Irish society is also reflected in the assessed taxes returns. Out of approximately 700,000 households, 51,000 lived in houses with 5 or more windows, 3,600 of them in houses with 30 or more, and a small group of five to six hundred in mansions with more than 50 windows. A comparatively small number of persons (6,700) employed at least one manservant, about half that number (3,000) possessed a four-wheel carriage. At the top of the pyramid a few hundred families employed four or more menservants and possessed at least two carriages.[90]

The income pattern, in so far as it can be ascertained, was also sharply pyramidal. About the close of the eighteenth century a considerable amount of information about the mass of the people who formed the base of the pyramid, artisans, cottiers and labourers, began to be published, some social investigators even trying to compile specimen budgets for labourers and cottiers (since these omit expenditure on religion or alcohol they are obviously incomplete). All this material shows that there were considerable variations in working-class income. For instance, while a labourer in County Londonderry was paid 7d. to 8d. a day, a good carpenter could earn at least 3s. 3d.; and while in Clare a labourer was paid 8d. a day, a thatcher or an expert ploughman could command 3s. 3d. The remuneration of a farm servant varied with the standard of 'diet' provided by his employer. The remuneration of a labourer or cottier was affected by the number of days he worked, in some areas it was higher in summer than in winter, it was said to be higher in the vicinity of towns and to have increased after

[89] *Commons' Jn. Ire.*, xv, p. cccxxxvii; J. McParlan, *Statistical survey of Mayo*, p. 66, J. Dubourdieu, *Statistical survey of the County of Down*, p. 33. It was stated in the eighties that persons in 'the rank next above the poorer people' lived in 2–3 hearth houses and that 'those of the highest rank' lived in houses with above 20 hearths (J. Howlett), *An essay on the population* (1786).

[90] *Second report of the committee . . . on . . . the public income and expenditure of Ireland*, appendix, pp. 87–8 H.C. (376), 1812, v.

the formation of the militia. It was also believed that agricultural wages tended to fall when provisions were dear because then farmers were inclined to cut down the number of their employees.[91] Obviously too, the income of the cottier or labourer who paid by his labour for his cabin, potato ground and grass, and who often kept a pig and poultry, depended on the productivity of his holding (Tyrone was probably not the only area where farmers were accused of giving the 'rough ground' to cottiers 'who must put up with it or want').[92] His family earnings were also important. Boys worked in the fields and the budgets show that without the woman's earnings from spinning and poultry many households would have had a deficit. If a County Meath cottier had a 'careful and industrious wife', he could, it was said, 'live in some degree of comfort and credit', but a public-spirited agricultural improver was scandalized to find that in parts of King's County the women only worked at harvest time and then regarded the money they earned 'their exclusive right for dress and finery'.[93]

The general picture which emerges is that all over Ireland the bulk of the labouring classes and probably very many small farmers were living near subsistence but that subsistence for an Irish rural family permitted some degree of comfort. The cabin if often dirty was usually warm, their clothing was hard-wearing, their diet (potatoes, meal, milk and eggs with perhaps 'great feastings of pork, beef and mutton' at Christmas and Easter)[94] satisfying if monotonous, and with the social framework taken for granted, they seem to have unquestioningly accepted their lot. It is impossible to quantify that very important historical factor, happiness, but it is significant that contemporaries were impressed by the cheerfulness of the Irish country people. They enjoyed music, dancing, every kind of sport, and conversation— 'when the glass goes round the difficulty is to find a listener'. An English economist touring Ireland was struck by the number of people he saw talking and laughing round their cabin doors and pronounced that 'with all their idleness, dirt and nakedness

[91] J. McEvoy, *Statistical survey of County Tyrone*, pp. 143–4.
[92] Ibid., p. 31.
[93] R. Thompson, *Statistical survey of the county of Meath*, p. 340; C. Coote, *Statistical survey of the King's County*, p. 23.
[94] J. McParlan, *Statistical survey of the County of Leitrim*, p. 63.

they look a much happier people than I have seen in any part of England or Scotland'.[95]

It is hard to generalize about the economic condition of that great section of Irish society, which contained some of the most dynamic elements in the community, the middle class. It comprised great diversities of talent and varieties of income and middle-class incomes attracted far less contemporary attention than working-class earnings or landlords' rentals. The net incomes of businessmen, which in individual instances must have fluctuated widely, are especially hard to ascertain. A large manufacturer in the poplin industry claimed that his net profits were about £2,500 per annum.[96] A successful Waterford merchant in the provision trade had c. 1790 a net income of about £900. An apparently well-informed essayist stated that a man with a capital of £3,000 engaged in the upper class of manufacturers (or who, to put it another way, would probably employ a foreman at about £100 a year) would expend annually on the rent of his 'villa', housekeeping, at least a couple of servants and a jaunting car £120 per annum, and hospitality would cost him another £70. It would be reasonable to assume that his income would be about £300.[97] The earnings of professional people who enjoyed much the same way of life as many businessmen are easier to ascertain. The typical income of a beneficed clergyman of the church of Ireland might be taken as about £150, a curate would probably receive £75; the catholic parish priest had on average £65; the presbyterian minister £80.[98] In the army, at the end of the century, a subaltern's pay was £100 per annum, a major's £250, a major-general's £700.[99] The lowest-paid government clerks received about £50 a year, a senior clerk or secretary to a board about £500. Curran in his first year at the bar earned £143. Fitz-gibbon, the son of a successful barrister, estimated that his earnings during his first ten years at the bar averaged £800 per

[95] *Gent. Mag.*, 1751, pp. 465–8; H. Townsend, *General and statistical survey o̥ County Cork*, i, pp. 82–8; *Memoirs and correspondence of Francis Horner* (1843), p. 57.
[96] T. Reynolds, *Life of Thomas Reynolds* (1839), i, p. 69; L. M. Cullen, 'The overseas trade of Waterford as seen from the ledgers of Courtney and Ridgeway' in *R.S.A.I. Jn.*, lxxxviii, pp. 165–78.
[97] T. Wallace, *An essay*, pp. 61–5.
[98] See below, pp. 162–3, 170–1, 175.
[99] *Commons' Jn. Ire.*, xix, pp. dxxv–vii.

annum. Another young barrister, rather too fond of amusement but keen on his work, was, according to his influential father, earning about £600–£700 a year.[100] An attorney with 'an extensive and lucrative practice' estimated his professional income at £1,000 per annum.[101] A successful medical man, Henry Quin, was said to have left personal assets valued at £30,000 and an estate worth £2,000 a year, the gains of his professional career.[102] William Drennan, a medical man specialising in obstetrics, after practising for some years in Newry, was earning about £290 per annum. Eager for metropolitan life he came up to Dublin but during the last decade of the century never seems to have earned much over £200 per annum. Drennan was diffident, and his radical politics may have damaged his practice but his qualifications were good and he had useful connections.[103] His finances, incidentally, exemplify an important aspect of middle-class economics. He had useful, if small, private means. As for farmers, the 'strong' farmer (probably farming between 100 and 300 acres) was able to live comfortably, an agricultural expert calculating that on reasonably productive land a farmer, using conventional rather than modern methods, might make annually twenty-eight shillings an acre.[104]

It is clear both that the middle-class income range was wide and that there was a striking disparity between middle-class and working-class incomes, the lowest middle-class income being to that of a labourer or a cottier at about 2:1. The middle-class Irishman had that margin which permitted social mobility upwards and could command a share of the luxuries and amusements which filled the advertisement columns of his newspapers. There was also a great disparity between typical middle-class incomes and those of the larger landowners, some of whom had in the second half of the century very large rent rolls. In 1765

[100] Curran's fee book (R.I.A. MS 12 B¹ 10); J. R. O'Flanagan, *Lord Chancellors of Ireland* (1870), ii, pp. 161–2; J. Beresford to Auckland, 13 Oct. 1788 (Add. MS 34428).

[101] *Copies of the claims laid before the commissioners under the act 40 Geo III, c. 34 and of the evidence*, p. 433, H.C. (87), 1805, vii.

[102] *Hibernian Magazine*, 1791, p. 287.

[103] W. Drennan to Mrs McTier, 4 Jan., 28 Dec. 1793, 2 Jan. 1800; to S. McTier, Jan. 1795. (Drennan papers, 459, 536, 596, 818 and 'budget' with 1081.)

[104] R. Thompson, *Statistical survey of the County of Meath*, p. 79; J. Archer, *Statistical survey of Dublin*, pp. 26–35.

Lord Kildare had, according to himself, an income of £17,000, and he expected to inherit an additional £2,000 on his mother's death. Lord Fitzwilliam, from his Wicklow estates, had an income of about £20,000 per annum. Lord Palmerston derived from his Irish properties at least £6,000 a year; and in 1790 a well-informed traveller estimated the incomes of Lord Donegall, Lord Bective, Lord Kingston and Hercules Rowley of Summerhill, as respectively £35,000, £20,000, £20,000 and £16,000 per anuum. Lord Clare was said to have an income of £7,000 and at the end of the century it was estimated that the average income of thirty great Irish landlords was just under £14,000 per annum.[105] It need scarcely be added that it was not easy to say what proportion of a landlord's estimated income was at his absolute disposal. There were jointures, dowries, children's allowances, mortgage charges, arrears of rent and possibly expenditure on improvements to be taken into account. The marquis of Downshire was a landed leviathan with about 100,000 acres and, it was rumoured, an income of £24,000. But at the close of the century, according to an episcopal neighbour, the marquis had debts totalling £80,000, having purchased a borough and spent about £10,000 on a mansion which was reputed to be 'the most expensive and inconvenient building in the north of Ireland'.[106] Nevertheless, when all qualifications are taken into account, many Irish landowners enjoyed substantial incomes sometimes running in the case of the larger landlords into five figures.

Land was the main source of wealth and the landed interest dominated most aspects of Irish life. A landed estate was not only a gilt-edged security, it conferred status and guaranteed a respected and coveted way of life to its owner. A landed gentleman was able to move freely amongst men of birth and breeding, he passed much of his time in rural pursuits, the *res rusticae* praised in the classics; the management of his estate prepared

---

[105] Kildare to Holland, 20 June 1765 (Add. MS 51246); for the rental of the Fitzwilliam estates in Wicklow see W.W.M.R. 221 f. 89; for Palmerston's income see B. Connell, *Portrait of a Whig Peer* (1957), pp. 352–79; for estimates of other landed incomes see C. Abbot, A tour; *Sketches of Irish political characters* (1799), pp. 299–300; for Lord Clare see A. Marsden to C. Abbot, 28 Jan. 1802 (P.R.O. 30/9/1); D. Large, 'The wealth of the great Irish landowners 1750–1815', in *I.H.S.*, xv, pp. 21–47.

[106] *Annual register*, 1777, chronicle, p. 31; T. Percy to wife, 4 Jan., 1 Aug. 1799 Add. MS 32335).

him for politics, local or national, and field sports, his usual pastimes, provided a useful training should duty or inclination impel him to serve his country in arms. Above all, he had independence. He was at liberty to develop his talents, assert his opinions, obey his conscience and, within wide limits, order his life as he saw fit. Naturally different life styles were adopted by landed gentlemen. Francis Hardy, in his life of Charlemont, an elegiac tribute to the pre-union Irish world, described two M.P.s each of whom might be regarded as the *beau idéal* of an Irish country gentleman, Denis Daly and William Brownlow. Denis Daly, head of a great Galway landed family, 'united beauty and dignity of person with great private worth, great spirit, extensive erudition and penetrating genius', Eloquent in debate, he 'read with the ardour of a lover of literature' and built up a very valuable library. He was good-humoured, and 'above the practice of satire, if ever he resorted to it, it was only to check the satirist, and with delicacy make him feel that he himself was vulnerable'. William Brownlow was a much respected county M.P. though 'he laid no claim to oratorical powers'. However, he stated his views with brevity, and on occasion with fire, and his assiduous attention to his parliamentary duties during a session of late sittings seriously undermined his health. He was a keen musician and an improving landlord, praised by Arthur Young for the way in which he laid out his demesne and his intelligent generosity to his tenants. 'His manners were more polished than familiar.' He had a composure and dignity, which in Hardy's opinion, 'contributed to that gentlemanly-like air which distinguished the Irish house of commons', and which, Hardy thought, was sadly lacking in the post-union house.[107]

Denis Daly and Brownlow, men of character, political integrity and taste, were in their general behaviour level-headed conventionalists. But independence and a substantial assured income permitted a landed gentleman to become a flamboyant eccentric. Beauchamp Bagenal of Dunlecky, an M.P. and volunteer colonel, when making the grand tour, 'exhibited the native, original character of the Irish gentleman at every place he visited. . . . His person was fine—his manners open and generous

---

[107] F. Hardy, *Memoirs of the . . . earl of Charlemont* (1810), pp. 145–7, 370–1; 'W. Brownlow to his constituents', 9 May 1768 (P.R.O.N.I. D. 1606).

—his spirit high and his liberality profuse. . . . He had fought a prince—jilted a princess—intoxicated the doge of Venice—carried off a duchess from Madrid—scaled the walls of a convent in Italy—narrowly escaped the inquisition at Lisbon.' Back in Ireland, a strong whig, 'prodigally hospitable, irregular, extravagant, uncertain, vivacious, the chaise, the turf, the sod, the bottle, divided a great portion of his intellect between them and left for the use of parliament only so much as he could spare from his other occupations'.[108] Bagenal is a striking example of the idiosyncratic individualism which independence promoted amongst the Irish gentry. It might emerge in the exuberant, high-spirited conviviality which Sir Jonah Barrington enjoyed and chronicled with the inveterate anecdoter's determination to make an immediate impact rather than with any concern for fine balancing and shadowing. It also sometimes manifested itself in intense devotion to the public service or in evangelical piety.

It was the independence of the landed man that William Drennan, a poet and a political radical, craved.

> The world he knew well, yet he felt some disdain
> To turn such a knowledge to traffic and gain,
> The gentleman scrupled to call to his aid,
> The craft of a calling and tricks of a trade.
> To live on the public and live at your ease,
> To retain independance, yet pocket the fees,
> Is a problem, which, tho' he threw down in despair
> May prove easy to him who the circle can square.[109]

Drennan, who had the instincts and education of a gentleman, obviously considered himself to be one, as indeed did many other Irishmen who were certainly not landed. For instance, Dermody, the poet, the son of a poor schoolmaster, when his kindly patroness, Lady Moira, offered to apprentice him to a bookseller, turned the offer down, declaring that 'it was not a situation for a poet and a genius who was born to be a gentleman'.[110]

---

[108] J. Barrington, *Historic memoirs of Ireland*, ii, pp. 27–8.
[109] W. Drennan, *Fugitive pieces in verse and prose* (1815), pp. 123–4.
[110] Lady Moira to Col Napier, 5 June 1803 (P.R.O. 30/64/1).

The line between gentlemen and the rest was drawn subjectively. Even Barrington, a believer in gentlemanly values,
mentions that there were the 'half-mounted gentlemen' (yeomen
farmers) who were 'occasionally admitted to the society of
gentlemen—particularly hunters'.[111] The very fact that the
limits of gentility were ill-defined ensured that the concept of
a gentleman had all the greater influence in determining the
prejudices, manners and conduct of many Irishmen. This was
obvious for instance in their attitude to money. A gentleman,
it was felt, should not be too concerned about money. He should
take his resources for granted, live with spirit and spend
generously. Being in debt was by no means the deepest form
of disgrace. In Ireland, a well-informed lawyer remarked,
'almost every man lives beyond his income' (though indeed
there were exceptions: James Bernard, a Cork M.P., though
he had an immense fortune lived at the rate of £300 per annum,
his tailor's bill being £6 a year).[112] It was a landed gentleman's
duty, and not a disagreeable duty, to maintain his status. All
over the British Isles the landed world displayed a propensity
for conspicuous consumption, expressed most conspicuously in
building. A country house was a massive embodiment of a
family's place in the county, reflected the owner's taste,
provided a centre for the estate and a base for social life. A house
could be costly—Miss Edgeworth said that some gentlemen 'at
last were obliged to sell an estate to pay for a house'—and it
required an expensive setting—gardens, plantations, lakes and
cascades:

> Here stands the mansion eminently bright,
> Pouring effulgence on the ravish'd sight.
> By sixteen steps we gain the welcome door,
> The sixteenth levels with the spacious floor.
> The polish'd front forms thirteen casements long,
> Four rais'd in height deserve sublimest song.[113]

Extravagance, or spending in a civilized and spirited fashion

[111] J. Barrington, *Personal sketches of his own times* (1827), i, pp. 26–8.
[112] A. Browne, *A comprehensive view of the ecclesiastical law of Ireland* (1803), p. 158;
Gent. Mag., 1790, p. 374.
[113] *Hibernian Magazine*, 1790, pp. 374–5; R. L. Edgeworth, Memoirs (1821), ii,
p. 6.

available resources (including borrowings), was bound to spread through a society in which the landed classes enjoyed overwhelming predominance. In 1778 a travelled clergyman comparing the living styles of a Dublin and a London merchant, observed that while the latter might provide his guest with 'a stinted dinner' with a glass of port, the former would have a table 'not only plenteously but luxuriously spread with a choice of wines'—moreover, during the entertainment he would 'betray no attention to the counter' but leave his business to take care of itself.[114] In the same year another Irish writer (presumably a southerner) pointed out that the English and Irish in Leinster and Munster were an agreeable blend of gentlemen, yeomen and traders, 'who being intermixed hinder them from being too much attached to trade or idleness, they are sprightly, agreeable, polite and hospitable'. He sharply contrasted them with the Ulster business middle class, 'a low plodding race', lacking in polish, inhospitable and always talking about how to make money or 'take in a person'.[115] At the close of the century it was remarked that in Dublin 'the entertainments of private individuals were in general more splendid than those of the same class of persons in England', though it was also remarked that in Ireland even liveried servants sometimes waited bare-footed.[116] Irishmen in general were proud of their country's reputation for hospitality and enjoyed being generous hosts, though as the century drew towards its close manners seem to have become more restrained. About 1780 it was observed that the bottle in Ireland 'circulates freely but not to excess'. An Irish gentleman in one of O'Keefe's plays, *The Toy*, remarks 'our hospitality is polished down of late days very genteelly. We're not so ready now to lock doors, hide hats and canes and nail our guests to their chairs as we used to do. No—now the third bottle sneaks back to the bin with a "What would you rather not".'[117] Certainly during the eighteenth century Irish gentlemen and those who regarded themselves as genteel spent vigorously and generously

[114] J. Campbell, *Philosophical survey* (1778), p. 401.
[115] *Hibernian Magazine*, 1778, pp. 149–50.
[116] W. Elliot to G. Elliot, 10 May 1796 (Minto MSS, N. L. Scotland); C. Abbot, A tour.
[117] W. Hickey, *Memoirs*, ed. A. Spencer, iv, pp. 149–50; *The Toy*, act xi, scene i,

on the pleasures and luxuries of life, a pattern of living which may have diverted an undue proportion of the national income from productive investment to immediate consumption.

The influence exercised by the contemporary conception of the gentleman is also shown by the place in both Irish and British social life assigned to the challenge and the duel. A duel was a breach of the sixth commandment and the laws of the land. It was a most irrational method of settling a dispute and could lead to a promising life being cut short over a trivial disagreement. But it was strongly believed that a gentleman should have such a sensitive regard for his honour—his reputation for courage and sound judgement on matters of social conduct—that he should not hesitiate to hazard his life in its defence. The duel was a test of a man's claim to be a gentleman and it was governed by a legalist etiquette, which meant that a quarrel and a meeting could be talked about and analysed and might even lead to another duel. As late as the beginning of the nineteenth century, duelling seemed so closely connected with the rules of good behaviour accepted and observed by Irish society that a sensible man of the world could only insist that men who quarrelled over the dinner table should not be allowed to fight when still in their cups, that seconds should always try and effect a reconciliation and that if a rencontre was unavoidable, the parties should be placed at least ten yards apart and instructed to fire simultaneously.[118] It is scarcely surprising then that many of those who played an active part in Irish public life, including a lord lieutenant (immediately after relinquishing office) and two chief secretaries, were involved in duels. What reflects the strength of the prevalent code of gentlemanly conduct is that a number of leading radicals, men who believed in rationality and humanity as guiding principles in politics, took part in affairs of honour; Tone, as a young man, was a second in a fatal duel and later condemned Napper Tandy for fumbling over a challenge; Drennan fought a duel; Hamilton Rowan was involved in several affairs of honour; Arthur O'Connor and Thomas Addis Emmet nearly had a hostile meeting after their release from Fort Saint George; Bagenal Harvey, the leader of the Wexford insurgents in 1798, some years earlier

---

[118] *General rules and instructions for all seconds in duels*. By a late captain in the army (1801).

had a duel with a fellow barrister over a political argument; in 1792 Matthew Dowling, a well-known radical attorney, exchanged shots, 'happily without any ill effects', with the chief secretary's private secretary over a quarrel at the theatre, and shortly afterwards a hundred citizens entertained Dowling and his second, Hamilton Rowan, at a public dinner.[119]

[119] *Fortescue MSS H.M.C.*, i, p. 569; *Cal. Home office papers 1773–6*, pp. 15, 88; *Horace Walpole's correspondence*, ed. W. S. Lewis, pp. 93, 97; *D.E.P.*, 4, 15 Dec. 1792.

2

Administration and politics

Almost all Irishmen who claimed gentility shared an absorbing interest in politics. The great majority of the population, engaged in a strenuous never-ending endeavour to secure subsistence, was of course not in touch with the methods by which political ideas and news were communicated, newspapers, pamphlets, county meetings, clubs and dinner tables. But in addition to the great landed families, a substantial number of middle-class men, minor landowners, large farmers, professional men and businessmen, as freemen, freeholders or burgesses, possessed a share, albeit a minute one, in political power. Even if, as was probable, his vote had to be cast in accordance with the declared will of a landlord or borough owner, an elector could pride himself on being a member of a political élite. Theoretically, he exercised independently a privilege and a responsibility, and convention required that at election times he should be approached with courteous deference. Politics offered opportunities for serving the public, winning distinction and gaining valuable prizes. It was in the political arena that great territorial families competed to improve their local or national status, and political news and political gossip, often spiced with malice, were prominent features in the newspaper press, that great and growing source of information and entertainment.

It may indeed be argued that politics loomed disproportionately large in Irish life, absorbing to an undue degree the attention of the aristocracy and the middle classes and diverting them from other worthwhile pursuits. After all, it was generally held that the state had only a limited range of functions. It existed to defend the community, to preserve order, to dispense justice and to protect property. The strong individualism of the age and its emphasis on self-reliance made men quick to suspect and resent encroachments by the state on what they conceived to be their rights. The enjoyment of property and power of bequeathing it was one of those rights and a guarantee of individual independence or liberty, and there was a feeling that state intervention in social or political matters, entrenching on property rights should be only reluctantly, if at all, permitted. But *laissez faire* was still in the process of becoming a clearly formulated orthodoxy which would provide guide-lines limiting government action in many spheres. Irish businessmen and landowners often combined a belief in the virtue of individual enterprise with a determination to obtain state assistance for an industry or an economic project, and individuals or groups frequently approached the Irish parliament for assistance— sometimes in the form of a direct grant, sometimes in the shape of fiscal legislation, providing a tariff or bounty. As for the Irish parliament, when a social or economic problem was thrust on its attention, it reacted in the manner of a benevolent landlord, applying without much regard for theory what seemed to be the obvious remedy. As a result the range of state action reflected in legislation seems remarkably wide, and those who wish to trace the evolution of legislation relating to state intervention in the spheres of education, public health, poor relief, transport, or regulation of incomes, will find its origins embedded in the eighteenth-century statute book. But it should be quickly added that the scope and effect of many of these measures was very slight. Irish parliamentarians did not have the investigatory techniques, the social theory, the blue books, the blueprints, the drive for sustained intervention on a significant scale. There was indeed much economic legislation. Some of it was ill-enforced. Some measures (Foster's corn law for instance) simply accentuated prevalent economic trends others (protective tariffs for Irish industry for instance) did little to divert them. Finally, much of the economic legislation of course was fiscal, and though taxation appeared to contemporaries to be an irritating burden, even at the close of the century, when it had risen to £3,500,000 per annum, it represented only a very small proportion of the national income. Even that grim and much debated group of statutes, the penal laws, though they had a great influence on some Irish catholics at critical points in their careers (for instance when they were choosing a profession or hoping to acquire land), nevertheless had comparatively little effect on the day-to-day lives of most Irish catholics during the second half of the eighteenth century.

Parliament discovered only too often that a well-intentioned effort to promote economic development could involve it in a conflict of economic interests. For instance when the felt-makers asked for an export duty on rabbit skins, the furriers asserted that there was a glut of skins and that an export duty would be against the interests of gentlemen with rabbit burrows on their estates; when the glovers requested that the export of lamb and sheep skins should be discouraged, the skin dealers retorted by requesting the removal of obstacles to their export trade; when the tanners asked for protection against English competition, the shoemakers pointed out that they had to use English leather because Irish leather was being brought to market in an 'unmerchantable' state; when the Irish iron manufacturers secured protection, the wire and steel manufacturers complained that the price of iron had at once been increased by 35 to 40 per cent; when it was suggested, with considerable backing from the linen trade, that bounties should be given on the export of linen to foreign countries, influential groups of merchants in Belfast and Lisburn attacked the proposal on the grounds that 'only a very few merchants would benefit by it' and that it might lead to the withdrawal of the British bounties on Irish linen. When the paper manufacturers obtained an additional duty on imported paper, some leading Dublin printers protested, stating that a duty on paper 'affects the literature of the country, the progress of education and moral instruction' and that the paper manufacturers, having secured a monopoly, were increasing prices by 30 per cent. The paper manufacturers retorted that they were making a large capital investment and employed a large labour force 'projectors, builders, machinists and artificers'.[1]

In 1780 following a judicial decision the Irish parliament had to handle a clash of interests in which economic, ethical and legal factors were nicely balanced. Many Irish tenants held their land on a lease for three lives, perpetually renewable on the payment of a fixed fine within a stipulated period. It was characteristic of an easy-going society that it had become accepted by the courts that even if the fine was tendered late the lease should be renewed, but in 1779 the British house of

---

[1] *Commons' Jn. Ire.*, x, pp. 62–137; xi, pp. 108, 162; xi, pp. 212, 308, 322–3; xii, p. 212; xiii, p. 189; xiv, pp. 189–90; xvi, pp. 189, 193.

lords held that if the fine was not paid in time the lease lapsed. This, a large number of Irish attorneys specializing in land business declared, 'threw the kingdom into the utmost confusion and ferment'. The attorney-general declared that 'the English were not well informed' and Grattan introduced a measure to relieve the tenants. It was not an occasion when the signs of deep-seated social conflict can be discerned. Only a limited number of tenants were immediately affected; many of them were men of substance (Grattan's opponents spoke of them as 'land jobbers' and declared that his bill would do nothing to help poor tenants) and the head landlords had never expected to recover control of leased lands. Two major issues of principle were involved—should long-standing custom or the letter of the law prevail; and was it proper for parliament to overrule the courts by retrospective legislation. The house of commons and the British privy council agreed on the heads of a bill, which provided that a tenant would not lose his right to the renewal of his lease by late payment of a fine, and that his landlord would be entitled to adequate compensation for the delay. The measure passed the house of commons by 92 votes to 57, and was carried in the house of lords, after assiduous whipping by both sides, by one vote.[2]

One area into which the state was hesitant to advance was the wide and controversial field of social welfare. Eighteenth-century Irishmen were thankful that the Elizabethan poor law, demoralizing to the poor and burdensome to the rate-payer, had not been extended to Ireland.[3] Though poverty and distress aroused sympathetic concern it was widely and firmly held that their relief should be left to private charity and voluntary effort. Benevolence was a virtue which the eighteenth century held in high regard and its practice was frequently observed with admiration. In an account of Lady Fitzgibbon, the wife of the lord chancellor, it was said 'that not one subscription is set on foot for any humane purpose but what

---

[2] *H.J.*, 24 July, 14, 16, 21 Aug. 1780; *D.E.P.*, 16 May, 3 June, 12 Aug. 1780; P.C. 1/12/26–7; *The English reports*, ii, pp. 506–14. The case of *Bateman* v. *Murray* illustrates the complications surrounding land ownership in Ireland. Not only was an important point of law involved but it seems that the father of the respondent (the tenant) when acting as agent for the landlord had behaved in an improper, not to say fraudulent, manner.

[3] *Account of the proceedings of the governors of the house of industry* (1801).

has constantly her honoured name in the list. Nay, we are informed that her private charities exceed those that example requires should be made public. Beauty all mankind admire; but when it is joined with an extreme benevolence it renders the possessor not only an object of admiration, but of reverence and general esteem.' Lord Bandon, on his wife's birthday, gave sixty entire suits of clothes to his labourers. 'Oh', exclaimed a local newspaper, 'may so convincing a proof of tenderness and compassion for the naked, excite in them sentiments of grateful acknowledgement and affectionate attachment to their generous benefactor.' When there was distress amongst the artisans in the liberties in 1778 ladies and gentlemen appeared at court in dresses of Irish manufacture, and in 1760 it was noticed with approval that Dublin catholics when they gambled on Sunday gave their winnings to the poor.[4] In Dublin and a few other places voluntary effort provided some hospital accommodation for the sick poor and there were a number of charitable societies but to a very great extent the relief of distress was left to individual benevolence.

At the very beginning of the century however, poverty in Dublin was conspicuous enough to call for parliamentary action, and an act of Queen Anne's first Irish parliament established the Dublin workhouse. It was supported by local taxation and was intended to house beggars and foundlings. The later type of inmate soon seems to have predominated, and in 1772 it was enacted that the workhouse should be exclusively a foundling hospital. In the late fifties it was found to be extremely badly managed, with its accounts in disorder and the children starved and neglected. A Dublin parish clergyman, William Tisdall, who had strong political connections, took the lead in calling for reform. Two house of commons committees inquired into the administration of the institution and the governors adopted a series of regulations which it was expected would put it on a satisfactory footing. But the house of commons committees, which in 1791 and 1792 investigated the running of the hospital, reported that its finances were in confusion, that the mortality rate for children admitted and either lodged in the hospital or put out to nurse, was extraordin-

[4] *Hibernian Magazine*, 1778, p. 367 and 1794, p. 193; *Cork Courier*, 17 Jan. 1795; *D.J.*, 8 May 1760.

arily high and that 'it requires great reform'. Sir John Blaquiere, an ex-chief secretary, took up the question and introduced a bill constituting a new governing body for the hospital. He pointed out that though the existing board, composed of *ex officio* and co-opted members, was 300 strong, it was hard to secure a quorum of 21 for a board meeting, 'except when some office or employment was to be given away'; and he proposed to entrust the management of the hospital to a much smaller board of 19 nominated directors, armed with considerable powers. Unfortunately the bill became a party issue. The lord mayor and aldermen, who were *ex officio* governors (and, it was suggested, conscientious attenders when patronage was on the agenda) petitioned against the bill as encroaching on the city's rights, and Grattan and other members of the whig opposition, suspicious of the executive, and perhaps too ready to see the possibility of 'a job' in the new scheme, attacked the bill, trying to show that if allowance was made for the number of children in general who died before the age of four and the fact that many of the children admitted to the hospital were suffering from venereal disease, the death rate was less horrifying than Blaquiere asserted. The bill failed to pass but in 1797 still another house of commons committee reported that conditions in the hospital were appalling and recommended that the physician, surgeon and apothecary be dismissed. In the following year it was enacted that the hospital should be managed by nine named persons who were given power to fill vacancies by co-option.[5] The other Irish foundling hospital, the Cork hospital, had a less lurid history. It was founded in 1735 to accommodate beggars and foundlings, supported by local taxation (a tax on coal), opened in 1747 (the governors going about the task of finding a site and erecting a building in a leisurely fashion), and soon became exclusively a foundling hospital.[6]

Until well after the middle of the century the two foundling hospitals were the only institutions for the relief of the poor supported by public money. In the late sixties, Richard

[5] 2 Anne, c. 19, 11 & 12 Geo. III, c. 11; *Commons' Jn. Ire.*, vi, pp. xcvi, ccccxiv; xiv, pp. cci, ccxcix; *Parl. Reg. Ire.*, xi, pp. 257–60, 307–13, 413–16; 38 Geo. III, c. 35.

[6] *First report of the commission for inquiring into the condition of the poorer classes in Ireland*, appendix C, part i, pp. 29–30, H.C. [35], 1836, xxx.

Woodward, an English clergyman, who had been appointed dean of Clogher, urged with lucidity and force that a national system of poor relief should be introduced into Ireland. The poor (by which term he meant 'not those idle vagrants who are a pest to society but those who though willing to work could not subsist by labour'), he boldly argued, had a moral right to relief. The welfare of society demanded that private proprety should be respected, but 'the poor being restrained by law from any of the rights of nature . . . should be provided with a subsistence in time of distress'. He suggested that in each county there should be a house of industry in which the helpless poor would be lodged and if fit to work provided with employment. Beside it should be a house of correction where idle beggars 'would be kept close to some laborious work'. An elderly labourer, still capable of a light day's work might have his reduced wages supplemented by outdoor relief. The scheme would be financed by a tax on landed and personal incomes, which Woodward calculated would amount to about 1 per cent. The scheme, he persuasively explained, would suppress beggary, be less expensive to the community than indiscriminate almsgiving, distribute charity more equitably (Woodward believed that the pertinacious beggar got more than his due share of alms) and spread the burden more fairly—the destitute, he thought, depended to a great extent on the farmer and even the cottager, and if some landed gentlemen were generous, the 'avaricious or hard hearted' could avoid contributing.[7]

Woodward secured the approbation of the Dublin society for his plan and in 1772 parliament enacted that in every county and city a corporation was to be formed (consisting of *ex officio* members, justices of the peace, subscribers and in the cities members of the governing body) and this corporation was to establish a house of industry which was to be supported by grand jury presentments and subscriptions. In this house beggars were to be detained and 'helpless' poor persons lodged.[8] The act was immediately implemented in Dublin, and as the governors were well placed for exercising influence, from 1777

[7] R. Woodward, *An address to the public on the expediency of a regular plan for the maintenance and government of the poor* (1775); *An argument in support of the right of the poor in the kingdom of Ireland to a national provision* (1772); and *A scheme for the establishment of county poor houses in Ireland* (1768).

[8] 11 & 12 Geo. III, c. 30.

the Dublin house of industry was receiving parliamentary grants. But the act was not applied very extensively, only eight houses of industry (three of them being supported entirely by voluntary subscriptions) being established by the close of the century.[9] Woodward noticed with regret that when it was a question of a grand jury voting money for the support of a house of industry, 'gentlemen in general thought it proper to decline from a conviction county charges were burdensome, especially on the lower people'. Opposition to the imposition of a poor rate was vigorously expressed in the house of commons in 1778 when a bill was introduced providing for the levy of a rate on Dublin householders for the support of the house of industry. According to Colonel Browne (a conservative) the bill had 'a great deal of a Jesuit in it, being pregnant with evil and carrying a poor rate in its belly', and Bradstreet (a liberal) denounced 'all legal permanent provisions for the poor' which were 'so many incentives to idleness by blunting the spirit to industry'. Though it was strongly urged that a rate was the most equitable way of meeting the cost, the bill was lost by 66 to 64.[10]

But the Dublin house of industry continued to receive a large parliamentary subsidy and as a result fell under the scrutiny of the commissioners of accounts. Towards the close of the century they reported that the accounts were badly kept, that the secretary had absconded with a large sum of money and that 'one rotation of governors frequently defeated whatever good had been done by a former set'. Pelham, when chief secretary, took a keen interest in the house, and in 1797 he introduced a bill which passed swiftly through all its stages, providing that the corporation should elect seven persons to act as governors. His successor, Castlereagh, shared his interest in the house and in 1800 an amending act was passed vesting the management of the house of industry in five governors appointed by the lord lieutenant—a very early instance of the Irish state intervening directly in the administration of social welfare (albeit on a miniscule scale).[11]

[9] 5 Geo. III, c. 20; 15 & 16 Geo. III, c. 31; 21 & 22 Geo. III, c. 13; 25 Geo. III, cc. 39, 40. *Poor (Ireland), A return of the corporations . . . in Ireland instituted for the relief of the poor*, H.C. (291), 1828, xxii.
[10] *Hibernian Magazine*, 1778, pp. 289–90, 353–5.
[11] *An account of the proceedings of the governors of the house of industry in Dublin* (1801), p. 18; *Commons' Jn. Ire.*, xv, pp. lxv, dxxi,; xix p. dlxxv.

Some attempt was made to provide relief for the sick poor, partly at public expense, by legislation passed between 1766 and 1785, which applied to twenty-six counties. In each county an infirmary was to be maintained, managed by a corporation consisting of the bishop of the diocese, the incumbent of the parish in which it was situated, and subscribers. The state was to contribute £100 per annum towards a surgeon's salary and the grand jury was empowered to make an annual grant. By the beginning of the nineteenth century every county had an infirmary but benevolent intentions were vitiated by a lack of sustained supervision. A survey of the system in 1788 shows that the average number of patients in an infirmary was only ten, the buildings were usually wretched and the patients neglected. Many of the surgeons were elected by voters who had paid a year's subscription merely to qualify, and a surgeon often practised midwifery and might be away from his infirmary for weeks on end attending a lady previous to her lying-in.[12]

The efforts of the Irish parliament—such as they were—to deal with poverty reveal a wide gap between the public-spirited M.P.s, who manufactured legislation, and the ordinary county gentlemen who were expected to implement it. The former drafted impressive plans, the latter believed that benevolent individuals would readily and adequately respond to distress and strongly disliked paying taxes. Moreover to eighteenth-century Irishmen poverty, while always with them, was not alarming (it was not until the early nineteenth century that 'the condition of Ireland question' aroused profound anxiety). The destitutes were divided into two broad categories. The helpless poor, children, the aged, sick and infirm, 'real objects of charity', for whom what seemed a considerable amount of private and public help was provided, and those 'who chose to live in idleness by beggary'.[13] For the beggar, lazy and drunken, aggressive, plausible, and liable to spread infection, the best treatment was punishment or corrective training (compulsory hard, routine work in the austere environment of a workhouse). That a man genuinely seeking work could be long

[12] *Commons Jn. Ire.*, xii, pp. dccclii–iii; *Accounts of the presentments passed by grand juries of Ireland . . . in the year 1807*, H.C. (205), 1808, xii.
[13] 11 & 12 Geo. III, c. 30, preamble.

unemployed does not seem to have been recognized though it was accepted that an industrious artisan might be out of work during short periods of dislocation caused by a political crisis or when a particular trade was suddenly exposed to severe competition. Admittedly from time to time, and especially in the last decade of the century, it was stressed that large sections of the rural population were suffering seriously from under-remuneration. But it was expected that living standards would be raised by the economic expansion which it was generally believed was inevitable, and in any event, as a well-known Irishman wrote,

> How small, of all that human hearts endure
> That part which laws or kings can cause or cure.

There were two spheres in which it was believed that the state should intervene vigorously and decisively—defence and law and order. There was not an Irish army, but there was what was termed the Irish military establishment, a number of cavalry regiments and infantry regiments or battalions whose pay and maintenance were a charge on the Irish revenue. The units on the Irish establishment frequently changed. Four regiments of horse remained in Ireland continuously for many years, but this was exceptional. A regiment stationed in Ireland usually stayed for a few years and moved to Great Britain or was sent overseas. Until the close of 1769 the force on the Irish establishment numbered 12,000 (2,000 being stationed abroad); from January 1770 it was raised to 15,000 (3,000, the Irish contribution to imperial defence, being stationed abroad, and 12,000 retained in Ireland for home defence). After the outbreak of the great French war in 1793, the Irish military establishment expanded rapidly until by 1800 the forces maintained by Ireland totalled about 60,000. But the number employed on foreign service was not increased, the importance of home defence being strongly emphasized in the Irish house of commons.

Ireland not only maintained some units on overseas service, it also became a major source of military—and naval—manpower. Until well past the middle of the century recruiting in Ireland was restricted. It was taken for granted that it would be dangerous to enlist catholics, and it was also held that it would 'cause infinite prejudice to the kingdom to take any considerable number of protestants'[14]—in any event working-class protestants could probably find more attractive forms of employment. Officers were discouraged from enlisting Irishmen, regiments on the Irish establishment tending to recruit in England, with the result that only about one in twenty of the rank and file of the whole army was Irish. (There was a minor scandal in 1728 when it was discovered that the Royal Scots had sent Irishmen it had recruited over to Scotland and then brought them back to Ireland wearing bonnets and enlisted them as Scots.)[15] In the *annus mirabilis* 1759, when the French were threatening a counter-stroke against the British Isles, Pitt, the great driving force behind the war effort, believed that many thousands of men could be raised from the Irish protestant community, 'a zealous, brave and flourishing people'. He was surprised how slowly recruiting in Ireland went forward. 'As to the zeal of His Majesty's protestant subjects in Ireland,' he wrote, 'no doubt can possibly be entertained of the sincerity of it. But the total efficacy of that zeal . . . cannot but administer here much just grounds of wonder and concern.' Accepting that 'the looms and manufactures are most deservedly tender points to the proprietors of lands in that opulent kingdom', Pitt sharply pointed out that it would be scarcely prudent for 'the protestant people of Ireland', to rely on the prompt arrival of reinforcements from Great Britain and to abstain from raising additional forces until an invasion took place. The lord lieutenant, in his correspondence with the great war minister dwelt on the difficulties of recruiting in Ireland. In the north the nobility and gentry gave little help; the south was 'very bare' of protestants. A subscription (for bounties) would not, he thought, be 'palatable', and the device of granting commissions to those who brought in a certain number of recruits would not be feasible. It would be looked on in Ireland as 'an ungenerous way to treat young gentlemen who are willing to enter the army', and would annoy those who thought that their parliamentary influence entitled

---

[14] Carteret to Newcastle, 27 Jan. 1726, 27 Mar. 1728 (S.P. 63/387,390).
[15] J. C. Leask and H. M. McCance, *The records of the Royal Scots regiment* (1915), p. 120.

them to recommend their sons and other relations for first commissions. Finally, the lord lieutenant impressed on Pitt that once the additional men were raised they must not be drafted from Ireland. Many government supporters 'would think themselves hardily dealt with, should they see the forces they have been instrumental in raising for their own defence employed in purposes which have no relation to it'.[16]

Before the Seven Years war ended it was suggested that the manpower resources in Ireland should be tapped on a wider scale than was customary—it being proposed that seven catholic regiments should be raised for the service of the king's ally, the king of Portugal. Nearly ten years later in January 1771, during the Falkland Islands dispute, regiments stationed in Great Britain were allowed to recruit in the three southern provinces (a tacit permission to enlist catholics) and two years later the 47th and 48th foot, before leaving Ireland, were allowed to recruit in the south and west. In 1775, with war impending in America, arrangements were made to recruit 'at large' in Ireland, though the lord lieutenant seems to have hoped that the men required might be obtained in Ulster.[17] Throughout the war the north apparently remained the best Irish recruiting area, the southern catholics in time of economic stagnation being 'less easily tempted from their bogs, their misery and their potatoes', than 'the manufacturers' of the north. In 1784 an inspector of recruiting for Ireland was appointed, and in 1787 all regiments were allowed to recruit in Ireland. At this time Orde, the chief secretary, was still uncertain if catholics should be recruited, though, he admitted that 'there is at present a necessity of not being very exact in that respect'. He was afraid that if there was an avowed change of policy the catholic clergy would try and discourage recruiting and that the catholics would begin to ask for commissions, raising 'an awkward question'. About the same time the Irish quarter-master general prepared a memorandum on recruiting which implied it would be inexpedient to pay much attention to the theological opinions of potential recruits. 'One

---

[16] W. Pitt to Bedford, 2, 21 Nov. 1759; Bedford to W. Pitt, 1, 30 Nov. 1759 (S.P. 63/416).
[17] *Cal. home office papers 1770–2*, pp. 100, 123, 186; *Cal. Home office papers 1773–75*, p. 320.

cannot be surprised', the memorandum declared, 'that there are few candidates for the sword in these commercial, manufacturing and enlightened times', and most of the Irish recruits were either 'grown up vagabonds or young boys'—the latter good material.[18] From the outbreak of the war in 1793 strenuous efforts were made to raise recruits and during the Revolutionary and Napoleonic wars Ireland may have provided about one-third of the rank and file of the regular army.[19]

Irishmen were also to be found in large numbers in the commissioned ranks. Irish protestants were bred in what was in some respects a frontier tradition: a military commission carried social prestige, and with the Irish government possessing a fair share of military patronage, a moderate amount of political influence might secure for a young Irishman an ensigncy or a cornetcy. By the middle of the century one army officer in four was Irish, and by the beginning of the nineteenth century the proportion of Irishmen in the commissioned ranks had risen to one in three. For many protestants, and, after 1793, for some Irish catholics, a military commission opened up a career which blended public service with a congenial social life. The army officer commanded men, travelled (if only within the British Isles), was respected, had an active club-life (even if his means were limited), and might win renown. At the beginning of the century Cadogan, the son of a Dublin barrister, was Marlborough's quarter-master general; at its close Hutchinson, the son of a provost of Trinity college, was Abercromby's second-in-command in Egypt, and Arthur Wellesley was distinguishing himself in India where Beresford was also serving. Blakeney, a Limerick man, distinguished for his defence of Minorca, was honoured by a statute in Dublin, and Eyre Coote, a member of a very well-known Irish family, received the thanks of the house of commons for 'the indefatigable pains he has taken to surmount the difficulties involved in the affairs of the Carnatic'.

The army loomed large in eighteenth-century Ireland. It absorbed a high proportion of the Irish budget. It contributed to the pageantry and vivacity of Irish urban life. It was largely

---

[18] Memorandum of Irish Q.M.G., 1787, T. Orde to Yonge, 4 Aug. 1787 (W.O. 1/611); H.O. 100/28/f.99.

[19] See Inspection returns for 1812, W.O. 27/106–8.

responsible for the preservation of law and order. Ireland's laws, an M.P. wrote, 'owe their force to the army, which I may say is a part, and the most essential part, of her police'.[20] A troop of dragoons or a detachment of foot was the final resort of the magistracy when confronted with organized violence on a dangerous scale. A commission in the army provided a career for many Irish gentlemen and from the middle seventies enlistment in the ranks was, for a growing number of poor men, a path to a livelihood, adventure, glory, death or disablement.

The law, the product of centuries of legislation and accumulated precedent, was greatly revered. It enshrined liberty, the prized possession of Englishmen and Irishmen, and if until 1782 Ireland lacked a habeas corpus act, Irishmen enjoyed the benefit of trial by jury and proudly participated in the rich heritage built up by the two great mutually sustaining systems, common law and equity. Admittedly as time went on they could scarcely help perceiving a vivid contrast between the intellectual strength and subtlety of the law and the crude inefficiency of much of the machinery by which it was maintained—absentee or ineffective justices of the peace and a ramshackled police and prison system.

The commanding dignity of the law was well represented by the judiciary, the lord chancellor and the common law judges.[21] Until 1783 each of the three common law courts had three judges; in that year the number in each court was raised to four (thus more than meeting the criticism that five circuits could not be adequately manned by nine judges). From shortly after the accession of George I no Irish judge had been removed from the bench by the crown and in 1782 it was enacted that the common law judges should have tenure during good behaviour and could be removed on an address from both houses of the Irish parliament. The lord chancellor had a salary of £7,000 and from about the middle of the century the income of the common law judges ranged from £3,250 (for the chief justice of the king's bench) to £2,150 (for puisne judges). In 1796 they were granted considerable increases so that their salaries ranged from £4,000 to £2,500. Their incomes and

[20] C. F. Sheridan to ——, 5 Oct. 1787 (N.L.I. MS 15920).
[21] For the Irish bench see F. E. Ball, *The judges in Ireland 1221–1921* (1926).

status lodged the judges firmly in the ruling world of Ireland. Many of them indeed belonged to it by birth. Between the accession of George III and the union two lord chancellors and thirty-four common law judges were appointed. Three out of the thirty-six, a lord chancellor and two chief justices of the common pleas, were Englishmen (all appointed in the early years of the reign); of the thirty-three Irishmen at least nineteen belonged to well-established families. For instance, Hewitt was the son of the lord chancellor, Gore was the son of a judge, Smyth was the son of a bishop, Tenison, Hamilton, Fitzgibbon and Downes were sons of M.P.s. Other judges clearly came from substantial backgrounds—a family must have had some resources to give a son a legal education—but Carleton's father, a Cork merchant, failed in business, Finucane was the son of an apothecary and Yelverton, though his father was described as 'generosus', entered Trinity as a sizar and maintained himself for some time after graduation as an usher in a school.[22]

The fact that between 1760 and 1801 no fewer than eight judges (including two lord chancellors) were ennobled is a sure indication of the respect with which contemporaries regarded the bench. This respect was not undeserved. A future judge could be helped on his advance to the woolsack or the bench by family influence and political connections—of the thirty-three Irish judges who have been referred to, thirty sat in the house of commons before receiving a judicial appointment, but the house of commons was a good testing-ground, and parliamentary experience could prove of considerable value to a judge. Moreover, when promoting members of a highly competitive and critical profession, the government was bound from self-interest to pick men of ability. Enough material survives to show that members of the bench could be learned, acute and humane. In political trials, judges (usually men of strong opinions) could be surprisingly fair and though individual judges were on occasion severely attacked and ridiculed, the judges of the superior courts as a body were respected.

The common law judges on circuit twice a year administered throughout Ireland civil and criminal justice but all over the country a vast amount of judicial business was continuously

---

[22] *Sketches of Irish political characters* (1799), pp. 13, 15.

handled by the justices of the peace, unpaid amateurs, usually country gentlemen. There were in Ireland at the close of the eighteenth century about 3,000 J.P.s, not an excessive number if absenteeism is taken into account—some magistrates having property at a distance from the county in which they held the commission of the peace, others being peers or M.P.s.[23] Justices of the peace granted warrants and took depositions. A single justice could hear and determine some petty criminal charges, two or more justices acting together had a more extensive jurisdiction, and the general or quarter sessions, which all the justices in the county could attend, had a very wide criminal jurisdiction, covering some felonies.[24] The system aroused relatively little comment in Ireland. The conspicuous and powerful role in the administration of justice assigned to the unpaid magistracy was accepted as natural, considering the part the county gentleman was expected to play in local public life. Early in the nineteenth century an embittered radical lawyer implied that J.P.s were often biased, arbitrary and ignorant—he was on the point of publishing a guide to their duties.[25] Theoretically a justice of the peace ought to have been acquainted with a considerable body of law, including the many statutes under which he was empowered to take action. Many J.P.s probably relied largely on common sense, scraps of legal lore and experience, though a conscientious magistrate could consult alphabetically arranged guides for justices of the peace. A magistrate's behaviour was bound to be greatly influenced by temperament and local conditions. An easy-going, sympathetic administration of the law might, in times of stress, be replaced by a flustered resort to strong measures. To what extent J.P.s in general exerted themselves in times of crisis is hard to say. During the period of acute tension in the late nineties active magistrates thought that many of their colleagues were not of much help. Norman Steele of Moynalty in Meath gave the chief secretary the names of 'the only four magistrates I have confidence in amongst those

---

[23] For the number of justices of the peace in each Irish county at the close of the eighteenth century see J. W. Stewart, *The gentleman's and citizen's almanack*, 1795–8.

[24] For the duties and powers of a justice of the peace see R. Bolton, *A justice of the peace for Ireland*, ed. R. Travers (1750), and L. MacNally, *The justice of the peace for Ireland*, 4 vols. (1812).

[25] L. MacNally, op. cit., i, pp. 1–5.

I have met and who are likely to make any use of the army'. The Revd Charles Warburton in County Armagh and Lord Cavan in County Londonderry complained in 1797 that men of property were deserting their houses and retreating into the towns. In Leinster Major Hardy, who commanded a militia regiment stationed in Wicklow, regretted that some of the magistrates were 'young at United work and though well disposed are fearful of giving offence'. Further south Robert Uniacke wrote that between his house and Dungarvan, eight miles to the west, and Waterford six miles to the east, there was not a single justice of the peace. Admittedly at Dungarvan there were two J.P.s, a clergyman 'frightened to death, and a layman crippled by gout'. In Westmeath, a very active magistrate grumbled about how 'all those who wished to conceal their offences from further investigation go to Mr Bond' —a J.P. in a neighbouring county.[26] A number of the more energetic magistrates were clergymen. At the close of the century just over 10 per cent of the magistracy were in orders and the clerical justice was likely to be resident, educated, public-spirited and acutely conscious of the dangers menacing the established order—after all tithe was one of the targets of the rural rioters. Unfortunately with the majority of the population, either catholics or dissenters, the clerical magistrate did not represent for most Irishmen an overawing fusion of spiritual and legal authority.

The weakness of the unpaid magistracy compelled the government to supplement it by paid professionals. In 1787 the lord lieutenant was empowered to appoint in certain disturbed counties, a barrister to act as 'a constant assistant' to the justices of the peace at general sessions, and in 1796 he was empowered to appoint an assistant barrister in every county. Besides being present at general sessions the assistant barrister, sitting in his own court, heard and determined civil bill cases. For almost a century a civil bill action had provided a cheap and simple method of deciding disputes concerning small debts. It had indeed proved so popular that the increased

---

[26] Cavan to ——, 13 Mar. 1797; C. Warburton to ——, 3 Apr. 1797; N. Steele to Pelham, 7 Apr. 1797 (I.S.P.O. 620/29/62, 172, 306); J. Hardy to Cooke, 19 Jan. 1798 (620/35/48); R. Uniacke to ——, 12 Nov. 1797 (620/33/46); T. Whitney to Pelham, 7 July 1797 (620/31/210).

business at assizes had tended to keep the assize judges away from Dublin for the whole vacation. The creation of efficient local courts both eased the burden on the assize judges and facilitated litigants.[27] The Irish police system was long-established, elaborate and weak. Its principal officers, both of medieval origin, were those of constable and watchman (responsible for the peace at night). The justices of the peace appointed a petty constable and watchman for each parish, seneschals of manors (or in their default the justices of the peace) appointed petty constables for their manors, and grand juries appointed a high constable for each barony.[28] Theoretically the constables and watchmen were chosen annually by the J.P.s from amongst the inhabitants but since the duties were onerous and substitutes were accepted, constables and watchmen during the eighteenth century were semi-permanent, paid officials. The constable, with powers accumulated over centuries, had a definite legal status. But in practice parish constables and watchmen were untrained, ill-supervised, poorly paid and therefore part-time, policemen. They were relatively few in number with geographically narrowly circumscribed zones of operation and the whole system provided a feeble and unsure support for law and order. If the peace was seriously threatened either by tough criminals or a disorderly mob, a vigorous magistrate, relying on the help of servants and friends might take successful counter-action. Often however magistrates and revenue officers were reduced to calling for military aid and small military detachments were continually being employed on police duties.

In 1784 a modest attempt was made to strengthen the system, grand juries being authorized to appoint four constables in each barony for the protection of public works and 'the maintenance of a good police'. Since the constable's salary was not to exceed £2 per annum he could scarcely be expected to devote himself exclusively to police work. A few years later, however, in 1786 the Irish administration—an administration directed by a few men very conscious of the importance of

---

[27] 27 Geo. III, c. 40,, 36 Geo. III c. 25; W. Disney, *A short history of the establishment of assistant barristers* (1799), p. 3.

[28] E. Bullingbrooke, *The duty and authority of the justices of the peace and parish officers for Ireland* (1788); 2 Geo. I, c. 10, 6 Geo. I, c. 10, 7 Geo. II, c. 12, 23 Geo. II, c. 14.

maintaining order—stimulated by the anti-tithe disturbances in Munster, introduced and passed a measure which faintly foreshadowed the creation of the Irish constabulary in the following century. An act for 'the better execution of the law', having repealed the act of 1784, empowered the lord lieutenant to divide any county into districts—consisting of baronies or half baronies. In each district there was to be a chief constable appointed by the lord lieutenant and sixteen sub-constables appointed by the grand jury. The county was to meet the expenses of the force, the chief constable being paid £50 and the sub-constables £12 per annum.[29] The act was immediately applied to four counties (Cork, Kerry, Kilkenny and Tipperary) and some years later a further seven counties were divided into districts. The act of 1787 was strongly criticized in the house of commons, as providing the government with the means 'to dragoon' the country and with extensive county patronage. It was an act, Todd Jones declared, 'suited not to France where it would not now be tolerated, but the meridian of Turkey'. Fitzgibbon retorted that it was better to have the public peace maintained by the civil power rather than by military force, and a few years later M.P.s from the counties, where the act was in operation, strongly approved of the new police system. It had been 'a common observation', Day declared, that Ireland had good laws but that they were never executed. However, he said, as a result of the 1787 act, Kerry was as well policed a county as Middlesex.[30] In 1792 a cheap alternative to the 1787 system was provided. It was enacted that the grand jury of any county (except the thirteen specifically exempted) might in every barony or half barony appoint eight constables, who were to be paid £4 per annum—obviously this type of baronial constable was not expected to be a full-time policeman. At the close of the century the county police in Ireland were thinly spread and not very effective. In the Athboy area (County Meath), shortly before the '98 insurrection, the police could not attend to their duties because they had to find other work, the chief constable having failed to pay them. If the Tipperary conditions were scandalous, constables keeping unlicensed whiskey houses and making no effort to preserve the peace, they were only a little better in Westmeath, where, it was said, the chief constables 'though they perform each matter well that is put into their hands—do not go about and inquire into the state of the district'.[31] From its sheer size and rapid growth, Dublin constituted an especial police problem, and in 1778 it was enacted that the lord mayor and aldermen should appoint an alderman 'to be president and guardian' of the policing of each parish. Assisted by a committee of householders, elected at a vestry meeting, he was to appoint constables and watchmen and have them properly 'clothed and armed'. The alderman was also empowered to enter licensed and unlicensed houses selling alcohol, and arrest all persons suspected of being 'robbers, thieves, or loose, idle or disorderly persons'. A conglomeration of small parish police forces was an inadequate means of preserving the peace of a large city, and in 1786 Fitzgibbon introduced and carried a police bill for Dublin, modelled on a measure for London which in the previous year had failed to pass at Westminster. The Dublin police act of 1786 set up a centralized police force under government control. The metropolitan police district was defined as the area lying within the Circular Road, together with Phoenix Park. Within that district three magistrates were appointed by the lord lieutenant, 'police commissioners for the preservation of the peace'. They were to have under their command a high constable, four chief constables and eighty constables (forty of whom were for night duty) and 400 watchmen, and they could call on the parish constables for assistance. There was to be a central police office and four divisional offices 'for transacting the business of a justice of the peace'. The expense of the force was to be met by a police rate. From the start the new police force was a subject of violent political controversy. Grattan described the 1786 bill as 'a bill of patronage not of police' and the force was attacked as being inefficient, lazy, officious and exceedingly costly. (It is only fair to add that it was also said that its activities were responsible for an influx of pickpockets, horse-stealers and house-breakers into the neighbouring counties.)[32]

---

[31] Norbury to A. Marsden, 13 Apr. 1803 (I.S.P.O. 620/50/39); G. Rochfort to ——, 2 Apr. 1798 (620/36/116); W. Tomkins to Castlereagh, 24 May 1798 (620/37/149).

[32] Parl. Reg. Ire., vi, p. 350; W. Wainwright to Fitzwilliam, 11 Mar. 1787 (W.W.M. F. 89).

The city liberals were very sensitive to any increase in government influence, rate-payers were hypercritical and the commissioners, who were engaged in an administrative experiment, were almost bound to make mistakes and certainly failed to practise rigid economy. In 1795 a compromise was arrived at, embodied in a bill introduced by the attorney general, which transferred the control of the force to the city authorities and provided for a wide measure of decentralization. A superintendent magistrate and two divisional magistrates, appointed by the corporation and approved by the lord lieutenant, were to be in charge of the metropolitan police district. They were to have under their command a high constable, two chief peace officers and fifty constables. In each parish the church wardens and vestry were to elect a watch committee which would appoint two constables and two sub-constables and watchmen to keep the peace at night.[33]

The Irish prisons were a grotesque aspect of eighteenth-century life. Each county and city of a county had a gaol, supervised by the grand jury, a body which held short and busy meetings at fairly long intervals. Many towns possessed a small local prison—a bridewell or dark hole. In Dublin there were not only Newgate, the great city prison, but the Bridewell, where some women criminals, minor offenders and lunatics were confined, and five debtors' prisons—the Four Courts marshalsea (the king's bench debtors' prison), the city marshalsea (for small debts), Saint Sepulchre's prison and Saint Thomas' marshalsea, and 'the Black dog', a prison near New Hall Market where both debtors and criminals were held, which was by 1783 in a ruinous condition. In addition there were at least three sponging-houses. The prisons held a miscellaneous population: persons awaiting trial, felons awaiting execution or transportation, lunatics, debtors and prisoners serving a sentence of imprisonment. This final category was comparatively small. Prisoners sentenced to hard labour were, it was pointed out in 1782, a nuisance, there being no way of employing them;[34] a prison being still regarded as a place of detention rather than an institution in which punishment could be combined with reform. The penalty for many offences

[33] 35 Geo. III, c. 36.
[34] *Commons' Jn. Ire.*, xi, pp. cxxx–cxxxiv, cccxxix.

was death, to which the humane alternative was transportation. At the beginning of the eighteenth century transportation to 'any of Her Majesty's plantations beyond the seas' received legislative sanction, and towards the middle of the century an average of about 130 convicts and vagabonds were being annually sent to America. During the war of Independence when transportation to America was 'found to be attended with various inconveniences', it was enacted that male convicts might be employed in improving Dublin harbour, and this legislation was continued after the war ended. Nevertheless, in the middle eighties convicts were again sent across the Atlantic, about 180 a year on average being shipped. During most of the century the high sheriff of each county made his own arrangements with a ship's captain for transportation but in 1786 the lord lieutenant was empowered to take the necessary steps for transporting convicts to His Majesty's plantations in America or to 'other places out of Europe'. A few years later a most awkward imbroglio occurred. When a cargo of eighty convicts from Ireland arrived off Newfoundland the admiral commanding the station would not permit them to be landed, directing the captain of the convict ship to proceed to Portsmouth. The result was an agitated correspondence involving the home secretary, the chief secretary, and the English and Irish lord chancellors. If the convicts were detained at Portsmouth writs of habeas corpus might be sought. If they were sent back to Ireland, it might be argued on their arrival that their sentence had been executed, and that they should be released. On hearing that the ship had sailed from Portsmouth the Irish government sent out a revenue cruiser to intercept it and persuade the captain to stay off the Irish coast until the legal conundrums were settled. Fortunately an ingenious legal solution was found. It was decided that as Newfoundland was not a plantation the convicts had by arriving there not been transported, so they were returned to gaol in Ireland. Shortly afterwards the Irish administration reluctantly, because of the expense, decided to dispatch convicts to the new penal settlement in New South Wales.[35]

Certainly the Irish prisons about the middle of the century

---

[35] 2 Anne, c. 12, 6 Anne, c. 11; *Commons' Jn. Ire.*, iv, pp. cclii, xiii, p. cccli; *Fortescue MS H.M.C.*, i, pp. 539-49, 551-2.

could have done little to improve their inmates. They were badly constructed, dark, damp, dirty, airless and insanitary. Since there were comparatively few compartments all types of prisoners were herded together. Debtors were sometimes compelled to rub shoulders with felons and children were locked up with hardened criminals, and 'consequently exposed to the most extreme degree of corruption and depravity'.[36] Prisoners sometimes had to sleep on a damp floor without bedding; in winter they were cold; they sometimes did not get their scanty bread allowance. As might be expected disease was rife and there were no special quarters for the sick. The number of prison officers in comparison to the number of prisoners was remarkably small—for instance in Newgate in 1783 where there could be up to 200 prisoners, the two gaolers were managing with half a dozen assistants. Discipline was naturally maintained by rough methods. Prisoners were sometimes kept in irons or confined in dungeons—the cells in Naas prison being so dark 'that there is no seeing without candles and [so] damp and filled with smokey vapours that candles will with difficulty burn'. On the other hand as whiskey could be easily smuggled in (it was handed through windows which looked into the street) and as indeed many gaolers owned a whiskey shop, spirits were easily available. There was much hard drinking and drunken violence. The gaoler was entitled to levy fees from prisoners and if a prisoner when the time came for his release was in debt to the gaoler, he might continue in detention. The corollary was that a well off prisoner could by a financial arrangement with the gaoler make himself comparatively comfortable in prison. The different levels of goal accommodation is simply illustrated by statistics from the Four Courts marshalsea. In 1786 nineteen prisoners between them occupied thirty rooms. Another twenty rooms were occupied by 114 prisoners with 'their numerous families'.[37]

The condition of prisoners—the Irish prisons in 1797 had about 1,600 inmates confined in concentrated misery in the centre of both the metropolis and every county town—challenged eighteenth-century benevolence. Many respectable and influential people, either as debtors—in Dublin there were

[36] *Commons' Jn. Ire.*, x, p. dxxxiv.
[37] Ibid., xi, p. cccxi; xii, p. lxxv.

about 1,500 arrests for debt in 1785[38]—or when visiting friends imprisoned for debt—gained first-hand experience of prison conditions. Moreover, charity was invigorated by self-interest. Prisons, it was recognized, were breeding-grounds for contagious disease, and it is significant that one of the first steps to be taken towards prison reform was the appointment in 1750 by the court of king's bench of a medical inspector for Newgate, 'to prevent contagious disease being brought into court' (the first medical inspector contracted gaol fever four times, but survived).[39] Early in the reign of George III the first of a long series of prison reform acts was placed on the statute book. It provided that in every gaol there should be distinct rooms for male and female prisoners, that the insane should be separated from the other prisoners, that the gaoler's fees should be examined by the grand jury and publicly exhibited, and that the incumbent of the parish in which the gaol was situate should distribute the prisoners' bread allowance and arrange when necessary for a sick prisoner to have medical attention. Fourteen years later a further measure empowered the justices at quarter sessions to take steps to improve the conditions of their local prison. They could direct that rooms should be scraped and washed and supplied with 'fresh air by hand ventilators'. They could also order that bathing tubs should be supplied, that a room should be set apart for the sick and that a medical man be appointed. The expense of these improvements was to be met by the grand jury. John Howard, who in 1778 paid the first of seven visits to Ireland, was much impressed by this legislation. But he soon discovered it was largely inoperative, a view confirmed by parliament in 1782 when it empowered the judges on assize to inquire into the execution of the acts and, if necessary, make orders and impose fines.[40]

In the seventies about the time the second prisons act was passed, Newgate was rebuilt. The grand jury and the Dublin corporation petitioned parliament on the grounds that it was 'a receptacle for criminals from all over the kingdom'. The corporation added an argument bound to strike home to M.P.s

[38] Ibid., xi, pp. ccccxiii–ccccxv.
[39] Ibid., viii, p. clxx.
[40] 3 Geo. III, c. 28, 17 & 18 Geo. III, c. 42; *Parl. Reg. Ire.*, viii, p. 443.

sitting in College Green—that 'an epidemic originating in the gaol had carried off many of the inhabitants of Dublin'. Parliament voted £3,000, the total cost of rebuilding amounting to £15,000. The money was not well spent. The new building was badly designed, passages and staircases being too narrow and there was insufficient provision for separation, debtors and felons, 'the highest and the lowest offenders', being confined together. The sewage was defective; the cells were 'stinking shocking places'; the bars on the windows were set in wood not in stone, and the walls, composed of small stones and bad cement were crumbling, so that escapes could be prevented only by stationing a sergeant's guard of military in the gaol. It was 'dirty beyond description' and the fire in the common hall 'generally encircled by the desperadoes of consequence', to the exclusion of the sick and feeble. The administration of the gaol at the beginning of the eighties was a standing disgrace to the capital. Whiskey was brought in large quantities from a shop in which the gaoler was said to have an interest. Intoxication was universal, there were frequent affrays, and some unfortunate prisoners were paying heavily for the privilege of sleeping in a vault 'to get away from the ruffians in the common hall among whom if they went to sleep they would be stripped and their clothes given for spiritous liquor'.[41]

In John Howard's opinion, Newgate was 'in every respect the very reverse of a perfect and well regulated gaol'.[42] Howard, whose strength lay in his ability to convey in plain language a powerful impression of conditions which he had investigated closely with a complete disregard of distaste and danger, devoted considerable attention to Irish gaols in his *State of the prisons*. He twice appeared before committees of the Irish house of commons and suggested the measure introduced by Hely-Hutchinson in 1783 which abolished the payment of gaol fees by prisoners who were acquitted, the gaoler being compensated by an allowance from the grand jury. The critics of this measure argued that it threw an unfair burden on the rates and an attempt to modify it in 1788 was narrowly defeated.

In 1785 the prison reformers, amongst whom Richard Griffith and Peter Holmes were prominent, secured the

[41] *Commons' Jn. Ire.*, xii, pp. dxxv, dccxxxiv–v; xv, p. cccvii.
[42] Ibid., x, p. dxxxiii.

appointment of a house of commons committee on gaols, which published some vivid evidence; and in 1786 they secured the enactment of a major prison reform measure 'for the avowed purpose of conjoining the exercise of humanity with the principles of true police'.[43] This measure was amended and improved in 1787 and in the same year a committee of the house of commons, which inquired into the Dublin gaols, emphatically declared that the Dublin corporation must take immediate steps to reform the city prisons. The corporation responded quickly by appointing a committee of aldermen and common council men to supervise the city prisons. The legislation of 1786-7 provided a sensible set of prison rules—cleanliness was to be enforced, the gaoler was not to sell spirits to prisoners, there was to be separation of the sexes, and three categories of prisoners, debtors, persons charged with capital offences and persons charged with lesser offences were to be kept apart. It was laid down the prisoners were to be supplied with blankets and bedding, that in each prison there were to be well-secured exercise yards, baths and a common hall with a large fire to which each category of prisoners was to be admitted in rotation. To prevent the legislation becoming a dead letter an inspectorate was instituted. The grand jury was to appoint an inspector and a surgeon for each prison. The inspector was to be the clergyman who distributed the bread allowance or 'some other fit and discreet person', and was to be responsible for seeing the regulations were obeyed. There was also to be an inspector-general, appointed by the lord lieutenant, who was to visit prisons, advise grand juries and report to parliament.

The legislation of 1786-7 provided minimum standards of prison administration and rudimentary machinery for enforcing them. The first inspector-general, Sir Jerome Fitzpatrick, a medical man who had written a work on disease in prisons, threw himself into his work with great enthusiasm, until he left Ireland in 1793 to become inspector of military hospitals in England. His successor, Foster Archer, a Cork clergyman with an interest in journalism, wrote concise, telling reports and made a pioneering effort to compile judicial statistics. Fitzpatrick, shortly before he left Ireland, described in glowing terms the change in prison conditions which had occurred in

---

[43] Ibid., xii, p. dccxxxvi.

recent years. Extortion had been put down, intoxication greatly diminished, the sick were being humanely treated, cleanliness and separation between the sexes and different categories of prisoner were being strictly enforced. Thirteen gaols had been rebuilt, four had been improved and eight were being rebuilt. He also drew attention to the fact that the Dublin Bridewell had been turned into a penitentiary, where criminals, especially the young, might be reformed by imprisonment 'accompanied by well regulated labour and religious instruction'. By 1793 a few of the inmates had been placed in trades in Dublin but with the outbreak of war the male convicts from the Bridewell were enlisted in the forces. About the same time the chaplain of Newgate, who in the middle eighties had been a severe critic of its administration, declared that 'subordination and discipline reigned' and that the divine service was regularly performed in the chapel (which Howard had found to be unused), many felons attending 'with propriety and decency'.[44] Generally speaking the progress of reform was slower than Fitzpatrick implied. As Howard put it, 'there is a spirit of improvement, but it has to struggle with the vice of persons from the highest to the lowest who make a job of public institutions' (ironically enough Howard's 'steady friend' in Ireland was Hely-Hutchinson).[45] Moreover, the spirit of improvement fluctuated. Prison reform bills, introduced by Richard Griffith in 1788 and 1789, failed to pass. In 1794 a society for the reform of the criminal poor was founded in Dublin, the members taking an especial interest in the Bridewell. But after a few years 'when the novelty of visiting prisons was satisfied by repetition' the society rapidly declined.[46] At the close of the century Fitzpatrick's successor noted that in a few prisons prisoners were still kept in irons. In one (Limerick city) fees were extorted from prisoners who had not been indicted. At least half a dozen prisons were conspicuously dirty, in some spirits were still available. In Monaghan gaol the bread allowance was being irregularly distributed, the inspector (a local clergyman) being careful to avoid

[44] Ibid., x, p. dxxxiii; xv, p. ccccviii.
[45] J. Field, *Correspondence of John Howard* (1855), p. 140.
[46] *Commons' Jn. Ire.*, xv, p. ccccviii; *The inspector general's report on the state of the prisons in Ireland*, H.C. (239), 1808, ix; *The inspector general's report on the state of the prisons for the year 1818*, p. 32, H.C. (534), 1819, xii; J. W. Stewart, *The gentleman's and citizen's almanack* 1798, 1800.

a meeting with the inspector-general. In eight or nine prisons the water supply was defective—at Kilmainham, Archer remarked, 'the Sabbath is so strictly observed by those that take charge of the forcing engine that the gaol is invariably without water on Sunday'. But it is only fair to say that there were also many conscientious inspectors as well as humane gaolers, Archer emphasizing how, when Carlow gaol was 'vastly overcrowded, . . . from the attention and professional skill of Mr Graham, who is both surgeon and inspector of the gaol, no epidemic sickness prevailed within it'. Archer also reported that some of the new gaols, built by contract or lump work were constructed of inferior materials. Twenty-five years later all Irish prisons were to be condemned out of hand as having been built before sound principles of prison architecture had been evolved. Early in the new century a strong committee of inquiry summed up the Irish prison situation by reporting that though the acts of 1786 and 1787 'had not been fully carried into execution' (from their own report rather an understatement) solid improvement had been achieved; and it obliquely indicated that one reason for reform being retarded was the lack of public spirit and administrative drive shown by many Irish country gentlemen.[47]

The machinery for the maintenance of law and order in Ireland was at the close of the eighteenth century clearly defective. Its inefficiency was strikingly illustrated by the low conviction rate at assizes—suggesting either a reckless proclivity to prosecute or that the guilty often escaped, or probably both. Well-organized criminal activities which had some popular support, such as smuggling or illicit distillation, could, especially in the more desolate areas, be conducted in defiance of magistracy and police. In an agricultural country with small urban centres a weak and inefficient system for law enforcement largely manned by amateurs could, with community backing, cope with ordinary crime, but it was certainly not devised to withstand extraordinary strains. And during the later eighteenth century it was intermittently subject to severe strain by endemic agrarian trouble. In Ulster during the summer of

---

[47] *Commons' Jn. Ire.*, xvii, p. dcix; xviii, p. cclxi; xix, pp. dcccviii, dccxxii; *Report from the commissioners appointed to inquire into . . . state prisons and other gaols in Ireland*, pp. 32–3 H.C. (265), 1809, vii.

1763 bodies of oak-boys (their badge was an oak leaf) assembled with banners and bands ('drums, horns, fiddles and bagpipes'). They were determined to resist exorbitant county cesses, insisting that no money should be spent on by-roads or 'private roads'. They also attacked tithe, especially small dues, and an oak-boy manifesto, published in County Derry, denounced the 'high flying clergy' 'who would overset the Church of God . . . and our most undefiled Church of Scotland' and impose on Ireland a popish pretender. Some gentlemen were compelled to agree to support the oak-boys' objectives and a number of clergymen and of tithe farmers found in Londonderry 'a city of refuge'. But the supporters of lawful authority quickly asserted themselves. Lord Hillsborough, the great County Down magnate, hurried over from England and tried to mobilize public opinion by the novel course of writing to the newspapers. Pointing out that all the freeholders he had talked to lamented the disturbances which discredited 'the once civilized province of Ulster', he called on his neighbours to assist him in keeping the peace. A few energetic magistrates with small military detachments dispersed crowds of insurgents; near Newtownlimavady the Revd James Knight, rector of Drumbagh and a sometime fellow of Trinity, at the head of three companies of foot defeated a large party of oak-boys, and parties of dragoons patrolling the countryside restored order. The government was less successful in its legal campaign. Though a number of insurgents were brought to trial at the autumn assizes most of them seem to have been acquitted and there was only one capital conviction. At Enniskillen when Robert Crawford, said to be worth £2,000, was charged with being an oak-boy colonel, he declared that he had been 'forced which is the general plea' and after a trial lasting six hours, was found not guilty.[48]

Similar trouble surged up again in 1770. The earl of Donegall leased some large holdings to Belfast businessmen, who seem to have raised rents and changed the use of the land from arable to pasture, evicting tenants. When a man accused of houghing cattle as a protest was arrested and lodged in Belfast gaol, a large body of men calling themselves Hearts of Steel descended

---

[48] *Free. Jn.*, 9, 26, 30 July, 2, 6, 13 Aug., 11 Oct. 1763; *Exshaw's Gentleman's Magazine*, Nov. 1763; J. Morrison to —— ,30 Sept. 1763 (W.W.M. Bk.).

on the town, secured his release and burned the house of a well-known liberal who was one of Lord Donegall's new lessees. Disturbances directed against tithe, cess, and what were regarded as unfair leases spread through the counties of Antrim, Down, Armagh, Londonderry and Tyrone. The government was alarmed, military reinforcements were hurried to the north and in 1772 it was enacted that persons charged with certain offences in the disturbed counties could be brought to trial in Dublin, since 'wicked persons' expected to be acquitted by the petty juries in these counties. This act was repealed in the autumn of 1773, all by then being quiet.[49]

Munster from the early sixties was disturbed by levellers or whiteboys as they tended to be called (their uniform being a shirt worn over their clothes). By 1762 their activities, which included breaking down the fencing of deer-parks and enclosures, raiding houses and maltreating the unpopular, were attracting considerable attention. Usually they tried to avoid contact with the military but in November 1764 a small party of dismounted dragoons, escorting prisoners to Kilkenny, were attacked by a large party of whiteboys armed with 'guns, swords, bill hooks and hatchets', and overwhelmed. It was said that the main causes of discontent were the cost of potato patches, hearth money and tithes. The aims of one group of whiteboys was summed up in the dying declaration of Darby Brown, one of five men executed at Waterford for burning the cottage of a tenant near Cappoquin. They had agreed, he said, to pull down the ditches erected on commons, 'for trespassing on which our cattle have often been pounded'; 'to do all in our power to hinder anyone from taking the little concerns we held, when out of lease'; 'not to permit tithe farmers to meddle with tithe but to pay it direct to the parson'; and 'to be true to Sive and her children'.[50] This last proviso expresses in language drawn from the mythology of folklore the feeling of simple men that they belonged to a large, historic and oppressed community. In eighteenth-century Munster, with much of the land owned by protestants and county administration a protestant monopoly, some catholics, even though economically

[49] G. Benn, *History of Belfast*, i, pp. 611–20; 11 & 12 Geo. III, c. 65.
[50] *Pue's Occurrences*, 15 Mar., 13 July 1762, 13 Oct. 1764, 19 Apr. 1766; *Letters of George III*, ii, p. 313.

comfortably off, must have seen themselves as belonging to the oppressed community, and this combined with the general lay dislike of tithe, explains the presence of men of some substance amongst the whiteboys. This was to Munster protestants anomalous and alarming, and convinced some active magistrates that they were confronted by a well-organized catholic conspiracy, which could rely on French aid (it was reported that the whiteboys in Kilkenny swore 'to be true to the king of France in order to make Ireland their own').[51] The Irish administration issued a *démenti*, emphasizing that in its opinion the disturbances were not religious in origin, and two vigorous Tipperary J.P.s may have been disconcerted to find in the papers of a parish priest whom they arrested documents from his bishop directing him to suppress the levellers if they appeared in his parish.[52] However the parish priest of Clogheen in Tipperary, Father Nicholas Sheehy, was suspected of being a leader of the whiteboys, and in February 1766 he was brought to trial in Dublin on a charge of high treason. He was found not guilty, but was immediately rearrested, charged with being concerned in the murder of a crown witness in his parish, and sent to Clonmel to be tried at the assizes. Sheehy and four other men charged with the murder were found guilty and executed. Since Sheehy was in orders and three of his fellow accused 'lived in affluence . . . and associated with the gentlemen of the neighbourhood', the trials naturally aroused intense interest. Some active J.P.s, eager to secure convictions, put considerable pressure on witnesses, and strenuous efforts were made to obtain evidence for the defence. The assize judges were respected lawyers; it was said that steps were taken to secure impartial juries, but the evidence was conflicting to a degree which suggests the possibility of perjury, and given the climate of County Tipperary opinion it was almost impossible for the legal machine to work with impartial precision in a case so packed with political and social implications. It was rumoured that French officers had landed in the south of Ireland, that Sheehy had admitted to having been engaged in criminal activities and that the murdered man had been seen alive in Newfoundland. Many protestants regarded Sheehy as a danger-

---

[51] *Pue's Occurrences*, 19 Apr. 1766.
[52] *London Gazette*, May 1762; *Pue's Occurrences*, 8 May 1762.

ous conspirator, while to the Tipperary peasantry he was a martyr. To a not unsympathetic observer, Sheehy was 'a giddy, officious, but not ill meaning man, with somewhat of a quixotic cast of mind towards the relieving of all those, whom he fancied to be injured or distressed', and therefore it is not unlikely that he may have had contacts with the whiteboys and have condoned their activities, even if he was, to use his own ambiguous phrase, 'innocent of the facts for which I was sentenced'.[53]

In the middle eighties the whiteboys, or rightboys, were again conspicuously active in Munster and south-west Leinster. They began by opposing tithe, the rates charged and the methods of collection. They then advanced to attacking the fees and dues paid to the catholic clergy, declaring them to be excessive and fixing maxima. They also tried in some areas 'to raise the rates of labourers, to confine the labour of the peasantry to their own respective parishes, to prescribe bounds to the hearth money and other taxes, to determine the rent, value and mode of taking lands, in short . . . by a sort of agrarian law', to place all property owners in 'subjection to the will of the mere peasantry'.[54] The movement spread rapidly from parish to parish, the whiteboys demonstrating their power by moving about the country in armed bands, holding at times great gatherings, posting up threatening notices, raiding houses, inflicting savage punishments on unpopular persons, tithe proctors or tithe farmers, erecting gallows and menancing with brutal violence protestant clergymen and catholic priests. In one instance in County Tipperary they stormed a rectory and severely wounded the rector—'the said outrage', a proclamation declared, 'proceeded from professional not personal prejudice', being intended to intimidate the protestant clergy.[55] Many country gentlemen, though warned by the defenders of ecclesiastical rights that an attack on tithe was a threat to property in general, seem to have felt little sympathy with the clergy, whom they regarded as rentiers whose income rights lacked the sanctity attached to real and personal property. The

[53] Exshaw's Gentleman's Magazine, 1766, pp. 127, 191, 244–8, 370–6; Pue's Occurrences, 15 Feb., 18 May., 19 Apr. 1766; A. O'Leary, Defence . . . (1787), p. 20.
[54] An address to the nobility and gentry. By a layman (1786), p. 22; A candid inquiry into the causes and motives of the late riots in the province of Munster (London) 1767, p. 7.
[55] Dublin Gazette, 30 May 1786.

County Cork J.P.s were said to have displayed 'inactivity and inexertion'.[56] Emergency legislation was quickly enacted—an act against tumultuous assemblies, a county police act and a measure enabling ecclesiastical persons to annul contracts for tithe made under duress, and providing a speedy procedure for recovering tithe arrears for 1786.[57] The government sent General Lord Luttrell (who had shown himself in the house of commons unsympathetic to the claims of tithe owners) to take command of the forces in Munster; active magistrates exerted themselves; the military in a few small engagements put parties of insurgents to flight and the troubles died down.

All these waves of agrarian trouble had features in common. Starting with local incidents, the disorder, spreading by con- tagious example, flared up over wide areas. Neighbours would be drawn together by concrete grievances, a sense of injustice or severely felt economic pressures. A subtle, scarcely perceived irritation may have been provided by price movements. The later eighteenth century was an era of rising prices and in such an era unorganized and ill-informed labour may find it difficult to keep remuneration in line with the cost of living and even those who may be making a net gain will probably resent the increases which hit them. In the disturbed areas the bolder spirits by dramatic acts of defiance, the imposition of oaths, nocturnal activity and savage assaults, and by occasionally bringing large numbers together in great gatherings, would create an impression of power and drive which would sweep the quiet and timid into their ranks. It is hard to estimate the magnitude of these disturbances. Sensational incidents of direct action are reported but the statistical returns which would indicate how far the general pattern of crime was altered by the great outbursts of agrarian trouble are not available. According to a parliamentary return, at the summer assizes of 1786, 126 'rightboys' were brought to trial (104 in Munster) and 26 convicted (20 in Munster).[58] The scanty newspaper reports for the 1763–5 assizes in the disturbed areas also suggest

---

[56] D. Trant, *Considerations on the present disturbances in the province of Munster* (1787), p. 6. Trant was about the time he published his pamphlet appointed an assistant barrister in County Tipperary (*H.J.*, 21 Sept. 1787); *Cork Evening Post*, 18 Dec. 1786.

[57] 27 Geo. III, cc. 15, 36, 40.

[58] *Commons' Jn. Ire.*, xii, pp. dxxviii–dxxix.

that only comparatively small groups of agrarian rioters were brought to trial and few convicted.

In 1787 a large Cork landowner, Richard Longfield (who seems to have been biased against clerical tithe owners) told the house of commons that the Munster disturbances were being absurdly magnified in Dublin. He himself had seen few signs of unrest. It was immediately pointed out that Longfield, living in a prosperous part of County Cork, 'in the midst of his tenantry with a number of servants and dependents', was in a position very different to that of a small landowner wondering every night if his house would be attacked.[59] The bishop of Cloyne, having spoken of Munster in 1786 as being 'in a state of savage anarchy', gave seventeen specific instances of clergymen in the dioceses of Cork and Cloyne being menaced in a terrifying way by armed bands (though not apparently in any instance being subjected to personal injury) and the catholic archbishop of Cashel, when insisting that his church had also suffered at the hands of the insurgents, wrote of six named parish priests being menaced and of fifty chapels being nailed up in Munster and Kilkenny.[60] For the victims these incidents were undoubtedly painful. But the number of incidents cited and the assizes reports, while they indicate grave disorder in certain areas, scarcely suggest a well-planned, sustained assault on the established order. Alarmed conservatives seem to have visualized a general strike against tithe, possibly developing into a great social mutiny. But in fact the insurgents' aims were vague and limited; their organization was cohesive only on a local level and they were easily discouraged by determined action by energetic magistrates and small packets of disciplined troops.

There was a third important sphere into which the state was advancing, though only tentatively, and to a great extent ineffectually, education. In the sixteenth century the state had founded a university and directed the established church to provide a national network of primary and secondary schools, supplemented by royal schools founded in the seventeenth century. During the eighteenth century parliament at least

---

[59] *Parl. Reg. Ire.*, viii, pp. 22–4.
[60] R. Woodward, *The present state of the Church of Ireland* (1786), pp. 97–104; Butler, *A Justification of the tenets of the Roman Catholic religion* (1787) pp. 25–7.

subsidized two institutions of higher education and was considering large-scale intervention in Irish education. The apex of the Irish educational system in the eighteenth century was the university of Dublin, Trinity college, which grew in numbers and expanded architecturally. At the beginning of the century a large new square, one side of which was formed by the great ponderous library and the other three by red-brick terraces, was built to the east of the college. Before the middle of the century, a dining hall with a graceful pilastered front, had been built to the north-east of the library square, and during the second half of the century the west end of the college was rebuilt, the older buildings being replaced by a fine Palladian front on College Green, with inward turning wings, terminating on the south side by a large public theatre and on the north by a chapel, opened during the '98 rebellion, which formed parliament square. The sweep and style of the square were on a scale and of a magnificence unusual in academic life, and reflected Trinity's position as the university of the Irish governing world. University and parliament were separated by only a small stretch of grass: many M.P.s were Trinity graduates, undergraduates if gowned were admitted to the galleries of the house of commons, and two outstanding eighteenth-century provosts, Francis Andrews and Hely-Hutchinson, were prominent politicians. Andrews, one of the few lay fellows, was M.P. for Londonderry and a leading privy councillor. A cultured man of the world and bon vivant, he was responsible for building the provost's house, an elegant urban mansion, befitting a peer or M.P. rather than the head of an academic community. Hutchinson, a successful lawyer, on Andrew's death in 1774 successfully pressed for the provostship to be treated as a political prize, and then won it. Hutchinson's efforts to turn the university constituency into a close borough, his autocratic use of the provost's powers (or of the powers which he believed the provost to possess), and his tendency to discuss and settle academic problems from the standpoint of a man of the world, rather than that of a hidebound don, made him very unpopular amongst the fellows. During his term of office there were two bitterly contested elections in college, each followed by an election petition and the second by a visitation which ended in the provost being censured for what seemed to be a partial use of his quasi-paternal powers for political purposes. Hutchinson survived these storms. He managed twice to secure a parliamentary seat for a son, he obtained a peerage for his family, and he realized some of his plans for the 'improvement and enlargement' of the college. Anxious to broaden the curriculum, so that Trinity graduates would be accomplished gentlemen as well as scholars, he urged that composition in Latin and English should be encouraged, that modern languages be taught, that senior and junior common rooms, 'supplied with newspapers, tea and coffee' be established, and a riding house built. His educational policy, he pointed out, would make 'young gentlemen of fortune . . . more capable of receiving improvement from their travels', and would enable graduates who became tutors in private families, to be 'more useful to their pupils' ('It is well known', the worldly-wise provost remarked, 'what beneficial consequences are frequently derived to the tutors from such connections').[61] Hutchinson's approach to higher education aroused the contemptuous ridicule of a senior fellow, Patrick Duigenan, a man of great and quaint erudition, rough manners and a talent for crude and humorous vituperation. Duigenan attacked the provost for being illiterate, greedy, vain and married, painting a grim picture of the college paths and gardens, hitherto sacred to 'the sober academick', invaded by the provost, his daughters, military officers on prancing horses and 'his infant children, their nurses and go-carts'.[62]

Though Hutchinson was 'almost stung to death by obtruding into the hive of the academics',[63] by bringing a powerful mind trained in politics to bear on academic matters he conferred considerable benefits on the college. He encouraged the professors to lecture, secured a government endowment for two chairs in modern languages, arranged for the college estates to be surveyed and rents to be raised, was largely responsible for the legislation which established the school of physic on a satisfactory basis, and was instrumental in securing large building grants from parliament, being convinced that 'great public

---

[61] *An account of some regulations made in Trinity college, Dublin* (1775); Hutchinson's History of T.C.D. Bk. 12 (T.C.D. MS 1774).
[62] P. Duigenan, *Lachrymae academicae* (1777), p. 155.
[63] *Correspondence of Edmund Burke,* viii, p. 19.

buildings raise the reputation of a seminary of learning, attaching the students to the place of their education, and to the country in which they have received it, and contribute in a considerable degree to raise that national emulation so favourable to the cultivation of science'. The great public theatre, completed in 1788, a few years later provided a setting for a visitation to decide a number of matters in dispute between the provost and a strong group of fellows. The visitation may be said to have ended in a draw, with the visitor, the lord chancellor, exhorting both parties to keep the peace, but the fellows soon began a vigorous campaign to ensure that Hutchinson's successor should be chosen from their own ranks. Two deputations of fellows were sent to England and when Hutchinson died his successor was a senior fellow, Richard Murray, the author of a textbook on logic.

The staff comprised seven senior fellows, who with the provost formed the board, the governing body of the college, fifteen junior fellows, who were tutors and lecturers and filled some of the chairs, and ten non-fellow professors, two of whom (the regius professor of divinity and the professor of feudal and English laws) were sometime fellows, and six of whom were connected with the medical school. Vacancies amongst the fellows were filled on the results of a competitive examination, conducted publicly and viva voce. On election a fellow (with rare exceptions) was obliged to take orders, and celibacy was a condition of holding fellowship. But there was no machinery for discovering whether or not a fellow had married. Many of them did marry while in office, their wives continuing to be known socially by their maiden names—a custom bound to be productive of ribald humour. Of course once a fellow resigned he could admit he had committed matrimony and of the eighteenth-century fellows rather over half left college on securing ecclesiastical preferment—in most instances a college living. Of the remainder, a few resigned, some died young, a few were deprived of fellowship. Of the men holding fellowship during the century only about one in four spent a full lifetime in academic work.

The life of a junior fellow was fairly exacting. He was expected to teach his own pupils in his chambers and he might have to give university lectures. Trinity, a comparatively recent foundation, which functioned under the eyes of parliament and parents, was an efficient educational institution. There was for each of the four undergraduate years an examination at the beginning of each term, conducted viva voce, with premiums for the best answerers, and all undergraduates had to take a number of these examinations before graduating. The undergraduate course, comprising classics, mathematics and philosophy, was comprehensive within conventional limits, and undergraduate enterprise supplemented it. In 1770 the College Historical society was formed, an undergraduate debating society which encouraged the study of history, awarded medals in oratory and composition and bred an awareness of contemporary issues. Hely-Hutchinson strongly supported the society, but after his death its sturdy independence was regarded by the board as a threat to discipline and at the close of 1794 the society was expelled from college. Within a few months it was allowed to return only to be expelled again in 1815.

In the nineties the undergraduate course was criticized by a contributor to a liberal newspaper who deplored the excessive importance attached to formal logic, the limited range of classical authors studied, and the absence of modern languages, chemistry, anatomy, botany, medicine, electricity, oratory, history and poetry. He also thought the fellows over-remunerated and their lectures dull. About the same time the course was cautiously criticized by Robert Burrowes, the headmaster of a Royal school and sometime fellow. He began by emphasing that the universities should 'not be repositories of the half-formed theories of the day, nor . . . mausolea of deceased pedantry'. He suggested that lucid, compact textbooks specially prepared for undergraduate use should replace the recommended portions of major works, and wanted two subjects added to the course, chemistry and political economy, which would include both economic theory and history.[64]

During the last thirty years of the century the number of undergraduates seems to have nearly doubled, there being at the close of the century between 500 and 600 names on the books. The entrance registers throw some light on the social composition of the undergraduate body, a completed entry

---

[64] Letters in *D.E.P.*, Sept. and Oct. 1795; R. Burrowes, *Observations on the course of science taught at present in Trinity college, Dublin* (1792).

for an undergraduate giving his father's name and description. The description (which was in Latin) might be either a profession or occupation, or it might be indicative of status—peer, baronet, knight, armigerous or gentleman. On the basis of the father's description the undergraduate body at the close of the eighteenth century can be divided into four categories. The first the sons of persons of recognized social position; the second the sons of professional men, clergymen, lawyers, soldiers, with a sprinkling of civil servants and a few artists, a musician, a sculptor, a painter; the third the sons of businessmen, most of whom were described as merchant; the fourth of sons of persons of relatively humble occupations—largely farmers, with a land steward, and a minor civil servant (a tide-waiter). In considering the first category it might be argued that the term 'gentleman' is vague; and that unlike the other qualifications indicating social status, its applicability is to some extent subjective, though in a status-conscious community the fear of ridicule must have provided a check on youthful presumption. Again some of the fathers are described by terms, *mechanicus*, *sartor* (tailor), *fabor lignarius* (carpenter), which might conceivably mean a master or a journeyman. But where other evidence is available, it seems they meant the former, that is to say, a shopkeeper or manufacturer—Theobald Wolfe Tone's father for instance, who was a successful coach-builder, being described as *mechanicus*. So the undergraduates concerned have been placed in the third category. Apothecaries (*pharmacopolae*) and schoolmasters (*ludimagistri*) present problems. Apothecaries might be considered as being on the fringe of the professional world, but they have been classed with businessmen. If it appears that a schoolmaster was a graduate he is treated as a professional man. If there is no evidence he graduated, it has been assumed he was on the level of a village schoolmaster and his sons have been placed in category four. Finally, it need hardly be said that the four categories do not correspond closely to economic groupings. A well-off merchant must have had a larger income than many army officers or clergymen, and a substantial farmer might have been considerably better off than a small businessman. Accepting therefore that the categories employed have only a limited significance, taking the entrance for the last quarter of the century (1775–1800) of the undergraduates whose fathers' status or occupation is given, slightly over 45 per cent belonged to the first category; 31 per cent to the second; over 14 per cent to the third; and 9 per cent to the fourth. It is scarcely surprising that the undergraduate body was largely recruited from landed and professional families and its composition reflects how in eighteenth-century Irish society land and the professions overshadowed commerce and manufacturing—'trade'. But the fact that almost a quarter of the undergraduates had businesses or farming backgrounds shows that there was some degree of social mobility. For instance, Thomas Gannon, whose father was described as 'operarius' (labourer or small farmer), entered as a sizar in 1800 and was elected to fellowship in 1813. Curran's father was a seneschal of a manor court (a very lowly judicial office) and it was only through the generous kindness of a well-off clergyman that Curran was able to go to a grammar school. When at Trinity, in addition to his sizarship, he received 'scanty remittances' from home; when reading for the bar in London he lived very economically, earned something by literary work and apparently received some financial help from his clerical benefactor.[65]

Trinity college was the only Irish university, though by the close of the century there were two other institutions in Ireland affording education on the higher level—the Royal college of Saint Patrick, Maynooth, and the Royal college of surgeons, founded in 1785 as both an examining and teaching institution, with a wartime market in the army and navy. If the peak of the Irish educational pryamid was narrow, the strata below were wide, sprawling and not always easily distinguishable. Sixteenth-century legislation had imposed on the clergy of the established church the duty of maintaining an 'English', that is to say a primary school, in each parish and a diocesan or grammar school in each diocese; and Charles I had founded and endowed five grammar schools, the royal schools, in Ulster. Towards the close of the eighteenth century rather less than half of the beneficed clergy maintained a school, and as for the diocesan schools, out of a potential of thirty-four, only fourteen were

---

[65] C. Phillips, *Recollections of Curran* (1818), p. 15. An English traveller reported that the annual allowance for a pensioner was £80 and for a fellow commoner £150 (C. Abbot, A tour). These estimates seem rather high.

functioning and of these eight could scarcely be regarded as efficient—for instance the Clogher school room had neither floor nor ceiling. Of the Royal schools, Armagh, under the eye of the primate, had a good reputation; Enniskillen had new buildings and an able headmaster with three competent assistants; and Raphoe had a keen headmaster, anxious to improve the buildings. Cavan was in decline, and Dungannon had only a few small boys. However, the headmaster of Dungannon, the Revd William Moore, was comfortably off, having arranged to have the school estate undervalued and then to obtain a lease of the lands on very advantageous terms. But at the beginning of the nineteenth century the primate intervened and school's fortunes began to improve.

There were also a number of endowed schools of private foundation—nine grammar schools, a dozen 'English' or primary schools and the charter schools. Of the grammar schools, Kilkenny, with a headmaster nominated by the board of Trinity college, was flourishing. The place of the parish school was to some extent taken by the 'pay' school. Throughout Ireland a large number of private school masters, in barns or even under hedges, for small payments, instructed children in at least the rudiments—reading, writing and arithmetic. The teachers were themselves products of the system and many of them were remarkable men, avid scholars, prepared to teach a wide range of subjects, proud of their vocation, enthusiastic and capable of kindling great enthusiasm in some of their pupils—there were said to be countrymen taught in the pay schools who knew Latin and Greek. Some of the teachers prided themselves on being custodians of the Gaelic tradition, some were men of light and leading amongst their neighbours, letter writers, amateur attorneys, secretaries of radical clubs. Of course they were a variegated body, unorganized and uninspected. According to a harsh critic some pay-school masters gave undue attention to those pupils whose parents provided generous hospitality. Moreover, work in the fields must often have competed with education for the children's time and many small farmers and labourers must have found even the small payments required a formidable demand on their resources. Nevertheless the pay schools, in which, early in the nineteenth century, about 400,000 children were being taught, are a striking example of what can be achieved by private enterprise in the educational sphere and their existence vividly demonstrates a widespread respect for learning amongst the Irish country people and the determination of many parents to obtain, even at a heavy cost to themselves, advantages for their children.[66]

Some of the more successful pay schools must have formed a part of an obscure but very important segment of British and Irish education, middle-class private schools. At the close of the century there were a good many of these scattered throughout Ireland divided into classical schools (schools in which the classics predominated, though a wide range of subjects might be taught), 'mercantile academies', which concentrated on modern languages, mathematics and even book-keeping, preparing youth for trade 'foreign and domestic', and schools for young ladies. In 1800 there were in Dublin and its suburbs at least sixteen classical schools, eight mercantile academies and four schools for young ladies. Cork had at least five private schools, Belfast four, and there were many others. The advertisements for these schools suggest what middle-class Irish parents were looking for. For their daughters, ladylike accomplishments, of which French was the most important academically; for their sons a good education which would prepare for the army, the navy, the university or the counting house (business). The product aimed at seems to have been 'the sound scholar, the finished orator and the polished gentleman'. Abraham Shackleton, however, the headmaster of the famous school at Ballitore and a member of the Society of friends, warned parents that he 'would not teach that part of the academic course which he conceived to be injurious to morals and subversive of sound principles, especially those authors who recommend in seducing language, the illusions of love and the abominable trade of war'. Parents were clearly concerned about health. The Revd Mr Marane, a Tipperary parish priest, emphasized that his academy (classical and mathematical) was housed on a dry site, near a small river with

[66] Report of the commissioners of Irish education inquiry 1791, printed in *Endowed schools, Ireland, commission evidence*, ii, pp. 341–79, H.C. (2336), 1857–8, xxii; *Report of the commissioners of the board of education*, in H.C. (142), 1809, vii; P. J. Dowling, *The hedge schools of Ireland* (1935). For a hostile account of pay-school teachers see *Association for discountenancing vice and promoting religion, reports*, 1800.

facilities for bathing. Other headmasters emphasized 'an extensive playground', 'an airy house', sea bathing and goats' whey for 'delicate young gentlemen', and a separate bed for each boy. At Jones's classical school in Crumlin this was an extra, but at Rathmines school not only had each pupil his own bed but boys were made to wash their hands and face every day. Parents were also concerned about the cost of education. A middle-class father must often have found the school fees, which ranged from 24 to 40 guineas per annum for a boarder, and which could be increased by extras—charges for washing, mending, hair-cutting, stationery, fencing and winter coal— a severe burden, and one headmaster advertised his school, in a phrase calculated to appeal to many middle-class parents, as 'cheap and genteel'. Some schools stressed that their fees were comprehensive, or that they prepared their pupils as speedily as possible. Admittedly one headmaster, Barry of Rathmines school, came out strongly against sending boys 'immature in age' to the university. But Barry was clearly aiming at a prosperous clientele, and it may be added that a critical visitor to his school pronounced that everything there 'is constructed for shew—the doctor gave audience in his study profusely decorated with gilt calf and morocco, globes etc. but the boys' dining hall into which I peeped was dark and dirty'.[67]

Towards the close of the eighteenth century there was increasing attention given to education in Ireland. Not only was great importance attached to the influence of education on the individual character (a well known country gentleman educated his sons on the principles expounded by Rousseau in *Émile*) but education was seen as an instrument of social improvement, a panacea perhaps all the more valued because its effects were immeasurable. Thomas Percy, bishop of Dromore, and an eminent man of letters, having dwelt on the outstanding characteristics of the Irish peasantry—'naturally open, generous and good natured, exceedingly hospitable and liberal of their little store' but lawless and lazy—and then having asked how 'whole nests of rioters and robbers' are changed into 'rising nurseries of virtuous and useful subjects'—

---

[67] *D.E.P.*, 9 Dec. 1786, 8 Jan. 1791, 12, 14 Jan. 1792, 18 Sept., 19 Aug. 1800; *Dublin Chronicle*, 25 July 1789; C. Barry, *Plan for Rathmines school* (1790), p. 3; Journal kept in Dublin, 5 Oct. 1801 (R.I.A. MS 24 K 14).

answered the question by declaring that 'the only charm to work this prodigy is contained in one word—education'.

Drennan, the celebrated radical publicist, believed that a plan of public education might 'give a new turn to the national character'—an idea expressed more prosaically by an advocate for Sunday schools who reminded his readers that every family is disturbed by 'the infidelity of servants, the drunkenness and negligence of tradesmen, and the continual dread of nocturnal assault'. Sunday schools, which would teach reading and writing and provide religious instruction supervised by the clergy of the established and Roman catholic churches, would inculcate subordination and cleanliness and 'qualify youth for the future relations of the community'.[68]

The government from an early date was alive to the importance of education and indeed could have claimed to be ahead of public opinion. In 1786 Orde, the chief secretary, gave notice that he was going to introduce into the house of commons an education bill, and in 1787 he adumbrated 'a general system', the first, he suggested, to be introduced in any country. Orde may have received some assistance from the provost. Hely-Hutchinson was convinced that composition as taught at Eton, where three of his sons had gone, was an essential element in education, encouraging elegance of expression and decision. Hutchinson wanted an equivalent of the great English public schools to be founded in Ireland. On Orde's arrival he approached him on the question and was delighted to find that the new chief secretary contemplated tackling Irish educational problems.

The plan which Orde laid before the house of commons in 1787 in scope and detail was worthy of Pitt himself. There were to be parish schools, maintained by a tax on church benefices, tithe proprietors and the more opulent landowners. Above these, maintained by the funds hitherto granted to the charter schools, were to be four provincial colleges, offering a modern and vocational education not only to those who were to be manual workers but to the future 'mariners, merchants and tradesmen'. Grammar-school teaching would be given in

---

[68] *Address to the public relating to Sunday schools* (1786); R. L. Edgeworth, *Memoirs*, i, pp. 177–9; T. Percy, *A sermon* (1790), pp. 7–13; W. Drennan, *A letter to Lord Fitzwilliam* (1795), pp. 8–10.

the diocesan schools, revived and reduced in number, and the
school system was to be crowned by two well-endowed 'great
schools' where youths destined, it was hoped, to win distinction
in politics and the professions would receive a first-class
classical education. Though pupils of all denominations would
be accepted throughout the system, Orde felt that the children
who were to be maintained as well as educated at the expense
of the state should be 'brought up in the religion of the state'.
There were to be numerous bursaries and scholarships, and
Orde emphasized that 'throughout the whole plan was left a
possibility for boys of genius to raise themselves from the lowest
to the highest rank'. This aspect of the scheme was strongly
criticized by Stephen Dickson, a medical professor of Trinity, as
liable to produce 'a swarm' of indigent, unemployed scholars.
It was a mistake, he argued, 'to increase the competition in any
employment disproportionately to the profits arising from the
exercise of that employment'. Another critic, William Drennan,
attacked Orde's scheme of 'education by statute' for its in-
flexibility and for placing education under the control of the
established church and state. 'Establishments', Drennan was
certain, 'are always decaying. Individuals are always in a state
of progressive amelioration.' The right course therefore was for
the state to assist 'the manufacture of mind' by grants to
individuals or private institutions engaged in education.
'Encourage but not endow', he wrote.[69]

Orde's scheme met with a favourable reception in parliament,
though Arthur Browne, M.P. for Trinity, complained that the
university had not been consulted—'a fresh instance of that
disrespect which coxcombs from Eton and Westminster were
too apt to show them'. After outlining his scheme in a very
lengthy speech, Orde recommended one immediate step—the
appointment of a statutory commission to inquire into educational endowments in Ireland. The commission, a pioneering
body in this field, made a nationwide survey and produced a
comprehensive, crisp report. But Orde left Ireland in 1787,
Hely-Hutchinson was ageing and nobody else took up the
subject of education in parliament until Edgeworth, who
believed the source of 'all the internal distractions of the

[69] *Parl. Reg. Ire.*, vii, pp. 486–505; *Trans. R.I.A.*, iv (polite literature), pp. 15–71;
Hutchinson's History of T.C.D., Bk. 10 (T.C.D. MS 1774).

country' was the education of the poor, secured the appointment of a commons committee on the education of the lower orders. This committee reported that in many of the schools in which the poor were being taught, the teachers were incompetent and the textbooks—for instance lives of highwaymen—highly unsuitable. The aim of the state, the committee enunciated, should be to rescue the rising generation, and 'give to this country a people fit to inhabit a civilized nation'. Parish school masters, licensed by justices of the peace, were to be provided with a house and £7 per annum together with bonuses based on examination results and to be inspected and controlled by the neighbouring gentry.[70]

With the functions of the state limited by public opinion, the Irish administrative machinery was, by later standards, on a small scale, the civil administration together with officials attached to the superior courts and the houses of parliament amounting in all to approximately 3,500: a total which includes the crews of the revenue cruisers (500), the drivers belonging to the ordnance wagon train (1,000) and messengers and domestic staff in government offices.

At the head of the Irish administration was the lord lieutenant, a great officer of state, entrusted by patent with many of the powers of the crown in Ireland. In practice, he was a member of the British administration of the day, and on the more important appointments and administrative questions was expected to consult with the prime minister and the secretary of state responsible for Irish affairs (until 1782 the secretary for the northern department, from then the home secretary). The lord lieutenant was always a peer, usually rich and of considerable political weight. Of the eighteen holders of the office between 1760 and 1800 twelve attained cabinet rank, of the others, three had been ambassadors; Townshend was a successful soldier and Northumberland, the son of a baronet, having inherited an earldom, acquired a dukedom.

During the early Hanoverian period the lord lieutenant was obliged to live in Ireland only for the biannual parliamentary session, being represented in his absence by three lords justices. The lords justices were expected to keep the lord lieutenant informed and received instructions from the secretary of state

[70] *D.J.*, 9, 26 Feb. 1799.

and the treasury. Nevertheless, the office of lord justice gave to the magnates who held it prestige and some patronage and the system threw into bold relief the political weight which pertained to the leader of a great parliamentary interest. In 1758, the then lord lieutenant, the duke of Bedford, suggested that he should be empowered, when absent from Ireland, to appoint a deputy who should be 'free from all Irish connections',[71] and though this suggestion was not acted upon, early in the reign of George III it was decided that the lord lieutenant should be permanently resident, Townshend, appointed in 1767, being the first of the succession of lords lieutenant who stayed in Ireland continuously during their tenure of office.

Townshend was faced with a formidable opposition, and from thenceforth an analysis of Irish political dynamics favoured in official circles was that the great borough interests, the Irish aristocracy, instinctively or deliberately, were intent on obtaining complete control of power and patronage in Ireland, and that the crown and its representatives were committed to resisting aristocratic domination. Both Townshend and Buckingham when confronted by a formidable parliamentary opposition, claimed to be fighting the aristocracy. William Knox, a civil servant profoundly interested in imperial problems, considered that the government of Ireland until early in George III's reign was 'purely aristocratical' and that the principal source of 'all maladministration in Ireland' was aristocratic influence. Westmorland in 1792 warned the British government that its catholic policy might, by driving the majority of protestants into opposition, enable the aristocracy 'to take the administration entirely from the hands of the British government' with the result that Ireland would probably become 'an engine in the hands of English opposition'. At the close of the century, Cornwallis saw himself struggling against the overgrown parliamentary power of 'five or six pampered borough mongers'. A few years earlier, during Fitzwilliam's term of office as viceroy, Cooke, an influential civil servant, with a proclivity for penning political *aperçus*, found the key to a series of sensational events (including his own dismissal) in a whig campaign to establish aristocratic control in Ireland and

[71] Bedford to Pitt, 4 Jan. 1758 (S.P. 63/417).

then form a government 'that will be able to support the corresponding party in England against the king or any other set of men'.[72] This dramatic interpretation of Irish politics was bound to be highly satisfying to men in office as providing them with a significant historic role. But it was a considerable over-simplification of the situation. Even during the reigns of George I and George II, when, according to this theory, aristocratic predominance was established, with lords justices acting for an absentee lord lieutenant, important administrative decisions had to be referred to England by the lords justices, who in any event did not represent the totality of the Irish aristocracy. Later in the century, the great interests, while always powerful, never managed to form a cartel against the Irish administration. It is significant that a chief secretary, immediately after designating the aristocracy as 'the natural enemies of Mr Pitt's government', proceeded to discuss arrangements for enlisting the support of Lord Loftus, one of the largest borough owners.[73]

The duties of the lord lieutenant were manifold. He represented the 'dignified' aspect of the state, and the viceregal court at Dublin, if not on the scale and magnificence of Versailles or even Saint James's, had sufficiency of pageantry, ceremonial and colour to draw the fashionable within its orbit and to impress the general public. The lord lieutenant opened and prorogued parliament in state, held drawing-rooms and levees, gave banquets and balls and occasionally visited the provinces. He had a steward, 'a gentleman of rank and a friend', to superintend the household, a comptroller to check his accounts, a chamberlain, a gentleman usher, gentlemen of the bed chamber, gentlemen at large and A.D.C.s. He had an orchestra, 'the state music', and on state occasions was escorted by the battle-axe guard ('the yeomen being respectable citizens of Dublin').[74]

---

[72] *Cal. home office papers 1765–69*, p. 496; *Fortescue MSS H.M.C.*, i, p. 420; W. Knox, *Extra-official state papers* (1789), pt. ii, appendix, pp. 1–2; Cornwallis to H. Dundas, 1 July 1799 (W.O. 1/612); Westmorland to Dundas, 2 Jan. 1792 (Westmorland corresp.); E. Cooke to E. Nepean, 27 Jan. 1795 (P.R.O. 30/8/327).

[73] *Fortescue MSS H.M.C.* i, pp. 492–3.

[74] *Report of the select committee on civil government charges with minutes of evidence and appendix*, H.C. (337), 1831, iv. For salaries of members of viceregal household in 1801 see P.R.O. 30/9/9, f. 2.

A suitable setting for the viceregal court was provided by apartments in Dublin Castle including the Presence chamber and Saint Patrick's Hall, with its ceiling decorated by paintings showing Saint Patrick converting the Irish, the Irish chieftains submitting to Henry II, and George III supported by Liberty and Justice. In 1782 the lord lieutenant was provided with a second official residence in the semi-rural surroundings of Phoenix Park, and in the same year his salary, which in 1762 had been raised from £10,000 per annum to £16,000, was again increased to £20,000.

The salary was large but so were the expenses of the office. The lord lieutenant was expected to find kitchen utensils, linen and plate. It was necessary, it was said, for him to employ eight upper servants and twelve footmen, 'as they walked in the procession' when he opened parliament. During the parliamentary session he was expected to provide a number of tables—one for the principal officers of the household, the board of green cloth (at which a considerable amount of wine was consumed), another for the pages and yet another for the battle-axe guards and the soldiers on guard at the castle. On a number of days in the year, wine had to be given liberally to the household officers and servants, and some of them were entitled to free coal allowances.[75] At the close of the century there was a short era of comparative austerity. Cornwallis, who was appointed lord lieutenant in the summer of 1798, was a widower, not very rich and a hard worker. Owing to the emergency he dispensed with balls and levees, and lived in the lodge in Phoenix Park 'without ceremony, with his aides de-camp, like a general officer'. Guests were expected to leave as soon as dinner was over, and then the lord lieutenant, after glancing at the newspapers and conversing (very often on professional topics) with the members of his 'family', went early to bed. Cornwallis prided himself that his expenditure did not exceed his income, though 'I live remarkably well and the style of my table has been much commended'. According to his splenetic predecessor, Buckingham, Cornwallis had isolated himself in the Park and was doing little entertaining. 'His table', Buckingham wrote, 'is of eight covers for himself

---

[75] T. Rhamshay to T. L. O'Beirne, 9 Dec. 1794 (W.W.M. F. 28/57).

and his family, and twice a week he has twelve covers, this . . .
leaves him completely uninformed of everything.'[76]
The lord lieutenant had a number of practical and important
duties. He was responsible for recommending names for a
number of appointments in church and state. He had to
discuss and finally decide on a great many issues, he was the
main link between the Irish executive and the British government. By his patent, which described him as 'commander and
captain general of the army', he was theoretically responsible
for the defence of Ireland. There was however a commander-
in-chief in Ireland, a professional soldier, and it was recognized that, though the lord lieutenant had a supervisory
authority and might express his views on military policy, the
training, inspection, discipline and disposition of the units
stationed in Ireland should be left to the commander-in-chief.
There was an area in which the lord lieutenant and commander-
in-chief might clash, military patronage. In the early seventies,
Harcourt, a viceroy who had to strive vigorously to maintain a
government majority in parliament, assumed that military
patronage was a matter for the lord lieutenant, with the
commander-in-chief in an advisory role. Eliott, a soldier with
high professional standards, resented the viceroy's claim and
after a short tenure of the Irish command resigned to become
governor of Gibraltar. His successor, Irwine, an Irishman,
handsome, witty and a favourite at court, fought the patronage
issue with suave persistence. He disavowed any intention of
interfering with the lord lieutenant's political arrangements.
'My principal view', he explained, 'was to take care that each
regiment had good field officers.'[77] He made sure his case was
placed before the king and in the end secured a royal ruling
directing that all recommendations of the commander-in-chief,
whether or not approved of by the lord lieutenant, were to be
transmitted to the king, that the Irish deputy adjutant general
and deputy quarter-master general were to be appointed not
by the lord lieutenant but by the crown and that the commander-in-chief was to be shown all communications relating
to military matters from the secretary of state to the viceroy.

[76] J. Moore, *Diary*, i, pp. 327–30; Cornwallis to Brome, 7 Apr. 1799 (P.R.O.
30/11/277); *Fortescue MSS H.M.C.*, iv, p. 369.
[77] General J. Irwine to Rochfort, 26 Sept. 1775 (S.P. 63/420).

This decision convinced Harcourt that he should leave Ireland as soon as possible,[78] and though the lord lietutenant until the close of the century had some influence over commissions and promotions in Ireland, the growing emphasis on military efficiency, strongly supported by the king and at the close of the century by the duke of York, was bound to weaken the influence of the lord lieutenant in the military sphere.

The lords lieutenant, who held office in Ireland during the last decades of the eighteenth century, were all men of marked personality, vigorous and intelligent members of a powerful aristocracy. They expressed themselves on paper with fluency and pungency, and their letters provide a well-informed, frank and fascinating survey of politics. Viceroys frequently indulged in what Irishmen might consider unfair comment. A lord lieutenant would find the mechanism of politics in Ireland familiar but he had to handle problems from a new angle. Formerly a participant in the struggle for power and patronage he now had to be an arbitrator amongst contentious contenders. Viceroys were very conscious of the difficulties of their position. The Irish parliament was a restive body and if the government failed to maintain a majority its incapacity would be publicly demonstrated. Then as the century progressed viceroys were confronted with a wide range of urgent problems and understandably were inclined to the belief that their colleagues in England underestimated their difficulties and were neglecting them.

The office of chief secretary had, as the name implied, a relatively recent and comparatively humble origin. In the seventeenth century the chief secretary was the viceroy's principal personal assistant. By the eighteenth century, however, he controlled a department in Dublin comparable to the secretaries of state's office in London, and he sat in the Irish house of commons where he was regarded as the authoritative exponent of the administration's policy, though in debate he was often overshadowed by Irish office-holders who were better acquainted with the issues under discussion and with the tone of the house. After 1767 a chief secretary spent most of his term

[78] For correspondence dealing with the relations between Harcourt, when lord lieutenant, and the commander-in-chief in Ireland, see S.P. 63/420.

of office in Ireland, though unlike the viceroy he might pay visits to England for consultation and relaxation. Harcourt in 1776, when complacently evaluating his work as lord lieutenant, emphasized that much of his success was due to his chief secretary, Blaquiere,[79] who had undoubtedly shown a mastery of official business and 'management', and it was becoming clear that a successful chief secretary might be considered to be the lord lieutenant's junior partner. Of the twelve chief secretaries who held office between 1760 and 1782, none ever sat in the cabinet, though eight are in the DNB; of the ten between 1782 and 1800, five became cabinet ministers and nine attained the DNB. Increasing responsibilities may have raised the standard for the office of chief secretary; they certainly intensified the strain on the holder, and sickness, which forms such a noticeable strand in the political correspondence of the period, took its toll. Windham, appointed in 1783, had to resign because he could not stand 'a life of close confinement, constant application, anxious thought and late hours in hot rooms'. Within a few months he was suffering from 'languour and debility', and when, convalescing in London, he went to his club for a relaxed dinner, an Irish peer who was looking for a blue ribbon, insisted on sharing his table. Pelham, who arrived in 1795, was dogged by ill health, 'a weakness in one of my eyes and a giddiness in my head', his ailments being intensified by absence from home. A middle-aged bachelor, Pelham was deeply attached to his family, and sighed for an Utopian age when air travel, ballooning, would enable his relations to come to Ireland for a ten-day visit. He was succeeded by Castlereagh, who in February 1800, during the union debates, was put out of action for a short term by a severe bout of influenza.[80]

The chief secretary's office, the mainspring of the Irish administrative machine, was responsible for conveying the lord lieutenant's instructions to other offices and corresponded with the local magistracy. In 1777 it was divided into two departments, each in charge of an under-secretary, and in 1797 a yeomanry department headed by a senior clerk was formed.

[79] Harcourt to C. Jenkinson, 29 Apr. 1776 (Add. MS 38209).
[80] The Windham papers (1913), pp. 40–1; T. Pelham to Chichester, 4 Apr. 1795, 16 Apr. 1798 (Add. MS 33130).

Two other offices, historic but small, were responsible for formally authenticating and promulgating acts of state, the Privy seal office and the Privy council office. There were seven financial departments, the Revenue board controlling customs and excise, the revenue side of the exchequer, which by archaic methods collected a small amount of money from historic sources and assisted in keeping a check of receipts and expenditure, the Stamp office (1774), the Post office (1784), the Lottery office (1780), the Treasury (1793) which supervised the management of the revenue and issue of public money, the Commissioners of accounts (1771) and the Commissioners for the reduction of the national debt (1797). There were five departments concerned with the maintenance of the army in Ireland, the Muster-master general's office, the Ordnance, the Barrack board and board of works, the Commissariat (1798) and Comptroller of militia accounts (1799). The Muster-master general was responsible for keeping up-to-date muster rolls of the units stationed in Ireland, the Ordnance provided the army with arms, munitions and equipment—a vast number of items, from heavy artillery to drums and halberds—and from 1764 controlled the Royal Irish artillery; the Barrack board and board of works which not only built and maintained military barracks throughout Ireland but was responsible for the upkeep of government buildings in Dublin, was an organization which dwarfed any contemporary business concern. In the mid-eighteenth century four parliamentary committees reported unfavourably on its management and at the beginning of the nineteenth century it was found to be a department in which slackness and dishonesty were prevalent. There was also a department, the Wide Streets commission, concerned with metropolitan amenities and two departments concerned with economic development, the Linen board (1711), which provided useful, if scarcely necessary, assistance to a successful industry, and the directors of inland navigation, appointed in 1800, to perform the function of the inefficient and extravagant Corporation for promoting inland navigation (1752–77). The registry of deeds, founded at the beginning of the century as an instrument in the campaign against catholic landowners, provided a useful system of recording land transfers, and there was a small department concerned with ecclesiastical finance, with a novelty in eighteenth-century official life, an official, its treasurer, 'without any profit or emolument'.[81]

From its foundation by the Normans the Irish administration had been evolving slowly, without ever undergoing the ordeal of a searching inquiry into its shape or functions. Vestigial procedures were firmly embedded in the structure and if newly perceived needs led to the creation of new offices there had been little or no pruning. There were some 'perfect' sinecures and a number of offices so well remunerated that the holder could enjoy a reasonable official income while arranging for his duties to be executed by deputy. Many officials were wholly or partly remunerated by fees, a source of income which rose during the century both from increasing business and the tendency of officials to raise the level of fees charged. Consumers might resent this but ultimately yielded. It was pointed out for instance that Dublin merchants would not receive satisfactory service from tide-waiters unless they paid the fees demanded. The refusal of M.P.s to pay the fees demanded by the officers of the house was a rare instance of successful consumer resistance.[82] Fees led to an erratic relationship between remuneration and responsibility and strengthened the proclivity of office-holders to regard a post as a productive estate held on a life tenure. Recruitment and promotion were largely governed by the favour of senior officials, by the endeavours of the administration to maintain its parliamentary position and by the widespread belief that society should endeavour to save from indigence members of well-established families. Civil service posts carried at least a modest degree of status (after all the clerks in some offices were entitled to an Esq.) and it was assumed that most of them could be filled by any moderately educated middle-class man, with preferably the breeding or at least the appearance of a gentleman. Lady Kildare expressed the feelings of many of her contemporaries when, asking for 'a small employ' which would save her nephew and his family from perishing, she added, 'I don't mean a place of trust of money: board of works or anything not unbecoming a gentleman to execute.'[83]

---

[81] *Valor beneficiorum ecclesiasticorum in Hibernia* (1780), p. v.
[82] *Commons' Jn. Ire.*, xii, p. 34; xv, pp. 86, cccciii.
[83] *Lothian MS H.M.C.*, p. 349. Sir E. Newenham when he purchased a revenue

But as the century progressed the forces making for efficiency and economy in the public service slowly gathered momentum. The principles of technology and *laissez-faire* economics, both of which emphasized the importance of obtaining the maximum result at the minimum cost, began to be applied to the machinery of government; the public frequently manifested what an Irish politician characterized as 'an ignorant impatience to be relieved from the pressure of taxation'[84] and politicians, who professed to be shocked by maladministration, acted on their professions. That a new era was dawning was indicated by parliament's continuously calling for returns and accounts and by the appointment of committees of inquiry. One such committee, a committee of inquiry into revenue administration, was appointed on Grattan's initiative in November 1783. The government was inclined to be well-disposed towards this committee; the lord lieutenant anxious to prevent the formation of a strong parliamentary opposition, being ready to gratify Grattan in 'every little instance of vanity or caprice'. And Grattan was able to argue that his ideas on revenue administration reform were similar to those adumbrated by the prime minister.[85] The committee recommended that collectors should reside in their districts, that superannuation allowances should be granted only after twenty years' service 'without censure' and that senior offices should be filled only by promotion from subordinate posts. About the same time the commissioners of imprest accounts, who in 1784 were empowered to audit the accounts of all bodies receiving government grants, began not only to insist that accounts should be properly vouched for but to investigate 'the efficacy and due execution of the several works and the prices charged'. In their printed reports they severely commented on the conduct of a number of bodies, including the police commissioners, the Dublin house of industry, and the board of Trinity college, which had woefully underestimated the cost of buildings for which it had received public money.[86]

A range of important administrative duties was entrusted

post from its holder seems to have regarded it as an investment (E. Newenham to W. F. Pitt, 11 Sept. 1784 (P.R.O. 30/8/329)).

[84] *Parliamentary history*, xxxii, p. 445.

[85] Rutland to Sydney, 17, 26 Mar. 1784 (H.O. 100/12). *Commons' Jn. Ire.*, xi, pp. 99, 226; *Parl. Reg. Ire.*, ii, p. 111.

[86] *Commons' Jn. Ire.*, xii, p. ccccvi; xvii, p. lviii; xv, p. dxxii; xvii, p. dcclxxxvii.

to local authorities—the parish vestries, the governing bodies of cities and towns and the grand juries in the counties. The vestries, besides performing ecclesiastical duties, were responsible for providing coffins for paupers and were supposed to provide a fire engine and 'the implements for working same'.[87] During the eighteenth century there were in Ireland 117 boroughs with at least the remnants of municipal institutions. About twenty of these had governing bodies which performed a moderate range of essential municipal functions; about fifty others at least managed a market or maintained a court in which civil actions for small accounts could be heard, arranged billets, or kept a pound or a black hole, repaired a pier or employed a bell-ringer; the remainder seemed to exist merely for the purpose of returning members to parliament.

The Irish grand jury had both judicial and administrative functions. At assizes it not only examined bills of indictment but it also, in what were termed presentment sessions, fixed and apportioned a county rate, the county cess, to meet the cost of the local services for which it was responsible—roads, bridges, gaols, court houses and county infirmaries. The twenty-three members of a grand jury were selected for each assize by the high sheriff who was appointed for a year by the crown. The great county interests exercised considerable influence in the selection of high sheriffs and the sheriff when choosing grand jurors had to respect the feelings of the local landed world. Grand jurors were usually large landowners, it being strongly felt that a grand jury should represent the property of the county. As might be expected the high sheriff's choice of jurors occasionally aroused unfavourable comment. It was said that sometimes men with large properties were passed over in favour of lesser landlords. High sheriffs were known 'to give preference to their relations and friends where there might have been gentlemen of larger property'. In County Cork the high sheriff it was said, used a convivial technique for selecting grand jury men. It was the custom for him to invite twenty-three gentlemen to dinner on the day preceding the assize and acceptance of the invitation was taken as indicating willingness to serve. Sir John Newport stated that after winning a bitterly

<hr>

[87] *Parochial rates, Ireland*, H.C. (370), 1828, xxii; E. A. Stopford, *A handbook of ecclesiastical law and duty* (1861).

contested election for Waterford city, he was not summoned to serve on the grand jury, though clearly eligible, until the assize judge intervened.[88]

During the eighteenth century Irish county administration was rarely publicly criticized. The construction and management of county prisons slowly improved in response to parliamentary and philanthropic pressure. The county roads—supplemented on some stretches by turnpikes—were generally during the century regarded as adequate. It is true that roads were sometime planned to benefit the estates of influential landlords, but the landlord concerned probably believed that what was good for his estate was good for the county, and it is pleasant to see a great county magnate, Lord Downshire, co-operating amicably with a radical M.P., Todd Jones, over the building of a road which ran through the latter's small estate.[89]

It is true that the grand jury, an unrepresentative body, imposed taxation (by the close of the century £400,000 per annum) and administered a fair amount of patronage, granting contracts and appointing county officers (their secretary, the county treasurer, the clerk of the crown, clerk of the peace, gaolers and high constables). It was also becoming clear that the grand jury during the assizes had far too much to do: grand juries usually disposed of indictments by examining informations rather than hearing witnesses, nevertheless they could only give a perfunctory attention to the bulk of the presentments, and the judge's fiat tended to be a formality.

There were occasionally complaints in the press about how grand juries, formed by 'the state mechanism', taxed their counties to pay for jobs, 'gew-gaws' to ornament a court house or a road which was an avenue to a gentleman's seat. In one county, Mayo, it was suggested that gentlemen should form an association with a stock purse for the purpose of traversing all presentments which they believed to be jobs; in another, Wexford, about twenty-five gentlemen, including some of the best-known names in the county, publicly promised not to agree

---

[88] *Report from the select committee on grand jury presentments of Ireland*, H.C. (283), 1814–15, vi.

[89] J. H. Andrews, 'Road planning in Ireland before the railway age' in *Irish Geography*, v, pp. 17–41; J. Slade to Hillsborough, 18 Mar. 1786 (Downshire papers, P.R.O.N.I.).

to any presentment for a road or bridge which was not certified as necessary by at least three persons resident in the barony. At the close of the century, in January 1798, it was urged that a house of commons committee should be appointed to inquire into county taxation. Predictably, conservatives pointed out that it was not the time to expose to criticism machinery which on the whole worked well. If grand juries might occasionally be 'actuated by *little interests* . . . no human institutions could be found to act with invariable correctness'. The motion was rejected but it marked the beginning of a movement which culminated precisely a century later with the Irish local government act of 1898.[90]

The Irish parliament being of medieval origin, the electoral system which returned the members of the house of commons had slowly been shaped and settled as counties had been shired and cities and boroughs (centres, or potential centres, of commerce and industry) had been chartered. The result was that by the close of the seventeenth century the Irish house of commons consisted of three hundred members chosen by one hundred and fifty two-member constituencies, thirty-two counties and one hundred and eighteen counties of cities and boroughs (including one university constituency, Dublin university, the borough of Trinity college, Dublin).[91]

The county franchise at a glance seems simple, the possession of a freehold worth at least forty shillings per annum clear. In fact it was highly complicated by the varieties of property which were regarded as freehold. A tenant in fee or in tail or a leaseholder for life or lives (i.e. on an indeterminate lease) was a freeholder. Other forms of freehold were the possession of certain offices (including a rectory or a vicarage), or the ownership of a rent charge, a mortgage, or tithes. The county franchise had an intelligible justification. A freeholder, it might be presumed, had a substantial stake in the country which would guarantee his independence. But the nature of the

[90] *D.J.*, 5 Dec. 1775; *D.E.P.*, 19 July 1780, 11 Apr. 1781, 15 Sept. 1791; *Commons' Jn. Ire.*, xvii, p. 207; *D.E.P.*, 24 Jan. 1798.

[91] For the Irish parliamentary system in the eighteenth century see E. Porritt, *The unreformed parliament* (1903), ii, pp. 185–529; J. Newport, *The state of the borough representation of Ireland, 1783, 1800* (1832); E. M. Johnson, 'Members of the Irish parliament, 1784–7' in *Proc. R.I.A.*, lxxi, section c, pp. 139–246; W. E. Hudson, *Elective franchise and the registration of electors in Ireland under the reform act* (1832).

qualification and its complexities invited argument, litigation and fraud, and from early in the eighteenth century, parliament, moved by a generally felt sense of political propriety, which M.P.s might individually flout when engaged in a hard-fought contest, strove by legislation to ensure that only the genuinely qualified would be enfranchised and that voting would be conducted in an orderly fashion.[92] A series of about a dozen acts culminated in a great consolidating statute passed in 1795. The 1795 act for regulating elections provided that freeholds should be registered, that registrations must be made not longer than eight years before the election at which the right to exercise the franchise was claimed, and that freeholds of less than £20 annual value should be registered at least six months before the election. A conveyance proved to have been made with the object of fraudulently qualifying voters was to be deemed an unconditional grant, and bribery at an election incurred the penalty of £500 fine. At a contested county election, the returning officer, the high sheriff, was to nominate deputies and at the place where the election was to be held erect booths as polling stations for each barony or half barony. Over each booth he was 'to cause to be affixed in large legible characters', the name of the area it was to serve. A riot was not to be an excuse for closing the poll, but if there was a serious disturbance polling could be suspended until it ceased. The eighteenth-century acts regulating registration and conduct of elections evince a strong desire to make a theoretically sound system work properly. They also show the difficulties of the task when the complexities of the franchise, political human nature and the level of local administrative competence are taken into account.

In many county elections there was an unopposed return, informed opinion being confident in advance what would be the outcome of a contest. It was assumed that in any county there was a limited number of families whose acreage and general local status entitled them to make a serious claim to represent the county. Tenants when voting usually accepted the advice of their landlord, and many lesser landowners were

---

[92] It was on one occasion alleged that in County Cork persons 'whose disunited tatters exhibited penury itself and whose despicable mansions were doorless huts' had voted as £10 freeholders (*D.E.P.*, 7 Oct. 1783).

ready and proud to agree with a great local magnate on electoral matters. It was then often comparatively easy to arrive at a balance of power in a county. The representation might be divided between two well-established and respected landed families; or a great magnate, the duke of Leinster in Kildare, Downshire in County Down, or Lord Shannon, 'the colossus of Castlemartyr',[93] in Cork, might be allowed to have the nomination of one member, the other seat being filled by a candidate put forward by the gentlemen of the county, the lesser interests. But, as in Europe, the balance of power could be upset. There might be uncertainty as to which of several landed families had the best claim, or the best chance of winning a county seat. Moreover, as on the greater stage, success and power might provoke opposition. The dominant position in local politics assumed by a great county magnate, with strongly developed political instincts and some skill in manipulating patronage, could arouse the resentment of lesser interests, and a coalition against him might be formed, claiming to be the 'independent interest' and with a popular cry, the freedom of the county. The supporters of the predominant interest could retort by pointing to past services to the county and stressing the value of loyalty in public life.

A contested county election was exciting and expensive. Preliminary election tactics are neatly illustrated by a book-seller's advertisement which appeared at the beginning of a general election in the early eighties. He offered for sale 'the candidate's memorandum book'—a ledger in which the electors' names could be entered alphabetically with freehold and landlord—and 'the candidate's cheque book', in which could be entered the names of electors with 'their connections and such objections and disqualifications as can be urged against them, together with some arguments and vindications to be of-fered in support of the votes objected to'.[94] The fact that an elector could vote for two candidates or give a plumper, encour-aged the formation of alliances between candidates and could lead to recriminations. Polling could be prolonged for weeks. Landlords brought their tenants to the poll in feudal array. Candidates provided cockades and ribbons for their supporters

---

[93] *D.E.P.*, 6 Sept. 1783.
[94] Ibid., 24 July 1783.

and were expected to provide them with subsistence on at least polling day, which involved a lavish expenditure on food and drink. During the general election of 1768 it was reported that cooks and waiters had been hired in Dublin at vast expense to dress food and serve it to electors in the contested counties. And one county candidate, it was reported, had provided for his supporters thirty oxen and eighty sheep, besides poultry, fish, wine and other liquors. Politics became highly infused with alcohol— it was said that at this general election 'many people who perhaps had never tasted spirits before had died suddenly by excessive drinking', and high living and political tension inflamed tempers. There was faction fighting and duelling—one Cork county election, it was estimated, led to twenty-two duels—and a contested county election was frequently followed by a petition alleging gross malpractices on the part of the victors— manipulation of the polling arrangements, polling unqualified voters (even papists), a sheriff acting throughout as 'the devoted friend and avowed partisan' of a candidate and 'every species of corruption and undue influence'.[95]

However, in spite of its rowdiness, absurdities and illegalities a county election drew the freeholders, peers, clergy, landed gentlemen and tenants together on an important public occasion. Many voters might be subject to unfair pressure, others might be offered improper inducements, nevertheless, with its wire-pulling, high spirits, canvassing, public debate and private talk about issues and personalities the county election was, in a limited way, an expression of the political will of the enfranchised community.

The 117 parliamentary boroughs which were theoretically urban centres, ranged in the eighteenth century from large and prospering cities to small villages, in a few instances dwindling down to a geographical point.[96] For example in Carysfort there was only one house and Clonmines had no inhabitants. No town of any importance was not represented but some boroughs had declined in importance and a number of small places had

[95] D.J., 16 July 1768; Pue's Occurrences, 2 Aug. 1768; D.E.P. 7 Oct. 1783; Commons' Jn. Ire., ix, pp. 311, 316; xi, p. 50; xiv, p. 30.
[96] The act (21 George II, c. 10) which permitted burgesses and freemen to vote though not resident did not apply to the counties of cities and towns but in fact in these constituencies non-residents seem to have been allowed to vote.

been chartered either in a mood of unjustified economic optimism or merely with the object of giving the town or a local magnate parliamentary influence. One hundred and six of the boroughs possessed a governing body. In Dublin this consisted of the board of aldermen and the common council, in the other boroughs it was composed of aldermen and burgesses sitting together or simply of burgesses. The Dublin common council was elected by the guilds and participated in the selection of aldermen. The members of the governing bodies of the other boroughs were (with a few insignificant exceptions) chosen by co-operation; in every borough, except Dublin where there were triennial elections for the common council, the members of the governing body held office for life, and after 1747, neither they nor freemen were obliged to be resident. Traditionally the freedom of a borough could be claimed by birth, servitude (apprenticeship) or possibly by marriage, and it could be obtained by special grace. Admission to the freedom of a city or borough was administered by the governing body and during the eighteenth century many governing bodies, refusing to acknowledge any right to freedom, exercised a discretionary power of rejection of admission. Current legal opinion towards the close of the century seems to have favoured this practice; an outstanding member of the Irish bar, John Fitzgibbon, stating, about 1788, that the governing body of Belturbet had the right to grant or refuse the freedom as they pleased. A cruder method of limiting the number of freemen may have been adopted at Ballynakill, a borough which by the end of the century had fallen under the control of Lord Drogheda, a man of property, influence and drive, who in the course of an exceptionally long life was to hold numerous offices and acquire a step in the Irish peerage and a United Kingdom barony (married to the daughter of Lord Hertford, it was suggested that he had acquired as part of his wife's dowry, the Conway 'faculty of asking'.) At the general election of 1790 John Barrington, the head of a family which had represented Ballynakill in the first half of the century, and his son Jonah, then an enterprising young barrister, supported by twenty-seven persons claiming to be freemen, challenged the patron's candidates. According to the Barringtons, the sovereign refused the freemen's votes, and when called on to produce the records of the corporation he 'produced a new book, recently made up and bound' in which the names of the Barrington supporters were not recorded.[97]

In respect to the parliamentary franchise the boroughs can be divided into four main categories. There were those boroughs, thirteen in number, in which the parliamentary franchise was exercised by the householders (and in four of them, in addition by the freeholders) in the borough. There were five boroughs in which the voters were the freeholders of the manor. Thirdly, there were those boroughs in which the privilege of returning members to parliament was vested in the governing body of the borough—the chief officer (mayor, sovereign, provost or portreeve) and the burgesses, usually about a dozen in number; and finally there were the boroughs in which the franchise was possessed by the burgesses and freemen. In the nine boroughs which were counties of cities or boroughs, in addition to the freemen, the forty-shilling freeholders also possessed the parliamentary franchise. Of course owing to the tight control exercised by governing bodies over admission to freedom, the distinction between burgess boroughs and the smaller freemen boroughs tended to be obliterated, the freemen in the latter often dwindling to a handful or becoming an extinct species.

In practical politics the boroughs were divided into two categories—the close, pocket or, to use the polite contemporary term, private boroughs—boroughs in which admission to the parliamentary franchise was firmly controlled by a patron (or in some instances shared between two patrons), and those boroughs which were 'open', at least to the limited extent that one, or at the most two families or interests, did not hold unchallenged sway. The burgess boroughs with a very small electorate could easily fall under the control of a powerful interest; in fact many burgess boroughs were controlled from the time they were chartered. For instance Belfast, when erected into a borough in 1613, was a small urban centre, built by Lord Chichester, the great local landlord, and dominated by his castle. Naturally then the governing body, the sovereign and twelve burgesses, was always composed of the relations, friends and dependants of Lord Donegall, the head of the Chichester family. The burgess boroughs and the freeman

[97] *Fortescue MSS H.M.C.*, i, p. 210; *Commons' Jn. Ire.*, xiv, p. 47.

boroughs which can be grouped with them, numbered about seventy (forty-eight burgess boroughs and approximately twenty-three freeman boroughs). To these might be added those manor boroughs (four in number) in which the lord of the manor had been able, with electoral purposes in mind, to control strictly the creation of freeholds, and a few very small household boroughs which could be easily controlled by their proprietor—the borough of Randalstown (as distinct from the town) was only a small strip of ground and Knocktopher, with one resident voter, did not give much trouble to its patron.

The close borough was a smooth running electoral machine, producing predictable M.P.s with the minimum of friction. All the patron was required to do was to keep the electorate up to strength by nominating the necessary persons for co-option or admission to the freedom, and arrange that at an election the returning officer and a few burgesses should be present. Many of the municipal corporations maintained their existence purely so as to be able to perform their electoral functions. The situation at Jamestown, a freeman borough chartered in 1622, was not untypical. The governing body was kept in being by two members of the King family meeting in the village twice a year, the officer known as the town serjeant being in attendance at their meetings.

A vivid contrast to boroughs of this sort was offered by Dublin, the conspicuous example in Ireland of an open borough. Its electorate of three to four thousand freemen was one of the largest in the country, and the guilds, the law courts and the exchange provided foci for political discussion. There were strong interests in Dublin—the Castle, commanding the allegiance of office-holders in the law and the revenue, the aldermen with their civic patronage, the city liberals, well organized and with influential press support. But none of these interests possessed anything approaching predominant power in a Dublin election, and a candidate's reputation, his personality, his canvassing ability, the temper of the public mind and the major political issues all played a part.

At a general election political excitement in Dublin was accentuated by the existence in the city of another important constituency, the University of Dublin. The university electorate was small, the fellows and scholars who had attained their majority, but it might be expected to display intelligent independence and in fact during the century the university M.P.s included some men of outstanding political and intellectual calibre. For about fifteen years the history of the university constituency and to some extent that of the college as a whole was dominated by the efforts of Hely-Hutchinson, appointed provost in 1774, to obtain at least one seat for a member of his family. Persuasive and overbearing, he boldly employed his powers as head of a house and as returning officer to achieve his objectives. His 'electing craft' in fixing the college election for the same day as the city's so as to ensure the absence from Trinity of an influential opponent, impressed Napper Tandy, himself an expert tactician.[98] Nevertheless Hutchinson's election campaigns in college constituted one of the less fortunate aspects of a successful career. In 1776 his son, Richard, secured one of the college seats only to be unseated on a petition. In the general election of 1790 the provost's third son was returned by a narrow majority and retained his seat by the casting vote of the chairman of an election committee. In 1797 he retreated to the borough of Naas.

Hutchinson's partial and short-lived success shows how even in an open borough a determined man or family, given a foothold, could build up a strong interest. In all the counties of cities and boroughs except Dublin, by the close of the century local landed families possessed considerable influence. In Cork Lord Shannon and the Longfields could influence many freemen. In Londonderry, a few landed families fought for the representation, one of them, the Hills, having the backing of the revenue influence after George Hill in 1788 married the daughter of John Beresford, the chief commissioner. In Limerick for years the Perys predominated, then towards the close of the century, the Smyths and their relations the Verekers, built up a powerful interest and, after sharing power with the Perys for some time, at a by-election in 1794 they were able to defeat Sir Henry Hartstronge, the brother-in-law of Speaker Pery. According to the defeated party, 'all the estates, revenues and privileges of the city of Limerick had been grasped . . . by one man', voters were intimidated by mobs of Smyth supporters, and 'strangers, foreigners and enemies to the freedom of Limerick' (including the officers of the garrison) admitted to the freedom. The Pery interest however proved resilient and in 1812 a long legal battle began which resulted in a majority for Spring-Rice, the young husband of Lady Theodosia Pery, at the general election of 1820. In Waterford three families, the Alcocks, Burtons and Carews left 'the citizens with little other choice than to select two of them'. It should be added however that, given a fairly large constituent body, there was always the possibility that the predominance of a patron might be shaken. The Dalys were accepted as being the patrons of Galway (a county of a borough), but the electors, it was said, 'had a testy pride' and 'would not be disposed of like bullocks at Ballinasloe fair'.[99]

But even in a well-managed closely controlled borough the unexpected could occur. Baltinglass, a freeman borough with an electorate of about thirty, situated on Lord Aldborough's property, seemed to be a model pocket borough. But the Stratfords were eccentric and quarrelsome, and with the family influence divided, the borough had several contested elections. In 1776 the earl's brother, Francis Stratford, indubitably a sometime sovereign, claimed that he was still in office and tried to secure the election writ and act as returning officer. However, the earl's nominee as sovereign obtained the writ by robbing the Revd Francis's messenger. At the election of 1797 the earl found his three brothers allied against him and with one of them acting as returning officer the others were elected as members. In Dundalk, Lord Clanbrassill's borough, a quarrel between Lord Clanbrassill and his agent, who as bailiff was the returning officer and could control the admission to the freedom, brought about a constitutional crisis, lasting over a decade, which led to an election petition and to litigation which ended in the house of lords.[100] Again, Tralee, a burgess borough, was considered to be controlled by the Denny family but it was said that once when Sir Edward Denny put forward a candidate whose politics did not meet with the approval of the electors, he was informed there would be

---

[99] (J. R. Scott), *Irish parliamentary representation*, by Falkland (1790), p. 38.
[100] W. Ridgeway, *Report of cases in the high court of parliament*, ii, pp. 445–503.

opposition.[101] The city of Clogher (a very small town) it might be thought was a borough under the unchallengeable control of the bishop of Clogher, whose palace and park were beside the town and who nominated the seneschal of the borough, who acted as returning officer. Nevertheless, there seems to have been some uncertainty respecting the boundaries of the borough and in 1783 the bishop's nominees were opposed by candidates who presumably relied on a larger electorate than had been customary. The seneschal, the Revd Hugh Nevin, the bishop's curate, disqualified a number of voters and returned the candidates backed by his patron.[102] However, in 1800, when there was a by-election involving both seats, there were again four candidates, two 'unionists' (a general and revenue commissioner), Charles Ball, the anti-unionist pamphleteer, who was very anxious to get into parliament, and John King, a major in the Fermanagh militia. The Revd Hugh Nevin, by now a prebendary, returned the unionist candidates. Ball and King petitioned against the return on the grounds that the votes of qualified electors had been rejected and an election committee decided in their favour. Another episcopal borough, Irishtown, had all the marks of a pocket borough. It was on the outskirts of Kilkenny, overshadowed by the cathedral. It was the practice of the bishop of Ossory to recommend for the freedom as many of his friends as he thought proper; the burgesses were nearly all clergymen; parliamentary elections were held in the palace yard and at the time of the union, the then bishop of Ossory, Hugh Hamilton, an able mathematician, claimed the union compensation for himself on the grounds that the control of the borough 'had given the bishops of Ossory such additional consequence and obtained for them such attention from government, that with the exception of two bishops (who lived a very short time after their appointment) for a century past, all have been translated to much more eligible bishoprics'. Nevertheless in 1776 Eland Mossom, grandson of a dean of Ossory and son of a sometime M.P. for Irishtown, along with his brother-in-law, Richard Wheeler, stood against two government supporters, presumably backed

---

[101] *Report of the commissioners to inquire into the municipal corporations of Ireland*, p. 423, H.C. (23), 1835, xxvii.
[102] *D.E.P.*, 28 Aug. 1783.

by the bishop. Mossom efficiently organized non-resident freemen, who supported him, and polled well, though the other two candidates were returned. Mossom and Wheeler presented a petition against the return but this was dropped on Mossom being returned for Kilkenny city.[103] Even in a manor borough the predominant interest could be opposed. Lord Granard was both lord of the manor of Mullingar and the principal landowner in the area, so it is not surprising that two of his sons were in 1761 candidates for the manor borough of Mullingar. What is surprising is that there was a third candidate, John Nugent. The Forbeses were returned and Nugent petitioned. Evidence relating to the qualifications of the voters, fourteen in number, fills columns of the house of commons journals—it being alleged that a Forbes supporter was married to a catholic and that some of those who voted for Nugent did so in virtue of freeholds situated outside the manor boundaries. The petition failed and from then on Lord Granard kept a tight hold on his borough.

There were some freeman boroughs which, though considered to be closed or tending to become closed, had a fair number of freemen—places such as Athboy, Clonmel, Maryborough, Trim, Wexford, Fethard (with 550 houses and about 900 freemen, almost all non-resident), Bandon and Navan.[104] In the first of these the prevailing interests were towards the end of the century challenged in election contests—though never successfully. In some places while the dominant family was not challenged at least a simulacrum of freedom was preserved. In 1790 the portreeve and electors of Navan, a borough controlled by the closely related Ludlow and Preston families, in a published address thanked their M.P.s, John and Joseph Preston, for their services. The Prestons correctly responded by thanking the electors for returning them. At Bandon during the general election of 1783, Mr Bernard, who partially owned and largely controlled the town, on leaving the court house after his unopposed return for the borough, was received by the Bandon Independent volunteers. Having congratulated the new M.P. they conducted him to a tavern

---

[103] *H.J.*, 4, 14, 29 May 1776; *Further proceedings of the commissioners under the union compensation act of Ireland*, p. 34, H.C. (89), 1805, vii.

[104] J. Newport, *State of the borough representation* (1832), p. 24.

where he was 'elegantly entertained', the day concluding with a firework display.[105]

In the larger household or pot-walloping boroughs, as might be expected, attempts were made from time to time to challenge the patron's power. At Antrim, controlled by Lord Massereene, Skeffington Thompson came forward on three occasions 'in support of the violated rights and liberties of the borough', with in 1783 the backing of over 100 electors. Lisburn, a prosperous town, where the liberal electors were organized in a constitutional club, in 1783 returned two popular candidates in defiance of the lord of the soil, the marquis of Hertford. But by the next general election Lord Hertford reasserted control, one of the new members returned being his son-in-law. At the same general election of 1790 in the borough of Downpatrick the influence of the lord of the manor, Lord de Clifford, regarded as the patron of the borough, was challenged by a very great county magnate, the marquis of Downshire, a supporter of the administration, who backed two candidates in opposition to Lord de Clifford's friends. The victory of the latter was greeted as a popular triumph. 'I never', a liberal reporter wrote, 'saw so many happy faces—and indeed the temptation the poor fellows withstood would astonish you, for handfuls of gold were offered them.'[106]

There were three household boroughs in Waterford— Dungarvan, Lismore and Tallagh—all of which were contested in the later decades of the century. The duke of Devonshire, as heir of the great earl of Cork, was considered to be the patron of each of these boroughs. But the Devonshire influence, presumably because the duke was an absentee, was not exercised vigorously. Indeed it was rumoured that the duke, finding that maintaining an interest in Tallagh (a borough with an exacting electorate) was too expensive an operation, had transferred it to Lord Shannon.[107] In Dungarvan, Godfrey Greene, a member of a well-known Kilkenny–Waterford family managed to win a seat in 1776. By 1790 a member of another

---

[105] *D.E.P.*, 19 Aug. 1783, 6 May 1790; J. Newport, *State of the borough representation*, p. 51.

[106] *D.E.P.*, 23 Aug. 1783.

[107] E. M. Johnston, 'Members of the Irish parliament, 1784–7', in *Proc. R.I.A.*, Section c, vol. lxxi, p. 228.

well-known County Waterford family, John Beresford, had built up an interest in the borough, according to William Greene, a prejudiced witness, by the shameless use of revenue influence. Revenue officers, Greene asserted, had purchased freeholds through a confidential friend of Beresford and a number of them were voting out of a small piece of ground. It was also said that 'a low revenue officer, a creature and dependent' of Beresford, had been installed as returning officer. The result was that at the general election of 1790 Greene was ousted and the representation divided between the Devonshire and Beresford interests.[108] At Lismore, where Sir Henry Cavendish and Sir Richard Musgrave were in 1790 the candidates favoured by the patron, Robert Paul stood and came third on the poll. He petitioned and an election committee, accepting his contentions that Sir Henry Cavendish had obtained 'a colourable majority' only by tampering with the registry books and polling non-residents, almsmen and menial servants, seated him in place of Cavendish.[109] At Tallagh in 1783 John Hobson, 'well known to the principal inhabitants of the borough', and who was a friend of Lord Shannon, managed to win a seat. But in 1790 he was defeated by Egan, a rising young barrister, who managed to secure the support of those electors on whom 'money or drink could operate'—many of his supporters 'displaying on the hustings evident symptoms of intoxication'.[110] It perhaps should be added that there was one household borough, Swords, a small town near Dublin, where the prevalent interest was laconically summed up in one word, 'money'. About 1760 John Hatch who spent nearly £8,000 in buying and creating tenements, built up a powerful interest in Swords, and another north County Dublin landowning family, the Cobbes, allied by marriage to the Beresfords, possessed considerable influence in the borough. But a large number of voters, probably at least about half of the total electorate, regarded themselves as independent. Their attitude seems to have been summed up by one elector who explained that he appreciated at an election the opportunity, of bringing himself to 'the notice and good offices of

---

[108] *Commons' Jn. Ire.*, ix, p. 297; xiv, p. 11; xvi, p. clxxxvii; *D.E.P.*, 26 Aug. 1783.
[109] *Commons' Jn. Ire.*, xiv, pp. 30–1.
[110] Ibid., xiv, p. 46.

gentlemen whom he had it formerly in his power to serve by a free and unbiased suffrage'.[111]

Complex, defective and absurd as the electoral machinery was, it produced a house of commons which until late in the century seems to have satisfied the public and which certainly was regarded by most M.P.s with self-congratulatory approval. It was not of course until the later decades of the century that it was easy to obtain an over-all picture of the constituency pattern. Moreover two of the most respected elements in society, landed property and intelligence, were undoubtedly well represented in the house of commons. A high proportion of the M.P.s were university graduates, about one in five had been called to the bar, a somewhat smaller proportion had been in the army and amongst those who sat in the house during the later eighteenth century were a medical doctor, a few merchants, rather more bankers, a few experts on national economics, some keen agricultural improvers, two dramatists and two provosts and two fellows of Trinity. But of course the overwhelming majority of the members were connected with the landed interest, the professional and business members usually belonging to landed families or purchasing themselves into the landed world. In 1790 no fewer than twenty-six sons of peers (twenty-one of them heirs) were M.P.s, and if brothers and paternal uncles of peers are added close relations of the peerage amounted to well over a sixth of the house. The house of commons itself was to a great extent an hereditary body, the same families coming in, generation after generation, so much so that at the close of the century about half the members were the sons of past or present M.P.s.[112] Understandably towards the close of the century there were complaints that the Irish parliament when coping with commerical and industrial problems was handicapped by a lack of first-hand knowledge. M.P.s were, to quote a tactfully-worded petition from a Dublin business group, 'removed . . . by their high rank and station from the difficulties that attend pecuniary transactions in detail, more especially among the manufacturers and middle

[111] J. Newport, *State of the borough representation*, p. 10 and *Further proceedings of the commissioners under the union compensation act of Ireland*, p. 15, H.C. (89), 1805, vii.

[112] R. B. McDowell, 'The Irish parliament of 1790', in *Bull. Irish committee of historical sciences*, no. 18.

orders of traders'. A Belfast man put it more bluntly—'it is for want of commercial knowledge that we are lost.'[113]

The Irish house of lords at the beginning of the eighteenth century had a membership of 125, consisting of 22 spiritual and 103 temporal peers. The annual average of creations during the first sixty years of the century was 1.3, but with an acceleration of political activity during the reign of George III it rose to about 3.5. As a result the Irish peerage almost doubled during the century, being composed at the union of 22 spiritual and 225 temporal peers (including 5 royal earls) together with eleven peeresses in their own right. The recipients of Irish peerages can be divided into two categories, grantees active in Irish life and persons living and working outside Ireland. From early in the seventeenth century the award of an Irish peerage, an honour undoubtedly more impressive than a baronetcy, had been used by the crown as a means of gratifying Englishmen and Scotsmen without inflating the English or the British peerage. Indeed on one occasion George I was said to have professed himself more ready to grant an Irish peerage than a K.B., adding for good measure that he could make a lord but not a gentleman; and George III, it was rumoured, when he would not permit a Welsh baronet to make an avenue from his house to Saint James's Park, softened the refusal by the offer of an Irish peerage.[114] But if some British recipients of an Irish peerage regarded it as a *pis aller* or a stepping-stone, others may have appreciated the advantages of being able to combine the social prestige of a peerage with a house of commons career. During the eighteenth century about sixty Irish peerages went to British M.P.s and landowners and about twenty were conferred for what might be termed imperial services, the grantees including nine admirals, three distinguished soldiers, one colonial and four Indian governors (Clive, Macartney, Shore and Pigot) and four diplomats. Some of the peers in this category were in fact Irishmen, for instance Macartney, General Blakeney, the defender of Minorca, two admirals

---

[113] *Commons' Jn. Ire.*, xvii, p. 59; *Short strictures upon the constitution, manufactures and commerce of Ireland* (1792), p. 11.

[114] *Horace Walpole's correspondence*, ed. W. S. Lewis, xxiv, p. 227; N. W. Wraxall, *Posthumous memoirs*, i, pp. 67–8. At the close of the century, the lord lieutenant, Camden, was trying to raise the value of an Irish peerage by resisting demands (T. Pelham to Portland, 1 Aug. 1797, H.O. 100/70).

(Aylmer and Shuldham), Holyroyd, the economist and friend of Gibbon and Nugent, an outstanding Irish adventurer in British politics. Nugent, the son of a County Westmeath landed gentleman, was a facile versifier with a penchant for marrying wealthy women. Entering the British house of commons in 1741 he was throughout a long career almost 'uniformly in favour of the administration', was created an Irish baron in 1767, promoted to be an earl in 1776 and died in 1788 worth, it was said, £14,000 per annum in landed property.

The peerages conferred on residents of Ireland naturally went to families with political influence and property. Nearly all the peerages in this category (122 out of 144) were granted to M.P.s or wives of M.P.s (fifty-four of them being obtained by M.P.s who sat for counties), and most of the newly-created peers who were not M.P.s had considerable county influence. It was customary too when a candidate was recommended or was putting himself forward for a peerage to emphasize with his other qualifications that he had a large landed property. For instance the average income from land of a batch of eight peers recommended by Cornwallis was said to be £7,500 per annum. About the same time it was calculated that the resident Irish peers had a total income derived from land of £786,000 per annum (with absentee peers having an additional £131,000).[115] It is also worth noting perhaps that about sixty of the resident Irishmen, who were created peers during the eighteenth century, were the sons or husbands of an heiress (some indeed were in the happy position of being both), the creation of a peerage setting a seal on the merger of two landed fortunes. On the other hand few great landed families remained unennobled. A striking exception was of course Thomas Conolly of Castletown, who was conspicuous at the close of the century as being untitled though he was one of the greatest Irish landowners. In fact he was trying quietly to secure the revival in his person of his maternal uncle's English peerage.[116] Some of the newly created peers, besides being landowners, owed their promotion to the peerage, primarily or partly to professional or even business success. During the century six lord chancellors, six judges, three distinguished soldiers

115 *Cornwallis correspondence*, ed. C. Ross, iii, pp. 224, 253–6.
116 Portland to Castlereagh, 25 Oct. 1800 (Portland correspondence).

(two of whom were also M.P.s), a bishop (the brother of a speaker) and two archbishops obtained Irish peerages. James Alexander the first Lord Caledon, who went out to India as a servant of the East India company returned to Ireland a nabob, purchased a large estate and entered parliament. Lawless, the first Lord Cloncurry, was a woollen merchant and manufacturer, the earl of Milltown was the heir to a huge brewing fortune, and three newly created peers and the husband of a new peeress in her own right were successfully engaged in banking (John Gore, the first Lord Annaly, was for a short time a partner in an unsuccessful bank). The peerage also illustrated that social mobility could work downwards as well as upwards. The fourth Lord Aylmer, having 'fallen into poverty and being unable to support his rank as a peer', was in 1783 granted a pension of £400 per annum. The third earl of Kerry having inherited in Ireland estates worth £20,000 per annum died possessing only a single farm there, having attempted to redeem an extravagant career by investing in assignats.[117] The third Lord Mountmorres left the family estate to his sisters and his half-brother and heir henceforth seems to have lived in comparatively humble circumstances. The Smythe family, shortly after it acquired the viscountcy of Strangford in the peerage of Ireland, lost its estate in the civil war, and the fourth viscount, who was a clerical pluralist in the diocese of Derry, was in 1784 disabled by act of parliament from sitting in the lords, after it had been proved that he had approached the plaintiff in an important appeal coming before the house for £200 which he said he needed if he was to attend the house. His son, the fifth viscount, having served abroad as a soldier, took orders and secured a living. In 1788 'at the instance of the peers of Ireland' he was granted a pension of £400 'to maintain one of the oldest titles amongst them, destitute of patrimonial support'. The pension he forfeited some years later by a display of independence during the regency disputes.

A peerage was the most glittering prize and solid gain to be won in Irish politics. For a landed family it was a formal recognition of its place in county and national life and it ensured its holders a permanent voice and vote in parliament. A peer also possessed an elevated and secure status in Irish

[117] E. P. Fitzmaurice, *Life of Shelburne*, pp. 5–7; *Gent. Mag.*, lxxxviii, p. 286.

society, local and metropolitan, emphasized by patent, precedence and privileges (an Irish peer attending at the bar of the British house of commons was accommodated with a chair, and if he were of the rank of earl or higher, his wife might be visited by the queen). At a time when birth, breeding, rank and the possession of inherited landed property evoked deep respect, the Irish house of lords, to an admiring antiquarian, seemed to represent all that was 'truly great and truly noble'. Since nobility in the British Isles was limited to the relatively small number of peers (and to some extent to their wives and heirs), and carried a considerable degree of political power, the British or Irish peer was bound to be far more conspicuous and influential than the continental nobleman, while his status, being clearly created by writ or patent, did not provoke the bitterness and jealousy aroused by theories of nobility by blood. Nevertheless, the Irish peers, one of their number proudly asserted, belonged to families distinguished by descent and achievement, 'many of them younger branches of the greatest houses of Great Britain', and, as a result of their position and privileges, inspired by 'that species of pride which is the greatest if not the only incentive to honour and that generous conduct by which the peerage ought to be distinguished'.[118] This tribute admittedly comes from a biased source but it might be noted that a great Irish radical club, the Dublin society of United Irishmen, at its first meeting chose as its chairman the brother of a peer.

Though the aristocracy was the apex of Irish social life and the hope of securing a peerage was an important factor in many a political career, the house of lords was overshadowed by the house of commons in the hurly-burly of Irish political life. The former house provided a decorative setting for state occasions, such as the opening or prorogation of parliament, with the peers robed and the lord lieutenant attending 'with the usual ceremonies of grandeur'. But its day-to-day proceedings attracted on the whole little attention. At many of its sittings only a small number of peers were present, the lords' debates were sparsely reported in the press and nearly all the political drama of the age was concentrated in the house of commons. This is

[118] Lord Egmont, *The question of the precedency of the peers of Ireland in England stated* (1739), pp. 74–80; J. Lodge, *Peerage of Ireland* (1789), i, preface.

understandable. Constitutionally the commons monopolized financial business and bills were usually first debated in the commons. County M.P.s and the members for some of the larger boroughs had constituents whose interests could not be ignored while many peers who had relations or 'friends' in the lower house, must have felt that they need not exert themselves in their own chamber. Moreover, conflict in the lords was bound to be dulled by the sheer weight of government influence in the house. Debates tended to be dominated by a few able lawyers and one or two high ecclesiastics who supported the government. Peers in general had an inherent respect for rank, authority and the *status quo*. Many of them wanted a ribbon or a step in the peerage (trivial advantages possibly, but families were keenly competitive in the honours sphere) and bishops were often hoping for a translation. Nevertheless, from the beginning of George III's reign there were always a few independent critics of the government in the lords and during Townshend's stormy administration the independents, reinforced by peers such as Shannon and Lisle, who had quarrelled with the viceroy, were able on one occasion to muster nine votes (with proxies eighteen) against twenty-six (or with proxies thirty-six) government supporters. During the American war the opposition in the lords was infinitesimal (three or four strong) but in July 1782, when the tide seemed to be running strongly in favour of the liberals, a bill for the disfranchisement of revenue officers was almost carried in the lords by receiving 15 votes against 19—the minority protesting that its rejection might 'induce an opinion that this house is disposed to become an obstacle to that general reform' which had begun in Great Britain. Again, it is not surprising that during the regency crisis the administration momentarily lost control of the house, its supporters being reduced to about twenty peers who were outnumbered by two to one by those who supported an administration in *posse*. But once it was clear the prince of Wales was not going to become regent the situation rapidly reverted to normal. Though in the years immediately following the regency crisis there was a strong whig party in the commons, the opposition in the lords during the nineties never mustered more than seven votes, including proxies, until the union debates when over twenty peers opposed the government.

A minority in the lords had one advantage. It could record its views at length in the journals of the house in the form of a protest, a privilege which independently minded peers used to the full. From the early sixties almost every protest against the administration's policy was signed, and many of them were probably drafted by Lord Charlemont, throughout a long parliamentary career the embodiment of the whig conscience in Ireland. Proud of being an Irishman, overflowing with *noblesse oblige*, Charlemont from his entry into public life was convinced that 'a permanent and respectable opposition' was essential as a check on the ever-encroaching power of the executive. 'Wholly independent', he saw himself as 'a standard to which upon an emergency men might resort'.[119] Charlemont was frequently joined by the first and second dukes of Leinster; during the American war he had the support of Ireham, head of a family, the Luttrells, which followed a complex course in politics, and he was stoutly supported by Powerscourt, by the first earl of Moira, a convivial peer, and by Mountmorres, a generous, erudite eccentric, who wrote on a wide variety of topics. Later the liberal causes in the lords were supported by Arran, Granard, Dickson, bishop of Down, an old friend of Fox, by Mountcashell, perhaps influenced by his wife, a pupil of Mary Wollstonecraft and a vehement liberal, and by Mountgarret, 'a man of strong intellect and violent disposition', a powerful debator, who shortly before his death in 1793 became a supporter of the administration.[120]

The members of the Irish parliament, peers and commoners, were very conscious of their constitutional importance, responsibilites and dignity. Parliament was convened and prorogued with traditional pomp and circumstance. From the early thirties it sat in an impressive building, which, with its ionic colonnaded front, great octagonal house of commons, barrel-ceiling house of lords, well-proportioned corridors and committee rooms, contrasted strikingly with the cramped, ramshackled quarters in which the imperial parliament conducted its business. Each house had its clerks and officers, whose ability is commemorated by two massive publications, the journals of the house of lords in eight volumes and the

---

[119] *Charlemont MSS H.M.C.*, i, 7.
[120] *Gent. Mag.*, lxiii, pp. 581, 678; lxvii, pp. 717–18, 885.

journals of the house of commons in nineteen volumes—each of them well-planned, well-printed, well-bound and superbly indexed. The work of the two houses exercised considerable influence over some areas of Irish life. Parliamentary struggles were exciting and from the early eighteenth century they thrilled the capital and sometime stirred the country. The eighteenth century granted rhetoric a respected place amongst the arts. From early in the century Dublin university had possessed a chair of oratory and two of its holders, Lawson and Leland, published treatises on their subject. From the early seventies the Irish parliamentary debates became a major feature of the Irish newspaper and periodical press—an important debate occasionally squeezing out almost all other news. Since the Irish newspapers also reported at length the British parliamentary debates, the reader, when the British and Irish sessions coincided, found a very large proportion of his paper occupied by political debate. In an age when news tended to be scrappy, the parliamentary reports offered intellectual stimulus and entertainment. Important issues were expounded from differing standpoints. High rhetoric might be followed by colloquial exchanges and many M.P.s emerged from their speeches as distinctive, forceful personalities. Parliamentary reporting greatly stimulated interest in politics. It also apparently provided an incentive to M.P.s. In 1780 a shrewd observer, Hely-Hutchinson, told the house of commons that by the publication of their debates 'the liberal spirit of your members is supported—it gives a spur to emulation—our rising geniuses receive the tribute due to their merit, and liberty and knowledge is diffused to the remotest part of the kingdom'.[121] The great issues which dominated public debate during the last quarter of the century offered superb opportunities for argument on general lines, expounded in glowing and ringing tones with a liberal employment of metaphor and emotion-charged personification. 'It is a common observation', Fox wrote, 'the Irish orators are too figurative for the English taste.'[122]

The house of commons also managed to get through a large

<hr />

[121] *Hibernian Magazine*, 1780, p. 566.
[122] J. Russell, ed., *Memorials and correspondence of Charles James Fox* (1853–7), iv, p. 442.

amount of humdrum but useful business in a matter-of-fact fashion. The legislative output, including many what would later be termed local acts, was considerable, and the attention of the British house of commons was drawn to the way in which the Irish house dealt with the public accounts, it being 'the practice for each gentleman to have the printed paper in his hand and check it article by article'.[123] But probably only a small number of M.P.s were so conscientious. A journalist's complaint that the business of the nation was being left to about twenty M.P.s, the other members treating the house 'only as a place of rendezvous', is borne out by the numbers dividing on the less spectacular issues and on one occasion an M.P. suggested that the house should adjourn early as there was a ball at the castle—incurring the ire of Fitzgibbon, who ironically remarked that nothing should be allowed to debar the dancing gentleman from attending his favourite fandangoes'.[124]

Relations between the administration and parliament were usually amicable, largely because the government regarded parliamentary management as one of its principal duties. Though most of parliament's legislative output contained nothing which, from the administration's standpoint, involved questions of policy, nevertheless it was essential for the government to be assured of a majority in both houses. Every session parliamentary approval of the estimates had to be secured and the supplies voted; on occasion support had to be mustered against a vote of censure or a proposal which might have seriously weakened the administration or the connection with Great Britain. In building up and maintaining a majority the government could rely on two strong and very different forces, reverence and patronage. Men in public life, peers and M.P.s, were profoundly influenced by loyalty to the crown, by the conviction that authority ought to be upheld (especially in time of war or internal emergency), by a desire to co-operate with the government for the public weal, by respect for those men in high office who had weight and experience and finally, by the gratifying sense of being on goods terms with those who controlled the official machine and by perhaps being admitted to the closet (the contemporary equivalent of visiting the

---

[123] *Parliamentary history*, xx, p. 330.
[124] *H.J.*, 2 Apr. 1784; *Hibernian Magazine*, 1780, p. 334.

corridors of power). Powerful as these feelings were they could be counter-balanced and even in some instances overborne by other strong presuppositions—the belief that independence was the dignified, constitutional and morally respectable attitude for an M.P. to assume, and that it was his duty to scrutinize severely the activities of the executive, always prone to disregard the rights of the subject, and often inclined to be prodigal with public money.

While public men were swayed by principles, emotions, prejudices, arguments, friendships and dislikes, the government was continually employing a potent concrete force, patronage, to attract support. The crown in Ireland had at its disposal a considerable quantity of patronage, ecclesiastical, military, civil and legal. Of course all of it could not be used for political purposes. Many eighteenth-century politicians were good churchmen and in any event a scandalous use of ecclesiastical patronage for secular ends would have jarred on public opinion, so when ecclesiastical appointments were being made by the crown, the interests of the church as well as the government's needs had to be taken into account. The use of military patronage for political purposes was also sharply limited by the demands of efficiency, voiced by influential soldiers and by the king himself, and by the workings of the purchase system. Many posts were automatically filled by promotion up a departmental ladder, others by the heads of the office. But with all these limitations the amount of patronage at the disposal of the government was large—civil service and legal salaries amounted to £285,000 per annum and to these must be added fees totalling about £152,000 per annum. In addition there was the pension list amounting in 1790 to £98,000 a year.

Patronage was bound to be a potent force in a comparatively poor country, 'a country not so remarkable for industry as it is for the number of younger sons'.[125] A politician was often concerned not only to secure patronage for himself, but also for his dependents and, if he were the leader of a parliamentary group, for his followers, the great man's 'tribe'.[126] Patronage both as a factor influencing political behaviour and as covering a variety of personal objectives of intense concern to many

[125] J. Lees to J. Blaquiere, 16 Oct. 1774 (S.P. 63/438).
[126] *A serious and affectionate call to the electors of Ireland* (1761), p. 7.

individuals looms large in contemporary debate and correspondence. It was important for a lord lieutenant to extract the maximum political profit from the patronage at his disposal, which never seemed sufficient for his requirements. 'There are many things undoubtedly in the gift of a lord lieutenant,' a viceroy wrote, 'but there are ten times more suitors.'[127] Individuals closely watched the patronage flow and urged their claims in tones ranging from the apologetic to the arrogant. John Claudius Beresford, pushing his father's claim to a post immediately after he heard of the death of the holder, 'poor Lord Shannon', remarked sententiously but probably sincerely, 'mankind are such selfish animals that they cannot help thinking in the midst of their grief who will gain the succession to the employments of the deceased.' Lord Aldborough, asking for a British peerage, assured the lord lieutenant that as 'I seldom ask unreasonable matters, therefore I am very pertinacious of what I do make a point of.'[128]

Patronage in fact is talked about so much that it is possible to overrate its political importance. A parliamentary placeman could, and, at least sometimes, did follow the dictates of conscience and vote against the government on the well-grounded assumption that the lord lieutenant would hesitate before taking the drastic step, dismissal. 'I consider myself,' the prime serjeant declared in 1780 'with respect to my estates in this country when compared with the emoluments I enjoy under the crown, as free to speak my sentiments as . . . any other man in this house.' More than one placeman could well have boasted, 'I am the servant of the crown in Ireland but I will not be the slave of the minister.'[129]

Though Irish peers and M.P.s resented it and tried to avoid dwelling on it, for the greater part of the century the Irish parliament was a subordinate legislature. The declaratory act,

---

[127] *The private correspondence of David Garrick* (1832), ii, p. 194.

[128] J. C. Beresford to Auckland, 4 Dec. 1799 (P.R.O. 30/8/113); Aldborough to Portland, 16 May 1783 (Portland papers, Nottingham).

[129] *Hibernian Magazine*, 1778, p. 694; *Parl. Reg. Ire.*, vi, p. 289. Early in 1794 a liberal newspaper published a list of placemen (102) and pensioners (7) in the house of commons. The list includes the names of 18 army officers, whose careers of course were not entirely dependent on political influence and 11 placeholders who held posts (mostly connected with the courts of law) on what their holders at least probably regarded as permanent tenure (*D.E.P.*, 13 Mar. 1794).

passed at Westminster in 1720, emphatically enunciated that the British parliament had power to make laws binding Ireland and that the Irish house of lords was not a court of appeal. To Philip Yorke (the future Lord Hardwicke), a lawyer of great intellectual power and political weight, it seemed obvious that 'the subjects of Ireland were to be considered in two respects, as English and Irish, that the Irish were a conquered people, and the English a colony transplanted hither and as a colony subject to the law of the mother country'.[130] Except for a well-argued protest by the Irish house of lords, the declaratory act went unchallenged in the Irish parliament for sixty years, partly perhaps because the imperial parliament did not exercise obtrusively its power to legislate for Ireland. Besides being subordinated to the British parliament, the Irish parliament until 1782 had to exercise its legislative powers under the restrictive procedure prescribed by Poynings' law. Bills having been first drafted in the Irish privy council were then transmitted to England and only after their final form had been settled in the privy council there could they be laid before the Irish parliament for approval or rejection. In fact by the beginning of the eighteenth century the Irish parliament had devised a procedure which enabled it to shape legislative measures. The 'heads of a bill', in fact a bill, could be introduced into either house and, after passing through the normal parliamentary stages in that house, be submitted to the Irish privy council to begin its career under the procedure proscribed by Poynings' law. Of course the Irish council or the British privy council could modify or reject 'the heads' of a bill.

Finally, in practice the competency of the Irish parliament was, in an important respect, severely limited. External affairs, except when Anglo-Irish relations were being debated, rarely came under its cognizance. The British government and the Irish administration treated imperial and foreign concerns as 'reserved subjects' which the Irish parliament must not be allowed to trench on. But these subjects had a considerable influence on Irish life at a time when Ireland formed part of 'the European bottom' of 'Great Britain's vast empire on which the sun never sets and whose boundaries nature has not

---

[130] *Several speeches in the house of commons in England, in a letter from a gentleman there to his friend here* (1721) p. 9.

yet ascertained'.[131] Ireland was slightly larger than Scotland
and by 1800 its population was almost one-third of the total
population of the British Isles. When Great Britain was at war
with a European power Ireland was of immense strategic
importance. If the dignity of history permitted the Low Countries to be called the cockpit of Europe, then Ireland might
be termed the back door of Great Britain, and there was from
the sixteenth century the menacing possibility that an enemy
expeditionary force, aided by Irish discontent, might establish
secure bases in Ireland and threaten England's western flank.
It was axiomatic in British strategic thinking that Ireland must
be protected from invasion, and since an invading force might
slip through, it was important to ensure that the inhabitants of
Ireland were loyal or subdued. Ireland however was not an
entirely negative factor in British strategy. Squadrons based on
southern Irish ports could afford protection to ships on the
great imperial trade routes between the British Isles and the
East and West Indies when in the danger zone off the European
coast. Cork, with its superb harbour and rich agricultural
hinterland, was a great victualling port for the British armies
campaigning in America, and as the century progressed
Ireland became an important recruiting ground for the army
and navy.

During the eighteenth century the British empire formed a
great economic community with, in theory, many activities
harmonized or co-ordinated by skilfully devised imperial
commercial legislation. In practice imperial economic planning
was less complete, less effective and more influenced by
interested pressure groups than the ideal demanded, and Ireland was forcibly fitted, without much regard for Irish susceptibilities, into a pattern conceived at Westminster. Ireland
was not permitted to import a very wide range of colonial and
East Indian products except through Great Britain and permitted to export directly to the colonies only a severely limited
number of products. Also certain Irish industries (wool, glass,
beer) were subjected to disabilities which prevented them
competing with British industry outside Ireland. On the other
hand Ireland was assured of a supply of colonial products and

[131] *An account of Ireland in 1773. By a late chief secretary* (G. Macartney) (1773),
pp. 55, 127.

of a limited colonial trade, had a market on favourable terms in Great Britain and the colonies for its great staple, linen, and enjoyed the protection of the British navy. Irishmen fully appreciated the value of belonging to an empire with rich and varied resources which they had helped to build up. 'The whole extent of a mighty empire is our country', the leading Irish historian declared in 1782.[132] But from the middle of the century Irishmen were viewing with growing resentment the restrictions imposed on their trade and industry by the imperial government. They may have exaggerated the effect of the restrictions; they certainly were confident that with a more free and flexible system Ireland would be able to develop its potentialities far more fully and make a much greater contribution to the empire.

Ireland had many ties with the empire. From the seventeenth century Irishmen were emigrating to the British colonies in North America as free settlers or indentured labourers. During the first three quarters of the eighteenth century emigration from Ireland to the American colonies was continuous, if fluctuating, reaching a peak of about 8,000 a year in the early seventies. It was largely from Ulster and predominantly protestant. The absence of landlords and weakness of anglicanism rendered, the American colonies attractive to Ulster presbyterians and when rents tended to rise or the linen industry was slack, an experienced farmer or weaver with a small competency, who often came of emigrant stock, would be tempted to try his fortune in one of the congenial and expanding communities on the other side of the Atlantic. During the War of Independence emigration was halted, but in 1782 Grattan prophesied that once the war ended a great wave of migration would sweep towards America, with 'her wide range of territories, cheapness of living, variety of climate and simplicity of life'.[133] In fact large-scale emigration from Europe to the United States did not begin until after Waterloo. But from 1783 there was some emigration from Ulster. In 1792 an observant tourist noted that a large number of emigrants were annually leaving for America from Belfast and Londonderry. In 1800 it was reported that many weavers had emigrated from

---

132 T. Leland, *Sermons* (1788), iii, p. 205.
133 R. J. Dickson, *Ulster emigration to colonial America* (1966), especially chs iv, v.

Monaghan and amongst those who at this time left the neighbouring county of Cavan for the United States was William
James, who arrived in the United States with a small amount
of money, a Latin grammar and a desire to visit the battlefields
of the revolutionary war. He prospered as a manufacturer and
banker and was the grandfather of William and Henry James.[134]
The United States were also a continuous inspiration to
liberals all over Europe. The Americans had asserted their
rights, backed them in arms, had enunciated liberal principles
and embodied them in constitutional forms. Ulster radicals
were told in a letter from Pennsylvania that 'the lowest here
(unlike those of poor Ireland) are well fed, well dressed, and
happy . . . they stand erect and crouch not before any man.
This my friend is due to the enjoyment of liberty in her proper
extent.'[135] When Priestley was preparing to leave Europe for
the United States the Dublin society of United Irishmen
assured him they wished they could 'participate in your
feelings on first beholding nature in her noblest scenes and
grandest features, in finding man engaged in rendering himself
worthy of nature, but more than all in contemplating with
philosophic prescience the coming period when those vast
inland seas shall be shadowed with sails, when the Saint
Lawrence and Mississippi shall stretch forth their arms to
embrace the continent in a great circle of interior navigation,
when man will become more precious than fine gold and when
his ambition shall be to subdue the elements and not to sub-
jugate his fellow creatures; to make water, fire and earth and
air obey his bidding and to leave the pure aetherial mind as
the sole thing in nature free and incoercible.'[136]

A number of well-known Irish radicals emigrated to the
United States. Matthew Carey, the editor of the *Volunteer
Journal*, settled in Philadelphia and became the father of
American protectionism. Blennerhasset, a member of the
Dublin society of United Irishmen, after emigrating in 1796,

---

[134] J. Bromwell, *History of emigration to the United States* (New York, 1858); C.
Abbot, A tour (P.R.O. 30/9/23). Abbot writes of an annual emigration of three to
five hundred from Belfast and six to seven thousand from Londonderry. The
Londonderry figures seem greatly exaggerated. C. Coote, *Statistical survey of the
County of Monaghan* (1801), pp. 48–9; L. Edel, *Henry James: the untried years* (1953),
p. 21; H. Grattan, *Speeches* (1822), i, p. 117.
[135] *N.S.*, 14 Aug. 1794.   [136] Haliday pamphlets, 669.

became an associate of Burr. Edward Hudson, a state prisoner in 1798, was a pioneer in American dentistry. John Daly Burke, who was said to have fled from Ireland for political reasons, was one of the earliest American dramatists. Bailie Warden, an Ulster insurgent leader, became American consul in Paris and a prolific author. Two members of the national executive of the United Irishmen, Thomas Addis Emmet and W. T. MacNeven, had distinguished careers in New York, Emmet at the bar and MacNeven as a medical man and author of works on chemistry. John Campbell White, a member of the Ulster executive, was delighted with America, 'a young country where political and religious liberty are enjoyed to the utmost extent and where no more taxes are levied on the citizen'.[137] It may be added however that two famous Irish radicals who visited the United States, Tone and Hamilton Rowan, were unfavourably impressed by the crudity of American manners, and Rowan, who pronounced America to be 'a heaven for the poor and industrious but a hell compared to any part of Europe for any other rank of society', was very annoyed to find in America the same veneration for the constitution and abuse of its critics which he had met in Great Britain. A younger man, Thomas Moore, was also disillusioned when he visited America in 1805. Shocked by the rude familiarity and party rancour which he encountered, he doubted for a moment 'the soundness of that liberal creed of politics . . . in which I may be almost literally said to have begun life'.[138]

North of New England lay Newfoundland, with its rich fishing banks, which were an important objective in the Anglo-French wars. Irish sailors helped to man the fishing fleets which sailed annually for the banks, Irish factors supplied the fishermen with necessities—often driving a hard bargain, and by the middle of the eighteenth century Waterford shipping was carrying fish caught off Newfoundland to continental markets. Many Irishmen finally settled on the island, forming an important element in the colony. They were accused of introducing faction fighting and certainly introduced catholicism —James O'Donnel, the first catholic bishop of Newfoundland,

---

[137] J. C. White to ——, 4 Dec. 1804 (P.R.O.N.I. D 11).
[138] A. H. Rowan, *Autobiography* (1840), p. 292; T. Moore, *Poetical works*, ii, pp. 202–5.

came from Tipperary. At the close of the eighteenth century the disturbances in Ireland had repercussions in Newfoundland. The United Irishmen's movement inspired a widespread oath-bound conspiracy which included men of the Royal Newfoundland regiment. Before a rising could take place the conspiracy was discovered, largely through the efforts of Bishop O'Donnell, and crushed, some of the military conspirators being court-martialled and executed.[139]

In the seventeenth and eighteenth centuries the West Indian islands, which supplied Europe with a luxury, sugar, which had become a conventional necessity for many Europeans, were strenuously fought-for prizes. From early in the seventeenth century Irishmen were sharing in the English effort to secure control of a number of islands and there were large Irish settlements in Saint Kitts, the Barbadoes and Montserrat. Admittedly some of the Irishmen who went to the West Indies in the middle of the seventeenth century were catholics, transported from Ireland as politically obnoxious to its rulers. But others, catholics or protestants, servants or plantation owners, boldly sought a career in a zone of quick profitability, if high mortality. Catholics of well-established families in the west of Ireland were attracted to islands where religious disabilities mattered little. Indeed at the close of the seventeenth century the Irish Jacobite wars spread to the West Indies when in the summer of 1689 the 'Irish papists' in Saint Kitts drove out the English and handed over the English part of the island to the French. However, in time all the English speaking settlers happily merged. 'In the West Indies', an Irishman wrote, 'we all live very socially and never trouble ourselves about religion.'[140] But it was observed during the eighteenth century that 'the national partiality which is made an accusation . . . against Scottish and Irish gentlemen was attended with good consequences for many of their young compatriots who came out to seek a fortune in the islands.'[141]

---

[139] C. Pedley, *The history of Newfoundland* (1863), pp. 23–91, 210–17, 476–9; C.O./194/42 and 44.

[140] *Cal. of state papers, colonial series, America and West Indies 1689–1692* (1901), pp. 73–4, 111, 129; A. Gwynn, 'Documents relating to the Irish in the West Indies' in *Analecta Hibernica*, iv, pp. 140–286; J. O'Brien to D. O'Brien 8 July 1793 (I.S.P.O. 620/15/7).

[141] E. Long, *History of Jamaica* (1772), ii, p. 286.

At the close of the eighteenth century trade with the West Indies account for about 5 per cent of Ireland's export trade, and the strength of the connection between Ireland and the West Indies was frequently demonstrated. When planters and merchants trading with Jamaica decided to raise a regiment for service there, seven Cork firms were amongst the subscribers. When in 1780 a great hurricane devastated the islands, subscriptions for the relief of the sufferers were organized in the cities of Dublin and Cork, and by the catholics of Dublin and a shipload of supplies was sent to the island by the Dublin subscribers.[142]

Irishmen were also involved in building up British commercial and military power in India. From the early eighteenth century Ireland was forging links with India, or at least with the East India company, by supplying the company's ships with beef and staves. But very little Irish capital seems to have been invested in East India stock. This is scarcely surprising. The East India company proprietors or stock holders were concentrated in London and the surrounding area. In 1772 only one Irish resident (Peter Hamilton of Fahy) was listed amongst them. In 1798 there were two, Marmaduke Cramer of Dublin, an attorney and lottery commissioner, and Sir Charles des Veaux of Indiaville, Queen's County. Des Veaux, the son of a Huguenot refugee who had settled in Ireland, went to India as a writer in 1762. He rose to be a member of council at Madras and on his returning to Ireland became M.P. for Carlow. By 1805 the number of East India proprietors resident in Ireland had increased to nine—including Lord Castlereagh, whose great-uncle, Sir Robert Cowan, son of a Londonderry alderman, had been governor of Bombay in the early eighteenth century.[143]

Des Veaux was not the only member of the Irish house of commons to have worked in India. Griffith of Millicent, M.P.

[142] *H.J.*, 15 Jan., 26 Feb. 1781; *D.E.P.*, 8 Mar. 1781. There were Negroes either from Africa or the West Indies working in Irish households. During the general election of 1783, a black servant of Lord Granard came forward to vote as a freeholder in Longford. After his case had been argued 'with great ability and humour by the gentlemen of the long robe . . . Mungo was allowed to vote' (*D.J.*, 23 Aug. 1783); for subscriptions towards raising the regiment in Jamaica see *Public advertizer*, 18 Nov. 1779.

[143] *List of the names of these members of the United Company of merchants of England trading to the Indies who stood qualified to vote in the company's books 1753–1805.*

for Askeaton, who in the eighties was an active liberal, had made a fortune in the East Indies; Thomas Maunsel of Plassey, County Limerick, M.P. for Kilmallock, had gone out to India as a writer in 1750 and James Alexander, who sat for Londonderry before being created Lord Caledon in 1790, had been a servant of the East India company and had accumulated a very large fortune. The other well-known Irish nabob, Robert Gregory, a chairman of the East India company, did not become an Irish M.P. though he sat at Westminster for fifteen years. But he bought a large estate in County Galway and was noted as an improving landlord. A third returned Anglo-Indian, Robert Brooke, had a much less happy time in Ireland. Having served with distinction in the company's Bengal army, Brooke on his return to Ireland threw himself into promoting an industrial development scheme at Prosperous, County Kildare. Having lost a large sum of money (his own and the public's) he returned to the company's service and was appointed governor of Saint Helena. Other Irishmen who served with distinction in India included Mornington, the governor general, his brother the future duke of Wellington, Eyre Coote, a testy general but a splendid soldier in an emergency, Philip Francis, Hastings's antagonist, Macartney, the governor of Madras, Hugh Boyd, who went out as Macartney's secretary and became one of the first English language journalists in India, Gore Ouseley and William Marsden, both well-known orientalists, and Francis Macnaghten, judge of the supreme court in Madras and Calcutta, whose wife was the daughter of a chief justice of Bengal, Sir William Dunkin of Clogher. Sir William, according to Hickey, 'if he had a fault, it was that of being too fond of the pleasures of the table, which was to be accounted for from early habit and having resided the greater part of his life in the country part of Ireland, in the society of men who were all hard drinkers, as was the general practice in those days in the sister kingdom, but now much left off amongst the higher classes'.[144] It should perhaps be added that Hickey—himself no anchorite—who was the lively chronicler of the society which was settling down in the exotic oriental world with eighteenth-century British aplomb, was the son of a Dublin man, a Trinity college graduate.

[144] W. Hickey, *Memoirs* (1932), iv, p. 25.

But despite the number of Irishmen conspicuous in India during the eighteenth century, there were relatively few in the company's civil service, writers' petitions and applications for admission to Haileybury, from Irishmen amounting to about during the eighteenth century, there were relatively few of them in the civil service of the company writers' petitions and applications for admission to Haileybury amounting to about 3 per cent of the total. The explanation for this may be that Irish families with influence exercised it at the Castle rather than in Whitehall or in Leadenhall Street.[145] The proportion of Irishmen in the military service of the company was much higher. Possibly about 15 per cent of the officers in the company's army were Irish, and the Irish proportion of the rank and file enlisted in the company's European regiments rose from over 10 per cent in the middle of the century to almost 50 per cent at the beginning of the nineteenth century. The total number of men sent out from the British Isles was comparatively small. Their effectiveness in Indian warfare was of course greatly disproportionate to their numbers.[146]

Ireland could not trade directly with India. The East India company's charter gave it a monopoly of trade between the British Isles and the zone lying between the Cape of Good Hope and the Straits of Magellan—a monopoly firmly maintained against all non-company shipping. But Indian commodities were imported into Ireland through Great Britain, and of them, tea was by the end of the eighteenth century beginning to exercise a profound influence on Irish life. Tea was first taxed in Ireland by the revenue acts of 1727; about the middle of the century the annual consumption in Ireland was about 120,000 lbs. By the beginning of the nineteenth century it had risen to nearly 3,000,000 lbs.[147]

Compared with the rich and mysterious Hindustan, the most

---

[145] Writers' petitions, 1749–1805 (India office library J/1/1–30). In 1793 it was agreed that the lord lieutenant could nominate annually three cadets (Camden to Portland, Feb. 1798, H.O. 100/80).

[146] The material provided by V. C. Hodson in *List of the officers of the Bengal army 1758–1834* (4 vols., 1927–47) shows that of the officers commissioned between 1758 and 1815 whose national background is known (78 per cent) just under 15 per cent were Irish. For the recruits for the company's European regiments from the British Isles see Embarkation lists, India office library, L/Mil/9/85–106.

[147] *Tea, coffee etc. return* . . . H.C. (14), 1865, 1. Smuggling seriously affects the value of the return.

recent of the British colonies, the newly-founded penal settlement at Botany Bay, must have seemed insignificant and raw. In 1791, three years after the first fleet arrived in Botany Bay, the first shipload of Irish convicts sailed from Cork for Australia, and it has been estimated that about a fifth of the convicts transported between then and 1815 were Irish. Many of these convicts were defenders or United Irishmen, and in March 1804 over 300 Irishmen gathered near Paramatta and began seizing arms, their cry being 'death or liberty and a ship home'. The rising was quickly suppressed, eight of the leaders being executed and 'about forty of the worst' sent to the coal-works. Shortly afterwards the 'most determined United Irishmen' were accused by the governor of being active in illegal distillation.

Irishmen also played a part in the early administration of the colony. John Thomas Campbell, the son of a vicar of Newry, was secretary to governor Macquerie; Nicholas Divine, the first principal superintendent of convicts, came from County Cavan. Another superintendent of convicts, Andrew Hume, the son of a presbyterian minister from County Down, helped to set up the flax industry (and after being charged and found not guilty of rape) became a successful grazier. One of the surgeons in the first fleet, Dennis Considen, who claimed to have discovered eucalyptus oil, was an Irishman, another surgeon in the first fleet, Thomas Jamison, who carried out the first successful vaccination of children in the colony, was a graduate of Trinity college Dublin. A third Irish medical man, Jacob Mountgarrett, a naval surgeon from County Armagh, was said to have been the first man to grow wheat in the colony (and was also rumoured to have been one of the first bush rangers).[148]

---

[148] *Historical records of Australia, 1st series*, i, p. 674, ii, p. 129, iv, pp. 563–78, v, pp. 571, 654; *Australian Dictionary of biography*; A. G. L. Shaw, *Convicts and the colonies* (1966).

3
Intellectual and religious life

During the eighteenth century Ireland could be taken as forming part of the British cultural, intellectual and social world. At the same time the Irish catholics had many links with continental catholicism and the bulk of the country people in the south and west still spoke Irish and cherished remnants of Gaelic culture. Contacts between Great Britain and Ireland were numerous and multifarious. A number of landowners had estates in both islands. Lord lieutenants and chief secretaries formed long-lasting Irish friendships. Great Britain was Ireland's principal market, by the close of the eighteenth century taking about 80 per cent of Ireland's exports. Great Britain was also the source of about 70 per cent of Ireland's imports, supplying Ireland with British manufactures, coal and the products of the East. By the eighteenth century the flow of emigration from Ireland to Great Britain had begun. Irish labourers went over to assist with the English harvest and, according to Castlereagh, it was the money earned on these annual expeditions which enabled the emigrants to pay their rent.[1] Towards the close of the century Irish harvesters were to be found as far as Lincolnshire, where the presence of the 'poor Irish' stirred up organized hostility amongst local labour.[2] There was also permanent emigration from Ireland to England. In the eighties large numbers of Irishmen were working in the London and Lancashire silk industries; Irish shoemakers were much esteemed in England.[3] In 1771 when there were rumours of war Dublin shipwrights went to work in British naval yards and stayed in England.[4] At the close of the century there were noticeable Irish working-class colonies in London and Liverpool. In London it was customary for

[1] Castlereagh to J. King, 11 June 1799 (P.C. 1/44/A158); E. Willes, copies of letters (Add. MS 29252).
[2] F. J. Cartwright, *Life of Cartwright* (1826), i, pp. 186–7.
[3] *Commons' Jn. Ire.*, xi, pp. ccccxlv, dccxxvi.
[4] Ibid., viii, p. 497.

chair-men to be sturdy Irishmen and Irishmen were also known to be pertinacious and ingenious beggars. On a higher level there were a number of Irish businessmen in England. Some of the principal mercantile houses in Liverpool were said to have been founded by Irishmen and the Royal Exchange in London had 'an Irish walk'. The metropolis acted as a magnet to many Irish men of letters, publicists, painters, playwrights, actors and politicians, who seem to have found there opportunities and stimulus lacking at home.[5] As early as 1704 the Irish community in London was large enough for a society to be formed for the relief of the Irish poor and eighty years later it merged with the Benevolent society of Saint Patrick (founded 1784), established to provide non-denominational schools for the Irish poor in London.[6]

Most of the working-class emigrants from Ireland were devout catholics and their catholicism both held them together and made them an important element in a religious minority. Generally speaking however Irishmen merged easily into British life. Coming from a somewhat different society they may have had an intensified awareness of the world around them and the gusto of new arrivals eager to become established. But they do not seem to have felt themselves to be aliens nor did they jar. Johnson, a discerning observer, remarked that 'the Irish mix better with the English than the Scots do; their language is nearer to English, as a proof of which they succeed very well as players, which Scotchmen do not. Then Sir, they have not that extreme nationality which is found in the Scotch.'[7]

Recreation and education brought many Irishmen temporarily to England. The fashionable went to English spas for health and pleasure. Hely-Hutchinson, the well-known provost of Trinity, went to Buxton; at Tunbridge Wells, Lady Fitzgibbon, 'a very smart lady', attracted the attention of the prince of Wales, and it was said, 'almost estranged him from the other Fitz'; Bath, Beresford wrote, was 'a little Dublin to an

---

[5] James Barry the distinguished Irish painter and John Hickey the best-known Irish sculptor of the period spent most of their working lives in England.

[6] J. Aitken, *A description of the country for thirty or forty miles round Liverpool* (1795), p. 336; J. W. Wallace, *A general description of Liverpool* (1795); Journeys from Dublin to London 1761, 1762 (Add. MS 27951); *The benevolent society of St Patrick* (1822).

[7] J. Boswell, *Life of Johnson*, ed. G. B. Hill (1924), ii, p. 242.

Irishman', and the landlord of the Hop-pole in Worcester, on the direct road between Holyhead and Bath, thought it worthwhile to advertise in a Dublin newspaper. During 1798 it was said that both Bath and Clifton were benefiting from the disturbed state of Ireland and during Humbert's invasion of the west Pelham warmly sympathized with the anxieties of the many Irish who were staying in Brighton.[8]

Education led to a number of Irishmen going to England at some time in their lives. During the last half of the eighteenth century over 250 Irish boys went to either Eton or Harrow (the Etonians outnumbering the Harrovians by almost three to one). One distinguished Irishman attended both schools. Richard Wellesley, the eldest son of the earl of Mornington, was sent to Harrow in 1770. 'A tiny but intrepid insurgent',[9] he played a leading role in a barring-out, was expelled and went to Eton where he was followed by his four brothers. A few Irishmen attended Oxford and Cambridge (the combined entrance averaging about 10 per annum between 1752 and 1800—approximately two-thirds going to Oxford).[10] A number went to the Scottish universities which were more congenial to the northern presbyterian than Trinity college, Dublin. On average approximately a dozen students from Ireland matriculated at Glasgow every year. But the most influential educational link between England and Ireland was forged by the regulations governing admission to the Irish bar. Before being called, an Irish law student had to spend eight terms (two years) at an English inn of court, and during the second half of the eighteenth century over 1,900 Irishmen entered at an English inn. What this implied varied with the individual student. For all it meant was of course paying the fees and eating the dinners. But if George Ponsonby, a future Irish lord chancellor, when he went to London entered the office of a special pleader and 'read law, a thing seldom done by the generality of students', another future judge, Hussey Burgh, an admirer wrote, 'did not wear away his constitution by

[8] Sheffield to Eden, 5 Oct. 1788 (Add. MS 34428); J. Beresford to Auckland, 29 Mar. 1795 (Add. MS 34453); *D.J.*, 3 Apr. 1784; *D.E.P.*, 12 May 1798; Castlereagh, *Memoirs and correspondence*, i, p. 345.

[9] W. T. M. Torrens, *Marquess Wellesley*, i, p. 26.

[10] J. Foster, *Alumni Oxonienses 1715–1886*, 4 vols. (1887–8); J. A. Venn, *Alumni Cantabrigienses, Pt. II, 1752–1900*, 5 vols. (1940–53).

pouring over Coke or Littleton, but he studied history and constitutional law and enjoyed the pleasure which his rank in life afforded him and his peculiar taste in the liberal arts led him to'.[11] For all students, the intent as well as the easy-going, there was the exciting and broadening experience of life in a great capital.

Occasionally an Irish student decided to stay on in England and at the close of the century about a dozen Irishmen were practising at the English bar, the best known being James Adair, the recorder of London. Edmund Burke, who began his studies at the Middle Temple in 1750, soon drifted from law to literature, convinced that in London 'a man who writes can't miss . . . of getting some bread, and possibly good'.[12] Grattan, having returned to Ireland after four years in the Middle Temple, was soon tired of Dublin, 'with all its hospitality and all its claret', and was sighing for 'the splendid and enraptured scenes of London'.[13] His sentiments were echoed ten years later by a young Irish peer, Mornington, when he wrote from Dublin, 'I need not say how I pant for London.'[14] Mornington, who in addition to his seat in the Irish house of lords had, from 1784, a seat in the British house of commons, hesitated for a time between concentrating on College Green or Westminster. In the end he devoted himself to British politics, becoming in 1799 governor general of India. Another Irish peer, Lord Moira, who was to be a successor of Mornington in India, also hesitated between Ireland and British and imperial spheres of action. When in 1793 Moira, a soldier, returned to active service, an Irish poet sadly addressed him:

> Ah could thy country claim thee for her own
> Could thou descend to low provincial care!
> But claims imperial, calls of high renown
> And more extensive plans thy bosom share.[15]

A third young Irishman, who, towards the close of the

---

[11] *Hibernian Magazine*, 1782, pp. 97–8; *Exshaw's Gentleman's and Citizen's Magazine*, 1784, pp. 169–71.
[12] *The correspondence of Edmund Burke*, i, p. 101.
[13] H. Grattan, *Memoirs of the life and times of . . . Henry Grattan*, i, pp. 152–3.
[14] *Fortescue MSS H.M.C.*, i, p. 249.
[15] *Anthologia Hibernica*, ii, p. 66.

century faced the problem of choosing on which side of the channel to make his career, was Robert Stewart, to become famous as Lord Castlereagh. After he left Cambridge, Robert Stewart considered his future with the dispassionate attention which twenty years later he was to give to European power politics. There were two things, he thought, which would incline an Irishman to enter British politics: 'the superior interest of the extended sphere', and great self-confidence. Stewart doubted if he himself had the ability to make his way in the highly competitive English world. 'I feel no confidence in myself', he wrote, 'beyond a general disposition to business.' So, admitting he would always regret 'that my lot had placed me in the narrower sphere', he decided 'to make Ireland, as nature had already decided, for my country and to consider England, though superior in every point of view, as secondary to me at least.'[16]

Throughout the century Irish intellectual, cultural and fashionable life was dominated by England, or rather it might be said by London and its outposts, which threw a long shadow over provincial England as well as over Ireland and the British colonies. An Irish writer acknowledged the influence exercised by a metropolis when pointing out that there were to be found in Cork 'every entertainment which has the authority of Dublin (which place takes its example from London)'.[17] Irish newspapers and magazines were largely filled by material taken from English journals; most of the works sold by Irish booksellers were produced by British authors. The Irish theatres presented the latest London successes (often by Irish dramatists). English fashions in dress were quickly adopted in Ireland, Irish 'dashers', it was said, riding post-haste to London to buy their breeches; a Dublin bootmaker announced that he had imported the best London boots and legs 'as many prefer the English to the Irish fashion' and ladies hats were advertised as 'worn in London'.[18] Irish middle-class parents seem to have been anxious that their children should not have a distinctive Irish accent—what a fellow of Trinity called 'a horrid brogue'.

[16] R. Stewart to Camden, 23 Mar. 1790 (Pratt MSS).
[17] T. Smith, *The ancient and present state of Cork* (1750), i, p. 406.
[18] Journal kept in Dublin, 31 Jan. 1802 (R.I.A. 24 K 15); *D.E.P.*, 21 Apr. 1810; *H. J.*, 31 Mar. 1801.

A prominent Irish educationalist, Thomas Sheridan, stressed how important it was for Irishmen to 'get rid of that disgusting tone called an Irish brogue, which pervades every sentence they utter and renders them a perpetual subject of ridicule to all English hearers' (sad to say an English critic discovered that Sheridan's phonetics revealed his nationality—the natives of Ireland having 'a brogue, a certain harsh gutteral enunciation').[19] The headmaster of a good Dublin school assured parents that his 'young gentlemen read every day to a *native of England* whose accent is approved of'; another headmaster emphasized that he himself had been partly educated in England; a third advertised for an assistant 'who understands Greek and Latin perfectly and speaks the English language free from provincial accent'; and the headmistress of an academy for young ladies in Cork wanted 'a protestant English lady' who would have, in addition to a knowledge of French, 'a polite acquaintance with her native language'.[20] Irishmen, an essayist declared at the end of the century, were so governed by England 'in everything, taste as well as politics, that they seem absolutely afraid to give the stamp of approbation to anything in the first instance and hesitate whether it has merit or not until they see an English review'.[21]

Though Irish intellectual and cultural life was largely derivative there was, towards the close of the eighteenth century, plenty of vitality. In 1800, for instance, Dublin, Cork and Belfast possessed subscription libraries. Dublin at the end of the century had five well-established newspapers and every country town of importance had at least one newspaper. Belfast for some periods had two and Cork for a short time half a dozen. Two well-known Irish magazines, Exshaw's *Gentleman's and London Magazine* and Walker's *Hibernian Magazine* ran for years and a number of other periodicals had an ephemeral existence, the most ambitious being the *Anthologia Hibernica* which published essays, articles on antiquarian topics, and vast quantities of verse. Half a score of Irish country towns

[19] A. Browne, *Miscellaneous sketches* (1798), i, p. 143; T. Sheridan, *A short sketch of a plan for the improvement of education* (1788); *A caution to the gentlemen who use Mr Sheridan's dictionary* (3rd ed., 1791).
[20] C. Barry, *Plan for Rathmines school* (1790), p. 11; *D.E.P.*, 14 Jan. 1792; *S.N.L.*, 7 Jan. 1800, *Cork Advertizer*, 11 Sept. 1800.
[21] A. Browne, *Miscellaneous sketches*, i, p. 142.

had a theatre, and travelling companies, often composed of well-known actors and actresses from the capital, offered a wide selection of plays ranging from Shakespeare to the latest London farce. The theatre was one of the great pleasures of Irish life, and Ireland, a country which revelled in quick and vivid conversation and the cut and thrust of debate, made a substantial contribution to the British theatre. A remarkable number of well-known eighteenth-century playwrights were Irishmen—Farquhar, Congreve, Goldsmith, Sheridan, Murphy, Macklin, O'Keefe, Kelly, the last three being also well-known actors. Ireland was a great recruiting ground for the stage and the two actresses who, at the close of the century, were conspicuous for a combination of professional and social success, Mrs Farren, who became countess of Derby and Mrs Jordan, who became the acknowledged mistress of the duke of Clarence, were both from the south of Ireland.

A lively awareness of the course of events, of political developments and of cultural and intellectual trends characterized Irish society—that is to say those Irishmen and women who bought books or at least read newspapers, went to the theatre and took part in affairs, professional, business or political. It is also fair to say that Irishmen who worked and wrote in Ireland did not produce much that was distinctive or of striking importance in the spheres of literature, learning or even politics. Irish magazines boldly reprinted large quantities of material from British periodicals. Most of the plays performed in Ireland were written for the British stage. The Irish essayists who wrote on literature and history, Mullala, Sherlock, Alley, were well read, sensible and commonplace.[22] There were, during the last decade of the century, a number of respected scholars and men of letters working and writing in Ireland, for instance Magee, the theologian, Browne the jurist, Kirwan, the chemist, but their fame was contemporary and to a great extent local. It is impossible from the Irish intellectual world to select a name which would rank with Blackstone, Adam Smith, Samuel Johnson, Bentham, Priestley, Paley, or Boswell. Even in politics it was Locke whom Irishmen studied at the

---

[22] Horace Walpole pronounced that Sherlock 'has no guile, on the contrary too much benevolence in his indiscriminate praise but he has made many ingenious criticisms' (*Horace Walpole's correspondence*, ii, p. 302).

university, and Burke and Paine who at the end of the century polarized their opinions.

There was a large output of poetry. Henry Murphy was the author of an epic, *The Conquest of Quebec*, and of another large poem, 'a complete system of poetical ethics'. Patrick Kelly wrote *Killarney: a descriptive poem* (which he accompanied by some verses addressed by an admirer to himself). The poems of Daniel Hayes, a Limerick gentleman, were printed posthumously. In the late eighties and early nineties John Anketell, Henry Boyd (the translator of Dante), Thomas Dermody, Thomas Dawson Laurence, William Preston, Samuel Shepherd and Edward Walsh all published collections of their poems. Shepherd, a clerical pluralist and a viceregal chaplain was a master of courtly verse, and William Preston, a dramatist as well as a prolific poet, produced, as he said himself, verse of 'a satirical cast' or 'of a moral or didactic tendency', 'light pieces of an airy and sportative turn', and a considerable amount of love poetry, the aim of which was 'to excite passion by exhibiting the perturbed state of an enamoured mind'. But though the poets wrote with feeling it must be admitted that little if anything of the vast quantity of verse they produced, conventionally correct in style and technique, is memorable.

It is not easy to draw up a cultural balance sheet for a community. In the preface to its first volume the Royal Irish academy frankly admitted that 'to the several advantages which Europe has within these latter centuries experienced from the cultivation of science and polite literature, this kingdom unfortunately has remained in a great measure a stranger', although it quickly added, this had been due to the working of historic forces and now a new age had dawned. The academy's secretary, William Preston, the poet, put it bluntly. 'The Irish', he wrote, 'with a number of good qualities, are taken collectively, an unlettered people.'[23]

For any weakness of creative vigour in Irish cultural and intellectual life during the latter eighteenth century several explanations may be advanced. The amount of time and energy absorbed by politics; the magnetic attraction of Great Britain and especially London for Irish writers and scholars, and the deep-seated divisions in Irish society. Catholics and

[23] W. Preston, *Poetical works* (1793), i, p. xv.

protestants were separated educationally, many catholics went abroad for their education and some preferred to live and work in catholic countries. Then, though contemporaries did not dwell on the fact, Ireland was a country of two cultures. The great bulk of the country people, farmers and labourers, still spoke Irish and were therefore the heirs of a great, if shattered and declining literary tradition. Gaelic culture in its heyday had been aristocratic. The literati, the bards, the poets, the jurists, were closely connected with the ruling world of the Gaelic princely families. Though Gaelic literature and learning ranged from lyrics to law tracts, from the vita sanctorum to collections of medical lore, its majestic core was formed by the sagas and one of its most characteristic products was the panegyric, commemorating in verbal baroque the achievements and lineage of a proud and powerful family. These writings reflect the ideals of a military aristocracy. They delight in conflict, and the hero is bold, enduring, generous, ruthless and cunning.

From the sixteenth century, with English rapidly becoming the language of politics, administration, science, business life and fashion, and English or Latin the language of theology, the Gaelic language, excluded from large areas of intellectual and practical life, narrowed, and by the eighteenth century was the medium of a popular culture, expressing itself in ballads, folk tales and proverbs. There were those who were loath to let a great tradition die. Poets lamented the decline and fall of the Gaelic ruling families; here and there a country gentleman entertained the surviving bards; there were schoolmasters who prided themselves on their knowledge of the language and keen scribes who devotedly copied manuscripts. All the evidence suggests that the English-speaking world in Ireland attributed little significance to the fact that the majority of the population still spoke Irish. The evidence admittedly is negative, but it is remarkable how rarely a reference to the prevalence of the Irish language over large areas of the countryside occurs in the newspaper press, or in contemporary pamphlets or correspondence. Apparently only once during the latter half of the eighteenth century was the language question raised in parliamentary debate. In 1796, when a bill regulating the franchise reached the lords, an amendment was inserted obliging a freeholder to take the registry oath in English. Permitting the oath to be taken through an interpreter, Lord Clare argued, would afford opportunities for perjury. When the bill was returned to the commons, several M.P.s, including Grattan, strongly attacked the amendment. It would, it was asserted, disqualify three-quarters of the freeholders in Connaught, a very large proportion of those in Munster and a large body in Ulster, and would convince the catholics that parliament intended to 'nibble away' the grant of the franchise made to them in 1793. Respect for catholic susceptibilities prevailed and the bill was lost.[24]

There was not amongst the Anglo-Irish in the eighteenth century a strong, sustained hostility to the Irish language—indeed a very popular drinking song, 'Bumper, Squire Jones', seems to have represented a fusion of the two cultures, being a free translation of a Gaelic ballad sung to a Gaelic air.[25] There was simply a lack of interest in a cultural tradition which had become associated with the lower orders and which, it was assumed, would disappear with the advance of civilization. It is not easy to discern to what extent Anglo-Irish culture was influenced by the Gaelic world in which it was set. Dramatists may have benefited by contact with a tradition which appreciated verbal fluency and the flashing phrase. Edmund Burke, a man of sensitive and capacious mind, probably derived his flair for the telling metaphor and his love of exuberant imagery from his contact with the Gaelic world, and boyhood visits to Munster must have helped to develop his sympathetic awareness of the variations of cultural experience. But the vast output of material which poured from Irish printing presses seems identical in style and tone with much of what appeared on the other side of the channel.

It might be thought that at a time when Ireland was engaged in a series of spectacular struggles to obtain its political rights an attempt would be made to strengthen its claim to possess a distinctive political identity by dwelling on its Gaelic tradition, the great Gaelic literary heritage, the wars waged by the Irish against successive waves of invaders and the existence of Irish as a living language. As O'Halloran of Limerick put it,

[24] *D.E.P.*, 22 Mar. 1796; *D.J.*, 17 Mar. 1796.
[25] J. Walker, *Historical memorials of the Irish bards* (1786), pp. 75–7.

if Irish gentlemen, most of whom had 'Milesian or Strong-bonean blood' in their veins, considered themselves as springing from a common stock, 'that love of letters, of liberty and of national glory, which fired out ancestors, will insensibly lead us to illustrate the great examples'.[26] In fact one leading figure in Irish parliamentary politics, Henry Flood, was credited with being an early exponent of cultural nationalism. After his death it was said that one of his 'favourite opinions . . . which he defended with passionate zeal, was that every circumstance which tended to distinguish the people of this country from those of Great Britain—which led Irishmen to think of themselves as a distinct people must serve the country', and he left a very large bequest to Trinity college, Dublin, for the encouragement of Irish studies by the creation of a 'professorship of or for the native Irish or Erse language', and by the collection of Irish books and manuscripts.[27] But there is no evidence that during his active political career Flood ever drew attention to Ireland's Gaelic past, and it may be added that, keen nationalist as he was, he was looking for a seat at Westminster, and seven years before his death he at last managed to enter the British house of commons. In short, a politically-minded Irishman, even if he was interested in Ireland's remote past or had a taste for antiquarian research, when discussing public issues spoke as a man who shared the British constitutional, historical and political traditions, and he was convinced that Ireland's separate identity was demonstrated and guaranteed by the sheer simple facts of geography.

Of course during the eighteenth century many intelligent men, very conscious that they themselves were living in a highly civilized epoch, were keenly interested in the history, literature and antiquities of the early inhabitants of the British Isles. The reception of Ossian revealed and encouraged a widespread interest in the Celtic past. Macpherson's verses might be stilted and his sources suspect, but he stirred his readers' imaginations by his picture of the British heroic age. Irish poetry seemed to Horace Walpole, a sophisticated critic, to

---

[26] S. O'Halloran, *Insula sacra* (1770).
[27] *D.E.P.*, 10 Dec. 1791. The bequest was held to be void as contrary to the statute of Mortmain (E. Hayes, *Reports of cases argued in the court of exchequer in Ireland* (1831), pp. 611–41).

'contain natural images and natural sentiments elevated before rules were invented to make poetry difficult and dull'.[28] A number of enthusiastic pioneers, archaeologists, philologists, and antiquarians, often amateurs and inevitably largely self-trained, strove hard to collect manuscripts and antiquities, and to unravel the complex threads of pre-Christian and early Christian history.

Outstanding for his decisiveness as a scholar and his vigour as an organizer of research and publication was Charles Vallancey. Vallancey, an officer in the Royal engineers, who ultimately rose to the rank of lieutenant-general, was a scientific soldier, publishing in 1757 a translation of a French work on fortification. Employed in Ireland in constructing fortifications and surveying the country, he became an enthusiastic antiquarian. He strove to show that the early inhabitants of Ireland, Phaeno-Scythians, were highly civilized, 'a polished people', and he bolstered his theories by a vast display of faulty philological learning. Having read one of Vallancey's major works, Sir William Jones, the orientalist, remarked, 'Do you want to laugh? Skim the book over. Do you wish to sleep? Read it regularly.'[29] Vallancey might be dogmatic, wrong-headed and irritable, but his industry, range of interests and zest made him a very stimulating influence in Irish intellectual life. One of Vallancey's admirers was Charles O'Conor, a man of learning and a readable popularizer. O'Conor, a catholic landed gentleman, with a small estate in County Roscommon, was the senior representative of one of the greatest Gaelic princely families. Living among a Gaelic-speaking people, the friend and patron of the surviving bards, he was an assiduous collector of Gaelic manuscripts, and spending half the year in the country and half in Dublin, he had a wide circle of friends, including Lord Moira; his publisher Faulkner; Delany, the dean of Down; Curry, the catholic publicist; Leland, a fellow of Trinity, who made him, 'free' of the college library, and Burton, an art patron and well-known improving landlord, 'the greatest friend Ireland has met with through the lapse of six centuries'.[30] O'Conor had an enthusiastic admiration for the vanished Gaelic

[28] *Horace Walpole's correspondence*, xv, p. 61.
[29] *The letters of Sir William Jones* (1940), ii, p. 769.
[30] C. O'Conor to T. O'Gorman, 30 June 1785 (Add. MS 21121).

world. Its heroes, he wrote, were 'in no respect inferior to those of Greece and Rome, except in want of an historian'. The early Gaelic inhabitants of Ireland were 'a singular people', 'in their infancy martial and free, in their progress an industrious and legislating people, in their prosperity learned, religious and hospitable'—though he admitted 'in every period fractious and turbulent'. He was a man of his age in that Gaelic society, as he presented it, seems perhaps more Augustan than Homeric or primitive (the Celtic system of government was, he explained, 'a mixed monarchy . . . in general too much under the control of aristocratical principle').[31] But he had high standards and worked with a strong sense of purpose. His aim being, his son recorded, 'to disarm persecution' by drawing the attention of the ruling world to the achievements of their Gaelic predecessors and reminding them of the vicissitudes of human history.[32]

Others keenly interested in early Irish history and literature included Ledwich the antiquarian, O'Halloran, a distinguished surgeon who turned to history, and Barnard the bishop of Limerick, a member of Johnson's circle in London, who wrote on the Scottish settlements in Britain. Sullivan, a fellow of Trinity College, collected Gaelic law tracts, Matthew Young, another fellow, was interested in Gaelic poetry, Scottish and Irish; Cooper Walker published works on ancient Irish dress and armour and on the Irish bards, and his friend, Charlotte Brooke, in her *Reliques of Irish poetry*, translated a number of Gaelic poems, clothing them 'in the vesture of modern rhyme'[33]—it may be added that the translations of Irish poems which occasionally appeared in the magazines, in vocabulary and versification, conformed to current conventional modes. Country gentlemen, such as Ralph Ouseley of Limerick or Green of Greenville in County Wicklow, reported on archaeological finds; even a busy lawyer, Arthur Browne, found time when visiting the archbishop of Armagh on official business to ride into the country to inspect an ogham inscription, and Townshend, when lord lieutenant, on being shown a sword, probably it was thought Phoenician, which had been found in

[31] C. O'Conor, *Dissertations on the history of Ireland* (1766), pp. 48, 51, 232–3.
[32] C. O'Conor, *Memoirs of the life . . . of the late Charles O'Conor* (1796), p. 309.
[33] Miss Brooke, *Memoir* (1812), p. xli.

a Tipperary bog, said he would use the pattern for his regiment.[34]

This antiquarian enthusiasm strongly promoted the formation of the Royal Irish academy in 1785. The eighteenth century attributed considerable practical and symbolic importance to the academy, the society in which men of learning and men of taste met to exchange ideas and extend the frontiers of knowledge. About the middle of the century there was in Dublin a society, the Physico-Historical Society, which might have become a great focus of Irish intellectual life. Founded in the early forties and composed of clergymen, country gentlemen and dons, interested in 'the rarities of art and nature', it aimed at publishing a survey of each Irish county, the eclectic nature of its approach to the task being illustrated by the offer of a member to procure for the society 'an old Gaelic manuscript and some sulphurous water' from County Leitrim. The society was responsible for the publication of work on five counties, but soon an ominous note appeared in the minutes, 'that this society proceed to no business until the accounts of this society are settled', and it seems to have ceased meeting in the early fifties. Twenty years later another body which might have developed into an academy was constituted, when in 1772 the Royal Dublin society appointed a committee 'to inquire into the ancient state of the literature and other antiquities of Ireland'. It was composed of prelates, peers and M.P.s but the driving force must have been supplied by the two secretaries, Charles Vallancey and Thomas Leland. The committee received a most encouraging letter from 'the College of Lombards' in Paris, expressing its pleasure that a scheme for collecting the material for a history of 'old Ireland' should be 'projected and patronized by the men under whose influence modern Ireland makes so distinguished a figure', and at first the society in a short burst of energetic activity located a number of Gaelic manuscripts, then it languished and ceased to operate; possibly owing to the irascible Vallancey reacting unfavourably to Edward Ledwich's waspish comments.[35]

---

[34] R.I.A. Trans., viii (antiquities), pp. 5, 12; P. Luckombe, Tour of Ireland (1780), p. 165.

[35] For these societies see preface to vol. i of R.I.A. Trans. and R.I.A. MSS 24 E 7, 24 E 28.

This society helped however to prepare the ground for the establishment of the Royal Irish academy, a body with about ninety members, which aimed at encouraging work in science and literature as well as antiquities 'uniting what is pleasing with what is useful'. The first secretary, William Preston, indeed complained that 'the taste of too many who have leisure and the inclination for literary pursuits, has taken an unhappy turn towards the minute spirit of antiquarian research, whose only object is to rake into the dust and rummage old collections of lumber for exploded trash and obsolete absurdities'. The published transactions of the society do not support his assertion, the antiquarian section being overshadowed by the other two branches, Preston himself contributing several articles to the polite literature section, including 'Thoughts on lyric poetry' with the principles he laid down illustrated by an ode of his own composition.

But though the Gaelic past fascinated antiquarians and on occasion inspired a poet, and even though the bulk of the country people spoke Irish, the Gaelic tradition did not noticeably influence the comfortably established, intellectually alert eighteenth-century Irishman. What did give a distinctive note to Irish cultural life, politics and society, was religion, the denominational pattern. This was highly anomalous. In Ireland the struggle between the reformation and the counter-reformation had coincided with the advance of the Tudor monarchy, and by the time the royal authority was effectually extended over the whole country, the catholic church had secured the allegiance of the bulk of the population. But the crown assumed that the religious polity it favoured in England should be adopted in Ireland, with the result that the established church was anglican and was the church of only a small proportion of the population. The situation was further complicated by the formation of a large Scottish colony in Ulster, the Scots importing presbyterianism. Irish religious statistics for the seventeenth and eighteenth centuries are merely estimates based on defective materials, and the first reliable religious census was that of 1861. However an indication of the denominational balance at the close of the eighteenth century is given by the (unreliable) religious census of 1834. According to it 10·7 per cent of the population adhered to the established church, nearly 9 per cent were presbyterian and almost 81 per cent catholic. Members of the establishment amounted to about 16·5 per cent of the total population of Ulster, about 14 per cent of the population of Leinster, being particularly strong in the Dublin area where they formed about a fifth of the population, but they comprised only about 3 to 5 per cent of the community in the south and west. About 45 per cent of the Irish anglicans and approximately 99 per cent of Irish presbyterians were in the province of Ulster. Over half the presbyterians in Ireland were concentrated in three dioceses, Down, Connor and Dromore, and these three dioceses were the only ones in which protestants outnumbered catholics. The catholics amounted to four-fifths of the population, in the south and west outnumbering protestants by about nineteen to one.[36]

This denominational balance, which was one of the most striking features of Irish life, gave a distinctive quality to each of the three great religious bodies. The members of the Church of Ireland, undismayed by their relative paucity of numbers, took the status and privileges of their church for granted. They firmly believed that the Church of Ireland, catholic and reformed in doctrine and discipline, reverential and rational, with its dignified ceremonial and sober piety, was the institution best fitted to bring Irishmen into the way of Christian truth. They were also convinced that anglicanism, with its loyalty to the crown, its balance of liberty and order, its respect for subordination and avoidance of extremes, was the natural ally of the eighteenth-century British and Irish state. The British constitution, a distinguished divine declared, was 'the model of government approaching nearest the ideal of perfection',[37] and such a state was indeed a fitting partner for the church. With a membership which comprised the governing world and the vast majority of Irish landlords, the Church of Ireland was in a position to instruct and inspire powerful sections of Irish society, and it could expect that in due time it would be able to influence directly the mass of Irishmen. Contemporary intellectual and political trends were, it seemed, working in its

---

[36] *First report of the commissioners of public instruction in Ireland,* H.C. [45], 1835, xxxiii. R. Woodward in his *The present state of the Church of Ireland* (1786) was of the opinion that the members of the established church amounted to an eighth of the population.

[37] T. Campbell, *A sermon* (1794), p. 68.

favour. Enlightenment and the penal laws might be trusted to change the denominational balance. The position of the established church was so secure that during most of the century its members did not feel strongly constrained to embark on a vigorous campaign for the conversion of Ireland. Admittedly early in the century, towards the close of Queen Anne's reign, the house of commons and convocation deliberated on 'the proper methods for the conversion of the popish natives of this country' to the established church. It was suggested that Irish-speaking clergymen should be appointed as evangelists, that Trinity college should provide teaching in Irish, that Irish bibles and catechisms should be widely distributed, and that there should be parish charity schools at which attendance should be compulsory, in which the children 'shall be taught gratis to speak and read English'. There was general agreement that a drive should be made to convert the natives, but there were differences of opinion over important issues. There were apprehensions that missionary zeal might make light of ecclesiastical discipline and jurisdiction (an attitude which half a century later was to influence the establishment's reaction to methodism). Some, notably the Revd John Richardson, a fervent and intelligent advocate and organizer of evangelicalism, were in favour of preaching and teaching in Irish. To give the Irish an opportunity to hear prayers in their own language, which they preferred to Latin, was, Richardson wrote, 'like giving sight to the blind'. But there were others who felt that protestantism and the English language were natural allies, and that 'to keep up a difference of language will keep up a difference of religion'—to which Richardson retorted that if the Irish natives conform to the established church they 'would more readily fall in with our customs and language'. Discussions over details and finance delayed the beginning of the great missionary enterprise, and the movement, which was to some extent at least a facet of the high church revival of Queen Anne's reign, waned swiftly at the beginning of the Hanoverian age, and Richardson, whom parliament in 1711 had recommended to the queen, ended his life almost forty years later as dean of Kilmacdaugh.[38] Forty years after his death, Richardson's

[38] J. Richardson, *The church catechism explained and* . . . *rendered into Irish* (1712), pp. 45, 54, 105, 109.

views on the evangelization of Ireland were confirmed by a leading catholic ecclesiastic, Father John Walsh, the superior of one of the Irish colleges in Paris. In a memorandum to the Holy See, he pointed out that the existence of two languages in Ireland was the most formidable barrier against the spread of heresy, adding how fortunate it would be if people in France 'ignorait la langue des journalistes et des nouveaux législateurs'.[39]

At the beginning of George II's reign, a large-scale, if less ambitious, scheme for the conversion of Irish catholics was launched. In 1733 a group of influential Irishmen was incorporated and empowered to found boarding schools in which the children of catholics were to be taught protestant principles, reading and writing. They were also to receive vocational education in agriculture, a trade or housewifery. The scheme, it was hoped, would 'rescue thousands of poor children from the dangers of popish superstition and idolatry, and their bodies from the miseries of beggary and idleness'. Parliament regularly made large grants to the chartered schools, but after a hopeful beginning the scheme made little progress. While there were forty-four schools in 1748, forty years later there were only thirty-eight with four 'nurseries', containing to about 1,500 children. When the schools were inspected in 1788 by two well-known prison reformers, Howard and Fitzpatrick, they were found to be in a scandalous condition. The funds were being misappropriated by the masters, the children were underfed, overworked, ill-educated and often sickly and living in disgusting conditions.[40]

The failure of the charter schools not only illustrated the harm that could be done by a combination of faulty administrative planning and negligence, it also strikingly demonstrates the lack of sustained and urgent interest in a major project for the conversion of the Irish catholics amongst eighteenth-century Irish protestants. Few clergymen of the Church of Ireland would have gone as far as Paley's friend, Law, bishop of Elphin, who thinking it 'a hopeless task to make his flock protestant', distributed throughout his diocese a short work

[39] *Archivium Hibernicum*, vii, pp. 4–5.
[40] *A view of the rise of the incorporated society* (1748); *Commons' Jn. Ire.*, xii, pp. dcccx–dcccxxx.

on ethics by a catholic divine. But though it was accepted by Irish churchmen that 'our reformation from popery . . . is the main fundamental subject of controversy in this part of the Christian world', and that the Church of Ireland clergy must be ready to handle the main points in dispute, the list of books recommended in 1790 by the Irish bench to Trinity college students preparing for orders, does not include a work dealing specifically with the protestant–Roman catholic controversy.[41] Most members of the establishment in fact seem to have regarded the situation in Ireland with complacency, or were prepared to accept calmly that the progress of truth, if certain, would be slow.

The more active and conscientious churchmen had plenty to absorb their energies. Keeping the complex machinery of their church functioning and trying to improve it was bound to occupy much of their time. The Church of Ireland had inherited the old diocesan and parochial framework of the medieval church and possessed the pre-reformation property of the church—tithes, church lands, glebes, church buildings. This was an impressive and immense inheritance—with large liabilities. As a national church, responsible for the religious welfare of the whole population of Ireland, it was in duty bound to maintain an organization of churches and clergy covering the whole country. If, as its critics were bound to suggest, the established church possessed resources which were large in comparison to the number of its adherents, these resources were by no means excessive in relation to the duties it claimed it must fulfil. The scarring civil wars of the seventeenth and eighteenth centuries had inflicted serious losses on the Church of Ireland. Church lands and tithes had in places passed into lay ownership and many parishes were without churches or glebes. Slowly during the eighteenth century efforts were made by the Church of Ireland to repair its deficiencies. In several dioceses the restoration of the cathedral was handled with brisk common sense. In Down, in 1790, the chancel of the great ruined abbey church at Downpatrick was sensibly converted into a compact cathedral. In Clogher, Bishop Stearne built a cathedral described by his successor as

---

[41] Gent. Mag., lxxx, p. 380. A. St George, The archdeacon's examination of candidates for holy orders (1751), p. 19; T.C.D., board register, 24 May 1790.

'a neat respectable parish church'. In Limerick about the middle of the century, Saint Mary's cathedral was repaired and enlarged, 'three elegant brass branches' being erected to supply light in winter, and the arches of the choir were glazed which 'renders it [the cathedral] warm and it is now one of the largest and most convenient churches in the kingdom'. In Cork the decayed medieval cathedral was replaced by 'a well looking modern one built of handsome white stone'. In Cashel the medieval cathedral on the rock had been allowed to fall into ruin, and in the sixties a solid, sober cathedral church, on 'a not inelegant plan' was erected in the town. In Waterford at the end of the seventies the medieval cathedral being ruinous was pulled down and replaced by a graceful, cool classical church 'executed with skill and strict economy'—as the protestant inhabitants pointed out when they successfully applied for a parliamentary grant towards the work.[42] In some parishes, especially in the urban areas new churches were built. A dozen parish churches were erected in Dublin during the century of which the most striking was Saint Werburgh's, with a front which, it was said, 'displayed bold elegance and delicacy' and an interior which inspired 'awful sentiments—it is capacious'.[43] In Cork four parish churches were built in the first half of the century; in Drogheda Saint Peter's was renovated about 1740 on an impressive scale. At Hillsborough, a new church with a fine organ and stained-glass windows, built at the expense of the earl of Hillsborough, was opened in 1773. The cathedral at Downpatrick being in ruins, the new church at Hillsborough was attended by the bishop, the earl when in residence, and the borough corporation, in their furred robes, preceded by a heavy silver mace. In Belfast a new church, dedicated to Saint Anne (the countess of Donegall's Christian name was Anne) with a 'high and beautiful steeple'—unfortunately disproportionately large for the church, was built in 1777. In Limerick about the middle of the century Saint John's was thoroughly repaired and the medieval church of Saint

---

[42] G. W. O. Addleshaw and F. Etchells, *The architectural setting of anglican worship* (1948), pp. 198–9; *Stopford-Sackville MSS H.M.C.*, i, p. 279; J. Ferrar, *History of Limerick* (1787), p. 160; Beaufort, Tour (T.C.D. MS 4038), p. 68; Bowden, *A tour through Ireland* (1791), p. 150; *Commons' Jn. Ire.*, ix, p. 356.

[43] R. Pool and J. Cash, *Views of the most remarkable public buildings*, pp. 87–9, and H. A. Wheeler and M. J. Craig, *The Dublin city churches* (1948).

Munchin's was improved by the addition of a gallery and a vestry room and by 'stuccoing and beautifying'; and towards the end of the century a gentleman touring the south was impressed by 'the neat appearance of the rising spires' of the churches being built by Archbishop Agar of Cashel.[44]

A number of parishes secured parliamentary assistance towards rebuilding their churches and in 1758, 1765 and 1782 parliament placed large sums at the disposal of the board of first fruits for building new churches and from 1786 an annual grant was made to the board for that purpose—it being thought that 'the performance of divine service will contribute to promote virtue and industry' and extend the protestant religion. As a result between 1785 and 1782 over seventy new churches were built and between 1786 and 1806 the board made grants towards the building of 210 churches and 209 glebe houses and towards purchasing 73 glebes.[45]

In spite of these efforts to remedy deficiencies, at the beginning of the nineteenth century of the 1,150 benefices with cure of souls in the established church, 17·7 per cent were without a church and 57 per cent lacked a glebe house.[46] In the absence of a church communion was sometimes administered in a gentleman's parlour,[47] but the absence of a glebe house provided many incumbents with an excuse for non-residence. There were very many instances of an incumbent living outside his parish boundaries but nevertheless close enough to perform his duties—not a very satisfactory arrangement. Thirty-four per cent of the incumbents however were non-resident in the fullest sense of the term, being resident on another benefice (often in a distant diocese), performing other duties, acting as a vicar general or master of an endowed school or absent with or without leave 'at Bath or some other English pool of Bethesda'.[48] In 1805 a Cloyne incumbent was staying

---

[44] D. A. Beaufort, A tour (T.C.D. MS 4038) p. 71; G. Benn, *History of the town of Belfast* (1823), p. 113; C. T. Bowden, *A tour through Ireland*, pp. 150–1.

[45] *Commons' Jn. Ire.*, viii, pp. 141, ccxxix; x, p. 238; xi, p. 69. *Papers relating to the established church in Ireland*, pp. 126–7, H.C. (78), 1807, v. The number of churches built between 1758 and 1782 with parliamentary assistance was probably between 70 and 100.

[46] *Papers relating to the established church in Ireland*, H.C. (78), 1807, v.

[47] For an occasion when this practice was followed see W. Bingley, *An examination into the discontents in Ireland* (1799), p. 48.

[48] S. Anketell, *Poems* (1793), p. x.

in Italy 'for the health of his daughter' and the vicar of Kil-fenora, having fled from his living in 1798, had not yet returned. When a clergyman was non-resident his duties were performed either by his curate or by a neighbouring incumbent or curate, and there were instances of an incumbent of a small living acting as curate in a neighbouring parish. The low value of many livings excused pluralities, one of the causes of non-residence. It might of course be said that some of those who held more than one benefice, if not the bloated pluralists of cliché, were in fact comparatively well off. They would probably have retorted that their resources were not in excess of their needs.

Allowing for non-residence the number of Church of Ireland clergy performing parochial duty was approximately 1,280 (just over 800 incumbents and about 475 curates). They were grouped in 22 dioceses, presided over by four metropolitans and 18 bishops (the somewhat top-heavy episcopate being a diminished reflection of the celtic church order). It may be added there were 30 cathedrals (of which 16 were parish churches), with dignitaries, canons and prebendaries—some with cure of souls, others enjoying 'a perfect sinecure'.[49] There were enormous varieties of income amongst this clerical body. The rector of Armagh was said, in the mid-eighteenth century, to be worth £1,000 per annum; at the other extreme there were a number of livings worth only a few pounds a year. In the eighties it was stated by an apologist for the establishment that the average income of an incumbent varied between £250 in the diocese of Clogher and £115 in the diocese of Dublin, and that the average for the incumbents of a group of dioceses from which he obtained material, was £150 per annum (reduced by the expenses of tithe collection to £133 per annum). But he seems to have excluded in his calculations the glebe income and pluralities, nor does he refer to the cost of a curate.[50] Curates' incomes, it may be added, were relatively uniform. An act of 1719 fixed the maximum stipend which a bishop could direct to be provided when he licensed a curate at £50 per annum, a figure raised in 1800 to £75; and curates seem usually

[49] *Second report from the commissioners on ecclesiastical revenues and patronage, Ireland*, H.C. (589), 1834, xxxiii.
[50] Petition of the rector of Armagh (S.P. 63/417 f. 200); R. Woodward, *The present state of the church of Ireland*, pp. 42–3.

to have received about the statutory maximum. A saddened curate with literary ambitions who failed to obtain preferment, wrote of their pitiful incomes and remarked that 'the epithet Reverend . . . a poor shred of sacerdotal respectability' had a touch of absurdity when applied to a curate. But a bishop noted that his curates were allowed by their rectors a stipend, 'as hath alas tempted most of them to marry, and it is not uncommon to have curates that are fathers of eight or ten children'.[51] Taking everything into account most of the clergy of the Church of Ireland had, or could look forward to, moderate, but definitely middle-class incomes, 'accompanied by the necessity of preserving a respectable and liberal appearance'.[52]

A few incumbents and the members of the bench of bishops had substantial incomes. The bishops' incomes varied considerably from the seven or eight thousand a year enjoyed by the archbishop of Armagh and the bishop of Derry to the £2,000 a year of the bishop of Ossory, the average episcopal income in the late seventies being about £2,300.[53] This was not excessive if it is taken into account that a bishop was a peer of parliament and a local magnate. At the close of the century O'Beirne of Ossory, one of the ablest men on the bench, said that his income (£2,300 a year) was insufficient. He would, he wrote, either have 'to shut myself up' in his palace (a wretched barracks needing improvement) or 'live amongst the very numerous gentry who are proverbial for their extravagant living'—fortunately his dilemma was resolved by his translation to Meath.[54] A previous bishop of Ossory who was translated to Clogher was delighted with his new post. He had a palace which was 'far from a disreputable place of residence', with a well-planted demesne. 'My beef, mutton, veal and lamb', he wrote, 'are all as good in their kinds as can be, the farm is to produce pigs, poultry, cream and butter, hay, oats and straw. The decoy gives me teal and wild duck, the warren supplies me with as excellent rabbits as I ever tasted, the pigeon house with pigeons, the water furnishes carp, tench, trout, eels, perch and pike, the venison in the park is remarkably good and a

[51] S. Anketell, Poems; A sermon on the distressed curates of the establishment (1787); T. Rundle, Letters . . . with introductory memoirs, i, pp. clxi–clxii.
[52] An address to the protestant clergy (1787), p. 32.
[53] A. Young, A tour of Ireland, ii, p. 112.
[54] T. L. O'Beirne to Portland, 31 July 1795 (Portland papers).

most extensive range of mountain . . . yields . . . an astounding
profusion of partridge, hares and grouse.' He also had a
borough under his control and a diocese in 'the highest order',
with a most respectable body of clergy, 'many of them learned,
all of them conscientious and exemplary'. Contemplating his
condition, Hotham could not but feel gratitude to the Supreme disposer of all events and to his influential friends, and
he looked forward both to enjoying 'the great prize' he had
won and to being of some service to the public by 'the exertion
of that degree of common sense which God has given him'.[55]

Hotham and O'Beirne together were representative in two
respects of the eighteenth-century Irish bench. To begin with
Hotham was English and O'Beirne Irish. It was taken as
axiomatic throughout the century that a substantial number of
episcopal vacancies in Ireland should be filled by Englishmen—
a practice which would strengthen the connection between the
two kingdoms and the two branches of the anglican communion,
and at the time of union nine members of the Irish episcopate
were of English or Scottish origin and of the thirteen Irishmen
on the bench four were graduates of Oxford or Cambridge.
Again, O'Beirne undoubtedly owed his place on the bench to
his own abilities. A man of great versatility, having been born
and educated as a catholic, he became an anglican, served as a
naval chaplain, translated a French farce for the English stage,
acted as chaplain and private secretary to two viceroys; as a
bishop he published a number of theological works and was a
very competent diocesan administrator. Hotham, who inherited a baronetcy and whose distinguished Yorkshire family
was prolific in men of affairs and courtiers, had been a royal
chaplain before coming to Ireland. In 1800 the Irish episcopate
included a peer (the bishop of Derry), five sons of peers, the
grandson of a peer and the son of a bishop. It also included six
sometime viceregal chaplains, of whom two, Bennet, an expert
on Roman Britain and O'Beirne had a reputation for learning.
Three other members of the bench were scholars of some
distinction. Percy of Dromore, the editor of the *Reliques* and two
sometime fellows of Trinity college, Dublin, Hamilton of
Ossory, a mathematician and philosopher and Stock of Killala,
a classicist.

[55] *Stopford-Sackville MSS H.M.C.*, i, pp. 279–80.

With birth and scholarship conspicuously represented in its ranks, the episcopal bench was bound to secure considerable contemporary respect. Its members behaved with decorum, were generous in helping good causes and performed their duties adequately by the not over-exacting standards of their time. Even Hervey of Derry, whose physical and mental restlessness, boundless self-assurance, extravagance, absenteeism and radicalism, were bound, especially in conjunction, to arouse criticism, was an active beneficient bishop, commemorated by an obelisk. One bishop, the energetic O'Beirne of Meath, was at the beginning of the nineteenth century profoundly concerned about the condition of the established church, with its clergy rendered lethargic by security and its laity indifferent to its interests. But his remedies were not dramatic—the closest possible contact with the church of England, the building of glebe houses and churches and the enforcement of clerical residence. The attitude of the bench in general was probably expressed by Brodrick, the archbishop of Cashel, in his reply to the question what steps if any should be taken to strengthen the church. Brodrick in his reply made two points—that 'a due regard to the regular and steady execution of the laws . . . will . . . gradually promote the discipline of the church and secure permanently its interests'; and that though 'it is not to be denied that there are circumstances in the church establishment which, in theory, must be viewed as defects . . . it is not so certain that these are found in practice to be attended with the evil consequences that might be expected from them'.[56]

For a bishop or beneficed clergyman obtaining his income was a task requiring time and planning. A bishop had to consider the terms of his leases; an incumbent, if he had a glebe, had to farm or set it, and the collection of tithe, a major source of clerical income, was usually a complicated and frequently a contentious business. Tithe, the right of the church to one-tenth of the fruits of the earth, rested, its defenders were quick to assert, on the strongest of foundations. It had been established by the Jewish law and had scriptural sanction; its payment had been ordered by early councils and confirmed by Christian rulers. 'A multitude of sage legislators,' one of the great Irish

[56] *Papers relating to the established church in Ireland*, p. 331, HC (78), 1807, v; H. Dutton, *Statistical survey of the County of Clare* (1808), p. 189.

champions of tithe wrote, 'whose names adore the history of
the most enlightened nations upon earth . . . have for many
years given their deliberate sanction to the ancient system of
tithes.' It was a fair tax, varying with payer's income and in
practice it was levied at a rate well below the theoretical 10 per
cent. Not only did tithe sustain religion, but by entwining the
interests of the clergy with those of their parishioners, it
strengthened the bonds holding society together. Tithe guaranteed the maintenance of a well-educated, because decently
supported, parochial clergy and were it abolished the clergy
would become 'a degraded, debased and servile herd of
teachers'.[57] Finally, tithe was a form of property. It was taken
into account when land was bought and sold and when rents
were being fixed, and a challenge to tithe was, its defenders
emphasized, a threat to property in general and especially to
landed property and rent.

But though the upholders of the tithe system could deploy a
powerful array of arguments, it was widely resented. There
was the customary repugnance to taxation, and if agricultural
prices rose the tithe payer was probably acutely conscious of the
increase in tithe due to the proportion of his total income it
represented; if prices fell he probably was annoyed at having
to pay at all. Then there was the resentment of the actively
employed against the rentier. It was remarked that even
landlords, a social group prone to protect property rights,
showed 'supineness' when tithe was attacked. They even, it
seems, criticized it themselves, it being remarked that in at least
one county (Clare) tithe was spoken of contemptuously in
'common table-talk before servants'.[58]

In 1736 the house of commons resolved that tithe of agistment
should not be claimed, since levying it would stimulate
emigration and would 'occasion popery and infidelity to gain
ground'. Of course this resolution had not the force of law
(indeed it was explicitly stated it was to be followed by
legislation) but it was regarded by Irish tithe payers as morally
binding, and in 1800, just two months before the enactment of

---

[57] R. Woodward, *The present state of the church of Ireland*, 8th ed., p. 7; W. Hales,
Observations on the political influence of the doctrine of the pope's supremacy (1787).

[58] *The insurrection . . . in the province of Munster* (1787), p. 35; H. Dutton, *Statistical
survey of the County of Clare* (1808), p. 129.

the union, a bill was quickly passed barring claims to tithe of agistment. Seventeen spiritual peers and two lay peers (one of whom was a dean), though for the sake of peace they did not vote against the bill, protested against a measure which transferred property from one set of men to another.

The opposition of the house of commons to tithe of agistment not only deprived the clergy of a source of income but increased popular hostility to tithe. The poor farmer when he had to pay tithe on his potatoes would be acutely aware that a better-off neighbour was avoiding tithe on his grazing land. The assessment and collection of tithe frequently caused friction. Its range varied, local custom deciding which articles were titheable—in some parishes apparently tithes included small dues which in England would have been regarded as oppressive. In Ulster and much of Leinster, where the glebes were large, tithe was not charged on potatoes. In Munster potatoes were titheable. The parson's 'viewer' and the tithe payer might differ in opinion; when tithe was paid in kind the tithe owner and the tithe payer could make difficulties for each other—where as was more usual, it was paid in money, a modus had to be agreed on. Tithe proctors and tithe farmers—some tithe owners, shirking from a distasteful and difficult operation, farmed their tithe—were in the eighties denounced as extortioners. They may well, when collecting an upopular tax under a system abounding in anomalies and dubia, have pushed their claims too hard, especially when dealing with the poor and ignorant. Tithe was bound to be very strongly resented by dissenters, catholic and protestant, who had no wish to pay for a church whose ministrations they rejected. Protestant dissenters, a presbyterian minister wrote 'don't like to give more than a tenth of their labour for nothing'. During the great debate on tithe in the eighties O'Leary, the principal catholic publicist, commended by his co-religionists for his 'discreet zeal',[59] cautiously refrained from challenging the right of the clergy of the established church to tithe, but he took the opportunity to dwell on how the Irish catholics supported their clergy by their voluntary contributions.

Irishmen were however in the eighties given a foretaste of the strenuous and searching debates of the next decade by the

[59] Monument in Saint Patrick's church, Soho.

controversy which arose, the Munster tithe disturbances. Richard Woodward, the bishop of Cloyne, a disturbed diocese, was interested in social problems and at the close of 1786 published a vigorous piece of episcopal pamphleteering, *The present state of the Church of Ireland*, which in a fortnight ran into a fourth edition. The established church, he argued, was an essential part of the political constitution, its members alone could be cordial friends to the constitution; and the preservation of the establishment was 'interesting to the landed gentry, the protestant government and the British empire'. It is hardly surprising that Woodward's uncompromising assertion of the supreme value of the alliance of Church and state should have produced strong reactions from catholic and presbyterian non-conformists. James Butler, the catholic archbishop of Cashel, by family, status and temperament a natural conservative, with pained indignation dwelt on catholic loyalty to crown and constitution. Father O'Leary, reminding his readers that until the sixties catholics could scarcely breathe in County Cork, sneered at Woodward's privileges, impugned his veracity and with some subtlety challenged the moral basis of the rights of the establishment. Two northern presbyterian ministers joined in the fray, William Campbell and Barber. Both denied that the established church was an essential element in the constitution, Campbell pointing out that neither Athanasius nor Thomas à Becket had contributed much to the peace of the community. Barber made it very clear that the presbyterians were 'not in love with their chains' and that in his opinion the sooner the ecclesiastical establishment, with all its privileges, dignitaries and tithes, was abolished the better. Both Campbell and Barber made it plain that the northern presbyterians were prepared to contemplate sweeping constitutional change and were convinced they had the right to participate in shaping their country's future. It is also noticeable that the tithe controversy stimulated controversy concerning aspects of the established order amongst those who might be expected to have a conservative bias. For instance in the house of commons when critics of the tithe system pointed out how harsh was the incidence of the tax on the small farmer or cottier, the defenders of ecclesiastical rights retorted that the real oppressors of the poor were middlemen and landlords.

Other methods of ensuring a provision for the clergy of the established church were suggested. Grattan in 1788 outlined in the house of commons a scheme for replacing tithe by a parochial rate, varying with the price of corn. This was essentially a conservative proposal, substituting a more popular (or less unpopular) tax for tithe. But Grattan, gripped by his own denunciatory vehemence, proved an unpersuasive advocate for a compromise solution. His brilliant exposition of the faults of the existing system was bound to stiffen the clergy's reluctance to surrender their historic and legally unchallengeable rights, and tithe remained an embittering problem for another half century.[60]

Tithe must have been for many sensitive clergymen a painful subject, driving a wedge between them and many of their parishioners. But it was a right they had an ex-officio duty to maintain, and tithe was an important portion of the property which placed them in a cherished position of independence and enabled them to render to the community valuable service in the secular as well as the spiritual sphere. At the close of the century about 300 clergymen were in the commission of the peace and some of them, being constantly resident, were outstandingly active magistrates. Again a number of Church of Ireland clergymen were inspectors of prisons or held municipal office. Bristow, vicar and for many years sovereign of Belfast, was a stately figure with his gold-headed cane and chain of office, and played a leading part in the administrative and charitable life of the town—presiding over the distribution of soup to the poor, helping to manage the dispensary, presenting a pulpit to the new catholic chapel and making a house-to-house collection for the sailors who fought at Camperdown. In Limerick, the Revd Deane Hoare, 'with a clear head and a good heart . . . laboured much to bring every charitable bequest to light' and took a leading part in managing the infirmary. In Dublin James Whitelaw was a pioneer in the compilation of social statistics; in Tyrone, Skelton gave his parishioners free medical advice and medicine (discovering that his charitable activities had reduced the income of the local medical man, he made him an allowance). Beaufort, the rector of Navan was a cartologist, William Traill, the rector of

Lisburn, a sometime professor of mathematics at Aberdeen, was so active in municipal affairs that a successor regretted that 'the great scholar's energies in Lisburn were chiefly directed to the paving of the streets'. Hugh Hamilton, a theologian and a mathematician of repute, when dean of Armagh, besides starting Sunday schools, founded a charitable loan scheme to assist indigent tradesmen, planned a new piped water-supply for the town and acted as treasurer of the county infirmary— when he decided that divine service should be regularly performed in the infirmary, 'unwilling to impose a new duty on his curate, he undertook it himself'. Many Church of Ireland clergymen were keen agricultural improvers and the serious-minded John Jebb, later bishop of Limerick, considered that 'a parish minister should possess an active bustling disposition, with some turn for agricultural pursuits and much fondness for introducing habits of sobriety, industry, cleanliness and comfort among the lower orders'.[61]

The presbyterians were geographically concentrated and ecclesiastically close-knit. With the exception of a few con-gregations scattered through the south and west, they were settled in Ulster, predominantly to the east.[62] Since Ulster was the most prosperous Irish province, with the eastern section its most prosperous zone, prosperity and presbyterianism were connected. Admittedly landed families of presbyterian stock tended to drift into the established church, the test act, military service, marriage and education inclining them to anglicanism. But many substantial farmers, and successful business or professional men were presbyterian, and the re-latively high Ulster living standards meant that many of the poorer presbyterians were well off compared to their equivalents in other parts of Ireland. The presbyterian clergy were con-spicuous and respected members of the community. They were not wealthy—many of them during the eighteenth century had incomes of only about £40 per annum, and in 1800 the average

---

[61] G. Benn, *History of Belfast*, ii, pp. 16, 26, 152; *U.J.A.*, 2nd series, p. 149; W. Carmody, *Lisburn cathedral* (1926), pp. 56–7; J. Ferrar, *History of Limerick* (1787), p. 227; H. Hamilton, *Works*, ed. A. Hamilton (1809), i, pp. xiv–xv; J. Jebb and A. Knox, *Thirty years, correspondence* (1834), i, p. 152.

[62] For Irish presbyterianism in the 18th century see J. S. Reid, *History of the presbyterian church of Ireland*, 3 vols (1867), and J. C. Beckett, *Protestant dissent in Ireland 1687–1780* (1948).

income of a minister belonging to the synod of Ulster (including *regium donum*—his share of the government grant to the presbyterian churches) was £83. Graduates of a Scottish university, Irish presbyterian ministers were trained in a strenuous educational tradition and they admired and to a great extent impressed on their people a respect for erudition and intellectual athleticism. Of course every presbyterian minister was not a man of learning, but John Leland, a Dublin minister, produced a comprehensive reply to all the leading deists, and William Crawford of Strabane rebuked Lord Chesterfield for the moral tone of his *Letters* and published a two-volume history of Ireland. John Cameron of Dunluce wrote an epic on the life of Christ which at least reached a second edition, James Porter of Greyabbey was one of the most sparkling Irish political satirists, and many Ulster ministers in sermon or pamphlet showed themselves to be relentless and resourceful dialecticians. It is also worth noting that amongst the sons of the eighteenth-century Irish manse were William Drennan, the radical publicist, Alexander Haliday, long the leader of the cultural life of Belfast, Adair Crawford, the chemist, William Conyingham Plunket, the lord chancellor, and Francis Hutchenson, the Scottish philosopher. Very conscious of the value of education, Irish presbyterians, though proud of their intellectual links with Scotland, wanted to have facilities for training their clergy at home in the north of Ireland. An academy approved in the eighties by the synod of Ulster, where candidates for the ministry could obtain instruction, flourished for a time in Strabane and in 1795, the foundation of a university in Ulster, under presbyterian direction, situated possibly in Cookstown, was mooted.

During the eighteenth century Irish presbyterians were divided over a fundamental issue: should standards of belief be enforced amongst christians? Extreme latitudinarians were not prepared to subscribe to formularies drafted by fallible men, if a statement of their faith was demanded they would give it in their own words. The orthodox stressed that creeds and confessions were required to preserve the truth and ensure mutual understanding. Hard debate ended in a compromise. In 1726 the synod of Ulster placed the non-subscribing ministers in a single presbytery, the presbytery of Antrim, which maintained a connection with the synod though its ministers did not sit in it. Throughout the century the controversy created tensions amongst Irish presbyterians. Many of the more intellectual ministers were latitudinarians, consciously enlightened and eager to reconcile religion with modern thought. The laity on the whole seem to have been in favour of orthodoxy, and the prevalence of moderatism in the synod of Ulster contributed to the growth of the secession churches in Ulster. The seceders left the established church of Scotland as a result of disputes over patronage. This cause of schism did not exist in Ireland but secession congregations were formed in Ulster, evangelical in outlook and drawn from the less prosperous sections of society. The seceders in Scotland split over the attitude to be adopted to the Scottish burger oath, and this secession divided the Irish secession church into burgers and anti-burgers and it certainly reflected the strength of the 'dividing spirit'[63] amongst Ulster presbyterians. Thus by the close of the eighteenth century there were three presbyterian churches in Ireland—the synod of Ulster (with about 180 congregations), the secession church and the Reformed presbyterian church.

All these churches believed in the same ecclesiastical polity— a hierarchy of committees, the congregational session, the presbytery and the synod. It was a system which bred a strict regard for legal forms, business capacity, debating ability and occasionally contentiousness. The synod of Ulster, as can be seen from its records, was ceaselessly engaged in regulating the relations between ministers, congregations and presbyteries, the synod and its committees clearly striving after equity and forebearance. Men familiar with this system were likely to be whigs or liberals—and even, to some extent, equalitarians, presbyterianism after all emphasizing the parity of ministers. But equalitarianism was severely qualified. Responsibility and power in each congregation were largely vested in the ministers and elders and from 1733 the ministers of congregations belonging to the synod of Ulster were chosen by a 'synodical majority' of the congregations, that is to say by a majority of two-thirds of those who paid two-thirds of the stipend.

Though respect for constitutional order was a strong element

---

[63] A sermon by the late Reverend Robert Craighead (1739).

in presbyterianism, Irish presbyterians were in the eyes of the law dissenters, and in the seventeenth and early eighteenth centuries they were subject to harassment by the civil and ecclesiastical authorities. This ceased with the Hanoverian age but the validity of presbyterian marriages was questionable until 1782, and until 1780 presbyterians were excluded from office under the crown and the commission of the peace by the test clause inserted in the popery act of 1704. Moreover, they had to pay tithe and see the anglican church enjoying the prestige and privileges of establishment. The disabilities endured by the Irish presbyterians were not very severe and were non-existent in the economic sphere. But they were bound to harden denominational loyalties and to stimulate the presbyterian into scrutinizing critically the established order. The middle-class presbyterian in fact could enjoy the feeling of being an outsider without suffering the discomforts associated with under-privilege. But along with a touch of alienation, there was amongst Irish presbyterians a strong tendency to see themselves as part of the established order. They were, the synod of Ulster pointed out to George III in 1761, 'the main strength of the protestant interest in Ulster and they had been encouraged by the crown to settle there. In Scotland, their intellectual home, presbyterianism was established, and in Ireland from 1690 the presbyterians had received an annual grant from the crown. The *regium donum*, considerably increased in 1784 and 1792, not only provided a welcome addition to ministerial incomes, but was important as an official acknowledgement of the value of presbyterianism to the community. Presbyterians, a representative of the synod of Ulster was quick to point out, regarded the grant not as a favour but as meeting 'a claim of right and justice upon the state'. Presbyterians might pride themselves on being independent and enlightened; they were far from being socially disruptive.

The catholic community was an unusual non-conformist body. It included the bulk of the population and prided itself on being historic and hierarchical. After the defeat of James II in Ireland the Irish parliament, determined to protect protestantism, strove to reduce to vanishing point the power of catholicism in Ireland. The attack developed along three lines— religious, political and economic. On the religious front a series of devastating blows were directed against the catholic ecclesiastical organization. The catholic bishops and regular clergy were expelled from Ireland. Secular priests (limited to one per parish) could only reside if registered, which involved subscribing to an oath which they felt unable to take.[64]

At first attempts were made to enforce this legislation. For some years there were only two catholic bishops in Ireland (one of whom was bed-ridden); arrangements were made to deport regulars; some priests were arrested, a few died in prison. But the enforcement of the legislation directed against the catholic ecclesiastical organization was largely a matter for the local magistracy, and though occasionally justices of the peace might be impelled into action by a strong sense of duty or a wave of panic, or by reports from a zealous protestant, on the whole Irish country gentlemen seem to have been anxious to avoid unpopularity and to keep on good terms with their neighbours, with whom they would want to have economic, social and sporting relations. So, from early in the eighteenth century the catholic church was functioning in Ireland to a great extent normally and with considerable success. Of course catholic ecclesiastical buildings had to be inconspicuous. Chapels were 'plain', though as early as 1730 a scandalized protestant ecclesiastic noted that the mass house at Mullingar had 'an aisle, three galleries and a spacious altar piece, painted and set off with images, flower pots and gilded candle sticks'.[65] Until well into the century bishops and priests were careful to attract as little attention as possible. As late as 1756 the archbishop of Armagh and a group of his clergy assembled to discuss diocesan business were detected, arrested and taken to Dundalk gaol. But it is significant that a local peer, 'treating them with the greatest politeness promptly released them'.[66] In the early decades of the eighteenth century the Irish catholic church had built up a strong nationwide organization. In 1731 the house of lords requested the bishops of the established church to report on the state of popery in their dioceses, and their flustered and unhappy reports show that there were in

[64] M. Wall, *The penal laws 1691–1760* (1961).
[65] *Lords' Jn. Ire.*, iii, pp. 207–10.
[66] J. Brady, 'Catholics and catholicism in the eighteenth century', in *Archivium Hibernicum*, xvi, p. 90. The peer was probably Lord Clanbrassill.

Ireland 1,440 priests, 60 religious houses and 890 mass houses, of which over a quarter had been built since 1714.[67]

What Irish catholics had to cope with was the humdrum, exacting and never-ending task of finding the resources with which to maintain their church. Their clergy were educated abroad, three-quarters of them in France, where there were seven Irish seminaries, partially endowed by the French crown.[68] When they returned to work in Ireland they depended on the contributions of the faithful. Parish priests received marriage and mortuary fees and a 'stated' contribution of one or two shillings a year from each family in the parish—the more opulent families however contributing about a guinea each. A parish priest's income varied with the size and wealth of his parish, and also, a bishop bluntly emphasized, was in proportion to the energy the priest put into collecting his dues. 'The strident, imprudent and importunate beggar', the bishop wrote, would obtain 'a tolerably handsome provision' from his parish; 'while the timid and bashful or rather silent supplicant will often fare very ill'.[69] At the end of the century the average income of a parish priest, 'exclusive of the expense of keeping a curate', was approximately £65, and they generally dined for about half the year in private houses. A curate usually received from his parish priest free lodging and diet, a horse and an allowance of £10 per annum. As for the bishops their incomes, derived from parishes held *in commendam* and small contributions from their parish priests, ranged from £100 to £550 per annum, the average being about £300.[70]

Finance, as might be expected, could arouse ill-feeling between clergy and people. To the clergy it must have seemed that some of their parishioners measured their generosity rather strictly. On the other hand during the great tithe agitation in the south, 'the incensed rabble' tried to regulate the fees of the catholic clergy. The bishop of Limerick wrote that many of his parish priests were unable to pay him their annual contribution, according to the archbishop of Cashel fifty catholic churches were 'nailed up' and the bishop of

[67] *Lords' Jn. Ire.*, iii, pp. 207–10.
[68] P. Boyle, *The Irish college in Paris 1578–1901*, p. 137.
[69] *Castlereagh correspondence*, iv, pp. 54–5.
[70] Ibid., pp. 97–173.

Killaloe, when preaching against 'the irregular conduct' of the lower orders, was interrupted and told that 'if he confined himself to religion and morality he would be heard but that he must not say anything against Captain Right'. About thirty years earlier Nicholas Sweetman, bishop of Ferns, had thought it necessary to warn some of his clergy against demanding from the poor people 'claret or any wine' at christenings, weddings and funerals. Sweetman's notes on his diocese also show that a few of the faults associated with the privileged world of the eighteenth century had seeped into the catholic church. Some of his parish clergy were easy-going and negligent and one parish priest, it was said, 'minded dogs and hunting more than his flock'. Sweetman's contemporary Anthony Blake, archbishop of Armagh, conducted himself like a self-indulgent prelate of the ancien régime, travelling to his diocese from time to time in an 'elegant carriage'. A man of family, a member of one of the Galway 'tribes', he preferred living with his relations in Galway to residence in his diocese, and for years he success-fully resisted the attempts of his indignant clergy to compel him to resign or reside.[71]

But it would be unfair and misleading to dwell too long on the tensions and flaws within the church. Irish catholics, both clergy and laity, could pride themselves at the close of the century at having, through their resilience and generosity built up a church with 1,026 parish priests, 400 curates (200 of whom were regulars), about 190 regulars living in 53 houses and 120 nuns in 16 convents.

On the political front catholics were excluded from parlia-ment and from the municipal corporations, from the franchise, parliamentary and municipal, from grand juries, from petty juries in actions arising from the penal laws or between protes-tant and catholic, from state and municipal office, from the commission of the peace, from the bar and from becoming solicitors or attorneys. These political disabilities were enforce-able—they could only be evaded by perjury in the face of alert competitors—and were enforced, with the result that the

---

[71] J. Butler, *A justification of the tenets of the Roman catholic religion* (1787), pp. 22–7; 'The diocesan manuscripts of Ferns during the rule of Bishop Sweetman (1745–1786)', in *Archivium Hibernicum*, iii, pp. 100–5, 111, 117; L. F. Renehan, *Collections of Irish church history* (1861), i, p. 110.

catholics were shut off from the prizes and pleasures of political life and could not exercise any direct influence on Irish politics. The economic disabilities were largely connected with landowning. The possession of land and social and political power were so closely intertwined that the obvious way of weakening catholicism was to prevent the amount of land in catholic ownership increasing and offering the catholic land-owner the choice between conformity and the fragmentation of his estate. So large did landed property loom in the minds of contemporary legislators (themselves landed magnates or country gentlemen) that little attention was given to other forms of wealth and no economic disabilities were imposed on the catholic tenant-at-will (including the grazier who often wanted a short tenancy) or businessman. The catholic business-man might, if he lived in a corporate borough, suffer some harassment as a result of the exclusion of catholics from the guilds. But by paying quarter-age he could enjoy the economic benefits of guild membership, and as the century progressed the guilds became of little importance in economic life, and though the catholic was debarred from the law and the army he could practice medicine. Thus the catholics could prosper in agricultural, commercial, industrial and to some extent, professional life, and they formed an important section of that vigorous, thrusting force, the middle classes.

The attack on catholic landowning was to some extent limited by respect for property rights. Once the Jacobite war was concluded direct confiscation was ruled out and inheritance rights were interfered with only to a limited extent. But by two acts, passed in the first decade of the century, 'framed upon a principle, generally true that influence follows property', a number of disabilities were imposed upon catholic landowners. A catholic was debarred from purchasing land either in his own name or through trustees. A catholic could not inherit land from a protestant unless he conformed. If he failed to conform the inheritance was enjoyed by the nearest protestant heir. A catholic could not take a lease of land for more than thirty-one years or upon a rent less than two-thirds of the improved yearly value. Lands possessed by a catholic on his death were subject to gavelkind amongst his sons. If the child of a catholic conformed to the established church, the court of chancery was empowered to grant him or her a suitable allowance from the parent's estate, and if the eldest son of a catholic conformed, his father became only a life tenant of any lands he held in fee. These provisions were meant to ensure that a catholic child should not 'from fear of being cast off or disinherited . . . or for want of a fitting maintenance, or future provision be compelled or necessitated to embrace the popish religion or be deterred from owning or professing the protestant'.

No public department was entrusted with the execution of this legislation, and the initiative in enforcing it had to be taken by private individuals, protestant informers. Catholic landowners, whose position was analogous to the possessors of substantial capital in a modern predatory state, often took steps to avoid the incidence of the laws, by the creation of trusts, vested in protestant trustees, by obtaining leases on terms that were more beneficial than legally permissible, by instigating collusive discoveries or by inducing younger sons to abstain from exercising their rights under gavelkind. Admittedly the protestant discoverer had a powerful incentive, if he won his case he secured the benefit arising from the attempt at avoidance he had discovered. But the prize had to be gained by legal proceedings which might prove protracted and expensive, and the catholic defendant might, on occasion, win in the courts. It was, for instance, held that a discoverer who was a convert failed because his certificate of conformity had not been filed in time, or because he was not clearly identified with the person named in the certificate. It was successfully argued that the value of a property at the time of leasing could not be properly ascertained because the lease had been granted a number of years back. A catholic pleading a pardon successfully managed to demonstrate that the correct—and perhaps strained—interpretation of the procedure implied that the suit against him had not begun before the pardon was granted. And in 1745 the lord chancellor showed his disapproval of an undutiful son (who had married imprudently against his father's consent) by granting him as a conformist the smallest allowance possible out of his papist father's estate. However the catholic litigant suffered from the application of the legal principle that remedial legislation was to be construed strictly. The courts assured in 1754 that the land legislation affecting catholics was 'not to be considered as penal but for the advancement of religion and must be extended to promote that end'; and years later, though it was accepted that a great part of the legislation was penal, yet it was still held that certain important clauses 'are for the advancement and promoting the peace and quiet of the kingdom and are therefore to be construed as best answer to that end'.[72]

In an age when the family and a family estate meant so much and were so closely linked, this legislation was bound to cause much distress to catholic landlords and must have exasperated the successful catholic businessman who, for the sake of security or social advancement, wanted to invest in land. Moreover, not only was the catholic gentleman liable to be injured by the penal land laws, he must have been conscious that his faith rendered him in some respects an outsider in county society. Unable to be a sheriff, grand juror or justice of the peace, he must have felt his exclusion from local power and the camaraderie of local politics and administration. Understandably, then, catholic landowners tended to conform to the established church. Conformity not only protected an estate against division but enabled its owner to assume his proper place in county society. By the close of the eighteenth century it is noticeable how many of the great Gaelic or Anglo-Norman names are represented amongst the protestant gentry—O'Brien, Macnamara, Kavanagh, Butler, O'Neill, and an M.P. could observe in 1778 that there were many in the house, 'good protestants and worthy members, whose fathers were catholics'.[73]

The economic and social reasons for conformity are obvious. But it is, of course, unfair to assume that because it is in a man's interest to perform a certain action, his motives for doing so are necessarily entirely self-interested. Some public-spirited catholic gentlemen may have been anxious to be in a position to perform the duties incumbent on the possession of landed property. Others may have been strongly influenced by the intellectual climate of the time. The prestige of protestantism stood high, especially in the British Isles. Latitudinarianism

[72] G. E. Howard, *Several special cases on the laws against the further growth of popery in Ireland* (1775), pp. 25, 75, 90, 102, 201, 204, 281–92, 360.
[73] *H.J.*, 17 June 1778.

was prevalent throughout western Europe. This was forcefully brought home to one intelligent Irish catholic gentleman in the early sixties. Daniel O'Conor, the brother of Charles O'Conor of Belanagare, when visiting London was delighted to meet Hélvetius, the philosopher, 'who', he found, 'had all the simplicity and all the condescension of a great man, joined to the easy politeness of a Frenchman'. When O'Conor mentioned the Irish penal laws Helvétius asked, 'why do not the Roman catholics become protestants?' 'They are attached to their religion and besides they would not be admitted into the protestant church without swearing away the most essential articles of the Roman catholic faith.' 'And where the Devil would be the great harm in that, surely you are not so idle as to have any regard to these fooleries? Is your brother a protestant?' 'No.' 'Is he bigotted to his religion?' 'Sir, he is too enlightened to be a bigot.' 'And why does he not turn protestant? Why don't you become a protestant yourself and protect yourself against the penal laws?' 'Sir, the O'Conors have made it always a point of honour to adhere to the religion of their ancestors.' This, O'Conor wrote, 'I said sternly to put an end to a disagreeable dialogue.'[74] O'Conor, though saddened, was unshaken. But other catholic gentlemen might have been more influenced by Helvétius's approach, and of course, once the decision to conform was taken, becoming a protestant would appear not apostasy but a transfer of allegiance from one Christian church to another. Unfortunately conforming catholic gentlemen were not given to producing apologias. However, Sir Michael Creagh, who, having been the Jacobite lord mayor of Dublin in 1688, in 1730 was active as a protestant discoverer, did publish the reasons for his change of religious allegiance. He had become a protestant after 'seeing a good part of the world in thirty-six years' time and examining their religious principles and particularly the gross errors and absurdities of the Church of Rome', and he was anxious to show that his change of faith 'was not the effect of any advantage or profit'. So he produced a summary of the differences between Roman catholicism and anglicanism which he thought proved that his 'sentiments were pursuant to truth, reason and scripture'.[75]

[74] Daniel O'Conor to C. O'Conor, 7 Apr. 1763 (O'Conor papers, R.I.A.).
[75] Papers of Sir M. Creagh, in S.P. 63/395.

Two very different Irishmen, a brilliant preacher and a genial politician, attempted to explain to the eighteenth-century public their change of the religious allegiance. Walter Kirwan, a catholic priest, educated at Saint-Omer, conformed to the established church in 1787, was appointed incumbent of a small Dublin parish, and became famous for his eloquent and moving sermons, often delivered on behalf of charitable causes. Before his conversion he saw a general change taking place in the climate of religious opinion, 'the day of emancipation from the fetters of mysticism, bigotry and religious credulity' was dawning. Though he did not 'set up for a Stoic' he felt that he had 'more than a common desire of being useful to society', his aims being to 'enlarge and enlighten the understanding of men, banish religious prejudice and diffuse through society the great blessings of peace, order and mutual affection'. By becoming a member of the established church, he thought that he was simply placing himself in a better position for realizing those aims and inculcating the 'pure morality of the gospel'.[76] Robert Nugent, a man of letters and a man of the world, an avid and successful wooer of wealthy widows, and a dexterous parliamentary debater, saw his conversion from catholicism, which occurred early in his career, as a triumph of intelligent conviction over superstition, and he described his spiritual Aeneid in exhilerating couplets.

Remote from liberty and truth,
By fortune's crime, my early youth,
Drank error's poison'd springs.
Taught by dark creeds and mystic law,
Wrapt up in reverential awe.
I bow'd to priests and kings.

Soon reason dawn'd with troubled sight.
I caught the glimpse of powerful light,
Afflicted and afraid,
Too weak it shone to mark my way,
Enough to tempt my steps to stray,
Along the dubious shade.

---

[76] W. B. Kirwan, *A discourse on religious innovation to which is added his letter . . giving his reasons for quitting the Roman catholic church*, 2nd. ed, 1787.

Restless I roam'd, when from afar
Low Hooker shines, the friendly star
Sends forth a steady ray,
Thus cheer'd and eager to pursue,
I mount, till glorious to my view,
Locke spreads the realms of day.[77]

The belief that catholicism was out of touch with the progressive tendencies of the age was expressed crudely by Jeffrey
French, the son of a Jacobite and catholic mayor of Galway, who
was called to the English bar, acquired a plantation in Jamaica
and in 1741 became a British M.P. When his nephew, fresh
from Saint-Omer, arrived in London, French called on the
boy at his lodgings, and advised him to abandon immediately
catholicism, 'a mean, beggarly, blackguard religion' and buy
a copy of Cocker's *Arithmetic*. He then 'stepped into his chariot
and drove away'—an Irishman who had made a success of
life.[78]

Though the Irish catholic church, relying on the voluntary
system for the support of its clergy, independent of the state
and regarded askance by many in authority, resembled in some
important respects the dissenting bodies, a vast accumulation
of tradition, pressing hard on its members, inhibited the
growth of a full non-conformist consciousness. The daily life
of the church was regulated by canon law, with its roots in the
Middle Ages, and considerable energy was expended on
litigation both in Ireland and at Rome, often over historic
disputes, for instance the appointment of the warden of Galway.
Church and state were, in catholic tradition, two divinely
appointed institutions, which should work in harmonious
partnership. During the eighteenth century over most of
western Europe the catholic church, with possessions and
privileges, was an essential and conspicuous part of the established order. Almost all the Irish catholic clergy had been
educated in the Bourbon monarchies, where the poorest priest
was a member of the first estate. Many of the bishops had held
office in a seminary and so had a respected status in the
academic hierarchy. A few of them were connected by blood

[77] *A collection of poems in six volumes* (1758), pp. 210–11.
[78] J. Foot, *Life of Arthur Murphy* (1811), p. 9.

with the Irish peerage and others were men of property, albeit on a modest scale. Catholic ecclesiastics were quick to censure agrarian rioting and illegal oath-taking by 'the low bred and ignorant',[79] and for nearly seventy years they maintained an unflinching, if doctrinaire loyalty to a lost cause. Irish Jacobitism, it might be argued, derived its strength from the conviction that the values cherished by catholic Ireland were involved in the conflict between James II and William III, rather than from fervent attachment to the Stuart dynasty. Nevertheless, the Irish church accepted until 1766 the claim advanced by James II that the crown had the right to nominate to Irish sees.

The Irish catholic gentleman was usually sustained by intense family pride. If his activities were circumscribed and his competitive powers limited by his exclusion from national and local politics, he could draw compensation from the past by dwelling on the length of his pedigree and the achievements of his ancestors. Genealogy isolated him from the mass of the population, catholic and protestant, and might be of practical importance if he or his sons enlisted in the service of a foreign power. He was bred in a tradition which stressed the virtues of order and obedience. A young Irish catholic of good family passing through London at a time of lively political debate was shocked by 'the licentiousness that the English called liberty', and saw 'with horror, nay contempt for the nation, their mistaken sense and notion of things. Royalty despised, subordination unknown, and unbounded pride and contempt for all other nations. Inhumanity, ferocity—in a word barbarism unknown to the rest of Europe renders the inhabitants, I mean the lower sort of people of England, the most odious. I believe the better sort of people, well bred in all countries, so don't comprehend them in the above critick'.[80] The well-established leaders of the catholic community welcomed effusively any gesture of goodwill from crown and parliament and they were clearly anxious to be permitted by the removal of the disabilities to assume fully their natural role in society. Nevertheless, the working of the penal laws and years of strain left their scars on Irish catholicism. It was deficient in an element which

---

[79] An essay on the rosary (1772), p. 56.
[80] M. J. O'Connell, The last colonel of the Irish brigade (1892), i, pp. 19–20.

contemporaries regarded as essential to a well-balanced community, a strong landed interest, to provide stability and leadership. One result of this was that the ecclesiastical organization,
especially at parish level, was clearly the creation of popular
effort. The catholic church was built by local subscriptions, the
clergy were recruited from the farming class and paid by
household dues, the catholic schoolmaster was maintained by
the parents of his pupils. The existence of such an organization
nourished self-reliance and democratic instincts in the catholic
community. Along with these feelings went a sense of alienation
from the state and the ruling world and an understandable
sense of grievance. In some catholics this sense of grievance
did not decline with the progressive abolition of the penal laws.
Instead each remaining disability seems to have bitten deeper
and the sense of being the inevitable victim of inequity was
strengthened by repeated retrospective surveys of the Irish past.
Irish catholicism then at the close of the eighteenth century
was both a conservative force and a challenge to the established
order. Tendencies compounded in varying proportions in
different groups and individuals within the community.

The penal laws were not only deficient, at the time of their
enactment they were already almost archaic. They were a
product of the great age of theological disputation and of
religious war, an age which had ended before the beginning of
the eighteenth century. It would be a mistake to assume that
it could be safely said during the eighteenth century, 'we are
all latitudinarian now'. The doctrinal issues which had divided
the great Christian denominations were by no means dead,
and were still, in some circles at least, being heatedly discussed.
The overwhelming majority of politically-minded men in the
British Isles were convinced Christians, and usually loyal
adherents of the denomination to which they belonged. But they
were intensely aware of being members of a highly civilized
society: they felt that all men of intelligence and goodwill
recognized and accepted certain fundamental truths, sound
general principles and a common morality, and that with the
spread of enlightenment and rational argument a wide measure
of agreement would be reached. Against this background the
penal laws were bound to appear at best an ugly necessity,
averse to the spirit of the age, justifiable only if dangerous

doctrines continued to dominate the catholic mind. The system was inevitably resented by the Irish catholics, handicapped and frustrated, and about the middle of the century they entered on what proved to be a seventy-five year campaign for the removal of their disabilities. Since at the outset the catholics counted for little in the Irish political balance and had to rely for success almost entirely on propaganda, they were fortunate in possessing two very skilful propagandists, Dr John Curry and Charles O'Conor of Belanagare. Curry, whose family had lost 'a considerable landed property' in the Williamite and Cromwellian confiscations, after studying medicine in France had built up a good practice in Dublin. 'Grown easy in his existence' he published a work on Irish history. Honest, with some analytical skill, he was essentially a forensic historian, striving to correct what he considered to be misrepresentations of past events which put the Irish catholics in an unfavourable light.[81] O'Conor, a landed gentleman with a small estate in County Roscommon, a remnant of his family's great possessions, was able, during a long life, to devote himself to Irish history and the catholic cause. The representative of the ruling family of Connaught before the Norman conquest, living amongst a Gaelic-speaking people, the friend and patron of the surviving bards, an assiduous pursuer of Gaelic manuscripts, he made himself an expert on Celtic history. His historical work, he hoped, would have political significance. His aim, his son wrote, was 'to reconcile the conquerors and the conquered' in Ireland by reminding all his fellow countrymen of the glories of the ancient Gaelic world, making them conscious of the vicissitudes of human society. In a series of pamphlets O'Conor pressed for a modification of the penal laws, which were inflicting grave economic damage on Ireland by encouraging the emigration of the more energetic catholic, tempted by the 'prospect of a more benign climate and more ascertainable property', and by discouraging catholic investment in agricultural improvement. Moreover, the laws were no longer necessary. Even if the court of Rome had in the past been guilty of political intrigue, the 'great charter of British liberties' had been obtained in the days of popery, and undoubtedly by the eighteenth century 'the political

---

[81] J. Curry, *Historical and critical review of the civil wars in Ireland* (1786), i, p. iv.

faith' of the Irish catholic was 'orthodox to our constitution'.[82]

By the close of George II's reign the Irish catholics realized that they required a permanent organization to press their claims and watch over their interests. In 1757 a small group met at the Globe tavern in Dublin to discuss the formation of a committee. Wyse of Waterford had an ambitious scheme, proposing that the committee should be composed of persons selected by the Dublin parishes and representatives (presumably laymen) chosen by the parish priests of the diocese. In fact a less elaborate procedure was adopted when two years later 'a number of gentlemen and traders' met on 29 March at the Elephant in Essex Street, and having agreed to take steps to obtain a mitigation of the penal laws, selected a committee. Its first move was a modest one. At the end of the year an address from the catholics was presented to the lord lieutenant expressing most fervent loyalty and the hope that the legislature would find means of rendering them useful members to the community. On the accession of George III the Dublin group organized an address to the new monarch from the catholics of Ireland. This address seems to have received widespread support, but Lord Trimleston, one of the most active and self-important of the Irish catholic peers, simultaneously organized an address from the nobility and gentry of Meath and Westmeath. Both addresses breathed the most effusive loyalty, both declared that the catholics looked forward to sharing in the happiness of the new reign, but the first address went a little further by hoping that 'we may not be left incapable of promoting the general welfare and prosperity of the kingdom'.[83] The addition of these few words indicate a difference of outlook amongst the catholics which was partly a matter of temperament. There were those who were eager for action, quick to see and seize opportunities of pressing for concessions, and there were those who were timid, or afraid of arousing hostility by precipitate action, or who may have instinctively found agitation, though necessary, distasteful. O'Conor bitterly complained that in discussions over tactics in

---

[82] C. O'Conor, *The case of the Roman Catholics of Ireland . . . vindicated* (1775), pp. iv, 16, 19.

[83] F. Plowden, *A historical review of the state of Ireland*, i, p. 321; *Exshaw's Magazine*, 1759, p. 634; *London Gazette*, 3, 7 Feb. 1761.

1759 the clergy and gentry 'upbraided the merchants as a presumptuous, low bred, ignorant multitude'.[84] But the division was not precisely along class lines. After all O'Conor himself was indubitably a country gentleman and one of the leaders of the forward group was Lord Taaffe, an Irish peer and an Austrian general, high in favour at the court of Vienna. Taaffe, when in England, attended the court at Saint James's (where his command of German was an advantage) and in Vienna he was able to introduce an influential Irish M.P., Andrews, the provost of Trinity, to a number of persons of position who treated him as if he were 'the viceroy of Ireland'. The result was that Taafe was able to conduct a friendly correspondence with Andrews on the prospects of obtaining concessions for the catholics. On the other hand Trimleston, inheriting both the family title and estates, had been practising medicine. Local or provincial feeling may have partly been responsible for the divisions in the catholic ranks. 'The secular gentlemen of Dublin', the archbishop of Tuam complained, 'assume an authority which I think they have no right to do: that is to put everything their wise heads suggest in the name of the kingdom'. 'I was always of the opinion', the archbishop continued, 'the more insignificant we appeared in the eyes of government, the better.'[85] Ecclesiastics were restrained not only by political caution. They were afraid that some catholics, influenced by the spirit of the age, might, in their eagerness to enjoy the benefits of the constitution, sacrifice catholic doctrine by accepting questionable views on the relationship of church and state.

Differences of opinion may have prevented the presentation of a remonstrance to the king, drafted about 1761, which asked for a modification of the penal laws, especially those relating to land. But soon Irish catholics were presented with an urgent issue on which they could unite and on which immediate action was called for. For years the non-freemen engaged in trade and industry in certain corporate boroughs had been resisting the claims of the guilds to collect quarterage. The guilds tried to enforce what they considered to be an equitable right as well as a useful source of revenue, but when the question came before

---

[84] C. O'Conor to J. Curry, 15 Dec. 1759 (R.I.A. MS B.I.I.).
[85] Archbishop of Tuam to C. O'Conor, 1 May 1778 (R.I.A. MS B.I.I.).

the courts the non-freemen won. So the corporations decided to obtain legislation confirming a long-established usage. Lucas took up their cause and between 1768 and 1778 seven quarterage bills were introduced into the house of commons. Three were withdrawn and four were apparently not transmitted to England by the privy council. These bills were vigorously opposed by the non-freemen. Petitions (clearly drawn up in concert) were presented emphasizing that the levy was contrary to 'the spirit of our happy constitution' and arguing that nothing 'should be established in favour of particular contracted societies which may tend to the injury of the great community'. The petitioners were represented by council, before the house of commons and the privy council and the catholic committee which was almost certainly the co-ordinating force behind the opposition to quarterage, provided financial backing for the non-freemen in fighting their case.[86] During the quarterage battle the committee, which had been languishing, began to meet at regular if rather long intervals. The catholic peers and well-established gentlemen from all over the country were admitted to membership, a London agent was employed and in 1774 a select committee of twenty-five (including three peers, a baronet and ten country gentlemen) was appointed. At the same time plans were made for securing subscriptions from all over the country, 'no part of the charge to fall on the poor'. Money, it was pointed out, was 'an ingredient, indispensably necessary', if efforts were to be made 'to subdue old prejudices and convince men in general how closely the public interest is connected with the relief of the Roman catholics'.[87]

One of the main arguments employed by the advocates of relief was that if the catholics could invest in agricultural land it would be of economic benefit to the whole community, besides giving them a stake in political stability. But that there were prejudices to be overcome was shown by the fate of three bills, the object of which was to enable catholics to lend on mortgage, the catholic creditor having no security but 'the hazard of personal engagements easily eluded'.

[86] M. MacGeehin, 'The catholics of the towns and the quarterage dispute in eighteenth-century Ireland', in *I.H.S.*, viii, pp. 91–114.

[87] 'The minute book of the catholic committee, 1773–92', ed. R. D. Edwards, in *Archivium Hibernicum*, ix, pp. 1–72.

With the beginning of the last quarter of the century the catholic question entered on a new phase. The intellectual climate had become unfavourable to penalization of theological opinion. In England the penal laws were falling into disrepute; in Ireland it was widely held that concessions to the catholics would promote economic growth and strengthen national defence. The Irish catholics at the outbreak of the American war had been quick to display their loyalty and by the close of 1777 the lord lieutenant, the earl of Buckinghamshire, and the British government agreed that something should be done to meet the Irish catholics' 'respectful complaints', though the lord lieutenant, who was inclined to be pessimistic, was afraid that any attempt to modify the penal laws 'would probably occasion a flame in the country'. In March 1778 Mr Talbot, 'a gentleman of considerable fortune and distinction', gave the chief secretary a draft relief bill. It swept away all the disabilities except exclusion from parliament and office under the crown (though it also provided that the king could dispense civil and military office-holders from taking the disqualifying oath). This draft may well represent catholic long-term aspirations rather than immediate expectations, and the relief bill introduced, towards the close of the session, by Gardiner, M.P. for County Dublin, and sponsored by the government was a much more limited measure. As it finally reached the statute book it merely abolished the special provisions in the act 'to prevent the further growth of popery' of 1704 relating to the holding and inheritance of land by catholics (including the gavelling clause and the clauses empowering an eldest son on conforming to turn his father into a life tenant), and it permitted catholics to take land on leases not exceeding 999 years. The debate in the commons on the heads of the bill was long and confusing: 'a multitude of amendments, alterations of amendments and amendments of those alterations'. Land law was a highly technical subject and in addition many M.P.s were apprehensive about the implications of the bill. The principles of papists, it was said, had not changed, and though some papists were liberal, 'we were to dread the common people under the influence of their priests'. Allowing papists the fee simple, Grattan pointed out, 'would in a few years throw the greatest part of lands' into their possession and he warned the house that the aim of the government was to balance the catholic against the protestants (he seems to have overrated the political subtlety of administration). It was suggested that the bill should be withdrawn and a committee appointed to revise the popery laws, and on the grounds that something should be done for the protestant dissenters a clause was added to the heads abolishing the sacramental test. Supporters of the bill were afraid that this clause would, by alarming the bench of bishops, prove 'a clog'. When the bill came before the Irish council some councillors disapproved of it *in toto*, others opposed the abolition of the test 'and more would have appeared against the presbyterian clause if they had not felt it might be more properly rejected' in England. The lord lieutenant was afraid that if the bill was returned from England without the clause repealing the test act the house of commons would reject it. He was over-pessimistic. The clause was deleted by the British privy council, but the house of commons accepted the argument that the catholics should not be disappointed because the presbyterians were compelled to wait for a session, and the bill passed by 127 to 84. The concessions were very limited and would, it was pointed out, 'benefit only the rich papist', but the work of demolishing the disabilities had begun.[88]

To Irish catholics the relief act of 1778, 'a great victory over the prejudices of those who called themselves true protestants in this country', was only an instalment and they expected that further concessions would be made in the near future. They saw 'the illegal spirit of intolerance . . . in all enlightened countries universally to be subsiding'; it was also obvious that a growing sense of nationhood would make it more difficult to maintain penal laws which harshly emphasized denominational divisions in Irish society. Conscious that the climate of opinion was changing in their favour, the catholic committee at the close of 1778 appointed a resident agent in England and started to raise money, the sinews of propaganda, by means of parish collections. But confidence was diluted with caution. When a hot-headed young catholic, Matthew Carey, advertised

---

[88] Buckinghamshire to Gower, 25 June 1778 (P.R.O. 30/29/3); Buckinghamshire to Weymouth, 15 Dec. 1777 (S.P. 63/458); Buckinghamshire to G. Germain, 3 June 1778, to H. Stanley, 29 May 1778; G. Germain to Buckinghamshire, 9 June 1778 (Add. MS 34523); Buckinghamshire to Weymouth, 4 Mar. 1778 (S.P. 63/459); *H.J.*, 19, 22 June 1778.

his forthcoming pamphlet, calling for an immediate repeal of 'the whole penal code', hinting that delay might provoke rebellion, the committee was quick to express publicly its disapproval of the seditious tendency of the advertisement.[89]

At the beginning of 1782 Luke Gardiner again brought the heads of a relief bill before the house of commons. It aimed at abolishing all catholic disabilities in respect of the inheritance or purchase of land and at removing all the disabilities imposed on catholic ecclesiastics (as a concession to protestant susceptibilities it provided that the disabilities would still apply to regular clergy not resident in Ireland at the time of the passing of the bill, and forbade steeples on catholic churches). Compared to the 1778 measure the bill was bold and generous and it aroused considerable parliamentary perturbation. Gardiner's drafting was severely criticized and his heads drastically reshaped (though unaltered in substance).[90] It is not unfair to assume that some of those who professed to be shocked by defective draftsmanship would not have been sorry if the measure had foundered on technicalities. Others attacked it on principle. One M.P. declared that while the catholics far outnumbered the protestants, the latter should not let landed property out of their hands; in the lords, Bellomont asked was the bill a *ne plus ultra*, and Tracton, an eminent lawyer, opposed it because it allowed catholics to influence elections. But the supporters of the bill spoke with the exuberant confidence of men who felt that they were moving with the prevalent intellectual tide. Langrishe declared that he would not hesitate to repeal any law 'which wore the face of impotent malice' and Woodward, the bishop of Cloyne, denounced those penal laws which were 'against national union, against national unity and against nature' (but though sympathetic to the catholics he was 'for keeping them from political power'). On the whole optimism outweighed apprehension. On an important division on the bill in the house of commons, it had 145 supporters against 56 opponents; and in the lords it was carried by 29

---

[89] 'The minute book of the catholic committee', pp. 32–3, 38, 60–3; *D.E.P.*, 10, 17 Nov. 1781.

[90] The bill as originally drafted by Gardiner swept away all disabilities except those specified in the bill. But in the bill as reshaped it was the disabilities which were to be abolished which were listed (see the heads of the relief bill in *H.J.*, 9 Jan. 1782, and 21/22 Geo. III, c. 24).

votes to 25.[91] Before the end of the session a supplementary bill permitting catholics to act as schoolmasters and guardians passed with little debate.[92]

The changing legal status of the Irish catholic raised an issue which was bound to stir up sharp controversy—relations between the state and a catholic church which was rapidly being relieved from disabilities. During the earlier decades of the century when the church was proscribed and lay catholics subjected to a wide range of disabilities, it was reasonable to suppose that Irish catholicism would wither away. But from early in George III's reign it had to be accepted that the catholics were a permanent section of Irish society, active in many areas of life. It also had to be faced that the catholic church, a dogmatic, well-disciplined, close-knit ecclesiastical body, with immense influence over its members, might constitute a threat to the authority of the state and obtain an unfair predominance in the community. All over Europe the secular power insisted on exercising some degree of supervision over the catholic church in its territory, often by claiming a say in episcopal appointments. In protestant countries, where the catholics formed a weak minority, the church had to accept the rules laid down by the state. In catholic countries, the state claimed by prescription rights in the ecclesiastical sphere, and though many churchmen would contest its claims on theological grounds, in practice it was hard for the church to defy rulers (Most Catholic or Most Christian kings) who declared themselves to be devoted sons of the church. In Ireland, however, the catholic church, the church of the great majority, had, for generations, though oppressed, not been controlled. Such a church would certainly react vehemently against any attempt to bring it under state control—especially that of a protestant state.

As early as 1778, Hervey, the bishop of Derry, whose long absences from his diocese enabled him to study continental ecclesiastical developments on the ground, pointed out to an influential Irish politician that if catholic relief, which the bishop supported, was granted, a new approach to the catholic question should be adopted. Hervey suggested that the crown

---

[91] *H.J.*, 1, 18, 22 Feb., 3 May 1782.
[92] 21 & 22 Geo. III, c. 67.

should be empowered to make catholic ecclesiastical appointments, that the catholic bishops and parish priests should be given 'an endowment in land'—40 acres for a bishop, 25 for a priest—and that the state should support a seminary in each province with the object of 'perpetuating the political orthodoxy of the Irish priesthood'. This policy, Hervey believed, would encourage the 'harmless' catholic and check abettors and partisans of the 'court of Rome'. A more practical politician than the bishop, Hely-Hutchinson, thinking along much the same lines, suggested during a house of commons debate that Irish candidates for the priesthood should be educated at home in an enlightened atmosphere. He wanted them to follow the undergraduate course in Trinity, sharing the life of the other undergraduates and attending 'a divinity professor of their own' for theological instruction. [93]

Hely-Hutchinson was severely criticized by Edmund Burke for his failure to understand the educational needs of men 'intended for celibacy and the function of confession'; and the catholic bishops were very disturbed by the suggestion that the crown should have the right of nomination to vacant sees in the Irish catholic church. It would, remarked Butler, the catholic archbishop of Cashel, 'by putting us on the same footing as bishops of the established church rob us of our people's confidence'. Troy, bishop of Ossory, the outstanding catholic prelate in Ireland, dismissed Hervey's scheme as inimical to the rights of the papacy and he correctly enough assumed that most M.P.s were 'indifferent about the mode of appointing our bishops'. When in 1793, Lord Tyrone talked of proposing that parliament should make financial provision for the catholic clergy, Troy, by then archbishop of Dublin, was afraid such a measure would lead to a decline of clerical zeal and lay generosity as well as giving the government an excuse to claim a say in catholic ecclesiastical appointments. [94]

The policy of supplementing the existing connection between the established church and the state, by linking the catholic church to the state and creating a dual—or if the presbyterians

[93] Bishop of Derry to S. Pery, 15 May, 21 July 1778 (*Eighth report H.M.C.*, *appendix*, pt. i, 197a–198b); *Parl. Reg. Ire.*, i, pp. 306–10.
[94] *Correspondence of the Rt. Hon. Edmund Burke*, iv, p. 411; M. P. McMahan (bishop of Killaloe) to Troy, 26 Mar. 1782; the Papal Nuncio, Brussels, to J. T. Troy (Troy 116/3).

be included, triple—alliance, won some favour in official quarters during the last decade of the century. It would be easy and unfair to say that this policy implied that the clergy, catholic and presbyterian, were to be bribed into becoming instruments of state policy. Rather, supporters of a triple alliance would have urged that the clergy, catholic and presbyterian, by being rendered independent of their congregations and attached to the state would be given the opportunity to exert themselves to the full in promoting religion and social morality in a highly civilized and progressing community.

During the last decades of the eighteenth century Irish catholicism was changing. Throughout Europe catholicism was under severe strain but in Ireland the closing years of the century were full of promise. With the penal laws almost gone, with a rising population and growing prosperity, Irish catholics could throw themselves into repairing the damage of the past and planning for the future. New churches were being built and new methods and agencies for carrying on the work of the church were being devised. Based on Dublin, the Trinitarian order in the nineties launched an ambitious scheme for the systematic teaching of the catechism. Large numbers of children were to assemble in their parish church, and divided into groups, be instructed by laymen, working under clerical directors. In Cork, Miss Nano Nagle, a wealthy lay woman, having established an Ursuline convent, decided that the only way to achieve her main objective, the teaching of poor children, was to found her own order, and in 1775 she set up the first Presentation house. In Waterford a group of young men about 1790 formed a society for religious and charitable work. It influenced Edmund Rice, a well-off merchant, who, at the opening of the nineteenth century, abandoned business and starting with a single school, built up, in less than ten years, a teaching order, the Christian brothers, which was to become a powerful force in Irish primary and secondary education. In Carlow, after fund-raising efforts stretching over nearly ten years, a diocesan college was opened in 1793 for the education of both lay pupils and theological students.[95]

---

[95] J. Dwyer, *The Trinitarian manual* (1795); P. MacSuibhne, 'The early history of Carlow college' in *I.E.R.*, 4th series, lxii, pp. 230–48.

But the most striking manifestation of renewed strength and confidence in Irish catholicism was the foundation in 1795 of a large national seminary, the Royal college of Saint Patrick, at Maynooth. The Irish colleges in France shared the fate of the French church, though an Irish ecclesiastic, Father John Walsh, tried to impress on the legislative assembly that there were sound strategic–political reasons for sparing the Irish colleges in Paris. The two-thirds of the Irish people who were catholics and excluded from political power would, he wrote, soon be inspired by 'the rights and dignity of man' to break their fetters. With Ireland independent, British power, which to a great extent was based on Irish provisions and sailors, would collapse. It was therefore in the interest of France to encourage Irish theological students to come to Paris and 'imbibe in our schools the principles which sooner or later will cause the germ of liberty so natural to man to burst forth'. But his plea in the end was unavailing, and in 1792 the colleges were closed.[96]

The Irish hierarchy was concerned about the loss of training facilities for their clergy and at the close of 1793 and the beginning of 1794 they approached the chief secretary and the British government with the aim of obtaining permission to found an endowed college (or colleges) for the education of the catholic clergy. Catholicism was seen in official circles as a conserving force and it was clearly desirable that Irish catholic priests should be educated in the king's dominions. Moreover, Grattan was convinced that 'if the catholic clergy can't have a catholic education at home they will have none at all or none that is not dangerous', and the provision of colleges for the education of the catholic clergy was one of the items in the programme which Grattan, as spokesman for the Fitzwilliam administration, recommended to the house of commons in January 1795. Fitzwilliam left Ireland in March, but the new Irish administration continued to sponsor the catholic education bill which received the royal assent in June. The act constituted a body of trustees (eleven catholic ecclesiastics, six catholic peers and gentlemen, the lord chancellor and three senior

---

[96] P. Boyle 'The Irish college in Paris during the French revolution' in *I.E.R.*, 4th series, xv, pp. 48–73.

common law judges) to manage the funds subscribed 'to establish and endow an academy for the education of persons professing the Roman catholic religion'. The government was authorized to pay £8,000 to the trustees—a sum which proved the forerunner of an annual grant. The trustees were empowered to appoint the 'officers' of the institution, and protestants were not to be admitted as pupils. The bishops' objective had been a seminary or seminaries, but yielding to the wishes of their friends in England, Edmund Burke and the duke of Portland, they agreed that the new institution should provide facilities for lay as well as clerical education. When the bill was before the house of commons, a group of catholics, whom Troy dubbed 'our liberality petitioners', remonstrated firmly against two of its provisions. They wanted appointments to the staff of the new institution to be made strictly on the results of public competitive examination, and they deplored the bar on taking protestant pupils as tending to 'perpetuate the line of separation . . . which it is in the interest of the country to obliterate'. The petitioners, when pressing for undenominational education, presumably had the laity in mind. But they possibly expected that lay pupils and clerical students should be educated together during the earlier years of the latter's course. In the event the lay school, which was founded at Maynooth in 1800 for the education of the sons of the catholic nobility and gentry, was almost completely separate from the seminary, and was closed in 1817. The great seminary at Maynooth, recruiting its students from all over Ireland, and in time recruiting its teaching staff largely from its own alumni, became a very powerful influence in Ireland. It gave the Irish church cohesion and provided it with a local intellectual centre, and it ensured that the Irish clergy should be educated in a thoroughly Irish environment.[97]

The first president of Maynooth was Dr Thomas Hussey, an outstanding representative of a new spirit in Irish catholicism. Born in County Meath and educated at Salamanca, in 1767 he became chaplain to the Spanish embassy in London, and moved for years on the fringes of diplomacy. Assured and

---

[97] J. Healy, *Maynooth College* (1895), pp. 661–2; *The correspondence of Edmund Burke*, vii, pp. 507–8; *Commons' Jn. Ire.*, xvi, p. 112.

ingratiating, Hussey had many contacts with the world of power and was well acquainted with many British politicians, including Burke. A man of—to use his own words— 'loyal and *royal* principles', he was vehemently opposed to Jacobinism, but on his return to Ireland he was very quick to resent any suggestion that catholics should be content with an inferior status in Irish society. He soon found an issue—that catholic soldiers were being compelled to attend protestant church services. The articles of war, not intended for a multi-denominational army, laid down that soldiers should attend divine service, and some commanding officers, actuated probably more by a respect for red tape than religious bigotry, did not see why catholic soldiers should be excused church parade if they were afterwards at liberty to attend their own services. The Irish administration certainly had no desire to force tender consciences, and Pelham, the chief secretary, in the summer of 1796 directed that militia men after parade on Sunday should be able to attend a protestant or catholic service. Hussey indignantly attacked 'the compulsion applied to whip the catholic soldier to protestant worship', and in the passionate pastoral he published early in 1797, shortly after becoming bishop of Waterford, he directed catholic soldiers not to attend protestant services, telling them their officers had no authority to order them to do so. In the opinion of the Irish official world, Hussey showed himself on this issue to be misinformed, impatient and ill-tempered. In fact he seems to have exaggerated his case, but what is significant is, that, unlike Irish catholic prelates in the past, he was neither defensive nor deferential.[98]

In the pastoral, Hussey warned his flock against attending protestant schools, reminding them they were not members of a small sect but of a great church, to which the most polished nations in the world were proud to belong. Looking back in anger, he dwelt on the persecutions the Irish catholics had suffered and survived, emphasizing that it was the poor who had protected and sustained the clergy. To a conservative catholic prelate the pastoral was 'unreasonable and reprehensible'.[99] In fact it portended the emergence of a church

---

[98] *Correspondence of Edmund Burke*, ix, pp. 140–3, 302–4.
[99] A. Cogan, *Diocese of Meath* (1870), iii, p. 212.

which would to some extent express the aspirations of the less privileged sections of Irish society, and make extensive claims for itself. That Irish catholicism might be developing into a more exacting and exclusive organization seems to have been dimly perceived about this time by an independent and tolerant M.P., Sir Lawrence Parsons. Writing to an old friend, a strong liberal, he pointed out that at the very time when protestant gentlemen were prepared to act as collectors at catholic charity services, and the youth of the university had declared themselves in favour of catholic emancipation, 'if a catholic fifer will put his foot within a protestant church, his bishop tells him he shall be damned'. Parsons tackled a catholic bishop who offered to explain the catholic attitude by showing him ecclesiastical documents: 'as if', Parsons angrily wrote, 'the ancient rubbish of the Vatican ought to be ransacked in these times for precepts of repulsion between our sects.'[100]

It is impossible to take the religious temperature of a country, especially when, as in western Europe during the eighteenth century, there is a strong tendency to stress the importance of rationality and restraint and to depreciate public outpourings of emotion. In Ireland, denominational loyalties were strong, and for many men their co-religionists formed the community which regulated and enriched their lives—when funds were being raised to rebuild Saint Mary's catholic church in Kilkenny, it was pointed out that 'a vast concourse of the country people frequent it on the Lord's day finding it most convenient for the worldly as the religious purposes'.[101] On the other hand the intensity of religious feeling in Ireland must not be exaggerated. At the opening of the century a bishop referred to the deluge of atheism and deism which had broken in on them. At its close a future archbishop, in an eloquent sermon, warned his hearers that 'the decline of Christianity—the decline of religion—the decline of morals—the threatened ruin of your country—all demand your most strenuous exertions'. Christianity was being ridiculed, church-going neglected, the observation of the Sabbath disregarded. About the same time a prebendary of Saint Patrick's pointed out that 'while most gentlemen have read Voltaire, Rousseau, Hume, Gibbon etc. it is a melancholy

---

[100] L. Parsons to P. Burrowes, 22 June 1795 (R.I.A. MS 23 K 53).
[101] W. Carrigan, *History and Antiquities of the diocese of Ossory*, iii, p. 125.

truth that few have perused the answers to those authors'.[102] These opinions may to some extent be discounted as rising from professional anxiety, and the comment of a London barrister that in Dublin 'the rich have all the intolerance of bigots without their piety', may be dismissed[103] as a tourist's ill-informed generalization.

The number of works on theological or religious subjects— sermons excepted—produced by Irishmen during the second half of the eighteenth century is not very great and it is hard to point to any Irish theological writer of even contemporary importance. The list of recommended books for divinity students drawn up by the bishops of the Church of Ireland in 1790 does not include any work by an Irish author and during the century Irish catholicism contributed considerably less to theological literature than did the much smaller English catholic community. Nevertheless the prevalent tone was one of reverence for and sincere acceptance of religious truth. Even in politically radical intellectual circles, where criticism of the established order flourished, there was remarkably little antagonism to religion. William Drennan was a keen, if critically-minded, presbyterian. Thomas Russell was an early example of an evangelically-minded soldier; William Steel Dickson, one of the most vigorous radicals in the north of Ireland, was a moderator of the synod of Ulster. When Thomas Paine, the political oracle of *fin de siècle* Irish radicalism, with insensitive common sense assailed Christian orthodoxy, he was answered in print by four Irishmen—two presbyterian clergymen, John Abernethy and William Stavely, an anglican clergyman, William Jackson, and a fellow of Trinity college, Whitley Stokes, all outspoken political radicals. Stokes, who was a member of the Dublin society of United Irishmen, was thanked for his answer to Paine by the board of Trinity college; Jackson, who had come back to Ireland early in 1794 as a French agent, wrote his reply when a prisoner in Newgate awaiting trial. Before leaving Paris he had been able to give Paine a sharp pre-publication rap over the knuckles. When Paine told him that he was writing a book against all revealed

[102] E. Synge, *Invisibilia* (1705), p. v; W. Magee, *A Sermon* (1796), p. 32; E. Ryan, *A short but comprehensive view of the Mosaic and Christian codes* (1795), p. ix.
[103] G. Cooper, *Letters on the Irish nation* (1799), p. 24.

religion which 'is nothing but nonsense and imposition', Jackson had retorted, 'I am sure Mr Paine you are a man of too good an understanding to write on any subject you are not thoroughly acquainted with'.[104]

Occasionally though, as might be expected, political radicalism was accompanied by religious unorthodoxy. A United Irishman, William Byrne, a member of the Leinster provincial committee, arrested in 1798, told the privy council that he was 'a catholic at least nominally' and that he thought 'every religion equally good'.[105] John Burke, a Trinity undergraduate, the son of a County Cork schoolmaster, who played a leading part in Dublin working-class debating societies in the middle nineties, was in April 1794 brought before the college board for expressing 'disrespectful' views on religion, and after being questioned was expelled from college. Before his interview with the board Burke had sent his tutor an Ode to Liberty which he had composed, and he believed that the real reason for his expulsion was political prejudice.[106] A far more distinguished Irish radical, Arthur O'Connor, seems, from his *magnum opus*, *Monopoly the cause of all evil*, to have been an extreme eighteenth-century latitudinarian, with an admiration for Bishop Hoadley, and a detestation of priestcraft. When managing the *Press*, shortly before the '98 rising, he printed in it extracts from Volney on religion, with the result, he triumphantly recalled forty years later, that two Dublin priests tried to get the circulation of the *Press* banned in their parishes—without success. Another radical newspaper, the *Cork Gazette*, also published extracts from Volney and its editor praised Paine's *Age of Reason*, and attacked the religious quackery practised by the priests of all sects. But these displays of heterodoxy were unusual and the great majority of leading radicals were more

---

[104] For J. Abernethy and W. Stavely see T. Witherow, *Historical and literary memorials*, ii, pp. 329, 377. W. Jackson, *Observations in answer to Mr Paine's Age of Reason* (1795). Stokes was thanked for his answer to Paine by the Board of Trinity college.

[105] William Byrne's examination before the privy council in I.S.P.O.620/36/9.

[106] J. Burke, *The trial of John Burk of Trinity College for heresy before the board o, senior fellows* (1794.) Burke was said to have emigrated to the United States (W. Ridgeway, *Trials* . . . (1795), p. 34). If so he may have become a playwright. But in 1799 it was reported that a Clare insurgent leader who had been captured was the John Burke who had been expelled from T.C.D. (*The Times*, 23 Jan. 1799).

or less attached members of the churches in which they had been bred.[107]

During the later eighteenth century Irish protestantism slowly became more earnest and active. The evangelical revival, with its emphasis on a correct understanding of doctrinal truth, its belief in the vital necessity of a deep personal awareness of salvation, and its warm insistent urgency, became in due time a strong force influencing many who would not term themselves evangelicals. The revival may be said to have begun in Ireland with the visits of the three great evangelical leaders, John and Charles Wesley and Whitefield. They were deeply impressed by the goodwill they met with. Whitefield, after his visit to Dublin, writing 'The congregations were large and hear as for eternity'. John Wesley, however, a severely practical idealist, after one preaching tour cautiously noted 'the waters too wide to be deep'.[108] Besides preaching all over Ireland he took steps to found methodist societies, whose members sustained each other's religious life, practising severe self-discipline, abstaining from idle talk and snuff-taking, and gave as generously as their means permitted towards building preaching houses and paying the preachers' very modest stipends. In 1752 Wesley held at Limerick the first Irish methodist conference, attended by ten preachers. In 1775 the Irish methodists numbered 5,000, by the close of the century they amounted to 20,000, and though it was not until some years later that they began to withdraw from the established church, they already were a distinctive body.[109]

Amongst Wesley's Irish followers were De Courcy, the curate of Saint Andrews, Dublin, who preached in the parish church-yard, Edward Smyth, vicar of Ballyculter, who after severely criticizing his principal parishioner for adultery, was deprived of his living for preaching in the fields and setting up a conventicle in a neighbouring parish, and Henry Moore of Dublin, who became Wesley's first biographer.[110] Moore, the son of a farmer at Drumcondra, had intellectual interests but was prevented from going to the university by his father's sudden

---

[107] A. O'Connor, *Monopoly, the cause of all evil* (1848), pp. 523–8, 549; *Cork Gazette*, 7 Dec., 23 Apr., 30 Mar. 1796.

[108] *A select collection of the letters of the late Rev. George Whitefield* (1772), ii, p. 410; J. Wesley, *Journals*, ed. N. Curnock, iii, 341.

[109] *Minutes of the methodist conference.*

[110] *Account of the trial of Edward Smyth* (1777).

death. Instead, he went to London and qualified as a 'carver'. He enjoyed some of the pleasures of London, Vauxhall, Ranelagh and the theatres—'the name of Garrick on a play bill would make my heart vibrate', he wrote, but after his return to Dublin he entered on a prolonged spiritual crisis. First there was a dawning awareness of the power of grace, succeeded by a wave of doubt as 'the infidel writers' he had read swept into his mind. Then, at last, one evening about the middle of February 1777, as he was crossing Dublin—'I felt I had been gently struck with lightning . . . I stopped and for a moment wondered what had happened to me, but I quickly found it was a healing visitation.' He immediately began to study the scriptures attentively; beginning by joining the methodists, he was soon visiting prisoners in Newgate and preaching in a disused weaving shed on the outskirts of Dublin. During the late seventies he was a preacher in the north of Ireland, and in the early eighties he left to carry on evangelical work in England.[111]

Methodism was the most striking manifestation of the evangelical revival, but there were evangelicals in the established church who were not methodists, for instance, William Howard, the subject of a well-known biographical tract by Joseph Milner, the evangelical ecclesiastical historian. Howard, who was mayor of Drogheda in 1755, after some years of dissipated living failed in business in 1770 and retreated to Yorkshire. There he became a fervent evangelical, and returning to Dublin, strove to convince his relations of the need for conversion.[112] About the time he returned to Dublin, Lady Moira, the fashionable Dublin hostess and the daughter of Lady Huntington, the evangelical leader, managed to arrange that Henry Peckwell, the evangelical preacher and one of Lady Huntingdon's chaplains, should give a course of sermons in the Magdalene chapel. A section of the congregation considered that Peckwell's views were methodist and subversive of morality and the establishment, and a group led by Lady Arabella Denny, who took an active part in Dublin charitable and church life, asked the archbishop of Dublin to silence him. Lady Moira strongly backed Peckwell and the dispute for a time divided a section at

---

[111] R. Smith, *Life of Rev. Henry Moore* (1854).
[112] *Some remarkable passages in the life of William Howard* (1785).

least of the Irish fashionable world.[113] Another learned and fervent evangelical within the establishment was John Walker, a fellow of Trinity, who having criticized the methodists for falling into theological error, decided in 1804 that he could no longer remain within an established church, and, resigning fellowship, with a small group of strict calvinists formed the Church of God.

There was also an intensification of religious activity amongst the presbyterians. The synod of Ulster rebuked some of its members for 'inattention to the affairs of the church', failure to attend the synod regularly. Congregational psalmody was encouraged; steps were taken to assist 'the frontier congregations' in the south and west; ministers were directed to visit gaols in their neighbourhood; and in 1792 the synod thanked Wilberforce for his efforts to end 'the unnatural traffic in human flesh'. The foundation of a university in Ulster under presbyterian direction, situated possibly at Cookstown, was mooted in 1795; an academy where candidates for the ministry could obtain instruction flourished for some years in the eighties at Strabane and in 1786 the presbyterians of Belfast founded the Belfast academy, a grammar school which provided some additional teaching on a higher level, with the Revd James Crombie, the minister of the first Belfast congregation, as its principal. In October 1798 some ministers of the Ulster synod united with some secession clergy and a few clergymen of the established church to form the Ulster Evangelical society to promote itinerant preaching throughout the province.

In the early years of the nineteenth century strict and earnest Irish evangelicals, highly conscious of their purpose and place in the scheme of things, nevertheless still saw themselves as a very small band. One keen young evangelical clergyman thought that in Dublin at the opening of the nineteenth century, 'religious society' consisted of about a dozen families and could be collected in a drawing room. Another young evangelical clergyman, Peter Roe, was slightly more optimistic. Visiting Dublin about this time, he perceived

---

[113] *Life and times of Selina countess of Huntingdon,* ii, pp. 196–8. Chapters xxiv–xxviii of this work are of great value for the beginning of the evangelical revival in Ireland.

'a rising spirit of religion . . .'; he went to several parties 'where not only cards were excluded but Christianity formed the topic of conversation'. About the time he visited Dublin, Roe, then a curate, was active in reviving the Ossory Clerical society for scriptural study, which had been founded in 1795. O'Beirne, when bishop of Ossory (1795–8), had strongly supported the society, intervening eloquently in its debates and entertaining its members to dinner. But when John Kearney, the provost of Trinity college, was appointed to Ossory in 1805, he let it be known that in his opinion the existence of such a society was likely to create divisions amongst the clergy. However, undaunted by episcopal disapproval a number of clergymen, some of them undoubtedly evangelicals, kept the society in being.[114]

In fact evangelicalism at the beginning of the nineteenth century was growing steadily in strength and in a generation was to become a potent force in Irish protestantism. Moreover, many of the clergy and laity who would not have regarded themselves as evangelicals, in what may be fairly called the party sense of the term, took religion very seriously and were clearly aware of the need for more vigorous and better organized Christian work. The list of subscribers to Edward Ryan's popular work on apologetics (a list which includes the names of Corry, Curran, Fitzgibbon, Grattan and Yelverton), and the membership of the Society for discountenancing vice and promoting virtue, evinced this. The Society for discountenancing vice was founded in 1792 by a small group concerned at 'the rapid progresss which infidelity and immorality' were making. The society strove to ensure that 'no house, no cabin in the whole kingdom, in which there is a single person who can read, shall be destitute of the Holy Scriptures'. It distributed thousands of tracts, assisted primary education, tried to discourage idleness amongst the poor and extravagance amongst the upper and middle classes, and it endeavoured to suppress window displays of 'obscene prints and pictures which directly tend to vitiate the virtue of youth'.[115] Amongst the members of the society were Richard Graves, William Magee

---

[114] *Brief memorials of Rev. B. W. Mathias* (1842), p. 205; S. Madden, *Memoir of the late Rev. Peter Roe* (1842), pp. 28–95.
[115] The Revd R. Burrowes, *A sermon* (1795). Appended to this sermon is a report of a committee appointed by the Society for discouraging vice for the purpose of composing a brief account of its activities.

and Joseph Stopford, all three clerical fellows of Trinity college. Stopford in the nineties was giving lectures in his chambers to 'candidate divines' on the duties of a clergyman. Graves, when in 1814 he became regius professor of divinity, instituted an annual voluntary examination for divinity students and in his first prelection stimulated his hearers to intellectual exertion by dwelling on the thorough training which was being given to students for the priesthood in Maynooth. Both Graves and Magee produced theological works which attracted contemporary respect. Graves in his *Essay on the character of the apostles and the evangelists* published in 1798, argued that the apostles were sober, sensible men, credible witnesses. Magee, a future bishop and archbishop, published in 1801 his *Discourses on atonement and sacrifice*, a work admired for its critical acumen and erudition. Two years earlier the composition of one of the most influential theological works produced in Ireland quietly began with a letter from Alexander Knox to the Revd John Jebb. Knox, Castlereagh's private secretary during the union struggle, was a profound and original thinker concerned to see religion steadily, and see it whole. Deeply influenced by the great Caroline divines, he readily emphasized the value of the Roman catholic and the calvinist contributions to Christian development, and though he could express himself with pungency and often humour, he was convinced 'that no good is ever done by direct attack on any body of people'.[116]

---

[116] J. Jebb and A. Knox, *Thirty years' correspondence* (1834), i, p. 129.

II

CONSTITUTIONAL CONFLICT

4

A restive parliament

In Ireland the early Hanoverian age was an era of political placidity. The very long intervals between parliamentary sessions, a judicious distribution of power and patronage, the absence of major issues, an unquestioning and generally satisfied acceptance of the constitutional pattern, the presence of a large and potentially dangerous catholic community, and sobering memories of civil war and abrupt reversals of political fortune, all contributed to the maintenance of political tranquillity. But by the middle of the century there were signs that this calm was breaking up. The great borough interests, whose support was essential for the smooth working of the parliamentary system, were becoming noticeably assertive, and alert independent M.P.s were calling for inquiries into the working of the government machine and raising constitutional issues—the increasing cost of pensions, the duration of parliament, and the power exercised by the Irish privy council under Poynings' law, of altering and rejecting bills. Bedford, the last of George II's viceroys, managed to handle with reasonable success the great interests ('he is a match for them . . . and laughs at these terrors', an admirer wrote, striving to form 'a broad bottomed union of parties . . . uniting and melting the different parties into one solid body, which by having the favours of government distributed by an impartial hand amongst them would be united in support of His Majesty's authority'). But his chief secretary, Rigby, a shrewd if notoriously self-interested politician, was alarmed to see to what an extent Irish M.P.s were being influenced by out-of-doors opinion. 'Scarce a man in parliament', he wrote, 'gives his opinion if he think it is not the opinion of the gallery, and popularity, as they call it, must take the place of service and reason. . . . No measure can be proposed in the house of commons now, that the first reflection is not, what will the people say out of doors.' Rigby almost certainly exaggerated the influence on Irish parliamentary life of what he termed the *vox populi*.[1] An old parliamentary hand, he was sensitive to the possibility of any change in the rules of the game at which he was so adept. But events showed that he was correct in assuming a growing interest in politics and an increasing determination to influence political action amongst Irishmen—or at least amongst the Irish middle classes. 'The country is numerous and wealthy', an able Irish lawyer wrote at this time, 'and they have been taught to think themselves injured by the present constitution.'[2]

In the last parliamentary session of George II's reign (1759–60) the Irish administration had to face severe attacks on two sectors of the financial front—pensions and army expenditure. The former was a conventional subject for opposition opprobium, both at Westminster and in Dublin, and though the house was heartily behind the war policy, there seems to have been a feeling that in the relaxed financial climate of wartime the administration required watching. The opposition, led by an indefatigable lawyer, Hely-Hutchinson, aided on occasion by Edmond Pery, an economic expert, was very persistent. In a division it could muster only about thirty votes and was usually outnumbered by nearly three to one, yet it constituted a definite threat; given a popular cause and favourable circumstances it might attract recruits and create serious parliamentary difficulties for the Irish administration. The session was also marked by a startling event, a sudden, crude expression of out-of-doors interest in politics. Rumours having spread through Dublin that there was to be a union or that parliament was to be abolished, at the beginning of December 1759 'a dangerous and insolent multitude' gathered in College Green, rabbled M.P.s, stormed the parliament house and installed a blacksmith in the speaker's chair and an old woman on the throne in the house of lords.[3] It was a sharp reminder that there were in Ireland untamed forces which might rudely interfere with the smooth working of the political machine.

The accession of George III, occurring during a great war, scarcely marked the beginning of an epoch. But the death of his

---

[1] Rigby to H. Fox, 31 Oct., 8 Dec. 1758, 14 Feb. 1758, 19 Dec. 1759 (Add. MS 51385).

[2] *Report on MSS in various collections H.M.C.*, vi, p. 77.

[3] C. W. Segrave, *The Segrave family 1066–1935* (1936), pp. 164–5.

predecessor had an immediate and striking effect on Irish politics. The parliament which had been elected in 1727, and which had continued for the whole of George II's reign, was automatically dissolved; and few days after the news of the king's death reached Dublin electioneering began.[4]

From the available evidence there seems to have been a poll in only about twenty-six constituencies (nine counties and seventeen boroughs) but a number of the members returned unopposed must have had to make contact with their constitutents, and one issue seems to have aroused widespread interest, the desirability of limiting the duration of parliament. The attorney-general, who was defending his Trinity college seat, at first refused 'to explain his sentiments in relation to limited parliaments', but after a rival candidate began to do well at the poll he declared that 'he thought limited parliaments were for the good of the kingdom' and was re-elected.[5] A number of other candidates pledged themselves to support a septennial bill and George Rochfort, a candidate for County Westmeath, argued that a 'short money bill' should be used to secure a septennial act. Rochfort also denounced the 'modern practice of entertaining the electors before and at an election', which he declared 'excludes all men of moderate fortunes'.[6] Rochfort was defeated but a far more famous liberal, Charles Lucas, was returned for the city of Dublin. Lucas, in some ways the harbinger of a new age, was a most unusual phenomenon in eighteenth-century Irish politics, a man of indubitably middle-class background, an apothecary in fact, who came to the forefront in Irish public life. Upright, earnest, emotional and plucky, an enthusiastic whig (he named his son Hampden), he was quick to resent infringements on individual liberty. In the forties he had vigorously attacked the aldermen of Dublin, a civic oligarchy, for encroaching on the rights of the commons (the representatives of the guilds). Having amassed a vast quantity of antiquarian lore, he charged 'their high-mightinesses our non-conscript fathers', with illegally extending their powers. Then, having, as he said, 'too much of a kind of political knight-errandry interwoven with my frame', he went on to attack 6 George I and Poynings' law, arguing that Irishmen, 'by

---

[4] *D.J.*, 4 Nov. 1760.   [5] *Exshaw's Magazine*, 1762, p. 182.
[6] *Pue's Occurrences*, 16 Dec. 1760.

the unalterable laws of our country, founded upon the great unerring laws of nature', should be subject only to their own legislature. And, though a strong protestant, proud of his British ancestry, he fortified his case by denouncing England's oppression of the native Irish during the medieval period.[7] Lucas was a very effective, if verbose and over-vehement, writer—his characteristic typography, distinguished by its excessive italicization and capitalization was well adapted to his literary style—and when a by-election for Dublin afforded him the opportunity he showed himself to be a shrewd political campaigner. But while he was busy canvassing, addressing excited gatherings in the different guild halls, he met with an abrupt check. The government had become alarmed, and when parliament met in the autumn of 1749 Lucas's publications were placed before the house of commons which directed the attorney-general to prosecute him for seditious libel. Lucas left Ireland and devoted himself to his profession, publishing in 1756 a bulky work on spas, in which he severely criticized the British medical world. He dedicated the work to the future George III, and the terms of the dedication show he was still keenly interested in politics. In 1760, announcing to the electors of Dublin 'the day of your deliverance is at hand', he came forward as a candidate for the city, declaring he was in favour of a septennial bill and a reduction in the pension list. He was returned, and though his origins and career sharply differentiated him from his fellow M.P.s, he played a leading and respected part in the house of commons until his death in 1771. Moreover, he founded a newspaper, the *Freeman's Journal* which was to be a watchful critic of men in power. It published wordy essays urging the highest standard of political morality, and the many letters it printed expressed explosively the indignation of the Dublin middle class on a wide range of issues—beggars, street lighting, strikes, the neglect of Saint Stephen's Green, the exorbitant demands by servants for vails (tips), the failure of military men to discharge their debts to Dublin shopkeepers and custom house abuses.[8]

At the close of the year (1761) the lords justices, the arch-

---

[7] *To the free citizens and free holders of Dublin* (1749); *Essay on waters* (1756), dedication; *Seasonable advice to the electors* (1760), p. 10.

[8] *Free. Jn.*, 17, 20 Sept., 22 Nov., 3 Dec. 1763, Apr., 14 May 1765.

bishop of Armagh (George Stone), Lord Shannon and John Ponsonby, raised an important issue. Was it judicious, they asked, to include amongst the 'causes' for summoning a new parliament which they had to certify to England, a supply bill? The Irish parliament, they pointed out, was jealous of its financial powers, and the prospect of a finance bill, drafted by the privy council, being placed before the house of commons, was already 'a subject of expectation in the minds of those who want to distinguish themselves in public concerns'. In urging caution, the lords justices reminded the lord lieutenant and the British government that public opinion was becoming a force which it would be dangerous to disregard. 'The people of all ranks here,' they wrote, 'as well as in other places are more curious and inquisitive into business than they were formerly, and are every day more prepared to take advantages of inaccuracies either of substance or form.'[9] The primate, Stone, having first assured his old patron, the duke of Newcastle, that he did not 'mean to vindicate myself at the expense of others', and then having proceeded to do so by explaining 'I did not lead but followed', emphatically warned the duke that it would be highly dangerous to ignore Irish opinion. 'I know', Stone wrote, 'Ireland may be curbed but I know too that its strength and its obstinacy are in very unequal proportions.'[10]

The lords justices' cowardice or caution shocked Lord Kildare, who after attending the Irish privy council remarked, 'I was extremely concerned to see that upon every occasion the opinion of the mob had so much influence upon the conduct of government'. In London, Henry Fox pressed for the immediate removal of the primate from 'the regency'; Pitt on the other hand was reluctant to criticize the lords justices. In the end the British cabinet decided to accept responsibility for maintaining 'a right hitherto allowed to be indubitable' and directed that a supply bill should be laid before the new Irish parliament when it met in October 1761.[11]

After this ominous prologue the first session of George III's

---

[9] The letter of the lords justices is printed in W. G. Hamilton, *Parliamentary logic* (1808), pp. 105–17.
[10] G. Stone to Newcastle, 6 Jan. 1761 (Add. MS 32617).
[11] Kildare to H. Fox, 20 Dec. 1760 (Add. MS 51426); H. Fox to Bedford, 30 Dec. 1760; R. Rigby to H. Fox, 2, 3 Dec. 1760, 8 Jan. 1761 (Add. MS 51385); Halifax to W. Pitt, 30 Mar. 1761 (P.R.O. 30/8/30).

first Irish parliament was tranquil. Members were conscious that the country was involved in a great imperial war. The lord lieutenant, Halifax, cultured and affable, was an experienced politician. His chief secretary, Hamilton, was a powerful, highly stylized orator, and he brought over as his private secretary an able young Irishman, Edmund Burke, who was at this time moving from literature to politics. Hamilton was soon on terms of intimacy with several leading Irish politicians—Andrews, Hutchinson and Pery—whom he impressed and flattered, and he was so conscious of his success in the Irish house of commons that he began to contemplate a permanent career in Ireland. If he and his Irish friends, he told Hutchinson, could build up a strong Irish parliamentary connection, 'we could paddle about the Irish channel very much to our advantage and amusement'. But another Englishman, Stone, the primate, who to some extent had already accomplished what Hamilton was contemplating, squashed the scheme by insisting that Hamilton should not be continued as chief secretary.[12]

Early in the session of 1761–2 the controversial finance bill, eloquently supported by Hamilton, was carried by a large majority (172 to 42); the government rode successfully a small parliamentary storm aroused by a proposal to recruit Irish catholics for the service of the king of Portugal, and critics of the administration decided not to debate the pension list, 'as a personal compliment to the lord lieutenant'. The heads of a bill limiting the duration of parliament were carried in the house of commons, but Halifax was sure that most M.P.s in fact did not want to see it on the statute book, and fervently hoped that the Irish privy council would reject it. But that body, also apparently influenced by a desire to avoid unpopularity, decided by one vote to transmit the heads to England. Understandably, it was not returned.

Before the second session (1763–4) of the parliament elected in 1761 opened, the new lord lieutenant, the earl of Northumberland, gathered that a number of Irish M.P.s were inclined to assert themselves by declaring that the house ought not to express an opinion on the peace of Versailles, a subject of

---

[12] *Twelfth report H.M.C.*, appendix, pt. ix, pp. 234–60; F. Hardy, *Memoirs of the political and private life of James Caulfield earl of Charlemont* (1810), p. 103.

vehement debate at Westminster, because it was a question which 'could not be laid parliamentarily before them'.[13] The viceroy therefore did not emphasize the subject in his speech from the throne. Nevertheless, later in the session, Pery attacked the peace as 'the most dishonest and disadvantageous that ever disgraced the annals of Great Britain' and Flood declared that Irish public opinion condemned it. It may be added in support of Flood's assertion that when Pitt retired from office in 1761 the citizens of Dublin expressed their regret at the resignation of a minister who had inspired the counsels and arms of Britain with that 'ancient, true, national spirit which must render the British name terrible to her foes in the utmost extremities of the globe'. The other great seaport, Cork, also voted an address to Pitt, thanking him for his 'faithful, wise and vigorous services' and some years later erected a statue to him with the motto, 'Nil oriturum alias nil ortum tale fatentes'.[14]

Before leaving for Ireland, Northumberland had been told that he could inform Irish politicians that the king did not intend to grant any pensions for life or a term of years, a concession to public opinion which would incidentally strengthen the influence of the crown. Nevertheless, early in the session a series of vigorous attacks against the pension list was mounted. John Fitzgibbon, a successful barrister, proposed an address which asserted that the payment of pensions was illegal, the revenues being voted for 'public uses'. He was defeated, but a resolution was carried in the committee of accounts drawing attention to the fact that the pension list exceeded all the other charges on the civil list taken together—a point which the attorney-general tried to brush aside as 'an entirely arithmetical operation'. Then, when Pery a week later moved that the house go into committee to consider the pension list, he was defeated by only 126 to 78, 'a large minority' as the lord lieutenant wrote. Undaunted by defeat, the opposition moved two addresses to the king lamenting the continual increase of 'the long train of pensions' and declaring that it was impossible for Ireland to bear the burden, 'deprived as we are of those resources for trade with which other parts of His Majesty's

---

[13] *Cal. home office papers 1760–65*, pp. 315–17.
[14] J. Caldwell, *Debates relative to the affairs of Ireland* . . . (1766), pp. 619, 644; *Exshaw's Magazine*, 1761, p. 540; *Pue's Occurrences*, 26 Apr. 1766.

dominions are blessed'. Both addresses were rejected, Flood characterizing the attitude of the majority as being 'a prostitution of our characters and a breach of our trust'. During the session the house passed the heads of a habeas corpus bill and a bill limiting the duration of parliament, the latter being rejected by the Irish privy council. It also secured a number of returns relating to the working of the barrack board and a resolution was moved but defeated, attacking the terms of the patent appointing the board. Northumberland, in the middle of a successful career which culminated in a dukedom, was anxious to know how he should cope with opposition in the Irish house of commons—should he be patient, 'by forbearance and management temporizing with the present evil', or should he assert the authority of the crown by dismissals? Halifax, now a secretary of state, though he resented the behaviour of the leaders of the great Irish parliamentary interests, counselled caution in 'this critical situation'.[15]

In the following session (1765–6) the heads of three important constitutional measures, a habeas corpus bill, a measure securing judges tenure on good behaviour and a septennial bill, were carried and Lucas introduced a place bill. Moreover an address to the king declaring the commons' 'earnest solicitude' for the return of the septennial bill from England was carried by an overwhelming majority. On the other hand the more extreme proposals put forward by the critics of the government, amongst whom Flood was conspicuous, were defeated. These included a resolution declaring that Ireland was entitled to annual parliaments by 'the express statute of Edward III never repealed'; an address to the king asking for a dissolution of parliament; a modification of Poynings' law; a resolution that a list of M.P.s, distinguishing those possessed of places or pensions, should be placed on the table of the house; and an address to the king on the state of the judicial bench, expressing approbation of our present judges who are natives of this kingdom and very critical of 'the persons of mean abilities and totally unacquainted with state and municipal constitution of Ireland' who had been sent over from England. Flood and Pery also strove hard but unsuccessfully to defeat an important

<hr />

[15] J. Caldwell, *Debates*, pp. 91, 208–9, 504; *Commons' Jn. Ire.*, viii, pp. 15, 73, 78, 105, 112, 124, 132, 142, 151; *Cal. home office papers, 1760–65*, pp. 324, 330, 334.

government measure, a temporary act to prevent the export of corn. Their opposition seems to have been largely provoked by a clause in the bill providing that its operation could be suspended by order of either the governor and privy council of Ireland or of the king in council in Great Britain. Ireland, it was angrily asserted, had a 'distinct and separate executive', and it was improper for the king to be directed 'to advise with his British privy council with respect to an act in which he is concerned merely as king of Ireland'.[16]

During the early sixties the Irish house of commons was, in the words of Pery, the member for Limerick who was coming to the front as an economic expert, 'engaged in a much larger circle of business'.[17] The legislative output was increasing, the employment of committees to investigate social and economic problems was growing, and public expenditure was being more minutely scrutinized. The independent M.P.s were often restive, and the constant critics of the administration, such as Flood, severe and indomitable, Pery, Osborne, Macaulay, French and Lucas, could command a fair amount of parliamentary support (usually mustering in the division lobbies about one-third of the members voting), and on a popular issue might even secure a majority. Moreover, there were signs it had growing out-of-doors backing. In 1763 a list was published for the information of the public of M.P.s who had voted in a division on the pensions list, with the offices and pensions enjoyed by government supporters indicated; and during the session of 1765–6 the commons of Dublin decided to set an example to the other cities and boroughs by resolving that Dr Lucas should be paid a salary of £300 per annum for his parliamentary services, and they also resolved that it should explicitly state that the freedom of the city was being offered to Flood for his defence of the rights of Ireland in the corn bill debates. The board of aldermen vetoed the first proposal and admitted Flood to the freedom simply on account of his 'character and abilities'.[18]

With the Irish house of commons showing that it might on occasion disregard the wishes of the government and display

---

[16] *Lords' Jn. Ire.*, iv, p. 360.
[17] *Eighth report H.M.C., appendix*, pt. i, p. 186.
[18] *Exshaw's Magazine*, 1766, pp. 110–16.

a will of its own, parliamentary management was by the beginning of George III's reign becoming a more exacting task. But for the first three sessions of the new reign all that was expected of the Irish administration was to keep the administrative and parliamentary machine running smoothly with the minimum of friction. In the later years of the decade, however, circumstances compelled the government both in Great Britain and Ireland to play a more positive role. The empire had made great gains in the Seven Years war and it could be assumed that its rivals would be quick to seize any opportunity which events might offer to revenge and reverse their defeat. Defence was bound to cost considerably more than it had earlier in the century and Britain was staggering under a national debt of nearly £60,000,000. However, 'it was a consolatory reflection to Great Britain that the members of her empire were in much happier circumstances than herself'.[19] Ireland, for instance, had a national debt of only £1,000,000 and an application of the principle that each part of the empire should contribute to imperial defence in proportion to its resources, suggested an increase in the military force maintained by Ireland. Even before the Seven Years war ended the possibility of keeping a larger body of men for the future in Ireland had been mooted and in 1767 it was decided that the force on the Irish military establishment should be raised from 12,000 to 15,000. This decision thrust an unusual role on the Irish administration, which would have to introduce into parliament an important, positive measure, which would involve a considerable increase in expenditure. The British government was convinced that 'the majority of gentlemen of property in Ireland who consult their own interest and the public good' would or should support the proposed augmentation of the forces, 'a measure of essential utility', which did not make unfair demands on Ireland.[20] Nevertheless it was decided that the scheme should be accompanied by concessions to Irish feeling and it was felt that, taking into account the growing complexities of Irish politics, the time had come when the viceroy must be resident in Ireland for the whole of his term of office. At the beginning of 1765 the cabinet already had decided that

---

[19] *Present state of the nation* (1768), p. 25.
[20] *Cal. home office papers, 1766–69,* pp. 218, 302, 313.

Northumberland's successor as lord lieutenant should 'reside constantly' in Ireland, but Hertford, who succeeded Northumberland, only remained in Ireland for the parliamentary session (he does not seem to have known that he was expected to do otherwise). However when his successor, the earl of Bristol, was appointed in the summer of 1766, the king laid down that he should reside in Ireland 'while he held office'. But a colleague wondered if Bristol's health could stand the strain of permanent residence in 'so turbulent and bacchanalian a state', and in the event Bristol never went to Ireland.[21] It seems however to have been intended that his successor would begin the new system, though it is indicative of the haphazard way in which cabinets were being conducted that Townshend himself seems to have been unaware of this. Fortunately, from soon after his arrival in Ireland he identified himself so strongly with the policy of his administration that he decided to stay on after the conclusion of his first parliamentary session.

Townshend was a member of a great political family. His grandfather had been Walpole's partner; his brother, the brilliant and short-lived Charles Townshend, was the chancellor of the exchequer whose bold attempt to make the American colonies contribute to imperial defence had such unforeseen and unfortunate results; and Charles's death at the very outset of his brother's strenuous term of office severed what would have been a valuable link between the British cabinet and the highly-strung viceroy. Lord Townshend had served as a soldier in Germany, in Scotland during the '45 and in North America, taking command of the Canadian expeditionary force after the death of Wolfe. He had also before inheriting the family peerage in 1764 sat in the house of commons, specializing in military questions. Experienced and diligent, he was sensitive, quick-tempered and subject to violent fluctuations of feeling. Townshend's opinions on men and affairs were often intelligent and always expressed with a fluency which, given his sharp changes of mood, could be damaging to his reputation. Moreover his social gifts—he was a caricaturist and satirist and, when relaxed, a genial, outspoken companion—could become

---

[21] *The correspondence of George III*, ed. J. Fortescue, i, p. 388; *Autobiography of Augustus Henry 3rd duke of Grafton* (1898), pp. 129, 157; *Additional Grenville papers*, ed. R. G. Tomlinson (1962), p. 336.

political liabilities. When he left for Ireland, Horace Walpole, with perceptive malice, remarked, 'Lord Townshend will impose upon them at first, as he has on all the world, will please them by a joviality and then grow sullen and quarrel with them'.[22] A year after he arrived in Ireland, Waite, an experienced official, was complaining that Townshend had 'no method, no idea of dignity or doing things at regular hours'. A year later he wrote, 'His Excellency familiarizes himself too much to all ranks and species of people. His good nature subjects him to be treated with great freedom. He walks about the streets like one of us, goes into a bookseller's shop, talks to everyone he meets whom he happens to know without considering that we are not used to such condescensions and have not the strength of mind to bear them with dignity. But with all his oddity and irregularities he is as honest a man as ever existed and has the most pure and upright intentions to all mankind.' Unfortunately, Waite had to admit that Townshend embroiled himself in an unpleasant discussion with Dr Lucas at a city dinner. The lord lieutenant remarked to Lucas that he (Lucas) could not possibly believe the doctrines enunciated in his paper the *Freeman's Journal*. The doctor grew warm and said he did not understand why his excellency addressed himself particularly to him and that but for his high station he should speak to him in a very different style. To which Townshend retorted, 'pray do not let my high station stand in your way'. In spite or because of his impetuous temper Townshend acquired considerable popularity. When he revisited Ireland in 1792 he was warmly greeted and for years his Irish friends dined together on his birthday.[23]

Townshend's task in Ireland was by no means an easy one. Unlike his predecessors, who had simply to watch over the routine running of an Irish parliamentary session, he was expected to push through the augmentation scheme and to control the shape in which the concessions the government was prepared to grant were to be enacted. While he was engaged in these delicate operations he had to cope with colleagues in England who were often ill-informed about Ireland and self-

[22] *Horace Walpole's correspondence*, xxii, p. 549.
[23] T. Waite to Weston, 28 Nov. 1769 (Add. MS 57928) and T. Waite to Weston, 4 June 1768 (Wilmot papers 47).

assured when it came to advising and criticizing the viceroy. At the outset the behaviour of his colleagues would have tried the temper of a more patient man. At the beginning of October shortly before leaving for Ireland he had a discussion with some of the cabinet which was so unsatisfactory that 'he burst into a justifiable rage'. It was then agreed that there should be a full cabinet on 7 October to decide on Irish policy and the lord chancellor came up from Bath to be present. But Grafton, who was to preside, had 'a match at Newmarket that morning' and sent a message that he could not arrive until eight in the evening. At eight a further message arrived that he had been delayed. The cabinet sat on until two in the morning but 'as companions not as statesmen'. There seems however to have been a meeting the next day, the day of Townshend's departure, at which it was settled that the British government would accept three bills, one limiting the duration of parliament, a habeas corpus bill and a bill giving judges tenure of office during good behaviour.[24] Acting on this Townshend in his speech recommended a measure securing 'the independence and uprightness' of the judiciary. This reference involved him in a long-drawn-out dispute with Shelburne, the secretary of state for the southern department, who in a couple of censorious dispatches reminded Townshend that at a cabinet meeting on the evening before he left London he had agreed not to mention the concessions in the speech from the throne, but rather refer to them in general terms in private conversation. To recommend the measures in the speech 'might draw in question the nature of the connection between Great Britain and Ireland which it has been thought sound policy to avoid'. Townshend defended himself vigorously. He was certain that it had been agreed that he might mention the concessions in his speech and he offered to resign. This episode, which illustrates how very easily misunderstandings could arise after unminuted discussions, frayed Townshend's nerves at a bad time.[25]

Early in the session the heads of the three bills were presented to the lord lieutenant. When the heads of the judges' bill were being considered in the house of commons Townshend suggested

---

[24] T. Whately to G. Grenville, 5, 8 Oct. 1767 (Add. MS 57817A); *Cal. home office papers 1765–69*, p. 199.
[25] Ibid., pp. 66–9, 213, 196–201, 212–15.

that a clause should be added empowering the crown to remove a judge on being addressed by both houses of the British parliament. But he was warned by his advisers not to insist 'upon anything of that sort' as it would certainly be rejected. The government also found that it was impossible to resist or modify a disagreeable financial proposal, a 20 per cent tax on salaries and pensions enjoyed by absentees, and finally in February the house of commons approved of a report from a committee on military expenditure which stressed the increasing cost of the forces on the Irish establishment and suggested possible economies.[26]

But at the beginning of February the government made a gesture which was expected to create an atmosphere of good-will. The bill limiting the duration of parliament (turned from a Septennial into an Octennial bill so as to meet Irish conditions) was returned. It rapidly passed through parliament, receiving the royal assent on 16 February, and the house of commons passed addresses expressing gratitude for the return of a bill 'so essential to the constitution and to the advancement of the protestant religion in this country'. Their gratitude was soon to be put to the test. At the time the Octennial bill was returned Townshend was informed that an enabling bill permitting the king to maintain 15,000 men in Ireland was about to be introduced into the British house of commons, a clear intimation that he should push forward with the augmentation plan. The plan was bound to arouse opposition. It involved increased expenditure, what the *Freeman's Journal*, the organ of Dublin liberalism, was quick to describe as 'a monstrous' expenditure, which would impose a heavy burden on the Irish protestants, 'a brave, loyal and hospitable people' who had come to Ireland to better themselves.[27] It was rumoured that the government's policy was to 'mow down all the influence and consequence of the gentlemen of the country' and secure an imperial contribution. It was argued that instead of augmenting the regular army, a protestant militia should be formed, the men being paid a shilling a day the cost to be met by tax on luxuries.[28]

---

[26] Ibid., pp. 196–7, 217–18, 234, 238.
[27] *Free. Jn.*, 14 May 1768.
[28] Blacklist of those who voted for and against an augmentation (Wilmot papers 47); T. Waite to T. Wilmot, 7 Feb. 1767 (Wilmot papers 44).

When the viceroy took soundings the results were depressing. In December 1767 he approached three leading politicians, Shannon, Ponsonby and the prime serjeant, Hely-Hutchinson. Shannon who was Master general of the Ordnance and Ponsonby, who was both speaker and first commissioner of the revenue, each headed an important parliamentary interest. The prime serjeant was, in Townshend's opinion, 'by far the most powerful man in parliament'. A self-made man, his forensic abilities and his marriage to an heiress giving him his start in politics, Hutchinson was in many ways the quintessence of an eighteenth-century public man, with the virtues and vices of the species exaggerated. A man of 'benevolence and enlarged spirit', having legal knowledge and good grasp of economic fact, he brought a hard common sense to bear on political problems. In touch with contemporary thought (he was an early admirer of Adam Smith and a friend of Burke) he advocated catholic relief and educational reform. A powerful debator, he was 'prepared to go out in all weathers'[29] and throughout his career he devoted himself to personal and family aggrandizement with a crude drive allied to a shameless shrewdness which disconcerted even contemporaries who were well aware that self-interest was a potent force in politics.

At first the triumvirate, Shannon, Ponsonby and the prime serjeant, though emphasizing the unpopularity of the augmentation scheme, were willing to support it, on the understanding that they should share in the disposal of Irish patronage, 'in proportion to the number of their friends and their weight in the country'—their immediate demands being carefully specified. By January the situation was grimmer. The triumvirate was not prepared to support the augmentation and the attorney-general, Townshend wrote, 'declines his assistance'. Townshend's immediate reaction was to recommend procrastination. The best time, he pointed out, to bring forward the augmentation scheme would be after the coming general election; and he began to consider the whole question of how the king's government in Ireland could be carried on. If the government was to be placed 'upon an honourable and lasting foundation', if the administration was to have 'vigour' (a

---

[29] *Correspondence of Edmund Burke*, iv, p. 411; F. Hardy, *Memoirs . . . James Caulfeild earl of Charlemont*, p. 73.

favourite term of Townshend's) then the lord lieutenant's authority must be strengthened by transferring to him the revenue patronage and by making quite clear that 'a system' of awards and punishments would be consistently observed.[30]

The British government, while it sympathized with Townshend's general approach, insisted that he should press on with the augmentation scheme, telling him that it must 'remain with the leading persons in Ireland to act as they can answer to their own consciences . . . for the evil consequences which may ensue from the failure of this measure'. Townshend retorted that he could not be 'so sanguine as to hope these sentiments were sufficient grounds upon which to carry a measure of this sort through parliament'. Nevertheless he dutifully went ahead, and on 19 April a viceregal message was delivered to the house of commons proposing an augmentation of the forces on the Irish establishment, since it was necessary that part of that force should be 'employed towards the necessary defence of His Majesty's garrisons and plantations abroad', and desirable that 12,000 men should be stationed in Ireland. The opposition produced a skilfully drafted answer to the effect that taking into account the size of the national debt it would be improper to decide a question involving heavy additional expenditure at so late a stage in the session, and the house by approving the answer by a majority of four (105 to 101) inflicted a dramatic defeat on Townshend's administration.[31]

The government must have been cheered by the fact that during the general election which occurred in the summer the augmentation question does not seem to have aroused much, if any, feeling, and a survey of the house of commons compiled with 'all possible exactness and impartiality' suggested that government business could be carried on even if a number of the great interests remained in opposition. Townshend was very conscious that he lacked the means of fixing fluctuating members and he wanted to consolidate his parliamentary majority by dismissing unreliable office-holders, rewarding friends with the vacant offices and using revenue patronage. But the British cabinet, Grafton's weak administration, confronted with difficulties in Middlesex and Massachusetts, was anxious not to

---

[30] *Cal. home office papers 1765–69*, pp. 219, 228, 230, 238, 291, 302–3, 306, 484.
[31] Ibid., pp. 235, 481, 500.

'come to those extremities if they could be avoided', and it expressed the hope that on 'mature deliberation' all Irish office-holders would support the augmentation scheme.[32] Townshend took considerable trouble to pave the way. He mentioned the economies by which the total cost would be cut down, and at the last minute he decided to bring the scheme to the attention of the house of commons by a vice-regal rather than a royal message. The reason for this was that in the text of the royal message supplied from England, there occurred the word 'insurrection', and Townshend pointed out 'infinite pains have been taken to persuade mankind that the object of this measure was against the Americans'. The viceregal message stated that the 'strictest economy' would be practised in military administration and that 12,000 troops would, except 'in cases of invasion or rebellion in Great Britain', be kept in Ireland, a stipulation criticized at Westminster by George Greville as weakening the prerogative.[33] These concessions and possibly the feeling that the measure was desirable overcame resistance and on 27 November the house agreed to the augmentation. But a few days before this victory the government suffered a resounding defeat on an issue of principle. One of the bills transmitted from England as a cause for holding a new parliament was a money bill, and this bill on the grounds that it did not take its rise in the house of commons was rejected by 94 to 71, the Leinster, Ponsonby and Shannon interests voting with the majority. Whether or not a distinction should be made between finance bills and other legislation was already a burning issue in imperial politics and the commons decision was as Townshend put it 'contrary to the constitutional dependence' in which Ireland stood to Great Britain. The lord lieutenant and the cabinet were in complete agreement that the rights of Great Britain should be asserted by following the precedent set by Sidney in 1692, when after the rejection of a money bill in similar circumstances, he entered a protest against this infringement of the rights of the crown in the journals of the house of lords, and prorogued parliament. Unfortunately the smack of firm government had to be delayed for a humdrum reason. A calculation, which Townshend quickly called for, showed that

[32] Ibid., p. 478.
[33] *Parliamentary history*, xvi, pp. 948–9.

it would be impossible to meet all the expenses of government from the hereditary revenue. So Townshend waited until the supply bills were safely through. Then on 26 December he suddenly came down to the house of lords, assented to the supply bills, delivered a protest against the rejection of the money bill and prorogued parliament.[34]

Shortly afterwards he went vigorously into action, dismissing Ponsonby and Lanesborough from the revenue board and Shannon from the office of master general of the Ordnance, and all three along with four of their associates from the privy council. A new revenue commission was set up, divided into two boards, customs and excise. This may have been administratively a sound decision. It certainly increased the number of well-paid posts available for M.P.s. On a less impressive level Townshend tried to conciliate the tradesmen of Dublin by holding a masquerade to compensate for the loss of custom they suffered from the abrupt termination of the parliamentary session.[35]

Hely-Hutchinson, a political pragmatist, dismissed the controversy over the money bill as 'a question of mere form'.[36] But Lord North saw the prorogation and the protest as part of the struggle to maintain effective imperial unity, an assertion of the principle that 'the vast bodies of British territories must have a head', a controlling power. Townshend himself, convinced he was fighting 'the dominion of aristocracy in Ireland',[37] was doggedly set on establishing his authority. Deficient in that suavity which counted so much in eighteenth-century politics he exasperated and exacerbated an opposition strong in numbers and debating power. As a result during the next two parliamentary sessions (February–May 1771 and October 1772) there were a number of strenuous debates. At the beginning of the first session Townshend in his speech tactfully ignored the circumstances of the last prorogation.

---

[34] *Lords' Jn. Ire.*, iv, pp. 539–40. As early as March the British government decided that a money bill should be transmitted as a cause for summoning a new parliament and the lord lieutenant and the privy council agreed to do so in June (Shelburne to Wilmot, 9 Mar. 1768; Waite to Wilmot, 2 June 1768) (Wilmot papers, 47).

[35] *Cal. home office papers, 1770–72*, p. 4.

[36] *Donoughmore MSS H.M.C.*, p. 265.

[37] *Cal. home office papers 1766–69*, p. 496.

The opposition was not prepared to let the matter drop and carried an amendment to the address to the king, proposed by Pery, declaring that the commons were 'ever tenacious of the honour of granting supplies', and did not wish their zeal in this respect 'to be construed into an invasion of Your Majesty's royal prerogative'. Townshend and the cabinet agreed that this amendment might be regarded as either an apology or a defiance. They wisely decided to treat it as the former and the issue was not pursued. A vote of thanks to the king for continuing Townshend in office was carried by only 132 to 107 and the opposition took the unusual course of trying to add satirical clauses to the address to the lord lieutenant. After the address had been debated Ponsonby abruptly resigned the office of speaker, 'not being able to bring himself to go up to the castle with the addresses of the house'[38] and the government was successful in securing the election of Pery as his successor— though as Pery had shown himself to be very independent this was only a qualified victory.

In the following session (1771), which began with a debate on the address to the lord lieutenant which lasted until three in the morning, the opposition, led by Flood, achieved a striking success, carrying by 123 to 101 a resolution to the effect that seven revenue commissioners were sufficient. A similar resolution was carried by 119 to 107 and they followed up these victories by moving that whoever advised carrying into execution the increase of the commissioners of the revenue advised a measure contrary to the sense of the house, and this motion was passed after a division, in which 216 members participated, by the casting vote of the speaker. But a motion that any M.P. who would accept a seat at the board would be guilty of a contempt of the house, was rejected, presumably as over-strong. Townshend attributed the government's defeat on the main issue to three reasons. The 'old and sage politicians of the country' were averse to administrative reforms which would tend to increase the hereditary revenue and so possibly render the crown independent of parliament. Other politicians were annoyed by the transfer of revenue patronage to the lord lieutenant and some members of the opposition were resentful 'merely because they could not obtain seats at the new board

[38] Bishop of Kilmore to ——, 7 Mar. 1771 (P.R.O. 30/29/1).

themselves'.[39] Townshend's analysis is probably correct enough
so far as it goes. But it is incomplete, since, understandably, it
ignores an important factor, the genuine concern of many M.P.s
with economy and efficiency. It is perhaps worth noting that
after examining the work of the new commissioners of accounts,
which had been appointed in October 1771 to audit the
accounts of a group of government departments, the house
decided that an increase of expense in auditing the public
accounts would not be unseasonable.[40]

Townshend's administration not only had to struggle with a
strong and unsparing parliamentary opposition. It was also
the target for a strident and sometimes savage press campaign.
During the early years of George III's reign the British and
Irish newspaper press was displaying a new, and to conventional politicians alarming, strength. The public was clearly
avid for political information, comment and gossip. Publicity
stimulated new forms of political activity, and politicians found
themselves working in a limelight which to many of them was
unwelcome. They undoubtedly had a grievance. Anonymous
journalists insisted on judging politicians, practical men in an
established system, by the highest moral standards, and while
moralizing continually indulged in crude and unfair scurrility.[41]
The behaviour of the press was commented on in the Irish
house of commons in 1773, when a stamp bill which imposed
a duty on newspapers and provided that the printer's name
should appear was being debated. Though the chief secretary
wanted the bill to be considered simply as a finance measure its
opponents saw it as a threat to the liberty of the press. On the
other hand there were supporters of the bill who saw that
'liberty is a wild beast, a beast of prey, till guided by reason'.
The great Dublin journalist, Faulkner, Hutchinson pointed out
'had been very *patriotic*, but as he was an honest man, he never
hurt private characters'. Other members criticized severely the
tendency of the press to dwell on men not measures, and to
'assassinate private reputations', a proclivity which undoubtedly

[39] *Cal. home office papers, 1770–72*, pp. 338–41.
[40] *Commons' Jn. Ire.*, vii, pp. 71, 460–1.
[41] A letter from Ireland to the *Public Advertiser* even suggested that the 1771
disturbances in the north of Ireland had been instigated by the Irish administration
'to make the English think the augmentation is necessary' (*Public Advertiser*, 29 Sept.
1773).

gratified the public. 'A labouring man', Tighe complained, 'now hardly goes to work until he had read the news.'[42] From the early sixties the American colonies were challenging the claims of the imperial parliament and defying the officers of the crown; and a few months after Townshend arrived in Dublin, Wilkes returned to England and there began a long, sensational struggle between authority and metropolitan liberalism occasionally backed by the mob. 'The spirit of the devil', an experienced Irish official wrote, 'has gone over the whole British empire and Satan seems to be hastening his kingdom.'[43] In Ireland, the *Freeman's Journal* printed justifications of the colonists and gave immense publicity to Wilkes. It was said that the Dublin aldermen absented themselves from the birthday levee at the Castle in 1770 out of sympathy with their London brethren, then embroiled with the court, and the following year it was proposed that the Guild of Merchants should present an address of thanks to Crosby, Oliver and Wilkes. The city conservatives mustered their supporters, 'a set of men', according to the *Freeman's Journal*, 'devoted to servile flattery and lost to all sense of honour' at a time when a whole empire groaned under ministerial tryanny, and the motion was defeated by 111 to 73.[44] From the moment the augmentation scheme was broached Townshend was under fire in the columns of the *Freeman's Journal*, and a number of letters attacking him were later reprinted in a volume entitled *Baratariana*, which ran into at least three editions. Written in the style associated with Junius (whom they anticipated by a year), these letters interpret Townshend's policy as part of a ministerial conspiracy against liberty and their satire still retains some bite. Townshend's second son, then a boy at Eton, consoled him by pointing out 'that a character of a man is so far from being impaired by the scurrilous abuses and contemptible defamations of the vulgar that it is if anything heightened'. Experience, he went on to say, 'daily shows us that the best and greatest of this country are constant marks for the folly and sometimes victims to the malice of the populace'.[45]

---

[42] *Hibernian Magazine*, 1775, pp. 23–5.
[43] T. Waite to T. Weston, 28 Nov. 1769 (Add. MS 57928).
[44] *Free. Jn.*, 7 June 1770, 11 Apr. 1771.
[45] John Townshend to Townshend, 25 Oct. 1772 (Townshend Misc., John Rylands Library).

Exasperating as the attacks on Townshend and his advisers may have been to the victims, there is little evidence of much public response. The Irish public in general does not seem to have been as hostile to the government as its opponents assumed and Townshend's own unpopularity seems to have been largely a legend created by his critics. Even a strong opponent admitted in the house of commons that though Townshend 'bullied and blustered he was merry and loved his bottle'. In a more serious vein Macartney, his chief secretary, argued that Townshend by 'patience and perseverance' had greatly strengthened the executive in Ireland.[46]

Harcourt, Townshend's successor, may have been chosen with Townshend's limitations in mind. A courtier and a diplomat, if a trifle pompous, he was shrewd, patient and conciliatory. He had in Colonel Blaquiere a highly competent chief secretary. Blaquiere had worked in a counting house, served in the army, being stationed for a time in Ireland, and later had been on Harcourt's staff when he was ambassador to France. A vigorous debater with a picturesque style, Blaquiere was good at managing men and he rapidly acquired a knowledge of Irish fiscal matters. On relinquishing office, having married an Irish heiress, he remained in Ireland and at the close of the century obtained a peerage as a reward for persuading English militia units to continue serving in Ireland.[47]

The new administration started with one advantage. Eighteenth-century politicians on the whole were glad to be on good terms with the government and Townshend's departure opened the way for his opponents to resume relations with the Castle. The duke of Leinster intimated that he would support the new administration; Lord Shannon, 'a cham of . . . high consideration in this country', was soon raising the 'particular points' he was concerned about, and even Flood appeared at a levee. Harcourt for his part was anxious to construct a broad-bottomed administration which would guarantee political placidity, and shortly after he arrived in Ireland, it was remarked that the new lord lieutenant had 'as yet shown a leaning to no party and hopes by that means to win them

---

[46] *Hibernian Magazine*, 1774, p. 319; *An account of Ireland in 1773* (1773), p. 54.
[47] Portland to Castlereagh, 11 June 1797 (letter book, Portland papers).

all'.[48] Harcourt attained a fair measure of success. Admittedly Ponsonby stood aloof; and the duke of Leinster in the end drifted into opposition partly out of principle (he disapproved of the stamp act) and partly out of pique—he considered himself to be 'neglected'. On the other hand the support of the Shannon interest was secured, James Dennis, a barrister who was 'devoted to and beloved by Lord Shannon',[49] being appointed prime serjeant in 1774. It may be surprising that Dennis's predecessor, Hely-Hutchinson, who had been prime serjeant from 1761 should have relinquished the office. The explanation is simple. He had secured a better post, the provost-ship of Trinity college, a crown appointment, hitherto not regarded as one of the prizes of politics. It had been customary for the provost to be drawn from the ranks of the fellows, and Francis Andrews, who died in 1774, had been a fellow for eighteen years before he became provost. The year after he became provost, Andrews, who was one of the few lay fellows, entered parliament as M.P. for Midleton, and a quick-witted man of affairs as well as a scholar, he distinguished himself in debate and became one of the confidential advisers of the lord lieutenant. Andrews's career may have suggested to Hutchinson the possibility of a politician becoming provost. He must have appreciated the fact that the provostship was a life appointment and been well aware that its holder would have considerable influence in the university constituency, both as returning officer and as the controller of much academic power and patronage. Given precedent and contemporary practice it was audacious to suggest that a busy practising barrister should become head of an academic house, but audacity triumphed, though Harcourt when submitting Hutchinson's name for appointment as provost felt obliged to justify his unorthodox choice. 'The government of a great university, situated in the metropolis', the lord lieutenant explained, 'requires greater experience, knowledge of the world and exertion, than perhaps are always found in the character of an ecclesiastic.' It was fortunate then that there was available a man such as Hutchinson,

---

[48] *Cal. home office papers 1773–5*, pp. 94, 119, 502; Harcourt to North, 20 Dec. 1772, 21 Oct. 1773, Harcourt to Rochfort, 20 Dec. 1772 (S.P. 63/438), *Eighth report H.M.C.*, appendix, pt. i, p. 193.

[49] W. Hunt, *The Irish parliament, 1775* (1907), p. 17.

'who possesses the accomplishments of a gentleman, as well as a scholar and [who] seems to have a peculiar turn for encouraging literature and the sciences'. It was also fortunate, the lord lieutenant reflected, that the man 'whom I had in my own mind selected as the most proper person should furnish me with the greatest facilities for my administration'.[50]

On being appointed provost Hely-Hutchinson, full of drive, ideas and self-assurance, set to work to improve the college as an educational instrument and turn it into a pocket borough. The fellows, slighted by his appointment, were inclined to regard some of his ideas with contemptuous suspicion and greatly resented his crude employment for electioneering purposes of the powers entrusted to him as head of a house for the benefit of the community. Hutchinson displayed arrogant audacity and great legal ingenuity; his opponents had plenty of spirit and a sufficient supply of the acrimony easily bred in a close academic community. There were many personal squabbles and some major engagements before the visitors and election committees of the house of commons, Hutchinson being accused of offences ranging from a serious and arbitrary misinterpretation of the provost's powers to stealing the college cook. It is only fair to add that the twenty years of Hutchinson's provostship was an era in the history of the college marked by rising numbers, building, improvements in the curriculum and the better organization of the medical school. In short if his appointment was a mistake and a scandal it at least had a stimulating effect on the college.

Harcourt not only satisfied (for the time being) Hely-Hutchinson and secured the support of the Shannon interest, he also won over the most powerful of the parliamentary critics of administration, Henry Flood. Flood for some years had been hesitating between two courses open to an eighteenth-century parliamentarian who was anxious to influence opinion and shape policy—independent criticism or office. At the beginning of Townshend's administration he had shown signs of friendliness to government, but Townshend's behaviour over the money bill had swung him into violent opposition. The Harcourt administration's readiness to give up the division of the revenue commission and to countenance an absentee tax

[50] Harcourt to Rochfort, 19 June 1774 (S.P. 63/438).

influenced Flood in its favour. Since however he had a high
sense of his own dignity and moral worth it was only after
prolonged negotiations that he became an administration
supporter, and an office-holder. In Harcourt's opinion 'however
great and exorbitant' Flood's terms might be, they were 'little in
comparison to the trouble he may give';[51] in 1774 he was made
a privy councillor, and in 1775 appointed a vice-treasurer for
Ireland in place of Jenkinson, one of a very long succession of
British politicians who had held that office. (Flood also was
anxious to become a British privy councillor but this request
was ignored.) Flood's intimate friend, Charlemont, the quintessence of political independence, was deeply pained by Flood's
acceptance of office. 'Flood,' he wrote, 'the champion of his
country, the bulwark of her liberties, her strong tower of defence
against all assailants—Flood, my friend Flood—the dear
partner of my heart and of all its councils—the author of my
hope and the pillar of my trust—Flood gave way.'[52] Fate
punished Flood cruelly. About the very time he accepted
office the political current began to flow strongly in favour of
opposition and as an outstanding lost leader, he was condemned
to sit for some exciting years in sullen silence amongst un-
congenial colleagues while younger men moved forward to
occupy his former place.

One of the main aims of Harcourt's administration was to put
Irish finances on a satisfactory footing.[53] Since the early sixties
Irish national expenditure had increased by about 12 per cent,
owing largely but not entirely to the augmentation, and by
the early seventies there was an annual deficit of well over
£100,000 a year (about 5 per cent of the total expenditure).
Though the immediate situation was not grave, a dangerous
trend was clearly developing and the Harcourt administration
aimed at making 'revenue and expenditure go hand in hand'.[54]
In its search for new sources of revenue the administration was
fortunate enough to discover a tax which might actually prove
to be popular, a tax on the net incomes derived by absentees
from their Irish landed property. An absentee tax, the lord

[51] Harcourt to North, 7 June 1775 (S.P. 63/438).
[52] *Charlemont MSS H.M.C.*, i, p. 38.
[53] Harcourt to North, 6 Dec. 1773 (S.P. 38/438).
[54] *Hibernian Magazine*, 1774, p. 600.

lieutenant pointed out, was widely supported in Ireland and Blaquiere when visiting London during the summer of 1773 spoke to British ministers about the possibility of introducing it. The cabinet was unenthusiastically acquiescent and the Irish administration was informed that if an absentee tax was put forward by independent M.P.s as part of a scheme for balancing the Irish budget, the British government would not 'risk the putting of the revenue on a sound basis by rejecting the tax'.[55]

Early in the session of 1773–4 Blaquiere in a long speech boldly surveyed the whole financial situation. He agreed with the government's critics that if deficits were allowed to accumulate the country would be ruined and he emphasized the government's determination to economize. Nevertheless defence could not be neglected at a time of international tension, when Prussia, for instance, 'had an army of 224,000 men on foot though it possessed but a span of territory', and he argued ingeniously that parliament by sanctioning a system of bounties and premiums which encouraged home manufactures, was responsible for a fall in the yields from import duties. In conclusion, having listed the new taxes under consideration, Blaquiere mentioned an absentee tax. On the whole the government's approach to fiscal questions met with a good reception. Flood praised its candour and called on the 'independent country gentlemen' to assist 'all its good intentions and not waste their time in useless opposition' and an attempt by Sir William Mayne to secure the appointment of a parliamentary committee on government expenses was defeated by 150 to 36. But one of the administration's critics, John Fitzgibbon, ended a powerful speech in which he attacked the restraints on Ireland's colonial trade on a very ominous note. Referring to the absentee tax, he said, it was the forerunner of a general land tax which the British government intended to impose on Ireland. The same view was voiced by the *Freeman's Journal*, the organ of Dublin liberalism.[56]

Before the question was broached in the Irish parliament opposition to an absentee tax was being organized in England. Early in September the earl of Bessborough had written to Lord

[55] Harcourt to Rochfort, 9 Nov. 1773 (S.P. 63/438); *The correspondence of George III*, ed. J. Fortescue, iii, p. 32.
[56] *Hibernian Magazine*, 1774, p. 671; *Free. Jn.*, 20 Nov. 1773.

Rockingham, the leader of the whigs, saying that he had heard from Lord Hertford that if the Irish parliament passed the heads of a bill 'taxing the estates of absentees they will pass it here'. (All three peers were large landowners in Ireland.) Rockingham though scandalized was not unduly disturbed. He did not believe, he wrote to Burke, that 'the privy council here *will dare* to advise assent' to 'a violation of the liberty and freedom with which every man in this constitution has a right to the usufruit of his property'. Burke was equally indignant but far less optimistic. An Irishman, who had embarked on a career in England, he had both an intense affection for Ireland and a strong attachment to England. To him the connection between the two countries, which formed the centre of the empire, was of inestimable value to them both, and he conceived the absentee tax to be a measure which tended 'in its principle and example to the separation and derangement of the whole contexture of this empire considered as a well ordered, connected and proportioned body'. It would interfere, he declared, with that 'free communication' so necessary to the maintenance of 'the united strength of a great and compact body'. It also tended to discourage 'mutual intermarriage and inheritance; things which bind countries more closely together than any laws or constitutions whatsoever'. 'What', Burke asked, 'is taxing the resort to and residence in any place but declaring that your connection with that place is a grievance? Is not such an Irish tax as is now proposed a virtual declaration that England is a foreign country, and a renunciation on your part of the principle of *common naturalization* — which runs through this whole empire?' Burke was prepared to grant that the restraints imposed on Irish trade at the time he was writing were mistaken and oppressive. But, he warned his Irish friends, 'an injury is not always a reason for retaliation; nor is the folly of others with regard to us a reason for imitating it with regard to them'.

Burke however was by no means confident that an absentee tax could be defeated. He was afraid that if the tax was suggested in the Irish house of commons by an opposition M.P. (perhaps Flood, who would 'have the merit of coming over to a government entirely in an Irish interest'), accepted by the Irish administration and assented to by the British cabinet, the

British public would remain quiescent. There was, Burke had to grant, 'a superficial appearance of equity in this tax, which cannot fail to captivate almost all those who are not led by some immediate interest to an attentive examination of its intrinsic merits'. Perturbed by these fears Burke, immediately on receiving Rockingham's letter, hurried to Bessborough's house to discuss the possibility of 'an early, prudent and vigorous opposition', and he probably assisted in drafting a letter of remonstrance to North, signed by Rockingham and four other peers who were large landowners in Ireland, protesting against an 'unprecedented imposition', 'as far as we can find without parallel in any civilized country'. They had not, they complained, 'hitherto considered residence in England, 'the principal member of our British empire', 'an act of delinquency to be punished or as a political evil, to be corrected by the penal operation of a partial tax'. North replied stating briefly that if the Irish parliament sent over to England a well-devised financial plan it would not be rejected even though it included an absentee tax. On receiving this answer Rockingham with amazing 'spirit and activity' began to organize a widespread protest movement. As Burke was careful to explain, 'a life of disinterestedness, generosity and public spirit,' were Rockingham's 'titles to have it believed, that the effect the tax may have upon his private property, is not the sole nor the principal motive of his exertions'.[57]

Appointing as his secretary for the campaign William Hickey, the famous memoirist, Rockingham circularized the Irish landowners resident in England, warning them that opposition 'to be effectual must be early; and it must be made in England as well as in Ireland', and requesting them to be ready to attend a meeting in London. The response on the whole was satisfactory, most of those contacted being vehemently hostile to 'a measure which runs totally counter to liberty'. What is interesting is the reason why some of those who replied to Rockingham were unwilling to support him. Lord Clare, an Irishman and an active M.P. at Westminster, declared that the objections to the absentee tax would be conclusive only if the Irish parliament could devise other measures which would balance the budget. The duke of Chandos wrote bluntly that

[57] *Correspondence of Edmund Burke*, ii, pp. 458–91; *Annual register*, pp. 219–20.

he always assumed that his property both in England and Ireland was liable to taxation. Lord George Sackville, having pointed out that in Ireland 'the resident gentlemen, the merchants and the substantial housekeepers' bore almost the whole burden of taxation, and that to tax articles of general consumption would drive the common people to despair, argued that a general land tax would be 'both just and eligible'. However, he admitted that the Irish house of commons 'would vote any man an enemy to his country who would adopt such an idea'.[58]

But the great majority of absentees reacted predictably, and as indignation against the absentee tax mounted the prime minister became uneasy. At the end of October, in a characteristic letter to Harcourt, he began by dwelling on the growing strength of the opposition to an absentee tax. 'Friend and foe', he wrote, 'joined in condemning and abusing it'. Shelburne was saying that a minister who assented to it deserved to be impeached and Mansfield had warned the cabinet that if the tax passed they could expect similar proposals from all the colonies 'who will be very earnest to load with new impositions such of their country men who think proper to reside in Great Britain'. Then, with what may be described as conscious decency, North went on to say that the government in the face of 'all the noise and clamour on this side of the water' would adhere to its promise to accept the absentee tax if it were 'blended and connected with the rest of the plan' for settling Ireland's fiscal difficulties. Harcourt immediately saw what North was hinting at, and realizing that the suggestion of an absentee tax was damaging the government in England, he quietly started 'to divert the progress of the tax'. Though he thought it advisable to observe 'strict neutrality' on the issue, his friends, he boasted to North, worked like slaves to defeat the proposal. When on 25 November Oliver, M.P. for County Limerick, moved that a tax of two shillings in the pound should be imposed on the net produce of the lands of absentees there was a vigorous debate which cut across the customary lines of division, and, after an amendment substituting one shilling for two, was rejected by 119 to 107, the original motion was rejected

<hr />

[58] For Rockingham's correspondence with Irish landowners over the question of the absentee tax see W.W.M. R 3.

by 120 to 106. The rejection of an absentee tax was, Harcourt sententiously remarked, an example of 'the capriciousness, and instability . . . and that wild and inconsistent conduct which every lord lieutenant has encountered'.[59]

A few weeks after the absentee tax had been disposed of the Irish administration was again in serious difficulties. When the tontine and stamp bills (the latter a measure with ominous American associations) came back from England it was discovered that a number of alterations had been made in the heads which had been transmitted, and the house of commons promptly rejected both bills. According to Harcourt, who resented being thrust into a new crisis, the government's friends bitterly complained that the alterations were 'wanton, unnecessary and unkind'; the secretary of state retorted that the heads as sent over were full of absurdities, and in the event the house of commons passed new heads with the corrections made in England incorporated. The administration besides securing new sources of revenue managed to strengthen the revenue machinery by pushing through a bill which empowered revenue officers to obtain 'writs of assistance' (which it was thought would enable them to obtain military backing). Thus at the close of the session of 1773–4 Harcourt could congratulate himself that much had been accomplished towards achieving his 'great object, the putting the revenues of this country on a footing equal to the expenses of government'.[60]

[59] North to Harcourt, 29 Oct. 1773 (S.P. 63/437); Harcourt to North, 9, 12, 19, 26, 30 Nov. 1773 (S.P. 63/438).
[60] Harcourt to North, 6 Dec. 1773 (S.P. 63/438).

5

The American war and the volunteers

During the long recess which followed the Irish parliamentary session of 1773-4 discontent in the American colonies and the determination of the home government to assert its authority produced a series of incidents which formed a grim chain of causation leading to armed conflict at Concord in April 1775. Ireland and America were linked by innumerable family ties and Irishmen settled in the colonies were conspicuously involved in the War of Independence. Early in the war a young officer serving in America, in a letter published in the *Hibernian Magazine* stated that the troops which 'kept up the spirit and life of the rebellion were totally Scotch and Irish',[1] many of the latter being tenants forced by eviction to emigrate. Some years later an Irish M.P. went further, declaring that 'the Irish in both the British and American forces have distinguished themselves and borne away the laurels'.[2] At the beginning of the war the part Irishmen were playing in the American ranks was illustrated by the advance into Canada and death before Quebec of the American general, Richard Montgomery, an Irishman closely related to two Ulster M.P.s. More fortunate was James McHenry, a Ballymena man, educated in Dublin, who after being Washington's secretary became secretary of war. McHenry was one of the four Irishmen who sat in the constitutional convention, and it may be added that two of the signatories of the declaration of independence were born in Ireland (though they both left it in childhood). Irishmen were also to be found in the loyalist ranks, as might be expected since the loyalists formed a substantial proportion of the population. Almost a quarter of the loyalist claimants for compensation who stated their country of origin were Irish and amongst the American corps in the service of the crown were two specifically

[1] Lt. Ridsdale in the *Hibernian Magazine*, 1776, p. 216. Ridsdale was twenty years later the author of *An ode . . . on the victory obtained by lieutenant general Johnson at Ross* [1799].

[2] *Hibernian Magazine*, 1778, p 232.

Irish units—the Loyal Irish volunteers, a company formed at the close of 1775 by the Irish merchants in Boston and the Volunteers of Ireland, a provincial corps, raised in 1778 by Lord Rawdon.[3]

The opposition throughout the British Isles tended to see the American war as a continuation of the political struggle in which they were engaged. Shortly before the first shots were exchanged Chatham in an impressive appeal for imperial reconciliation declared that 'the cause of America is allied to every true whig. They will not bear the enslaving of America. . . . The whole Irish nation, all the true English whigs, the whole nation of America, these combined make millions of whigs averse to the system.'[4] The Irish whigs or 'patriots' were bound to sympathize with the American cause. Ireland and the colonies had both accepted British parliamentary supremacy; but both Irishmen and the colonists had resented the way in which that supremacy was exercised and they were both sensitive to the danger of taxation without representation and quick to make a distinction, practical if illogical, between financial and other legislation. As early as 1765 Gerard Hamilton had thought it necessary to assure his friends in Ireland that 'there is not at present whatever there may be in prospect, the faintest idea of taxing Ireland'. But he had to admit that in a recent debate George Grenville and Charles Yorke had both asserted 'without any reserve' the right of the imperial parliament to impose taxation on Ireland. In 1774 Richard Rigby (who enjoyed a valuable sinecure in Ireland) in the debate on the Massachusetts regulation bill went if anything further, declaring that 'we have a right to tax Ireland if there was a necessity to do so in order to help the mother country'—a declaration which, it was said, produced 'contortions' in the countenances of Irish M.P.s who were in the gallery. Rigby must have felt that he had been indiscreet because the next day he explained that 'no parallel could be drawn between Ireland and the colonies, for Ireland has a parliament'.[5]

---

[3] W. Brown, *The king's friends* (1965), pp. 287–341; H.Q. papers of the British army in America: order book of General Howe (P.R.O. 30/55/107).

[4] *Parliamentary history*, xviii, p. 159.

[5] *Eighth report HMC, appendix* p. 190; *Parliamentary history*, xvii, p. 1287, xviii, pp. 62–4.

With Ireland and the colonies sharing constitutional grievances and objectives, many Irishmen naturally sympathized
with the American cause. In the summer of 1775 an intelligent
Irish M.P. wrote from Dublin 'here we sympathize more or less
with the Americans, we are in water colour what they are in
fresco. The language of your ministerlings has made us what
we are.' Lord Midleton, a young Irish peer closely connected
with the English opposition, wrote from Cork, 'we are all
Americans here except such as are attached securely to the
castle or are papists'. And Skelton, a clergyman of the established
church with affinities to Dr Johnson, writing from Ireland to
William Knox, an Irishman, who was under-secretary for the
colonies, complained, 'here are none but rebels. . . . All our
newspapers abound with intelligence favourable to rebels. . . .
The king is reviled, the ministry cursed, religion trampled
under foot.' But Skelton himself was very hesitant when he
attempted to say how the American situation should be
handled. In 1774, though he termed the Americans 'downright
rebels', he felt that 'if they were to be taxed by the parliament
of England they may bid adieu to the thing called property.
How wisdom shall make its way between the horns of this dilemma with justice in tow I am too far off to see.' By 1777 he
had come to the conclusion that 'all colonies have a right to aim
at independence when they can. Our American colonies however have set up too soon, at an improper time for themselves,
ungratefully, dishonestly and impoliticly.' The same hesitancy
was evinced by an Irish M.P., Thomas Waite, who was
under-secretary. At the beginning of 1775 he was sure that it
was an opportune moment 'to go to war with the refractory
spirits in the colonies'. But six months later he was almost
convinced that the sooner Great Britain got rid of the American
colonies the better. The rebels, he argued, would never work
any constitution framed for them by the imperial government.[6]

As Midleton indicated, the Irish catholics, in so far as they
were politically articulate, supported the government's American policy. Towards the close of 1775 a group of influential

[6] R. J. S. Hoffman, *Edmund Burke: New York agent* (1956), p. 585; Midleton to
Townshend, 16 Aug. 1775 (N.L.I. MS 52); *Knox MSS H.M.C.*, p. 446; Waite to
G. Macartney, 15 Jan., 27 Aug. 1775 (Add. MS 51389).

catholics presented a memorial to the Irish government expressing their horror of rebellion and offering to encourage recruiting. The government readily accepted catholic recruits, a step which both helped to bring regiments in Ireland up to strength and intensified the opposition of Irish protestants to the war. When an administration supporter in the house of commons argued that 'it was better to export papists than protestants', Barry, the M.P. for Cavan retorted that 'if papists were trained as soldiers they would be the more dangerous'; and a satirist in the *Hibernian Journal*, an organ of Dublin liberalism, published a letter from 'Thady Flaherty', supposedly a catholic recruit, stating that Sir Boyle Roche, a genial humorist, famous for his Irish bulls, who was busy recruiting in the west of Ireland, 'calls us all cousins and that America is the new Eden, and that we get the estates we lost by our fidelity here if we go and kill the heretics there'.[7]

The newspapers reflected Irish sympathy with the American cause. The colonists' manifestos were published, the *Freeman's Journal* reprinted Paine's *Common sense*, one of the most popular expositions of the Americans' case, and much of the press comment on the progress of the war was pro-American. Opposition to the war was also voiced at public meetings. In the early summer of 1776 the citizens of 'the opulent and commercial city' of Cork in a petition to the king, having emphasized that their American trade was destroyed and their West Indian trade almost ruined, called on him to dismiss his ministers and sheath the sword. Almost simultaneously about 250 of the principal inhabitants of Belfast including over half a dozen of those who were to be conspicuous liberals in the nineties, implored the king to put an end to civil war and demanded 'a speedy and happy restoration of that old constitutional system', which had united Great Britain and her colonies.[8] During the latter half of 1775 the Dublin liberals exerted themselves strenuously. In July the guild of merchants (the most influential of the guilds) thanked Wilkes, leader of the London liberals, Lord Effingham, who had resigned his commission rather than fight the Americans, and the peers who had opposed the New

---

[7] *H.J.*, 6, 18 Sept. 1775; *Hibernian Magazine*, 1775, pp. 686–7; catholic petition (S.P. 63/438).

[8] *B.N.L.*, 7 Nov. 1775; *Free. Jn.*, 24 June 1776.

England bills and the establishment of popery in Canada—the Quebec act had given civil liberty to the Canadian catholics and protected their ecclesiastical endowments.[9] On 20 August the sheriffs and common council of Dublin expressed their regret that, owing to the refusal of the aldermen to co-operate, the city corporation was unable to petition against the unconstitutional measures which were being pursued against America. Ten weeks later a meeting of Dublin parliamentary electors instructed the M.P.s for the city to oppose a change in the position of the custom house, a land tax, 'any act tending to give the papists more power than they had' and grants in aid of the measures being pursued against their fellow subjects in America. Towards the close of the year 3,000 freeholders, freemen and merchants of Dublin signed an address to the king urging him to promote that policy of reconciliation with America 'on which the happiness, strength and glory of Your Majesty's empire (hitherto the admiration and envy of the world) so greatly depends'. The liberals of County Dublin deputed Napper Tandy (who also was active in the city agitation) and Joseph Fuller to request the high sheriff to summon a county meeting to consider the war with America. After repeated applications they at last secured the reply that the sheriff, believing that he was appointed 'to preserve and not disturb the peace of the county' was not prepared to 'give colour to the assembling together of many thousands'. Undiscouraged by this rebuke, the country liberals held 'a respectable meeting' of freeholders which expressed its sympathy for the Americans, exposed to the horrors of war for endeavouring to defend their liberty and property.[10] The Dublin liberals also expressed their feelings on convivial occasions. The Free citizens of Dublin, dining with Tandy in the chair, had as toasts: 'Our fellow subjects in America now suffering persecution for attempting to assert their rights' and 'May the gates of Temple Bar be speedily decorated with the heads of those who advised the employing military force to enslave our fellow subjects in America.'[11] Napper Tandy was already conspicuous among the group, including Edward Newenham and

[9] H.J., 19 July 1775.
[10] H.J., 30 Aug., 25, 30, Oct., 29 Nov., 15 Dec. 1775.
[11] H.J., 19 July 1775.

Henry Howison, which was from the middle seventies directing Dublin liberalism. The son of an ironmonger, Tandy first joined his father's business, then he became a merchant, and by 1776, when he was about thirty-nine, he was of sufficient standing to be elected a representative of the guild of merchants on the common council. Fervent, fluent and flamboyant, an indefatigable organizer and a rumbustious orator, Tandy soon became an inspiring radical leader and an object of ridicule among conservatives. Years after the event, Tandy wrote, 'when America revolted against Great Britain my heart rejoiced within me, and I should at that time have joined her standard if not prevented by our poor friend Humphreys'.[12] He was not the only Irish radical leader of the nineties who at this time thought of leaving for America. William Drennan, then a medical student at Edinburgh, saw America 'as indeed the promised land I wish to see before I die', as well as the place to which he would emigrate if he failed an important exam-ination. Attending church, he heard with disgust 'a virulent prayer to the father of mercy against poor America', and he refused to subscribe to a fund for raising recruits, getting a grim pleasure from seeing his acquaintances 'emptying their pockets (and what more could be asked of a Scotchman) in the support of the war'.[13] Another well-known northern radical, the presbyterian minister, William Steel Dickson, who in 1798 was the United Irishmen's military leader in County Down, preached vigorously against 'the unnatural, impolitic and unprincipled war in America'. His sermons, which he published, aroused the ire of Ulster conservatives, so that whenever some of them 'got warm round their bottle' they agreed, Dickson wrote, that 'I ought to be d—— as hanging was too good for me'.[14]

The reaction to Dickson's sermons shows that Irish opinion was not unanimously favourable to the American cause. However it was sufficiently pro-American for Burke to hope that when the Irish parliament met in the summer of 1776 it would declare itself against the war by 'a pathetic address' to

<hr />

[12] J. N. Tandy to J. Tandy, 28 Prairial, Year 10 (S.P.O.I. 620/12/144).
[13] W. Drennan to Mrs McTier, 14 Nov., 13 Dec. 1777, 20 Jan. 1777 (Drennan papers, 9a, 17, 20).
[14] W. S. Dickson, A narrative . . . (1812), p. 8.

the king, a letter to both houses of parliament and, not least effectively, by 'a suspension of extraordinary grants' for troops employed overseas. Ireland, Burke asserted, had 'the balance of the empire, and perhaps of its own fate for ever, in its hands', and he urged Rockingham and Devonshire to persuade their Irish friends, Leinster, Conolly and Ponsonby, to throw their parliamentary weight against the war.[15] The Irish administration on the other hand was very anxious to secure Irish parliamentary support for the British government's American policy, and Harcourt in his speech from the throne emphatically drew attention to the commercial concessions which the British parliament had recently made to Ireland. Irish rape-seed, he pointed out, was now admitted into the English market, Ireland had been allowed to export directly the clothing and accoutrements required by troops on the Irish establishment stationed abroad; and Irish-owned ships had been made eligible for the bounties granted to boats engaged in the Newfoundland whale fishery. These concessions, the lord lieutenant expected, 'would form such a system of agriculture and improvements as will, I trust, secure riches and plenty to the people of Ireland'. Nevertheless during the debates on the address Ogle and Yelverton argued that it was impossible to call the Americans rebels without admitting that the British parliament had the right to tax Ireland; Ponsonby compared the war to 'the social war of the Romans'; Newenham warned the house that if Ireland supported the British war effort, not a yard of Irish linen would in the future be sold in America; Yelverton stressed that it would be unjust 'without the proper evidence for parliamentary information' to declare the Americans to be rebels and Conolly told the house that when he voted for the augmentation, 'a venerable member', Dr Lucas, had 'tapped me on the shoulder and said "Young man, you know not what you are doing, you are putting a sword in the hands of the British minister which when he has got, he will cut the throats of your American brethren and when that is done, he will turn it against ourselves." Blaquiere wearily replied that he would not enter into the question who were the aggressors, for the original dispute was lost in the consequences; but that he could only call the Americans rebels: 'America had

---

[15] *The correspondence of Edmund Burke*, iii, pp. 218–19.

drawn the sword of rebellion against her sovereign and America must be subdued'. The government, having defeated by 99 to 49 an opposition amendment to the address, urging peace negotiations with the colonists, set to work to secure parliamentary support for an important war measure—the dispatch of troops from Ireland to America. Parliament was informed that the government planned to send 4,000 of the troops stationed in Ireland across the Atlantic, replacing them by 4,000 Hessians who would be paid by Great Britain. This plan was naturally attacked by the opponents of the war and was also criticized by country gentlemen, who felt that German mercenaries could not be used for maintaining law and order. Were magistrates and revenue officers, Ogle asked, to learn German?[16] In the event the government gave up the plan of stationing Hessians in Ireland, and the house agreed to the dispatch of reinforcements to America, a decision which, in the lord lieutenant's opinion, indicated to the world at large Ireland's attitude to the war. This transfer of troops involved the Irish government in an awkward parliamentary imbroglio. Two finance bills came back from England with alterations, including the deletion of clauses indicating that parliamentary sanction was required for the removal of the 4,000 men. This 'gave occasion to the most violent heats', Hussey Burgh arguing that the British ministers should be taught that 'if they altered bills they would risk part of the supplies', and Ogle moving that the altered bills should be burned by the public hangman. The house of commons, jealous of its rights or claims, promptly rejected the bills, but the government managed to carry revised heads of bills incorporating the changes made by the British privy council.[17]

Another war measure which was vigorously criticized in the house of commons was an embargo on the export of provisions. In February a proclamation had been issued forbidding the export of Irish provisions (except corn) to all places, except Great Britain and the colonies which were not in rebellion. This embargo was ostensibly to prevent supplies reaching the king's enemies. Its object in fact obviously was to keep down prices at a time when the government was purchasing very large

---

[16] *Hibernian Magazine*, 1775, pp. 609–10, 722–3.
[17] Harcourt to North, 26, 30 Nov., 21, 28 Dec. 1775 (S.P. 63/438).

quantities of foodstuffs in the south of Ireland for victualling the fleet and the forces in North America. Irish provision merchants naturally resented being cut off from their continental markets and must also have resented the imposition of a check on war profits and profiteering. Though food prices rose in Ireland during the late seventies, it was widely believed that the embargo had damaged the Irish economy; and it was attacked in the house of commons as 'overbearing, arbitrary, illegal and partial'. But the government managed to defeat an attempt to censure it by the not very satisfactory majority of 89 to 66.[18]

Harcourt prided himself on how successfully he and his chief secretary had managed government business in the house of commons; the dispatch of 4,000 men to America, was, he wrote, 'one of the most knotty points a lord lieutenant could attempt'.[19] But a high price had to be paid for parliamentary support at this critical time. In 1776 twenty-two new Irish peerages were created and eight Irish peers obtained a step in the peerage. Fourteen of the newly created peers and five of those who gained a step were influential and active in Irish parliamentary politics. Moreover at the close of the session of 1775-6 the lord lieutenant and chief secretary produced long lists (totalling about forty names in all) of persons to whom it would be advisable to grant pensions. Admitting that the cost, about £11,000 per annum, was high, Blaquiere argued that it was trifling compared to 'the important, if novel but necessary idea, of securing to the king's government a proper majority' in the parliament which would be chosen at the general election of 1776. Blaquiere thought that his arrangements would guarantee the government 138 votes, 'as great a power as a government ever commanded in parliament'.[20] The British government agreed to most of the proposals but Harcourt did not remain in Ireland to meet the new Parliament. After more than three years in office he looked forward to retirement, hoping to pay a visit to France; he was annoyed by his defeat in the dispute over the powers of the commander-in-chief and

---

[18] T. M. O'Connor, 'The embargo on Irish provisions, 1776-9' in *I.H.S.*, ii, pp. 3-11.

[19] Harcourt to C. Jenkinson, 29 Apr. 1776 (Add. MS 38210).

[20] Blaquiere to J. Robinson, 15 Dec. 1775; Harcourt to North, 4 May 1775 (S.P. 63/438).

he felt that having played with good luck he wanted to leave a winner.[21]

It was not easy to find a suitable replacement for Harcourt. Dartmouth, who had considerable political weight, was unwilling to go to Ireland, and Rochford, who had been a secretary of state, would only go if it were agreed that the viceroy should not be permanently resident. Hillsborough and Buckinghamshire were both very willing to accept the office of lord lieutenant, but the king dismissed their claims contemptuously. Buckinghamshire had been 'knocking at every door'; Hillsborough was a man of poor judgement and his appointment would encourage all the Irish resident peers to compete for the office. But in the end, *faute de mieux*, Buckinghamshire was appointed. He had been a competent ambassador at the court of Saint Petersburg, was a man of presence and had a sense of dignity which led to an immediate stiffening of etiquette at the viceregal court. His chief secretary was Sir Richard Heron, an attorney who had held offices attached to the courts of law. An affable man, he lacked parliamentary experience and did not distinguish himself in debate.[22] Buckinghamshire and Heron formed a reasonably competent team, but neither was in the first flight, and they were doomed to have to cope with a major emergency.

Buckinghamshire's wife was a sister of Thomas Conolly whose sister-in-law was the mother of the duke of Leinster, and Buckinghamshire, who was afraid that in the near future it would be impossible for the Irish government to find the resources required for the purchase of parliamentary support, felt that these family ties would be a source of strength to the administration.[23] When he wanted to relax he retired to Castletown, Conolly's seat near Dublin, and Conolly seems to have been largely responsible for the appointment of Hussey Burgh as prime serjeant, a move which greatly increased the government's debating strength. Burgh, an expert in constitutional law, was said to have introduced a new style of advocacy to the Irish bar, and according to Buckinghamshire,

[21] Harcourt to North, 29 Mar. 1776 (S.P. 63/438); Harcourt to C. Jenkinson, 29 Apr. 1776 (Add. MS 38210).

[22] *Abergavenny MSS H.M.C.*, p. 15; Buckinghamshire to G. Germain, 2 Feb. 1777 (Add. MS 34523); J. Beresford, *Correspondence*, i, p. 14; *Gent. Mag.*, 1806, p. 94.

[23] Buckinghamshire to C. Thompson, 3 June 1780 (Add. MS 34523).

'the liberality of a gentleman and the intelligence of a scholar are happily blended in his conversation'. But Burgh's feelings, the lord lieutenant was doomed to discover, were 'exquisitely sensible, a circumstance most amiable in society but seriously inconvenient in business'. Buckinghamshire about the same time brought forward Foster, later speaker and an acknowledged expert on Irish economic problems.[24] After being eighteen months in Ireland Buckinghamshire was congratulating himself that he was on good terms with Leinster, Shannon, Ely and Tyrone, heads of important connections, as well as being in touch with a number of respectable independent peers and M.P.s. He admitted that 'the immediate friends of the late administration were disquieted at my not placing an implicit confidence in them' but he accepted this as inevitable—'a jealousy of temper almost characteristic to the gentlemen of this kingdom', he wrote, 'is a very serious impediment to every political transaction'.[25]

One important senior official who was undoubtedly annoyed by the change of administration was John Beresford, who had been made a revenue commissioner by Townshend. Beresford had a good grasp of fiscal matters, was a strong upholder of the British connection and had a proclivity for firm government. Early in the new viceroyalty he detected a symptom of weakness—the omission in the speech from the throne at the opening of parliament in October 1777 of any reference to the American war. The omission aroused unfavourable comment in government circles in England, the king remarking that 'the gentlemen who supported the war before will think themselves given up'.[26] The American issue was indirectly raised in the Irish house of commons when Daly (whom Buckingham had hoped to secure as a supporter) attacked the embargo. Ireland, Daly declared, was 'being converted into a magazine to support the unnatural war with the colonies', and the south and west of the country were being reduced to a deplorable condition. Later Hutchinson,

---

[24] *Hibernian Magazine*, 1779, pp. 657–8; Buckinghamshire to C. Thompson' 12 Oct. 1779, Buckinghamshire to Sir Henry Clinton, 28 Mar. 1779 (Add. MS 34523), Buckinghamshire to G. Germain, Sept. 1778 (Add. MSS 34523).

[26] J. Beresford, *Correspondence* 1854, i, p. 17; G. Germain to Buckinghamshire, 23 Oct. 1777 (Add. MS 34523).

[26] J. Beresford, *Correspondence*, i, p. 17; G. Germain to Buckinghamshire, 23 Oct. 1777 (Add. MS 34523).

on behalf of his Cork constituents, complained that the Irish provision trade was losing important foreign markets. Another debate on the provision trade raised an awkward constitutional issue. It was pointed out that provisions for the forces were being exported from Cork without paying duty. The administration had a good answer—the provisions were not dutiable. But an admission was made which Yelverton (that 'viper' to an administration supporter) sprang on. The revenue commissioners had acted under the authority of the British treasury, who, Yelverton asserted, 'are usurpers if they pretend to act here'. 'His Majesty', he declared, 'does not rule over this kingdom as king of Great Britain but solely as king of Ireland.' The prime serjeant, though he defended the government's action, granted that the orders of the British treasury were in Ireland 'so much waste paper', and Flood, Hely-Hutchinson and the prime serjeant all left the house before the division. The opposition also pressed the government hard on retrenchment. In November a debate initiated by Grattan on this subject was 'carried on with great warmth for nearly six hours' but 'afforded no amusement as almost all the argument was founded upon arithmetical calculation'. The pension list, 'a junto of the worthy and the unworthy', came in for strong criticism and the chief secretary felt it necessary to promise that representations on the subject would be made to the British government.[27]

During the early summer, while the session was still in progress, an edge was put on Irish parliamentary debate by events at Westminster. With the empire weakened by rebellion and threatened by its European rivals, it was imperative to encourage loyal and profitable co-operation between the territories which still adhered to the crown. A few important officials, Sackville Hamilton, the Irish under-secretary, William Knox, an Irishman who was under-secretary for American affairs, and Charles Jenkinson, a man of great official experience and great influence behind the scenes, were all convinced the time had come to promote Irish economic development by making modifications in the imperial commercial system. Hamilton in a long memorandum suggested that Ireland should

---

[27] Ely to Buckinghamshire, 16 Apr. 1779 (Add. MS 34523); *Hibernian Magazine*, 1777, p. 822: 1778, pp. 228, 229, 376.

be permitted to trade freely with the British colonies; and Jenkinson, who had the Irish question 'much at heart' thought that the restrictions on Irish commerce were unnecessarily harsh. Finally, North himself, when early in 1778 he took steps to open the negotiations with the American colonies, on the basis of course that they remained within the empire, implicitly accepted that the whole imperial system could be critically examined and reshaped.[28]

In April 1778, Nugent, an able Irishman and a government supporter, persuaded the British house of commons to consider in committee the legislation regulating Irish trade. It was the first occasion on which parliament had reviewed Ireland's position in the imperial economy, and the result was highly satisfactory to Nugent and his supporters. The committee, under the chairmanship of an Irish peer, Lord Midleton, agreed to resolutions recommending that Ireland should be granted a direct export and import trade with the colonies in all articles except woollen goods and tobacco, and that Irish sail-cloth, cordage and cotton yarn should be admitted into Great Britain.[29] The supporters of these resolutions not only sympathized with Ireland. They were also concerned about the future of the British empire. 'There is', Burke wrote at this time, 'a dreadful schism in the British nation. Since we are not able to reunite the empire, it is our business to give all possible vigour and soundness to those parts of it which are still content to be governed by our councils.' 'Justice to others', he argued, 'was not always folly to ourselves', and expediency as well as justice demanded that Ireland's economic growth should not be discouraged. Goodwill was the cement of empire and a prosperous Ireland would be both willing and able to contribute to imperial defence.[30]

The committee's resolutions were approved of by the house on 8 and 9 April and four bills based on them were immediately introduced. But the new departure in commercial policy aroused vigorously-voiced alarm throughout the British

[28] Lothian MSS H.M.C., pp. 301–4; Knox MS, H.M.C. various collections, vi, pp. 234–8; C. Jenkinson to Buckinghamshire, May 1777; C. Thompson to Buckinghamshire, 21 Mar., 26 Apr. 1777 (Add. MS 34523).
[29] Parliamentary history, xix, pp. 762–6.
[30] Correspondence of Edmund Burke, iii, pp. 426, 431–3.

industrial world, and the neo-imperialists soon learned how deeply ingrained were protectionist prejudices. Petitions from a number of industrial areas poured into parliament, protesting against 'a change in a great system of commerce which has been so long and so successfully a rule of conduct in this kingdom'. It was asserted that in Ireland taxes were low and labour cheap, so that it would be easy for Irish manufacturers to undersell their British competitors. The result would be, the merchants of Bristol declared, 'that a torrent of mischiefs, unthought of and unforeseen would pour upon this kingdom'. 'Even upon the most liberal principles', the merchants and manufacturers of Glasgow stated, 'the commercial privileges of Great Britain should only be extended to those parts of the empire where the people paid taxes in proportion to those levied upon the inhabitants of Great Britain.' As for the economic ills which Irishmen were said to be enduring, the main cause of these was the penal laws, 'their narrow, mean system of policy . . . their protestant popery and odious intolerance'.

Nugent retorted that the attitude of the petitioners was 'mean, unmanly, ungenerous, despicable and even diabolical'. Burke, tackling the economic arguments against concession, pointed out that Ireland was in comparison to its resources taxed as heavily as Great Britain. 'You tax candles in England,' he explained, 'but there are 200,000 houses in Ireland in which probably a candle such as you tax is never lighted.' And Welbore Ellis, the son of an Irish bishop, reminded the house that 'competition far from being the ruin was the life of trade'. But the opposition to concession, expressed so vehemently by the petitioners and some influential M.P.s, was too strong to be disregarded, and the supporters of the bills were forced to compromise. The proposal that Ireland should be permitted to import directly from the colonies was dropped and though Ireland was now allowed to export directly to the colonies, this concession was accompanied by an impressive list of exempted articles. For the rest it was provided that Irish-built ships should be regarded as British-built in respect to certain fishery bounties and Ireland was permitted to export spun yarn to Great Britain. In the closing debate Burke emphasized that he regarded the concessions which were being granted as 'nothing more than a prelude to others which will grant a greater freedom of trade', and North admitted that 'he wished the favours, if he might make use of such an expression, intended to be granted by the bills had been conferred in that graceful manner which would have tended most to rivet the affections of both England and Ireland'. North clearly saw the unhappy circumstances which would almost certainly ensue from whittling down a generous offer. But his perception was stronger than his will and the government failed to give a firm lead during the Irish debate. Indeed, a week before he made the speech which has just been referred to, North had written what was for him a firm letter, pointing out to the king his own 'insufficiency'.[31]

The British debates on the Irish trade bills, had an electrifying effect on Irish opinion. In parliament, Ponsonby, implying that the aim of the concessions (such as they were) was to increase Ireland's taxable capacity, compared the British ministry to American savages who fattened their prisoners before eating them; and Bradstreet, who sat for Dublin, emphasizing that 'beggarly Glasgow and the *loyal* town of Manchester had more weight in the scale than the interest of this kingdom', called on Irishmen not to consume the manufactures of those two towns.[32]

The policy of economic retaliation received widespread and powerful support. In the summer of 1778 members of the Society of free citizens of Dublin were reminded that each of them on admission had bound himself to wear only Irish manufacture and a number of Dublin clubs decided to drink Irish in preference to British porter. On a more impressive level, in 1779 the committee for the relief of distressed Dublin artisans, a committee which included some of the leading businessmen of the capital, sanctioned a plan for the co-operation of retailers, wholesalers and manufacturers in pushing the sale of Irish manufactures. Some weeks later an aggregate meeting of the citizens of Dublin (at which Napper Tandy and John Binns played a prominent part) approved of a declaration against the importation of any English goods which could be manufactured in Ireland, until 'an enlightened policy actuates the inhabitants

---

[31] *Parliamentary history*, xix, pp. 1100–27; *D.J.*, 19 May 1778; *H.J.*, 20, 27 May 1778.
[32] *H.J.*, 8 June 1778; *Hibernian Magazine*, 1779, pp. 246, 307.

of certain British manufacturing towns'. Many grand juries sometimes supported by the freeholders of their county issued declarations against the importation of British manufactures. Many of these declarations, though they advocated positive action for putting pressure on Great Britain, had as a theme the value of co-operation between the kingdoms. The prosperity of the British empire, the grand jury and freeholders of County Galway declared, 'must depend on the union and harmony of its component parts, founded upon the broad and generous basis of equality'. If Ireland were permitted to export coarse clothes, the grand jury and freeholders of Wicklow pointed out, 'it would enable the Irish to purchase the better sort of English manufactures'. As might be expected crude self-interest and violence played some part in the movement. The Dublin city grand jury while emphasizing the importance of wearing Irish manufactures, felt it necessary to exhort Irish manufacturers to bring their goods to market well-finished and 'upon the cheapest terms a reasonable profit will admit', and the journeymen in the liberties were advised not to be 'jealous of workmen coming in from the country . . . they will assist you in conquering your rivals the importers'. It was also on occasion hinted that the importation of English goods might be discouraged by tarring and feathering and 'the boys' were advised to keep a sharp look out for English goods which might be landed at the out-ports and sent to Dublin by road.[33]

This wave of resentment against the trade restrictions, British mercantilism, British predominance and British arrogance, though disturbing, might be expected, sooner or later to die down. But it was accompanied by a much stronger manifestation of public feeling, organized in a fashion which had alarming implications—the formation of armed associations—the volunteers. The entry of France (June 1778) and later (June 1779) Spain into the war, transformed it so far as Great Britain was concerned, from a trans-atlantic conflict into a war on two fronts, the American and the European, and exposed Ireland to the danger of invasion at a time when, owing to the demands of the American theatre, the military forces in Ireland were below the safety level. The threat of

[33] *Free. Jn.*, 16 Feb., 13, 29 Apr., 25 May, 1, 26 June, 12 Oct. 1779; *H.J.*, 27 May, 1, 22, June, 21 Sept. 1778.

invasion was bound to have a striking effect on Irish social life. The peacetime distribution of the army in Ireland was largely conditioned by the need to employ military detachments in support of the civil power. In wartime however, strategy dictated that the forces in Ireland should be concentrated in the south in readiness to repel attacks on the south or southwest. During the Seven Years war there had been available a second line force, the Irish militia, composed of protestants, formed into units and armed under commissions of array; and some of the Ulster units of this force almost smelt powder in February 1760, when they assembled at Belfast after Thurot's small expeditionary force had captured Carrickfergus. The militia act of 1755 had expired in 1767 and the heads of a militia bill, which were approved by the house of commons in 1776, though recommended by Blaquiere who thought that militia detachments could be employed in support of revenue officers, were not returned as a bill from England.[34] In the spring of 1778 a number of M.P.s, including Edmund Butler, who thought that a French expeditionary force might rely on the assistance of 'the papist whiteboys', urged the formation of a protestant militia. Though Daly argued forcefully that what was required was an increase in the number of regulars, 'soldiers, not people consulting their own ease', the heads of a militia bill, modelled on English militia legislation were passed. When they were being considered by the Irish privy council, it was pointed out that if a militia were constituted, it would be hard to find recruits in the south and west and in the north the rank and file would be unreliable if ordered to defend rents and tithe. Nevertheless the heads were transmitted and before the close of the session a militia bill was enacted. But the government, lacking the necessary financial resources, did not implement it.[35]

Faced with the possibility of invasion and well aware that as the army was concentrated, local crime and disorder would rise and spread, the Irish upper and middle classes displayed their reliance on private enterprise and a robust readiness to assume responsibility. Voluntary local military corps had

---

[34] J. Blaquiere to Weymouth, 28 Feb. 1776 (S.P. 63/438).
[35] *Hibernian Magazine*, 1778, pp. 583, 636, 693; Buckinghamshire to Weymouth, 21 Apr. 1778 (S.P. 63/59).

already been formed from time to time for home defence and maintenance of law and order. It was later asserted that the volunteer movement of the seventies started when the inhabitants of Carbery, Bantry and Bere in West Cork formed a corps in 1774.[36] About the same time Sir Vesey Colclough formed companies of horse and foot at Enniscorthy, which later claimed to be the first volunteer corps in Ireland. In the autumn of 1775 the light horse and foot 'militia' of County Wexford (including Sir Vesey Colclough's infantry) assembled to preserve law and order at the execution of two whiteboys. In 1776 the protestant inhabitants of Birr and Roscrea formed companies to suppress the whiteboys.[37] But it was in 1778 that the rapid, nationwide formation of volunteer corps began. In March the first Belfast company was formed; by June there was a Lisburn company and three corps in Londonderry.[38] By the beginning of July there were said to be thirty-eight volunteer corps in the counties of Cork and Tipperary; two months later the First Dublin company elected the duke of Leinster as its commander; and the growing popularity of the movement was indicated by the launching of an insurance scheme to cover volunteers killed in action against a foreign invader.[39]

Usually about company strength (30–100 men) the volunteer corps were formed either by neighbours binding themselves together or by a local landowner enlisting his tenantry. It may be said at once that it is impossible to state with certainty what was the strength of the movement when it was in full swing. In 1780 Grattan spoke of 40,000 volunteers and the available evidence suggests that this was not an outrageous oratorical flourish. Towards the close of 1779 a highly competent administrator estimated that the volunteers numbered at least 25,000 and at the 1783 Dungannon volunteer meeting 272 Ulster corps were represented which suggests that then there were about 20,000 volunteers in the province. Reference to the Leinster volunteers suggest there were about 5,000–10,000 volunteers in that province, and the other two provinces, being overwhelmingly catholic, probably had relatively few volun-

---

[36] A. Griffith, *Six letters addressed to the Rt. Hon. the Countess of* —— (1780), p. 20.
[37] *H.J.*, 10, 27 July 1778; *Hibernian Magazine*, 1776, p. 215. In neighbouring areas other corps were under arms (*H.J.* 2 Feb., 29 Mar. 1776).
[38] *B.N.L.*, 17 Mar., 26, 30 June 1778.
[39] *H.J.*, 12, 26 Oct. 1778.

teers.[40] So it is probable that when the movement was at its zenith there may have been approximately 40,000 volunteers.

The strength of the movement is impressive, especially when it is taken into account that recruitment was limited by economic and religious factors. Many volunteers were expected to provide their own uniforms and equipment, and though subscriptions were raised to assist volunteers who could not equip themselves, every volunteer must have felt obliged to pay his share of the social expenses of the corps. Indeed, some members of the Castledermot corps resigned because of the admission of 'servants and others of low rank' to the corps. Probably it was the difficulty of arriving at a generally acceptable level of expense which led to the formation in Londonderry of three corps, for 'young gentlemen', citizens, and tradesmen (skilled artisans) respectively.[41] The other factor which limited recruitment was religion. Legally catholics were not permitted to bear arms and this together with protestant feeling formed a barrier to their enlistment. Admittedly there was not a consistent policy of exclusion. In Kerry from the outset catholics seem to have been admitted to the Dingle volunteers, in Cork city, during an invasion scare in the summer of 1779 a number of catholic gentlemen were allowed to join the local volunteer corps, and the city of Armagh volunteer cavalry from its formation in 1782 admitted catholics, 'an instance of liberality which at that period was not very common'. Disputes in Sligo and Meath show that in those counties the admission of catholics was a controversial issue. A Sligo corps when inviting other companies in the county to join them at a review, specified that 'none but the protestant part of any corps would be accepted as men and brethren'; and this illiberal message, it was reported, was treated with contempt. On the other hand the gentlemen of County Meath resolved that as it was not lawful for papists to carry arms, it was improper for any volunteer corps in the county to attend a review with persons of that persuasion or for any gentleman to have under his command 'any number of papists'. The commanding officers of several Wexford volunteer corps adopted a similar attitude.

[40] H. Grattan, *Speeches* . . . (1822), i, p. 41, and figures given in *H.J.*, 11 July, 6 Aug. 1781; *Free. Jn.*, 5, 7 June 1781; J. Beresford, *Correspondence*, i, p. 77.

[41] *H.J.*, 20 Dec. 1779; *B.N.L.*, 26 June 1778; *Free. Jn.*, 4 Nov. 1779; *D.E.P.*, 15 Nov. 1781.

On hearing that the Wexford Roman catholics intended to raise a volunteer corps, they drew their attention to the fact that it was illegal for catholics to carry arms—adding that 'many disagreeable quarrels, disputes and jealousies have arisen in other counties from an intermixture of corps of different religious persuasions'.[42] In short, good nature very strongly tempered by caution, governed the attitude of volunteer corps to their catholic neighbours, and the force was overwhelmingly protestant, being, as an Irish clergyman told Dr Johnson, 'composed of the most affluent and respectable inhabitants of the kingdom, from the knights of the shire to the most opulent freeholders in each parish'.[43]

It is hard to say what was the military value of the force. It was composed of units with strong local ties who elected their own officers—though in the north an attempt was made to group companies in at least six battalions, and Fitzgibbon in 1782, with outspoken realism, declared that 'it would be ridiculous and absurd to expect that the volunteers, not under the control of military law, nor commissioned by the king, not provided with camp equipage, magazines of provisions or with military stores . . . could keep together so long as an ardent general might deem necessary'.[44] However, the matter was never put to the test, and on the one occasion on which a volunteer corps was in action against a foreign foe the volunteers won a decisive victory. In 1779 when a French privateer anchored off Larne, the Larne volunteers by taking possession of commanding points held it in the bay until a frigate coming down the lough from Belfast compelled it to strike its flag.[45]

On the many other occasions when volunteer corps went into action it was to perform police duties. Volunteer corps were active in suppressing agrarian disturbances, and arresting dangerous criminals. Volunteers escorted prisoners to gaol, guarded French prisoners of war, protected the cargo of a wreck, put down local riots and acted as fire brigades. In Dublin the volunteers sent out for a time a night patrol which

[42] *Free. Jn.*, 11 Sept. 1779; *D.E.P.*, 19, 21 Sept. 1780, 12 July, 25 Oct. 1781; *D.J.*, 5 July 1781; *Correspondence of Edmund Burke*, iv, p. 95.
[43] T. Campbell, *Strictures on the ecclesiastical and literary history of Ireland* (1789), pp. 336–7.
[44] *Parl. Reg. Ire.*, i, p. 449; *B.N.L.*, 4 May 1779.
[45] *B.N.L.*, 4 May 1779.

not only arrested disorderly persons but reported some night watchmen for being 'drunk and incapable of doing their duty'; and when there were labour troubles in Dublin the Liberty volunteers expressed their horror of combinations, the Lawyers corps offered rewards to informers against journeymen combinations, and the Tailors guild thanked the volunteers for their spirited determination to put down combinations.[46]

For some years volunteering loomed very large in Irish life and clearly provided an outlet for strong emotions. It gave the upper- and middle-class Irishman an opportunity of displaying his public spirit and conspicuously occupying an honourable place in the community. On national and civic occasions the volunteers, in gorgeously faced uniforms with glittering accoutrements, paraded and lined the streets. Gentlemen were referred to by volunteer rank, captains and colonels abounding in Irish society. Not only did individual corps have their drills and parades but during the summer reviews would be held of neighbouring corps, companies from over a wide area meeting for joint manœuvres, which might include a sham fight, conducted 'with an éclat which would have done honour to any regular forces in the universe'. Something of the feeling generated by these great gatherings is conveyed by an account in the *Hibernian Magazine* of the great Belfast review of 1782, attended by about 4,000 volunteers, 'where discipline prevailed, hospitality furnished the table, and through which temperance supported by freedom, mirth and good humour preserved an unbounded sway'. The volunteers were in camp for a week, their tents of 'the best sail canvass', fortunately proving waterproof since the rain fell in prodigious torrents every night. 'The routine of camp discipline was enforced without the smallest relaxation or indulgence', and it was inspiring to see how 'a body of wealthy, independent men, bred in all the comforts of life, submitted to such restraints without repining, rather struggling who should mount the guards and expose themselves to the inclemency of the night'. When the companies were on parade 'the ranks dressed uniformly firm, not a man out of line, whether the movement was fast or slow'.[47]

---

[46] *H.J.*, 5, 14 Aug. 1778, 8 Nov., 4, 21 Dec. 1780, 14 Feb. 1781; *D.E.P.* 26 Dec. 1780.
[47] *Hibernian Magazine*, 1782, pp. 445–7; *H.J.*, 11 July 1781.

Even on a sad occasion the volunteers could make an impressive show. 'All the volunteers of Limerick', wrote Lady Roche, 'made a most martial appearance when they attended the funeral of a brother volunteer . . . the procession was closed by a corps commanded by the speaker's son and it was with difficulty I could recognize amongst them some honest traders of my acquaintance and some good hack horses which I knew through the splendour of their dress and the richness of their furniture.'[48] Popular admiration for the volunteers was demonstrated not only by the multitudes of spectators at their displays but by the manufacture of pottery and textiles with volunteer motifs and by the publication of a spelling book 'with the most accurate and pleasing representations of the manual exercises of the volunteers . . . which, while it delights the boy may probably lead him to make this exercise his infant sport, and thus happily engage his body and his mind.[49]

Preparing to defend his country, the volunteer could see himself as an eighteenth-century equivalent of the citizens of ancient Greece and Rome, whom the country revered, and the movement seemed to offer a striking demonstration of loyalty to crown and country and of the courage, public spirit and organizing abilities of Irishmen. Ireland, Lord Charlemont told his men, was 'an object of veneration to all Europe'. A northern newspaper when advertising *An essay on field fortification*, went further. Ireland, it declared, was 'a community to which the eyes of all men are directed', the volunteers having 'excited the admiration of the world and inspired Irishmen with confidence in the natural strength and security of their country'.[50] Volunteering not only had a most invigorating effect on the Irish political mind, it also provided machinery for political education and agitation. A volunteer company was not only a military unit, it was a social club which could easily turn into a political association. The committees which planned the great reviews were meeting at the time when English liberals were trying to devise machinery for ensuing county co-operation in putting pressure on parliament.

Two very distinguished and very different Englishmen,

[48] Lady Roche to ——, 18 Apr. 1783 (Scrope Bernard papers).
[49] *H.J.*, 20 Aug. 1781.
[50] *Free. Jn.*, 3 July 1781; *B.N.L.*, 10 July 1781.

Samuel Johnson and Jeremy Bentham, expressed strong opinions on the Irish volunteer movement. When in 1781 an Irish clergyman visiting London explained that the volunteers, far from disturbing the peace, were maintaining law and order, Dr Johnson angrily asked, 'What do you not call it disturbance to oppose legal government with arms in your hands, and compel it to make laws in your favour? Sir, I called it rebellion—rebellion as much as the rebellions of Scotland.' Sobering down he added, 'the times are altered for power is nowhere. We live under a government of influence not of power.' Bentham writing forty years later saw the movement in another light. Its success was a striking proof that democracy was neither socially disruptive, nor subversive of the rights of private property. The volunteer movement, Bentham argued, was an example of a democracy based on universal suffrage. Though many volunteer officers were aristocrats or men of means, they were elected by the privates in their corps; and neither religion nor want of property was a bar to membership of the movement. The results of volunteer predominance were 'tranquility, harmony, morality, felicity unexampled. Such as they were—behold another miracle—by the evidence of all parties in one voice their existence was acknowledged. People's men triumphed in their golden age and recorded it. Aristocrat whigs, even after they had succeeded in destroying it—in substituting to it the iron age—trumpeted it, calling it their own work. So conspicuous was it, so uncontestable, that not even could the most zealous monarchalists and tories forebear confessing its existence.'[51] The volunteers themselves would have resented being called rebels, though they thoroughly appreciated the influence that armed and embodied citizens could exercise over government and parliament. Most of them saw themselves as members of a *corps d'élite* rather than the forerunners of radical democracy. If, by supplying political self-confidence, cohesion and camaraderie to the respectable sections of Irish society, they anticipated anything, it was the Reform bill of 1832, the great charter of the responsible middle classes.

The rise of the volunteers, the growth of a military force, in the private sector, created obvious problems for the Irish

---

[51] *Dr Campbell's diary of a visit to England in 1775*, ed. J. L. Clifford (1947), pp. 94–5; *Works of Jeremy Bentham*, ed. J. Bowing, iii, pp. 613–16.

administration. Buckinghamshire, when he realized that the volunteers had 'insensibly' become a large force, ineffectually tried to secure control of the movement by arranging that volunteer officers might accept commissions from the crown. This attempt to turn the armed societies into 'legal and regular' formations having failed, the viceroy in the autumn of 1779 played with the idea of replacing the volunteers by a militia. But by then an attempt to undermine the volunteer movement would have aroused dangerous hostility and in any event the funds required for a militia were not available. The lord lieutenant himself admitted that in the circumstances of the time the volunteers were 'a necessary evil'. 'At present,' he wrote, 'considering the various military services to be provided for, and the check which the riotous disposition of the common order of men too universally calls for, without these bands the kingdom would be without police and in no degree in a state of defence.' Fortunately, he believed, once the war ended, the expense and fatigue involved in membership of a corps, would 'soon put a period to their existence'.[52] Therefore the official attitude was to accept the assistance of the volunteers, without pronouncing on their legality and they were provided with 14,000 muskets and bayonets from the ordnance stores.

At this time defence was a matter of urgent concern to the Irish administration. During the summer of 1779 it was reported that a French expedition against Ireland was being mounted in the Breton ports, and the lord lieutenant was informed that Cork, where enormous stores of provisions for the use of the forces were being accumulated, was a probable target. An intelligence report, transmitted to Buckinghamshire, stated that the French were preparing an expedition against Ireland, aimed at Cork or Galway, composed of 32,000 infantry and 1,600 cavalry. On landing the invaders intended to declare themselves in favour of Irish independence, religious freedom and free trade. In June the news reached Cork that sixteen French ships of the line and a large number of transports had arrived in Bantry Bay.[53] It was a false alarm but it heightened the suspense.

[52] *Lothian MSS H.M.C.*, p. 345; *Stopford-Sackville MSS HMC*, p. 257; Buckinghamshire to Weymouth, 12 June 1779 (S.P. 63/465).

[53] *H.J.*, 11 June 1779; Weymouth to Buckinghamshire, 23 June 1779 (S.P. 63/465); North to Buckinghamshire, 2 Aug. 1779 (Add. MS 34523).

The apparent imminence of invasion brought painfully home to the government Ireland's military deficiencies. For some years men had been drawn from Ireland for America; many recruits were found to be unfit and though young recruits 'were treated with temper and coolness and every method taken to conciliate their affections', desertion was a serious problem, high bounties tempting men to desert and re-enlist in another unit. In 1778 the forces in Ireland amounted to only 9,000 'effectives' (of which over 1,000 were invalids); and in the following year Irwine, the commander-in-chief, estimated that he had only 8,000 men at his disposal. To face a French and Spanish invasion with 3,000 men (the force he had concentrated in the south) was, he remarked, 'no trifling undertaking'.[54] In the early seventies, the importance of King Charles' Fort near Kinsale had been stressed by Vallancey, the only senior army engineer in Ireland. The fort, which Vallancey pronounced, would 'not have disgraced a Vauban or a Cohorn', with 'a good engineer and a spirited commander', could hold out for a considerable time, and an enemy general who landed in the south would be reluctant to advance with such a strong point untaken in his rear. But in the spring of 1779 Vallancey was dismayed to discover that cannon sent from England for the defence of the fort and the fortifications at Cork and Waterford had been dispatched without their gun carriages and were lying on the Dublin quays. However, efforts were being made to strengthen Ireland's defences. 'Floating batteries' were stationed in Dublin bay and King Charles's fort, Duncannon fort and the defences at Cork harbour were in time improved and a relatively large force encamped at Clonmel, strategically well placed to cope with a landing on the south or south-west coast.[55] In fact Ireland was not a target in 1779. When, towards the close of the campaigning season, combined fleets of the two Bourbon powers put to sea, they hovered in the English channel, accomplishing nothing and at the end of the year France and Spain directing their efforts in Europe southward, began a long siege of Gibraltar, where, in consequence of his dispute with Harcourt, Eliott was fortunately in command.

[54] Report in S.P. 63/459, f. 282; J. Irwine to Cunningham, 16 July 1779 (S.P. 63/463); J. Irwine to Buckinghamshire, 30 Sept. 1778 (S.P. 63/461).

[55] Commons' Jn. Ire., ix, pp. dcxii–xiii, ccix–xii; C. Vallancey to Weymouth, 11 May 1779 (S.P. 63/463).

During the spring and summer of 1779 Buckinghamshire was not only preparing to meet invasion: he was also, with the rise of the volunteers and the agitation against the commercial restrictions, facing novel forces, continuously thrust on his attention by a newspaper press becoming steadily more contemptuous of authority. There were, Buckinghamshire wrote, 'essays in the public prints which have affected me with more terror than 10,000 soldiers'; and when he asked his Irish advisers what steps should be taken to check press attacks on government policy, their advice was to do nothing. Buckinghamshire was reluctant to add to the cabinet's burdens. 'A most painful reflection', he wrote, 'too frequently occurs to me, that my administration should exist at a period when of all others, England was most oppressed with difficulties which this country instead of relieving was obliged to increase.' Nevertheless, 'with the whole Irish nation making a push for relief', from early in 1779 he was pressing his colleagues to pay attention to the Irish question, emphasizing that working out an Irish policy in detail would take time. But North procrastinated. 'If the empire of Great Britain is dissolved', Buckinghamshire bitterly wrote, 'it is owing to His Majesty not having a prime minister'. North and some of his colleagues were in fact considering a plan, which North declared would be 'infinitely more to Ireland's advantage than a few commercial concessions'—a union. Buckinghamshire agreed that this was the 'only measure which can produce permanent tranquillity, substantial opulence and diffuse civilization in Ireland' but, he pointed out, 'many prejudices and many local interests must be surmounted' before it could be carried.[56] The suggestion of a union certainly demonstrated North's ability to think imperially. Also, the consideration of such a sweeping solution was a reasonable excuse for postponing discussion of other more pressing Irish issues.

Parliament showed itself to be more alive to the urgency of the Irish situation than the cabinet. Newhaven, an Irish peer and a Westminster M.P., endeavoured to get the house of

[56] Buckinghamshire to Weymouth, 25 Nov. 1778 (S.P. 63/461), 29 Apr. 1779 (S.P. 63/464); Buckinghamshire to H. Stanley, 1 Nov. 1779 (Add. MS 34523); *Lothian MSS H.M.C.*, p. 349; *Stopford-Sackville MSS H.M.C.*, i, p. 254; Buckinghamshire to C. Thompson, 21 Aug., 13 Nov. 1779 (Add. MS 34523).

commons to consider again the restrictions on Irish trade and on being criticized for not producing a specific remedy for Irish distress, urged the house to allow Ireland to import sugar directly from the West Indies. Sugar was a sensitive subject in eighteenth-century politics—there was a strong West Indian interest in the house of commons—and North, arguing that the house should wait and see the results of the 'indulgences' granted in the previous session, secured the defeat of the proposal. Two minor concessions however were made to Ireland in the course of the session. The prohibition on Irish tobacco entering Great Britain was abolished and a bounty was given on imported Irish hemp. Moreover it was decided that the whole cost of the units on the Irish establishment serving in America should be paid by Great Britain, 'a concession', the lord lieutenant pronounced 'of the first magnitude'.[57]

Early in May 1779 Rockingham, the whig leader, raised the subject of Irish distress both in an audience with the king and in the house of lords.[58] At the beginning of the audience Rockingham, to show that he was not influenced by personal considerations, mentioned that his own Irish rents were being paid. The king adroitly seized the opportunity presented by this remark and kept the discussion for most of the time on the marquis's private affairs.[59] In the lords, Rockingham, influenced by Burke, took a very moderate line. He referred only briefly to the armed associations and emphasized strongly how much the woollen industry was affected by Irish depression and the non-importation agreements. During the debate great sympathy was expressed for Ireland and Townshend (an ex-viceroy) and the duke of Richmond both stressed, in the latter's words, that 'all local distinctions were creatures of prejudice and selfishness . . . [and that] Ireland and England were in fact the same nation and people'.[60] At the close of the debate it was resolved to request the government to furnish returns relating to Irish trade and a similar motion was passed by the house of commons. These requests were transmitted to Buckinghamshire who promptly took action. He asked the

[57] *Parliamentary history*, xx, p. 270; *Stopford-Sackville MSS H.M.C.*, i, p. 256; North to Buckinghamshire, 13 Oct. 1777 (Add. MS 34523).
[58] *Parliamentary history*, xx, pp. 136, 248, 269, 635–42, 651–3, 661.
[59] *Correspondence of Edmund Burke*, iv, p. 67.
[60] *Parliamentary history*, xx, pp. 635–51.

revenue commissioners and about a dozen leading Irish politicians to state what they considered to be the causes of Irish distress and by the middle of July he had received their replies. Flood's answer was short and acid. He had not, he wrote, been supplied with any official information, and since the objections to change in the existing commercial system had arisen in England, they 'must be better known to the ministers and parliament of that country and it might be presumptuous for us to point them out'. But the other replies constitute a remarkable series of succinct and expressive state papers. Their authors agreed that the principal cause of Ireland's depressed condition was the commercial restraints—more especially the limitations imposed on the colonial trade and the woollen industry. But these restrictions, which had been imposed with the aim of 'humbling a nation hardly cool from rebellion and then but slightly joined in affection with Great Britain', had long been outmoded by changing circumstances. Ireland, it was emphasized, was Great Britain's close partner and best customer. 'There is little to be got by trading with a poor country, much by trading with a rich one', so Britain was the loser by the restrictions. Ireland, with the commercial disabilities abolished, would be able to contribute considerably to the prosperity of Great Britain and to 'the commonwealth and commerce of the empire'.[61]

With commendable dispatch Buckinghamshire sent the appreciations of the Irish situation he had collected to England. He realized how important it was for the success of his administration that the British cabinet should make up its mind on the Irish trade question before the next meeting of the Irish parliament (which was bound to meet in the autumn of 1779). But during the summer of 1779 the decision-making process was working badly in Whitehall and Downing Street. A prime minister, suffering from nervous exhaustion, at the head of a cabinet, which had 'no system, no steadiness and little concert'[62] and which was on the point of losing two of its members (one of them the minister responsible for Irish business), was coping with a war on two fronts separated by the Atlantic.

[61] G. O'Brien, 'The Irish free trade agitation of 1779' in E.H.R., xxxviii, pp. 564–81, xxxix, pp. 95–109.
[62] Lothian MSS H.M.C., p. 351.

When the Irish parliament assembled early in October 1779 Buckinghamshire had no concessions to announce and had been given no indication of what would be the British government's attitude to Irish demands for a revision of the commercial regulations. All he could do was to insert in his speech from the throne a platitudinous reference to the king's concern over Irish distress and to arrange that Foster, a government supporter, should propose that the house of commons go into committee on the condition of the country. It was hoped that if the administration took the initiative on these lines there would be an interval during which instructions might arrive from England. Members had been living and moving in a discontented and assertive country, they shared the feelings of the political community and were not prepared to wait until the British government made up its mind what was a reasonable pattern for Anglo-Irish trade. Early in the session M.P.s were reminded of what the public expected from them by two large demonstrations in College Green. On 4 November ten Dublin volunteer corps (one of them commanded by the duke of Leinster) paraded in College Green before an immense crowd of spectators. The pedestal of King William's statue was decorated 'with labels in large capital letters', one of which read 'A short money bill' and another 'A free trade or else'. There were 900 men on parade and the precision of their firing, it was said, was not surpassed by any army in Europe. Ten days later there was a cruder display of public feeling when some thousands of artisans, assembled it was rumoured by printed hand bills, beset the parliament house demanding a free trade, and a party of rioters, trying to find the attorney-general, stormed his house in Harcourt Street and swept through the Four Courts.[63]

In the debate on the address in the house of commons Grattan made a powerful attack on the trade restrictions, and an amendment demanding a free trade, drafted by Hussey Burgh, who had broken with the administration, was carried unanimously. This was a bad shock for the government, and the opposition, realizing its strength, did not stop at this point but went on to apply pressure by employing parliament's financial powers. They insisted on a six-months' money bill and

[63] *Hibernian Magazine*, 1779, pp. 554-5.

argued (in face of a deficit) that no new taxes should be granted until the commercial restrictions were removed. Their 'watch word', Hussey Burgh declared, should be 'to grant taxes when the British ministers proclaim a free trade'. In November Sir Richard Heron on behalf of the government agreed to a six-months' money bill, to the disgust of some supporters of the administration and of one potential supporter, the young John Fitzgibbon. 'By proper solicitation', the under-secretary said, 'the proposal for the six-month money bill could have been defeated', and, he added, in any event 'it should not have passed without a division though Sir Richard had been a single member to divide.' There was a division on the 24 November when by 170 to 47 the house resolved that it was inexpedient to grant new taxes. When administration supporters declared that this decision would soon lead to 'a total annihilation of the revenues of the country', opposition M.P.s replied with cheerful confidence that a tax could be imposed on official salaries or that the army or the custom house officials could remain unpaid and that 'the blood-suckers who had devoured the nation' would have to be satisfied with the rapine they had made. When the government argued that for the sake of the public credit the loan duties at least should be voted for two years, La Touche, the banker, rose and said that he and his correspondents with money in the funds would be content with a six-months' money bill.[64] Simultaneously outside parliament an attempt was being made to challenge the validity of British legislation binding Ireland by a Dublin merchant who entered at the Custom house woollen goods for export to Holland. The revenue commissioners were afraid that if they tried to enforce the prohibition on export they would be defeated by the Dublin mob and, on a higher level, by a Dublin jury. For the moment a clash was avoided by some opposition leaders, including Grattan, being persuaded to advise 'the persons engaged to drop the business at present'.[65]

The attorney-general, Scott, and Beresford attributed the Irish administration's catastrophic loss of power and prestige, as might have been expected, to the viceroy's weakness and

[64] *Hibernian Magazine*, 1780, pp. 165–6, 333, 453; J. Beresford, *Correspondence*, i, p. 107; *Stopford-Sackville MSS H.M.C.*, i, p. 261.
[65] J. Beresford, *Correspondence*, i, pp. 86–7.

reliance on private connections which were linked to the English opposition, and which had deserted him in an emergency. With the self-satisfaction of Cassandras whom events had justified, Scott and Bereford strove with 'heart and soul to work through this storm even with Sir Richard Heron'.[66] But while trying to muster support for the administration they too pressed for 'an efficient extension of our trade'—as well as a new lord lieutenant and chief secretary.

When the British parliament met on 27 November, the opposition mounted a vigorous attack on government mismanagement in a number of spheres, including of course Ireland. The cabinet's criminal negligence in respect to Ireland had, Burke declared, 'changed a mere question of commerce into a question of state'. At last stirred into activity, North at the beginning of December introduced resolutions which indicated the line he was going to take on the Irish question, resolutions on which, he wrote, 'depended the salvation of the empire'. On Thursday 9 December, he at last started to tackle the question in earnest. 'Paper upon paper' was asked for and a dozen clerks were set to work preparing returns. Finally on Sunday, with a senior civil servant at his elbow, North worked until long after midnight on his speech for the following day, which gained him 'great credit'.[67] He boldly placed a fundamental change in the principles governing Anglo-Irish commercial relations in the context of contemporary economic thinking. 'The world', he said, 'was now more liberal than heretofore.' The restrictions on the export of woollen goods and glass from Ireland were to be repealed and Ireland was granted freedom of trade with the British colonies on the reasonable condition that the Irish parliament imposed duties equivalent to the British on articles of colonial trade. In this new settlement Great Britain was, North stressed, being wisely generous. Irish linen still retained its privileged position in the English market and Ireland was being allowed to share the advantages of Britain's overseas empire, though 'an exclusive right was the very essence of colonization'. The concessions were enacted effortlessly, which may appear surprising in the light of what happened in 1778. Shelburne's explanation was that British manufacturers, who were 'in general a wise and liberal set of

[66] Ibid., i., p. 65   [67] Ibid., i, pp. 118–19.

men', had been taken by surprise in 1778 and had formed an exaggerated opinion of the dangers of Irish competition. And a member of the government, Dundas, having defended its delay in making concessions to Ireland by reminding the house of its own attitude in recent sessions, frankly confessed that he had changed his mind on the question, converted by 'Burke's solid reasonings'.[68]

The concessions were welcomed in Ireland. When they were explained to the Irish privy council every member declared himself satisfied, except a small but influential group, the speaker, the provost, Flood and Brownlow, 'who sat sullenly and opened not their mouths'. The two houses voted addresses of thanks, the lords expressing their determination to try and defeat the attempts of misguided men to raise groundless jealousies in the minds of the people, the commons adroitly avoiding the implication that the concessions removed all grounds of discontent. In a number of urban centres there were rejoicings and though the lord mayor of Dublin was afraid that an illumination in Dublin would cause 'a mob riot' (a handbill had been distributed declaring that there should be no illuminations until 'our constitution is made free') on 28 December the city was illuminated and 'Mr Guinness, the Castle brewer', provided the populace with a hogshead of porter.[69]

Lord North had hoped that after the commercial concessions were granted it would be possible 'to keep out of sight' constitutional issues.[70] But the concessions had come too late to restore placidity to Irish politics, Anglo-Irish relations in general were being examined and debated, and before the session ended three great constitutional issues were raised. In April Grattan proposed a resolution affirming Ireland's legislative independence. His speech was a powerful one, its argument being that a great surge of national feeling was sweeping Ireland towards that liberty which was the country's birthright. A liberty, which Grattan did not fail to stress, should be enjoyed in close association with Great Britain, 'common trade, common liberty will give strength to our constitution and make both nations immortal'. The government did not meet his

[68] *Parliamentary history*, xx, pp. 650, 1215.
[69] *Stopford-Sackville MSS H.M.C.*, i, pp. 264–5; *London Chronicle*, 30 Dec. 1779; *D.J.*, 30 Dec. 1779.

motion with a direct negative, the attorney-general employing a parliamentary device by moving that the question should be postponed until 1 September. In the end after a debate which lasted until six in the morning the simple adjournment was voted—M.P.s being obviously averse to committing themselves to the defence of 6 George I. Shortly afterwards Yelverton moved the heads of a bill amending Poynings' law by removing the Irish privy council from the legislative process. He collected substantial support, being defeated by only 130 to 105. Ten days later Hussey Burgh introduced the heads of an Irish mutiny bill, according to the attorney-general 'the most dangerous and important motion that ever came before the parliament of Ireland'. If Burgh's bill passed it would be an implicit denial of the right of the British parliament to legislate for Ireland, if it was rejected military discipline might collapse, with justices of the peace and juries refusing to enforce the British mutiny act. In committee a compromise was reached. Burgh's bill was so shaped as to confirm the articles of war regulating the army in Ireland, without precisely duplicating the British mutiny act. As transmitted from Ireland it was intended to be a temporary act, requiring regular parliamentary renewal, but in England it was changed into a permanent measure. Though the lord lieutenant pessimistically warned the cabinet that the Irish house of commons would almost certainly reject a permanent mutiny bill, it was accepted in this form at the close of a long and exhausting session.

From well before the termination of the session volunteer corps throughout the country were vigorously asserting in published resolutions Ireland's constitutional rights; corps in Ulster, Cork, Waterford and Galway thanked Grattan for his patriotic exertions, and Grattan in ringing phrases re-echoed their sentiments. 'Liberty', he declared, 'is a native of the north, translated into the south and now flourishing in every part of the kingdom.' There were however those who felt that military formations should not intervene in political debate. The officers of the Coleraine corps and the committee of the Lisburn corps expressed their confidence in parliament. As a result the rank and file of the Coleraine corps printed a protest against their officers' action and twenty-one of the Lisburn corps seceded

[70] North to Buckinghamshire, 9 Dec. 1779 (Add. MS 34523).

from the corps. The committee of the corps of Dublin volunteers refused to summon a meeting of the corps, requested by
Napper Tandy, for the purpose of voting an address to Grattan.
Tandy protested, the corps, meeting under the chairmanship
of the duke of Leinster, expelled him and a number of his
supporters seceded and formed a new corps, the Independent
corps. Tandy set out his version of the dispute in a strongly
worded letter to the duke. 'Let', he wrote, 'such as bask in the
sunshine of a court . . . enjoy the wages of their prostitution';
he, Tandy, 'uninfluenced by power and unawed by fear', would
persevere in his chosen course.[71] Another great magnate, Lord
Glenawly, when the Rathfriland corps subscribed to resolutions,
which, *inter alia*, denounced the perpetual mutiny act, recalled
the muskets he had issued to it. Scandalized, the Belfast and
Newry volunteers requested 'the honour of arming the corps
afresh.'[72] It is clear that many volunteers, far from feeling that
when under arms they should abstain from politics, considered
their corps to be a useful pressure group, though as the recess lengthened out and the excitement generated by the
parliamentary session of 1779–80 died down, the volunteers
desisted for a while from publishing their opinions on political
issues.

It was during the session of 1779–80 that there definitely
emerged an Irish school of parliamentary oratory, vehement,
high-flown, highly coloured, and very ready to resort to
personification. It had several brilliant exponents, but its grand
master was undoubtedly Grattan, a poet before he became a
politician. A barrister with little enthusiasm for a legal career,
'called to the bar without knowledge or ambition in my
profession', Grattan had for some years been preparing
himself for public and more especially parliamentary life,
reading history, helping the patriot leaders to prepare political
polemics for the press and attending the galleries at College
Green and Westminster, listening to the debates as a pupil
and critic (he found the British house of commons far more
enthralling than the London theatre).[73] He entered the Irish

---

[71] *D.E.P.*, 25, 27 Apr., 6, 16, 18, 27 May, 19 Sept., 10 Oct. 1780; *H.J.*, 28 Apr.
1780; *B.N.L.*, 5 Sept. 1780.
[72] *D.E.P.*, 9 Dec., 1780; *B.N.L.*, 9 Feb. 1781.
[73] H. Grattan, *Memoirs of the life . . . of . . . Henry Grattan*, i, p. 257.

house of commons in 1775 at an opportune moment. During the next six or seven years a series of issues which lent themselves to epic treatment were to be debated, and Grattan soon showed himself to be a superb orator, capable of producing rhetorical masterpieces in the grand style. He had the good fortune that his entry into the house of commons coincided with the beginning of regular parliamentary reporting in the Irish press so that his speeches, which read well, reached a wide out-of-doors audience. Grattan's vocabulary, supplied by a glowing imagination, was unusually rich and vivid; he found with apparently effortless ease the scintillating phrase and the telling metaphor; he could by 'happy amplification' develop a theme in 'a series of thoughts rising upon one another',[74] and the strenuous animation with which he advanced his arguments suggested the happy straining of a successful athlete breasting the tape. In imitation of his hero, Chatham, he was prepared to take oratorical risks, asking rhetorical questions, freely apotheosizing his audience, speaking with fervent passion and readily indulging in personification—a device which if often moving could sometimes dangerously oversimplify. Appealing both to the intellect and the emotions, fusing poetry and political dialectics, Grattan as a speaker delighted and dominated first the Irish and later the United Kingdom house of commons, winning the unstinted admiration, if seldom the votes, of his fellow M.P.s. To them Grattan's speeches were magnificent products of the culture they all shared, striking proofs that contemporary parliamentary debate need not fear comparison with the achievements of Demosthenes and Cicero. Moreover, Grattan, though often in a protesting minority, did not jar on his hearers. A rational liberal, he had conservative instincts, and for all his oratorical vehemence, well-illustrated by his love of antithesis, he was essentially a man of the centre. He revered the constitution, respected the house of commons, supported the British connection and saw the Irish gentry as the natural leaders of their country. He might denounce defects in the constitutional machinery and corruption, but it was clear not only from what he said but from his unspoken assumptions and the very style and texture of his speeches that he was ardently anxious to preserve those values which he himself, his

---

[74] W. G. Hamilton, *Parliamentary logic*, p. 6.

friend and mentor Burke, and most M.P.s would denote by the term civilization.

In one respect Grattan's influence was limited. He never held office and during a parliamentary career stretching over forty-five years he was in close political contact with an Irish administration only for three short periods totalling in all about three years. This of course was partly due to the general political situation during his parliamentary career, summed up in the well-known lines

> Naught's permanent among the human race,
> Except the whigs *not* getting into place.

But it was also a matter of temperament. A man of great sensitivity, Grattan found it hard to face 'the infinite littleness of life'. Detail was not his forte; he preferred the highly coloured, sweeping survey of a problem. He had seen Chatham, 'more like a grave character advising than mixing in the debate', and he prided himself on his aloof independence. A watchful critic, detached from party, the advocate of fundamental principle, he was the country gentleman *par excellence*—and with the added advantage of being highly articulate. His role was a valuable one but it carried an inevitable handicap. His opponents and critics must have felt that Grattan, unconstrained by official routine and free from the immediate responsibility of dealing with the results of a decision, was, as he spoke, moving in a rarefied political atmosphere. However, Grattan, 'the most upright and temperate of demagogues',[75] could be regarded by his contemporaries as the conscience of the house; and even though M.P.s knew well that the dictates of conscience must be subject to the practicalities of politics they may have been glad that idealism had a voice.

[75] *Fortescue MSS H.M.C.*, i, p. 163; H. Grattan, *Memoirs of the life ... of ... Henry Grattan*, i, p. 235.

6

An Anglo-Irish settlement

By the summer of 1780 Buckinghamshire had been well over two years in Ireland and his nerves were sorely strained. 'The most painful part of my situation', he wrote, 'is the necessity at times when my mind is particularly agitated to listen with apparent temper to capricious reasonings', and he had, he said, become dependent 'on the cheerful circulation of claret' for two or three hours after dinner. He resented being written to by the secretary of state 'in the style which Dr Busby with a birch under his arm would have used to a king's scholar' and his own letters show signs of despondency and weariness.[1] He had warned his colleagues in England well in advance that the Irish situation was becoming critical and, he had then, in his own opinion, coped successfully with the difficulties of a very stormy parliamentary session. But he had been unlucky, so it is not surprising that at the close of 1780 he was replaced by a young and rising politician, the earl of Carlisle, a man of fashion and ability, who for the sake of his wife and children was pursuing an official career which kept him away from gambling tables.[2] Carlisle's chief secretary was William Eden, who in 1778 had, along with Carlisle, been a commissioner for negotiating with the American colonies. Eden, shortly before being appointed chief secretary, having stressed that intelligent men must not be influenced by 'the contagious delirium incident to national questions', had expressed the hope that Great Britain would abandon 'the rusty and rugged armour of monopoly', and by the application of free trade principles (he was an admirer of Adam Smith) make Ireland 'a jewel in our crown and not a thorn in our side'. Eden, when assessing his own character, decided that 'I love business and . . . possess the spirit of perseverance' and while he was in Ireland he displayed immense administrative energy. He conducted an

---

[1] Buckinghamshire to Irwine, 2 June 1780, Buckinghamshire to Barrington, 1 Apr. 1780, Buckinghamshire to C. Thompson, 10 Dec. 1780 (Add. MS 34523).
[2] Carlisle to Gower, 31 Dec. 1773 (P.R.O. 30/29/1).

endless succession of interviews (on a single day during the parliamentary session between 8 a.m. and 2 p.m. he saw fifty-three gentlemen) and he grappled successfully with a mass of official detail. On his arrival Heron told him that he should regard the Irish public accounts, which few gentlemen understood, as 'your grammar, which you must study as much as your leisure will admit'. Eden was 'very alert in examining and stating the different accounts of the different boards', he enforced attendance in public offices and endeavoured to infuse 'a little activity, method and economy' into the working of the Irish revenue departments. He entertained generously—his 'manner of living', the lord lieutenant pointed out, 'greatly exceeded the scanty provision made for the chief secretary'— and he built up friendships with some influential Irish politicians, contacts which during the next couple of decades played a useful part in holding together the British and Irish official worlds.[3]

As usual many Irish politicians were prepared to welcome a new administration. 'All is honey', Beresford explained, 'until something is refused to individuals',[4] and Carlisle and Eden fortunately had not to meet parliament for about ten months. Admittedly they had to be prepared to cope with an unprecedented and unpredictable factor in Irish politics, that 'self-embodied army' the Irish volunteers, and during the summer of 1781 there were a number of spectacular displays of volunteer power at reviews and at sham fights, held all over Ireland. But only one of these gatherings put forward a specific political programme, the Birr review demanding an assertion of legislative independence, and amendment of Poynings' law, an annual mutiny bill and security of tenure for judges.[5] And when a Franco-Spanish attack on Ireland seemed to be impending in the summer of 1781 volunteer corps in all parts of the country offered their services to the lord lieutenant who thanked them in terms, which, he thought, would 'cement the good understanding between crown and people'.[6]

---

[3] W. Eden to Loughborough, 24 Feb. 1782 (Add. MSS 34418); R. Heron to W. Eden, 31 Jan. 1781; W. Eden to C. Jenkinson, 29 Jan. 1781 (Add. MS 34417); J. Beresford, *Correspondence*, i, p. 188; *Lothian MSS H.M.C.*, pp. 386, 390; *Carlisle MSS H.M.C.*, p. 528.

[4] J. Beresford, *Correspondence*, i, p. 150.   [5] *Free. Jn.*, 11 Sept. 1781.

[6] *Carlisle MSS H.M.C.*, pp. 520, 534; Carlisle to Hillsborough, 24 Sept. 1781 (S.P. 63/463).

At the close of the volunteer campaigning season Carlisle and
Eden had to face a more familiar problem, a parliamentary
session, the Irish parliament meeting early in October. Carlisle
was optimistic. 'I have effected', he wrote, 'what I may say
without vanity my predecessors never did effect—the uniting
together of all the great factions in support of the government',
together with almost all the independents. Moreover, he
considered he had achieved this remarkable result without
making a single promise since his arrival in Ireland. 'Death
and a thousand accidents', he added, 'must occur to make it
practical for me to meet all demands.' Eden, who was in the
front line, was not quite so happy about the situation. At the
beginning of the session he thought he could count on 130 'as
devoted friends to the government as Irish politics can admit'.
But this had been attained by mortgaging 'even eventual
patronage'. Eden was, according to his opponent Charlemont,
an able 'man-monger'. But when building up a government
majority he had not to rely only on patronage. His task was
eased by a shift in policy which made it less difficult for M.P.s
to support the administration without jeopardizing their
popularity. Concessions to Ireland had already been made
under Buckinghamshire, dubbed by Burke 'the hero of non-
resistance', and Carlisle and Eden, who a few years previously
had been engaged in trying to conciliate the American rebels,
now accepted that positions which the Irish government had
hitherto tenaciously clung to were untenable. To enforce a
British enactment binding Ireland would be as easy, Eden said,
'as to carry the Liffey over the Wicklow hills'. After all,
Carlisle argued, if the connection was being newly formed
could Great Britain demand from Ireland more than 'the
admitted interference with any new law proposed in the parliament of that country, the judicial appeal to the English courts
(which the Irish are more tenacious of than we can be) and the
full acknowledgment of her being comprehended as part of the
empire in all transactions or treaties with foreign powers'. But
though a whig might scornfully declare 'omnipotence is completely impotent and poor supremacy has nothing left to
surrender', the British cabinet still made a despairing effort to
maintain the old constitutional restrictions, Carlisle being
instructed at the beginning of the session 'to divert or prevent

the whole class of what are called constitutional questions as they cannot produce any advantage to the true interests of either kingdom'.[7]

But the Irish administration did not think it politic to be obdurate. Eden decided not to oppose the heads of a habeas corpus bill and of a bill giving security of tenure to judges, and both passed easily. When Grattan in February moved an address assuring the king that 'the kingdom of Ireland is a distinct kingdom with a parliament of her own, the sole legislature thereof', the attorney-general, emphasizing that he did not intend to discuss the question of right, argued that the issue should be postponed. And though the address was rejected by 137 to 68, it seems to have been generally assumed that Ireland was legislatively independent. In Bushe's phrase, 'Ireland's free and uncontrollable right of legislation is by all acknowledged'. When the mutiny act was denounced as 'perpetual', Langrishe, an administrative supporter, defended it 'not on principles of preference but on principles of accommodation'. It was an adequate if not an ideal solution to the problem. When Yelverton introduced a bill for the amendment of Poynings' law, Eden's attitude was, 'I have not declared that I will or will not oppose it but I will freely discuss it'.[8]

Indeed the debates over Poynings' law developed into a controversy between Yelverton and Flood as to how the procedure for transmitting Irish measures to England was to be improved. Flood for some years had been a sullen and un-cooperative office-holder, in his own eyes 'a man of too much situation to be a mere placeman'. 'I voted with them [the government]', he later explained, 'in matters of importance when they were clearly right; I voted against them in matters of importance when they were clearly wrong; and in matters of small moment I do not vote at all. And why? I scorned by voting in such matters to seem to pay court.' This attitude may have been a dignified one, but it was unlikely to be tolerated for long by his colleagues in the Irish administration. During the session of 1779–80 he had co-operated with the opposition

---

[7] *Correspondence of Edmund Burke*, iv, p. 359; W. Eden to Loughborough, 16 Mar. 1782 (Add. MS 34418); Carlisle to Gower, 23 Mar. 1782 (P.R.O. 30/29/1); *Charlemont MSS HMC*, i, p. 148; Hillsborough to Carlisle, 29 Sept. 1781 (Add. MS 34418).

[8] *Parl. Reg. Ire.*, i, pp. 35, 110, 177.

and Buckinghamshire at the close of the session was contemplating dismissing him. During the summer of 1781 Carlisle decided that Flood should be told 'that in consideration of the very high and lucrative employment he holds under the crown, I expect a decisive conduct from him'. Carlisle soon heard that Flood 'resents the manner in which I have directed he should be talked to', and at the beginning of the session in November 1781 Flood 'threw away the scabbard', declaring in debate that 'they should not trust any minister that countenanced a perpetual mutiny bill'.[9] Very shortly afterwards he was removed from office. Uncompromising and authoritative, marshalling his arguments with compelling force, Flood immediately attempted to assume the leadership of the opposition and, as far as possible, of the house. But the pathos of his position was soon apparent. While he had been a silent member of the administration, younger men had come to the front, and Flood's assumption of effortless superiority did not go unchallenged. Scott, the attorney-general, asked him to observe 'good manners and parliamentary order' and 'not to break in upon a man's discourse every minute'. Flood was also discomforted to find that 'after a service of twenty years in the study of a particular question', Poynings' law, 'it was taken out of his hands and entirely wrested from him'. Flood's solution for the question was a declaratory act, stating that the intervention of the Irish privy council in the legislative process was based on a misinterpretation of the law. Yelverton's solution was an amending act. Yelverton's bill provided that all bills which were passed by the Irish parliament should be transmitted to the king under the great seal of Ireland and such bills as were returned to Ireland under the great seal of Great Britain should receive the royal assent in parliament. The weight of legal opinion in the house favoured Yelverton's plan and Flood was reduced to pointing out that a non-practising lawyer could take a more enlarged view of the subject 'than a man tied down to the minute distinctions common in the courts'.[10] There was another

[9] Ibid., i, p. 170; *Carlisle MSS H.M.C.*, pp. 510, 515; W. Eden to Loughborough, 4 Nov. 1781 (Add. MS 34418).

[10] *Parl. Reg. Ire.*, i, pp. 170, 186. One of Scott's speeches in reply to Flood was, according to Eden, marked by 'many turns and expressions of imperfect taste, but upon the whole it was fully suited to the taste and disposition of the audience' (W. Eden to Loughborough, 30 Nov. 1781 (Add. MS 34418).

issue on which he competed with Yelverton, that of confirming past British legislation relating to Ireland (it was clear that if this were not done a denial of British legislative supremacy would cause legal confusion). Flood introduced a bill for 'quieting possessions held under English acts of parliament', which, according to Carlisle, was 'selfish in its purpose, coarse in its interest, and unqualified by any civil expression whatever towards the other country'.[11] The bill, sponsored by Yelverton (and apparently Grattan) for 'confirming statutes made in England', on the other hand, stressed that 'whereas a similarity of laws, manners and customs must naturally continue to perpetuate that affection and harmony . . . which subsists between the peoples of Great Britain and Ireland', it was desirable to promote the navigation, trade and commercial interests of Great Britain as well as of Ireland.[12]

Carlisle and Eden were anxious that the British government should accept Yelverton's bill amending Poynings' law, but Loughborough, the lord chancellor, who combined a good legal brain with considerable political acumen, argued that in the event of concessions being made to Ireland they should be accompanied by conditions and by 'an ultimatum of demand on the part of Ireland'. In short, he favoured 'a contract' between the two countries which should, for instance, settle what forces Ireland would maintain, 'put some restraint upon her volunteers' and provide 'against her interference with the general affairs of the empire'. The whole question of Anglo-Irish relations must not, Loughborough wrote to Eden, 'be left to the caprice of adventurers in politics whose vanity will make them stir every point upon which there can be any mark of subordination'.[13]

While brisk debate on large constitutional issues went on in parliament the Ulster volunteers began to bestir themselves. Just after Christmas delegates from eleven companies of the First Ulster regiment (Lord Charlemont's) met at Armagh, and having resolved that 'to restore the constitution to its original purity' effective measures should be taken 'to root corruption

[11] *Carlisle MSS H.M.C.*, p. 556.
[12] 21 & 22 Geo. III, cc. 47, 48.
[13] E. Cooke to Eden, 15 Mar. 1782; Loughborough to W. Eden, 16 Mar. 1782 (Add. MS 34418).

and court influence from the legislative body', they suggested that a meeting of delegates from all the Ulster volunteer corps should be held. On 15 February 1782 delegates from 143 Ulster corps assembled in Dungannon. Charlemont, with the assistance of a small group, which included Flood and Grattan, had prepared resolutions for the assembly which began its work by resolving that 'a citizen by learning the use of arms does not abandon any of his civil rights'. It then in a series of resolutions asserted the legislative independence of Ireland, and demanded the amendment of Poynings' law, a limited mutiny bill and a bill securing the independence of the judiciary. They also resolved to use every constitutional means to attain their objectives and to support at every ensuing election only those candidates who accepted the programme they had outlined. The Dungannon resolutions were a manifesto round which men could rally, expressing in specific terms and ringing phrases, the political ideals of public-spirited, liberal protestant Irishmen.[14] They did not however call for immediate decisive action and the Dungannon meeting achieved its contemporary renown not by what it did but because of its place in a dramatic sequence of events.

The Irish parliament adjourned for four weeks on 14 March and during the adjournment North's government, overwhelmed by catastrophe and hard pressed by a strong parliamentary opposition, resigned and was replaced before the end of March by a ministry composed of whigs and Chathamites, headed by Lord Rockingham. The new government was conscious that it had come to power in a crisis and it was determined to resolve as quickly as possible the problems created, aggravated or ignored by North's administration. From its formation the cabinet had the Irish problem in mind, but on 8 April, the day on which the new ministers who were in the commons took their seats for the first time on the front bench, Ireland was violently thrust on their attention by Eden, highly incensed by the unceremonious speed with which Carlisle was being replaced. Varying the metaphor he had already used, he told the house it 'might as well strive to make the Thames flow up Highgate hill as attempt to legislate for Ireland', and he called for the immediate repeal of 6 George I, being confident that

14 *D.J.*, 10 Jan. 1782; F. Dobbs, *A history of Irish affairs* (1782), pp. 51–2.

'a sensible and judicious people like the Irish' would always realize that the interests of the two countries were inseparable. He was backed by some other M.P.s, Courteney, Luttrell and Newhaven, all with Irish backgrounds, but Fox, having censured Eden for coming post-haste to embarrass the government and having made some play with his transformation into an Irish patriot, asked the house to give the government a little time 'to determine with precision on the plan to be offered to both countries'. He was supported by the most distinguished Irishman in the house, Burke, who wanted 'a clear and solid settlement' of Anglo-Irish relations, and who spoke of a reciprocal compact before anything was granted'.[15] This in fact was Fox's policy. Though he believed that it was 'downright tyrannical' for a legislature to make rules for the internal government for a people not represented in it, he made a distinction between internal and external legislation, because he thought that ideally 'a great superintending power', to be used for the good of the empire at large, should be lodged in the British parliament. Speaking however with the candour of a man who had not been in power, Fox admitted that Great Britain's legislative supremacy had been employed, so far as Ireland was concerned, as 'an instrument of oppression'. Therefore he thought it should be relinquished at once. His attitude to Poynings' law was similar. In the abstract there was something to be said for permitting the two privy councils to play a part in the legislative process. But their powers had been abused, so it was necessary to accept the modifications of Poynings's act proposed by Yelverton. These constitutional concessions to Ireland, Fox insisted shortly after he took office, should form part of a general settlement, 'a treaty to settle finally the connection between the two countries'. 'What I want to guard against', he wrote, 'is Jonathan Wild's plan of seizing one part in order to dispute afterwards about the remainder.' Probably influenced by the Scottish union, Fox seems to have visualized a treaty covering all political and economic issues of common interest being negotiated between British and Irish parliamentary delegations. One question, which he specified, was defence. Some clear understanding, he felt, should be

[15] *Parliamentary history*, xx, pp. 1241–64; *Charlemont MSS H.M.C.*, i, p. 400; *Correspondence of Edmund Burke*, iv, p. 440.

arrived at with Ireland on what 'we are to expect from Ireland in return for the protection and assistance she receives from those fleets which cost us such enormous sums and her nothing'.[16]

On taking office Rockingham and Fox wrote to Charlemont expressing their intention to devise 'a new system of connection' and their hope that Charlemont and his Irish friends would co-operate with them. 'Why', asked Fox, 'should not the whigs unite in every part of the empire to establish their principles so that no faction shall be able to disturb them?' To give time for consultation on the future of Anglo-Irish relations the two British ministers urged Charlemont to secure an extension of the Irish parliamentary adjournment which had begun on 14 March. Charlemont, having consulted Grattan, replied expressing unbounded delight at seeing the whigs in office and explaining why it was quite impossible to postpone the meeting of parliament at which Ireland's reasonable demands were to be pressed—'the nation was to the last degree anxious'.[17] Portland, the new lord lieutenant, who arrived in Dublin on 14 April two days before parliament reassembled, at least managed to persuade Grattan to substitute for a declaration of rights an address to the throne. But the wording of the address turned out to be so aggressive that Portland requested the speaker and provost to draft an alternative version. This too was unsatisfactory so at the very last minute Portland's cousin, George Ponsonby, agreed to move on 16 April a very short address, thanking the king for taking Irish grievances into consideration.[18] Grattan, not to be baulked, promptly moved an amendment six times as long as the address, assuring the king that though the crown of Ireland was annexed to that of Great Britain, Ireland was a distinct kingdom, and urging that the declaratory act should be repealed, Poynings' law amended and the perpetual mutiny act replaced by a statute with a limited duration. 'The people of Ireland', the amendment asserted, 'never expressed a desire to share in the freedom of England, without declaring a determination to share her fate

[16] *Memorials and correspondence of Charles James Fox*, ed. Lord John Russell, i, pp. 411–13; *Parliamentary history*, xxiii, pp. 20–6.
[17] *Charlemont MSS H.M.C.*, i, pp. 53–9.
[18] Portland to Shelburne, 16 Apr. 1782 (H.O. 100/1).

likewise, standing or falling with the British nation.' Grattan
moved his amendment in a sparkling speech, which swept his
audience with him. 'You not only excel modern Europe,' he
told the house, 'but you excel what she can boast of old.'
Ireland, 'a country in which', according to Grattan, 'every
living man has a share in the government', had attained full
political maturity and was determined to enjoy freedom, which
he emphasized was enshrined in British forms. 'This nation', he
declared, 'is connected with England not only by allegiance
to the crown but by liberty—the crown is one great point of
unity, but Magna Carta is greater—we could get a king anywhere but England is the only country from which we could
get a constitution.' Grattan's amendment was carried unanimously, and even the newly-arrived secretary, who described
Grattan's speech as 'splendid in point of eloquence, all declamation; very little, and what there was, weak argument',[19]
admitted that he evoked admiration and support from his
entire audience.

After this drastic declaration of rights by the Irish house of
commons the Irish administration was convinced that the only
course was concession, and Grattan, the hero of the hour, wrote
reassuringly to Fox, stressing that the address, which 'defined
our desires and limited them', displayed 'a veneration for the
pride' as well as a love for the liberty of England and if Ireland's
demands were granted, 'your administration in Ireland will
certainly meet with great support. I mean national as well as
parliamentary.'[20] The British cabinet, with America vividly in
mind, retreated quickly. In the middle of May both houses at
Westminster agreed to resolutions which declared that 6
George I should be repealed and that the interests of both
countries were inseparable and should be placed on 'a solid
and permanent basis'. By the end of June a bill repealing the
6 George I received the royal assent and in the following month
the royal assent was given to Irish bills amending Poynings' law
(Yelverton's act), securing the independency of the judiciary
and limiting the duration of the mutiny act. The response of
the Irish house of commons to the government's declaration of
policy was on 27 May to vote an address to the king expressing

---

[19] *Memorials and correspondence of Charles James Fox*, i, p. 398.
[20] Ibid., i, pp. 403–9.

its pleasure at hearing that he 'disclaimed the little policy of making a bargain with his people' and asserting its determination 'to stand and fall with the British nation'. This address was carried by 211 votes to none (the tellers for the noes being two barristers, Bradstreet and Walshe). The house also agreed to vote £100,000 towards raising men for the navy and empowered the government to withdraw 5,000 troops from Ireland for general service.

A comprehensive settlement of Anglo-Irish relations had still to be worked out. Fox considered that the Irish administration should take the initial steps and Portland, having recovered from the shock of meeting Irish patriot feeling in full tide, considered that he was in a good position for opening discussions. Not only could he claim to have persuaded the British government to concede Ireland's demands but by making a number of removals and appointments which almost constituted a change of administration, he had shown his sympathy for the group which had been pressing Ireland's constitutional claims.

The attorney-general, John Scott, a doughty upholder of the administration in the commons since 1774, the prime serjeant, Brown, Lees, the under-secretary for war who had been Townshend's private secretary, and Maurice Copinger, the council to the revenue, were replaced respectively by Yelverton and Hussey Burgh, the well known 'patriots', by Francis Sheridan, whose cousin was already in the front rank of whig orators at Westminster, and by George Ponsonby, Portland's cousin. Ponsonby was a leading member of a powerful interest which had more than one link with the English whigs, and which, Portland thought, might become 'the nest egg of a real whig party' in Ireland. It was thought that Carleton, the solicitor-general, was going to be succeeded by an able whig lawyer, John Forbes. But Carleton, 'a very sensible and very amiable man', 'managed in the tempest to keep all his masts standing', and remained solicitor-general until placed on the bench in 1787. Another old servant of the crown who seems to have been unruffled was Hely-Hutchinson. He reflected that if he had 'several acquaintances' in North's administration, it was 'more than a compensation' that he had a good friend, Burke, in Rockingham's. Scott, understandably, considered himself disgracefully used. A tough debater, he was, his diary reveals, introspective, ambitious and prepared to sacrifice much to professional success—'in this guttling country, the man who should distinguish himself for eating, drinking and sleeping least might run before everybody'. After his dismissal, making up his mind 'to trust none, rely on none, confide in none, give up my time to none, quarrel with none, intermeddle with none, speak ill of none, find fault with none, get drunk with none', he threw himself into hard work. As for Lees he seems to have started drinking heavily.[21]

To a young M.P. with strong conservative instincts, the dismissals seemed intended 'totally to unhinge government in Ireland and erect a kind of mobocracy, by which they [Portland and his advisers] hope to rule parliament'.[22] But Portland thought that his attempt to provide the Irish administration with a new 'face' (as Fox put it) would be of considerable help when it came to negotiating a settlement. At the beginning of June, Portland assured Shelburne that he was confident that he would have the assistance of influential Irish politicians, including Grattan, in carrying through parliament a measure providing for the acknowledgement of 'the superintending power and supremacy of Great Britain in all matters of state and general commerce', and for an imperial defence contribution from Ireland. Shelburne, the secretary of state, was delighted. The news was a vindication of the government's Irish policy. 'Bargains and compacts', he told Portland, 'may accomplish little objects—great ends must be obtained by a noble and more generous policy'. But at the end of June Portland had to explain with 'disappointment and mortification' that there was no immediate prospect of discussions on the lines he had indicated. In fact Portland had been playing a part in a wry political comedy. The intermediary, who, the duke believed, could get the discussions started, was William Ogilvie, a Scotsman, who had married the widow of the first duke of Leinster. Portland seems to have been pardonably impressed by the ducal connection. But Ogilvie, a Scotsman,

---

[21] Portland to Northington, 18 Sept. 1783 (Add. MS 39716); Orde to W. Pitt, 4 Oct. 1784 (P.R.O. 30/8/329); *Correspondence of Edmund Burke*, iv, p. 434; J. Scott, *Diary* (privately printed, T.C.D. Press B.4.11); J. Beresford to W. Eden, 14 Apr. 1783 (Add. MS 34419).

[22] *Carlisle MSS H.M.C.*, p. 629.

who had entered the Leinster household as a tutor, was not an M.P., was regarded as 'officious' and carried no weight in Irish political circles.[23]

The Irish parliamentary session of 1781–2, which attained its climax with Grattan's great speech on 16 April, was one of striking constitutional achievement. But at the close of May, when the commons were debating the address of thanks to the crown, the general attitude of gratitude, goodwill and success was slightly marred by a few M.P.s who doubted if a decisive victory had been obtained, Walshe pointing out that the 6 of Geo. I was only a declaratory act and what was needed in addition to simple repeal was that the British parliament should 'unequivocally and expressedly' state that it had not power to legislate for Ireland. The British parliament, Flood pointed out, 'might at some future period change its mind'. The house of commons rejected, almost unanimously, an attempt to amend the address. But Flood kept insisting on the importance of securing strict legal guarantees of Ireland's rights. He was not, he emphasized, hostile to the British connection (indeed he was soon to obtain what he had long wanted, a Westminster seat),[24] but he was always a severe critic of other men's work and hypercritical of the achievements of his successors in the leadership of the country party.

The difference between the simple repeal with which Grattan was satisfied and a British act of renunciation demanded by Flood, though it involved a fine point of constitutional law, generated great heat—fuel being added to the flame when in September Lord Mansfield in the king's bench, in the case of Holland v. Barry, pronounced judgement in an appeal from the Irish king's bench. A group of volunteer delegates from Ulster and Connaught meeting in Dublin professed to be satisfied with simple repeal, but the Ulster delegates were severely criticized in the north for assenting to this declaration. The delegates of the volunteer corps of Connaught approved of an address to the king stating that all jealousies were at an end, a minority protesting against what they considered to be a declaration in favour of simple repeal. The Lawyers corps of

---

[23] *Parliamentary history*, xxxiv, pp. 877–82; *Memorials and correspondence of Charles James Fox*, i, p. 431; Portland to Shelburne, 6 June 1782 (H.O. 100/2).

[24] H. Flood to Chatham, 12 Sept. 1767 (P.R.O. 30/8/32).

Dublin approved by 77 votes to 21 a long opinion to the effect that the repeal of 6 George I left the law as the legislature deemed it to be at the time the declaratory act was passed. The liberals of Belfast were acrimoniously divided.[25] Taking the country as a whole, opinion as expressed by volunteer meetings was strongly behind the demand for a renunciation act, a demand often accompanied by angry protests against the government's decision to raise six fencible regiments, it being argued that the enlistment of these 'mercenaries' cast a slur on the volunteers. The agitation filled the newspapers with addresses and protests, and the newly arrived lord lieutenant, the impressionable and tense Lord Temple, having quickly consulted almost every prominent Irish politician, informed the cabinet that if the demand for renunciation was resisted his administration would lose the support of even 'the simple repeallers' and British authority in Ireland would be imperilled.[26] The British government responded by introducing a bill declaring the right of the people of Ireland to be bound only by laws enacted by the parliament of Ireland and to have all suits begun in an Irish court finally decided in Ireland, and this measure received the royal assent ten days before Temple was recalled from Ireland, following the fall of Shelburne's administration.

By the spring of 1783 Irishmen could survey with pride, with 'an enthusiasm of happiness',[27] their recent political triumphs. All the positions which successive administrations had so tenaciously held as bastions of British authority had suddenly fallen. British parliamentary supremacy, so far as Ireland was concerned, had vanished, and the liberties of the subject had been ensured. Unlike the American colonies Ireland had managed to win both legislative independence and maintain its connection with Great Britain; and it had attained its objectives without using military force. Admittedly the volunteers had exercised considerable influence. But they had remained in the background and Irishmen had the gratifying feeling that they had soldiered for liberty without having to draw the sword. The atmosphere was heady enough for Irishmen to feel that they were living through a revolution, a revolution of course in the

[25] B.N.L., 12, 17 Oct. 1782; D.E.P., 12, 14 Sept., 23, 28 Nov. 1782.
[26] Fortescue MSS M.H.C., i, p. 166
[27] Parl. Reg. Ire., i, p. 367.

restrained style of 1688. At the beginning of the following decade (and two years after the fall of the Bastille) an angry young Irish radical was to dismiss the revolution of 1782 as 'the most bungling, imperfect business that ever threw ridicule on a lofty epithet'.[28] But in the eighties Irishmen prided themselves on having acquired British liberty and on having established an independent kingdom, linked by a common crown to Great Britain. It was not an easy matter to reconcile Irish autonomy and imperial unity, and the constitutional position after 1782 was complex and contained elements which suggested that Ireland was to some extent still subordinate to Great Britain. Shelburne in recommending the settlement of 1782 with Ireland to the house of lords emphasized that 'the king, therefore, as the executive power of this country, will still hold the sovereignty of that, and all acts of state flow as before from His Majesty in his privy council of Great Britain.'[29] Yelverton's act provided that the royal assent to Irish bills should be signified under the great seal of Great Britain, and in the debates over Yelverton's measure in the Irish house of commons, the employment of the British great seal in the Irish legislative process aroused no comment. The point on which Flood, who was critical of Yelverton's handiwork, fastened was the failure to provide for the royal assent or dissent to Irish bills being pronounced in parliament. The old French formulae, he said, were 'sacred relics of Agincourt and Cressy'.[30] Later the ingenious, but hardly convincing, argument was advanced in Ireland that though the British great seal was used by the king to signify his assent to an Irish bill, he gave the assent as king of Ireland, and that 'the annexation of the great seal of England . . . was merely evidence of the bill's having been confirmed and approved by the Irish monarch'; it was important, 'not to mistake the usual proof and symbol of the royal volition for the royal volition itself'. But both Fitzgibbon, a future lord chancellor, and Parsons, an independent M.P., stressed that the employment of the British great seal in the Irish legislative process was a valuable guarantee of Ireland's connection with Great Britain.[31]

---

[28] T. W. Tone, *Life of T. W. Tone* . . . (1826), i, p. 346.
[29] *Parliamentary history*, xxiii, p. 43.
[30] *Parl. Reg. Ire.*, i, p. 391.
[31] Ibid., ix, pp. 67, 82, 121.

The question remained an academic one. On more than one occasion it was suggested that the veto should be employed. Indeed one lord lieutenant, Buckingham, who was irritable and irritating, was anxious that the right should not lapse by disuse.[32] But ministers were well aware that the rejection of an Irish bill would probably arouse violent indignation and Irish bills after being transmitted invariably received the royal assent. They were, as in the past, laid before the British privy council, which referred them to the law officers. However, though the law officers occasionally drew attention to the implications of a bill or to defects in its drafting, only one measure out of eighteen years' legislative output failed to secure the royal assent.[33] The British government of course could rely on the Irish administration exerting itself to block measures, thought to be detrimental to imperial or British interests, in their progress through the Irish parliament.

The great seal of Great Britain was also the instrument under which the lord lieutenant was appointed, which suggests, in fact correctly, that he was a member of the British administration of the day, appointed on the advice of the prime minister. In 1792 a group of radical lawyers challenged in the Irish courts the validity of the lord lieutenant's appointment, arguing that a patent under the British great seal ('a mere cake of wax' in Ireland) could not have 'any weight in a judicial decision in an independent kingdom'. The attorney-general replied that for six hundred years the lord lieutenant had been appointed and the king's will made known under the English or British great seal and chief baron Yelverton and the chief justice of the common pleas refused to allow the matter to be pursued further in their courts.[34] The status of the Irish executive was also suggested by the procedure for signifying the crown's decision on a number of administrative questions—the issue of public money, appointments, pension grants, the regulating of public

---

[32] The bill Buckingham suggested should not be returned was the preservation of sheep bill (1788) which, he pointed out, was ungrammatical and unconstitutional (it threw the onus of proving his innocence on the accused) (Buckingham to Sydney, 2 Apr. 1788, H.O. 100/23).

[33] In 1785 it was decided to 'respite' an act for preventing doubts concerning parliament . . . on the demise of the crown (P.C. 1/31/78). For material relating to the consideration of Irish bills by the privy council see P.C. 1/31/3, 1/31/78, 1/44/156.

[34] *Society of the United Irishmen of Dublin* (1794), pp. 135–87.

departments—authorization being conveyed by a royal warrant, countersigned by three British lords of the treasury.[35] Between 1790 and 1794 the Irish whigs, arguing that public money was being dispensed on the authority of British ministers and Irish ministers, the lord lieutenant and chief secretary, who were 'fugitive', introduced responsibility bills providing that all Irish expenditure would be authorized by Irish officials, who, it might be presumed, would be permanently resident. These bills failed to pass, the government's supporters arguing that with the lord lieutenant and chief secretary accountable to the Irish parliament, parliamentary control over expenditure was well secured.[36]

There was another important sphere, foreign affairs, including peace and war, in which constitutional conventions, and the absence of any machinery through which the Irish state could act, ensured that the British government acted for the whole empire. The Irish parliament could, if it disapproved of a war, refuse supplies, but it is hard to see what positive steps it could take. Early in 1782 when Portugal refused to agree that the Methuen treaty covered woollen goods from Ireland, a bellicose M.P., who shared the widely held view that the British ministry was not sufficiently active in maintaining Ireland's interests, moved an address to the crown stressing Ireland had 'the vigour and resources' to maintain her rights. But calmer councils prevailed and in the end the British government secured satisfactory concessions from Portugal. In 1783 the British cabinet decided that the peace treaties should not be submitted to the Irish parliament—to do so would create a bad precedent and 'have a great tendency to raise ill humours between the two countries'.[37] But in 1787 the commercial treaty with France was laid before both houses of the Irish parliament; addresses approving the treaty were voted and the necessary consequent fiscal legislation enacted. In 1790 when Great Britain was nearly at war with Spain and in 1793 at the beginning of the great French war, supplies were voted unanimously by the Irish house of commons. In January 1797 Camden, who considered he had to mention the breach with

---

[35] For the procedure see T 14/17–18.
[36] Parl. Reg. Ire., x, p. 384.
[37] North to Northington, 3 Nov. 1783 (Add. MS 38716).

Spain and the failure of the Malmesbury negotiations with France in his address from the throne, was uncertain whether or not he should place the correspondence relating to these two questions before parliament—it had of course already been laid before the British parliament. Portland, the secretary of state, gave indecisive advice and at such a critical moment Camden felt he could not adjourn parliament to await an answer to the problem. So on the advice of 'His Majesty's servants in this kingdom', he placed the correspondence before parliament. He was sure that if he had not done so a motion asking for papers would have been moved, and he was confident that the papers were 'in the nature of a manifesto to persuade the world of the rectitude of the conduct of ministers'.[38] The whig opposition, developing the implications of the lord lieutenant's action, debated foreign policy at length, urging the house to support a very different policy to that of the government.

[38] Camden to Portland, 16 Jan. 1797 (H.O. 100/69).

7
Parliamentary reform and protection

In the early eighties Ireland was politically buoyant and restless. A series of constitutional debates characterized by close argument, intense feeling and high rhetoric, with in the background the volunteers arrayed and alert, and a great Atlantic war in progress, had terminated dramatically by what appeared to be complete capitulation on the part of the government and the imperial parliament. Political thinking had been stimulated, Irishmen had learned to work the machinery of agitation, they had seen parliament lagging behind the public and had at last realized what a limited control the intelligent and respectable public seemed to exercise over the house of commons.

During the first two decades of George III's reign even those who regretted that the house of commons was not more responsive to enlightened public opinion accepted the existing political framework. It had long been taken as axiomatic in political thinking that the British constitution, a remarkably successful blending of the three accepted forms of government, monarchy, aristocracy and democracy, had attained as high a degree of perfection as might be expected of any human institution. The eighteenth century was not excessively charitable in its comments on public men, but there was a strong tendency to blame human nature rather than the system for the failings of politicians. Nevertheless the critics of the administration felt that steps should be taken to reduce the parliamentary influence of the crown by reducing the amount of patronage at its disposal, and they encouraged the electors to direct their representatives to support sound policies. It was noted with approval by James Burgh, one of the earliest English advocates of parliamentary reform, that many Irish constituencies in 1768 instructed their representatives to vote for the Octennial bill. M.P.s for Dublin city and Dublin county were from time to time given directions by their constituents.[1] Some M.P.s even

[1] J. Burgh, *Political disquisitions* (1774), i, p. 202.

announced that they welcomed such directions. Sir Edward Newenham told his County Dublin constituents that he regarded himself as 'their delegated servant' and two years later he requested their instructions on the catholic relief bill. James Wilson, a successful candidate for County Antrim, undertook if returned to inform his constituents about forthcoming legislation and he suggested that the protestant clergy might assemble the freeholders in their parishes and convey their opinions to him. Richard Sheridan, an unsuccessful candidate for Dublin in 1782, stated 'that he was perfectly convinced that nothing could so perfectly banish corruption from parliament as an unqualified deference in the representative to the sentiments of his constituents', and Grattan told the house of commons that an M.P. was the servant of his constituents 'whose commands he was as much bound to obey as the servants of the crown the regal authority'. There were however those who did not want to see M.P.s treated 'as if they were puppets' and Brownlow, a leading county member declared that constituents had 'the right to address but not to compel' their representatives.[2]

Efforts were also made to secure the election of M.P.s who would support popular policies. At the general election of 1776 Hugh Boyd, a County Antrim landlord, who became a successful political journalist in London, stated that if the electors of Ireland put their shoulders to the wheel they could 'extricate the political machine from the bogs and filth which have hitherto clogged its operations'.[3] At the same time it was emphasized that if the electors were true to their country 150 honest M.P.s would be returned, and it was suggested that 'gentlemen of virtuous and independent principles' should inform the lower classes of electors of their rights.[4] Six years later a committee appointed by the Dungannon volunteer convention exhorted electors to disregard their landlords and vote only for men whose conduct merited their approval. 'An upright house of commons is all that is wanting.'[5] At the general election of 1783 in three boroughs, which might be regarded as

[2] *D.J.*, 4 May 1776, 4 June 1778; *Free. Jn.*, 11 Jan. 1776; *H.J.*, 12 Nov. 1779, 16 Jan. 1782; *Observations on the parliamentary conduct of the Rt. Hon. John Foster* (1784), p. 15.
[3] *The miscellaneous works of Hugh Boyd*, ed. L. D. Campbell (1800), i, p. 14.
[4] *Free. Jn.*, 18 May, 23 Apr. 1776.   [5] *Hibernian Magazine*, 1782, p. 221.

close, the controlling interest was actually challenged by an organized liberal opposition. In Lisburn, a pot-walloping borough, a constitution club was formed to mobilize the liberal vote and support electors who 'should be injured in property or person for voting as their consciences dictate', and two well-known liberals, Sharman, a country gentleman and Todd Jones, a barrister, were returned against the candidates supported by the great local landlord, Lord Hertford, who however recovered control at the general election of 1790. In Belfast, indubitably a close borough, during the 1783 election a number of citizens gathered, 'a gentleman of the town' was proposed and a liberal lawyer asked all the candidates to promise to support reform. But the two sitting and non-resident M.P.s, who refused the test, were elected by the five burgesses who were present. At Carrickfergus, a freeman borough with a large electorate, Waddell Cunningham, a successful Belfast businessman and a declared supporter of parliamentary reform was supported by about 100 members of the Belfast constitution club, wearing cockades inscribed 'Freedom of election'. As a result of their activities Cunningham was returned against the influence of Lord Donegall only to be unseated on the grounds that his Belfast supporters had by threats and 'unlawful entertainments' intimidated and intoxicated many of the voters.[6] It may be added that in 1783 a bold attempt was made to emancipate Dundalk, long regarded as a pocket borough of Lord Clanbrassill's. Lord Clanbrassill and his agent Read disagreed over the way in which the affairs of a volunteer corps should be conducted. 'Lord Clanbrassill's principles seem to have been monarchical, Mr Read's republican.' The dispute spread from the military to civil sphere and Read contrived to have a number of new freemen admitted at Dundalk with the aim, he declared, of 'laying the borough open'. At the general election of 1783 the candidates supported by Clanbrassill were opposed. But their return was upheld by the house of commons, and in 1792 a decision of the house of lords severely limiting the number of freemen in Dundalk re-established the patron in firm control.[7]

[6] See R. B. McDowell, *Irish public opinion*, p. 97; *D.E.P.*, 12 Aug. 1783. The liberal candidate at Belfast was probably also Waddell Cunningham (S. S. Millin, *Sidelights on Belfast history* (1932), pp. 36–7).

[7] *A succinct detail of some late proceedings at Dundalk* (1782), and see p. 115.

The very efforts which were made in the seventies and eighties to bring opinion to bear on parliament helped to make clear to many liberals that public spirit, however vigorously and intelligently exercised, could be rendered ineffectual by the workings of the parliamentary system, and that what was called for were drastic alterations both in the pattern of the constituencies and the qualifications for the franchise. From the sixties it was being urged that the number of county M.P.s in the British house of commons should be increased, and a speech of John Wilkes urging this reform was prominently displayed in the *Freeman's Journal*.[8] In the Irish general election of 1776, Lewis Francis Irwin, an unsuccessful candidate for County Sligo declared himself to be in favour of 'an equal representation of the people', and delegates appointed by the electors of County Antrim asked the candidates for the county to subscribe to a declaration binding them not to accept place or pension and to strive for 'a more fair and equitable representation of the people in parliament'. Two candidates took the test and one of them, James Wilson, was returned. But from the middle seventies the struggle against the commercial and constitutional restrictions increasingly absorbed the energy of Irish liberals and it would have obviously been tactically unwise while asserting the rights of the Irish parliament, to have emphasized the defects of the Irish house of commons. Nevertheless it was noticeable during these years how parliament continually lagged behind liberal or 'patriot' public opinion, and how frequently members of the public expressed unqualified contempt for their representatives. In the house of commons, it was said there could be seen courtiers and placemen standing ready 'with the bowstring at the command of the government to strangle the political or commercial liberties of this country'. M.P.s, who were pensioners or placemen, it was remarked, were just as much enlisted in the government's service as 'the poor soldier who signs for sixpence a day'.[9] Division lists, with offensive explanatory notes, were appearing in print in the newspapers and in 1783 there was published the first realistic

[8] *Free. Jn.*, 21 Mar. 1776. In 1775 an Irish gentleman, Christopher Nicholson of Balrath, bequeathed John Wilkes £350 on account of his sufferings for the cause of liberty (*H.J.*, 28 Aug. 1775).

[9] *D.E.P.*, 24 Dec. 1782; *D.J.*, 4 June 1776; *B.N.L.*, 31 May 1776.

survey of the Irish constituencies with seats divided between patrons and the people.[10]

If the defects of the parliamentary system were clear, so was the remedy. While the struggle against the restraints was developing in Ireland, a widespread parliamentary reform movement, generated by the American war, war taxation and administrative bungling, was gathering strength in England. The English reformers were much impressed by the Irish volunteers. 'Was it love of Ireland', a Yorkshire meeting was asked at the close of 1779, 'that made Lord North anxious to hurry the Irish bills through parliament? No. It was 64,000 bayonets planted at his breast.' The Irish liberals too were quick to acknowledge that reformers in Great Britain and Ireland had a common cause. It was the duty of each kingdom, they stressed, to help the other in its efforts to restore 'to its ancient purity and vigour a decayed, enfeebled and sickly constitution'.[11]

The first great sustained effort to win parliamentary reform was in both Great Britain and Ireland characterized by moderation and reason. Its leaders stressed that their aim was simply to remove blatant defects in the electoral system, making only such changes in the arrangement of the constituencies and the franchise as were required if the house of commons was to reflect intelligent public opinion. These changes, they ceaselessly reiterated, would be strictly in accordance with the principles of the constitution, and this first generation of parliamentary reformers presented themselves not as political innovators but as constitutional renovators. Moreover they did not regard parliamentary reform as a prelude to extensive changes in other spheres. Admittedly Francis Dobbs, a soldier, a barrister, an M.P., a playwright, an ambitious historian and an ardent theologian, convinced that 'a more equal representation of the people is unavoidably blended with other subjects', prepared for the delegates attending the Dungannon volunteer convention of 1783 a comprehensive programme of reforms. It included not only a redistribution of seats and extension of the franchise to every man who paid hearth money but also the codification of the criminal and civil laws, the creation of

<hr>

10 *D.E.P.*, 22, 25 Jan. 1783.
11 C. Wyvill, *Political papers*, iv, p. 12; *VJ.*, 15, 22 Oct. 1783.

provincial and district courts, free trade, and the abolition of tithe and all direct taxes. Dobbs's state religion would have had bishops, a very short form of subscription for the clergy, and a simple liturgy based on the Lord's prayer, the ten commandments and the sermon on the mount. Besides maintaining this latitudinarian church, the state was to pay all the clergy, catholic and protestant, in the country.[12] But Dobbs was prevented from adumbrating his ideas at Dungannon, being debarred from sitting in the convention on the grounds that he had become a fencible officer, and reformers in general had less ambitious plans for the immediate post-reform era. Their main objective was to redress the constitutional balance and by strengthening the democratic pillar of the constitution'[13] to diminish the influence of the crown over the legislature and to weaken the power of the aristocracy, of the great interests, 'the Venetian nobles' in the county constituencies.[14] The elimination of corruption would be followed by a welcome reduction in taxation. What was even more important, a reformed parliament was expected to be very ready to protect and promote Ireland's economic interests. In Ireland political liberalism was often accompanied by a keen concern with economic development and Irish liberals were acutely conscious that the unreformed house of commons would be dangerously susceptible to British influence when economic questions were under consideration. The government, it was said, 'might prevail with that virtuous assembly under any absurd pretence of justice or gratitude or generosity' (for profligate parliaments are always remarkably sentimental).[15] A reformed parliament, it was hoped, might set up a board (modelled on the Linen board) to supervise and encourage the woollen industry, would impose a stiff absentee tax and stimulate Irish industry by tariff manipulation.

Though most of the advocates of parliamentary reform relied on sober, matter-of-fact arguments, a novel and compelling note was struck by a young pamphleteer, William

---

[12] F. Dobbs, *The true principles of government applied to the Irish constitution* (1783).

[13] *Commons' Jn. Ire.*, xi, p. 199.

[14] R. Geoghegan, *An utilist to the aggregate body of the Irish nation* (1784), p. 26.

[15] *Arguments to prove the interposition of the people to be constitutional and strictly legal* (1783), pp. 15–17.

Drennan. Drennan, the son of a leading Belfast presbyterian divine, had graduated in medicine at Glasgow and was practising in Newry. A man of poetic sensibility and strong ethical convictions, from an early age he was passionately eager to be able to share in shaping the destinies of his country. 'A sort of aristocratical democrat', as he put it himself, he realized that he was not altogether suited to public life. He thought that in many ways he resembled Rousseau, 'in reserve of countenance —the awkward timidity—the short-sightedness . . . really frank and open—apparently sullen and shut up . . . social yet solitary—without address, art, dissimulation, prudence—hating vulgarity, loving the vulgar—gentle in manner yet a stern republican, flexible in every other thing. His spirit tuned to a flat key—yet much latent enthusiasm—fonder of the fair than he appears.'[16] Though Drennan was fundamentally a new light presbyterian and a rational liberal, very forward-looking—'the world is yet', he wrote, 'too young in experience to repose on any plan of government'— he had a quick command of emotive and often evocative imagery. 'You are all native Irish', he told the Ulster liberals, 'under the control of an English pale. Every rotten borough is nothing more or less than a feudal castle', and his *Letters of Orellena, an Irish helot,* which appeared in pamphlet form in 1785 are a reminder that the reform movement coincided with the Romantic revival. To Drennan parliamentary reform was 'not merely the removal of an evil', it would prove a transforming spirit in Irish social life. 'The public mind, by being frequently brought into action, must grow better informed; the latent powers and energies of every individual that enjoyed the blessing would be brought into action, for there is a sympathy between the noble principles of our nature. The heat of public spirit would foster and bring into the light of day those seeds of science which at present generate but to die in the breasts of indolent and unambitious men. The republic of letters . . . would arise to illuminate the land. The mines of labour would be open and the mists of superstition would dissolve away. We would all live like Christians and behave as countrymen.'[17]

[16] W. Drennan to Mrs McTier, 17 Oct. 1794, 24 Feb. 1796 (Drennan papers, 530, 598).
[17] *Letters of Orellena* (1785), pp. 40–1.

With parliamentary reform apparently a constitutional and reasonable cause, Irish reformers at the beginning of the eighties were confident they could quickly attain their objectives. Reform seemed to be pre-eminently a question on which the popular will should prevail—a people was certainly entitled, it was held, to correct the defects in its own constitution. In Ireland, the people, sometimes a nebulous concept, were represented in a concrete and respected form by the volunteers, and it was the volunteers who made the opening moves in the first Irish campaign for parliamentary reform. At the end of May 1782, a Dublin unit, the Liberty corps, meeting with their colonel, Sir Edward Newenham, an ebullient liberal in the chair, resolved that 'a more equal representation of the people in the national assembly will give stability and add lustre to the rights and liberties of Ireland'. About a month later Sir Edward Newenham in a letter to his County Dublin constituents suggested a simple scheme of reform. Dublin was to return four M.P.s and every county and the university were to be given one additional member. A reformed parliament, Newenham wrote, would reduce the taxes 'only too successfully applied to feed the avarice . . . of the betrayers of the interests of their country'.[18] Shortly afterwards, at the very end of the session of 1782 Newenham introduced a bill for the more equal representation of the people in parliament.

Until the late autumn of 1783 much of the energy of the politically-minded in Ireland was being absorbed first by the renunciation agitation and then by a general election. Even so in March 1783 delegates from the Munster volunteer corps, meeting in Cork, resolved that the majority of the house of commons was returned by venal boroughs and that parliament would never be virtuous until a more equal representation of the people was obtained. It was also resolved, with seven corps dissenting, that any candidate that would not sign a test promising to obey the instructions of his constituents and declaring he had not used any undue influence to secure election was unworthy to represent the province. Three months later delegates from thirty-eight corps present at a Belfast review agreed that the more equal representation of the people in parliament deserved the consideration of every Irishman. At the

[18] *D.E.P.*, 1 June, 11 July 1782.

end of June the Ulster Regiment suggested that there should be a meeting of volunteer delegates at Lisburn to discuss how the defects in the constitution should be remedied. The Lisburn meeting, at which forty-five corps (including two in Belfast) were represented decided that a meeting of representatives of the Ulster volunteers should be held at Dungannon at the beginning of September to consider 'the most constitutional means of procuring a more equal representation'. The Lisburn delegates also appointed a committee of correspondence under the chairmanship of Colonel Sharman.[19] This committee promptly wrote to half a dozen prominent English reformers, requesting advice on some issues which were bound to arise when a scheme of reform was being drafted—the ballot, the duration of parliament, compensation for borough owners, the pattern of the constituencies (should the decayed boroughs be abolished or enlarged?), and qualifications for the franchise. To this last question a simple and sweeping answer was given by the duke of Richmond an earnest advocate of universal suffrage. Political equality and economic inequality were both, he asserted, 'founded in nature', so he earnestly advocated universal suffrage. Thinking specifically of the Irish situation he went on to argue that 'the same principles which go to civil liberty lead equally to liberty of conscience'. But he admitted he knew nothing about 'the present temper and disposition' of the Irish catholics. Another distinguished English reformer, Richard Price,' sensible that he was breaking tender ground', also referred to the catholic question. Keeping in mind that 'the efforts of enlightened men should be governed by a regard to what is most practical', he was against universal suffrage. The right to vote, he thought, should be granted only to those possessing a property qualification, and catholics who were qualified should be allowed to vote. 'The danger from the papists', he wrote, 'is perhaps more produced by the penal laws against them than by their religion.' Privately he pointed out that, owing to the distribution of property in Ireland, the protestants would have a secure majority in the electorate. Wyville, the Yorkshire reform leader and Jebb agreed with Price; Jebb, impressing on a Belfast liberal that were the catholics enfranchised 'industry would flourish more

[19] *B.N.L.*, 13 June, 1 July, 5 Aug. 1783.

abundantly, commerce be expanded . . . [and] you would set a glorious example to the popish states.'[20]

The conscientious application by British liberals of enlightened principles to the Irish situation met with a mixed reception from Irish reformers. Sir Edward Newenham thought that 'it would be the highest absurdity to give two million people the power to destroy the half million who had fought and bled to support the free constitution in church and state we now enjoy. Their principles and ours can never be in unison. We are for freedom, they are for depotism. They have an old claim to our estates. We give them full exercise of their religion. If they had the power we should not have a similar liberty.'[21] But a younger reformer, Todd Jones, told his Lisburn constituents that 'the catholics are our brethren and are entitled to the rights of citizens. If we refuse them this extension Ireland remains divided, with neither party strong enough to cope with external opponents or accomplish any considerable domestic reformation.' (To reassure the timid he explained in a footnote that the catholics agreed that only the comparatively small number of catholics who possessed a high property qualification should be enfranchised.)[22] A year or so later William Drennan, having impassionately called on protestants and catholics 'to unite as a sacred compact in the cause of your sinking country— for you are all Irishmen', coolly analysed the practicalities of the situation. In each denomination there were 'the select few', who aimed at reform and 'the multitude', inflamed by sectarian animosity (the ugly side of that religious fervour which strengthened their moral stamina). The Irish catholic body was in a peculiarly unhappy condition. Its 'superior and middle classes', whose duty it was to instil toleration into the minds of those below them, were relatively small. But Drennan was able to assure his readers that enlightened catholics were 'too wise to wish for a complete extension of civil franchises to those of their own persuasion'.[23]

Early in September, 500 delegates representing 276 Ulster

---

[20] *A collection of letters which have been addressed to the volunteers of Ireland on the subject of a parliamentary reform* (1783); Price to Joy, 23 Sept. 1783, Jebb to Joy, Sept. 1783 (Joy MSS).

[21] Sir E. Newenham to B. Folsh, 13 Oct. 1784 (P.R.O. 30/8/329).

[22] T. Jones, *Letter to the electors of the borough of Lisburn* (1784), pp. 54–5.

[23] *Letters of Orellena*, pp. 29–30.

corps gathered in the presbyterian meeting house atDungannon, constituting, according to the bishop of Derry, 'a very eminent figure in the debates' until compelled to retire by gout, a more 'faithful, honest, and spirited representation of the people' than any senate he knew. Having received a report from the committee of correspondence, emphasizing the great interest taken in their proceedings by the English reformers, the delegates resolved that freedom was the indefeasible right of Irishmen and Britons and that only those were free who were governed by laws to which they had assented either in person or through their representatives. They then called on the volunteer armies of the other provinces to join with them in a grand national convention, which would, by producing an extensive plan of reform, extend to 'thousands of our fellow citizens, a franchise comprehending the very essence of liberty'. The meeting also published for the consideration of the national convention a draft scheme prepared by the committee of correspondence. It suggested a redistribution of seats with compensation for borough patrons; the enfranchisement in the counties of all protestants resident for twelve months who were either forty-shilling freeholders or who possessed £20 worth of property; the enfranchisement in the boroughs of these two classes and householders rented at £5 per annum; annual parliaments; vote by ballot; the exclusion from the house of commons of pensioners and place holders (though six officeholders would sit in the house to explain public business). As for catholic enfranchisement, the scheme suggested that the vote might be given to those catholics whom the national convention judged worthy to exercise it.

Volunteer provincial meetings in Munster and Connaught endorsed the Ulster resolutions and representatives of the Leinster corps meeting at the Thorsel in Dublin agreed to take part in the National convention. At the Leinster meeting two issues were raised which revealed significant differences in opinion. Colonel Henry Hatton (son-in-law of the earl of Arran, a borough owner) pressed the assembly to resolve that 'it is only through the medium of parliament that we hope for constitutional redress'. This provoked other delegates to point out that 'the sacred majority of the people was at all times fully competent to correct the abuses which might arise in the constitution', John Talbot Ashenhurst, who was to be a prominent Dublin radical in the nineties, citing Dr Jebb in support of this opinion. In the end Michael Smith, a talented barrister who was to become a baron of the exchequer, produced a platitudinous compromise. 'Parliamentary reform', it was resolved, 'could best and most constitutionally be obtained through the medium of the legislature'. Then Peter Burrowes, a fervent and candid liberal, asked the assembly to face the catholic question. He argued that in general the suffrage should be granted to 'those and none but those who are likely to use it for the public good'. He dismissed Richmond's scheme contemptuously as 'giving the right of election to the mob', but he thought that those catholics who possessed the necessary property qualifications should be enfranchised. He secured some support, but several delegates tried to avoid a vote on the question by declaring that they had not been authorized by their corps to vote on it and the only step taken was to direct a committee appointed to investigate the state of the constituencies to compile religious statistics.[24]

The Dungannon meeting and the Munster provincial assembly elected the county delegates from their province to the convention. The delegates from the other two provinces were chosen by the volunteers of each county or their representatives and a few urban centres also elected delegates.[25] With the Irish landed world largely supplying the leadership of the volunteer movement, it is scarcely surprising that the great majority of the 186 delegates were men of 'status and property'. They included many well known country gentlemen, over 40 M.P.s and four peers. Admittedly one of the peers was the bishop of Derry, the most outspoken radical in the assembly (Charlemont sourly commented that 'the extreme volubility of his tongue and of his ideas affects his hearers rather with surprise than with pleasure, and seldom, if ever, with respect') and there were a few keen reformers from the north, including Colonel Sharman, Henry Joy, the prosperous proprietor of the Belfast News-Letter, William Todd Jones, a barrister and William Bruce, the minister of the First presbyterian church in Belfast, a man of fine bearing, proud of his descent from 'the royal blood of Scotland' and a strong liberal in both theology and politics. But Charlemont had taken steps to ensure that 'turbulent spirits' would be controlled by 'a strength of prudent men'. He was a sincere reformer but he had a strong dash of whig caution and he was not prepared for the sake of parliamentary reform to run the risk of civil war, or of what the bishop of Derry euphemistically called 'a little confusion'. Charlemont might be highly strung and highly fastidious but he had plenty of political acumen and he successfully persuaded a number of his friends who were moderates to have themselves elected as delegates.[26]

On 10 November the delegates to the Grand national convention gathered at the Royal Exchange in Dublin and marched across the centre of the city, through streets lined by the volunteers presenting arms, to the Rotunda where they deliberated for the following three weeks. The convention showed a due regard for form, Charlemont was elected chairman, secretaries were appointed, it was agreed that each delegate should subscribe a guinea, a volunteer guard was mounted and the spectators kept under firm control. On the second day the divisive question of catholic enfranchisement was raised. One member, the popular George Ogle, informed the convention that Lord Kenmare and others had stated that 'the catholics disavowed a wish for being connected with the business of election' and simply wanted to be allowed to enjoy in peace the concessions they had recently received. The next day the bishop of Derry produced a resolution of the catholic committee stating that 'we do not so widely differ from the rest of mankind, as, by our own act to prevent the removal of our shackles'.[27] The division amongst the catholics made it possible for protestant reformers to argue that they should avoid the catholic question until the catholics themselves knew what they wanted.

The convention appointed a committee, under the chairmanship of Robert Stewart, to prepare a scheme of reform. This

---

[26] For the proceedings of the volunteer convention see *H.J.*, 12 Nov.–3 Dec. 1783, *Charlemont MSS H.M.C.*, i, pp. 123–33.

[27] Ogle's statement seems to have been based on a communication from Sir Boyle Roche, who believed that he was expressing the sentiments of the leaders of the catholic body though he had not been authorized to do so (T. R. English, *The life of the Rev. A. O'Leary* (1822), pp. 107–14).

committee floundered badly until Flood was called in as a consultant. Under his masterful management a plan was quickly evolved. It provided that all voters were to be resident and registered and in county elections the poll was to be taken in all baronies simultaneously. The boundaries of decayed boroughs were to be enlarged and the franchise granted to protestant freeholders and thirty-one-year leaseholders. The duration of parliament was to be limited to three years, M.P.s were to take a bribery oath, pensioners at pleasure were to be excluded from the house of commons and members accepting a pension for life or a place under the crown would have to seek re-election. When the convention discussed the scheme in detail a few amendments were suggested, it being suggested for instance that non-residents might vote at county elections, and that there should be vote by ballot and annual parliaments. But Flood, making it aggressively clear that every point raised on the floor of the house had already been considered by the committee, bore down all opposition. The scheme having been approved, Charlemont thought that the next step should be to submit it to county meetings. But Flood, who had at last secured a seat at Westminster and was anxious to get over to England, prevailed on the convention to authorize him to present the scheme immediately to the house of commons. A day or two before he took this step, the bishop of Derry gave a large dinner party, and after Grattan had left but 'before the bottle had made a very considerable impression upon the company', he proposed that the whole convention in uniform should escort the bill to the house of commons—a suggestion promptly and successfully resisted by Edgeworth.[28]

At this stage the reform movement, which had been advancing with purposeful and apparently irresistible drive, came up against an almost irremovable obstacle, the house of commons. Those who benefited by and believed in the existing system were very well represented in parliament and a rallying point for men of conservative instincts was provided by the Irish administration. Northington, who had replaced Temple in June 1783, could easily be underrated. Devoted to the pleasures of the table and gouty he seemed to the supercilious Mornington

<hr />

[28] R. L. Edgeworth, *Memoirs*, ii, pp. 63–4.

to be polite but 'hustled headed'.[29] However his correspondence suggests that he was equitable and sensible. Facing the prospect of a parliamentary session as well as the growing reform agitation, he exerted himself to build up a strong administration, with 'a little cabinet' to manage parliamentary business (Yelverton, Sheridan, Foster and John Forbes, a whig barrister and M.P.). Northington started the negotiations which brought Foster, an economic expert, into office as chancellor of the exchequer and he managed to win the goodwill of Grattan, who though he approved of parliamentary reform in principle, was strongly opposed to the reform agitation which culminated in the volunteer convention. Grattan attended a confidential dinner or two and was regarded as a friend of the administration (Cooke rather maliciously remarked that Grattan had now a stake in the country). Still Grattan was not an easy ally. He was always a reforming whig, or, as Portland irritably remarked, he was dangerously influenced by 'popularity', and he pressed the lord licutenant to accept a scheme of retrenchment which would appeal to the independent country gentlemen, but which, he assured Northington, was 'not of a sort to affect the patronage of government'.[30]

Northington also secured Scott and Fitzgibbon as prime serjeant and attorney-general. Grattan showed a 'disinclination to this arrangement' and Forbes declined to accept office once Fitzgibbon, whom he regarded as anti-whig, was brought into the administration.[31] Their attitude was understandable. Scott had in the recent past been a bold, and at times boisterous leader of the government party in the house of commons; Fitzgibbon was already showing signs of developing into an indomitable and acrimoniously outspoken defender of authority. A very successful lawyer, who when he became lord chancellor was a very competent judge, and a pugnacious parliamentary debator, Fitzgibbon was courageous and clear-headed in council and his arrogance, if rude and irritating, enabled him

---

[29] *Charlemont MSS H.M.C.*, i, p. 100; *Fortescue MSS H.M.C.*, i, p. 221.
[30] Northington to W. Windham, 6 Oct. 1783; T. Pelham to W. Windham, 14 Sept. 1783 (Add. MS 37873); Northington to Portland, Portland to Northington, 18 Nov. 1783 (Add. MS 38716); E. Cooke to W. Eden, 4 Sept. 1783 (Add. MS 34419).
[31] Northington to W. Windham, 6 Oct. 1783 (Add. MS 37873); J. Forbes to J. Adair, 30 July 1794 (Add. MS 53802).

to bear down opposition. He held tenaciously a coherent political faith, enunciated with hard logic and reinforced by a harsh interpretation of Irish history from the Middle Ages. Fitzgibbon believed in British political and cultural values and in the British empire. He was certain that the connection between Great Britain and Ireland was of essential importance to both islands and he was sure it would be imperilled by catholic emancipation and parliamentary reform, long before the close-of-the century circumstances convinced him that the connection could only be maintained by a union. But what rendered Fitzgibbon a formidably outstanding figure in Irish politics was neither the clarity of his opinions nor his professional and parliamentary abilities. It was his tone and temper. When trouncing political error and iniquity he expressed himself with a moral anger and provocative vehemence more characteristic of an embittered radical than a contented conservative. In fact Fitzgibbon was far from contented. The son of a self-made man, he drove himself hard, and he prided himself on being, where Ireland was concerned, a political realist. Consequently he tended to view men and movements in Ireland with an exceptionally strong mixture of moral and intellectual contempt. He was not only defiantly hostile to agitators, radical, catholic and agrarian, but he violently attacked Irish politicians, the great aristocratic connections and the Irish whigs for being prepared to hazard the connection and indeed the whole social system for the sake of office, and he severely rebuked the Irish landlords for being selfish and negligent in their dealings with their tenancy. (It may be added that privately he criticized English politicians for failing to handle the Irish problem firmly.) Fitzgibbon's savage indignation with the follies of mankind (and perhaps self-dissatisfaction) naturally vented itself on his immediate environment, 'this giddy country'.[32] If he had long survived the enactment of the union he might have found that the wider political world of the United Kingdom had its faults and failings.

Though in 1783 Fitzgibbon, Beresford and Cooke obviously disliked the whig wing of the Fox–North coalition and grumbled

---

[32] Fitzgibbon's opinions are expressed with characteristic vehemence in letters printed in 'Some letters from the Sneyd muniments' in *Bull. of the John Rylands library*, xxxv, pp. 226–31.

about how English politics were weakening government in Ireland—there must, Cooke emphasized, be a government in England, 'which will give ground for gentlemen here on which they can stand'—nevertheless 'the old and tried friends' of the Irish administration would probably have agreed that the position in the autumn of 1783 was considerably better than it had been in the summer of 1782.[33] Northington could certainly rely on their wholehearted support in resisting parliamentary reform. He himself regarded the volunteer convention with concern rather than apprehension. He thought it was composed of 'a heterogeneous set' and he must have been reassured by a conversation that his chief secretary, Pelham, had with Charlemont shortly before the convention met. The meeting, Charlemont told Pelham, 'need not be so dreadful to him as it was composed of men who knew their duty and would do it'.

Though two members of the British cabinet were greatly alarmed, Fox declaring that if the convention did not speedily dissolve, 'government, and even the name of government must be at an end', and Portland advising the lord lieutenant to be ready to use military force to arrest the reform leaders, Northington remained calm. He claimed that through his friends in the convention he was 'able to perplex its proceedings' and he took vigorous steps to instil spirit into the parliamentary opponents of reform.[34] When, on 29 November, Flood introduced the convention's scheme into the house of commons he met with determined resistance. With the convention still in session Flood's opponents had a considerable debating advantage. They could abstain from discussing parliamentary reform and dwell instead on the importance of preserving parliamentary freedom. Was the house of commons, the attorney-general asked, to be reduced to registering the edicts of an armed assembly? The house rose to the occasion by rejecting the bill by 158 to 49. It was a gratifying display of political courage, but based of course on calculation. During the sittings of the convention M.P.s had plenty of opportunities of gauging what the convention's reaction was likely to be.

---

[33] W. Cooke to W. Eden, 25 Sept. 1783; J. Fitzgibbon to W. Eden, 11 Oct. 1783; J. Beresford to W. Eden, 17 Oct. 1783 (Add. MS 34419).

[34] Portland to Northington, 18 Sept. 1783 (Add. MS 38716); *Memorials and correspondence of Charles James Fox*, ii, pp. 163, 174, 184–7; *Charlemont MSS H.M.C.*, i, p. 120; Northington to C. J. Fox, 17 Nov. 1783 (Add. MS 38716).

When the convention assembled on Monday 1 December, the members were seething with indignation. But even the more extreme liberals seem to have had no idea of how that indignation could be expressed effectually. Throughout the convention's long and animated debates not a word had been said about what should be done if parliament proved obdurate and Charlemont and his supporters were determined to prevent precipitant action and wind up proceedings as quickly as possible. 'Policy not passion', Edgeworth declared, 'should dictate their resolutions', and the convention's indignation found pacific outlets. An address to the king was approved stating that their desire to remedy the 'manifest perversion of the parliamentary representation' should not be 'imputed any spirit of innovation'; the electors in each county were requested to appoint a committee which would arrange the constituencies in their county in accordance with the convention's plan and the counties and urban centres were exhorted to promote the plan by petitions to parliament and instructions to M.P.s. The delegates seem to have felt that they were terminating with dignity the first stage of a great movement. But to a lively-minded undergraduate it was pathetic to see 300 of the leading gentlemen in Ireland flying 'like deer to their counties, to return no more, after making a foolish profession of their pacific intentions; foolish, because it was evident that their anxiety was how they should reach their homes, without attachments and incarceration'.[35]

The country's response to the convention's call was impressive enough, twenty-two counties and cities or towns petitioning for parliamentary reform. Backed by this display of public opinion, Flood in March 1784 again introduced a reform bill, emphasizing that 'his idea was to restore the constitution by moderate measures, not to introduce novelties but to take them away'. The opponents of his bill made great play with what they considered to be its defects in detail, dwelling on points which reformers complained should have been raised in committee. The bill, its critics argued, narrowed the constituent body, violated chartered rights, enfranchised 'a dependent body of men', the thirty-one year-leaseholders, transferred a mass of electoral influence from borough owners to landlords

[35] T. W. Tone, *Life*, i, p. 351.

in the surrounding countryside and, by insisting on voters being resident, destroyed 'the generous idea' that an M.P. was a representative of the whole kingdom and not the fettered deputy of a small community. The existing constitution, under which Irishmen enjoyed liberty and commercial freedom, had put them in possession of every blessing that could render a people happy and flourishing. Denis Daly, a respected country gentleman with a good parliamentary style summed up the theme of many conservative speeches by a Shakespearian quotation (boldly torn out of context),

> Better 'Bear the ills we have
> Than fly to others which we know not of.'[36]

The house rejected Flood's bill by 159 to 85 and a month later the Irish administration inflicted a decisive parliamentary defeat on another powerful popular agitation. Parallel with the parliamentary reform movement, a tariff reform movement had developed. In the past Irish businessmen had not infrequently looked for state financial assistance from subsidies. It is therefore not surprising that in 1783–4, with widespread unemployment in the textile trades of the south of Ireland, the newly emancipated parliament should be asked to erect tariff barriers against foreign, or in fact British, competition. From the autumn of 1783 protection for Irish industry was being clamorously demanded by clubs, parishes, trade associations and volunteer corps. The Irish brigade, a Dublin volunteer corps, reminded the man who wore the manufactures of another country, that while 'he studies to trim himself elegantly the manufacturing poor of this city are naked and starving'; the Kilkenny horse rangers resolved that any shopkeeper detected selling foreign goods should be considered an enemy to his country, the workers employed by the Dublin coachmakers pledged themselves not to repair any British-built carriages, the journeymen tailors of Dublin bound themselves not to work up British cloth, the inhabitants of Dublin, Cork and Belfast entered into non-importation agreements, though it was maliciously observed by a court journalist that the citizens of Belfast had carefully avoided pledging themselves to non-importation. 'They will

not consume English fabrics,' he pointed out, 'but they forget
to tell us how many people in other parts of Ireland they will
supply with English goods from clandestine importation '[37] The
protectionist movement seems to have derived most of its
support from the south of Ireland and its most energetic organ
in the press was the Dublin *Volunteer Journal*, edited by Matthew
Carey. Carey, the son of a wealthy Dublin baker, had worked
for a time as a printer in Paris under Franklin. After he returned to Dublin his father put up the capital required to start
the *Volunteer Journal* in 1783. Carey later wrote, 'I was miserably
qualified for such an occupation which required no small
degree of tact, of experience of the world and of course of
prudence, in all of which I was greatly deficient.' But he admits
he had 'a superabundance of zeal and ardour' and, he might
have added, a vigorous and virulent pen.[38] He professed the
main articles of the radical creed of the following decade—
parliamentary reform and catholic emancipation, measures
which were essential if Irishmen were to resist successfully
English influence in Irish political life. 'Let all ranks of oppressed Irishmen ask', Carey wrote, 'whence flow their wrongs.'
And he immediately supplied the answer—From the blasting
connection with England; 'No English connection', the
Volunteer Journal declared in the spring of 1784 'is the
prevailing exclamation'. On both political and economic
grounds a fervid protectionist, Carey implied that direct action
might be used to discourage English imports. He referred to
tar as 'that convincing and adhesive argument of popular
rhetoric in favour of patriotic and non-consumption agreements'. The *Volunteer Journal* attacked the leading anti-
protectionist John Foster by publishing a crude woodcut of a
man hanging with the caption 'Beneath this gallows lie contemptuously scattered the unhallowed remains of Jack the
Bloodsucker . . . That for which he suffered was to destroy by
famine 40,000 lives.'[39] During 1784 attempts were made in
Dublin to intimidate by mob violence the importers or vendors
of English goods, the rioters, according to the lord lieutenant,

[37] *V.J.*, 12, 23 Apr., 10, 21, 26 May 1784; *B.N.L.*, 30 Apr. 1784; *V.E.P.*, 29 Apr.
1784.
[38] *New England Magazine*, v, p. 409.
[39] *V.J.*, 1, 10 Mar. 1784.

attacking not only the importers of English goods but also men who accepted low wages, worked at trades to which they had not been apprenticed or who had come up from the country to work in Dublin.[40] In October 1783 the house of commons appointed a committee to inquire into the state of Irish manufactures. This committee heard about thirty witnesses, textile merchants and manufacturers and a couple of Dublin hatters. The great majority of the witnesses favoured high duties on textile imports and export duties on some raw materials. Irish industry, it was argued, was being retarded by British competition, the British manufacturers having 'great ingenuity and vast capitals'. In addition their products had considerable prestige, possibly unfairly acquired. 'As we take our fashions from England,' a manufacturer explained, 'the latter end of her fashions would generally be preferred to the first of our own.' And McLoughlin, a woollen draper, complained that English cloth was not as well finished as might appear at the first glance, but 'the colours have a great effect'. The Irish textile industries, it was strongly asserted, could supply the Irish market adequately, if encouraged by protecting duties. On being asked to define a protecting duty, Richard McCormuck, a woollen manufacturer explained it meant a duty which 'would effectually secure a preference to this country so that a piece of other goods would not be sold while there was a piece of Irish to be had'. Another woollen manufacturer, on being asked if the Irish manufacturers wanted a monopoly, explained that while it would be creating a monopoly to give a preference to the Dublin manufacturer, giving a preference to the industry of the whole country was not granting a monopoly. Though it looks as if tariff reformers marshalled witnesses for the inquiry, some of the evidence presented weakened the protectionist case. To begin with the inferiority of some Irish manufactured goods was revealed. For instance a cotton printer complained that Irish cotton was not as good as English; on the other hand a cotton manufacturer complained that his cotton, after it left his hands, was not finished properly. Significantly too, northern industrialists, who appeared before the committee, were decidedly averse to a tariff which might jeopardize the position enjoyed

---

[40] Rutland to Sydney, 19 Aug. 1784 (H.O. 100/14)

by Ulster linen in the British market, which it was pointed out took 17,000,000 yards of Irish linen annually. The Irish linen trade always had to face the possibility of serious Russian and German competition and might be ruined by an Anglo-Irish tariff war. As for the suggestion that an export tax should be imposed on linen yarn for the benefit of the linen manufacturer, a Dungannon linen merchant bluntly said this scheme 'originated with the woollen manufacturers to bring us into their scheme which in my opinion would prove fatal to this country.' When this witness's attention was drawn to the industrial distress in Dublin, he unsympathetically attributed it to the difficulties confronting industry in a metropolis where rents were high, provisions dear and the artisans were 'tempted to drunkenness from the convenience of brandy and whiskey shops and ready to join combinations'.[41]

The committee reported at the beginning of March by laying the evidence before the house of commons, and a month later, its chairman, Luke Gardiner, M.P. for County Dublin, opened a protectionist campaign by moving that a high additional duty be laid on an important category of woollen imports. Gardiner at this time was quick to emphasize that in general he agreed with Adam Smith, adding however, 'I must insist that he should grant me that the people must at all events be employed.'[42] The British government's attitude to the Irish protectionists' demands had already been expresssed towards the close of 1783 by North, then home secretary. 'We have', North wrote, 'the right to expect that no prohibition of British manufactures should pass the parliament of Ireland.' Also, it was unreasonable to expect that British duties on Irish manufactures should be lowered, when it was considered that the 'the principal weight of supporting the empire lies on Great Britain'. 'The surest way', North declared, 'of preserving an uninterrupted harmony between the two kingdoms would be to prevent fresh and new demands on the part of Ireland to the prejudice of British trade and manufacture. If every session of the Irish parliament is to be signalized by some commercial advantage gained over Great Britain, jealousy and ill humour will gradually arise, the old attachment between the two coun-

[41] *Commons' Jn. Ire.*, xi, pp. cxxxv–ccvi.
[42] L. Gardiner to ——, 4 June 1784 (Orde papers, N.L.L.).

tries will gradually decay and our merchants and manufacturers will begin to call for protection and retaliation.'[43] The two principal administration spokesmen in the house of commons, Foster and Fitzgibbon, argued that as a result of the non-importation agreements 'manufactures had declined in quality and increased in price', and that when protective duties were being discussed, 'the whole trade with England and not a part should be considered'. Gardiner was supported by Todd Jones, John Doyle, Lawrence Parsons, who seemed to think that Ireland's status demanded that Irish duties should be raised to the British level, and Richard Griffith, who compared the condition of the distressed Irish artisans with those endured by 'the Esquimaux in North America or the Hottentots'. A majority, composed of M.P.s who were convinced free traders, or who were susceptible to government influence or who sympathized with the consumer, rejected Gardiner's motion by 123 to 49, and he realized that it was futile to persist.[44]

The setbacks sustained by the allied causes of protection and parliamentary reform during the session of 1784 left some Irish radicals remarkably undaunted. Early in June an aggregate meeting of the citizens of Dublin resolved that the people of Ireland had a right to frequent elections and an equal and adequate representation, that a majority in the house of commons was returned for 'indigent boroughs' by the mandates of a small number of individuals, and that a committee should be appointed to draw up an address to the people of Ireland requesting their co-operation in attaining an equal representation of the people in parliament. Napper Tandy and Pemberton wanted to 'appeal to' rather than 'request' the people but their suggestion was indignantly opposed by John Keogh as implying civil war. The disturbing problem of catholic enfranchisement was dealt with by a resolution stating that 'to extend the right of suffrage to our Roman catholic brethren, still preserving in its fullest extent the present protestant government of this country would be a measure fraught with the happiest consequences to our liberty'. This resolution was vigorously criticized by Joseph Pollock, a barrister and radical publicist, the candid friend of any group with which he was

[43] North to Northington, 7 Oct. 1783 (Add. MS 78716).
[44] Parl. Reg. Ire., i, pp. 128–43.

associated. The resolution, he said, when moving its rejection, was disingenuous. Most of those accepting it thought that it meant that only catholics possessing a high property qualification should be granted the franchise. In fact it implied equal voting rights for catholics.[45] Pollock was overwhelmingly defeated but Richard Griffith of Millicent, a leading Kildare liberal, denouncing the resolution as 'an absolute contradiction in sense', withdrew from the reform movement. Griffith thought that if the catholics were granted the vote, within a century they would predominate and the connection with Great Britain would be destroyed. He thought reform could be carried without their support and that the reform cause was being seriously damaged by its association with catholic enfranchisement.[46] William Drennan, a leading northern liberal, to some extent agreed with Griffith. 'The Roman catholic question', he wrote in the autumn of 1784, 'was our ruin—but if the reformers had not pretended a wish for an alliance with them on the grand question, government would have anticipated the volunteers and made the catholic volunteer act against the protestant.'[47] To George Tandy, a leader of the Lisburn radicals, the catholic question was 'the rock upon which we have split', and he was delighted to hear that Napper Tandy hoped to persuade the catholics to renounce their claim to the franchise. This, George Tandy wrote, 'would be a glorious thing and endear them to their protestant brethren'.[48] The catholics however remained silent. But if they disappointed Tandy in not disembarrassing the reformers by temporarily relinquishing their claim to the franchise, they also disappointed a leading conservative catholic, Lord Kenmare. A popular and improving Kerry landlord, with a rental of about £10,000 per annum, the holder of a Jacobite peerage (which even in official circles was treated as a courtesy title), Kenmare was not acutely conscious of being underprivileged and he was contemptuous of the Dublin catholic shopkeepers who were clamouring for reform though most of them were not in possession of a freehold. In the autumn of 1784 he seems to have wanted to obtain from the

[45] V.J., 9 June 1784.
[46] Ibid., 23 Aug. 1784.
[47] W. Drennan to Mrs McTier, [1784] (Drennan papers).
[48] Napper Tandy to G. Tandy, 2 Oct. 1784, and G. Tandy to Napper Tandy, 19 Oct. 1784 (P.R.O. 30/8/330).

catholics a declaration of confidence in the Irish administration, but he found that 'our people are still frightened of shadows and when pressed by the heads of the clergy and me to disavow this claim of election franchise the answer we get is "shall we reject the offers of our most ancient enemies"'.[49]

The committee appointed by the Dublin aggregate meeting presented the address it had prepared to another aggregate held at the end of June. This address, having dwelt in detail with the misdoings of the legislature, suggested a plan of action. Every county and large urban centre should elect delegates to a congress which would 'deliberate, digest and determine on' measures 'to reestablish the constitution on a pure and permanent basis'. The aggregate approved of this address and appointed a committee headed by Tandy to convoke the congress.[50]

At this point the reform movement, which was losing impetus, came up against a conservative reaction led by the Irish government. From the close of 1783 the more conservatively minded members of the Irish administrative world had been greatly cheered by British political developments. The coalition ministry had been forced to resign; Pitt had become prime minister with the king's open support and had won a hard-fought general election. Pitt's self-assurance, conspicuous ability and success had an invigorating effect on those Irish office-holders who were by instinct and principle strong supporters of the British connection, Beresford, Fitzgibbon, Foster, Cooke. Other placemen, such as the Ponsonbys, who had ties with the English whigs, acquiesced more or less reluctantly in the situation; Sheridan, the under-secretary for war who owed his appointment to Portland, explaining to his brother Charles Brinsley, the whig leader, that the circumstances of the two countries were so different that it would be absurd to extend British party distinctions to Ireland. He had the grace to add 'you will say this is a good plan for people in place. . . . But I give you my word it is not my reason for thinking as I do'.[51]

Pitt, when he turned his mind to Ireland, brought to bear on

[49] Kenmare to B. Roche, 30 Sept. 1784; Kenmare to ——, 23 Oct. 1784 (P.R.O. 30/8/328).
[50] *V.J.*, 28 June 1784.
[51] T. Moore, *Memoirs of the life of . . . Richard Brinsley Sheridan*, i, pp. 409–11.

its problems a powerful political intellect, capable of effectively combining a mastery of broad principle with a grasp of detail, and in the summer of 1784 he rapidly formulated a coherent Irish policy—the resumption by the Irish government of complete control over all military forces in the country; the conciliation of 'a moderate, respectable' section of Irish opinion by 'a prudent and temperate reform' of parliament (with the franchise restricted to protestants) and a generous settlement on a permanent basis of Anglo-Irish commercial relations. He pointed out to the Irish administration, which was bracing itself to resist parliamentary reform, that if, as was probable, a reform bill was carried in England, 'the tide would be too strong to be withstood in Ireland'. Moreover once reform was granted in Ireland, 'the arms will then drop out of the hands of the volunteers' and it would be possible to replace them by a militia under government control.[52]

Pitt's attitude to parliamentary reform in Ireland startled the the new lord lieutenant, the duke of Rutland and his chief secretary, Thomas Orde. Rutland was a near contemporary and fervent admirer of the prime minister—'I can never', he wrote, 'have a thought or view in politics separate or distinct from his interests and fortunes.' Handsome, well-read, dashing and convivial, he shared with the chief secretary an interest in art, Rutland being a discriminating collector and Orde an accomplished caricaturist. Orde, who had been for some years an M.P., was industrious and capable of conceiving large-scale solutions for Irish problems, though time, ill health and lack of drive—Pitt remarked that Orde's temper was 'not decisive'— prevented him realizing his intentions. Orde himself admitted that he was 'liable to great agitation', and both he and Rutland were convinced that they were facing in Ireland a dangerous political crisis, perhaps even impending revolt.[53] They were profoundly disturbed by the reform agitation together with the continuing activities of the volunteers, by rumours of catholic disaffection, French intrigue and rioting in Dublin,

---

[52] *Correspondence between . . . William Pitt and Charles duke of Rutland* (1890), pp. 77, 81.

[53] *Rutland MSS H.M.C.*, iii, p. 321; *Country life*, cxx, p. 1501; *Correspondence between . . . William Pitt and Charles duke of Rutland*, p. 126; T. Orde to W. Pitt, 20 Apr. 1785 (P.R.O. 30/8/328).

'the cry of the mob and the factious spirit of the Dublin news-paper press'.[54] Though the volunteers, with Ireland no longer at war, were declining, they still in 1784 numbered about 18,500 effectives and some corps were showing signs of political radicalism.[55] The Ulster regiment, the Belfast volunteer corps, the Dublin Independents, the Liberty corps, a County Longford corps and the Newry corps announced that catholics would be admitted to their ranks. The Belfast corps invited residents in the town to attend drills without purchasing a uniform and the Dublin Liberty corps decided that weekly drills should be held at which 'the sons of freedom' who attended would be instructed in the use of arms free of expense—a decision which, according to the lord lieutenant greatly annoyed the old established Dublin corps, 'who pictured themselves as being gentlemen in manner and appearance'.[56]

Orde believed that there was a great conspiracy on foot to overthrow the existing order and break the British connection, directed by 'needy, disappointed villains', the leaders of the protectionist agitation and the reform movement, who were hoping for French assistance, and he also saw an alliance being formed between the northern dissenters and the catholics, the priests in the south being active in spreading discontent.

Naturally anxious to discover the plans of the conspirators, Orde during the summer of 1784 pressed the British government to secure information about French naval and military depo-sitions; an expert in London roguery was brought over ap-parently to ferret out information in the manufacturing areas of Dublin, and Orde was in touch with some potential in-formants including 'a naturalised foreign merchant' in Dublin, the eloquent capuchin preacher, Arthur O'Leary, and a con-servative newspaper editor, Francis Higgins. Higgins produced a young gentleman from Trinity college who claimed to have heard a well-known radical saying in a tavern that negotiations with France were being conducted by the bishop of Derry and who believed that Carey of the *Volunteer Journal* was receiving French money.[57]

---

[54] T. Orde to ——, 24 Apr. 1784 (H.O. 100/12).

[55] For the strength of the volunteers see Orde papers 15891 (3).

[56] *V.J.*, 30 Apr., 5, 24, 28 May 1784; *D.E.P.*, 29 Apr., 29 June 1784; Rutland to Sydney, 19 May 1784 (H.O. 100/13).

[57] T. Orde to W. Pitt, 16, 18, 24, 25, 26, 31 Aug. 1784 (P.R.O. 30/8/328); T.

The information which the Irish administration managed to secure relating to seditious activity was insubstantial and unsubstantiated. This is scarcely surprising. The Irish radicals, though they may have indulged in reckless talk, were essentially law-respecting and law-abiding, as can be seen from the letters of a few well-known reformers, intercepted and copied when in the post. But Rutland and Orde were clearly over-impressed and deeply disturbed by what was to conventional politicians a novel and frightening phenomenon, an organized and strident popular agitation for major objectives. Believing Irish politics, and indeed Irish society, to be in a highly unstable condition, they naturally considered that for the Irish administration to take up the question of parliamentary reform would be 'little less than lunacy'. The lord lieutenant forcefully pointed out to Pitt that a reform confined to protestants would leave the catholics dangerously discontented, and 'if you admit the catholics to vote your next parliament will be composed of papists'. Though he frankly admitted that the Irish parliamentary system did not bear the smallest resemblance to representation, Rutland did not see 'how quiet and good government could exist under any more popular mode'. Orde, stressing the interests involved, the catholics, the protestant dissenters, the supporters of the government, asked rhetorically 'what can prevent confusion, what can preserve a unity of government but to do nothing?'[58] Slowly Pitt gave in to his Irish advisers. When in November 1784 Orde visiting England strove to convince the prime minister of 'the impracticability' of an Irish reform bill, 'he met with nothing unexpected in his partial adherence to his original ideas and his delicacy on the point of consistency'.[59] But early in 1785 Pitt was defeated on the reform question at Westminster and by the close of 1784, when considering Ireland, was more and more concentrating on economic issues.

During 1784 he was successful in persuading his worried Irish colleagues not to take precipitant action against the reformers, and he discouraged a suggestion that the bishop of

Orde to ——, 23 Sept. 1784 (H.O. 100/14); Rutland to Sydney, 21 Aug. 1784 (H.O. 100/14).

[58] *Rutland MSS H.M.C.*, iii, p. 148; *Correspondence between . . . William Pitt and Charles duke of Rutland*, p. 16; T. Orde to W. Pitt, 16 Aug. 1784 (P.R.O. 30/8/328).

[59] *Rutland MSS H.M.C.*, iii, p. 157.

Derry, who had been issuing a series of vehement pronounce-
ments attacking the house of commons, and hinting at forcible
action, should be prosecuted.[60] Pitt also reminded the Irish
administration that a distinction must be drawn between assemblies which attempted to usurp the place of parliament and
meetings 'to concert legal measures'. In spite of Pitt's warning
the Irish administration appears to have contemplated preventing the reform congress being held because it tried to secure
the opinion of the judges as to the legality of such a gathering.
Earlsfort, the chief justice of the king's bench, who as attorney-
general had been a sturdy upholder of the executive power,
refused to help. He said the question was a matter for the law
officers. In Earlsfort's opinion the reformers were 'such a
mangled, misshapen mass that if they meet they will grow
ridiculous and nothing will make them formidable than
treating them as if they were so'.[61] But Fitzgibbon, the attorney-
general, could not resist the temptation of attempting to deflate
the self-importance of the Dublin reform leaders by a legal
stroke. The committee appointed by the aggregate meeting to
prepare for a congress had written to the high sheriffs requesting
them to call county meetings to elect delegates.[62] When the
sheriffs for the city of Dublin summoned such a meeting,
Fitzgibbon wrote telling them that if they held it he would
prosecute them for a breach of duty. He reinforced his letter by
arriving at the meeting backed by a number of conservatives,
including a phalanx of government clerks and revenue officers.
The sheriffs (in Tandy's opinion 'a pair of poltroons') overawed,
quickly adjourned the meeting and withdrew.[63] A few days later
an unofficial gathering of citizens in the Weavers' hall, with
Sir Edward Newenham (prepared for legal martyrdom) in the
chair, elected delegates and a meeting in County Roscommon,
directed that the attorney-general's letter to the sheriff be
burned by the hangman. Fitzgibbon, who Newenham thought

---

[60] The letter on which the Irish administration wished to ground a prosecution
was probably the one in which the bishop wrote of a long-suffering nation striking
like lightning a 'rapacious oligarchy' which imposed laws 'subversive of liberty'
and taxes contrary to the will of the people (*B.N.L.*, 20 July 1784; *Later correspondence
of George III*, ed. A. Aspinall, i, p. 75).

[61] T. Orde to W. Pitt, 4 Oct. 1784 (P.R.O. 30/8/328), Earlsfort to ——, 4 Oct.
1784 (P.R.O. 30/8/327).

[62] *D.J.*, 2 Sept. 1784.

[63] Napper Tandy to G. Tandy, 2 Oct. 1784 (P.R.O. 30/8/330).

had 'all the low arts and cunning but not the judgement of Loyola', prosecuted the gentleman who had conducted the Roscommon meeting and Stevens Reilly, the sheriff for County Dublin, who had held a county meeting to elect delegates. The former prosecution failed on a technicality; and Reilly was sentenced by the court of king's bench to a week's imprisonment and a fine of five marks.[64]

Some high sheriffs agreed to hold county meetings to elect delegates; others said they were willing to do so if approached by the freeholders of their county; a few declined to take action and the high sheriff of Queen's County, Henry Moore, sent a letter to the committee which it returned, being unable to believe it could have come from a gentleman. In Limerick, Louth, Meath, and Wexford county meetings and in Counties Cork, Down, Kerry, Kilkenny and Monaghan the grand juries approved of their high sheriff's refusal to call a meeting to elect delegates to the congress. In Counties Cork, Kerry and Limerick large numbers of freeholders agreed with the grand jury. Over two hundred County Dublin freeholders published an address declaring that a county meeting was acting *ultra vires* in sending delegates to another assembly. In Dublin city about 1,100 freemen and freeholders signed an address to the king expressing their abhorrence of attempts to create discontent. In Antrim the grand jury, though it approved of reform, disapproved of the congress.[65] In the city of Londonderry where reformers were sneered at as 'Nappers', a hundred citizens subscribed to a declaration stating that they were 'perfectly contented with our present happy constitution' and that the city delegates to the congress had been elected at a very small meeting.[66] Even Trinity undergraduates at this time inclined towards conservatism. At a meeting held to decide whether delegates should be elected to the congress it was resolved by 108 votes to 40 that 'the students of the university possess collectively no power to decide on political questions'.[67]

[64] E. Newenham to B. Franklin, 9, 12 Oct. 1784 (P.R.O. 30/8/328); *D.E.P.*, 30 Sept., 12 Oct. 1784.
[65] *D.E.P.*, 29 July, 30 Sept., 9, 20, 30, Nov. 1784; *D.J.*, 26 Aug., 4, 9, 16, 25 Sept. 1784; *D.E.P.*, 17 Aug., 20 Oct. 1784; *V.E.P.*, 24 Aug. 1784; *B.N.L.*, 27 Aug., 3 Sept. 1784.
[66] *H.J.*, 21 Jan. 1785; R. Black to W. Bruce, 6 Sept. 1784 (P.R.O. 30/8/329).
[67] *D.E.P.*, 11 May, 26 Oct. 1784.

After the excitement it aroused, liberal hopes and conservative alarm, the meeting of the reform congress proved to be an anti-climax. According to a list published in the liberal press by the beginning of 1785, 27 counties and 13 urban centres were represented by 165 delegates. Over 40 of the delegates failed to make an attendance, three of them declining to serve, and in an important division only 51 are recorded as voting.[68] Amongst the non-attendants was the bishop of Derry. He had not been well and he wanted the congress to postpone meeting 'until we can see how my friend Mr Pitt fulfils his engagements' and then to meet at some place, such as Athlone, 'removed from Castle influence'.[69] The delegates included not only the bishop but two other peers, four baronets, twenty-eight M.P.s and a number of well-established country gentlemen. Their proceedings were decorous and dull. At the outset several delegates rose to say that they disapproved of holding a congress, since 'they relied upon the professions of the English ministry, the wisdom of the Irish parliament and the justice of our cause'. The congress spent its time working over a plan of reform which did not differ essentially from that sanctioned by the volunteer convention, as might be expected, when it is taken into account that Flood played an active part in the congress. The congress also issued an address to the people, which expressed the hope that king and parliament would gratify the wishes of a loyal country. 'Time', the address declared, 'will lead us to success', and the Irish public was exhorted 'to keep alive the spirit but let prudence regulate the spirit of your zeal'.[70]

These proceedings irritated two forward-looking young Ulster delegates, Hamilton Rowan and Todd Jones, who both expressed their dissatisfaction with the congress in letters to the press. Archibald Hamilton Rowan, the well-off heir to a County Down estate, had returned to Ireland in 1784 after ten years of wide travel and enjoyment of fashionable life. At Cambridge he had been a pupil of Jebb, the academic and political reformer. Jebb failed to make Hamilton work but he corresponded with him after he left the university and influenced him politically.

---

[68] *D.J.*, 12 Feb. 1785; *H.J.*, 11 Feb. 1785.
[69] Bishop of Derry to G. Fitzgerald, 4 Oct. 1784, to C. Lyster, 14 Oct. 1784 (P.R.O. 30/8/329).
[70] *D.E.P.*, 5 Mar. 1785.

At the reform congress Rowan was disappointed to discover that a majority of the delegates were not in favour of his 'three great objects', exclusion from the house of commons of all place-holders and pensioners, disfranchisement of the depopulated boroughs and the ballot, which 'would exempt the tenant from the too frequent tyranny of the landlord'. Jones, who supported these three measures together with annual parliaments and catholic enfranchisement, had so despaired of the congress that he put off going up to Dublin and gave a great ball (which he could ill afford) for his constituents. When he did enter the congress he found most of the delegates decidedly against catholic enfranchisement and he thought the address to the people 'too vague and general to appear as the sole product of an assembly which had sat too long'.[71]

To the exasperation of enthusiastic reformers it was clear that by 1785 the movement had lost the impetus it had possessed a few years earlier. Reformers were divided on the catholic question and were bound to be dispirited by their lack of success. 'Liberal and enlightened men', a Londonderry reformer wrote, 'are worn out with fruitless efforts to drag the mass of the people after them'.[72] The public-spirited country gentlemen, the readily accepted leaders of local liberalism, certainly considered parliamentary reform to be a political desideratum but they did not feel that the country's well-being depended on its immediate enactment. To a country gentleman or successful businessman life at this time offered many advantages, even with parliament unreformed. Grattan, the quintessence of a liberal country gentleman, when he was advocating parliamentary reform in 1784, declared that with all its defects the constitution was 'the best in the world' and he emphasized his determination to say nothing that would undermine the authority of a house of commons which he compared in flattering terms to the barons of Runnymede. It is understandable then why the reform cause did not command that degree of sustained enthusiasm required to overcome opponents, well entrenched in the legislature and buoyed up by

---

[71] *B.N.L.*, 22, 25 Feb. 1785. Jones's opinion that the majority of the delegates were averse to catholic emancipation was confirmed by another northern liberal (H. Joy to R. Joy, 24 Oct. 1784; 24 Oct. 1784, P.R.O. 30/8/328).

[72] R. Black to W. Bruce, 6 Sept. 1784 (P.R.O. 30/8/329).

self-interest, prejudice and a reasoned belief in the merits of the existing system.

It is noticeable that at first even strong supporters of reform gave comparatively little attention to the problem of how their objective was to be attained. Convinced their cause was reasonable and just, they were confident that parliament could be easily enough persuaded or shamed into accepting a reform of the representative system. Then, when the strength of unyielding conservatism became apparent, various methods for overcoming the obduracy of parliament were suggested. The king might be persuaded to set on foot an investigation into borough charters; there could be a general strike against taxation; or the counties might direct their M.P.s to secede from parliament. If the county members withdrew from the house of commons, the government would be left with 'a terrible shadow, an unreal mockery of representation'; if on the other hand the county M.P.s defied their constituents' instructions it would be clear that Ireland was a corrupt borough.[73] There was also an ingenious scheme to destroy parliamentary corruption by the use of up-to-date business techniques. A joint stock company, it was suggested, could be formed to purchase pocket boroughs, the stock-holders then selecting the M.P.s for the boroughs acquired by the company.[74] Above all, reformers hoped the volunteers would support parliamentary reform with decisive effect. But the volunteer movement had never worked out how and in what circumstances it should intervene in politics. Admittedly British political orthodoxy acknowledged the right of revolution— though it was taken for granted that after the glorious year 1688 it was highly unlikely to be exercised. Phrases were freely used which hinted at direct action. For instance it was pointed out that arms in the hands of citizens would 'facilitate' reform; 'some rhetorical flourishes of a firelock', it was said, would 'point the periods' of a patriotic orator; and the volunteers were told that 'the energy and perseverance which liberated this high minded nation from a foreign yoke will trample a domestic one under its feet'. But the volunteers were loyal,

---

[73] D.E.P., 12 Feb. 1784; V.J., 5 Apr., 21 May 1784; B.N.L., 20 May 1785, W. Drennan to Mrs McTier. [c. 1783] (Drennan papers, 58).
[74] An address to the people of England and Ireland (1783).

law-abiding men, who, as an official volunteer statement expressed it, had helped to win Irish constitutional freedom by their 'dignified conduct'.[75] Their presence and prestige, it was felt, were of value to any cause they espoused, but their leaders seem to have had no conception of what they should do if they failed to overawe.

[75] *An address to the volunteers of Ireland* (1781), pp. 11–14; *Letter from the committee of the Ulster volunteers to the duke of Richmond* (1783), p. 11; W. W. Steward, *The rights of the people asserted* (1783), p. 51; *D.E.P.*, 6 June 1783; *B.N.L.*, 6 Jan. 1784.

8

Pitt and Ireland

Pitt when he became prime minister was deeply conscious that Britain's 'power and pre-eminence' was in eclipse, and was calmly confident that it was his responsibility—it might be said his hereditary responsibility—'to unite and correct what yet remains of our reduced and shattered empire'. Though a realist, he was not content to be simply a pragmatist. Unlike many contemporary politicians he did not restrict himself to keeping the administrative machine functioning and meeting problems as they presented themselves. He was not 'one of those who thought that if a session passed without anything material being done, it was a circumstance of pleasure and self-congratulation'.[1] Rather, he was prepared to survey the whole field, isolate major issues, and attempt to cope with them by well-planned, comprehensive measures. By the close of 1784, he was immersed in the preparation of a grand design which, he believed, would dispose of a number of issues likely to breed contention between Great Britain and Ireland, promote the prosperity of both nations and strengthen the empire.

When the old imperial system was collapsing at the close of the seventies, Lord North's ministry had attempted to readjust Anglo-Irish commercial relations by hastily improvised legislation, covering a limited range of issues. It was hoped that mutual goodwill and co-operation between the British and Irish administrations would settle the many conflicts of interest in the economic sphere bound to arise between the two countries. But within a few months of the Irish parliament expressing its gratitude for the commercial concessions of 1780 the difficulty of ensuring economic harmony between Great Britain and Ireland was vividly illustrated by measures relating to two important commodities, sugar and linen. Protectionists within and without parliament called for a duty on British refined sugar

[1] *Parliamentary history*, xxiii, pp. 549, 823; xxv, pp. 584, 587.

imported into Ireland, arguing that the expansion of Irish trade with the West Indies depended on the development of the Irish sugar-refining industry. The Irish administration recommended a duty of 5s. 10d. per hundredweight. La Touche suggested 16s. 7d. and the house of commons decided on 12 shillings. When the heads of the sugar bill arrived in London they were carefully considered by a committee of the board of trade. This committee was averse to establishing a precedent 'for gradually shutting up between the two kingdoms every branch of manufacture wherein there might be supposed to exist a competition' and favoured fixing the duty at a level which would both encourage the Irish refiner and permit the British refiner to retain a small share in the Irish market. Taking into account a number of factors, including the cost of raw material in Great Britain and Ireland, the effect of the English drawback on refined sugar exported, and the amount of raw sugar required to make a given quantity of refined (a much disputed matter) the board of trade decided on a duty of 9s. 2d.[2] The Irish house of commons accepted this figure, a decision which aroused much public indignation, the Dublin merchants corps declaring it was 'an overthrow of the refinery of this kingdom'. In November 1781, when the Irish administration recommended an increase in the duty on refined sugar to counter an increase in the English drawback, both Flood and Grattan unsuccessfully demanded complete protection for 'an infant and trembling manufacture'. Fitzgibbon remarked that they must protect the consumer—the sugar refiners were 'affluent'—and the attorney-general argued that the English share of the Irish refined sugar market had fallen and that it was undesirable to give a complete monopoly to the Irish refiners.[3] In the event the government prevailed and the issue lapsed.

In the summer of 1780, when sugar seemed likely to sour Anglo-Irish relations, the board of trade had to report on the heads of a controversial bill granting bounties on Irish linen exported to the American and African colonies and parts of

---

[2] Minutes of board of trade committee, 4 July 1780 (C.O./389/41). The membership of the committee included the earl of Carlisle, William Eden and Edward Gibbon.

[3] *Hibernian Magazine*, 1781, pp. 605–7; *Parl. Reg. Ire.*, i, pp. 84, 87, 95.

Europe. These bounties, a committee of the board of trade reported, were slightly higher than those on linen exported from Great Britain and seemed designed to encourage Irish competition with Great Britain in overseas markets with detrimental effects to the British export trade and British shipping, at a time when Ireland enjoyed 'a solid and permanent position in the British market for her linens'; a preference which incidentally militated against British woollen goods getting into certain continental markets. Great Britain could retaliate by lowering the duties on foreign linen and the committee regretted that Ireland should be embarking on 'an experiment tending to interrupt and hazard a great branch of commercial intercourse between the two countries'. However, it pointed out that in the immediate future Irish exporters would not be able to give long credit or send out 'full and well assorted cargoes', containing for instance metal and woollen goods.[4] So taking everything into account the bill was permitted to pass.

But far wider and potentially more contentious issues remained unsettled. For instance, according to the official interpretation of the navigation acts, colonial products could be exported from Great Britain to Ireland but not from Ireland to Great Britain. Not unexpectedly, it was suggested by Irishmen that a correct interpretation of the acts placed both countries in this respect on an equal footing. The question tended to be a rather academic one. Irish merchants were unlikely to export colonial products on a large scale to Great Britain, though, as Pitt was to point out, it might on occasion be advantageous to an Irish merchant with a surplus on his hands to be able to enter the British market. What was significant was that the official interpretation of the acts treated Ireland as an inferior country. Another question liable to embitter relations was East Indian trade. Ireland in practice preserved the East India company's monopoly by 'the clause in the revenue bill', but there was always the possibility that the company's rights might be challenged as being held under an English charter. The highly favoured position of Irish linen in the British market and the advantages enjoyed by Irishmen trading with British colonies both depended on British legislation,

[4] Report of the committee of board of trade, 17 July 1780 (C.O. 389/35).

which of course might be altered or repealed (however strongly Grattan and Flood might assert that Ireland participated in the colonial trade not by favour but by right). British import duties on Irish manufactures were generally considerably higher than the equivalent Irish duties on British imports.[5] Given British industrial superiority, this could not greatly affect Irish imports to Great Britain but 'the inequality of duties' was to Irishmen 'a badge of slavery'.[6] There was too, as has been seen, the possibility that Ireland might embark vigorously on a policy of industrial protection, and start a tariff war with Great Britain which would 'necessarily tend to separate each country farther from the other'.[7]

When he examined Anglo-Irish economic relations, Pitt was undaunted by complexities and controversy. He was sure that up-to-date economic thinking would provide an intelligent and fruitful solution to the question. 'The commercial points of discussion though numerous and comprehensive may certainly', he wrote, 'be ascertained and reduced to clear principles by diligent investigation.'[8] Pitt was profoundly impressed by the logical strength and lucid common sense of the theories associated with Adam Smith (*The wealth of nations* appeared when he was up at Cambridge), and he was exhilarated to see how a practical problem of considerable magnitude could be easily solved by the application of sound economic principles. His aim was basically simple and sweeping; the creation of a common market for the whole British Isles. But he had to take into account that two elaborate tariff systems were in operation. The abolition of all customs duties on trade between Great Britain and Ireland, would, the board of trade pronounced, 'occasion the ruin of many of Your Majesty's subjects and introduce an immediate convulsion into the commerce of the two kingdoms'.[9] Nevertheless the scheme which Pitt drafted at the close of 1784, with the assistance of two Irish economic experts, Beresford and Foster, went a long way towards realizing his ultimate objective.

[5] *Correspondence between . . . William Pitt and Charles duke of Rutland*, pp. 57–65.
[6] Clare to T. Orde, 19 Apr. 1784 (P.R.O. 30/8/329).
[7] *Commons' Jn. Ire.*, xi, p. ccclii.
[8] *Correspondence between . . . William Pitt and Charles duke of Rutland*, p. 42.
[9] *Commons' Jn. Ire.*, xi, p. ccclii.

Pitt's plan, embodied in ten propositions, provided that no additional duties should be imposed on the products of Great Britain and Ireland when imported from one country into the other, and where the British and Irish duties on an article, the product of either country, differed, the higher duty was to be reduced to the lower level—though if there was a duty on an article in one country, a countervailing duty should be imposed on its import from the other. Foreign and colonial produce was to pass freely between the two countries, no bounties were to be paid on articles exported from the one country to the other and no new prohibitions were to be imposed on the export of raw material from one country to the other. Finally, Ireland was to make a contribution to imperial defence, it being provided that whenever the hereditary revenue exceeded £654,000 the surplus was to be apportioned to the support of the navy.

A convinced free trader, Pitt believed that intensified competition would encourage every zone in the British Isles to make the most profitable use of its resources, and that Ireland, with a guaranteed access to the British colonial market and the expanding home market, was especially bound to benefit. Indeed, he was prepared to accept that in some branches of industry Ireland might in time successfully rival Great Britain. 'But this', he told the house of commons, 'ought not to give us pain, we must calculate from general not partial views.' He would, of course, have said the same, *mutatis mutandis*, in Dublin, displaying an inherent readiness to take a broad, unprejudiced view of the whole field—or, as his critics would say, revealing an aloof disregard for the emotions and concerns of ordinary humanity. To the argument that each country would resent the loss important economic interests might sustain when exposed to brisk competition, Pitt had a ready answer—Great Britain and Ireland must for the future see themselves as 'one country in effect though for local concerns under distinct legislatures'. 'The wealth and prosperity of the whole is the object', he wrote, 'from what local sources they come is indifferent.' If it had been pointed out to him that each legislature would probably develop its own national or regional economic policy, Pitt could have optimistically explained that the growing influence of *laissez-faire* principles would provide a salutary check on government intervention in the economic sphere. Alternatively he would have been driven to accept that the management of a unified economy called for a single sovereign legislature.[10]

Rutland was most favourably impressed by the plan, except for one feature, which he did not believe to be essential—the contribution towards imperial defence. It was, he agreed, equitable, but impolitic and ill-timed, certain to suggest to Irishmen that the aim of the scheme was to lessen Great Britain's financial burdens. A senior Irish official, Sackville Hamilton, agreed with Rutland. Though Pitt's plan in general, Hamilton declared, was so comprehensive, liberal and so free from 'all intolerance, bigotry and enthusiasm in trade' that he could only compare it with the established church, the imperial contribution would destroy all the grace of the concessions. Grattan who supported the plan in general thought if the proposal for an imperial contribution was included, it would be defeated by 'the violent resentment of an exasperated people', and Orde warned Pitt that though he might imagine the arguments Grattan would employ he could not conceive 'the peculiar force his peculiar manner would give them among a peculiar people'.[11] But Pitt and the British cabinet were obdurate on this point. Pitt strongly believed that a country admitted to a permanent partnership in a great economic empire should accept a permanent obligation to share in its defence, and the form of grant proposed enabled Ireland to contribute 'in proportion to her growing means'. The Irish administration desperately looked round for a method of making the contribution palatable to Irish opinion. It suggested that the contribution should be spent in Ireland on the purchase of naval stores or that it should be used to provide ships for Irish coastal defence. The British government was prepared to consider the former proposal, the latter they rejected out of hand. The navy, the home secretary wrote, 'must be employed under the executive power of the empire for the protection of the commercial interests which are common to both kingdoms', or as Burke more eloquently put it, 'the great trident that was to move the world must be grasped by England alone'.[12]

[10] *Correspondence between . . . William Pitt and Charles duke of Rutland*, pp. 58, 63, 66; *Parliamentary history*, xxv, 324.

[11] S. Hamilton to ——, 22 Dec. 1784 (Orde papers, N.L.I.); *Rutland MSS H.M.C.*, iii, p. 179; T. Orde to W. Pitt, 12 Feb. 1785 (P.R.O. 30/8/329).

[12] *Parliamentary history*, xxv, p. 649.

On 7 February Orde, asking M.P.s 'to enter the temple of commerce and concord', outlined the propositions to the Irish house of commons. He had barely finished, when Brownlow impetuously (he afterwards admitted too impetuously) sprang up and asked was Ireland to become a tributary nation. During the next few days the law officers worked out a compromise—the contribution would be annually paid in peacetime whenever the Irish revenue equalled expenditure and in wartime without reference to the general financial situation. To meet an obvious British objection to this proposal they added that they believed that the taxes necessary to balance the Irish budget would be voted. Within an hour of the house of commons going into committee on the propositions, Rutland and Orde agreed to a compromise which the British cabinet reluctantly accepted though it was afraid it rendered the contribution 'precarious'. The house of commons welcomed the propositions, increased to eleven by the new arrangement for the defence contribution. A few M.P.s, including Flood, were reluctant to surrender the power to protect Irish manufactures by high tariffs but Grattan declared the scheme to be 'open, fair and just', it was approved by 109 to 0, and shortly afterwards the taxes which it was hoped would balance the Irish budget were voted.[13]

Though things had gone remarkably smoothly in Ireland, Pitt was well aware that he faced a severe struggle in England. In parliament there was an energetic opposition, 'an inindefatigable enemy, sharpened by disappointment',[14] in the country a number of important economic interests saw themselves menaced by the proposed concessions to Ireland. British industry might be powerful and expanding, but British businessmen were conscious they were living in a competitive world. They apparently believed that the margins on which their supremacy depended might suddenly diminish, they were quick to voice their apprehensions and they were certainly determined to use every advantage they possessed. At the beginning of 1785 a commercial committee assembled at Birmingham was disturbed to observe 'a spirit of rivalry and

<hr/>

[13] *Parl. Reg. Ire.*, iv, pp. 131, 139, 143, 207; *Rutland MSS H.M.C.*, iii, pp. 182, 188. The tellers were Lawrence Parsons and Alexander Montgomery.
[14] *Correspondence between . . . William Pitt and Charles duke of Rutland*, p. 105.

supplanting of our manufactures is now operating in various parts of Europe to a degree truely alarming', and shortly afterwards two industrialists from the Midlands, Wedgwood and Boulton played a prominent part in establishing the General chamber of manufacturers, meeting in London, which helped to mobilize opposition to Pitt's Irish plan. By the middle of May 1785 about sixty petitions against the plan had been presented to the house of commons. One very influential group, the West Indian planters, preferred not to petition. Instead they approached the prime minister directly and about the middle of March accepted as satisfactory, by 82 votes to 31, his response to their deputation (he had presumably informed them of his intention to insert an amendment into the propositions protecting their interests).[15]

The apprehensions of the British business community were brought to the attention of parliamentary committees by nearly fifty witnesses. It was asserted that the propositions constituted a serious threat to British trade and industry. If the existing duties were abolished or reduced, Irish manufacturers, who had undoubted advantages—lower living costs, cheap labour, abundant raw materials, cheap coal (either locally mined or easily imported from England), light taxation and no poor rates, would be able to undersell the British manufacturer in his home market and soon compete with him successfully abroad.[16] Robert Peel, the great cotton manufacturer, explained that a saving of 1 per cent was sufficient to draw an industry from one part of the empire to another and he was certain that if Irish printed cottons could come into England under the terms proposed by Pitt, 'the English manufacturer will have no alternative but either to quit his business or remove his capital to Ireland'.[17] Wedgwood, the great pottery manufacturer, also expressed similar views with melodramatic force. If English import duties on Irish manufacturers were lowered, 'from that moment we may date the decline of British manufactures', Great Britain's 'cork jackets', which kept the

---

[15] *Birmingham Gazette*, 7 Feb., 14 Mar. 1785; *Morning Chronicle*, 9, 15, 16 Mar. 1785; *Morning Herald*, 24 Mar. 1785; *London Chronicle*, 17 Mar. 1785; *General Advertizer*, 17 Mar. 1785.

[16] For the evidence given before committees of the British privy council, lords and commons see *Commons' Jn. Ire.*, xi, pp. ccccxxxv–dcccii.

[17] *D.E.P.*, 19 Feb. 1785.

country afloat.[18] Wedgwood shared with a number of other manufacturers the fear there would be a drain of skilled men, who would emigrate to Ireland carrying British trade secrets, and he thought it not unlikely that the Irish parliament would conduct economic warfare in what would later be called the Napoleonic fashion, concentrating for a period all the funds it was prepared to grant in bounties on a single industry, so enabling it to undercut its British rival.

There was, too, the possibility that trade might be diverted from British to Irish ports, and, more likely, that Ireland might become a great depot from which foreign goods would be smuggled into Great Britain. There were only a few points in Ireland, North pointed out, at which the revenue laws were strictly enforced. It may be added that during the debates on the propositions North reiterated the opinion he had expressed in the past, that Great Britain should grant every economic advantage to Ireland, if the two countries were 'perfectly united under one parliament', an approach also favoured by the General committee of manufacturers and by Wedgwood.[19]

The vast assemblage of practical detail which the experienced representatives of British business produced in support of their case tended to obscure two important points. Except perhaps for the leather manufactures, there was no recent instance in which an Irish industry had begun to compete successfully with a British; and their doom-ladened projections were based on a series of pessimistic hypotheses which attributed every advantage in the greatest measure to Ireland and every disadvantage in a corresponding degree to themselves. In the light of history their fears appear ludicrous. But they were genuine, and to conciliate British opinion Pitt made concessions or changes which extend the propositions from the eleven approved by the Irish parliament to twenty. There was a procedural defence for making modifications to the plan as originally proposed. Theoretically the Irish parliament had stated what it wanted and the British parliament was enunciating what it was prepared to give. But, accepting that the ten propositions was entirely the prime minister's own work, it could be argued that the additions made at Westminster were

---

[18] *A selection of letters of Josiah Wedgwood* (1965), p. 286.
[19] *Parliamentary history*, xxv, p. 633; and *Birmingham Gazette*, 7, 13 June 1785.

inserted for the purpose of clarification and were in accordance
with the broad principles of the original propositions. The
additional propositions and clauses protected the privileges
of the East India company, patent rights and copyright;
proposed that no drawbacks should be given on the export of
foreign spirits from Ireland to Great Britain, and that steps
should be taken to prevent the fraudulent export of foreign
produce through Ireland into Great Britain; suggested that
steps should be taken to prevent fishery disputes between the
two countries; declared that the collection of the hereditary
revenue should be permanently secured; and, in what became
the fourth proposition, laid down that all legislation relating
to shipping and colonial trade passed by the British parliament,
imposing restraints or conferring benefits on the subjects of
both kingdoms, should be re-enacted by the Irish parliament.
Uniform legislation on these matters was essential if the two
countries were to form an economic unit, and either a procedure
for permitting formal consultation in advance of joint action
had to be devised or the initiative left to the country more
closely concerned. The latter was certainly the easier, if in the
long term, the less satisfactory, course to take, and when the
fourth proposition had taken shape the opposition was quick
to assert that in an insidious way it revived the British claim to
legislate for Ireland. Sheridan in a glowing speech (which it
was said influenced Grattan) denounced 'tacking' a surrender
of Irish independence on to a commercial bill and Fox summed
up the propositions as a commutation of English commerce for
Irish slavery.[20]

This set the tone for the reception of the revised propositions
by the Irish house of commons. The Irish parliament, had, with
adjournments, remained in session until the British houses
concluded their debates (much to the annoyance of some M.P.s
who were dragged back from the country in high summer) and
on 12 August Orde introduced a bill based on the twenty
propositions. Grattan, in a speech pulsating with energetic
anger, having emphasized that Ireland had long been the victim
of British commercial jealously, implored the house not to
surrender the substance of a constitution for the shadow of a

[20] *Parliamentary history*, xxvii, 299, 451; *Journals and correspondence of Lord Auckland*,
i p. 79.

market. The fourth proposition was inspired by 'the remnant' of the North ministry, which 'had but one idea with respect to Great Britain, Ireland and America—coercion', and the scheme as a whole 'embodied a union, an incipient and creeping union, establishing one will in the general concerns of commerce and navigation, and reposing that will in the parliament of Great Britain'. The Irish parliament, Grattan declared, should exercise its powers 'for Ireland, with due regard for the British nation; let them be governed by a spirit of concord and with fidelity to the connection'. Flood, having shown that the plan was unfair to Ireland, implied that any trade agreement between the two countries was unlikely—'nothing that is subtle and intricate can ever be the foundation of settlement and concord'. Though government supporters urged Pitt's argument, that any treaty involved a limitation on sovereignty and that a procedure by which Ireland could denounce the agreement was provided in the bill, the fourth proposition proved a stumbling-block to many M.P.s and after a debate which lasted until 9 o'clock the following morning, the first reading of the bill was carried by only 127 to 108—tantamount to a government defeat.

It was the fourth of the twenty propositions which seems to have aroused the country—in so far as it was stirred. When the propositions were introduced in February only two petitions against them (both from groups in Dublin) were presented to the Irish house of commons but after the twenty propositions emerged from Westminster twenty-six hostile petitions including four from groups in Dublin were presented; and in these, though the economic aspects of Pitt's plan were mentioned, it was the constitutional issue which was emphasized—the propositions being denounced as 'highly insulting to the dignity of this free nation'. But only eight counties presented petitions, and when a Belfast town meeting dominated by the local liberals called on the freeholders of Ireland to display their opposition to the propositions by electing delegates to provincial assemblies, there was no response.[21]

Pitt was distressed that 'prejudice and party' should have made 'so many proselytes' in Ireland against the true interest of the country, although, ever resilient, he thought at first that the ques-

[21] B.N.L., 12 Aug. 1785.

tion might be raised again in the Irish parliamentary session of 1786. But shortly afterwards he decided the best approach to a settlement would be by 'urging separate questions on distinct points—construction of the navigation act, protecting duties and India trade'. During the session of 1787 the Irish parliament without much debate confirmed the official interpretation of the navigation laws when re-enacting British legislation on shipping and in 1793 the East India company's charter was confirmed by an Irish act. The act laid down that the company should provide 800 tons of shipping yearly for the purpose of carrying from Cork goods which might lawfully be exported by private individuals to the East Indies, and in 1794–5 attempts were made to introduce Irish linen goods to the Chinese market. But an agent at Canton reported that the Chinese had refused to purchase them at a reasonable price.[22] By the middle nineties the whig opposition was pressing for an Anglo-Irish trade settlement along the lines of the propositions but the British government was not prepared to tackle the issue when engaged in a great war. Finally, with the union, Irish manufactures were admitted freely into the British market without catastrophic consequences for British industry.

By the close of the session of 1785 the Irish parliament had disposed of two very important issues, big with far-reaching implications. It had rejected parliamentary reform and both Pitt's commercial propositions and industrial protection. With these momentous questions out of the way, peers and M.P.s could relax and enjoy public life. Already in the autumn of 1782 Irish politicians had been able to congratulate themselves that after having had the exhilarating experience of living through a revolution, they found the familiar landmarks still standing, the basic facts of political life unchanged, and their own powers and importance increased. The constitutional status of the Irish parliament had undoubtedly risen. It now met annually, its activities were extended, its legislative output was greater, M.P.s were busier and better reported than in the past. The government clearly appreciated that they needed to be handled with more attention, leading office-holders taking

[22] *Correspondence between . . . William Pitt and Charles duke of Rutland*, pp. 117, 118; *Rutland MSS H.M.C.*, iii, p. 243; 27 Geo. III, c. 23, 33 Geo. III, c. 31; *Fourth report on the affairs of the East India company*, pp. 468–9, H.C. (148), 1812, vi.

considerable trouble over speeches calculated to improve the morale of the government's supporters and influence out-of-doors opinion.

For many Irish politicians the middle eighties must have constituted the happiest epoch in Irish parliamentary history. They performed their duties with dignity, in stately surroundings, they had plenty of useful work to do, fundamental assumptions went unchallenged, yet from time to time there was a grand debate offering opportunities for sparkling oratorical displays in the best parliamentary tradition. For instance, Grattan's 'able and animated' 1788 speech on the tithe question was generously described by Fitzgibbon as the most splendid display of eloquence that the house had ever heard.[23] Moreover, though of course contemporaries could not be expected to realize it, Irish public men were enjoying the last years of the true eighteenth century—stable, secure, self-assured, with all conflict kept within bounds. There is an almost horrid fascination in watching from the safe standpoint of history a community—in this instance not only Ireland but western Europe—moving steadily closer to the precipice, and it is hard not to dwell on the incongruous contrast between the questions absorbing parliamentary attention and the fiery controversy over political and social rights into which the political world was soon to be flung.

Towards the close of 1788, during the parliamentary recess, a crisis developed in which were combined a medical tragedy, a constitutional problem with gave implications, and a political drama with farcical elements. Early in November it was clear that the king was insane and that steps must be taken to provide for the exercise of the regal functions. It was generally accepted that there should be a regent and that the regent would be the prince of Wales. But there were no provisions in law for establishing a regency and two very different methods by which the prince of Wales could be installed in office as regent were suggested. The government proposed that a bill should be passed constituting the prince regent and defining his powers, the royal assent to the bill being given by a commission under the great seal. The whig opposition argued that the prince had an obvious claim to be regent and that both houses of parliament should by address request him to assume office. It is understandable why the whigs stressed the prince's claim. It was taken for granted that once he became regent he would dismiss Pitt and appoint a whig administration. From the government standpoint, appointment by bill had the advantages that it enabled parliament to impose limitations on the regent and was the more time-consuming procedure.[24]

As might be expected the Irish administration agreed with their British colleagues that appointment by bill was the correct procedure to follow. Following the constitutional course chartered at Westminster maintained and even strengthened the connection between Great Britain and Ireland, since the royal assent to the Irish regency bill would be signified under the British great seal, which by the time the bill arrived in London would be under the control of the British regent. Thus the connection between two kingdoms, linked by a common crown, would be unimpaired by the disaster which had struck their sovereign. But Irishmen, who were concerned to preserve the status achieved by the Irish parliament in 1782, were bound to view very critically a procedure which involved a 'servile imitation of the proceedings of another country'[25] and underlined a stage in the Irish legislative process which implied a degree of subordination to Great Britain. It was also true that by requesting by address, the prince of Wales to assume the regency of Ireland the Irish parliament would demonstrate its loyalty to whig principles and to the party which would soon be in control of power and patronage.

Before the close of the year it was being said in Dublin that the viceroy would soon be replaced by a whig (Fitzwilliam, Spencer or Norfolk), it being asserted by the Irish whigs that since the lord lieutenant was commissioned under the British seal the British regent on taking office could immediately recall him.[26] Early in December, the lord lieutenant, Buckingham, prickly, petulant and flappable, was afraid that when the Irish parliament met he would be beaten. He was able to prorogue parliament until the beginning of February, but with the bulletins reporting the king's health steadily undermining

[24] J. W. Derry, *The regency crisis and the whigs 1788–9* (1963).
[25] *Parl. Reg. Ire.*, ix, p. 36.
[26] *D.E.P.*, 18 Nov., 4, 11, 13 Dec. 1788.

politicians' confidence in Buckingham's administration, he
splenetically watched government supporters, led by the
'four great rats', Shannon, Ponsonby, Loftus and Leinster,
preparing to leave the sinking ship. When parliament met, on
the second day of the session (6 April) the government sustained
a resounding defeat, being beaten on an important procedural
motion by 130 to 76. A few days later Grattan, having drawn
attention to 'the highest land mark in English annals', the
convention parliament of 1689, called on the house to follow
the example of that assembly and request the prince of Wales
to act as regent of Ireland. On 17 February the two houses
agreed to request the prince to take upon himself the government of the kingdom during the king's indisposition, and when
the lord lieutenant refused to transmit their address parliament
appointed commissioners (two peers and four M.P.s) to lay it
before the prince. But on the day the lord lieutenant refused to
transmit the address, at Westminster parliament was informed
the king was rapidly recovering. By the time the commissioners
arrived in London their mission was plainly superfluous and
their interview with the prince embarrassingly absurd. Buckingham, having endured 'hell', was at first out to punish all the
deserters who had joined the aristocratic combination which
had defied his administration on the regency issue, and his
opponents for the moment closed their ranks. Charlemont
urged them to form a united front in defence of Ireland's
parliamentary rights but some of his associates had a narrower
objective, and at the close of February many of the opposition
signed an agreement 'to oppose any government who turns any
one man out of his employment' for his vote on the regency
question. The lord lieutenant firmly refused to treat en corps,
but decided he must pardon some of the culprits—'however
bitter the pill I must swallow the mortification'. Loftus, Clifden,
some well known office-holders (including Hely-Hutchinson,
Blaquiere and Langrishe) and 'some insignificant rats' were
pardoned, but Leinster and Ponsonby continued in opposition
(pledged, it was said, to their friends in England). Shannon
wanted to revert to being a government supporter but his
wife was Ponsonby's sister and a fervent partisan, so 'for the
sake of his domestic peace' he remained in opposition.[27] The

[27] *Fortescue MSS H.M.C.*, i, pp. 398–434; *Charlemont MSS H.M.C.*, ii, p. 89.

government soon recovered its parliamentary position. At the beginning of March the opposition carried the third reading of a pensions bill in the house of commons by 130 to 98 and it was defeated in the lords by only one vote. By the middle of April the government defeated a bill disfranchising revenue officers in the house of commons by 148 to 93.

The behaviour of the Irish parliament during the regency crisis, when, as an M.P. admitted, it might be said that 'the pulse of the Irish parliament beats according to His Majesty's physicians',[28] provides plenty of material for a political cynic. But it is only fair to say that at the beginning of February, on the question whether the prince should be requested immediately to assume the regency, 76 M.P.s offered 'noble and manly'[29] support to the apparently tottering administration and of the 127 who supported the address, 63 had, on occasion at least, opposed the government in the recent past. When the king was rapidly recovering 19 M.P.s with opposition records, 15 of whom had not voted on the regency issue and 4 of whom had voted with the government, defied the Irish administration by voting for the pension bill. Again, of the 40 peers who in February voted to address the prince, only four, at the close of March, voted against the pension bill, though 10 of the 40 abstained on this issue. It perhaps should be added that of the four who quickly changed their allegiance three were spiritual peers, the senior being the archbishop of Cashel, one of the fastest movers throughout the crisis.[30]

Though statistics and charity may suggest that many peers and M.P.s had respectable motives for their actions during the regency crisis, the episode did not enhance the dignity of the unreformed parliament and offered arguments to those who wanted to diminish the influence of the executive. A large and heterogeneous band of politicians had acted together in opposition to the government in the early months of 1789 and many of them continued to co-operate after the crisis had been resolved, forming a parliamentary party with a large membership, a name, an organization and a programme. The party was

[28] *Parl. Reg. Ire.*, ix, p. 142.
[29] *Fortescue MSS H.M.C.*, i, p. 402.
[30] For house of lords and house of commons division lists see *D.E.P.*, 11 Feb., 9 Mar. 1786, 13 Mar. 1787, 26 Feb., 1 Mar. 1788, 17 Feb., Apr. 1789.

composed of great 'interests', which refused to resume relations with Buckingham—the Ponsonbys, linked to the English whigs, the friends of Lord Shannon, a conventional but potent parliamentary connection, together with many independent country gentlemen and some consistent critics of administration. They annexed the most respected contemporary political label, calling themselves the Irish whigs, and strengthened their cohesion by the formation of a club, the Irish Whig Club, the members of which regularly dined together. In August 1789 the club issued a declaration, setting out its principles and a programme. It began by stating that 'the great object of the society' was the preservation of the Irish constitution as settled in 1688 and 1782. It emphasized both that the Irish parliament was 'the only legislature of this realm', and that the connection with Great Britain was 'sacred and indissoluble . . . [and] necessary for the freedom of this kingdom in particular and the freedom, strength and prosperity of the empire in general'. It then listed the measures the whigs supported—place and pension bills, a responsibility bill, the disfranchisement of revenue officers and the reform of the Dublin police.

Published about a month after the fall of the Bastille, the whig manifesto embodied a conventional country party programme, its general aim being to combat the undue influence of the crown over parliament. 'The trade of parliament', Grattan declared, 'is like original sin—it operates through all political creation.'[31] It was soon apparent that the programme did not satisfy all the supporters of the whig opposition. Towards the close of 1789 Charlemont took steps to establish a whig club in Belfast, 'our political metropolis'. He had in Belfast an attached friend in Dr Haliday, the earl and the doctor, both men of very effusive feeling, being bound together by a common political creed and strong mutual esteem. Haliday set to work to promote Charlemont's wishes, but almost immediately there was a hitch. 'Many good whigs' in Belfast refused to join the proposed club, because many of its members were likely to be country gentlemen of 'superior rank and fortune'.[32] It was decided then, that two whig clubs should be constituted, a Northern whig club and a Belfast whig club. The first of these was formed in March 1790 and soon had a membership

---

[31] *Parl. Reg. Ire.*, xii, p. 132.   [32] *Charlemont MSS H.M.C.*, ii, p. 117.

of sixty. This included three peers, three sons of peers, well over twenty members of well-established landed families, two barristers, a dignitary of the established church, about ten Belfast businessmen, the secretary of the ballast board, a sometime distiller, a 'lately dubbed Esq', a couple of rich farmers and Michael Barber, 'formerly a merchant, now a gentleman at large'.[33] Its declaration differed in three important respects from that produced by the whig club in Dublin. It made no reference to the British connection—on the grounds that Ireland was receiving unfair and ruinous treatment from Great Britain. It referred to the unequal and inadequate representation created by the existence of venal boroughs, and it declared that no person should 'suffer civil hardship for his religious persuasion unless the tenets of his religion lead him to endeavour the subversion of the state'. Charlemont was much perturbed by this reference to the catholic question and Haliday tried to reassure him by pointing out that it was obvious that the catholics held subversive tenets.[34]

During the latter part of the session of 1789 and the sessions of 1790–2 the whigs conducted a series of well-sustained parliamentary campaigns against the administration. They denounced with wit and scorn the methods they alleged had been employed by the government to restore its parliamentary position after the regency debacle. 'Abuse, peculation and profusion', Egan asserted, 'are the epidemical diseases of office', and Curran sneered at 'the political music or hurdy gurdy men' hired 'to pipe the phrases of the viceroys'. (Stung by such attacks, Sir Boyle Roche, a government supporter, complained about opposition speakers' 'Billingsgate dialect'— and then retorted crudely in kind himself.) The government's behaviour, the whigs emphasized, was a powerful argument for enacting place, pension and responsibility bills. The government's conduct, Grattan angrily declared, was undermining respect for the constitution. While the radical was denouncing hereditary honours, the administration was selling peerages. The minister advanced ahead of the radical leveller 'like sin preceding the shadow of death'. Whig denunciations of current political practice must have strengthened the contempt

---

[33] Westmorland Corresp., 32; D.E.P., 27 Sept. 1789.
[34] Charlemont MSS H.M.C., ii, 118–20.

of the radically minded for the existing political order; they left the government's supporters seemingly unshaken. Langrishe, a respectable and respected office-holder, contended that though 'influence may appear', for some years past 'there had never been wanting a sufficient share of public virtue to assert the rights and maintain the interests of this country'; and Wolfe, who had succeeded Fitzgibbon as attorney-general, contrasted 'the pompous professions' of the opposition with the government's intentions. The Irish administration, he said, intended 'to govern the country according to the laws and constitution . . . to use our exertions to promote her peace and prosperity . . . to manage her revenues with the most rigid economy'.[35]

The whigs took a strong stand on three issues which were arousing considerable feeling in Dublin—the Dublin police, the mayoral election of 1790 and the use of fiats. The Dublin police act of 1786 had empowered the lord lieutenant to appoint three commissioners who were to be responsible for preserving the peace within the area bounded by the circular road. They were authorized to raise and equip a force of about 500, constables and watchmen, and to levy a rate for its maintenance. The act may be seen as a pioneering attempt to cope with the problems created by large-scale urbanization. Dublin liberals condemned the new police force as being 'extravagant, inefficient and unconstitutional'; in five successive sessions the citizens petitioned parliament against it and in 1791 a number of Dublin parishes and guilds held meetings to protest against the police. In parliament the whigs denounced the police act as an attempt to turn the city into a government borough,[36] and in 1789 when the opposition predominated in parliament, a house of commons committee reported instances of gross extravagance in the management of the Dublin police— expensive uniforms, superfine stationery and looking-glasses and a Wilton carpet for the commissioners' house.

At the civic election of 1790 the board of aldermen in selecting the sheriffs passed over the first three names in the list submitted by the commons, those of well-known radicals, Tandy, Ewing and Jackson, and sent down as their nomination

[35] Parl. Reg. Ire., ix, p. 405; x, pp. 75, 110, 210, 536.
[36] Ibid., ix, p. 411.

for the office of lord mayor, the name of Alderman James, a police commissioner. The commons on principle rejected him by a narrow majority and put forward instead the name of Alderman Howison. Both names were placed before the privy council which under the 'new rules' of 1672 had to approve the mayor. The government did not want to be involved in the dispute and twice the council referred the matter back to the corporation. Support in the commons for Howison increased as resentment against the aldermen mounted, and on both names being submitted for a third time, the council, as a step towards securing a decision from the courts, approved of James. The excitement in the city was intense. An aggregate meeting, with Hamilton Rowan in the chair and Matthew Dowling as secretary, passed resolutions attacking the privy council. Two volunteer corps (the Goldsmiths and the Independents) pledged themselves to defend the liberties of the city, and the whig club declared it would co-operate with its fellow citizens in defending the rights of the citizens (and became involved in acrimonious bickering with the lord chancellor). The commons, led by Tandy, who reminded them that the violation of charters had proved fatal to the house of Stuart, took steps to retain possession of the city regalia and the mansion house, and at the end of July James resigned and Howison took office.[37]

During 1790 and the previous year the whigs in parliament pressed the administration hard over another legal issue— fiats—which had aroused considerable feeling among the Dublin liberals. In 1789, Magee, the lively and pugnacious editor of the *Dublin Evening Post* (who may have been suffering from temporary loss of mental balance) attacked in his paper Richard Daly, the manager of the Theatre Royal, and Francis Higgins, the editor of the pro-government *Freeman's Journal*, in a style remarkably scurrilous even by contemporary standards. Daly sued him for libel and Higgins prosecuted him. During the proceedings, Earlsfort, the chief justice of the king's bench, who as attorney-general had been a defiant supporter of the authority in stormy days, issued fiats directing Magee to find very heavy security for the payment of damages which might be awarded against him, and Magee, being unable to do so, was committed to prison. Embittered by this treatment he

[37] *D.E.P.*, 20 July 1790; *H.J.*, 19, 26 Apr., 29 May, 19, 21 July, 4 Aug. 1790.

not only struck out savagely in the *Post* but tried to harass Earlsfort by encouraging riotous, popular fêtes in a field beside the chief justice's suburban retreat. Higgins won his case, the jury after some hesitation, on being given a firm direction by Earlsfort, finding Magee guilty, and Daly was awarded moderate damages. Magee after a period in prison continued to manage his paper with ability—the *Dublin Evening Post* both energetically advocating liberal policies and clearly earning a large advertising revenue. But its editor henceforth abstained from gross personal abuse. Magee's attacks on Daly, Higgins and Earlsfort were marked by rancorous and raucous buffoonery. But he seemed the victim of an excessive and unreasonable extension of judicial authority. The Dublin liberals took up his case, four of them (three of whom were to be prominent in the Dublin society of United Irishmen) signing an appeal for subscriptions to a defence fund, and Tandy accompanied Magee to court and advised him during the Higgins trial.[38] A group of whig barristers in the house of commons argued forcefully that if the way in which fiats were being employed in Magee's case was not unprecedented it ran counter to prevalent legal opinion, and in the future Earlsfort's practice was not followed.

Conflict in Dublin drew the whigs and the more advanced city liberals together. In March 1790 a meeting of freemen and freeholders, presided over by Tandy, endorsed the whig club programme, and in July the club elected Tandy a member in recognition of his efforts in defence of the constitution of Dublin. Immediately after the general election of 1790 liberals of various shades, including four future members of the Dublin society of United Irishmen, formed a committee to petition against the return of Wogan Talbot instead of John Finlay, the candidate supported by 'the independent electors'. In Dublin, two whigs, Henry Grattan and Lord Henry Fitzgerald, who were approved of by 'a delegated committee' of the guilds, presided over by Tandy (who it had been rumoured might stand himself), were returned by a majority of about two to one against two candidates supported by the aldermen.[39] On nomination day Drennan saw Grattan and Fitzgerald proceeding to the hustings at the head of a long procession

[38] *D.E.P.*, 14 July 1789.
[39] *Dublin Chronicle*, 16, 21, 26, 30 Jan. 1790; *D.E.P.*, 6 Nov. 1788.

interspersed with bands and banners—'Grattan advancing on his light fantastic toe, hope elevating and joy brightening his crest, his eye rolling with that fine enthusiasm without which it is impossible to be a great man; Fitzgerald a fine, tall young fellow bending to hear what Grattan is saying'. Behind them stalked Napper Tandy, 'in all the surliness of republicanism, grinning most ghastly smiles' and directing the cheers of the crowd, 'the many headed monster'. Drennan noted that though there were banners with mottoes recommending place and pension bills and even one aimed against slavery—'a negro boy well dressed and holding high the cap of liberty'—he looked in vain for a reference to reform. Another radically-minded medical man, Dr Robert Emmet, asked Grattan at this time 'was he a friend to a proper representation—his answer was— I and my friend here (Lord Henry Fitzgerald) are by no means averse to a reform in parliament. The people then, says the doctor, are enlisted under you as a party, that people who were once the principals and the nation is become a Ponsonby party.'[40]

[40] W. Drennan to Mrs McTier, 3 May 1790 (Drennan papers, 291). Twelve years later, Tandy, then an exile in France, expressed his disapproval of the French attempt to subdue the negro insurrection in Saint Dominque. 'We are all of the same family,' he wrote, 'black and white, the work of the same creator' (J. N. Tandy to J. Tandy, 1 Prairial, year 10 (17 June 1802) (I.S.P.O. 620/12)).

III

THE REVOLUTIONARY ERA

III

THE REVOLUTIONARY ERA

9
The French revolution and Ireland

At the beginning of May 1789 a few weeks before the Irish parliamentary session, which began with the regency crisis, closed, the States General met at Versailles. During the parliamentary recess the ancient regime in France collapsed and the National assembly set to work to manufacture a constitution and institutions adapted to a modern, liberal community. The French revolution was not only momentous in its immediate effects and implications, it was also highly spectacular. The stage was a great country, lying at the centre of European civilization: the participants spoke and acted as men and women conscious they were making history before the eyes of their contemporaries. Publicists and journalists strove hard to convey to the public what they thought was happening in France. In Ireland during the early nineties booksellers advertised a wide range of books on contemporary French politics, a number of which had been reprinted in Dublin—for instance the *Livre rouge*, Mirabeau's speeches, Dumouriez's memoirs, Camille Desmoulins *History of the Brissotins*, Mallet du Pan's *Considerations on the nature of the French revolution* and the constitution of 1793. One Dublin bookseller claimed to have advertised 'all the pamphlets on the revolution in France', another advertised 'the work from which the principles of the revolution in France were drawn', 'John James' Rousseau's *Inquiry*.[1] The Irish newspapers from the meeting of the States General, by providing extensive coverage of French affairs, and by printing at length the debates in the successive French representatives assemblies and the Jacobin club, enabled their readers to obtain a vivid impression of the personalities, ideas and style of French political life. Even the Dublin theatre found material in contemporary French events. As early as November 1789 the Theatre Royal staged 'Gallic freedom or the destruction of the Bastille'. A year later the Royal Amphitheatre presented 'a superb spectacle, called The civic oath . . .

D.E.P., 26 May, 11 June 1791.

portraying the whole of the business in the Champ de Mars'. In the spring of 1793 Preston's *Democratic Rage*, a tragedy based on the trial and death of Louis XVI was produced at the Theatre Royal. In Belfast, when in May 1793 *The Guillotine*, a play based on the death of Louis XVI was performed, though the author claimed he had 'strictly avoided every idea of party or of factions', it was greeted with conflicting cries. The boxes and pit cried 'Off, off', the gallery, 'Go on, go on'.[2]

But though the British and Irish public from the summer of 1789 watched with fascination events in France, they seem to have regarded the upheaval as a purely French crisis, which, if the glorious revolution was taken as a precedent, might soon be resolved by a general acceptance of a sensible constitution, modelled on the British. The first anniversary of the fall of the Bastille passed uncommemorated in Ireland, where the politically-minded were absorbed in a general election. But a few months later the publication of Burke's *Reflections on the revolution in France* in November 1790 marked the beginning of a great debate on the significance of the revolution in political and intellectual history. In March 1791 Thomas Paine published the first part of his *Rights of Man* (the second part appearing in February 1792), the best known and most effective reply to Burke. Burke and Paine were not unevenly matched as controversialists, though Burke with his strong, far-ranging intellect, erudition and experience, prophetic vision and poetic imagination was to occupy a far greater place in intellectual history. In the *Reflections* Burke not only denounced with a plethora of lurid detail the results of revolutionary mismanagement, but he endeavoured with intense urgency to bring home to his readers the complexity, variety and subtlety of the relationships which held together any historic and continuously-evolving community. The immense sweep of his argument, his profundity, his profusion of allusions, and his defiant assertion of what he regarded as self-evident but imperilled political truth, provided numerous targets for an assailant. Paine who prided himself on being rational, practical and progressive, might also be shallow and cocksure. But he was an irreverent and acute critic of both the established order and

---

[2] *Dublin Chronicle*, 14 Nov. 1789, 18 Nov. 1792; *H.J.*, 10 June 1793; *N.S.*, 23, 29 May 1793.

of Burke, and by outlining the faults of the old regime in France and the limitations of the existing order in Great Britain, by showing how the equal and natural rights of man were protected in the new French constitution and by sketching a programme of sensible social reform, he provided radicals with an iron ration of principles and objectives. Moreover, with exhilarating clarity, he brought to bear on politics the optimism which was such a striking feature of the century which was coming to its close. 'From what we now see,' he declared, 'nothing of reform in the political world ought to be held improbable. It is an age of revolutions in which everything may be looked for.'

A Dublin edition of the *Reflections* appeared by the end of November 1790 and eight Dublin editions were printed before the end of November 1790. Early in 1791 some of the replies to Burke had also been reprinted in Dublin. At the beginning of April the Whigs of the capital (the socially less distinguished supplement to the Whig club of Ireland) appointed a committee of thirteen to take steps to disseminate Paine's pamphlet. Within a few weeks a cheap edition of the *Rights of man* appeared under the auspices of the club, and by the end of the year there were thirteen Dublin editions of Paine's work. One member of the committee of thirteen, Richard Sheridan, a K.C., was most annoyed to hear that he had been placed on the committee, since he considered the *Rights of man* to be 'designed to level all distinctions . . . and to have in view a total overthrow of the constitution'; seven other members of the committee later joined the Dublin society of United Irishmen, the famous radical club, and in June 1792 Paine was elected an honorary member of that society.[3] His great rival had been already honoured in Dublin when the Board of Trinity college, acting with unusual speed for an academic body, five weeks after the publication of the *Reflections*, decided to confer an honorary degree on Burke, 'the powerful advocate of the constitution and the friend of public order and virtue and consequently of the happiness of mankind'.

[3] *D.E.P.*, 7 Apr., 3 May 1791; *Charlemont MSS H.M.C.*, i, p. 137. The thirteenth Dublin edition of the *Rights of Man*, and the eighth of the *Reflections* are in Haliday collection 601, 623. A Dublin bookseller, J. S. Jordan, claimed that the edition of the *Rights of Man* he had for sale was the one authorized by Paine for Ireland.

A number of Irish pamphleteers threw themselves into the fray, displaying ardour and ingenuity, if not much originality. Public opinion became sharply and acrimoniously divided over the revolution in France, and when the second anniversary of the fall of the Bastille came round it was enthusiastically and aggressively commemorated by radicals throughout the British Isles. In Dublin the volunteers, commanded by Colonel Tandy, paraded and fired a *feu de joie* and 'enlightened citizens' dined in various taverns. In Ulster the Bastille anniversary was celebrated at a number of centres: in Belfast the volunteers, the Northern whig club and the inhabitants, holding a parade and a dinner and voting an address to the National assembly, declaring 'it was good for humanity that grass now grew where the Bastille once stood'. Replies to this address came from Bordeaux and Nantes.[4]

The following year the fall of the Bastille was again commemorated in Dublin by a volunteer parade and dinners; and about ten weeks later at the beginning of October, when the lord mayor summoned a meeting to consider a subscription for the exiled French clergy, Oliver Bond, a well-known radical, argued that 'the business intended involved under the garb of charity a political question', and the meeting adjourned without taking action. At the end of the month when the news of Valmy arrived, Oliver Bond and James Tandy circulated handbills and inserted a notice in the press calling for a general illumination. But the magistrates having applied for military aid, sent patrols through the streets to prevent the mob smashing unlit windows, and few houses seem to have been illuminated. The next night however the whigs of the capital dined to celebrate the completion of the glorious French revolution. In the north of Ireland, there were rejoicings, to mark Brunswick's retreat at a number of places, including Belfast. Belfast had already in July celebrated the fall of the Bastille on a grand scale. There was a volunteer review and a great procession in which were carried the flags of the free nations, Ireland, America, France, Poland and Great Britain, followed by a grand standard on a triumphal car, showing the release of the prisoners from the Bastille, with on the reverse a picture of a volunteer

---

[4] *Dublin Weekly Journal*, 16 July 1791; *B.N.L.*, 19, 22 July, 2 Aug. 1791; *H.J.*, 12, 29, 31 Oct. 1791.

presenting Liberty to a shackled Hibernia. In an address to the National assembly the citizens of Belfast expressed their pleasure at seeing a creative spirit animating the whole mass of mind in France. They expected a great increase in human happiness from a revolution which 'calls into activity the whole vigour of the whole community, amplifies so largely the field of enter-prize and improvement and gives free scope to the universal sense of the empire [of France]'. 'If you will be free', they told the French people, 'you must be free.'[5]

To the British and Irish radicals the revolution was a great and inspiring experience. It meant the sweeping away of tyranny, privilege and corruption; a transfer of political power to the community at large (or at least to the active citizens); a simplification and rationalization of the whole process of government and an opportunity for the individual, free from unjust restrictions, to exercise his talents to the full. What the French accomplished in the years following the meeting of the States General showed what man (middle-class man, it might be subconsciously added) could achieve, and when their achievements aroused the ire of the European despots, the French in the words of a young Irish poet 'like the soldiers of Cadmus . . . at a moment of least expectation started up from the very ground' and became, 'pardon the expression', a 'mob of heroes'.[6]

By claiming their ideals of government were being realized in France, radicals put themselves in the awkward position of associating the attainment of Utopia with the evolution of an existing political regime. But for the less attractive features of the revolution they had an immediate excuse—the war. Radicals abhorred war, 'the dire campaign, the reeking plain', as a regal and aristocratic pastime, and they believed France was the victim of absolutist aggression. The organ of Ulster radicalism, the *Northern Star*, declared that in France 'the fruits of calm and philosophical deliberation have been blasted by the breath of savage war'. Two years later the *Star* commenting on 13 Vendémiaire, remarked, 'let matters go as they will,

[5] *Belfast politics* (1794), pp. 52–72.

[6] T. Dermody, *Justice or rational liberty* (1793), pp. 7–8. After publishing this Dermody joined the army, served as a private in the 108th foot, and then secured, through Lord Moira, a lieutenancy in the wagon corps and fought in Flanders (J. G. Raymond, *The life of Thomas Dermody* (1806), ii, pp. 115–23).

suffering humanity weeps, and the originators of a coalition against a people *then* calmly remodelling their internal government have another reason to regret their bloody machinations'. Another excuse put forward in the *Northern Star* for the excesses committed in France was that they were the result of the sudden emancipation of a people whose feelings had been blunted by a tyrannical system, in which 'torture and breaking on the wheel was a familiar spectacle'.[7]

Moreover the revolution, a creative and liberating force of immeasurable power, was too tremendous a phenomenon to be subject to the ethical standards applicable to humdrum political activity in humdrum conditions. France, Drennan wrote in the summer of 1792, 'is like a man in the crisis of a furious fever—a second convulsion comes on—Good God how he struggles—how the mercy of the human countenance is distorted—how the breast heaves for air—How the limbs twine with anxious jactation . . . Art is vain—but not nature— but not God—What a groan—He is dead—No—he lives—and the *agony* was the effort of regeneration.' The massacre of the prisoners in early September 1792 was, he thought, 'one of those things that must be openly condemned and perhaps tacitly approved . . . . If the boat which escapes from a wreck be sinking with the weight of men some of them ought to be thrown into the sea—it is no time to weigh nice points of morality much less of legal forms—Suspicion is a shrewd sign of guilt. . . . When the extreme danger ceases the amenability to law will resume its former place—Law is precedent which really cannot anticipate the circumstances which occur in revolution periods, and therefore all that is to be referred to is the instinctive decisions of the people.' There was never, Drennan was convinced 'a general insurrection of the people, call them mob, sans-culottes etc. or what you please, which was not justified by the necessity of the case, except perhaps religious mobs'.[8]

Convinced that France was evolving politically and socially in the right direction, Irish radicals accepted with surprising equanimity how fast the revolution devoured its children. When La Fayette and Dumouriez abandoned France in disgust, the *Northern Star* contrasted their conduct with that of their troops

[7] *N.S.*, 20 Apr. 1793, 15 Oct., 24 Dec. 1795.
[8] Drennan to S. McTier, 18 Aug., Sept. 1792 (Drennan papers, 340, 346).

who remained loyal to liberty. When the Hébertists and Danton were guillotined, the *Star* explained that the Hébertists were hostile to religion and that Danton despised morality. When Robespierre fell—'but a hair lost from the head of the French Samson'—the *Star* pronounced that the time had obviously come for him to retire and 'the energy and dignity of the people had never been more strongly marked'. In the following year, when it criticized the convention for passing the decree of the two-thirds, the *Star* quickly added, 'in the meantime their gallant armies heedless of domestic broils proceed from conquest to conquest'. Some years later, when Bonaparte overthrew the directory and sent the legislature packing, Drennan hailed the new French constitution as based on democracy and as 'a practical education for the people, who in the different graduations or classes will be well disciplined for the public service'. Though he was reluctant to make 'a military disciplinarian' the chief magistrate, he hoped that Bonaparte might prove 'the great pacificator of Europe', and that 'a succession of constitutions will probably emanate from public opinion in France each one improving on the last'.[9]

Irish radicals perceived a wide range of virtues in the French, 'the only nation great in proportion always to the occasion and elegant in the least even the names of the months so accurately descriptive and so beautifully true'. Both the *Northern Star* and Tone noticed with approval that the perpetrators of the September massacres while killing prisoners (whom they believed to be enemies of their country) held property inviolable. 'An Irish mob', Tone wrote, 'would have plundered but shed no blood. A Parisian mob murders but respects property. Which is best? I lean to the Frenchman. More manly.' Unlike most radicals Tone had an opportunity of seeing revolutionary France at close quarters. Arriving in Paris shortly after the directory took office he was pleased and exhilarated by much of which caught his attention in France—farming, the Pantheon, 'sacred to everything that is sublime, illustrious and patriotic', the dash, confidence and gaiety of the soldiery, the plainly dressed Council of five hundred who have humbled all Europe 'with their blue pantaloons and unpowdered locks'; and 'the figure

---

[9] *N.S.*, 20 Apr. 1793, 14 Apr., 21 Aug. 1794, 5 Oct. 1795; W. Drennan to Mrs McTier, Oct., 24 Dec. 1799 (Drennan papers, 797, 815).

and fashion of the women'. Even the very foibles of the French, he wrote, 'amuse me, while the singularities of an Englishman are almost always offensive'. He was deeply moved by the revolutionary spectacles he witnessed—the great official gatherings on the Champ de Mars, the patriotic ballets in the theatre (which in other circumstances he might have thought somewhat absurd) and the presentation by the municipality of sabres and firelocks to young men liable for military service, in an affecting ceremony before an altar to liberty. He soon realized however that the revolutionary enthusiasm, which had inspired the community with a strong sense of common purpose, was on the wane. It was a passion, Tone reflected, which could not last for six years of war. The directory had bitter opponents on the right and the extreme left. A substantial section of the public seemed apathetic. At the theatre the *chants civiques* were 'received with the utmost phlegm and sometimes worse', and numbers of young men with the strong backing of their women-folk were trying to evade conscription. But one factor in the situation cheered Tone and dominated his thinking on French and European affairs, the drive and *esprit de corps* of the French armies (conscripts included). Early in 1798, contemplating the sweep of French military achievement, Tone decided that 'the French revolution is but yet begun; the Hercules is yet in swaddling bands. What a people!' Some months earlier Drennan had noted 'among the curious circumstances of the day that the standing armies of France . . . the collected virtue as well as the power of the country' were the great support of the republic.[10]

The swift succession of French victories and the astonishing expansion of French power encouraged Irish radicals in the later nineties to expect an early triumph of their cause, achieved through French intervention. But with the increasing importance of the army and the decline in revolutionary ardour, French foreign policy began again to be influenced by strategic considerations and play of power politics rather than crusading idealism, and Irish radicals at the beginning of the new century were to have the disillusioning experience of finding that the liberation of their oppressed country was obviously a minor

[10] T. W. Tone, *Life*, i, p. 183; ii, pp. 9, 11, 41, 76, 80, 114, 118, 156, 176, 222, 479; W. Drennan to Mrs McTier, 24 Aug. 1797 (Drennan papers, 673).

matter to the first consul. France, Thomas Addis Emmet wrote in 1805, 'is the headquarters of fraud, deceit and despotism'. If the French supported revolution in Ireland, he believed, their aim would be to set up a government 'modelled on that of the protecting country', with the catholic church in a privileged position.[11]

To Irish conservatives, as to conservatives all over Europe, the revolution seemed a challenge to civilization, an awful and alarming example of what could happen to a country when it began to remodel its institutions recklessly and ruthlessly on erroneous first principles. French society in the early nineties seemed to be in a state of chaotic collapse and reports in the more conservative newspapers indicated in lurid detail that life in France was nasty, brutish and liable to be short. A proud and powerful monarchy had been overthrown and those classes which should naturally predominate in the political and economic life of a community depressed and penalized—young Robert Stewart, touring France in 1790, saw with shocked disapproval tradesmen and fisherwomen dictating to their employers, with princes, noblemen and men of property trampled under foot. The machinery of ordered government had been replaced by rough and dictatorial direction and the rights of the individual, especially the educated and propertied individual, were being disregarded in the interests of an ugly Utopianism. France, ruled by 'a few desperate and detested adventurers governed by a ferocious and sanguinary rabble', was 'one great scene of sacrilege, plunder and violence, one general shamble of promiscuous assassination and undistinguishing massacre'. A conservative portrayal of a France where 'Nero would have seen himself rivalled in malignancy and Helogabalus in buffoonery' inevitably became a caricature of civilized living.[12]

Surveying the results of revolution with fascinated horror, conservatives strove to discover why a highly civilized, chivalrous and prosperous society should suddenly disintegrate. They concluded it was a remarkable instance of the power of ideas.

[11] *U.J.A.*, 2nd series, iv, pp. 256–8.
[12] *Charlemont MSS H.M.C.*, ii, p. 151; R. Day, *A charge to the grand jury of the city o, Dublin* (1793, reprinted 1796), p. 12; T. O'Beirne, *A sermon preached on the 19 April 1793* (1793), p. 12; A. Knox, *Essays on the political circumstances of Ireland* (1798), p. 42.

The sound principles, ideals and traditions which had been cohering forces in French society had been corroded by a pernicious political philosophy. One revolutionary dogma, constantly proclaimed in France and fervently assented to by radicals all over Europe, equality, seemed to conservatives to be the root of much political evil. Conservatives perhaps perceived its implications sooner than some radicals, arguing that political and economic equality tended in practice to be closely related. Early in 1793 Sir Lawrence Parsons, a man of strong, stimulating intellect (Tone, whose opinions were very different, said that Parsons, 'one of the very few honest men in the house of commons', first turned his mind to the question of Anglo-Irish relations) published a clear, compact pamphlet in which he tried to demonstrate that inequality was requisite to social progress. Man, Parsons wrote, was 'a progressive animal' and 'the great stimulation to progress' was property. Property, acquired by industry and ability was 'the great prime mover everywhere'. Obviously all men could not progress equally, and this was just as well, because with a vast number of tasks of varying difficulties and importance to be performed, 'a great and various inequality' was absolutely necessary 'to sublime man to the highest degree we know he is capable of'. Political power was annexed to property because every man had a right to the acquisitions of his own labour, and ought to have the means to protect them. Parsons was also convinced that democracy was absurd. The peasant, who had spent his days digging the earth and who had been educated as 'a mere machine', could not be expected to understand political issues. Even a strong radical when he was ill did not 'call on the next digger of the earth to feel his pulse'. To anybody who thought the lot of the poor hard, Parsons had an answer—'let it be considered the right to political power has been forfeited by their own or their ancestors' imprudence and indolence, but that by contrary conduct they or their children may rise to the enjoyment of such power'.[13] Another M.P., who showed considerable independence during his political career, William Smith, an essayist and amateur philosopher, who in the early nineteenth century became a baron of the exchequer, also defended political inequality. Economic inequality, he pointed

---

[13] L. Parsons, *Thoughts on liberty and equality* (1793).

out, was natural, property having a tendency to split into fragments of unequal magnitude. Since few are talented, the poor will always exceed the comparatively rich, with the result that in a democracy the latter are exposed to pillage. But once an equal distribution of property was made, permanent natural impulses would continue to operate, and economic inequality would soon reassert itself, 'Thus forever', Smith wrote, 'the machine revolves, presenting us alternatively with the motive and the mischief'. But such an unhappy cyclic movement could be prevented by a balanced constitution on the British model, in which democracy was modified and controlled.[14]

Alexander Knox, a conservative publicist of considerable intellectual ability, who was in later years to be a profound and influential theological thinker, was very much afraid that if 'a democratic senate' were in control of the country, it would attempt to equalize property or fix a minimum wage. Of course Knox was aware that wages were regulated by the laws of supply and demand, but he was afraid that during a period of radical experimentation 'the poor desolate lover of order [would] see all that he held dear, the fruit of his industry, the reward of his ingenuity, his domestic comforts, his fireside delights carried off'.[15]

The Irish conservatives when they examined the premises on which the established order rested were undisturbed by political doubt and by the middle nineties they were observing with satisfaction that France was beginning to repudiate revolution. 'There can be no doubt', a highly intelligent Irish peer wrote towards the close of 1795, 'that most of those mischievous principles of universal application to all governments are renounced by the new constitution . . . namely equality, natural rights of men, insurrection, right of daily or rather hourly revolution,[16], and Alexander Knox sardonically pointed out that the influence of the British prime minister on parliamentary elections was trifling compared to that secured by the convention under the decree of the two-thirds. But it was also obvious that France by 1795 was a most formidable military power, prepared to employ the resources and audacity

[14] W. Smith, *The rights of citizens* (1791) and *The patriot* (1793).
[15] A. Knox, *Essays*, p. 223.
[16] Lord Mornington (see *Fortescue MSS HMC.*), iii, pp. 149–50.

derived from the revolution to realize the ambitions of the *ancien régime*. The French moreover continued to possess an undeniable, if in the eyes of conservatives undeserved, advantage. To many people throughout Europe they were still the champions of progress, and radical Irishmen might welcome French invaders as liberators. Attempts were made to bring home to the Irish public, especially the less-privileged, what a French invasion would mean for them. A conservative newspaper printed a long letter from a merchant in Venice describing conditions there under French military government.[17] A handbill published in Dublin reminded Irishmen of the great advances their country had made in the past twenty years as evinced by trade statistics, public buildings and canals. They had just laws and freedom of worship and received excellent value for the taxes they paid. Alexander Knox warned them that a French conquest would turn them into 'enslaved dependents of headstrong and haughty demagogues' and reminded them of how their ancestors had suffered at the hands of the Danes. Another northern conservative, George Hill, produced a handbill in which he suggested Irish farmers should ask themselves would a French invading army want meat 'while you had cows, bullocks and sheep'. 'Do you imagine', he asked, 'that they would busy themselves talking politics with men who could not understand their language, while an opulent country lay before them, from which by a little squeezing they might extract something better than their own paper currency.' A similar point of view was expressed poetically:

> In France do you see how Equality's plan
> Most wisely accords with their famed Rights of Man
> There all is confusion and bloodshed and hate
> And misery's equal with poor and with great.
>
> The farmer no longer can count on his cow,
> His ox, nor his ass, nor his house, nor his plough
> . . .
> And when they cry out they are starving for bread,
> The guillotine hastily chops off the head.[18]

---

[17] *D.J.*, 14 Feb. 1798.

[18] Handbill dated 26 Aug. 1796 (620/24/182); handbill enclosed in G. Hill to ——, 6 Dec. 1796 (I.S.P. 620/26/103); A. Knox, *Essays*; *D.J.*, 7 Jan. 1797.

10

The radical revival

The French revolution had a most invigorating effect on British and Irish radicalism. It may not have added significantly to the radicals' stock of ideas. Advanced liberals in both Great Britain and Ireland were already committed to constitutional changes which were bound to change the whole social tone of the community, and they accepted that a progressing society must be ready to undertake a drastic reorganization of many of its institutions on rational lines. But events in France inspired the advocates of change in all parts of the British Isles with verve, with a sense of being participants in a great European drive against tyranny and anachronistic privilege and the assurance that their cause would soon triumph. From the beginning of the nineties, Irish radicals, convinced that in the near future they would be in a position to intervene decisively in Irish politics, were active in proclaiming their principles, systematizing their ideas and disseminating their opinions. They had three immediate political objectives—parliamentary reform, catholic emancipation and the reduction or elimination of English influence in the government of their country. Living in a 'great era of reform', 'when the rights of man are asserted in theory and that theory substantiated by practice', they were convinced that Ireland could hope to obtain an efficient and upright government, only through 'a complete and radical reform in the representation'. But 'with a parliament thus reformed everything is easy'. Parliamentary reform was not only politically desirable. It was bound to have a profound and bracing effect on the moral and intellectual life of the whole community. The existing regime degraded all who were involved in its working. An organized system of corruption, Arthur O'Connor, an outstanding radical publicist, declared, stretched from the Castle to the cabin. 'There can never be', Drennan argued, 'any national morality, or what is the same thing, there can never be so much individual probity as to influence and regulate national character while a borough morality pervades the whole country and perpetuates its idleness, its poverty and corruption.' But the humblest man, when enfranchised, gained a sense of responsibility and a real place in the political community. His social status would be raised, his intellect developed and his moral stamina strengthened by the performance of his political duties, and parliamentary reform would 'prove a seed of sobriety, industry and regard to character'.[1]

It was not until 1794 that the Irish radicals, involved in the struggle for catholic relief, and in a series of exhausting legal tussles with the authorities, managed to formulate and publish a specific plan of reform. As early as December 1792, the Dublin society of United Irishmen, the most important and intellectually active radical club in Ireland, requested their committee of constitution to prepare a plan, and a fortnight later the society appointed a special committee of twenty-one members to draft a scheme. A number of questions were brought before this committee. These included the size and shape of the constituencies, methods of registration, the duration of parliament (one, two or three years?), the payment of M.P.s (should they be paid by their constituents or by the national treasury, and what should be their remuneration, one or two guineas a day or 'a small salary barely sufficient to defray the additional expense of residence in Dublin during the session'?), compensation for borough owners, the recall of M.P.s who had lost the confidence of their constituents, and an obligatory clause in leases, renouncing on the part of the landlord all claims on the vote of his tenant, and the number of M.P.s (when Emmet suggested 500, Drennan characteristically observed that this was too large as 'after a certain amount wisdom does not accumulate in the same ratio as wiseacres'). By far the most important and controversial question which came before the committee was the qualification for the franchise. The French constitution of 1791 had restricted the right of voting to active citizens, who had to possess a fairly high property qualification and though Irish radicals at the beginning of the nineties spoke of enfranchising 'the great body of the people', many of them

---

[1] *Society of United Irishmen of Dublin* (1794), pp. 3, 5, 9, 222; A. O'Connor, *The state of Ireland* (1798), p. 39; W. Drennan, *Letter to . . . Lord Fitzwilliam* (1795), p. 16.

stopped short of universal manhood suffrage. Malachy O'Connor, a member of the committee of twenty-one, a merchant with an interest in a plantation in the West Indies, bluntly stated that 'the house of commons should speak the sense of that portion of all the people where common sense, wisdom and virtue, are most abundantly found. This portion of the people consists of the middle ranks of society. The electors then of the house of commons should be the middle ranks of society.' He then suggested property qualifications which he thought would result in the enfranchisement of about one-ninth of the adult male population. Whitley Stokes, a fellow of Trinity, put the same point of view more gently. The object of framing a constitution, he laid down, was the public good. 'That', he wrote, 'is best to be procured by establishing such a legislature as is most likely to make the best laws, and such a one is more probably to be procured by having a small qualification than by letting every man vote.' Stokes also thought that indirect election might be desirable. 'The lower classes', he pointed out, 'are better qualified to choose an honest neighbour, than to judge of a member of parliament.' Another member of the committee, Chambers, a successful printer, would have granted the vote to freemen and householders, a proposal which, he said, would enfranchise 'every industrious mechanical man though in a garret'. Even Drennan, though he declared that 'it was the right of every commoner in this realm to have a vote in the election of his representative', felt that until Ireland had advanced considerably in knowledge and civilization it would not be advisable to give every a man vote. In the scheme he submitted to the committee he proposed granting the franchise to all taxable householders and to lodgers paying not less than an amount to be fixed by legislation. Though Drennan emphasized that 'the property here is not a qualification but only a mark of residence', his plan would almost certainly have left a considerable number unenfranchised.[2] Henry Sheares, a barrister and a prominent member of the society, though not a member of the committee of twenty-one, in his address to the electors of Cork cautiously stated that he was in favour of

[2] 'United Irish plans of parliamentary reform', in *I.H.S.*, iii, pp. 39–59. W. Drennan to T. A. Emmet, 21 Jan. (I. S. P. O. 620/15/2/7); *Caribbeana*, iv pp. 252–6.

'extending the elective franchise to the utmost limits which the collective wisdom of the nation shall deem safe'.[3]

But one member of the committee of twenty-one, Thomas Addis Emmet, an able barrister, at the beginning of January 1793 came out boldly in favour of universal suffrage, stating in his plan that Ireland should be divided into 500 electoral districts, 'as nearly as possible equal in population', and that every male aged eighteen or upwards should have a vote, to be given viva voce, in the district where he resided. By the end of the month the committee agreed by eleven votes to nine (Drennan voting with the minority) that there should be no property qualification for the franchise.[4] As a result of this decision the publication of a plan of reform by the Dublin society of United Irishmen was delayed for some time because the committee of twenty-one, when they completed their draft, warned the society 'that as individual representation was the basis of it, at present it would be imprudent to send it forth while there is such a charge of republicanism against the society'. The society did not begin considering the plan in detail until the close of December 1793; it discussed it during January 1794 and published it in February 'on a single sheet for the purpose of hanging up in cabins'. The plan provided that there should be annual parliaments, that representatives should receive 'a reasonable stipend', that pensioners and placeholders should be disqualified from being representatives and that a representative who was absent from duty should vacate his seat, that the country should be divided into 300 equal electoral districts, that arrangements should be made to hold all elections on the same date, and that every male of sound mind, aged over twenty-one should be entitled to vote in the district where he was resident, votes being given 'by voice and not by ballot'. When the society was discussing the plan Dr Reynolds, an Ulster radical, spoke in favour of the ballot 'which would be the most effectual means of destroying the influence of the aristocracy in this country, as poor men then might without injury to their families promise their landlords and yet serve their country by breaking their words'. But the opinion that 'it is by

---

[3] Henry Sheares, address to the electors of the city of Cork (*Cork Gazette*, 31 Oct. 1795).
[4] W. Drennan to S. McTier, 29 Jan. 1794 (Drennan papers, 464).

honest public actions that public principle is chiefly acquired and preserved' prevailed.[5] Clear, concise, comprehensive and easily comprehensible, the plan represented an unflinching application of radical principles. A few months before it was published, the British convention, meeting in Edinburgh, pronounced in favour of annual parliaments and universal suffrage, but about a year after it appeared the French convention, elected by universal suffrage in 1793, decided on a franchise restricted by property qualifications and of indirect election to the legislature. The United Irishmen of Dublin justified their decision on the franchise question in a manifesto drawn up by Emmet from material largely provided by Drennan, whose pen, according to himself, was 'deemed too florid and refined for the people'. If property was represented, the manifesto asked, 'why should liberty and life not be represented?' The poor man, who paid indirect taxes, was 'interested in the honest disposal of the public money' . . . and the need for universal suffrage was illustrated by the 'aristocratic' nature of much existing legislation, for instance, the game laws, the whiteboy acts, and the stamp acts which effectually debarred the poor from the civil courts.[6]

The arguments for universal suffrage were arguments for complete catholic emancipation. Without emancipation, the representation, even if reformed, would not be 'free, equal and entire'.[7] Justice and expediency, the rights of man and the balance of forces in Irish politics, alike demanded that all religious distinctions in civil life should be swept away and in stressing the supreme importance of union amongst Irishmen, Irish radicals displayed a warm and genuine awareness of the value to the country of sympathetic goodwill and mutual understanding. Union was, too, an emotively powerful term (defenders of the established regime were to try and annex the equally compelling term, 'loyalty'). Of course the union the radicals passionately urged meant at the outset at least a union or alliance against the privileged and conservative sections of Irish society, which could only hope to be included if they

---

[5] 'Proceedings of the Dublin society of United Irishmen' in *Analecta Hibernica* no. 17, pp. 104–6.

[6] *Society of United Irishmen of Dublin*, pp. 24, 28.

[7] Ibid., p. 24.

surrendered power and possibly principle. It is also probable too that when radicals spoke of all the barriers between protestant and catholic being beaten down, 'so far as civil matters are concerned', and 'the three great sects blended under the common and sacred title of Irishmen',[8] they disregarded the difficulty of drawing the boundary between the civil and the religious, especially when religious feelings were strong. Though Irish protestant radicals deeply and actively sympathized with the politically underprivileged catholic, they were little interested in catholicism. Drennan indeed regarded catholicism with something approaching aversion. Proud of being 'a protestant dissenter . . . zealously attached to that essential distinction, the right of private judgement', he stressed that the catholics were 'but a sect though a numerous one', and that the great difference between them and the presbyterians was that 'the catholics are still more religionists than politicians and the presbyterians are more politicians than religionists. The one still cherish their creed as the first objective; the creed of the other is general liberty and equality'—though Drennan characteristically added that presbyterians often failed to live up to their convictions.[9] Todd Jones was slightly more sympathetic to catholicism. In 1792 he wrote of how 'the genius of the catholic religion was dispelling the gloom of oppression and persecution' and raising temples to liberty; and Dr Ryan, a leading catholic, a United Irishman and an acquaintance of Fox, agreed with Jones. He was sure that 'if anything like phrenzy enters into the taste of the present day it is . . . strictly and purely political'. Denominational differences were rather jauntily dismissed by Tone, who pointed out that 'the emancipated and liberal Irishman, like the emancipated and liberal Frenchman, may go to mass, may tell his beads, or sprinkle his mistress with Holy water; but neither the one nor the other will attend to the rusty and extinguished thunderbolts of the Vatican or the idle anathemas which, indeed, His Holiness, is now-a-days too prudent and cautious to issue'. And when, in 1798, Tone heard that the pope had been dethroned and exiled from Rome, he reflected with satisfaction

---

[8] T. W. Tone, *Life*, i, p. 358.
[9] W. Drennan to Mrs McTier, 25 Nov. 1792; S. McTier, 21 Jan. 1794 (Drennan papers, 351, 463).

that these events marked the emancipation of mankind from the yoke of religious and political superstition.[10] In Ireland, as in other parts of Europe, radicalism fused with nationalism. Throughout the eighteenth century, in Irish parliamentary politics, opposition had often seemed a matter of trying to protect Irish rights against Great Britain. The first Irish reform movement was closely associated with an assertion of Ireland's constitutional claims, and in the nineties, the political relationship between Great Britain and Ireland offered to Irish radicals an example of that privilege on one part and subordination on the other which they were seeking to destroy. Ireland, it was said, was ruled by Englishmen and the servants of Englishmen, by an alliance between the Irish oligarchy based on land and the British administration. Ireland's economic interests were continually being sacrificed to Great Britain's, the relationship between the two countries was, it was implied, one of pure loss for Ireland, and nearly all Ireland's ills, most of which were the result of the country's economic retardation, could be traced to the British connection. Free from British domination, Ireland would 'in arts, commerce and manufactures spring up like an air balloon and leave England behind her at an immense distance'.[11] Ireland, Drennan believed, might become the great free port of the world,

> The vast Atlantic tide,
> Has scoop'd thy harbours deep and wide.

The United Irishmen were intensely conscious that Ireland was a distinctive country and a country which should shape its own political destiny. But, unlike many nineteenth-century nationalists, they did not attempt to fortify Ireland's claim to independence by strongly asserting that Ireland possessed its own cultural tradition, literature and language. The materials for cultural nationalism were abundantly available. Irish was still spoken over much of the country and many of the country people had a lively appreciation of Irish poetry and legend. Also Celtic lore was in fashion and for decades historians and

---

[10] C. Ryan, *Oration delivered at a numerous and respectable meeting . . . of the Roman catholics of the city of Dublin* (Cork, 1795), p. 20; T. W. Tone, *Life*, i, p. 358, ii, p. 464; W. T. Jones, *A letter to the societies of United Irishmen of the town of Belfast*, (1792), p. 81.
[11] W. Drennan, *A second letter to the Rt. Hon. William Pitt* (1799), p. 36.

archaeologists had been dwelling on the achievements of Irish civilization in the Christian and pre-Christian eras. Naturally enough then there were Irish radicals who displayed some interest in the Gaelic tradition. In October 1792 Edward Bunting, a gifted and wayward musician, who was a close friend of the MacCracken family, organized a harpers' festival in Belfast, at which ten masters of Irish traditional music played. The festival aroused considerable enthusiasm amongst the townspeople (though Tone, who was staying in Belfast, dismissed it with 'strum, strum and be hanged'), and Bunting was subsidized by a group of Belfast men in his travels over Connaught and Ulster collecting Irish airs. In 1796, a strenuous year in Ulster politics, he published his general collection of the ancient Irish music, and later some of his airs were to be popularized by Thomas Moore, who, while a Trinity under-graduate in the late nineties, was a keen radical. Bunting was a friend of Drennan, who was probably influenced by this friendship when he wrote of that 'instinctive sentiment of country . . . which I often hear with strange delight in the wild and almost savage melancholy of native music'.[12] The *Northern Star* reported in commendatory terms the harpers' festival, and praised the labours of Patrick Lynch, who was teaching Irish in Belfast and who gave some lessons to Tone's friend, Russell. A knowledge of Irish, the *Star* suggested, would be of value to the student of 'druidical theology and worship' and of use to the merchant and artisan who wanted to do business all over Ireland, and would promote the union of 'this neglected and much divided country'. The *Star* also commended to its readers *Bolg an Tsolair or the Gaelic magazine*, which aimed at bringing the beauties of Irish to the notice of Irishmen. The first (and apparently only) issue of the magazine, which was printed by the *Northern Star* office in 1795, consisted of a grammar and vocabulary together with a collection of Gaelic poems. The *Star* itself printed in 1796 'Erin go bragh', an exhilarating song with a Gaelic refrain, and 'Tara', a poem, which sang of

Glorious Tara Ireland's pride,
Seat of ancient heroes hail . . .[13]

[12] W. Drennan, *A second letter*, p. 4.
[13] *Trial of Thomas Russell, general in the late insurrection* (n.d.); *N.S.*, 20 Apr., 4 June 1795, 21 Apr. 1796.

John Boyd, the Newry poet, who contributed to the *Northern Star*, published in 1797 'The patriot', a long poem describing the defeat of the Danes by Brian, who calls on his countrymen to

> Act like your fathers and the Danes expell,
> Then liberty and peace with you shall dwell.[14]

But except in its theme the poem shows no awareness of the Gaelic literary tradition and could be the product of any contemporary English minor poet.

The occasions on which Irish radicals showed a sympathetic interest in the Gaelic world were few and far between. Their nationalism, like that of the Americans, was based on geography and a strong sense of common interests, and in their writings they referred very rarely to ancient or medieval Ireland, drawing their ideas and ideals from the British political tradition and from the American and French revolutions. Far from being anxious to stress a continuity of national tradition stretching back to the Gaelic past, they were inclined to think 'mankind have been too retrospective, canonized antiquity and under-valued themselves'. 'In associating,' the Dublin society of United Irishmen declared, 'we have thought little about our ancestors and much of our posterity.' The *Cork Gazette*, the Munster radical newspaper, which did not measure its words on any topic, was positively hostile to Irish. Lamenting the ignorance and superstition of the lower orders, it denounced the use of Irish as an obstacle to progress and hoped that parliamentary reform would be quickly followed by the introduction of universal education (which would presumably promote the use of English).[15]

The United Irishmen's determination to free Ireland from British control, and their vehement hostility to the British administration and those whom they regarded as its instruments in Ireland, should not obscure the fact that Irish radicals were well aware that Ireland and Great Britain were linked by innumerable ties. Drennan, a fervent Irish nationalist, spoke of 'the sociality of manners, language and law', which ought to unite Great Britain and Ireland, 'in any relation but that of

---

[14] J. Boyd, *Odes and elegies* (Newry, 1797).
[15] *Society of United Irishmen of Dublin*, pp. 33, 107; *Cork Gazette*, 16 Mar. 1796.

master and servant'. To Drennan, the England of 'Alfred, Edward and Locke' was far more significant than the England of Pitt, and he made it clear that to him a war between the two islands would be a civil war.[16] The United Irishmen were both convinced that Ireland should be independent and very conscious how much Great Britain and Ireland had in common. Did they then believe that there should be no political connection between the two islands? The question is not easily answered. The subject was a dangerous one to discuss in public, and in the event the Irish radicals were never in the position of having to take a final decision on the matter. Tone, as early as the summer of 1791, frankly said that the connection should be destroyed. But he made this pronouncement in a private letter, written when he had only just embarked on a political career, and when making the pronouncement he thought it advisable to practice what theologians term economy—a judicious reserve in communicating doctrine. Six months later the Dublin United Irishmen, addressing the English reformers, declared that 'we shall love each other *if we be left to ourselves*. It is the union of minds which ought to bind these nations together.' In the following year however the society in its addresses spoke with respect of the king and empire. From the middle nineties, with many radicals convinced that they could gain their ends only through invasion and insurrection, separation from Great Britain became part of the radical creed. Nevertheless, as late as the spring of 1797, a widely publicized radical manifesto answered the accusation that they were striving to get rid of the connection by stating that 'if that connection only existed in the manifold evils which have been heaped upon us by the present abominable administration, we sure should wish for a separation. But fellow subjects, connected as we are by the ties of blood—of a common language and polity—intimately connected as we are by our relative situation with each other and with the rest of the world, as well as by our mutual wants and redundancies—so far from wishing to lessen the ties of connection, we call upon, we entreat you to unite still further with us in the just and necessary work of reform.'[17] Even after the insurrection, MacNeven was prepared to admit that if 'we

[16] W. Drennan, *Second letter*, pp. 29, 50, 82.
[17] *N.S.*, 14 Apr. 1797; *Beauties of the Press* (1800), pp. 29–30.

had a free parliament, there might be a federal connection advantageous to both countries'. Emmet was perhaps expressing the same point of view in a different way when he said that 'if the government of this country be not regulated so as that the control may be wholly Irish, and the commercial arrangements between the two countries be not put on a footing of perfect equality, the connection cannot last'.[18]

Irish radicals were forward-looking and optimistic, but they spent little time discussing how Ireland would develop in the age of reform. Their immediate and absorbing concern was over-coming the formidable obstacles to reform, and contemporary liberal thinking, which exalted individual freedom, and strongly believed in the social value of private enterprise, guided by enlightened self-interest, did not encourage the production of blueprints for the organization of national endeavour. As Drennan put it 'any plan of reform once made would render every reform afterwards more easy'. There would obviously be great changes for the better. A drastic reduction in taxation would lead to a fall in the price of many commodities. County cess would be abolished or reduced; county government re-formed; tithe abolished and the church disestablished. There would be a national system of education: both Drennan and Emmet emphasized this, Drennan insisting that it should be subsidized but not directed by the state. The criminal law would be reformed. Emmet hoped 'to compare the crime with its punishment'; Henry Sheares urged 'a great simplification of the revenue laws', and Drennan asked for 'a bill that would remedy the intoxication of the populace'.[19]

Though Paine in the second part of the *Rights of Man* pointed the way towards the welfare state and in *Agrarian justice*—reprinted in the *Press*, the Dublin radical journal—suggested an inheritance tax on real property to subsidize a system of old age pensions and grants to young men setting out in life, the Irish radicals did not in the early nineties adumbrate any plans for directly improving the condition of the poor. They wanted to see 'a more equal distribution of the blessings and benefits of life', that every father of a family would be able to

---

[18] W. J. McNeven, *Pieces of Irish history* (1807), pp. 208, 217.
[19] W. Drennan, *Letter to . . . Lord Fitzwilliam*, pp. 43, 49, 53; H. Sheares, address in *Cork Gazette*, 31 Oct. 1795; W. J. MacNeven, *Pieces of Irish history*, p. 228.

acquire by his labour 'something beyond a mere subsistence, some little capital to provide in sickness, old age or misfortune a safeguard for his body and for his soul'. But this they hoped would be achieved by increased opportunities for employment and rising living standards, resulting from the growth and diversification of Irish industry which would follow the attainment of Irish freedom. The Dublin society of United Irishmen firmly declared that they were not levellers; by equality they did not mean 'the equality of property or the destruction of subordination'. Robert Thompson, a leading Belfast radical put this in concrete terms at a great reform meeting, when he explained that if they divided the land and money of Ireland equally each man would find himself with two acres and twenty-five shillings. All the rest of the national wealth would be lost, for who, for instance, could afford a coach and six. In the end, Thompson prophesied, the idle having wasted their shares, inequality would be re-established.[20]

Respecting property rights, the Irish radicals were slow to suggest modifications in the economic structure. The middle-class businessmen who provided much of the driving and directing power in the radical reform movement accepted the existing relationships between capital and labour in industry as axiomatic and in some instances they came into conflict with militant working-class groups. Thomas Dry, a clothier who was a very active radical in the nineties, in 1792 prosecuted a band of men who were trying to regulate wages and who broke into his house demanding 'burying money'. Abraham Creighton, a tailor, and a leading city politician, and a United Irishman, defied what he considered to be the tyranny of combinations, and half a dozen other members of the Dublin society of United Irishmen publicly opposed incipient trade unionism. William Sinclair, who played a leading part in the foundation of the Belfast society of United Irishmen, a linen manufacturer, with a great bleach green, in Tone's phrase, 'a noble concern' strongly resented local Luddism. 'All improvement', he complained, 'was resisted by the people.' The *Northern Star*, the powerful Belfast radical journal, also recognized that the working class had limited horizons. Realizing that working people

---

[20] *Society of United Irishmen of Dublin*, pp. 45, 55; *B.N.L.*, 29 Dec. 1792; *Press*, 2 Nov. 1797; S. S. Millin, *Belfast Politics*, pp. 108–14.

did not read newspapers, the *Star* suggested when the Belfast working weavers were discontented that handbills providing a digest of the laws against combinations should be distributed.[21]

From the middle nineties however, with the landed interest in radical opinion associated with oligarchic rule, political corruption and conservatism, and with the rural masses being mobilized behind the reform cause, some keen radicals began to scrutinize critically the Irish agrarian system. As early as 1794 the Revd Denis O'Driscoll, the editor of the pugnaciously radical *Cork Gazette*, defending himself when charged with publishing a seditious libel, asserted that he had advocated 'a proportionate not an equal partition of property', and that his agrarian principles were those of Locke. The *Gazette* pressed for a land tax which would hit only the landlord, and urged that middlemen should be eliminated and the land let directly to tenants on very long leases.[22]

In the later nineties radical leaders assumed that agrarian change was bound to follow invasion and rebellion. Tone in the summer of 1796 foresaw the possibility of 'a general massacre of the gentry and a distribution entire of their property'. He regretted that the Irish gentry had failed to assume the leadership of the national movement, and disappointed in the men of property, or at least of landed property, he turned without alacrity to the people, the labouring poor. In an address to the Irish peasantry, whose misery he painted in vivid colours, he pointed out how in France tithe, the game laws, corvée and the taxes which bore hard on the peasantry, had all been abolished, and that the lands of clergy and emigrants, perhaps three-quarters of the land in the country, had been confiscated and sold. The peasantry had been able to purchase clerical and noble land with depreciated assignats and 'almost all the lands of France are now the property of those who cultivate them'. But Tone pronounced that the rent the French peasant had had to pay was 'the least and lightest of his burdens', and that it was 'reasonable' when the land was let for

---

[21] *H.J.* 14 June, 23 Oct. 1780, 9 June, 29 Sept., 16 Nov. 1792, 2 May 1794; S.P.P. (Richard Dry). In *H.J.*, Thomas Dry clearly by mistake referred to as John. *N.S.*, 9 June 1792; T. W. Tone, *Life*, i, p. 148.

[22] *D.E.P.*, 1 May 1794; *Cork Gazette*, 11 Jan. 1794, 24 Feb. 1796; O'Driscoll was possibly for a time curate of the French church in Cork (W. M. Brady, *Clerical and parochial records of Cork, Cloyne and Ross* (1864), iii, p. 232).

its value.[23] Moreover, he did not suggest that there should be a general confiscation of landed property. The establishment of a peasant proprietory would be a probable consequence of the revolution but not a direct aim of the revolutionaries. Indeed, MacNeven, a leading United Irishman, when being examined by a house of commons committee immediately after the '98 insurrection, remarked that not very much land might have been confiscated, because if the revolution had looked like being successful 'many of the warmest friends of the British connection' might have joined the insurgents—after all they had readily enough in the past shifted their support from one administration to another. Thomas Addis Emmet, appearing before the same parliamentary committee, boldly declared that 'if a revolution takes place a very different system of political economy will be established from what had hitherto prevailed here'. But this merely seems to have meant that rents might be controlled, and even this, Emmet apparently thought, would be accomplished not by legislation but through the pressure of public opinion, with landlords realizing 'the increased value of the common people . . . in the democracy'.[24]

Arthur O'Connor, who from 1795 was to be one of the most outspoken of the radical leaders, was intensely interested in the land question. In his old age O'Connor declared that from infancy he had regarded himself as 'mere Irish', one of the conquered race. But he was also brought up to believe that he was descended from 'our ancient chiefs' and he might not have appreciated Mrs McTier's pen portrait—'an odd figure, tall, dark and penetrating, with that natural vulgarity of face you observe in the Irish'. Grandson of a very rich Cork businessman and a nephew of Lord Longueville, a county magnate, O'Connor inherited a reasonable property, was high sheriff of County Cork, 1791–2, and M.P. for his uncle's borough of Philipstown. To the self-assurance of a well-connected protestant landed gentleman O'Connor added a strong sense of intellectual superiority, a compound which could render him at times unbearably arrogant. He was consciously a man of the enlightenment (it is significant that when he married Cordorcet's daughter he added the philosopher's name to his own) and he

[23] T. W. Tone, *Life*, ii, pp. 148, 161, 302–4, 317–24.
[24] W. J. MacNeven, *Pieces of Irish history*, pp. 205, 222–3.

was proud both of his classical attainments and his grasp of economic theory. It was not until 1848 that he published his magnum opus, *Monopoly*, largely devoted to a denunciation of two blighting evils, priestcraft and primogeniture. *Monopoly* is a rambling, opinionated work (O'Connor pours scorn on Wellington, Napoleon and O'Connell, and refers complacently to himself as the Cassandra of the last half century, and a successful agricultural improver), but it shows that O'Connor, if not profound, was a restless and resolute thinker. When in 1798 he handled the land question at some length in his *State of Ireland*, he was primarily concerned not with the landlord–tenant relationship but with the size of landed estates. In O'Connor's opinion a system of laws (which he compared to the Newtonian system) governed human society. Property, he explained, was the machinery through which self-interest worked. Self-interest (checked to some extent by 'sympathy') was the force which regulated human society. Therefore those who possessed property would shape society and the rules of law which settled the ownership of property influenced decisively the nature of government. The existing property laws which had been evolved in 'the barbarous ages of Europe', encouraged the formation and preservation of huge estates. A landed system characterized by the predominance of great estates, was reflected in a constitutional system, in which political power was controlled by a landed oligarchy, entrenched in the house of lords. With the emergence of a large and powerful middle class and with society tending towards 'a cheerful, joyous state of general plenty and happy mediocrity', the existing agrarian and constitutional systems were outmoded. What, in O'Connor's opinion, circumstances urgently demanded, was a reform in the representative system, the abolition of the house of lords and of 'the monopolizing laws of primogeniture, entails and settlements', so that great accumulations of acres would disappear.[25]

It may be added that there are a few—very few in fact—indications that some of the rank and file in the radical movement were looking forward to drastic changes in the agrarian system. In 1797 a strong radical in Clady, County Tyrone, informed a friend in Washington that 'the multitude had a

[25] A. O'Connor, *Monopoly the cause of all evil* (1848); *State of Ireland* (1798), pp. 40–59.

mind to "take off the landlords and tyranic great men, and pay the rents into the public treasury" '—granting a salary to those who joined the people. An insurgent leader in Mayo said that as Lord Altamount had quitted his house, he should never enter it again 'nor should he ever again have a foot of his estate'. But if Lord Altamount gave a sum of money he might get back part of his house and 'a grasp of two or three cows or horses'. A paper, apparently drawn up in the late nineties by simple men, declared that 'large estates should be divided, giving to every person a competent share to enable him or her to get a comfortable livelihood'. It should be added that the writers of this paper considered that the 'beauty' of universal suffrage was that the poor man would have representatives who would watch with vigilance 'lest the labour or employment of the citizen or husbandman be made uncertain or unfashionable'.[26]

From the beginning of the nineties the Irish radicals agreed on their primary aim, a sweeping measure of parliamentary reform (which would include catholic emancipation). The next question was, how was it to be achieved? There seemed to radicals to be a simple answer to this question. They had immense faith in the power of enlightened public opinion, resoundingly expressed. Adept at working the machinery by which middle-class mass meetings registered support for liberal sentiments, embodied in resolutions and addresses, they were reluctant to admit that so far their efforts had made little or no impression on the parliamentary opponents of reform. 'If the people of Ireland', the Armagh society of United Irishmen declared in 1793, 'state their grievances and demand redress with firmness and moderation, with the determined calm and dignity of men inspired with a due sense of the justice and magnitude of their cause, their voice must be heard and their efforts finally crowned with success.' The Dublin society of United Irishmen suggested methods by which public opinion could be consolidated and brought to bear. Shortly after its foundation in 1791, it proclaimed that radical clubs throughout Ireland, 'points of union . . . acting in concert, moving as one body, with one impulse and one direction, will become not parts of the nation but the nation itself . . . expressing its will,

[26] H. White to C. S. Stephenson, 13 Feb. 1797 (I.S.P.O. 620/28/276); court martial of P. Agar (620/32/31); sheet in 620/43/6).

restless in its power'. Some weeks later the society called on the country to take steps to choose delegates to a national convention which would unite their 'scattered and insulated will into one momentous mass'. Once the nation's will was known, the crown, acting as a reforming *deus ex machina* might be expected to intervene on the people's behalf.[27] Convinced then, that Irish opinion enthusiastically favoured reform and the national will, when clearly expressed, must prevail, radicals in the early nineties optimistically busied themselves in arraying the volunteers and preparing for a great national convention, based on popular election.

As has been seen, the Dublin liberals had been active in 1790. In 1791 the Ulster liberals took the initiative with great energy and enthusiasm. In the summer the Belfast liberal leaders decided to have an impressive commemoration of the fall of the Bastille and in June a committee was set up to draft the resolutions to be approved by the town meeting which was to be held on 14 July. This committee consulted two political publicists living in Dublin, William Drennan and Theobald Wolfe Tone.[28] Drennan was celebrated in the north as the author of a brilliant political pamphlet, the *Letters of Orellena*. Tone, a younger man, good company, with a lively mind, wide interests and literary ambitions, was trying, not very hard and without much success, to build up a practice at the Irish bar. In 1790 he had entered politics by publishing *A review of the conduct of administration*, an attack on the Irish government along the lines developed by the whig opposition. The whig leaders congratulated him on the pamphlet and for a moment Tone optimistically thought they might put him into parliament. But though George Ponsonby always spoke to him 'with great civility' he soon felt neglected by the party he had tried to help (after all the whigs had a number of able lawyers in their ranks). Tone's next pamphlet, *Spanish war*, sharply criticized Grattan's approach to foreign policy, arguing that if the Nootka Sound dispute led to an Anglo-Spanish war, Ireland should not

---

[27] *D.E.P.*, 22 Jan. 1793; *Society of the United Irishmen of Dublin*, pp. 10, 56–61. Drennan, who composed the address of the Dublin society of United Irishmen in which crown action was mentioned, also referred to the intervention of the crown in favour of reform in his plan of reform.

[28] *B.N.L.*, 17 June 1791; S. McTier to W. Drennan, 2, 9 July 1791; W. Drennan to S. McTier, 3 July 1791 (Drennan papers, 302, 303, 304).

become involved. Ireland's independent parliament had the right to grant or refuse supplies, and Tone was convinced that 'the quarrel is English, the profit will be to England, and Ireland will be left to console herself for treasure spent and gallant sons fallen by the reflection that valor like virtue has its own reward'. At the end of August 1791 he published his best known pamphlet, *An argument on behalf of the catholics of Ireland*, in which he expounded with Euclidian force and clarity the radical solution for Ireland's problems. The cause of Ireland's economic retardation was that the Irish government was unduly influenced by England; this influence could be successfully opposed only by a reformed parliament; and no scheme of parliamentary reform would be 'honorable, practicable, efficacious or just' which did not include the catholics. Tone briskly disposed of the arguments for retaining the catholic disabilities (for instance that catholics were Jacobites), and though he believed that 'religion has at this day little influence on politics', he was prepared to agree that only catholic £10 freeholders should be enfranchised if, at the same time, 'the wretched tribe' of forty-shilling freeholders be struck off the register. His views may not have been very original but he expressed them with point and polish, and his pamphlet was a lucid and compelling radical manifesto.

Tone must have been immersed in considering and composing the *Argument* when he received the request for advice from the Belfast committee through his friend, Thomas Russell, an army officer of advanced political views, who was a popular figure in Belfast liberal circles. Tone responded by sending three resolutions summarizing the views he was to set out in his forthcoming pamphlet. In a letter accompanying the resolutions he stated, 'they certainly fall far short of the truth, but truth itself must sometimes condescend to temporize, my own unalterable opinion is that the bane of Irish prosperity is the influence of England [and] I believe that influence will ever be extended while the connection between the two countries continues'. But recognizing that his views were 'for the present too hardy', he had abstained from putting into the resolutions 'one word that looks like a wish for separation'.[29] A copy of

[29] *Commons jn. Ire.*, xvii, p. dcccxxxvii; T. W. Tone to T. Russell, 9 July 1791 (R.I.A. 23 K 53).

this letter was soon in the hands of the government (possibly because Russell, an admiring and indiscreet friend showed it to Diggis, an American adventurer who was staying in Belfast, and whose readily available political reminiscences greatly impressed the local radicals). Conservatives were to make great play with Tone's frank exposition of his opinions, which confirmed their belief that the Irish radicals would be satisfied with nothing short of complete independence, and the letter was given a much wider circulation than any of Tone's other works obtained. Some Irish nationalists valued the letter as providing irrefutable proof that from an early stage in his political career Tone was committed to the struggle for national independence. But it should be taken into account that the frequently quoted phrases appeared in a letter written to an intimate friend by a young man who had only recently begun to think seriously about political issues and who was not yet actively associated with any political organization.

On 14 July 1791 the Belfast volunteers accompanied by a number of the inhabitants marched through the streets. At the White linen hall an address to the French, drafted by Drennan, was approved. It called for 'a real representation of the national will' and the annihilation of all civil and religious intolerance in Ireland. A clause, which Drennan was keen to have included, emphasizing the desirability of political co-operation between protestants and catholics in Ireland, was omitted. Nevertheless, catholic meetings at Elphin and in Roscommon voted their thanks to the volunteers for their liberal declaration, and Drennan, always fertile in experiments, at once suggested that the Belfast volunteers should persuade other Ulster corps to agree on an alliance between reformers and catholics and place specific proposals before a group of leading catholics who would be at Ballinasloe fair in October.[30] This plan was premature but in October the Dublin volunteers were provoked by a grand jury into passing resolutions, which greatly pleased those catholics who were eager for action.

The Armagh grand jury, perturbed by serious sectarian rioting in their county, attempted to apply a partial (in both

---

[30] The reply of the volunteers to the catholics assembled at Jamestown and Elphin (620/19/28); W. Drennan to S. McTier, 9 July, 31 Aug. 1791 (Drennan papers, 305, 306).

senses of the word) remedy. They issued a notice deploring 'the rage among the Roman catholics for illegally arming themselves' and offering a reward for the conviction of persons illegally carrying arms. Shortly after this notice appeared the Independent Dublin volunteers met with Hamilton Rowan in the chair. They expressed both their regret that 'a part of the law which discredits our ancestors' should be enforced and the hope that catholics and protestants would unite to claim the rights of man. A few days later representatives of the protestant members of six other Dublin volunteer corps endorsed this declaration. It is significant that Hamilton Rowan and five of the six representatives were soon to become members of that famous radical club, the Dublin society of United Irishmen. A fortnight later 'the catholics of Dublin', assembled at Derham's tavern in Essex Street, with Dr William James MacNeven (another future member of the Dublin society of United Irishmen) in the chair. 'A few', wrote John Keogh, an astute Dublin catholic businessman, 'were timid at first as might be expected', but, he added, '*spirit* is getting very high'. The meeting thanked the volunteers for their reply to the Armagh grand jury and the volunteers were also thanked for their 'spirited and liberal' resolutions by the catholic inhabitants of Galway. With catholics and liberal minded volunteers publicly displaying effusive goodwill, it is easy to forget that their objectives, or at least their priorities, were different. In October William Sinclair, the Belfast liberal, writing to Charles O'Conor, a well-known Connaught catholic, stressed that parliamentary reform was 'a national cause' which catholics and protestants together should wholeheartedly support. But a month or so later John Keogh was suggesting to O'Conor that the Connaught catholics, while of course expressing gratitude to their northern friends, should 'at the same time keep clear of deciding about reform or other political questions'.[31] Keogh, though himself a radical reformer, saw that it would be bad tactics for the catholics, whose prospects were good, to allow the cause of catholic relief, which would attract support from conservatives, to be closely linked to parliamentary reform.

However, the signs of a *rapprochement* between protestant

---

[31] *H.J.*, 5, 24 Oct. 1791, 27 Feb. 1792; C. O'Conor Don, *The O'Conors of Connaught* (1891), pp. 298–9, 302.

liberals and politically conscious catholics were encouraging to those who wanted to see a catholic–radical coalition emerging in Irish politics. Obviously a club or society which would mobilize progressive opinion in support of a programme combining parliamentary reform and catholic emancipation was required, and Drennan had already in a printed broadsheet, circulated in the spring of 1791, provided Irish radicals with a scheme for a political club, a Brotherhood, blending liberalism and romanticism. Its aims were to be, in general, the rights of man and the greatest happiness of the greatest number, and, in particular Irish independence and republicanism. It was to have 'much of the secrecy and something of the ceremonial of freemasonry'. In communication with sympathizers in England, France and America, it would be 'a benevolent conspiracy', diffusing throughout the community radical teaching, 'until the trial comes'.[32] The powerful influence which energetic political clubs could have on events was being daily demonstrated in France, so it is not surprising that about the middle of September the Belfast radical leaders, 'the secret committee', which Tone discovered, 'directed the movements of Belfast', formed a club which was intended to be a centre of radical thought and action in the town.[33] They invited Tone and Russell, who had retired from the army and was living in Dublin, to visit Belfast and take part in preparing for publication the society's first manifesto. In early October they both arrived. Tone turned out to be one of the few Irish politicians who was happily at home in both Dublin and Belfast, and he greatly enjoyed the visit. He was present at a succession of breakfasts and dinners, went to the theatre, a coterie and a card club, and saw the sights, including a sail-cloth factory, a glass factory and a bleach green, and listened to the grievances of a successful businessman—lack of government help for the linen industry and the resistance offered by artisans to technological advance. His diary provides a vivid and lively picture of Belfast at a time of transition. A compact place, pulsating with economic, political and intellectual life, alert and industrious but not dour, which was in the process of changing

[32] W. Drennan to S. McTier, 21 May, end of Dec. 1791 (Drennan papers, 300, 312).

[33] See forthcoming edition of T. W. Tone's *Works*, ed. T. W. Moody and R. B. McDowell.

from being a busy market town to being a large aggregate of industrial and productive power.

On 18 October Tone attended a meeting of the new society of United Irishmen, eighteen members being present with Samuel McTier in the chair. Resolutions, which Tone had helped to draft, declaring the aims of the society were approved and in the ensuing discussion he and Russell emphasized how important it was for the northern radicals to co-operate with the Dublin radicals and the catholic committee (about whose proceedings the Belfast radicals knew very little).

Shortly before they founded their new political club with its clearly enunciated programme, the Belfast radical leaders had been taking steps to start a newspaper to propagate their views, the *Northern Star*, which began publication in January 1792. It was, as might be expected, run on extremely efficient lines. In September a committee composed of the investors in the new venture, ten Belfast businessmen, met with Thomas McCabe in the chair, and having decided that all their 'differences' would be settled by ballot, they elected a subcommittee, Robert Caldwell, Samuel Neilson (who acted as editor) and Robert Simms, to make preliminary arrangements. The subcommittee wrote to over fifty liberals scattered throughout Ulster, asking them to secure subscribers. Only half a dozen refused to support the new publication, though letters from Ballymoney and Limavady pointed out that the cost of a newspaper was 'a great bar to men in the lower ranks of life', and that few farmers or mechanics would buy one. The committee was also warned that some Donaghadee people who would change to the *Star*, were in arrears with their subscriptions to the *Belfast News-Letter*. On the whole however the new journal was greeted with great enthusiasm. Alexander Crawford, a well-known Lisburn radical wrote, 'whatever tends to cultivate knowledge of the rights of mankind, diffuse political information, and to promote unanimity and concord amongst Irishmen' deserved support, and a Derry correspondent thought that the new paper was certainly required since both the *Belfast News-Letter* and the *Derry Journal* had displayed 'a degree of delicacy which prevented useful local truths from appearing'.[34]

The *Northern Star* very well printed and produced, had a good

[34] Papers relating to *N.S.* in I.S.P.O. 620/15/8/1 and I.S.P.O. 620/19/42.

distribution system, with agents all over Ulster and in Dublin, London, Liverpool and Edinburgh. It gave a considerable amount of news, British, French, American and Ulster—its coverage of Irish affairs outside Ulster being comparatively narrow. Its comments sometimes extending into short editorials, expounded the radical approach with clarity and bite. It published some entertaining and stinging political satire, William Sampson's 'Hurdy-Gurdy', a mélange of verse and prose and 'Billy Bluff and Squire Firebrand' by the Revd James Porter, a series of dialogues between two blimpish Irish tories. Literary essays and poetry from time to time appeared in its columns. The product of an energetic, economically fast-advancing community, the *Northern Star*, intelligent, consistent, hard-hitting and readable, provided a tremendous stimulus for northern radicals, continuously reminding them that they were part of a great world-wide political and moral movement destined to early victory.

The Dublin radicals also decided at the close of 1791 to produce a newspaper, the *National Journal*. Its aims, according to its preface, were to promote union amongst men of all denominations and parliamentary reform, and it was written, it declared, not only for the politician and the man of letters but for the artisan, the mechanic and the husbandman. It was expected to begin publication on 1 January 1792 but it did not appear until March. Printed badly on poor paper, it ceased publication in June. It failed, according to Drennan, because the catholics did not like its editor; Carey, a working journalist, pointed out that it was conducted by university-bred amateurs.[35]

If the Belfast *Northern Star* was the outstanding Irish radical journal, the Dublin society of United Irishmen soon became the most distinguished radical political club in Ireland. Tone and Russell, on returning to Dublin, introduced themselves to Napper Tandy, the doyen of Dublin city liberalism, and told him about the formation of the new Belfast club. Tandy seized on the idea of having a fraternal society in Dublin and convened a meeting of catholics and protestants, eighteen in all, for 9 November. This gathering, having placed the Honorable

[35] H.O. 100/34 f. 79; W. P. Carey, *An appeal*, p. 31; W. Drennan to S. McTier early Nov. 1791, 30 Mar. 1792, June 1792 (Drennan papers, 209a, 328, 337).

Simon Butler ('the only man of fashion among us') in the chair,
adopted the Belfast society's declaration and founded the
Dublin society of United Irishmen.[36]

The Dublin society of United Irishmen was probably the
most influential, and undoubtedly the most conspicuous,
political club in eighteenth-century Ireland. Also, and this is
certainly unusual for a radical society, there is ample material
available relating to its activities and membership. The society
itself published a fair amount.[37] Drennan, one of its founders,
was a zealous and critical member and kept his Belfast relations
continually informed about what the society was doing and
hoped to achieve. The government, from shortly after the
society's foundation, was receiving regular reports on its proceedings from a member, Thomas Collins, a Dublin linen
merchant and apparently at one time a man of some means,
who had in 1790 gone bankrupt. He had wide contacts with
Dublin radicalism and by the close of 1791 became a United
Irishman and was soon reporting on the society to John Giffard,
the Dublin municipal conservative leader, and to Cooke, the
under-secretary. Collins had his failings. He continually
indulged in jeering facetiousness at the expense of the men whose
private proceedings he was reporting. He officiously offered his
advice on political problems to his employers and he suffered
from the occupational disease of a secret agent—a tendency to
magnify the dangers to be apprehended from the group he is
watching. But Collins's reports, systematic and written in a
clear flowing hand, bear the marks of a good business training.
With the reports he frequently enclosed his printed summons
to the meeting, giving the names of candidates for membership
with those of their proposers and seconders (when a motion
was made for discounting the use of a summons, Collins
successfully opposed it).

Candidates for admission to the society had to be proposed
and seconded, could be rejected by one black bean in five and
had to pay an admission 'fine' of one guinea in addition to their
subscription. About 400 members seem to have been admitted

---

[36] W. Drennan to S. McTier, 10 Nov. 1791 (Drennan papers, 311).

[37] For the Dublin society of United Irishmen see 'Proceedings of the Dublin
society of United Irishmen' in *Analecta Hibernica*, no. 17, pp. 3–142 and 'The
personnel of the Dublin society of United Irishmen, 1791–4' by R. B. McDowell in
I.H.S., ii, pp. 12–53, H.O. 100/34 f. 79.

between the foundation of the society and its dissolution in May 1794 but only about 200 of these seem to have attended regularly. Up to November 1792 the average attendance at a meeting was 56; during the winter of 1792–3, a period of great political excitement when the membership was steadily growing the average was about 90, but from April 1793 it fell to about 40. The membership, as might be expected, was composed of professional and businessmen with a sprinkling of country gentlemen. The aristocracy was represented by Simon Butler, a barrister, who was a brother of Lord Mountgarret. Lord Edward Fitzgerald thought of joining, but his brother, the duke of Leinster, 'negatived his desire with the greatest indignation'.[38] The membership of the society comprised no fewer than 26 barristers, more than twice that number of attorneys, 24 medical men (physicians, surgeons and apothecaries), 14 booksellers and printers (including two well-known liberal publishers, Patrick Byrne and John Chambers, both in business on a fairly large scale and both destined to emigrate after the '98 rebellion to America), half a dozen army officers, a schoolmaster, who seems to have been an educational reformer, and a fellow of Trinity college, Whitley Stokes. Stokes, a member of a great intellectual dynasty (with seven members in the *DNB*), and one of the few lay fellows, was a man of wide interests and generous enthusiasms. A professor of medicine, he advocated drastic precautions against contagious diseases and worked in a dispensary to relieve the sick poor. He catalogued, with considerable expertise, the college mineral collection, was one of the founders of the Dublin Zoological society, wrote replies to Paine on religion and Malthus on population, drafted a plan of parliamentary reform, and advocated the creation of small farms and the translation of the scriptures into Irish. In Tone's opinion, he was ideally suited to be head of a system of national education.

The businessmen included over 100 merchants (of whom 67 were cloth merchants), 31 textile manufacturers, an ironfounder (who claimed to have installed the first steam engine in Dublin), a pin-maker, tailors, jewellers, hatters, hosiers and butchers. The predominance of the textile trades is easily explained. Dublin was the great textile manufacturing centre,

[38] W. Drennan to S. McTier, [8 Mar. 1793] (Drennan papers, 396).

textile industrialists had been strongly protectionist and some of the textile merchants must have had links with Irish manufacturers. It may be added that Nicholas Butler, the jeweller, an active member of the society, had in the eighties vigorously promoted the sale of Irish goods by producing an emblematic button to be worn on suits of Irish cloth, and at least fourteen other members of the society had publicly supported the protectionist agitation. But the difficulty of reconciling different economic interests was illustrated early in 1793 when a resolution pledging the Dublin society of United Irishmen to confine themselves 'to the consumption of Irish manufactures only' was opposed by the importers of English cloth who were members of the society. Though 45 of the businessmen in the society at one time or another went bankrupt, a number of them were enterprising, successful and prosperous—men with a stake in the community. As for the working classes, as might be expected, they were not represented in the society's membership. The only employees admitted seem to have been a couple of clerks and an attorney's apprentice (son of a distiller).

The presence of so many professional men, and especially of a large contingent of lawyers is reflected in the formal fashion in which the society conducted its business. It had its officers (elected for three months), standing committees and procedure. It was laid down that 'every respect and deference shall be paid to the president', his chair was to be raised three steps above the members' seats and he was to be 'the judge of order and propriety', with power to insist on an apology and to fine. The society had its seal, bearing an Irish harp with the motto, 'I am new strung, I will be heard'. Its manifestos were carefully drafted, strictly scrutinized by the society and sometimes amended after discussion; and the moves in the society's legal battles were debated with professional zest. William Paulet Carey, in a vitriolic attack on the United Irishmen, declared that businessmen such as himself, 'the men from behind their counters', resented the way in which the professional men ran the society. But Carey was abnormally sensitive and many Dublin businessmen who played a part in civic politics were fluent debaters. What attendance figures suggest however is that interminable political theorizing may have bored a good many members.

The leaders of the Dublin society of United Irishmen, intelligent, intense political enthusiasts, expected it to be a political forum in which the details of their programme could be hammered out, a means of mobilizing liberal opinion and an intellectual generating force for Irish radicalism. At the outset they appointed a committee to consider what publications 'it may be necessary to republish and what others may be required to be confuted as injurious to the public good', and early in 1792 the society published a report on the popery laws, a close printed pamphlet listing the catholic disabilities. Towards the close of 1793 it was decided to publish all the society's addresses and other communications to the press in 'one neat volume', under the supervision of Drennan, Rowan and McNally, and this work, a small, well laid-out book of 200 pages, appeared in 1794 without a printer's name. In two years the society published 15 addresses. Written in a high-flown nervous oratorical style, elevated in tone, and pungent in argument, taken together they comprise an anthology of ideas and ideals for Irish radicals. The Dublin society also tried to influence opinion by its contacts with affiliated political clubs. There are known to have been United Irishmen societies not only in Belfast but in Armagh, Clonmel, Gorey, Limerick, Lisburn, Nenagh, Sixmilewater, Templepatrick and Tullamore.

I I

The catholic agitation

While during 1791 the radical agitation for reform was getting under way, another section of Irish society, already provided with well-tried machinery through which it could exercise political pressure, was beginning to stir. The Irish catholics for some years after the passing of the 1782 relief act had refrained from pressing for the abolition of the remaining disabilities. For the moment they were grateful for what they had received and perhaps sensed that the protestant mind needed an interval in which to adjust itself to the inevitability of further concession. But by the close of the eighties their instinctive urge to ask for more was stimulated by events outside Ireland. In the United States religious equality was accepted as politically axiomatic. At Westminster in 1789 and 1790 the disabilities of the English dissenter were debated when it was moved that the test and corporation acts be repealed, and at the end of 1789 the French national assembly decreed that French protestants should enjoy all civic rights. A fortnight after this decree was published in the Dublin newspapers the catholic committee decided the time had come for the Irish catholics to make an attempt to obtain the repeal of the penal laws and a select committee was appointed to plan a campaign against the disabilities. But in the spring the triennial elections for the general committee—held in Dublin and about thirty provincial centres—absorbed for a time the attention of community-conscious catholics and it was not until the beginning of 1791 that the newly constituted general committee was ready to move into action. At gatherings held to elect representatives to the committee, resolutions relating to relief had been formulated, so, when it came to assessing catholic opinion, the committee had plenty of material at its disposal. It decided to press for four concessions. Catholics were to be admitted to both branches of the legal profession, and they were to be eligible for the commission of the peace and jury service, both on grand and petty juries. In the counties a limited number of catholic freeholders were to be enfranchised—it being suggested that catholic £20 freeholders and catholic forty-shilling freeholders who rented a farm for at least £20 per annum, should be permitted to vote.[1] These may appear modest demands in what was a revolutionary era, but for many Irish protestants they represented the thin end of a dangerous wedge. They implied that Irish catholics should be allowed, albeit in a very limited degree, to participate in the political life of the community.

A subcommittee of thirteen, under the chairmanship of Lord Fingall, was set up to press the catholic demands. It included seven Dublin businessmen, three medical men and two country gentlemen, and it is of some significance that six of its members were later to join the Dublin society of United Irishmen. Within a few weeks a rift developed in the subcommittee, the two country gentlemen, Bellew and Strange of County Kildare, resigning and being replaced by Thomas Fitzgerald, a Kildare country gentleman, of liberal or radical opinions, and Dominick Rice who later became a member of the Irish bar and of the Dublin society of United Irishmen.[2]

These resignations almost certainly reflect a division in the catholic ranks between those who wanted vigorous action and the more cautious. The Dublin radicals were active in the forward party; the conservatives had a natural leader in Lord Kenmare, who had an inherent dislike of agitation and 'a contempt for many of the members who formed the committee'. However, since a respected peer was bound to carry great weight in Irish political life, the subcommittee was very anxious to have Kenmare's co-operation when approaching the Irish administration, and it went to considerable trouble to persuade Kenmare and his cousin, Lord Fingall, to accompany a deputation to the Castle on 14 March 1791. Kenmare had long been regarded as the leading catholic layman, the deference the committee had displayed had done nothing to lessen his sense of his status, and when the deputation met the chief secretary he automatically acted as its spokesman, stating or implying that the catholics were content to leave their cause

---

[1] 'The minute book of the catholic committee, 1773–1792', p. 151.
[2] Ibid., p. 124.

in the hands of the government. But other members of the deputation, apparently sensing in advance that this might happen, had armed themselves with a set of resolutions, approved by the committee, suggesting immediate and substantial concessions. Kenmare complained that he and Fingall had not seen the resolutions and that 'if we had foreseen them we should not have been present'. The public split in the deputation diminished the significance of the resolutions which it presented to the chief secretary, and in any event the session was too far advanced for anything to be done.[3]

Shortly after the session ended the general committee decided to overhaul its machinery in preparation for a renewed drive against the disabilities. Early in April a subcommittee of twenty-two, apparently dominated by the forward party, was set up to take the necessary steps to secure a mitigation of the disabilities and in June it was replaced by a slightly larger subcomittee of twenty-seven on which both the radicals and the conservatives were well represented. In addition two small subcommittees were set up, each composed of advocates of vigorous action—the one to handle publications, the other to examine the principles on which the general committee was constituted. In July the subcommittee of twenty-seven had an interview with the chief secretary at which they informed him that the catholics intended to petition parliament at the beginning of the session and sounded him regarding the Irish administration's attitude. Hobart was amiable but stressed that 'a matter of such importance' must be referred to the British cabinet.[4] Shortly afterwards the subcommittee, feeling that the Irish catholics should be represented at the point of final decision, persuaded Richard Burke, the son of the great conservative champion, to act as their agent in England.

Richard Burke was a high-minded, competent member of the English bar, with a number of political contacts. However, the main value of his appointment was that it publicly associated his father with the Irish catholic cause. Edmund Burke had a powerful and passionate loathing for political injustice and for

---

[3] Kenmare to R. Hobart, 15 May 1791 (H.O. 100/33); 'The minute book of the catholic committee, 1773–1792', pp. 127–8; A. Cogan, *The diocese of Meath*, iii, p. 189.

[4] 'The minute book of the catholic committee', p. 136.

many years he had regarded the penal laws as being both immoral and in a multiplicity of ways injurious to Irish society. Convinced that civil society, 'an institution of beneficence', 'a partnership in every virtue and all perfection', was of essential value to man, he was distressed to see the Irish catholics, who, he was sure would make good citizens and loyal subjects, debarred from playing that part in the Irish community which their status, property and intelligence warranted. Burke was concerned to maintain the connection between Great Britain and Ireland and to preserve the Irish constitution in church and state—a loyal anglican he regarded the established church in Ireland as 'one of the main pillars of the Christian religion' (as well as the church of 'the greater number of the primary landed proprietors of the kingdom').[5] Conscious that catholicism had a great and inherent respect for hierarchy and tradition, Burke was certain that if the Irish catholics were treated fairly many of them would rally to the defence of the existing order. But if they were kept amongst the unprivileged they would be forced into alliance with those who were striving to destroy existing institutions and introduce innovating democracy. Burke's policy was essentially a moderate one—full political rights for the Irish catholic, but within the existing constitutional framework and the established social order. He pressed however for a policy of concession to the catholics with intense, impatient, and at times violent, vehemence. This is understandable. With European civilization imperilled by the spread of revolution and revolutionary ideas, it was a matter of urgency to take steps which would stabilize Irish society. Opposition in these circumstances was exasperating, and what drove Burke from exasperation to anger was the quality of the opposition. The Irish protestant critics of concession claimed to be good conservatives, defending existing institutions, but Burke saw them as trying to hang on to positions which were indefensible morally as well as in terms of practical politics. Naturally then he explained their motives in the harshest terms. They were a monopolizing group with a corrupt, selfish, shortsighted leadership, clinging tenaciously to power.

At the beginning of November an energetic and impatient catholic group, the Catholic society of Dublin, 50 or 60 of the

[5] Edmund Burke, *Works* (1882), vi, p. 72.

most violent agitators, according to the lord lieutenant—'very good people' according to Drennan, produced a declaration which delighted radicals.[6] Having sketched in vivid, over-charged language, the 'mortifying and oppressive bondage' endured by Irish catholics, 'preserved in this land but as a source of revenue', the declaration demanded the abolition of 'the entire code'. From the Irish administration's standpoint this declaration was most inopportune. The government—the Irish administration and the members of the British cabinet principally concerned with Ireland—had been considering the catholic question and were formulating a policy which might arouse protestant apprehensions. In England the en-enactment of a catholic relief bill of 1791 which swept away almost all the disabilities, except those which debarred catholics from any share in political power, had shown that catholicism was no longer regarded as a menace to British society; and Burke, in his *Reflections*, the work which provided an intellectual basis for the conservative cause, had paid a tribute to the French catholic church as one of the enriching and conserving forces of the ancient regime. It is not surprising then that the British cabinet towards the close of 1791 had come to the conclusion that the Irish catholics, or a substantial section of them, should by a policy of generous concession be enlisted in the defence of the state and the established social order.

In Ireland Westmorland was conscious that a union between catholics and dissenters could prove very formidable. But it had not yet been formed, and he and Hobart were prepared to make concessions to the Irish catholics on the lines of the British measure of 1791—'however politic or impolitic upon the comparative strength of the professors such indulgence may be'. They were also acutely aware that any suggestion of concessions, at a time when change was in the air, might stir up protestant feeling. Westmorland pointed out that 'whatever scheme the English government may form it is not in our power to force anything upon this subject against the general sense of the parliament'. It was then, Westmorland wrote, 'most provoking that at the very moment I had reconciled most of our leading minds to the good policy of following

[6] Westmorland to Dundas, 21 Nov. 1791 (H.O. 100/33); W. Drennan to S. McTier, 10 Nov. 1791 (Drennan papers, 311).

England in like concessions', 'a mischievous publication' should appear.[7] When at the end of November a deputation from the subcommittee of twenty-seven waited on the chief secretary to present him with a list of the catholics' immediate objectives, Hobart asked them to disavow the declaration of the catholic society and 'to do away with the alarms the book had excited'. The deputation, while regretting that anything done by the catholics should be displeasing to the government, said they could not disavow a declaration which 'contained truths as to our situation which could not be disavowed', and they pressed the government 'to restore a deserving people to their natural rank in society'.[8] But when the more conservative catholics were warned that the good intentions of the administration might be thwarted 'by the folly of the catholic association', their response was more satisfactory. Archbishop Troy of Dublin, who believed that 'the influence of the catholic bishops should be cherished by every well wisher to legal subordination and peace', informed the chief secretary that catholics of rank and property were coming forward with declarations satisfactory to the government—and he also took the opportunity to emphasize to Hobart the desirability of enfranchising catholic freeholders. And at the beginning of December an address, signed by Kenmare and the bishop of Ardfert on behalf of the catholics of Kerry, was presented to the lord lieutenant, expressing abhorrence of writings and associations 'which might possibly sow the seeds of discontent and impatience amongst the lower classes of our persuasion'.[9]

With the conservative catholics in touch with the government and anxious to modulate the relief agitation, and the forward party eager for action, acute tension was bound to develop in the catholic committee. On 17 December when future policy was being discussed, the conservatives on calling for a division were defeated by 90 to 17. The minority thereupon seceded and, in consultation with Sir Hercules Langrishe, a government

---

[7] Westmorland to W. Pitt, 5 Mar. 1791, to Hobart, 19 Dec. 1791 (Westmorland correspondence); Westmorland to Grenville, 7 Mar. 1791 (Add. MS 59253).

[8] For the catholic delegation's interview with Hobart on 26 Nov. 1791 see I.S.P.O. 620/19/37.

[9] J. T. Troy to Hobart, 29 Dec. 1791 (H.O. 100/34); *H.J.*, 12 Dec. 1792.

supporter, and one of the earliest advocates of catholic relief, drew up an address to the viceroy.[10] In this address they emphasized that they would not presume to point out to the legislature what concessions should be granted—though they made it perfectly clear that they expected a relief measure. The address was signed by three peers (Fingall, Gormanston and Kenmare), the archbishop of Dublin, two baronets, nine Dublin merchants, and a number of country gentlemen, the signatories numbering in all 68. It was supported by addresses from three counties (Galway, Kilkenny, Mayo), the city of Kilkenny, a number of Kerry baronies, and by groups of catholics in Waterford and Carlow. A few days after the publication of the seceders' address the parishioners of the catholic Saint Michan's, Dublin, met and expressed their support of the general committee, stating that to put the catholics on the same footing as other dissenters would be only 'an equitable return' for the loyalty they had displayed. The other Dublin parishes followed suit, declaring that the committee was 'the only organ through which the voice of our people can be unequivocally heard'. The committee was also supported by addresses from four counties and over thirty urban centres, as far apart as Cork and Belfast, Carrick-on-Shannon and Navan—an impressive manifestation of Irish catholic opinion. Kenmare was naturally severely criticized, the parishioners of Saint Mary's, Dublin, who stressed their loyalty to the house of Hanover, referring to him as Sir Thomas Browne, and on 14 January the general committee, considering he had been responsible for the 'insidious and servile addresses', removed him from the subcommittee.[11]

In Burke's opinion the schism in the committee reflected a change in the social balance within Irish catholicism. 'The old standard gentlemen', whose 'pedigrees alone afforded them any hope of distinction' found themselves competing with 'a new race of catholics' who 'have risen by their industry, their abilities, and their good fortune to considerable opulence and

---

[10] H. Langrishe to R. Hobart, 19 Dec. 1791 (H.O. 100/34); D.C., 29 Dec. 1791. At the beginning of December Cooke had a talk with a member of the committee and suggested that the 'respectable' catholics in their petition should leave 'the mode of relief' to the government (E. Cooke to R. Hobart, 5 Dec. 1791, H.O. 100/34).

[11] H.J., 6 Jan. 1792; D.E.P., 17 Jan. 1792.

of course to an independent spirit'.[12] In fact, the second estate was being challenged by the third. As for the first estate it was divided—an archbishop and three bishops publicly supporting Lord Kenmare, and one bishop signing resolutions in favour of the committee. The division amongst the laity did not precisely run along social lines. For instance, some merchants, as has been seen, were amongst the seceders and some country gentlemen, including a baronet, Sir Thomas French, sided with the committee. What can be safely said is that the early months of 1792 saw the emergence of the catholic middle classes, the urban businessmen and respectable farmers, as an unmistakable and potent force in Irish public life.

About ten days after the schism in the catholic committee, which apparently made it easier for the Irish administration to find an acceptable immediate solution for the catholic question, Westmorland sustained a severe shock. On 26 December, Dundas in two dispatches communicated to the viceroy the views of the British ministry on the Irish catholic question. In the first dispatch Dundas, having laid down that the question should be 'divested from the prejudices arising from former animosities', directed Westmorland to recommend to the Irish parliament the relief of the Irish catholics from all disabilities connected with the practice of any trade or profession, and the repeal of all legislation which interfered with catholic education, penalized intermarriage between catholics and protestants, 'made a distinction between protestant and papists as to the use of arms', and prevented catholics from serving on grand and petty juries. On the admission of catholics to the franchise, Dundas, accepting that there were difficulties in either 'total exculsion or limited participation', came down in favour of the latter. If the catholics of 'consequence and property' were enfranchised, they would, Dundas argued, become 'sharers in the general predilection with which moderate men are accustomed to contemplate the existing government'. In the second and private dispatch Dundas put it squarely to Westmorland that if the Irish government expected to have British assistance in an emergency, it must keep in mind that 'the public and parliament of Great Britain should feel that the

---

[12] *Correspondence of Edmund Burke*, vii, pp. 9-10.

object for which their aid is demanded is one in which the Irish
government is founded in justice and policy in resisting the
wishes of the body of the people of Ireland'. Great Britain would
not be prepared to expend its resources in defending a mere
monopoly. Dundas emphasized that he was writing 'on the sup-
position of the empire remaining in a state of perfect tranquillity', a war of course would strengthen his case; and he ended by
hammering home that 'there cannot be a permanency in the
frame and constitution of Ireland unless the protestants will lay
aside their prejudices'. Westmorland, startled, told Dundas
that if the opinions expounded in the private dispatch were
known, the Irish protestants would band themselves together
and 'take the administration of Ireland entirely from the British government'. Even the public dispatch created difficulties
enough for the lord lieutenant. When he communicated it to
his confidential advisers—Fitzgibbon, Foster, Beresford, Parnell,
and Agar, the archbishop of Cashel, 'the first and natural
reaction' of the group was for resistance 'in nomine and in toto'.
But they were not prepared for outright opposition to the
British government, so after some discussion they agreed to
the proposals relating to the professions, education and intermarriage (though the archbishop was reluctant to abolish the
penalties on intermarriage). Parnell summed up his colleagues'
opinion when he remarked that these concessions, though
unpopular with protestants, 'might keep the country quiet until
the frenzy of reform had passed over Europe'. The proposal
that the catholics should be allowed to bear arms was rejected
as 'dangerous in the extreme', the lower classes in Ireland being
almost entirely catholic. Moreover, catholics of 'a decent rank
in life', could by using the prescribed procedure secure permission to possess arms. About jury service, the point was
made that in Ireland the grand jury was responsible for county
government, that therefore grand jury service afforded 'much
consequence to the protestant gentry' and that to ask them
to share the privilege would imperil the other concessions.
As for the suggestion that catholics might be granted a limited
admission to the franchise, the confidential advisers agreed on
'the impolicy of attempting it'. The proposal would arouse such
hostility in parliament that all the other concessions would be
jeopardized and if the franchise was granted even in a carefully

limited form, it would prove only the prelude to fresh demands from the catholics who would soon predominate in the county constituencies 'the pure and popular part of the government'.[13]

A few days after this meeting Westmorland poured out his feelings on the Irish situation in a long, impassioned letter to Pitt, reflecting the views he had formed during his two years as viceroy and presumably also the opinions he had absorbed from his Irish advisers. 'If Ireland', he wrote, 'was at the bottom of the sea it might be one thing, but while she exists you must rule her.' In short there must be a system or 'management that will render Ireland subservient to the general orders of the empire'. The existing 'Irish frame of government', he explained, was a protestant government, with the protestants in possession of land, magistracy and power. It had, like any other human institution, its faults, but through what other machinery could England govern Ireland, a country with a population half as large as its own? Catholic enfranchisement had obvious dangers. 'Do you believe', Westmorland asked, 'England can govern Ireland by the popularity of government . . . Is it not the very essence of your imperial policy to prevent the interests of Ireland clashing and interfering with the interests of England?' Moreover, a policy of favouring the catholics might drive the Irish protestants, who Westmorland insisted regarded concession with apprehension, into opposition, thus depriving the government of its most reliable allies in Ireland. The British government accepted the sharp contraction in its concessions policy suggested by the men on the spot, though Pitt explained to the viceroy that 'the idea of our wishing to play what you call a catholic game is really extravagant; we have thought only of what was the most likely plan to preserve the security and tranquillity of the British and protestant interest'. And Dundas irritably told Westmorland that the British ministers were entitled to 'complain of the spirit and temper which have manifested themselves in the deliberations of your friends in Ireland'. In the summer the Irish administration had expressed great alarm at the prospect of a coalition between the catholics and the dissenters. The British government had suggested

---

[13] H. Dundas to Westmorland, 26 Dec. 1791; Westmorland to H. Dundas, 11, 14, 21 Jan. 1792 (Westmorland corresp.).

a solution for the problem which had been treated with 'intemperance and jealousy'.[14]

As a result of the attitude adopted by the Irish administration the relief bill presented to the house of commons by Sir Hercules Langrishe (who was silently seconded by the chief secretary) was a very modest measure. Catholics were to be admitted to both branches of the legal profession (though they were debarred from taking silk); all restrictions on education abroad were abolished; catholic schoolmasters were no longer to be obliged to obtain the licence of the ordinary and the limitation on the number of apprentices that a catholic could employ was repealed. The bill itself offered little scope for discussion so members took the opportunity to speak about the catholic question in general. Langrishe stressed the house must be on its guard against a 'sudden or extravagant transfer of power or property'. Conservatives stressed the danger of 'shaking the props' which supported the constitution and wanted to know 'the ne plus ultra'. 'A line', Mr Ogle declared, 'must be drawn somewhere' and he reminded the house that 'everything you grant in compliance with the claims of the catholics is just so much lost to the protestants'.

On the other hand there were those who thought the bill did not go far enough. Colonel Hutchinson, a son of the provost, argued that the penal laws, which had been enacted in an era of clerical domination, were a disgrace and unnecessary in an age of reason, when 'the spirit of the catholic religion is softened and refined, the influence of the pope as feeble as the feeble and decrepit hand that wields it'. George Knox, a strong supporter of the British connection and protestant ascendancy, nevertheless attacked the disabilities because they unified the catholics and made them as it were 'one family'. 'When you took off the bonds of oppression', Knox declared, 'you broke the bonds of union.' Grattan, in a speech which Burke judged 'a noble performance', expressed the same opinion in a couple of pithy phrases—'it is not the opinion but the penalty which makes the fraternity'; and 'the repeal of the disabilities is the repeal of the passion that grows from it'. After summarizing contemptuously the penal laws in a series of staccato sentences, Grattan made a

---

[14] Westmorland to W. Pitt, 18 Jan. 1792; W. Pitt to Westmorland, 29 Jan. 1792; H. Dundas to Westmorland, 29 Jan. 1792 (Westmorland corresp.).

powerful appeal to his fellow members to place themselves 'at the head of the people for ever', by sweeping away the catholic disabilities. Grattan was clearly confident that the leadership of a strong and united Ireland would rest in the hands of the Irish gentry. He also seems to have been sure that religion, or at least denominationalism, was ceasing to be an influential force in politics. The catholic, he explained to the house, 'differs from you only in the forms of his worship and the ceremonies of his commemoration'; differences which Grattan clearly considered meant little to men with similar backgrounds who mixed freely in the ordinary affairs of life. He gave a concrete instance of what he meant by pointing out that a catholic granted a commission in the army would tend to adopt the outlook of his brother officers. The mess would count for more than the chaplain. It was an argument which Grattan generalized and crystallized when he remarked, 'you have tried the force of study to convert mankind, try the pleasures of the table'.[15]

The catholics soon made it clear that they would not be satisfied by Langrishe's bill. On 20 January the general committee decided to petition parliament for the suffrage and Richard Burke drafted a petition which he 'endeavoured to make as affecting as I could . . . nothing dry, crude or in a common manner'. It was certainly remarkably long, and though the catholic committee thanked him for uniting 'reason with eloquence and truth with spirit', Grattan and some other whigs, when they saw it suggested alterations, which its author indignantly declared, 'as a composition entirely destroyed it'.[16] Since the whigs would not present his petition unamended, Burke put it into the hands of O'Hara, the M.P. for Sligo, a family friend. O'Hara, on presenting the petition, explained that he was doing so 'as a personal favour' for 'a very particular friend'. This led to a procedural wrangle, it being asserted that a petition should be presented on behalf of the petitioners. Burke, excited by the debate and anxious to prompt O'Hara stepped on to the floor of the house. There was a general cry of 'into custody' and he quickly backed away. In the end O'Hara withdrew the petition and weeks later the general committee

<hr/>

[15] *Parl. Reg. Ire.*, xii, pp. 28–41, 58–64, 127–231.
[16] *Correspondence of Edmund Burke*, vii, pp. 45–7.

drew up a much shorter petition which was presented by Egan. It pointed out that to restore the catholics 'to some share in the elective franchise' would tend to strengthen the protestant state and 'afford protection and happiness' to the catholics. On 20 February David La Touche, a respected landowner and banker, took the unusual step of moving the rejection of the petition and his motion was carried by 208 to 25. The minority (with tellers) was composed of 18 whigs and 7 supporters of the administration.[17] The majority, which must have included a number of whigs, was determined to put an end to agitation by making it absolutely clear that the catholics were not going to be granted any form of political power in the foreseeable future. Even some of the minority which voted against the rejection of the petition, declared themselves to be against catholic enfranchisement. For instance, Francis Hardy, who saw nothing against 'a Roman catholic gentleman of property and respectability being entrusted with the franchise', nevertheless did not expect catholic enfranchisement to come for about a generation, when 'the grosser errors and doctrines of popery would be comparatively lost in the superior purity of the protestant religion'. The house of commons' decision was endorsed by the common council of Dublin. This body had in the past been dominated by the city liberals, but at the beginning of 1792 it called on the M.P.s for Dublin to oppose any measure which might subvert the protestant ascendancy. Grattan replied, declaring, 'I do not hesitate to say I love the Roman catholic— I am a friend to his liberty—but it is only as much as his liberty is entirely consistent with your ascendancy.' The commons council were unabashed by this 'set-down' (as Drennan termed it) and in March by 53 votes to 12 thanked the 209 M.P.s who supported La Touche; Cope, a conservative, pointing out that though many members of the catholic committee were loyal men, they could not answer for 'the mass of their people who are unenlightened . . . and are daily told they have not the Rights of Man'.[18]

Westmorland was greatly impressed by the obstinacy, bigotry

---

[17] For the minority see *D.E.P.*, 25 Apr. 1793. R. Smith is counted as an administration supporter.

[18] *D.E.P.*, 31 Jan. 1792; *D.J.*, 6 Mar. 1792; W. Drennan to S. McTier (Drennan papers, 321).

and feeling of almost every man amongst the protestants. However, he was satisfied by the general situation at the close of the session. The relief bill had passed, nevertheless protestant confidence in the government had been restored. The 'better sort of catholics' were grateful for the concessions, and the agitators were making little impression on the country. The time had come, he thought, for the British government to show its approval of the Irish administration, for instance by a blue ribbon for the lord lieutenant.[19] At the close of the British parliamentary session Hobart and Parnell discussed the Irish catholic question with Pitt and Dundas at Wimbledon. At first Pitt talked about finding 'a permanent system which they would stand upon' and Dundas asked why the catholic agitation should arouse so much apprehension if the catholics were a weak, unimportant element in the community. Hobart and Parnell strongly emphasized that the catholics would develop into a formidable political force only if it seemed that their claims were favoured by the British government, and Hobart felt at the end of the discussion that the British ministers agreed with 'an idea I threw out of the possibility of the present system in Ireland continuing as long as the system of popery which every hour was losing ground, and which once annihilated would put an end to the question'.[20]

But those conservatives who believed that a judicious blend of rationed concessions and sharp rebuke would put a stop to the catholic agitation were soon sorely disappointed. The rejection of the petition was a setback for the catholic cause, but a relief bill had passed and the committee must have been cheered by the support it received from catholics all over Ireland and by signs of protestant sympathy and British goodwill; and its members were stung into action rather than successfully snubbed by the contemptuous comparisons made between them and the seceders in parliamentary debate. Some of the seceders indeed returned to the committee shortly after signing Kenmare's address, and by June some 'respectable country gentleman' had managed to close the breach in the catholic ranks. Publicly both sides expressed regret for the rift.

[19] Westmorland to W. Pitt, 24 Feb. 1792; to Dundas, 4 Apr. 1792 (Westmorland corresp.); Westmorland to Pitt, 23 Apr. 1792 (P.R.O. 30/8/331).
[20] Hobart to Westmorland, 25 June 1792 (Westmorland corresp.).

Privately Lord Fingall and his friend (Lord Kenmare) assured the committee that they appreciated the 'propriety' of its behaviour and would not oppose in the future its efforts to obtain relief.[21] About ten of the signatories to the Kenmare address sat in the catholic convention of 1792 and if other catholic conservatives held aloof from active participation in catholic politics the forward party was probably thankful. The committee from early 1792 devoted considerable attention to fund-raising and propaganda—publishing resolutions and addresses in the newspapers and arranging for the printing of Burke's *Letter to Sir Hercules Langrishe,* the pamphlets of Tone and Todd Jones on the catholic question, and a speech of Grattan's on catholic relief. The committee also took steps to disembarrass itself of Richard Burke, who Keogh complained, had 'contrived to embroil them with everybody'. Burke's overbearing impetuosity and consequential manner could be charitably attributed to intense identification with his clients' cause, which he saw as being of the utmost importance in the European as well as the Irish context. The committee gave him a dinner before he left for England at the beginning of April and voted him 2,000 guineas for his services—which seemed to Keogh 'foolish generosity'. Back in England he annoyed the Irish catholic leaders by failing to supply them with information about his negotiations with the government (in fact he had nothing substantial to report), and in July the committee sent him a tactful letter dispensing with his services. It was so tactful that Burke apparently did not realize he had been discharged and when in September he returned to Ireland Keogh felt it necessary to give him his *congé* in an interview.[22] But Keogh seems to have done this so delicately that Burke, sensitive but imperceptive, still felt he had an official connection with the catholics. The result was that Richard Burke's feelings were unscathed and he and his father remained fervent adherents of the catholic cause.

In July the committee appointed Wolfe Tone as assistant secretary. By appointing Tone, a protestant barrister, the committee conspicuously demonstrated its liberality. They also obtained a remarkably efficient and energetic executive officer.

---

[21] 'The minute book of the catholic committee', p. 166.
[22] T. W. Tone, *Life,* i, p. 180.

It was still unusual for a political movement to employ a full time organizer, but Tone quickly realized the potentialities of his new post. He not only attended committee meetings and conducted a large correspondence but he threw himself into a wide variety of useful activities, ranging from folding circulars to undertaking long journeys through Ulster and Connaught on behalf of the committee. He managed while displaying a spirit of independence to win and retain the goodwill of Keogh (at times by applying flattery with a trowel). Theoretically Tone was the servant of the committee, but political awareness, a ready pen and social vivacity enabled him to move unobtrusively but quickly into the inner circle which was directing the catholic agitation. The catholic committee gained considerably by having the help of a full-time professional organizer.

After the rejection of their petition the committee took two drastic steps to demonstrate the strength of catholic opinion. On 17 March they approved of a declaration in which they stated that catholics were not required to believe that the pope was infallible, renounced all claims to forfeited lands in Ireland, and disavowed opinions wrongly attributed to catholics—that princes excommunicated by the pope could be deposed, that it was lawful to murder heretics and that faith need not be kept with heretics. The committee recommended that this declaration be signed universally throughout Ireland, and the meetings convoked for this purpose and the long lists of signatories provided an impressive demonstration of the unity and cohesion of catholic Ireland. In the early summer the committee put into operation a plan, suggested by Miles Keon, a Leitrim country gentleman, which would give the committee 'somewhat more of a representative and somewhat less of an individual character' by providing that county delegates should be chosen by 'electors', 'respectable persons', themselves selected in each parish at a meeting 'in a private house'. The electors were recommended to elect also 'associate delegates', resident in Dublin who could keep the county informed about the committee's work. This scheme, it was pointed out, by 'making attendance a duty', would bring a greater number of country gentlemen on to the committee at a time when it was beginning a great drive for two objectives—the franchise and a full participation in the benefits of trial by jury.[23] The committee's claim 'to speak the sense of the whole catholic people', was undoubtedly strengthened by its adoption of the new plan of election, a plan which also provided an interesting and challenging contrast with the electoral machinery for selecting M.P.s.

Westmorland was perturbed at the prospect of a representative catholic congress, and he consulted the law officers who gave a very cautious opinion. If the committee's objective was to overawe parliament, it was an illegal assembly. But it would be difficult to prove intention until the committee met and took action; accepting election to membership would not in itself constitute grounds for a prosecution—which, the law officers emphasized, would have to be conducted before a jury. On the general question of how best to deal with the catholic question Westmorland was diffuse and indecisive. He believed that the government should rely on protestant support. 'Great Britain', he wrote, 'may still easily manage the protestants and the protestants the catholics, but this to me is clear that you cannot support your government without the confidence of the protestants.' He was also sure that the catholic agitation could be easily checked. 'A big word from England of her determination to support the protestant establishment', he asserted, 'would see everything quiet.' At the same time he was anxious to stop the spread of disaffection by taking steps to conciliate the catholics. But, being in continuous official contact with a vigorous group of protestant conservatives, Westmorland was very conscious of the dour determination of Irish protestants not to concede the smallest share of political power to the catholics. However, towards the close of 1792 he perceived a miraculous change on protestant opinion. With the French winning (momentarily) sweeping victories against the coalesced powers, Irish protestants had suddenly become convinced that it was urgently important to encourage their fellow countrymen to rally to the defence of the constitution. Events were to show that Westmorland was right in seeing a shift in protestant opinion (his perception of course may have been sharpened by a wish to agree with the

---

[23] *A vindication of the conduct and principles of the catholics of Ireland . . . with an appendix of authentic documents* (1793), pp. 62–9.

British cabinet). By the end of 1792 he agreed that concessions to the catholics were expedient but was not prepared to say when or in what form they should be made.[24]

The catholic committee's bold attempt to redress the balance in Irish politics by calling on a new force, organized public opinion, to outweigh the old political interests, dismayed and deeply shocked many protestants. Early in August the London-derry grand jury protested against the circular letter, and at the close of the month the freeholders of County Limerick (appar-ently encouraged by the lord chancellor), denounced the con-voking of a popish congress, elected 'after the manner of the French national assembly', which would 'unite in itself the whole catholic power and influence of this kingdom'. During the autumn the freeholders of six and the grand juries of seventeen counties, together with the governing bodies of four urban centres, publicly expressed their disapproval of the congress.[25] When issuing its protest against the congress, the Dublin corporation, the lord mayor, aldermen and common council stated positively what they wished to maintain—a protestant ascendancy, which they defined as a protestant king of Ireland, a protestant hierarchy, protestant electors and government, the bench of justice, the army, the revenue, throughout all their branches and details, protestant, and this system supported by a connection with the protestant kingdom of Great Britain.[26]

There were signs that protestant opinion, even in groups which might be expected to be conservative, was not unanimous. In County Armagh only thirteen grand jurors signed the resolutions condemning the congress; in County Cork, though the Grand jury condemned the congress, a meeting of free-holders passed resolutions in favour of catholic relief, and the Cork city grand jury by 14 votes to 9 refused to censor the congress. In Mayo a minority of nine grand jurors published a protest against the anti-congress resolutions passed by the other fourteen members of the jury, and at a Wexford County meeting anti-congress resolutions were carried by 110 to 45 votes, after strenuous debates in which speeches against the resolutions

[24] Westmorland to Dundas, 7 June 1792 (H.O. 100/38); to Dundas, 11 Dec. 1792 (Westmorland Corresp.); to W. Pitt, 20 Oct. 1792 (Westmorland corresp.).
[25] It was said that 28 counties declared themselves against the proposed congress (D.J., 20 Sept. 1792).
[26] D.J., 15 Sept. 1792.

were made by Francis Hely-Hutchinson, a government[27] supporter, Sir Frederick Flood, a whig, Harvey, a United Irishman, Cornelius Grogan, who was to be an insurgent leader in 1798, and Edward Sweetman, who was to be a leading member of the new catholic committee.[28]

If the viceroy and conservative protestants were dismayed at the prospect of a popular catholic congress, the catholic leaders were afraid that the prestige of the new committee might be seriously diminished by the failure of some counties to appoint representatives. The catholic gentry of Galway and Mayo were said to be 'rather averse to the general committee from the bad spirit of aristocracy'—some of their leaders had been strong supporters of Kenmare, and Braughall, accompanied by Tone, went down to Ballinasloe to persuade them to elect delegates. Keogh, hearing that Munster was becoming apathetic, paid a visit to that province and he also attended a meeting of catholic bishops at Armagh, striving to 'create a confidence between the bishops and the laity'. Though he found 'old men, used to bend to power' were inclined to mistake 'all attempts for liberty as something connected with the robbers and murderers of France' he managed to get some help from them.[29] In the end all the counties sent delegates to the committee and two prelates, Troy of Dublin, and Moylan of Cork, attended a meeting of the committee and on behalf of the Irish clergy signed its petition.

The newly elected catholic committee met in Dublin at the beginning of December. The organizers had applied for the Rotunda, 'but the governors put off their answer on account of a thin meeting and Lord Charlemont with others declined attending', so the committee had to use a much smaller hall, the Tailors' Hall in Back Lane, which the United Irishmen were using for their weekly meetings. The committee, composed of representatives of the counties, the Dublin parishes and of 39 urban centres, together with a number of associated delegates, had about 230 members. Considerably over half were resident in Dublin. The Dublin members were principally businessmen, many of them merchants, amongst them being D. T. O.Brien

[27] *D.E.P.*, 11 Oct. 1792; *D.J.*, 28 Aug., 11 Sept. 1792.
[28] *H.J.*, 26 Sept. 1792.
[29] J. Keogh to T. Hussey, 2 Oct. 1792 (H.O. 100/38).

and John Comerford, who were said to be worth £60,000 and Edward Byrne, a merchant who was said to pay £100,000 yearly in customs duties.[30] The textile industries and brewing were well represented and the members resident in Dublin included three booksellers, an attorney's apprentice and a schoolmaster (all members of the Dublin society of United Irishmen) and a dozen medical men (of whom four were United Irishmen). In the list of country delegates there occur the names of a number of well-established catholic families and it is perhaps worth noting that twenty of the country representatives were within the next few years to be placed in the commission of the peace.

Led by a number of successful men, convinced of the righteousness of their cause and aware that the tide of opinion and events was running in their favour, the committee pressed forward with contagious enthusiasm spreading through its ranks.[31] They resolved on the first day of meeting (4 December) to petition the king. They then rapidly discussed and approved a petition (apparently prepared in advance by the sub-committee).[32] One important amendment was suggested. The petition asked for admission to the franchise and full admission to juries. Teeling, one of the delegates for county Antrim, proposed that the prayer be 'generalised'. His speech (of which Tone provides a staccato summary—'Golden opportunity, union amongst ourselves, dissenters with us, England, Scotland liberal, France. No danger of violence. What to do in case of refusal? Tell our constituents they, and not this body, will determine') was greeted with loud applause, and his motion was carried, it being decided to ask for full relief. The conservatives however achieved a small success. The original draft seems to have requested that the catholics be admitted to the rights of 'a free constitution' and this was amended to 'the constitution'—one conservative remarking 'the north and us

---

[30] *Hibernian Magazine*, 1793, p. 185; list of catholic committee (H.O. 100/34); W. Drennan to Mrs McTier, 30 Nov. 1792 (Drennan papers, 352); *Hibernian Magazine*, 1793, p. 185.

[31] Tone, who seems to have had in mind a history of the catholics' struggle in the early nineties, summarized the speeches made in the convention (T. W. Tone, *Life*, i, pp. 224–36, 252–67).

[32] The petition was signed by the members of the convention and by Archbishop Troy of Dublin and Bishop Moylan of Cork, on behalf of the bishops and clergy.

have different views'. The next question was—how was the petition to be transmitted to England? The customary method was to present petitions to the lord lieutenant for transmission, but Christopher Dillon Bellew (one of the seceders who considered that his party had been let down by the government) moved that a deputation from the committee should present it directly to the king. It was no offence, Devereux of Waterford pointed out, to present a loyal petition, 'and right to mark our abhorrence of the measures of our enemies here for they are the enemies of Ireland'. A few members hesitated, Theobald MacKenna urging that the petition should go through the Castle, 'no recollection of past piques should influence'. It was intimated to members of the committee that if the petition was presented to the lord lieutenant it would be immediately sent over to England. Messages passed between the committee and the castle and at one stage after the committee had allowed half an hour for an answer the members sat waiting watch in hand. The lord lieutenant was in fact prepared to transmit the petition but he considered it 'indecent' for the committee to expect him to commit himself to forwarding a paper before he had seen it.[33] As a result negotiations collapsed and on 7 December the committee elected a deputation to present the petition to the king. The deputation which was composed of two Dublin businessmen, Keogh and Edward Byrne, and three country gentlemen, Christopher Bellew, Devereux and Sir Thomas French, was instructed to adhere firmly to the spirit of the petition and 'to take an hotel and make a superb appearance'. On 8 December the catholic committee adjourned until it should be re-convoked by a subcommittee which it appointed before adjourning.

By snubbing the Irish administration the catholic committee showed its self-assurance. It also displayed cool political judgement by fending off the Irish radicals. The catholics of course appreciated the value of radical support. It was heartening to have the openly expressed sympathy of their protestant fellow-countrymen, and radical propaganda was directed with force and fervour against the penal laws. There were too a number of personal links between the two movements, twenty-

[33] Westmorland to Dundas, 7 Dec. 1792 (H.O. 100/38); T. W. Tone, *Life*, i. pp. 80–4.

five members of the catholic committee elected in 1792 being members of the Dublin society of United Irishmen. But it would have been highly disadvantageous to the catholic cause for emancipation to become too closely identified with radical reform. By the close of 1792 the former movement was much stronger and moving much faster. An avowed alliance with the radicals would have alienated English goodwill, startled some moderate protestants, provided ultra-protestant conservatives with potent arguments and very possibly split the committee (Tone soon realized that there were catholic conservatives to be reckoned with). The catholic committee, though it thanked the citizens of Belfast, did not publish this resolution; a communication from the four United Irishmen's societies of Belfast, suggesting that the catholics should demand complete emancipation was not even acknowledged, and when Drennan tried to find out if it had been received, 'Tone had like to have snapt off my nose'. Then, when the United Irishmen of Dublin on 6 December sent a deputation—Rowan, Butler, Chambers, Rice and Tandy—to the catholic committee to assure them they could rely on the society's support, Rowan confidently expected to be asked to address the committee. Instead the deputation was shepherded into an antechamber, and 'their further progress evaded by many plausible reasons'. The deputation retired hurt but according to Drennan, Rowan and Butler, though indignant, were afraid to take the matter up 'as the catholics are to a man very suspicious and apt to take dislikes, and they are now getting self-sufficiency as a body that has sat in spite of aristocratical power and are in a prospect of success'. Edward Sweetman even tried to persuade the Dublin society of United Irishmen to tone down its manifestoes while the question of catholic relief was in the balance. At the beginning of 1793 when the society was discussing a resolution pledging it to resist the impending prosecutions of Rowan and Tandy, Sweetman urged that the words 'legally and constitutionally' be inserted after 'resist'. His amendment was rejected by 55 to 45, the division, according to Collins, being along sectarian lines. At the beginning of February when the house of commons was discussing catholic relief, Sweetman wanted the society to issue a statement, declaring that their only object was to be governed by a king, lords, and commons which fairly represented the people. He explained that the society was rumoured to be two-thirds catholic and republican in principle, and this might injure the catholic cause. But his fellow catholic members did not support him, and a few days later he resigned from the society.[34]

The deputation, anxious to avoid a long sea crossing, travelled to London via Belfast and Scotland. In Belfast they were entertained by some of the leading citizens and 'the populace took the horses from their carriage and drew it through the town'. Haliday, now left stranded by the mainstream of Belfast liberalism, heard that the men who drew the carriage were hired, but he granted that the catholic ambassadors showed their good sense 'by condemning the extreme violence of the *Northern Star*'.[35] The deputation arrived in London about 24 December, and Dundas, at some inconvenience to himself, as his secretary made clear, presented them at the levee of 2 January where they met with 'what is called in the language of courts a most gracious reception, that is, His Majesty was pleased to say a few words to each of the delegates in turn'.[36] The deputation had two long interviews with Dundas who was sympathetic and non-committal. An old political hand, he declined to be drawn into any detailed exposition of the government's catholic policy—a breach of official form would irritate the Irish administration and afford the deputation an opportunity of pressing for further concessions.[37]

The catholic leaders were exhilarated by their reception in London. About the middle of January Christopher Bellew told Hobart that 'nothing short of being on a footing with other dissenters would satisfy the Roman catholics', and a week later a delegation from the subcommittee was sent to inform Hobart that 'nothing short of complete emancipation will satisfy the catholics'.[38] Tone, caught up in the great wave of confident

---

[34] *D.E.P.*, 6 Dec. 1792; W. Drennan to S. McTier, n.d., to Mrs McTier, 9 Dec. 1792 (Drennan papers, 357, 359); 'Proceedings of the Dublin society of United Irishmen' in *Analecta Hibernica*, no. 17, pp. 53–66.

[35] *H.J.*, 15 Dec. 1792; *Charlemont MSS H.M.C.*, ii, p. 208.

[36] T. W. Tone, *Life*, i, p. 89; E. Nepean to E. Byrne, 31 Dec. 1792 (H.O. 100/38).

[37] For the conversation the delegates had with Dundas see H.O. 100/42 ff. 57–59ᵛ.

[38] Hobart to Nepean, 15 Jan. 1792 (H.O. 100/42).

enthusiasm which was sweeping through radical Europe, was sure the Irish administration was tottering and that the time was ripe for the catholic leadership to stir up a nation-wide agitation set on total victory. But he soon found that 'merchants are no great hands at revolution' (and he added, forgetting his radicalism 'if ever the business is done it will be by the country gentlemen').[39] In discussion with Hobart the catholic leaders came up against the hard realities of the situation. There was bound to be, as Hobart pointed out, parliamentary opposition to catholic relief and he firmly refused to present a petition from the subcommittee requesting complete emancipation. Keogh, a master of the art of the possible, managed by adroit formula-finding to reconcile the views of the subcommittee and the chief secretary. In its final form the petition asked the house of commons to take the whole of the catholics' case into consideration, but it did not make any specific demands. And by entrusting the petition to the chief secretary the subcommittee implied it would acquiesce in the government's policy.

Hobart at the beginning of 1793 must have wished he knew precisely what that policy was. Though it was clear that the British government had decided that the Irish catholics were to receive a further substantial instalment of relief, when the Irish parliament met on 10 January 1793 the Irish executive had not been told exactly what concessions were to be granted. It was not until a fortnight later that Dundas wrote apologetically to say that though the cabinet had repeatedly considered the catholic claims, so many points had risen that he could not convey a final decision on the matter. (It must be taken into account that Great Britain was on the brink of a major war.) However, Dundas skilfully managed to give the Irish administration definite guidance by enclosing as a private communication the draft of a dispatch. In it he began by pointing out that in December 1791 he and the viceroy's Irish advisors had differed 'as to the best mode of resisting attempts to subvert the protestant establishment and maintain the frame of government'. Forgivably he added that his policy, generous concession, though turned down, had been vindicated by events. The concessions which in 1792, 'would have quieted the question are not now likely to do it', and the Irish government should

[39] T. W. Tone, *Life*, i, p. 241.

'weigh well the consequences of leaving behind any sore part of the question'. Dundas then suggested a list of concessions—enfranchisement, jury service and admission to civil offices (with, perhaps for the sake of calming protestant fears, the exception of those possessing political power).[40]

On 4 February 1793 Hobart presented the catholics' petition (cautiously saying that he did not consider himself pledged to agree completely with the petitioners) and a catholic relief bill.[41] The bill was a comprehensive measure. Catholics were granted the parliamentary franchise and permitted to hold all civil and military offices with the exception of the higher offices of state, judgeships, and the posts of high sheriff and general on the staff. They were also still debarred from becoming king's counsel. Catholics possessing a freehold with a £100 or £1,000 of personal property could keep arms on the same terms as protestants; catholic £10 freeholders and catholics possessing £100 worth of personal property might keep arms if they took the oath of allegiance and filed affidavits as to their property and catholics could take degrees in the university of Dublin.

Parliament treated the bill as a most momentous piece of legislation, and the number of M.P.s who spoke on the bill—72 in all—and the variety of opinions they expressed, illustrate vividly the perplexities of a privileged community, who seeing their position challenged by powerful upsurging forces were striving to control their destinies in an uncertain future. It was difficult, one county member remarked, for an individual firmly attached to the protestant interest to know how to steer himself, and an academic lawyer, Arthur Browne, confessed that he 'had scarcely been able to form a determination until the urgency of the time positively required me to do so'. His final conclusion was that emancipation should be gradually granted, and he was against 'enfranchising an enormous rabble'. The members who spoke on the bill can be divided broadly into three catagories—those who accepted the bill, those who thought it went too far, and those who considered it did not go far enough, Some M.P.s were hostile to the bill *in*

---

[40] Dundas to Westmorland, 23 Jan. 1793 (H.O. 100/42).
[41] For the debates on the catholic relief bill see *The proceedings of the parliament of Ireland, 1793*, 3 vols. (1793).

toto, their views being forcefully expressed by the speaker, Foster. When the bill was in committee, Foster attacked it, drawing his arguments, he emphasized, not from 'metaphysical speculation' but from a knowledge of human nature—'from what the protestants would do and have done and from what I myself would do if I were a catholic'. If the catholics were granted the franchise, admission to parliament, he was sure, would inevitably follow; then the protestants would be at their mercy and the connection with Great Britain would be broken. Foster's policy was 'to draw a line round the constitution' within which he would not allow the catholic. But the opponents of the bill did not call for a division on any of its three readings. Instead they concentrated their efforts on trying to restrict the extent of catholic enfranchisement. Duigenan, who delivered two erudite diatribes against catholicism and the bill, moved in committee that catholics should be permitted to exercise the county franchise only if £20 freeholders, and to vote in boroughs only if in possession of a £20 freehold or £1,000 worth of personal property. He was defeated by 146 to 74. At the other extreme George Knox urged that the catholics be admitted to parliament. 'Depend upon it', he said, 'a catholic peer and a catholic commoner with influence in the senate will be no republican or leveller.' Knox was defeated by 163 to 69. Of the minority 54 were whigs or independents. 33 government supporters. Several of those who favoured the admission of catholics to parliament voiced apprehensions over the enfranchisement of the forty-shilling freeholders, not, as Ormsby said, 'because they are catholics but because they are a multitude'. 'It is inconsistent with reason,' George Ponsonby, the whig leader, remarked, when supporting Knox's motion, 'not to give the great body of the inhabitants of any country under a reasonable government any portion of political power'. Lawrence Parsons, a very independent member, in a most forceful speech, argued in favour of admitting the 'first', the upper-class catholics, to parliament, and against giving the vote to the 'inferior catholics'. Were they, he asked, to risk the best constitution in the world by enfranchising a body of men, living in 'great poverty, in great ignorance, bigoted to their sect and their altars, repelled by ancient prejudices from you and at least four times the number of you'? And Graydon, a whig supporter of Knox's motion, unsuccessfully suggested that the qualification for the county franchise be raised for all voters to the possession of a £10 freehold (preserving the rights of existing forty-shilling freeholders). A young M.P. in a sensible speech answered one of the arguments against the enfranchisement of the catholic forty-shilling freeholders. They would not, explained Arthur Wesley (the future duke of Wellington), act as a body, under priestly direction, but would be influenced by 'their landlords, their opinion, good or bad of the candidates, and a thousand other matters'.

Those who accepted the bill varied considerably in their attitude towards it. Some looked forward to the time when the last restrictions on the catholics would vanish 'before the meridian blaze of modern principles'. On the other hand, Sir John Parnell, in a candid and gloomy speech, explained that though he disapproved of the bill he thought it must be passed, because 'England thinks the connection can be better preserved by a change of system'. Political experiments, Parnell thought, were always dangerous. But he hoped the catholics would gratefully 'embrace the constitution'. If they remained un-satisfied, 'I', Parnell declared, 'shall lament the generosity of this day'. Hobart himself complacently, and apparently quite sincerely defended the bill as providing a long-term settlement of the catholic question in Irish politics. Some years later, writing confidentially to Pitt, he outlined the situation in Ireland as he conceived it. The Irish catholics would always be hostile to the British connection and disaffected. But 'as you cannot extirpate them it is an evil which must be borne and the end to be aimed at was to make that evil as little dangerous as possible'. Though Hobart disapproved of 'the severe and cruel restrictions' imposed on the Irish catholics in the past, he strongly believed that in Ireland the state, the parliament and the church should be 'exclusively protestant'.[42] The 1793 relief bill, he told the house of commons, while not admitting the catholics to 'the state', gave them everything that could be safely conceded, and he was sure, would satisfy 'every rational catholic in the kingdom'.

Two other liberal amendments, the one making catholics eligible for the office of high sheriff, the other admitting them

[42] Hobart to Pitt, 2 Nov. 1799 (P.R.O. 30/8/328).

to the revenue board, were both rejected and the government accepted an amendment put forward by the ultra-protestants, it being provided that catholic voters and office-holders should take an oath, 'a pamphlet of an oath', prepared by Duigenan. This oath was comprised of the declaration which catholics could make under the act of 1774 with additional clauses stating that papal infallibility was not an article of the catholic faith and abrogating any intention of disturbing the existing settlement of property in Ireland or subverting the established church. When the bill was in the lords two important amendments were passed. In accordance with the liberal ideal that 'the youth of both religions should be educated together', it was provided that any new college to be founded was to be part of the university of Dublin and that neither its teaching staff nor student body was to be exclusively catholic. It was also decided that the qualification for keeping arms should be raised from £100 to £300 of personal property. Fitzgibbon remarking that he was against 'the lower order' of either religion being allowed to keep arms.

During the second reading debate in the lords Fitzgibbon delivered a powerful attack on a measure which he characterized as being 'an indiscreet and precipitate experiment'. Already disturbed and angered, he was intensely irritated by a speech in support of the bill by a broad-minded bishop, born and bred in England. Fitzgibbon vehemently argued that if the catholics were granted political rights, the catholic community, 'the descendants of the old Irish', would instinctively strive for predominance. The reign of James II had vividly illustrated how catholics when in power behaved and proved that the penal laws were 'a code forced on the parliament of Ireland by harsh necessity'. Concession, always dangerous, had become more hazardous because of the alliance between the catholic agitation and the democratic movements, and the connection between Great Britain and Ireland, so necessary to both countries, might soon be imperilled. A situation would then arise for which, Fitzgibbon warned the house, there would be only one remedy, a union with Great Britain. And, he gloomily prophesied, the very factors which would render a union necessary would militate against its success. Having demonstrated that the bill was a bad measure, he advised the house to pass it: after what had been allowed to take place, it was 'essential to the momentary peace of the country'.

Though to Irish conservatives the relief act of 1793 seemed the harbinger of momentous change, its immediate effects were not very striking. A few catholics were admitted to the commission of the peace and to serve on grand juries and some were commissioned in the army and militia. A small number of catholics were called to bar in the closing years of the century, Daniel O'Connell (called in 1798) being the first to come to the front. Between 1793 and the close of the century the average number of catholics entering Trinity college annually was about eight, only 7 per cent of all entrances, and it was not until the end of the first quarter of the nineteenth century that the catholic freeholders began in some counties to form a separate 'interest' at county elections. The borough corporations (with the exception of Tuam) remained until their abolition almost exclusively protestant bodies. Immediately after the passing of the 1793 relief act some of the Dublin guilds admitted a few catholics. The guild of merchants, the most influential guild, at first in July 1793 refused admission to thirty-three catholic applicants by 73 votes to 66 (Sir Edward Newenham, who had been in the eighties a strong liberal, being prominent in the majority); then in October the guild admitted eleven catholics to membership. But the following April it rejected the application of Ignatius Weldon, a well-established catholic merchant, by 83 votes to 55. Even more significant was a decision come to by the common council of the city in October 1793. When about thirty catholics petitioned for the freedom of the city, the common council rejected the first petition, that of Valentine O'Connor, a well-known catholic merchant, by 66 black beans to 29 white. A leader of the majority, Howison, declaring that 'he did not think that keeping catholics out of power, which it was likely they would abuse, was inflicting on them a punishment'.

In 1795 when the guild of merchants was electing its representatives on the common council, Thomas Braughall, a catholic who had been admitted to the freedom of the guild, tendered his vote. But, since there was a bye-law of the guild to the effect that a member of the guild who had not been admitted to the freedom of the city could not take part in a ballot for common council men, the master refused Braughall's vote. There was talk of legal proceedings and the catholics took counsel's opinion but the question does not seem to have come before the courts. About this time attention seems to have been drawn to 'a mandate' of the lord mayor, endorsed by the common council in 1675, forbidding the admission to a guild of any person not eligible for the freedom of the city, and it could be argued, though the case was a poor one, that catholics were not eligible for the freedom. What was more important than their eligibility, was the determination of a large majority in the common council to use its discretionary powers to prevent their admission to the freedom, and until 1835 no catholic was admitted to the freedom of Dublin (to be quite precise there was a rumour one was admitted, but it was agreed this could only have been due to inadvertence). With pressures for change mounting, the Dublin common council and the guilds from being the focal points for city liberalism were becoming strongholds of protestant conservatism. Symbolically, on the day that Valentine O'Connor's petition was rejected, Napper Tandy's resignation from the common council was accepted.[43] It may be added that the conservatives also asserted themselves in Cork municipal life. Just after the passing of the 1793 relief act three catholics were granted the freedom of the city but two years later when Edward Byrne was proposed for the freedom the court of D'Oyer hundred rejected him by 81 to 47.[44]

So great was the social, economic and professional strength of Irish protestantism that it was a generation or so before its political predominance began to weaken perceptibly, and its decline was a very slow process. But at the end of the eighteenth century many Irish protestants did not realize how many brakes on change were built into Irish society. They saw themselves on the brink of revolution and regarded their remaining privileges as a thin line of defence. To liberals the remaining catholic disabilities were futile concessions to protestant prejudice and panic, galling to the go-ahead catholic but scarcely significantly weakening the power of the catholic community. If these remaining restrictions had been,

---

[43] *H.J.*, 16, 20 July 1793, 29 Apr., 20 Oct. 1794; T. Braughal, payments to E. Lewins, 23 Dec. 1795 (I.S.P. O. 620/34/50); *H.J.*, 18 Nov. 1795.
[44] *D.E.P.*, 16 June 1795.

as the liberals in the house of commons proposed, swept away in 1793, catholic emancipation as a constitutional issue would have been removed from Irish politics. The course of Irish history might have been changed and would certainly have been simplified. However, the debates and divisions in parliament and out-of-door comment suggest that the relief act of 1793 represented the maximum which the majority of Irish protestants was prepared at the time to concede. It can of course be argued that if the Irish administration had agreed to accept complete emancipation, that would have tipped the parliamentary balance in favour of that policy. But Westmorland and Hobart, both cautious by temperament and conditioned by their Irish official environment, were reluctant to advance far ahead of Irish conservative opinion. The relief bill of 1793, the result of a number of forces—catholic pressure, the determination of the British government to conciliate the majority in Ireland, the hesitancies of the Irish administration, Irish protestant intransigence and protestant liberalism—was a compromise measure, in which almost every concession was soured by limiting clauses. Pitt could scarcely have regarded the relief act of 1793 with great satisfaction. Accepting that the Irish catholics, 'from their numbers and increasing property' would inevitably obtain complete emancipation, he was by the end of 1792 coming to the conclusion that the best solution for the Irish question was a union, which by giving security to the protestants would render catholic emancipation politically feasible. In the meantime, he confessed, Irish policy could only be 'a government of expedients'.[45]

But Pitt was thinking about a long-term solution. What immediately concerned the Irish administration was, would parliament accept the bill, and would it satisfy the catholics? In April the bill was safely through, and only then was the general committee reconvened. At its first meeting there were complaints that the committee had failed to attain its objective. 'The demand of the catholics', Edward Sweetman declared, 'was total. Why was the relief partial?' Keogh, showing that beneath his suppleness there was a vein of steel, vigorously argued that the deputation to London had put the case for full

---

[45] W. Pitt to Westmorland, 18 Nov. 1792 (Westmorland corresp.); S. Douglas, *Diaries*, ed. F. Bickley (1928), i, p. 35.

emancipation forcefully to Dundas, 'one of the ablest men in England, they being little practised', and that the relief act gave them as much as they could expect to get from the Irish parliament. Moreover, Keogh pointed out 'What is withheld must be obtained by the elective franchise.' He carried the committee with him. It agreed to thank the king, the lord lieutenant and Hobart, and it decided to request the duke of Leinster to permit the catholics to erect a statue of George III on Leinster Lawn. The address to the king thanked him for the substantial benefits the catholics had received, and Teeling failed when he tried to get a paragraph inserted declaring 'with all possible gentleness' the determination of the catholics to secure complete emancipation. MacNeven and Sweetman also failed when they tried to stop the committee thanking Hobart. The radicals however persuaded the committee to resolve that the catholics should co-operate with the protestants in trying to secure by 'all legal means' parliamentary reform. Only one member of the committee (Sir Thomas French) recorded his dissent but some others obviously disapproved of the resolution. Eighteen months later the catholic leadership was publicly divided over reform. One of the toasts suggested for a Dublin dinner to commemorate the meeting of the general committee was 'the last wish of the late catholic committee', parliamentary reform. It was opposed 'on the grounds of being prudently silent' and quashed by 29 to 25, with the result that the minority and majority dined separately but toasted one another.[46] To what extent the majority was composed of those who opposed the toast of reform from expediency or on principle cannot be determined. On 25 April the committee dissolved, having appointed a subcommittee to raise funds to pay off outstanding debts and to consider how catholic education might be improved. The dissolution of the committee suggested that the catholics were for the moment satisfied, and the 1793 concessions certainly made it easier for those catholics who were inherently conservative to accept for the immediate future the existing regime.

[46] *D.E.P.*, 16 Dec. 1794; W. Drennan to S. McTier, *post* 9 Dec. 1794 (Drennan papers, 536).

12

Radicalism and reaction

While the catholics had been developing a sustained and well-organized drive for relief, the Irish radicals had been both encouraging the catholics and strenuously striving to promote what they regarded as the more comprehensive cause of reform. During 1792 the Dublin society of United Irishmen produced six important addresses declaring their aims and ideals, and early in 1792 it publicly challenged parliament and the executive on two important constitutional issues, though, unfortunately for the radicals, political drama was interspersed with farce. During the commons debate on the catholic petition, Toler, the solicitor-general, who had a penchant for robust humour, entertained the house by offensive puns based on Tandy's distinctive and unattractive facial appearance. Tandy immediately sent a friend, Colonel Smith, to demand an explanation. Toler refused to apologize and suggested as a suitable place for a meeting the fields adjacent to Merrion Square. Tandy continued asking for an explanation, his aim, he later asserted, being to provoke Toler into challenging him, since he was afraid that if he sent a downright challenge he might be charged with violating the privileges of parliament, and that if he killed Toler he might be found guilty of murder.[1] This approach to a matter of honour could be misinterpreted, and after Toler had waited for a reasonable time, his second brought the matter before the house of commons. Tandy was ordered to the bar and was arrested in his home by the serjeant-at-arms. He went into the parlour to collect his hat and escaped by scrambling through a window. According to Drennan, Tandy had 'two horrors about him—a horror of Newgate —a horror of the bar of the house—and I much fear between ourselves—a third horror—of fighting'. Tandy's conduct dismayed his political associates and both Tone and Drennan saw that the society must at once remove the affair from the

[1] *Parl. Reg. Ire.*, xii, pp. 202, 231–2, 305–8; *D.E.P.*, 23 Feb. 1792.

personal to the public sphere and show the nation that 'we were not to be intimidated or put down so easily'. On 24 February the society resolved that undefined parliamentary privilege was a danger to the liberty of the subject and that it was quite prepared to face a constitutional inquiry into its proceedings. These resolutions were published but were ignored by the house of commons. A proclamation was issued offering a reward for Tandy's arrest, it being rumoured that 'when £50 was proposed in council as a reward for apprehending him, let it be 50 *pence* said the lord lieutenant'. On the day parliament was to be prorogued, Tandy surrendered himself and was sent to Newgate. He was accompanied by a large crowd and released soon after the house rose. Drennan, who did not join in the procession to Newgate, reflected 'Poor Tandy, after 18 years' struggle, against his own interest, in the public cause, has nearly lost his reputation as a gentleman in a quarter of an hour.'[2]

A series of legal battles ensued in which the leading barristers, who were United Irishmen, distinguished themselves. Tandy was prosecuted in the king's bench for sending a challenge to Toler. The defending counsel made great play with the laws of evidence and Tandy was found not guilty, a verdict greeted by the populace, who crowded the outer hall, with cries of 'Chair him, Chair him'. The verdict however might have been regarded as questioning Tandy's honour, so he went before a volunteer court martial which acquitted Colonel Tandy of cowardice but pronounced that 'the origins and termination of this affair have been equally imprudent and ill-advised'. Tandy then sued in the recorder's court (probably collusively) John Knight, who acting under the viceroy's proclamation had arrested him. The government refused to support Knight, who was found guilty and fined 6*d*., a verdict which radicals considered proved 'the inefficacy of a proclamation when it strikes at the liberty of the subject'. Finally Tandy sued, unsuccessfully, the lord lieutenant in the court of exchequer for issuing the proclamation, the aim of the action being to challenge the validity of the lord lieutenant's patent.[3]

The Ulster radicals were also active and during the summer

---

[2] W. Drennan to S. McTier, 24 Feb., *post* 24 Feb., 2 Apr. 1792 (Drennan papers, 326, 329, 403).

[3] *D.E.P.*, 19 Apr., 12, 30 June, 18 Aug. 1792.

of 1792 they achieved a striking victory over old-fashioned liberalism, or, as they would have said, obscurantism, in the Belfast zone. It was again decided to commemorate in Belfast the fall of the Bastille on a grand scale with a volunteer parade, a meeting and a dinner. Tone, Tandy and some members of the catholic committee came up for the celebrations and when Tone arrived in Belfast on 10 July he discovered that there was a disturbing possibility that there might not be unanimous support for the catholic cause at the meeting on the fourteenth. Late on the 13th, Neilson, the editor of the *Northern Star*, entering a room in the Donegall Arms, the principal Belfast inn, found a number of volunteer delegates from the country listening to Waddel Cunningham, a prosperous merchant, who was 'haranguing against the catholics and talking of some sedition that was to be broached the next day'. Neilson joined the party and forcefully answered Cunningham, but it was impossible to say how the country delegates had been influenced by the discussion and Neilson anticipated 'hot work'. On 14 July nearly 800 volunteers paraded, and while they were being reviewed a group of radical leaders, Tandy, his brother George, and Dr Crawford from Lisburn, Sinclair, Theobald McKenna and Tone, gathered in the adjacent field to discuss what course they should take on the catholic question at the meeting which was to follow the parade. Tandy and McKenna both seem to have feared a discouraging defeat, but Sinclair and Tone were for coming 'fairly forward'. At the meeting Henry Joy, the editor of the *Belfast News-Letter*, wished to insert in the address a statement that the assembly rejoiced in the gradual emancipation of the catholics and looked forward to the day when their entire enfranchisement could be safely granted, in place of a sentence declaring that a scheme of parliamentary reform which did not equally include all denominations of Irishmen would be unsatisfactory. Alexander Stewart, a barrister, supported him, arguing that there were bigoted catholics as well as bigoted protestants, and 'until this bigotry could be overcome it would be in vain to look for union'. But Steel Dickson, the presbyterian minister, in a robust speech ridiculed gradualism. When, he asked, was emancipation to come? Was it today or tomorrow, next month, next year, next century or happily in the next world? The meeting with only a few dissenting voices rejected Joy's amendment and then many of those present adjourned to a banquet with a most formidable toast list, described by Tone in exhilarated and impressionistic prose.[4] The following day, the radical leaders, flushed with victory, discussed organizing the northern reformers on the lines which had been adopted by the catholic committee, and later in the year Drennan was pressing his Belfast friends to bestir themselves and hold a reform convention of parochial delegates, which would 'embody and ascertain public opinion', at Dungannon. The convention, he thought, should start every day with prayer, and should draw up 'a few, simple, comprehensive principles, relative to the rights of man and the nation'. At first he urged that the convention should refuse to dissolve until assured reform would be granted (the delegates being granted a subsistence allowance). In early January, however, he recommended that the convention should, at the conclusion of its labours, appoint a permanent executive committee and provisional delegates to a National reform convention. Then, if by the close of the session parliament had not accepted radical reform, a national convention could be convened—'a final measure and a necessary one'.[5]

Drennan was addressing himself to willing listeners. In the later months of 1792 the reform movement, inspired and directed by the radicals, was rapidly gathering momentum in Ulster. Men felt 'the irresistible elasticity with which man long bent down into a beast of burden, shakes off the yoke of despotism', and they saw with delight 'the seeds of liberality vegetating with vigour in the genial warmth of restored fraternity'. The United Irishmen of Belfast published declarations in favour of the catholic claims and sent an address to the reformers in Scotland, 'the asylum of independence . . . renowned in arms and arts', the country where Reid and Beattie (the common-sense philosophers) had overthrown the scepticism 'which had reduced the universe to a shadowy idea' (and which was associated with a tory, Hume). In October the Northern whig club 'with only a solitary and feeble No from Dr Haliday', passed resolutions congratulating Ireland on the ignominious

---

[4] T. W. Tone, *Life*, i, pp. 155–6.
[5] W. Drennan to S. McTier, 15, *post* 17, 24, 31 Dec. 1792, 8 Feb. 1793 (Drennan papers, 360, 361, 364, 368, 388a).

flight from France of the enemies of liberty and demanding 'an honest and effectual reform in the representation', with equal rights for Irishmen of every denomination. Significantly enough the resolutions were inspired by one United Irishman, Drennan, and the chairman of the meeting was another, Hamilton Rowan.[6] At the end of October Belfast was illuminated and the volunteers fired a *feu de joie* to mark Brunwick's retreat. 'I have', Mrs McTier wrote, 'been all this day singing over the hills and far away, and Prussia and Brunswick skipping before my eyes.'[7]

Volunteer corps were being revived or formed throughout the province and on 26 December a Belfast town meeting held in the second presbyterian church, agreed that a 'military fund' should be formed by subscriptions from those who 'by age, infirmity or other causes' were incapacitated from joining the volunteers and that from this fund grants would be made to volunteers to buy arms and ammunition, which would enable 'our poorer brethren to act'. It was important Montfoad stressed, to arm 'the lower orders, the strength of the nation', though they must be careful to 'avoid being led with rashness into premature measures'.[8] The meeting also agreed that an Ulster reform convention should be held, and appointed a committee to make arrangements. During the next few weeks a number of meetings were held in connection with the forthcoming convention, the general plan being for parochial delegates to meet and select county representatives. There were some faint signs of conservative opposition. The County Down meeting to approve the scheme was attended by Lord Hillsborough, a great county leviathan, a man of strong public spirit with a high sense of his own dignity ('an insolent puppy', to Mrs McTier). Hillsborough said that 'it would be ungracious at this particular period to argue the question of reform', and he went on to tell the meeting that he had heard 'on good authority', that the French had opened the Scheldt in order 'to facilitate a scheme of General Doumorier' for the invasion of Ireland. This statement caused loud laughter, and Steel Dickson, the presbyterian minister of Portaferry, made much

[6] *Belfast Politics*, pp. 100–2.
[7] Mrs McTier to W. Drennan, n.d. (Drennan papers, 347).
[8] *Belfast politics*, pp. 112–13.

play with the idea that Hillsborough was treating the gathering as a collection of ignorant provincials. In spite of Hillsborough, County Down went ahead and elected delegates. Counties Tyrone, Derry and Donegal selected their delegates at a meeting in Londonderry city, and the County Antrim delegates meeting at Ballymena chose twenty-four representatives, together with the county M.P.s, and instructed them to keep in mind as a fundamental principle, 'we aim at reformation and renovation not revolution'. About the same time, the Fermanagh conservatives summoned a meeting to form an association in support of the constitution. When at this meeting resolutions in favour of reform were brought forward, 'the feelings of some noblemen and reverend gentlemen which could no longer be maintained within bounds, overbore by every indecent exertion the freedom of debate', and the high sheriff, directed by the earl of Enniskillen, closed the meeting. The 'people' then repaired to the commons and passed resolutions in favour of reform but Fermanagh was not represented in the convention.[9]

What is noticeable is the degree of support which the reform cause secured at this time from sections of society which might have been expected to have a conservative bias. Hillsborough himself acknowledged that the group which called the County Down meeting was composed of 'respectable names'—it included representatives of a number of well-known landed families, Hamilton, Price, Maxwell, Montgomery and Pottinger. And amongst those elected to the convention were Colonel Sharman, a sometime M.P. and well-known volunteer, who acted as chairman, Gavin Hamilton, a sometime high sheriff of County Down, and Alexander Stewart, a brother of the first Lord Londonderry. One well-known Ulster radical, William Todd Jones, who was elected a representative for County Antrim, declined to act on the grounds of health and finance, but took the opportunity to point out that not one catholic had been included in the Antrim delegation. The *Northern Star* retorted tartly that in a county where the majority of the people and almost all landed and commercial property was protestant, we should not 'fly to an extreme and reverse the order of society'.[10]

The Ulster reform convention which sat for two days in the

9 *N.S.*, 16, 26 Jan. 1793.　　10 *N.S.*, 23, 26 Jan., 9 Feb. 1793.

presbyterian church of Dungannon, the 'Mons sacer' of the province, was, according to the *Northern Star*, 'a very respectable and spirited body' (the first adjective possibly explaining the moderation which marked its deliberations. On 15 February the convention appointed a committee to prepare resolutions. The committee sat all night and by midday on the 16th presented the convention with a series of resolutions which were almost unanimously accepted. These resolutions affirmed the convention's attachment to the British constitution, as uniting the advantages and tempering the defects of the three simple modes of government, disapproved of republican forms of government, 'as not applicable to this kingdom'; rejected with abhorrence 'the principles which have a tendency to dissolve all governments and destroy every wise and salutary distinction in society'; declared that all boroughs should be disfranchised and a 'representation established on a fair and rational principle, by extending the franchise equally to persons of every religious persuasion, by elections frequently repeated and by a distribution of representatives proportioned to the population and wealth of the country'; approved the appointment of a committee empowered to recall the convention; thanked the volunteers and expressed indignant disapproval at the formation of a militia.

When these resolutions were being considered a number of points were made with an insistence which seems to have wearied his audience, by one of the County Down delegates, Joseph Pollock. Pollock, who was moving to the right, was afraid that a number of reformers, influenced by the Dublin society of United Irishmen, were developing 'a strong and dangerous disposition to republicanism'. Before heading for Dungannon he had a hurried consultation with the whig leaders, Grattan and Forbes, and he arrived with a complete set of draft resolutions in his pocket. He was anxious that the convention should stress the value of the British connection and the practical benefits conferred on Irishmen by the constitution as it stood. He wanted the convention to endeavour to attain its objectives by the constitutional course of petitions to parliament, and he opposed the resolution attacking the militia, arguing that the government was perfectly justified in raising such a force in wartime. On the other hand Dr Caldwell, who 'made some of the squires smart', wanted the assembly to pronounce in favour of biannual parliaments and the ballot. But it was argued that these were points for a national convention. Caldwell also proposed that the criticisms of the republican mode of government be omitted from the resolutions. He was supported by Dr James Reynolds from County Tyrone (a member of the Dublin society of United Irishmen) but successfully opposed by Steel Dickson, whose radicalism was indubitable. Dickson pointed out that it was necessary to meet the insinuations of 'the minions of a corrupt and seditious faction'. Caldwell received another lesson in political tactics when he urged that the meeting should fix a date for the National convention. Sinclair of Belfast pointed out this was inadvisable, since the catholics, who were certain to support reform, could not be expected to declare their views until the catholic relief bill was safely through parliament. Finally when Caldwell and Reynolds called on the convention to show its disapproval of the war 'entirely unprovoked on the part of France', some of the delegates stated they were not empowered to deal with that issue. In the end it was decided that after the convention closed, gentlemen might meet and pass a resolution condemning the war, a step which was immediately taken.[11]

'The delegates of the province of Ulster', the *Northern Star* pronounced a few days after the convention adjourned, 'speaking the voice of the people from Dungannon, have demonstrated to the world that the whole province is one great society of United Irishmen'. Privately the editor expressed himself more cautiously. 'The meeting', he wrote to Drennan, 'was rather led by the aristocracy but the people's spirit was infused into their resolutions . . . upon the whole I think the proceedings prudent and useful though not entirely up to my ideas.' Neilson was wise in having reservations. The convention's resolutions, though outspoken and clearly inspired by well-grounded conviction, were characterized by a restraint which suggests that many of those who agreed to them might, under changed circumstances, consider that parliamentary reform could be for a time deferred.[12]

[11] For the convention's proceedings see *N.S.*, 15, 20 Feb. 1793; J. Pollock, *Letters to the inhabitants of the town and lordship of Newry* 1793; the counties represented were Antrim, Down, Donegal, Londonderry and Tyrone.
[12] S. Neilson to W. Drennan, 17 Feb. 1793 (Drennan papers, 390a).

During the winter of 1792–3 it seemed possible or even probable that the cause of parliamentary reform might triumph in Ireland. Liberalism was on the march all over western Europe. In Ireland the catholics were employing democratic techniques to demonstrate the strength of their demand for further relief. In Ulster the liberals were preparing for the Dungannon convention. In the south numerous groups, including the Association for the preservation of the constitution, liberty and peace (sponsored by the whigs) were pressing for the reform of the representative system. It was rumoured that Ponsonby, Shannon, Conolly, Beresford, Leinster, Hutchinson, Burton Conyngham, Grattan, Corry and many country gentlemen were pledged to reform. If keen liberals saw reform as just, rational and inevitable, whigs, who had shown themselves tepid on the subject, now felt it necessary to conciliate vigorous middle-class opinion, and some late converts to reform may have been encouraged by the theory that a moderate reform scheme which gave additional M.P.s to the counties or which enlarged the boundaries of the smaller boroughs to bring in rural areas, would not weaken the power of the landed interest.[13] But it was obvious that if reform was enacted along with the measures of administrative and financial reorganization which were bound to accompany it, the influence of the Irish executive would be seriously diminished and the whole system of government thrown into disarray.

The lord lieutenant and chief secretary who had to meet the crisis, Westmorland and Hobart, were intelligent men with conventional views, who were both to attain cabinet rank (Westmorland indeed was to be a not very distinguished cabinet minister for thirty years). Neither had the capacity to impose their will on events, they both had an instinctive inclination to adhere to the status quo—'the business of government here', Westmorland remarked, 'is to keep everything as quiet as possible'.[14] But their basic conservatism was tempered by common sense and a high degree of deference to Downing Street. By the end of 1792 a slow realization that it might pay politically to conciliate the Irish catholics and British government pressure

[13] G. Knox to Abercorn, 19, 24 Jan. 1793 (P.R.O.N.I. T/2541/1B 1/3, 5); T. Knox to Abercorn, 11, 22 Jan. 1793 (P.R.O.N.I. T/2541/1B 1/5/2, 6).
[14] Westmorland to W. Pitt, 12 Oct. 1790 (P.R.O. 30/8/331).

had brought the Irish administration to the point of sponsoring a major catholic relief bill. About the same time a bold challenge from the radicals compelled it to take forcible action in another sphere with unexpectedly successful results.

In October 1792 Tone and McCormick, the Dublin poplin manufacturer, discussed over the dinner table the possibility of reviving volunteering in Dublin, and in November when a number of United Irishmen were dining well with Thomas Warren, a reputably rich catholic cotton manufacturer, the subject of volunteering was again raised. Hamilton Rowan was keenly interested, and Tone talked 'a great deal of tactics and treason' until he saw the glasses on the table doubling. On 17 November a small group of influential Dublin radicals, Tandy, his son James, Dowling the attorney, Bacon the tailor (a volunteer 'martinet'), Bond, Warren and McCormick met and decided to form a new volunteer corps, the first National battalion, which in name and uniform would be reminiscent of the French national guard. It was to be 1,000 strong, its uniform coat and trousers (they were to be *sans-culottes*) green; the device on the button, a shamrock crowned with the cap of liberty. The corps was to have 'a magnificent oriflame', inscribed 'in glowing capitals' with the words 'Universal emancipation and representative legislation', and Drennan looked forward to seeing a battalion defiling in French fashion before the Dublin United Irishmen. On 3 December the government was informed by Collins that the first National battalion was going to meet at the Tailors' Hall for the purpose of electing officers, and a few days later Colonel Jackson of the Merchants corps, at the request of some of its members, published a notice calling on the corps again to assemble as a military association in order to win reform.[15]

On 8 December there was a long and largely attended meeting of the privy council, the result of which was a proclamation, signed by twenty-three councillors, 'a grand, grand jury', which was rapidly distributed through Dublin. Skilfully distinguishing between the old and the new volunteers, it declared that 'ill affected persons', under 'the colour of laudable

---

[15] T. W. Tone, *Life*, i, pp. 195–202; ii, p. 133; *D.E.P.*, 7 June 1798; *H.J.*, 7 Dec. 1792. Excited conservatives visualized the volunteers taking possession of Dublin; see remarks of attorney-general reported in *Trial of William Drennan* (1794), p. 14.

associations' formed in the past for the defence of the country, were assembling in arms. It charged them to desist and directed the magistrates to act against them. A few of the national battalion met and called on the volunteers of Dublin to meet and discuss the proclamation and Hamilton Rowan, with one or two others, walked through the streets in their green uniforms 'huzz'd' by the mob. But some catholics concerned in the formation of the corps were reluctant to take action at this time (their affairs, Drennan tartly remarked, were 'in a good train without trying the military instrument'), and Tone had the excuse that he had to leave for England with the catholic delegates.[16]

On 14 December the Dublin United Irishmen agreed on an address to the volunteers, 'citizen soldiers', calling them to arms, and on 16 December the National battalion met in a hall in Cope Street, thanked the United Irishmen for their address and declared that they were attached to the principles and hated only the abuses of the constitution. The same evening four other volunteer corps, meeting with Colonel Tandy in the chair, resolved they would not be deterred from doing their duty as citizens and volunteers by the proclamation. A few weeks later one of these corps, the Goldsmiths, assembling in Ship Street for a parade, was warned by Alderman Warren that if they attempted to march through the streets he would arrest their officers. A hasty message was sent to a committee of the Dublin society of United Irishmen which was deliberating on reform, and several lawyers 'with Tandy at their tail' hurried across to Ship Street. After some legal wrangling, on Tandy's advice the parade dispersed 'in order to prevent the possibility of any disturbance from a numerous appearance of the populous'. Some weeks later the Dublin Rangers, marching to Drum-condra to breakfast with their colonel, had a scuffle with Alderman James who tried to disarm them. They 'gobbled up their breakfast' and dispersed before the military arrived. Lord Charlemont had a fruitless interview with Hobart, the delegates of the Dublin corps received from Simon Butler and James Whitestone diametrically opposite opinions on the legality of parading, and the Lawyers corps presented an address to the

[16] W. Drennan to S. McTier, 8, 9 Dec. 1792, 28 Jan., *post* 28 Jan., 25 Feb. 1793 (Drennan papers, 358, 359, 380, 381, 327).

lord lieutenant declaring they were going to discontinue their meetings as an armed corps, 'being perfectly convinced that any attempt to intimidate the legislature . . . is a criminal violation of the laws of the land'. From early in 1793 volunteer activity in Dublin ceased.[17]

The Northern radicals observed the collapse of volunteering in Dublin with some contempt; Samuel McTier, referring to the timidity of the Goldsmiths corps, confidently declared that if 'a scuffle' were to take place in Belfast between the volunteers and the military, within forty-eight hours there would be 10,000 armed men in the town. Some weeks later his assertion was unexpectedly tested. On 9 March there was a bad riot in Belfast. The men of the 17th Dragoons, incensed by the playing of 'an outlandish tune', 'ça ira', lost their temper and scuffled with the citizens. Windows were smashed and shop-signs (including one of Dumouriez who in a few weeks' time was to desert to the allies) pulled down. There was great alarm in the town and while the officers strove to get their men back to barracks, the volunteers mustered several hundreds strong at the Linen hall and the sovereign assembled a committee of the leading townsmen. Early the following morning General Whyte, who though that his position at this time resembled that of 'my late friend General Gage at Boston', arrived in Belfast. He sympathized with the committee, took prompt steps to restore discipline and insisted that the volunteers should disperse. Belfast seems to have been badly shaken by this sudden experience of violence and the volunteers went quietly home. When a few days later a proclamation was issued warning loyal subjects in Belfast not to assemble in arms, the *Northern Star* told the volunteers that it would be 'magnanimous to discontinue the use of arms for the present'. Shortly afterwards the Coleraine volunteers, when a magistrate showed them the proclamation, quietly dispersed and volunteer parades in Ulster ceased to be held. Down in Cork two volunteer corps, the True blue and the Cork union, having been informed by the mayor that their appearing in arms on His Majesty's birthday, 'would not be pleasant to the government', resolved that though they had the right to bear arms they would not

[17] *H.J.*, 16 Dec. 1792; W. Drennan to S. McTier, 28 Jan., 28 Feb. 1793 (Drennan papers, 327, 381); *N.S.*, 6 Feb. 1793.

hazard the peace of the city.[18] The volunteers, law-abiding men, many of them instinctively deferential to authority, quietly faded away, not even attempting to challenge the proclamation in the courts, and an imponderable and impressive force in Irish politics, big with potentialities, vanished from the scene.

At the beginning of 1793 however the government's ability to master the volunteers had still to be proved and it was also highly uncertain if it could impose its solution of the catholic question without yielding in the end to liberal or ultra-protestant pressure. So when on 16 January William Ponsonby, who in 1783 had opposed reform, asked the house of commons to consider the question, it seemed likely enough that a moderate reform bill would reach the statute book. 'Never, never, since I sat in parliament', Grattan enthusiastically declared, 'have I heard words which gave me more satisfaction . . . I feel myself young and my mind possessed with rapture little known in my time of life.' What was more significant was that Isaac Corry, a revenue commissioner, and 'a member in the confidence of the administration', supported Ponsonby's motion that the house go into committee to consider the state of the representation of the people in parliament. The motion was passed without a division and Charlemont noted with grim pleasure 'the ludicrous oddity and comical amazement of many long faces in the assembly'.[19] Sir John Blaquiere who considered parliamentary reform to be the main issue in Irish politics, convinced as he was that it would lead to 'the instant subversion of all order and perhaps to separation from Great Britain', also noticed that on 14 January reform was supported not only by the opposition but by many of 'the principal gentlemen of the administration'. Blaquiere, an old parliamentary hand, was confident, however, that there were still 'some men stout enough to hold out'.[20] The execution of the king of France, the war and agrarian trouble were bound to bias M.P.s against constitutional change and once the house was in committee the conservatives rallied. It was argued that the house should take

[18] S. McTier to W. Drennan, 30 Jan. 1792 (Drennan papers, 382); R. Whyte to E. Nepean, 8 Apr. 1793 (H.O. 100/46); *N.S.*, 13 Mar. 1793; *D.J.*, 26 Mar. 1793; *B.N.L.*, 7 June 1793.

[19] *Charlemont MSS H.M.C.*, ii, pp. 209–10.

[20] J. Blaquiere to Hawkesbury, 15 Jan., 16 Feb. 1793 (Add. MS 38228).

into account the good as well as the bad aspects of the existing system and when Forbes moved that a list of the electors in each borough be transmitted to the house he was defeated 137 to 38. The committee achieved nothing and it was not until the close of the session that George Ponsonby introduced a reform bill. This provided that every county and the cities of Dublin and Cork were to be three member constituencies and that the boundaries of every borough should be extended in every direction four miles from its centre. Within the extended boroughs the franchise was to be exercised by ten-pound freeholders, freemen by birth, marriage or servitude, and free-men admitted by the corporation who were five-pound freeholders.[21] The whigs defended their scheme as being in accordance with the principles of the constitution, a constitution which contained in itself the seeds of its own reformation. Under universal suffrage, Grattan explained, 'those who have nothing in land, farms or trade would return the parliament, that is those who have nothing in the common stock would make the laws and the man who receives alms would vote the taxes'. Under the whig scheme parliament would represent 'the propertied part of the community', and, Grattan added, the mass of property usually included the mass of talent. But in spite of the conservative arguments used in support of the scheme, when in 1794 it was presented to the house of commons it was rejected by 142 votes to 44, the majority genuinely believing that in France 'temperate reform was the rudiments of all that followed'.[22]

But if obdurate on reform, parliament, during 1793, showed that it could respond to intelligent public opinion. At the beginning of the session Westmorland believed that it would be highly desirable to give the friends of the government 'some popular ground to stand upon' by accepting a number of the measures in the opposition programme.[23] Four bills, incorporating reforms urged by leading whigs were introduced by members of the government and passed. The civil list act established a consolidated fund, regulated issues of public money and provided that the pension list should be gradually

[21] For Ponsonby's bill see *Parl. Reg. Ire.*, xiii, pp. 394–5; xiv, pp. 62–8.
[22] *Parl. Reg. Ire.*, xiv, p. 70.
[23] Westmorland to Dundas, 16 Jan. 1793 (H.O. 100/42).

reduced to £80,000 per annum. A place bill excluded from the house of commons persons holding a group of specified offices, pensioners during pleasure and any person holding a place created after the passing of the act. It also provided that an M.P. accepting an office of profit under the crown must seek re-election. A barren land act provided that barren land brought into cultivation should be exempted from tithe for seven years. A hearth-tax act exempted from hearth-tax occupiers of a house with only one hearth (with the qualification that the occupier of a holding worth more than £5 per annum could not claim this exemption). In addition a libel bill introduced by George Ponsonby was passed. Based on Fox's libel act of 1791, it empowered the jury in a libel case to bring in a general verdict. Finally, the East India act passed at the close of the session, to some extent met the whig case against the East India company's monopoly. In the debate on East Indian trade the whigs raised a larger and more pressing issue, the need for a comprehensive settlement of Anglo-Irish commercial relations, Grattan urging that Irish manufactures should be admitted into the British market on paying the same duties as were levied on British manufactures imported into Ireland. In fact the Irish whigs had come to accept Pitt's policy of 1785—assuming that the details were adjusted fairly from the Irish standpoint.

Besides trying to kill with legislative kindness the hostility of sections of opinion, the government during the session of 1793 increased its power by three important measures—a militia act, a gunpowder act (which made it an offence to import or transport arms or munitions without a licence), and a convention act. The convention act, which Fitzgibbon said 'in ten lines did no more than declare there should only be one parliament in Ireland',[24] declared unlawful assemblies purporting to represent the people or any section of the people, with the aim 'of procuring an alteration of matters established by law in church or state'. The administration's policy of controlled concession combined with firmness seems to have been widely acceptable. 'Our session', Hobart complacently remarked, 'has closed with prodigious advantage to the government.'[25]

---

[24] *D.E.P.*, 11 July 1793.
[25] R. Hobart to E. Nepean, 17 Aug. 1793 (H.O. 100/44); *Charlemont MSS H.M.C.*, ii, pp. 214–5.

Charlemont, the doyen of the whigs, was also pleased with the session. 'Our success', he wrote, 'has not been equal to my wishes, it has however greatly exceeded my expectations'; and the Irish whigs could congratulate themselves on the impression which their parliamentary pertinacity, aided by circumstances, had made on the statute book. The fact that measures which the whig leaders had emphasized were of the utmost importance, had been enacted made it possible for those of their followers who had an inherent wish to support the government especially at a time when established institutions were threatened to desist from systematic opposition. At the beginning of the session the whigs, when challenging what appeared to be a harsh exercise of parliamentary privilege, mustered 70 votes (against 154), but when, at the close of the session, Grattan opposed the second reading of the convention bill he was defeated by 128 to 27— 'most of the country gentlemen commonly in opposition supporting the government'. Though Charlemont asserted with pride 'our party keep together', Shannon, important for his borough influence, was again ready to support the government, as he said at the beginning of 1794, 'disinterestedly and without office or favour' (overlooking that he had recently accepted a seat at the treasury board) and according to an opposition newspaper, at the beginning of the session, there had been twenty-two desertions from the whig ranks to the government side of the house. The administration was also encouraged by Grattan's attitude. When opposing the convention bill, he had declared the proposed national reform convention to be unseasonable and inadmissible and he seems to have been favourably impressed by the concessions made in 1793.[26]

With party tension relaxed Hobart made overtures to the whigs. Supported by Fitzgibbon and Beresford he had a meeting with George Ponsonby and Bowes Daly (Grattan refused to meet Fitzgibbon). Hobart said he was anxious to 'tranquillize' the country and ready, without sacrificing his own friends, to bring some of the whigs into office. Ponsonby and Daly agreed on the importance of tranquillity but wanted the measures the whigs had been advocating implemented. In spite of the

[26] *Charlemont MSS H.M.C.*, ii, pp. 214–15; Westmorland to W. Pitt, 29 Jan. 1794 (P.R.O. 30/8/331); *D.E.P.*, 23 Jan. 1794.

failure of this *démarche*, Hobart's successor Sylvester Douglas, who arrived in Ireland in January 1794, observed at the beginning of the session 'a parliamentary calm'. When a few whigs tentatively criticized the war—George Ponsonby made it clear he was not pledged to support it indefinitely, Duquery wanted to know what were their objectives and Parsons moved for papers relating to the war to be laid before the house— Grattan declared that he supported the war effort to the utmost and Parsons was defeated by 128 to 9. Cooke was delighted. 'I never', he wrote, 'saw greater marks of chagrin painted on countenances than those of George Ponsonby, Curran, Duquery and Egan.' Cooke thought it essential to secure Grattan's support for the government. 'He is', Cooke wrote, 'very high minded, resentful and suspicious. He is however very steady and honourable.' A week later the chancellor of the exchequer showed polite deference to the great tribune by postponing his budget statement because Grattan 'whose presence he wished when any matter of importance was to be submitted to the house', was out of town for a few days, and when Grattan, in a speech distinguished by eloquence rather than economic argument, argued that Great Britain should be urged to lower the duties imposed on Irish manufactures to the level of the Irish duties on similar articles imported from Great Britain, the chancellor of the exchequer responded sympathetically and the motion was not pressed to a division.[27]

Not only was the short and uneventful parliamentary session of 1794, from the government standpoint, remarkably successful, but there were signs that out-of-doors agitation was dying down. Early in 1794 the government was cheered to learn that at two meetings of the catholic leaders, the second held at Dr MacNeven's being composed of 'persons of a more sanguine disposition', it had been decided to abstain from action for the present.[28] As for Irish radicalism, by the summer of 1794 it was, if not in decline, undoubtedly in disarray. In the previous eighteen months it had sustained a number of damaging blows. The convention act and the suppression or dissolution of the

---

[27] Westmorland to W. Pitt, 29 Jan. 1794 (P.R.O. 30/8/331); S. Douglas, *Diaries* i, p. 40; E. Cooke to E. Nepean, 7 Feb. 1794 (H.O. 100/51); *D.E.P.*, 3 Jan., 10, 13 Feb. 1794.

[28] S. Douglas to H. Dundas, 20 Feb., 1 Mar. 1794 (H.O. 100/51).

volunteers had left the radicals without the machinery on which they had relied for bringing public opinion to bear effectively on parliament. The war had given conservatives a cause to rally round, and if convinced radicals retained their faith and their sympathy for France, moderate men had a reason or good excuse for abstaining from agitation. Finally, all over the British Isles the authorities launched legal counter-attacks against conspicuous radicals.

When, at the end of February 1793 the Dublin society of United Irishmen published a series of resolutions criticizing a committee of the house of lords for acting *ultra vires* by examining witnesses on oath, Butler and Bond, the society's chairman and secretary, the signatories of the resolutions, were brought to the bar of the house and each fined £500 and sentenced to six months in Newgate. This threw a severe strain on the society, which generously accepted responsibility for the fines and with considerable effort raised the £1,000. A number of members also tried to alleviate the monotony of captivity by agreeing to give in rotation a dinner for eight in Newgate. Drennan, who sourly commented that 'the brother of Lord Mountgarret and the extensive merchant take all our treats in good part and with thankfulness', thought that many members resented Butler and Bond living remarkably well (their wine bills were large) while the society was striving to help them. His sister-in-law, the censorious Mrs McTier, was shocked to hear that Butler's mistress was to be seen in Newgate, dining unchaperoned, on 'fruit and all the rarities of the season'.[29]

A fortnight after Butler and Bond were committed to Newgate, Napper Tandy was in trouble. He was due to appear at the Louth assizes, charged with distributing a paper, 'Commonsense', violently denouncing the Beresford and Foster families. Some of his associates, including Simon Butler and McCormick, the catholic leader, advised him to forfeit his recognizances 'on the probability of his being found guilty and in that case the judge would inflict punishment without mercy in fine and imprisonment, and on the likelihood that other things were being kept in reserve for him'. (It was probably known that a

---

[29] W. Drennan to S. McTier, 9 Mar., 16 Aug. 1793 (Drennan papers, 396, 438); Mrs McTier to S. McTier, Apr. 1793 (Drennan papers, 416); 'Proceedings of Dublin society of United Irishmen', p. 85.

zealous magistrate was trying to persuade a prisoner in Kilmainham to swear that Tandy and Rowan were connected with the defenders.) Tandy left Ireland for America and ultimately France.[30] His departure was a serious loss since, though a target for conservative ridicule, he was an experienced municipal politican and a man of weight in the city—he had recently been re-elected a representative of the guild of merchants on the common council and a trustee of the Royal Exchange.

At the beginning of 1794 Hamilton Rowan was brought to trial for distributing a seditious libel, the Dublin society of United Irishmen's address to the volunteers, found guilty and sentenced to two years in Newgate. In June William Drennan was tried for being the author of the address to the volunteers (which, he said, 'I wrote as if I had felt the departed spirit of 30,000 of my countrymen stirring in my breast'). His counsel, Curran, concentrated on destroying the credibility of the principal prosecution witness, William Paulet Carey, on whom the crown relied for proof of publication by the accused. Pulverized, Carey gasped, 'I have been so baited with questions that I have been put beyond myself, I never was in a court before but once and then only a listener', and Drennan was acquitted.[31] Curran also secured the acquittal of the proprietors of the *Northern Star*, who were charged with publishing an address to the volunteers, on the grounds that it had already appeared in another paper, the more conservative *Belfast News-Letter*; six months earlier the proprietors of the *Star* were acquitted of publishing an address from the Jacobins of Belfast (a political club), it being argued by the defence that their responsibility had not been proved.

---

[30] *Trial of Francis Graham . . . for attempting to suborn Joseph Corbally, tailor, to swear that A. H. Rowan and Napper Tandy were at the head of the defenders*, 1794; W. Drennan to Mrs McTier, c. 16 Mar. 1793 (Drennan papers, 395); 'Proceedings of the Dublin society of United Irishmen', pp. 32–4.

[31] *Trial of William Drennan* (1794), p. 42. Carey was well rewarded by a payment of £1,000 plus a promise of government advertising for his paper and an annuity of £100 for his wife. His newspaper collapsed and the annuity ceased in 1795 but he received a few hundred pounds in addition to the £1,000. He practised as an auctioneer in Dublin, was involved in a dispute in his yeomanry corps, left Dublin and then, after settling in London, became celebrated as an engraver (I.S.P.O. 620/40/165; F. Higgins to ——, 13 Feb. 1797 (I.S.P.O. 620/18); *S.N.L.*, Nov. 1799; *DNB*).

In Ireland, as in England—Scotland was rather different—
the government was by no means sure of a conviction in a
political prosecution. Judges might be influenced by a fine
legal point, juries by argument and perhaps political bias. Still
sufficient convictions were secured to shake the movement and
create apprehensions. Drennan, a very sensitive if courageous
man, found his trial a great ordeal and after his acquittal, tired
of 'striving to live like a gentleman on £150 per annum in the
centre of a splendid city', he concentrated on the uphill task of
'trying to secure a competent professional income as a physician'. Easily offended, Drennan resented the way in which 'this
timid, staring people,' always left their defenders in the lurch
and 'one of the patriarchs' of Irish radicalism, he felt that his
political associates, though ready to use him as a writer, were
inclined to shove him civilly out of their company. Moreover, in
the autumn of 1794 he was drawing away intellectually from
the more extreme Irish radicals. At a time when they were
considering employing new techniques, Drennan felt 'a certain
nausea or indifference to politics' creeping over him. He
remained a radical, as can be seen from three striking pamphlets he published, he sent a poem to the *Press*, the organ of
extreme radicalism, 'lest they should think I did not like them',
and he retained his admiration for France. But when he
contemplated Irish politics, he was disgusted both by 'the cruel
system adopted by the upper ranks', and by 'the stupidity,
ingratitude and barbarity' of the lower orders. He wondered if
'a speculative republican may find a practical reform all the
wants', and he detested plots and conspiracies.[32] During the
stormy years 1796–8 he courageously visited friends who were
imprisoned, but he remained 'a mere spectator' of political
events. In 1800 he married and, returning to the north of Ireland, played a stimulating part in the cultural life of his native
province.

Six weeks after Rowan was sent to Newgate he was visited by
an Irish clergyman, the Revd William Jackson, who had
recently arrived in Dublin. Jackson had an unusual and varied
career. A devoted anglican, after ordination he had become a

---

[32] W. Drennan to Mrs McTier, late 1794, 25 Apr. 1795, early 1796, 24 Feb.,
14 Mar. 1796, early 1797, 25 Apr., 20 Oct. 1797 (Drennan papers, 536, 598, 600,
601, 648, 660, 678, 681).

journalist in London, editing the *Morning Post* and championing the cause of the notorious duchess of Kingston (that he regarded her as a much-wronged woman suggests a man of naive enthusiasms). A fervent liberal from the time of the American war, he was in Paris during the revolution and was selected by the French foreign office as a suitable agent to report on British and Irish opinion. Early in 1794 he arrived in London where he renewed acquaintance with Cockayne, an attorney.[33] Jackson talked freely, and Cockayne soon suspected that he was engaged in a scheme to aid the enemy—possibly smuggling contraband over to France. He immediately informed Downing Street of his suspicions and was instructed to keep a watch on Jackson. Early in April Jackson, accompanied by Cockayne, arrived in Dublin where he got in touch with MacNally, who he had known in London. MacNally over the dinner table introduced him to Simon Butler and Lewins, an attorney who was a member of the Dublin society of United Irishmen. Butler 'treated all ideas of invasion both with ridicule and reprobation',[34] but Lewins was more helpful and Jackson had talks with Tone in Rowan's apartments in Newgate. Tone drew up a short survey of the situation in Ireland which indicated that a French 'invasion in sufficient force would be supported', and there was talk of sending an Irish agent, who Jackson hoped would be Tone, to France. The government of course was well-informed about Jackson's contacts both by intercepting his letters in the post and through Cockayne, who was in a miserable condition. He disliked the double role he was playing and Jackson kept him up late talking—Cockayne was a moderate drinker, while Jackson, always extravagant, insisted on three bottles of claret a night. On 28 April Jackson was arrested at his hotel in Dame Street. Rowan, on hearing the news, a few days later escaped from Newgate, rode to Howth and took a ship for France.[35] Tone stood his ground. There was not enough evidence to convict him, his survey of the Irish situation, which the government had seized in the post, being in Rowan's hand.

---

[33] Cockayne's correspondence with the government is in P.R.O. 30/8/124.

[34] W. Drennan to S. McTier, 28 May 1794 (Drennan papers, 497).

[35] According to Drennan, Rowan, who had received permission to spend the anniversary of his wedding night with his wife, escaped from his house in Denmark Street (W. Drennan to Mrs McTier, 3 May 1794, Drennan papers, 490).

But there was the possibility of a prosecution, and in any event once Jackson was brought to trial Tone's professional prospects in Ireland would be blasted. Influential friends interceded with the government and Tone was allowed to leave Ireland for America. Jackson a year after his arrest was brought to trial, found guilty and just before being sentenced took poison and died in court.

With two leading members of the Dublin society of United Irishmen suspected of having aided the king's enemies, the government decided to strike at the society itself. Collins swore 'a most satisfactory information', and on the evening of 24 May Alderman Warren accompanied by the high sheriffs and a number of peace officers, entered the Tailors' Hall, called on the society to disperse and seized its books and papers.[36] The secretary, Collis, a barrister, protested indignantly, some of the members talked about adjourning the meeting to a tavern, and within a few months steps were being taken for 'the regeneration' of the society. A committee had been chosen on the last night of the meeting, and this committee elected a committee of twenty-one which started 'to reballot for the whole society as their names are on the list'. One name in five was rejected. Not only had many members been lax in their attendance but it had been suggested early in May that the government had infiltrated agents into the society. One of those considered for rejection was MacNally, later a useful government informant, but Drennan secured his re-election on the grounds he had 'not been treacherous and I don't think levity a good ground of objection'. While the scrutiny was in progress, Henry Sheares suggested that the society should be organized in 'sections', small local groups each of which would send a deputy to 'the council or central committee'. Drennan disapproved of this plan for 'petty, private, plotting meetings'. Butler was keen that the society should boldly challenge the right of the government to disperse its meetings by holding an advertised meeting at the Tailors' hall. He also encouraged Collis, to take an action against one of the high sheriffs. The difficulty of deciding between two contrasting schemes delayed the reorganization

---

[36] E. Cooke to E. Nepean, 26 May 1794 (H.O. 100/52); *D.J.*, 24 May 1794; 'Proceedings of the Dublin society of United Irishmen' in *Analecta Hibernica*, no. 17, pp. 127–8.

of the society.[37] Moreover, in the autumn of 1794 it seemed that a change of viceroy (Fitzwilliam replacing Westmorland) might lead to major changes in policy, including the abolition of the catholic disabilities. It was a time for Irish radicals, especially radicals who were catholics, to be politically subdued and the society was not in the event revived.

[37] William Drennan to Mrs McTier, 30 July 1794; to S. McTier, 2, 20 Aug. and 3 Sept. 1794 (Drennan) papers, 519, 523, 524.

13

Fitzwilliam's viceroyalty

In the summer of 1794 it seemed that Irish politics had entered a period of comparative calm. The parliamentary reform movement had stalled, the catholics appeared for the immediate future to be satisfied and if the outcome of the fierce conflict being waged on the north-east borders of France was uncertain, the naval victory of the glorious first of June ensured that war would be kept well away from Ireland. Conscious of the revolutionary menace, old parliamentary opponents in both Great Britain and Ireland were coming together. In Ireland Grattan energetically supported the government's war policy, in Great Britain Pitt and the Portland whigs finally coalesced. But what was expected to be an era of co-operation and broadly based government soon ended in Ireland with an unhappy misunderstanding, bitter recriminations and sharpened antagonisms.

When in July 1794 the Portland whigs, 'the old whigs' who accepted Burke's interpretation of the revolution, agreed to form a coalition with Pitt, it was obvious that Portland should be a secretary of state. Pitt at first thought of offering him foreign affairs, but Portland quickly explained that this was the post he would least like, and instead he went to the home office, thus becoming responsible for the supervision of Ireland.[1] Portland could not 'suffer the government of Ireland to be administered by any person in whom I have not implicit confidence', so it was agreed that his close friend Fitzwilliam, the new president of the council, should go to Ireland, once a suitable post was found for Westmorland. Both Portland and Fitzwilliam had important links with Ireland. Portland had Irish cousins, the Ponsonbys, and having been viceroy for a few critical months seems to have considered himself an authority on Ireland. Fitzwilliam had large Irish estates, was married to

[1] *Fortescue MSS H.M.C.*, ii, p. 597; Portland to W. Windham, 8 Oct. 1794 (Add. MS 37845).

a Ponsonby, and was the friend and political pupil of Edmund Burke. High-minded, public-spirited, frank and intelligent, Fitzwilliam seemed admirably suited to be lord lieutenant, though it must also be taken into account that he was inexperienced (at forty-six he had never held political office) and that his moral intensity was so strong it could dangerously colour his opinions and overbear his judgement.

The formation of a coalition can be a painful and acrimonious process, involving loss of career prospects and awkward compromises on policy. But in 1794 Pitt was able to bring the whigs into office without dropping any of his leading colleagues and both parties were in agreement on the great immediate issues, the war and the maintenance of order at home. Everything went so smoothly that apparently neither Pitt, Portland nor Fitzwilliam raised the question of how coalition principles were to be applied in Ireland. From the beginning however, Portland and Fitzwilliam seem to have assumed that the new arrangements implied a large transfer of office and power to the Irish whigs. Portland seems to have told William Ponsonby that he, the duke, had been entrusted with the direction of Irish affairs and the management of business in Ireland would be placed in the hands of his friends there, who, in Portland's opinion, could not be expected to act with Fitzgibbon, Beresford and the clerks (a term which covered the under-secretaries, Cooke and Sackville Hamilton). Portland apparently went on to say that he agreed with the Irish whigs' programme (including catholic emancipation.).[2]

The impressionable Fitzwilliam during the later months of 1794 invited and received a thorough indoctrination on Irish issues from his whig friends. When he wrote (in confidence) to Grattan telling him he was to succeed Westmorland, Gratton replied saying that Fitzwilliam's acceptance of the viceroyalty was 'our redemption'. On the same day as Fitzwilliam wrote to Grattan, Thomas O'Beirne who had been Portland's private secretary, and was beneficed in Ireland, informed Fitzwilliam that Grattan, George Ponsonby and Yelverton had met to discuss the news that he was coming over. They hoped the country was going to be put into a proper state of defence, the

---

[2] Report on the original propositions of the duke of Portland, enclosed in a letter from W. Ponsonby to Fitzwilliam, 4 May 1795 (W.W.M. F. 29).

catholics conciliated, the administration purified and Fitzgibbon removed. Charlemont wrote effusively to the nephew of his beloved Rockingham, telling him that 'a wise, good and respectable administration' would give 'a new and beneficent turn' to public opinion. The duke of Leinster referred bitterly to the way public money had been squandered. Thomas Conolly advised Fitzwilliam to abolish useless places, to trust to the good sense of the Irish landed aristocracy, and to grant catholic gentlemen of property the right to sit in parliament. O'Beirne, a man of forceful intellect, in later life distinguished as a vigorous diocesan, in a series of letters impressed on the lord lieutenant designate his poor opinion of men in office in Ireland, and the importance of entrusting efficient power to men who shared Fitzwilliam's principles.[3]

But before Fitzwilliam could assume control in Ireland Westmorland had to be removed, and Westmorland, though he had felt for some time that he had been long enough in Ireland, wanted the circumstances of his departure to indicate he had been a success there. Writing to Pitt, he stressed 'the mortification' he would suffer if offered anything below cabinet office. Pitt handled him with tactful firmness, and in the end he accepted a household appointment. But finding a suitable opening for Westmorland took some months and the whigs became impatient. It seemed to Fitzwilliam, that if Westmorland was to be removed from Ireland only on his own terms 'he might remain there in perpetuity'. Bickering broke out between Westmorland and Portland over fragments of patronage, one important vacancy raising a question of principle. The death of Hely-Hutchinson in September 1794 left vacant both the secretaryship of state and the provostship of Trinity. Hutchinson had been an energetic and enlightened provost but his autocratic habits and crudely conducted attempts to turn the university constituency into a close borough had led to violent dissensions within the college, culminating in the visitation of 1791. About a year before the provost's death the fellows had begun a campaign to prevent the appointment of another

---

[3] Fitzwilliam to H. Grattan, 23 May (Grattan papers, N.L.I); Grattan to Fitzwilliam, 31 Aug. 1794; Charlemont to Fitzwilliam, 1 Sept. 1794; Leinster to Fitzwilliam, 4 Sept. 1794; Conolly to Fitzwilliam, 30 Aug. 1794 (W.W.M. F. 29); L. O'Beirne to Fitzwilliam, 23 Aug. 1794 (Fitzwilliam papers, Northampton).

'alien' provost, sending successive deputations over to London. Westmorland made an adroit proposal. He put forward the name of his private secretary, Bennet, the recently appointed bishop of Cloyne. Bennet's appointment would reward a staunch administration supporter and, as he was an accomplished classicist, he was academically well-qualified. Burke protested vehemently against the appointment of 'a castle chaplain' and urged that a senior fellow be appointed. It would be scandalous, he declared, to treat the headship of great educational institution, the 'seminary of the church of Ireland', as 'a thing in the mass of promiscuous patronage'.[4]

By October Pitt was alarmed to realize that his whig colleagues assumed that Ireland was to be their own administrative preserve. At the back of his mind he doubted if it was wise for Fitzwilliam to go to Ireland, but he was anxious to maintain the coalition which was working well. There were however, he felt, three points on which he must insist. Suitable provision must be made for Westmorland and Douglas, the chief secretary; Fitzgibbon and the other Irish supporters of the administration were not to be displaced 'so long as they supported the system approved here', and any exclusive right 'to conduct the department of Ireland differently from any other in the king's service' was to be disclaimed. On 11 October when he raised the Irish question with his colleagues the whigs were shocked and angered. All their past resentment against Pitt's arrogant pursuit of power surged up and Fitzwilliam and Portland took 'a high and hot tone'. Fitzwilliam claimed that 'if I am to undertake the government of Ireland to the end of its better government I must have the power of electing the proper instruments'. Pitt countered this by saying that the removal of Fitzgibbon would be 'dangerous and impolitic'.[5]

For a short time it seemed as if the coalition might break up. But the gravity of the general situation (Holland was on the point of being overrun) had a sobering effect. Loughborough thought that the proscription of a few minor politicians was 'a miserable object at a period when proscription in all the

---

[4] A. Browne to T. Elrington, 28 Sept. 1793 (T.C.D. MS v, 2, 18); *Correspondence of Edmund Burke*, viii, pp. 11, 46–7.

[5] W. Pitt to Westmorland, 19 Oct. 1794, Memorandum in Chatham papers (P.R.O. 30/8/325); Portland to Fitzwilliam, 11, 14 Oct. 1794); W.W.M. F. 31); J. Beresford, *Correspondence*, ii, p. 41; *Correspondence of Edmund Burke*, viii, pp. 43, 56–8.

force of the term hangs by a very slender thread over all property and all legitimate power'. On 6 November Burke and Grattan, men of goodwill who were very anxious that Fitzwilliam should go to Ireland, discussed the crisis with Loughborough. On behalf of Fitzwilliam they explained that though he was determined to reform abuses he intended to proceed along temperate lines and that he and Portland did not think of Ireland as 'a thing separate from the general mass of the king's government'. Grattan and Burke also suggested that it would be advisable 'to begin the arrangement of Ireland as if it had been but this day thought of'.[6]

A week later Pitt, Grenville, Portland, Spencer, Windham and Fitzwilliam met at Downing Street to settle outstanding Irish issues. It was decided that the provostship should be filled by the appointment of a fellow. Fitzwilliam urged that William Ponsonby should be made secretary of state, but it was decided that the office should be annexed to the chief secretaryship and that Ponsonby should be appointed keeper of the signet. It was suggested that if the attorney-general, Wolfe, and the solicitor-general, Toler, were placed on the bench, George Ponsonby could be appointed attorney-general. But in the end it was agreed that if Toler could be placed on the bench, Ponsonby might serve for a time as solicitor-general under Wolfe. Fitzwilliam raised the question of reducing the number of revenue commissioners, but since 'it soon appeared he was by no means acquainted with the subject' (which indeed nobody in the room understood), it was decided he would collect information on the subject after his arrival in Ireland and then give his colleagues an opportunity of 'deliberating upon any measure he might propose'. At the close of this exhaustive discussion the catholic question was mentioned. 'It was considered a subject of much delicacy' and 'no decided sentiment as to the line it might ultimately be right to adopt upon it was expressed by any person present'. Fitzwilliam it was settled was to try to prevent the question being raised during the coming session and 'in all events . . . do nothing in it which might commit the king's government without fresh instructions from hence [England]'. Fitzwilliam himself recorded the decision on this last question

---

[6] Loughborough to E. Burke, 3 Oct. 1794 (W.W.M. Bk. 2005); *Correspondence of Edmund Burke*, viii, pp. 74–5.

in obscure terms on a scrap of paper . . . 'that the Roman catholic question not be brought forward by the government that the discussion of the propriety be left open'.[7] The record of the discussion suggests that Fitzwilliam was given a defined but difficult task. A man of strong convictions who had already committed himself on Irish issues, he was to represent in Ireland a coalition cabinet which, preoccupied with a menacing military situation, was inclined to go slow on domestic questions. The attitude of the British government was clearly shown at another conference on Irish affairs, which took place at the end of November, when Pitt, Sir John Parnell and Fitzwilliam met Grattan and George and William Ponsonby. The Irish whigs pressed for the reduction of the British duties on Irish products to the level of the Irish duties on imports from Great Britain, and they wanted measures to help the Irish silk, sail and cloth manufacturers and the Irish brewing industry. Pitt, though of course he favoured in principle lower duties, was not prepared during the war to undertake the reshaping of Anglo-Irish commercial relations and he pressed the Irish politicians to raise additional forces for home defence.[8]

Fitzwilliam landed at Balbriggan on 4 January, travelled up to Dublin and assumed office. Immediately he arrived in Dublin, O'Beirne, whom he had appointed as his private secretary, handed him a most secret memorandum. This emphasized that Fitzwilliam's friends in Ireland were contending not for 'places yielding emoluments', but for places which conferred power and it suggested that the undersecretaries, the law officers and Beresford should be dismissed.[9] Fitzwilliam soon swept into action. On 9 January Bowes Daly called on Beresford and told him that he was going to be removed from office because Fitzwilliam considered him to be 'the king of Ireland' from the amount of patronage he con-

---

[7] A memorandum giving an account of this meeting is printed in *Fortescue MSS H.M.C.*, iii, pp. 35–8. There is a manuscript copy in Add. MS 33118. Apparently during March 1795 a draft memorandum summarizing the proceedings at the meeting was circulated amongst the members of the cabinet who were present, who agreed on its final form (Portland to Pelham, 28 Mar. 1795, Add. MS 33101). In W.W.M. F. 29 there is a very short paper in Fitzwilliam's hand noting the heads of the discussion. This gives the date of the meeting.

[8] Memorandum of conversation, 27 Nov. 1794 (P.R.O. 30/8/331).

[9] Memorandum marked 'Most secret and for your lordship alone' (Fitzwilliam papers, Northampton, 46).

trolled. On the same day O'Beirne called on Wolfe and 'with every complimentary and panegyric address' asked for his resignation. In return for this Wolfe was offered the first vacant seat on the bench, the reversion of the office of registrar of deeds, and a peerage. He demanded that the viceroy should try and secure for him a chief justiceship and that the peerage should be conferred on his wife. The next day Toler was asked for his resignation. Understandably, he was 'prepared with his budget'—a peerage for his wife, a seat on the bench, and a promise of the place of chief baron. On 15 January, Milton, the chief secretary, told Cooke and Hamilton that they were going to be removed. Cook asked was his removal meant to imply that he was guilty of misconduct, and was he to receive compensation? Milton answered that misconduct was not alleged and the viceroy intended he should be granted compensation, though possibly 'we might differ as to the extent of it'.[10]

Beresford, who was offered a pension equivalent to his salary, was at first prepared to 'cheerfully acquiesce' in his removal from office if it convenienced Pitt. But he resented the way in which he had been treated and on being informed that Pitt had heard the news of his dismissal 'with great surprise and concern' he left at once for London. On his arrival he saw his old ally Auckland. Auckland was of course sympathetic but he was very seriously concerned about the general strategic situation and made a great effort to persuade Beresford that at such a critical moment he must not allow himself to be made 'a real or ostensible cause of disagreement'. He was successful and Beresford agreed that if it would be of help to the government he was ready to retire.[11] But Pitt had already written to Fitzwilliam complaining that the changes taking place in Ireland were 'in contradiction to the ideas which I thought were fully understood among us', and that he did not recollect 'any idea of Mr Beresford's removal being mentioned or even hinted before Fitzwilliam left for Ireland'. Fitzwilliam replied that he had told Pitt that Beresford should be removed. 'It struck me', he wrote, 'that as you made no objection or indeed reply

---

[10] Beresford to Auckland, 9 Jan. 1795 (P.R.O. 30/8/325); Cooke to Westmorland, 9, 10, 15 Jan. 1795 (Westmorland correspondence).

[11] J. Beresford, *Correspondence*, ii, pp. 57, 63; Auckland to W. Pitt, 7 Feb. 1795; J. Beresford to Auckland, 10 Feb. 1795 (P.R.O. 30/8/110).

and never resumed the subject again . . . it was a matter of indifference to you.'[12] The speed and extent of the dismissals caused perturbation amongst Fitzwilliam's colleagues in England. They felt that he was disregarding the spirit of the decisions which had been arrived at before his departure and their confidence in his political judgement was shaken.[13]

Fitzwilliam had measures as well as men in mind. An ardent supporter of a 'vigorous war', he thought it was absolutely necessary to win the zealous support of 3,000,000 of his Majesty's subjects, by repealing the remaining catholic disabilities. 'We must', he wrote, 'unite all the higher orders in one common cause.'[14] Before he arrived in Ireland the catholic leaders had already started an organized drive to get ride of the remnants of the penal laws. According to Fitzgibbon, as soon as Grattan returned from England in the middle of December, 'he sent for Mr Edward Byrne, and Mr Keogh, he pledged Lord Fitzwilliam to them for the unqualified repeal of all the laws which affected them . . . [and] directed them to pour petitions to parliament'.[15] Whatever Grattan may have said, a few days after he returned the rumour was flying through catholic circles that the British cabinet had agreed to emancipation. On 23 December a meeting of the Dublin catholics decided to circularize the catholics throughout Ireland, advising them to petition for the total repeal of the disabilities and by the middle of February the catholic petitions which had been presented to the house of commons, in Grattan's words, 'comprehend names that would reach from College Green to Holyhead'.[16]

When the Irish parliament met on 22 January, 'Grattan, the two Ponsonbys, Curran and Hardy were all on the treasury bench,[17] and Grattan, in an exhilarating speech indicated the lines on which the administration would proceed. He began with a philippic against France, 'her liberty was death, her state bedlam', then he called for a union of the property of the

---

[12] W. Pitt to Fitzwilliam, 9 Feb. 1795 (W.W.M. F. 5); Fitzwilliam to W. Pitt, 14 Feb. 1795 (H.O. 100/56).

[13] *Fortescue MSS H.M.C.*, iii, pp. 13–15; Portland to Fitzwilliam, 2 Feb. 1795 (W.W.M. F. 5).

[14] *The later correspondence of George III*, ed. A. Aspinall, ii, p. 339. Fitzwilliam to Portland, 23 Jan., 10 Feb. 1795 (H.O. 100/56).

[15] Fitzgibbon to Westmorland, 29 Mar. 1795 (Westmorland papers).

[16] *H.J.*, 29 Dec. 1794; *Correspondence of Edmund Burke*, viii, p. 150.

[17] J. Beresford, *Correspondence*, ii, p. 42.

country in defence of its laws. During the next few weeks the government's programme emerged in specific measures—an increase in the militia, a vote of £20,000 for the navy, an act regulating the issue of public money, a new Dublin police bill and a catholic relief bill introduced by Grattan. The introduction of the catholic relief bill was opposed by two ultra-protestants, Ogle and Duigenan, but on a division they mustered only one vote. Two important committees were appointed, each with a whig chairman; the one to inquire into the cost of collecting the revenue, the other to investigate the circumstances surrounding the sale of land adjacent to the new custom house by the Wide street commissioners. These inquiries it was hoped would contribute to administrative efficiency and the elimination of corruption. They might also incidentally help to discredit John Beresford.

In the house of commons the new administration was criticized by Duquery, a whig, and Parsons, an independent. Duquery attacked the war policy, arguing that 'peace should now be the only object of our deliberations'. Demanding retrenchment, he reminded 'the gentlemen now in power' of their past professions. Parsons asked if the administration was going to abolish sinecures, amend the convention act and introduce a reform bill. But Duquery and Parsons seem to have had little or no support in the house. A third M.P., Lord Edward Fitzgerald, who by 1795 may be counted as a radical rather than a whig, considered proposing that the house of commons should sanction a revival of volunteering. 'An armed people', he remarked to Drennan, 'would in any event have great power to negotiate.' Drennan, who was withdrawing from active politics, was not encouraging. He doubted 'if the people in the north would obey any such call at present'. To which Fitzgerald retorted 'they would be fools not to take up arms if called upon to do so by parliament'. The northern radicals displayed guarded goodwill towards the Fitzwilliam administration, which, Drennan thought would probably grant everything but 'the one thing needful . . . a reform'. In the middle of January the *Northern Star* declared, 'we shall not be niggardly in our applause', if the new administration repealed the gunpowder and convention acts, reduced the place and pension lists, encouraged commerce, protected industry, restored peace, and above all carried parliamentary reform and catholic emancipation. The administration's programme announced in the house of commons about a week later, fell far short of that adumbrated in the *Star*, which was soon drawing attention to the lord lieutenant's failure to mention parliamentary reform and to the unqualified support which Grattan and his friends were giving to an unpopular war.[18]

Meanwhile Fitzwilliam was striving to secure the support of the cabinet for his policy. A few days after landing he wrote to Portland: 'I tremble about the Roman catholics. I mean about keeping them quiet for the session. I find the question already in agitation.' A week later on 15 January, in a most important dispatch, Fitzwilliam emphasized that even the more conservative section of the catholics were expecting emancipation, and that 'not to grant cheerfully on the part of government all the catholics wish, will not only be exceedingly impolite but positively dangerous'. He asked Portland to discuss the matter with Pitt immediately, adding the startling remark, 'If I receive no very peremptory directions to the contrary, I shall acquiesce with a good grace to avoid the manifest ill effects of a doubt or the appearance of a hesitation'. About a fortnight later he reported that he thought that the catholic business would be carried easily if it had his full support. He had had a conversation with Fitzgibbon who agreed that with the viceroy's backing emancipation would be carried. The chancellor, with perfect temper, stated his grounds for opposing emancipation, which, Fitzwilliam wrote '*entre nous* tended exeedingly to confirm my own opinion'.[19]

Owing to bad winter weather Fitzwilliam's critical dispatch of 15 January was not received in London until the twenty-seventh and it was not until 8 February that Portland replied to Fitzwilliam, saying that he just managed on the previous day to get the cabinet to consider the Irish catholic question. This further delay after the arrival of Fitzwilliam's delayed dispatch was almost certainly due to Portland who, shy, hesitant, and attached to Fitzwilliam, must have shrank from what was bound to be a distressing discussion. On 7 February the cabinet

---

[18] W. Drennan to Mrs McTier, 12 Jan. 1795 (Drennan papers 537); *N.S.*, 15, 19, 26 Jan. 1795.

[19] Fitzwilliam to Portland, 8, 15, 28 Jan. 1795 (H.O. 100/56).

decided that it wanted more information on the probable effects of emancipation and Fitzwilliam was warned not to commit himself.[20] Fitzwilliam received Portland's dispatch communicating the cabinet's views two days after the relief bill was introduced by Grattan. This bill, Fitzwilliam explained to Portland, admitted catholics to all offices which were not 'regal or ecclesiastical'. Grattan had, Fitzwilliam added, suggested that the catholics should take the oath provided for them in the act of 1793, but Fitzwilliam himself had decided that catholics and protestants alike should take a new oath, so that 'the people may be made one people, one Christian people, binding themselves in one common cause by one civil oath'. Though Fitzwilliam considered himself to be fully authorized to decide how the catholic question should be handled, he thought that he could have Grattan's plan modified before it was disclosed in detail to the house. As the man on the spot he drove home the urgent necessity of finally settling the question and he made it plain that he would not be 'the person to put it off'.[21]

By the middle of February the cabinet was convinced it must halt their impetuous and imperious colleague. On 16 February Portland wrote two dispatches approved in draft by the cabinet, in which he developed the arguments against immediate emancipation. The existing ecclesiastical establishment would obviously be endangered, and even if a catholic establishment was substituted for the protestant one, tithe would probably be abolished. 'Take away this provision,' Portland wrote, 'and you may be assured the profession of the gospel would very shortly get into disrepute.' Again, one of the most striking features of the Irish electoral system was the corporation borough, and if the catholics' claims were granted, 'such oligarchies must seem odious'. Towards the end of February he sent off three further dispatches in rapid succession. The first directed Fitzwilliam to take effective steps to prevent the catholic bill proceeding further. The second (which Portland found painful to write) advised Fitzwilliam to give up the viceroyalty. To Portland, Fitzwilliam, who appeared to have fallen under the domination of an Irish group, presented a psychological problem. 'Forgive me', Portland wrote, 'if I dwell

20 Portland to Fitzwilliam, 8 Feb. 1795 (W.W.M. f. 5).
21 Fitzwilliam to Portland, 10, 12, 14 Feb. 1795 (H.O. 100/56).

too much on the state of your mind ... Do you feel the government of Ireland is really in your hands?' With a touch of hysterical hyperbole he told Fitzwilliam, 'At this moment probably the existence of the civilized world is in your power and at your mercy.' Two days after writing this 'miserable letter', he informed Fitzwilliam that the king wanted him to rejoin the cabinet, adding, 'I will retire, I will make any expiration or atonement that can satisfy you.'[22]

Fitzwilliam, completely taken aback by his colleagues' attitude, frustrated and deeply hurt, wished to leave Ireland at once. But he had to wait until his successor was on the point of arriving. In the interval he wrote two vehement letters to his friend Carlisle setting out why he had been recalled. It was not on account of his catholic policy, it was not even because he had dismissed Beresford and the clerks, it was because Pitt was determined to humiliate the whigs. Since Fitzwilliam circulated copies of these letters widely it is not surprising that they soon got into print, affording the public a highly-coloured view of the inner workings of government. Liberal and catholic Ireland, at a series of county and catholic meetings, expressed dismay at his recall, and when on 25 March he finally left Ireland he was escorted by a large number of gentlemen dressed in black, and the crowd took the horses from his carriage and drew it to the waterside.[23]

There was a sprawling aftermath to his viceroyalty. On his arrival in England he requested an audience 'in the closet', at which he handed the king a memorial justifying his conduct.[24] When he came out from the audience, Windham and Spencer were in the antechamber. 'The former', Fitzwilliam wrote, 'came up to me with an open countenance. I received him with decent openness. He is the only one who deserves the least degree of candour ... As for Lord Spencer, shame was upon his countenance and I did nothing to wipe it off. It was in its proper place.' A few days later he saw for the first time the

---

[22] Portland to Fitzwilliam, 16, 18, 21, 23 Feb. 1795 (H.O. 100/56; W.W.M. f. 5).

[23] The breadth of liberal support of Fitzwilliam is indicated by the names of the two secretaries of the Belfast meeting which voted an address to him, Campbell White and Charles Rankin (*D.J.*, 16 Mar. 1795). Subsequently White became a member of the provincial directory of the United Irishmen and Rankin the commander of a yeomanry corps.

[24] The memorial is printed in *The later correspondence of George III*, ii, pp. 336–40.

duke of Portland. 'We passed', Fitzwilliam wrote, 'with the coldest bow. Lord Grenville does not deign to lay his eyes upon me, and mine do not seek him.'[25] In May the opposition at Westminster raised the question of Fitzwilliam's recall and the government spokesmen in both houses replied that it was the prerogative of the crown to dismiss ministers and that it would be improper to reveal the private correspondence between the British and Irish administrations. In June Beresford, angered by a phrase in Fitzwilliam's first letter to Carlisle, suggesting he had been guilty of malversation, challenged Fitzwilliam. Having evaded a large crowd anxious to witness the duel, they were about to exchange shots in a field near Paddington when a magistrate bustled up and arrested Fitzwilliam. Fitzwilliam then felt he could apologize; Beresford accepted his explanation, they shook hands and Fitzwilliam exclaimed: 'Now thank God, there is a complete end to my Irish administration.'[26]

Fitzwilliam's viceroyalty was a personal tragedy—the tragedy of a sensitive, high-spirited man, set on the solution of a question and convinced he was right, quickly losing the support of his colleagues. To a considerable extent this was his own fault. His precipitate and spectacular dismissals were probably unnecessary. The political influence of the men he dismissed would have diminished rapidly once it was known that the viceroy attached little weight to their opinions. Fitzwilliam did not observe precisely the understandings he had entered into with his colleagues, he allowed himself to be overborne by moral indignation, he failed to keep in mind that he was a member of a coalition cabinet, and he does not seem to have realized that a cabinet (like other committees) resents being hustled. Portland admittedly was both dilatory and fussy, but he and the other members of the cabinet were carrying the responsibilities of a great war. What intensifies the tragedy is that if Fitzwilliam's tactics were faulty, his strategy was reasonable. He may have underestimated the strength of the parliamentary opposition to Grattan's relief bill. The distinguished M.P., Sir John Blaquiere, normally a government supporter, at the beginning of the session of 1795 privately admitted: 'I know not what to do—my principles are the king's

---

[25] Fitzwilliam to H. Grattan, 25 Apr. 1795 (W.W.M. f. 5).
[26] J. Beresford, *Correspondence*, ii, pp. 118–19.

government—they can be no other—but I would like to know whether this can be the king's government or not!'. Catholic emancipation, he was convinced, was meant to lead to parliamentary reform, 'that delusive and bloody phantom' and he sensed that 'moderate men were alarmed and frightened though nobody speaks'. Blaquiere was not alone in his fears. A strong committee which was organizing opposition to the relief bill, claimed (after Fitzwilliam's departure) to have had 140 supporters in the commons.[27] Nevertheless, Fitzwilliam's friends, with the prestige and influence of the administration on their side, would probably have managed to push emancipation through parliament.

The Fitzwilliam episode was seen by many liberals as a tragic turning-point in Irish history, the slamming of the door on a policy of intelligent and measured concession and the loss of the last opportunity to avoid a catastrophic sequence—a demand for reforms, conservative obduracy, bitter and resolute agitation, repression and insurrection (conservatives also saw a sequence, but for them it began with a ruthless determination to obtain revolutionary change). History does not permit controlled experiments. Before Fitzwilliam arrived deep-seated forces were at work which in conjunction were likely to produce a crisis. It is questionable but not impossible that this crisis would have been resolved or reduced by the adoption of Fitzwilliam's policy.

Fitzwilliam was succeeded by Lord Camden, who for some years had been a promising junior minister in Pitt's government, with Pelham, a Portland whig, as chief secretary. Pelham was well experienced in official business, sensible, moderate but decisive. He had a wide range of interests, busying himself in the Park with experiments in agriculture and gunnery, 'as a relaxation from the more wearisome toils of the desk', and his Saturday 'literary dinner', according to Vallancey, 'connected the few men of letters in this country and made them known to each other'.[28] But Pelham was continually troubled by ill health and as time went on he relied more and more on Camden's young relation, Castlereagh, who was intelligent and

[27] J. Blaquiere to Hawkesbury, 18 Jan., 19 Feb. 1795 (Fitzwilliam papers, Northampton, 48); J. Pollock to Westmorland, 15 Apr. 1795 (Westmorland corresp.).
[28] T. Pelham to Chichester, 16 Oct. 1797, to Lady Chichester, 23 May 1798 (Add. MS 33130); C. Vallancey to Pelham, 30 Sept. 1800 (Add. MS 33106).

remarkably equable and self-assured. After holding office for three years, Pelham was at last able to resign, leaving Dublin on the 23 May 1798, the day on which the rising began.

The new Irish administration which of course took office in the middle of a parliamentary session, had immediately to reverse, or at least clarify, government policy on the catholic question. When on 4 May Grattan moved the second reading of the emancipation bill, Pelham made it clear that in his opinion further concessions to the catholics would endanger the constitution and the British connection. However, he spoke in friendly terms of the catholics while dashing their hopes. The bill was rejected by 155 votes to 84; the minority being composed of whigs and habitual government supporters in a ratio of about three to one. It included, as the lord lieutenant remarked, several office holders, but taking into account the circumstances under which the bill had been introduced, he decided 'to suffer their conduct to remain unnoticed'.[29] One M.P. who was regarded as a government supporter, Arthur O'Connor, took the opportunity to announce his conversion to radicalism, in a speech which, Burke sadly wrote, 'though full of fire and animation was not warmed with the fire of Heaven'. According to O'Connor himself, when he rose near the close of a long debate 'the benches were strewed with snoring members, who soon started up to hear the truths I told them'. O'Connor promptly published his speech as a pamphlet. His uncle Longfield, who later assessed O'Connor in a simple, sweeping phrase—'of all the bad men I ever was acquainted with he is the worst', and who was on the point of obtaining a peerage, also acted promptly and by the next session O'Connor had been replaced as member for Philipstown by his cousin, Captain John Longfield. O'Connor thought of returning to parliament. In 1795 he was said to be considering standing for Dublin; in the following year he seems to have been making inquiries about a seat at Westminster and in January 1797 he came forward as a candidate for County Antrim, but by then he was deeply involved in plans for extra-parliamentary action.[30]

---

[29] Camden to T. Pelham, 10 May 1795 (Pratt MSS).

[30] A. O'Connor, *Monopoly* (1848), p. 544; *The correspondence of Edmund Burke*, viii, p. 245; Longueville to ——, 7 Nov. 1798 (I.S.P.O. 620/12/2); *D.E.P.*, 20 Oct. 1795; C. J. Fox to A. O'Connor, 28 Mar. 1796 (620/15/3/8).

The English whig ministers seem to have hoped that once the emancipation bill had been disposed of, the coalition, which had been formed in England, might, in spite of the Fitzwilliam misadventure, influence Irish political groupings. Portland thought that his protégés, the Ponsonbys, were not 'very fond' of the catholic bill and might continue to support the administration. Windham, a man of generous feelings, hoped that Pelham would 'still be able to preserve a good intelligence with Grattan and to satisfy him on men and measures, except immediate and unlimited concessions to the catholics'. Pelham himself just before arriving in Dublin, told Portland that he thought that Pitt should accept Beresford's removal, and declaring that administrative reforms were required in Ireland, warned Portland that 'I cannot defend a job even an Irish one'. Beresford returned to the revenue board but two well-known whigs accepted office. Lodge Morres, who was to have been Hamilton's successor as under-secretary, in 1796 became a treasury commissioner, and John Forbes, who was financially embarrassed, in 1796 accepted the governorship of the Bahamas. Cooke and Sackville Hamilton were reinstated as under-secretaries, Cooke becoming under-secretary for civil affairs in 1796 on Hamilton's retirement. In spite of the change of administration three measures sponsored by the whigs, the Maynooth bill, Forbes's responsibility bill and Grattan's Dublin police bill, reached the statute book by the close of the session of 1795 and Camden during the summer thought that Grattan was favourably disposed to the administration.[31]

But Grattan and the Ponsonbys bitterly resented the termination of Fitzwilliam's viceroyalty. They were certain that the policy of his administration would have united Irish society in a grave emergency by removing grievances and resolving tensions. Sore and frustrated, they saw their antagonists restored to office, and during the sessions of 1796 and 1797, their opposition to the Irish administration was characterized by scathing contempt, vehement urgency and considerable intellectual effort. But many of the measures advocated by the whigs in the early nineties had by 1796 been enacted, and the

---

[31] Camden to T. Pelham, 10 May 1795 (Camden papers c 29); Portland to T. Pelham, 28 Mar. 1795; W. Windham to T. Pelham, 21 Apr. 1795 (Add. MS 33101): T. Pelham to Portland, 22 Mar. 1795 (H.O. 100/56).

new whig programme, coherent and intelligent as it was, embraced a series of measures each of which was likely to have complex, far-reaching and unforeseeable consequences. Any M.P. whose liberalism had a dash of caution might reasonably feel that enough reform had been achieved and that the time were not propitious for bold political experiments. As for career-conscious M.P.s, they must have realized that the whigs were probably out of office for some time. Understandably then the whigs, though powerful in debate, were weak in the division lobby, their voting strength having fallen by about two-thirds since the beginning of the decade.

14

Agrarian trouble and militant radicalism

At the close of the session of 1795 Camden and Pelham could congratulate themselves on having coped successfully with the problems created by Fitzwilliam's incursion into Irish politics. The catholic question had been disposed of, and official and parliamentary relationships established which seemed to guarantee the smooth working of the political machine. Fitzwilliam, Camden with some complacency remarked, 'is as much forgotten here as in the more enlarged scale of London'.[1] But there were already signs that a situation was developing of the utmost gravity, that forces were at work which could cause the collapse of the whole existing political and social regime in Ireland. The country was by the beginning of 1796 clearly in a very vulnerable condition. Agrarian trouble, in the past sporadic, was from the early nineties continuously surging up. Radicalism, which early in 1794 seemed to be a discredited and rapidly diminishing force in Irish politics, was becoming a dangerously well-organized underground movement, The blend of agrarian and political discontent soon constituted a serious threat to lawful authority and an invitation to a revolutionary invader, at a time when, as a result of a great change in the strategic balance, France was passing from the defensive to the offensive.

From early in 1792 rural rioters, known as defenders were raiding houses for arms and administering oaths in Louth and Meath. The disturbances spread into Monaghan and Cavan, developing in the Meath–Cavan borders areas into faction fighting between catholics and protestants. In the summer of 1793 opposition to the militia ballot led to rioting in a number of counties—Carlow, Down, Kerry, Kildare, Leitrim, Mayo, Queen's, Roscommon, Sligo, Wicklow and Wexford.[2] Resist-

---

[1] Camden to H. Dundas, 9 June 1795 (W.O. 1/612).

[2] *A candid and impartial account of the disturbances in the county of Meath* (1794); *H.J.*, 31 June 1793 to July 1793; E. Cooke to ——, 27 June 1793; Westmorland to H. Dundas, 11 June 1793 (H.O. 100/44).

ance to the ballot is self-explanatory. As for the defenders, it was said that when they were asked what they were seeking 'they answer that they think each family ought to have at least ten acres for its support. They say something too about the articles of Limerick, yet do not seem perfectly acquainted with them.' There was also a picturesque rumour that in County Louth smugglers were stirring up trouble with the object of facilitating their operations. In March 1793 a house of lords committee reported that the defenders were eager to assist the catholic cause and 'talked of being relieved from hearth money, tithes, county cesses and of lowering their rents'.[3] Some protestants in the disturbed areas saw the defenders as the unattractive face of catholic agitation, and in 1794 several catholic merchants were brought to trial at Dundalk and Drogheda on conspiracy charges. The crown witnesses were unsatisfactory, and the accused were found not guilty. The defenders must have been conscious of being catholics but it was their economic griev-ances which propelled them into action. They were 'a plebeian association' and in Mayo were not only hostile to tithe but anxious to regulate the dues paid to the catholic clergy. One of the most active opponents of rural rioting in County Dublin was a catholic gentleman, who was described in popular parlance as being ready 'to put a defender on a spit and eat him' (he was said to be anxious to become a J.P.).[4]

The 1793 disturbances died down in the autumn but in 1794 there was widespread trouble in County Cork, the insurgents swearing 'to true to their parish law',[5] that is to say not to pay tithe or taxes; and at the spring assizes twelve men were found guilty of whiteboy activities. Then during the summer of 1795 agrarian discontent surged up in north Leinster (Kildare, Meath and County Dublin) and spread through Westmeath, Cavan, Tyrone, Longford and Roscommon into Connaught. Houses were raided for arms, Caleb Harman, a county M.P. for Longford, being killed when a band broke into his house. Cattle were houghed and active magistrates attacked. In Sligo

---

[3] Lords' Jn. Ire., vii, pp. 128–9; J. B. Nicholls, Illustrations of the literary history of the eighteenth century, vii, pp. 723–5; H.J., 2 Jan. 1793.

[4] Hobart to ——, 17 June 1793, Westmorland to H. Dundas, 12 July 1793 (H.O. 100/44); Trial of James Bird (1794), p. 10. The catholic gentleman, William Dillon, was appointed a justice of the peace after the passing of the relief act of 1793.

[5] E. Cooke to E. Nepean, 5 Feb. 1794 (H.O. 100/51).

and Galway rural rioters fought militia detachments. In Westmeath a party of revenue officers and police were overwhelmed and the high sheriff of Kildare when escorting prisoners to gaol with difficulty beat off an attack by a large crowd. The aims of these rural conspirators and rioters were simple— the abolition of tithes and taxes, a reduction in priests' fees, a higher price for labour, lower potato and meal prices and reduced rents for potato plots, for which, according to Laurence O'Connor, 'poor men had to pay a rent which swallowed all their earnings'. O'Connor, a schoolmaster and turnpike keeper, was tried at Naas for treason, it being alleged that he had been swearing men to be loyal to their brother defenders and to the French. He eloquently defended himself, defining loyalty as 'that union which subsisted at present amongst the poor', and denying any intention of 'dividing the lands'. His account of the sufferings of the poor moved Mr Justice Finucane, who in 'a colloquium' with the prisoner declared that he never let his land to middlemen. 'God bless your lordship for that,' O'Connor replied, 'you will feel the benefit of it, but you must allow there are few rich men like yourself in the country.' O'Connor was found guilty and executed, his head being placed over Naas gaol.[6]

In County Armagh economic rivalry was interfused with religious animosity and from the eighties there was intermittent sectarian rural rioting. Armagh was a prosperous farming county with a great linen industry. Farmers and labourers and their families often worked as spinners and weavers, combining agriculture and manufacturing industry. County Armagh, it was said, was 'a hotbed of cash' for the industrious farmer and weaver, with, incidentally, the result that 'many young apprentices get the handling of cash before they knew its real value' and drank heavily. It also meant that there was intense competition for land, in a county where the three major Irish denominations were each strongly represented.[7] A sequence of grim violence began in 1784, apparently with a drunken quarrel

---

[6] 'Comparison of the ... general objects and views of the United Irishmen and defenders', July 1795 (H.O. 100/58); *Hibernian Magazine*, 1795, pp. 351–5, 425–34. In 1798 there appeared in Dublin 'printed for the use of United Irishmen' *The Martyr of liberty: a poem on the heroic death of Laurence O'Connor.*

[7] C. Coote, *Statistical survey of County Armagh*, ch. x; *An impartial account of the late disturbances in the County of Armagh* (1792), p. 27.

(without sectarian elements), which developed into faction fighting, the factions, or 'fleets', taking a religious colour, protestant or catholic. The protestants seem to have taken the initiative, and their bands became known as peep o'day boys from their habit of raiding catholic houses for arms. The catholics termed themselves defenders, but were not lacking in aggressive qualities. There were attacks, counter-attacks scuffles between crowds, some of which were dignified as 'battles', and boycotting. In November 1788 there was an encounter between the Benburb volunteers on a march and a catholic crowd, the crowd attacking the volunteers with stones and insults, the volunteers responding by opening fire and killing two men—said to be innocent bystanders. In the summer of 1789 there was a bad riot at Lisnegade in which people were killed, and it seemed to the Revd Edward Hudson, an active magistrate, that 'party rage' had 'reached its zenith' in Armagh and south Down. Hudson condemned the inertia of the local gentry. 'If men of property unite', he wrote, 'it would be easy to strike out a method that would be effectual', and he suggested rewards should be offered for information, rents should be strictly collected in disturbed districts and 'private distillation' discouraged. In December an attempt was made to discourage Hudson. He was 'fired at with a musket loaded with slugs' and his horse shot. At the Armagh assizes in the following year two of the Benburb volunteers were fined, six peep o'day boys and five defenders sentenced to be whipped, and Ferdy McElvey, 'captain of a set called break-of-day boys', who was charged with shooting at Hudson, acquitted but ordered to find securities. It was thought that the magistracy (entirely protestant) was partial, and public-spirited protestants complained that the catholics allowed themselves to be bribed into not appearing as witnesses against peep o'day boys.[8]

The disturbances continued. In 1791 an ugly episode which attracted considerable attention occurred at Forkhill, where a protestant schoolmaster, anti-catholic in outlook, was brutally mutilated. In 1792 there were clashes between catholics and protestants to the east of Armagh in the Rathfriland area in south Down. The catholic committee sent up a deputation to

[8] *Charlemont MSS H.M.C.*, ii, pp. 79, 102–3; *Dublin Chronicle*, 23 July 1789, 17 Aug. 1790; *D.J.*, 14 Aug. 1790.

investigate which concluded that, though the catholics were 'marching about in military array and firing shots at unseasonable times', they never began an attack. However, the protestants were understandably apprehensive, so the deputation and a number of local gentlemen agreed that the catholics should be persuaded to cease parading, and that the volunteers should keep the peace impartially. In 1795 County Armagh was again seriously disturbed. Quarrels following a cock-fight and a dance developed into faction fights with a sectarian colouring. In September, after a riot at Loughall fair, trouble spread quickly through the surrounding countryside, roving bands of armed men skirmishing. 'Some of the quiet inhabitants' arranged a truce, but a column of defenders attacked protestant houses in the Loughall area. The protestants retaliated and a series of engagements took place, one of which 'the battle of the Diamond' on September 21 gained renown in folklore and in the history of Ulster denominational strife. The peaceable fled in panic to Rich Hill and Portadown, a couple of neighbouring small towns. The citizens of Armagh organized a town patrol to arrest stragglers from the rural fighting which might drift into the town, and a couple of energetic magistrates took out military parties in the hope of checking disorder.[9]

The protestants regarded themselves as the aggrieved party, claiming that during 1795 they had been subject to repeated attacks. This may be true. But in north-east Armagh they soon passed over to the offensive. They were probably somewhat in the majority in this area and they tried to drive catholics out by wrecking their houses and destroying their looms. The liberal *Dublin Evening Post* compared the Armagh catholics to the Moors driven from Spain and wrote of 60,000 people being banished. Keogh writing to Burke referred to Armagh as 'La Vendée of Ireland'.[10] These are palpable exaggerations, but it is not easy to measure the extent of the disturbances. Observers on the spot could differ sharply as is shown by a short correspondence in the *Northern Star*. Valentine Derry sent the paper some intelligence 'which cannot be contradicted' about the enormi-

---

[9] *H.J.*, 2 Feb. 1791; T. W. Tone, *Life*, i, pp. 63–5; *B.N.L.*, 13 July, 28 Aug. 1792; *N.S.*, 14 July 1792; R. Alliot to ——, 17 June 1795 (620/22/9); *D.E.P.*, 29 Sept. 1795.

[10] *D.E.P.*, 4, 29 Aug. 1796; *Correspondence of Edmund Burke*, ix, pp. 59–60.

ties committed by the peepo'day boys. Accompanied by a protestant gentleman, he had visited a couple of townlands near Lurgan and seen a number of wrecked houses. His companion promptly wrote stating that Derry had exaggerated the number of houses damaged and the extent of the destruction. Derry replied suggesting his companion's memory must be defective, but somewhat modifying his original statements. Statistical information is scanty. In July 1796 the *Northern Star* wrote of 700 families being driven from their homes (which would mean several thousand people). It is of course not clear whether they all left the county permanently. About the close of the year, a report from County Mayo in the north-west gave the total number of emigrants from the disturbed area as 1,360, a figure which also suggests that some thousands were driven from the county. Of the emigrants, in the opinion of a County Mayo landlord, 'decent, well behaved men and much more intelligent than the natives of this place', some had been plundered, some 'noticed' (i.e. had received threatening letters) and others, though they had not been injured, had left their homes from fear. He also observed that some at least had managed to sell their interests in their holdings'.[11]

In October Lord Gosford, the governor of County Armagh, found the county 'inflamed to the highest pitch of animosity', with the protestants openly talking of extirpating their opponents. Gosford at the end of the year held a meeting of the county magistrates at Armagh and gave them a vigorous allocution on the sufferings of the County Armagh catholics. Under his guidance the meeting agreed to resolutions deploring the 'uncommon disorders' and the oppression endured by catholics in the county, and appointed a committee of magistrates to receive information against disturbers of the peace, empowering this committee to spend money on 'secret service'. The Irish administration, which deplored disturbances that added to its wartime burdens and which could be used 'to raise the people against the government', also took steps to check disorder in Armagh. By amending the act against tumultuous assemblies, it extended the time in which persons in County Armagh, who had suffered in person or property, could make

[11] *N.S.*, 7, 11, 14 Jan. 15 July 1796; A return (I.S.P.O. 620/26/183); J. Cuffe to H. Pelham, 22 Oct., 25 Nov. 1796 (620/26/95, 145).

claims against the county; and at the April assizes of 1796 a number of rioters were prosecuted by Wolfe, the attorney-general. Wolfe, a man of transparent integrity, in a forceful address which he delivered at the beginning of the assizes, emphasized that the government was determined to exert its powers to the utmost in order to preserve the peace. The enormities committed, he said, could not be defended by asserting that 'men have been provoked to transgress the law by suffering injuries', and he dwelt on how misrepresentation, exaggeration and false suggestions could create a dangerously charged atmosphere. He concluded by declaring that once examples had been made 'it was the duty of every man to inculcate in the minds of all parties, forgiveness and oblivion'. He also exerted himself to ensure that 'the miserable wretches whose property had been destroyed by the banditti' should receive compensation. 'I thought', he wrote, 'it essential to the poor people, and I thought the burden would have a great effect to rouse the magistrates and men of property to union and action.' After the assizes the Armagh disturbances seem for a time at least to have died down. A government supporter, in the spring of 1796, optimistically declared that the county was never more tranquil and that the catholics who had been driven out by terror were beginning to return to their farms, and in July General Dalrymple, who was stationed in Armagh, pronounced the county quiet, though outrages were taking place 'on the confines'. But a couple of months later he spoke of the roads near Monaghan, being 'crowded with decent-looking people banished from this part of the county, going they know not where'.[12]

As a consequence of the Armagh disturbances the protestants began to form Orange societies or lodges.[13] These societies were generally composed of farmers and labourers but they received some countenance from vehemently protestant country gentle-

---

[12] Gosford to T. Pelham, 25 Feb. 1796 (I.S.P.O. 620/23/37); E. Cooke to H. Ogle, 7 Aug. 1796 (620/24/89); W. Dalrymple to E. Cooke, 7 July 1796 (620/24/20); Arthur Wolfe to ——, 5 Apr. 1796 (620/23/68); D.E.P., 2 Apr. 1796; I. Corry to ——, 20 Apr. 1796 (620/23/80); W. Dalrymple to E. Cooke, 10 Sept. 1796 (620/25/48).

[13] The formation of the first Orange lodges and the development of the order at the close of the eighteenth century is described by N. Senior in *Orangeism in Ireland 1795–1836* (1966).

men, who shared the feelings of their humble neighbours or felt they could exercise a steady influence. The societies spread through the province and there were a few elsewhere in Ireland. In 1797 the grand lodge of Ulster was formed and in the same year some protestant ultras in Dublin, including a few peers and M.P.s, formed the grand lodge of Dublin, which in the following year evolved into the grand lodge of Ireland. This body in November 1798 and 1800 produced constitutions for the order, providing rules governing admission of members, election of officers and proceedings at lodge meetings, and creating a national framework, county grand lodges, and a grand lodge of Ireland.[14] Clearly the leaders visualized a tightly knit, nation-wide organization, which could mobilize, discipline and direct mass opinion. But this ambitious conception only emerged at the very end of the century. During the later nineties Orangeism was localized and uncentralized. Nevertheless it attracted a considerable degree of attention. Conservative workingmen's political clubs were a novelty. Orangemen delighted both in secrecy and in demonstrating their power by great gatherings, marches and displays of ribbons. The movement was also well advertised by liberals and radicals who attributed immense, if malignant, importance to Orangeism. To them it was a revival of a primitive, hard and narrow approach to politics. To radicals it was also a serious competitor in a field in which they hoped to have a monopoly—the Ulster farming community. Naturally radical journalists magnified the importance of Orangeism by selecting the bigoted and brutal Orangeman as a stereotype for the Irish conservative. A false version of the Orangeman's oath was widely publicized and fear and hatred of Orangemen spread amongst the catholic country people in the south. For instance, a leader of the Cork United Irishmen appears to have been genuinely convinced that in his county the Orangemen intended to massacre the catholics (the latter were far more numerous but had been disarmed). The County Westmeath insurgents declared that they had taken up arms to defend themselves against the Orangemen. 'On being asked by the magistrates who the Orangemen were, they answered they did

---

[14] *Report from the select committee appointed to inquire into Orange lodges*, pp. 2–11, H.C. (377), 1835, xv.

not know and had never seen such persons.' In Wexford a group of insurgents called all protestants Orangemen and Orange-women and told their prisoners they would burn them to make an Orange pie.[15]

To upholders of authority the Orange movement presented a problem. The eighteenth-century governing world frowned severely on popular intervention in politics; moreover, even after the formation of lodges which might impose a measure of discipline, groups of Orangemen were spasmodically involved in illegal violence, robbing and threatening catholics. But the house of Orange was in the Irish protestant tradition associated with civil and religious liberty and the constitution in church and state. The Orangemen of the nineties, militant protestants, were very ready to defend the protestant establishment, and though their views tended to be parochial, given the general political situation, they were bound to be conservative. During an acute struggle it is difficult to be fastidious over the choice of allies. If Lord Blayney, who was critical of the Orangemen, asked 'why sanction a mob of any kind?' Thomas Knox, an M.P. and Lord Northland's eldest son, felt that the Orangemen must not be 'entirely discountenanced . . . for with all their licentiousness on them we must rely for our lives and properties'.[16] The Revd Charles Warburton, a vigorous magistrate, though he was thoroughly hostile to 'the ill-judging Orange societies', nevertheless when conditions were critical in Armagh, advocated trying 'to regulate and keep within proper bounds the zeal of those who call themselves Orangemen'. 'Upon principle I am an enemy to all kind of religious party', he wrote, 'but the enemies of our establishment have reduced us to make "divide" a justifiable measure.'[17] In fact the Orange movement afforded very little direct aid to the government. Admittedly in Ulster, Orangemen in substantial numbers joined the yeomanry and they formed loyalist cells in militia regiments.

---

[15] *N.S.*, 8 July 1796; *Press*, 12 Oct. 1797; examination of John Swiney (I.S.P.O. 620/48/47); *A concise account of the material events and atrocities that occurred on the part of the rebels* (1799), p. 53; court martial records, Waterford (620/70/7).

[16] T. Knox to ——, 13 Aug. 1796 (I.S.P.O. 620/24/106); Blayney to ——, 2 June 1797 (620/31/12).

[17] C. Warburton to E. Cooke, 27 May, 31 July 1797 (I.S.P.O. 620/30/212, 620/31/292); C. Warburton to Fitzwilliam, 2 Jan. 1799 (W.W.M. F. 30); E. Cooke to T. Pelham, 14, 27 July 1796 (Add. MS 33102).

But the spirit of militant protestant conservatism which Orangeism expressed and fostered, would probably have produced in any event the yeomanry recruits and fervently loyal militiamen. On the other hand the Orangemen's aggressiveness, by arousing intense resentment amongst the catholics sent recruits into the ranks of revolutionary radicalism.[18]

At the very time the government was faced with sectarian violence and conspiracy in east Ulster, it was confronted by another serious problem, also largely the product of the denominational pattern of the region, the rapid development of a secret, close-knit, militant radical organization. Frustrated by the failure of the volunteer revival and the reform movement, the northern radicals refused to disperse. Undeterred, but warned by the fate of the Dublin society of United Irishmen, three of the Belfast societies of United Irishmen unobtrusively continued their meetings and during the winter of 1794–5, many radicals in Ulster, 'mechanics, petty shop-keepers and farmers, who wanted a practical engine by which the power and exertions of men like themselves might be most effectually combined and employed', were forming new societies—which in time won a measure of middle-class support. The new societies took the name, by now well-known, of United Irishmen, and required members to take a 'test', a member binding himself by an oath to strive to form a brotherhood of affection amongst Irishmen of every religious persuasion and to endeavour to obtain an equal, full and adequate representation of all the people of Ireland. He also bound himself not to give evidence against any other member for any act or expression of theirs in pursuance of the spirit of the obligation. By the spring of 1795 the leaders felt that there was sufficient enthusiasm and activity in the movement to justify the preparation of a scheme for a nation-wide organization. On 10 May 1795 delegates from 72 societies met in Belfast and approved a constitution for the movement.[19] 'A society' was to have a minimum of seven and a maximum of thirty-five members; when its membership amounted to more than thirty-five, then it was to split into two

---

[18] For instances of Orange violence see Blayney to T. Pelham, 20 Nov. 1797; Capt. O'Beirne to T. Pelham, 3 June 1797 (I.S.P.O. 620/33/71, 620/31/27;) D. Seddan to ——, 25 Jan. 1798 (620/35/67).

[19] W. J. MacNeven, *Pieces of Irish history* (1807), pp. 76–8, 99–103.

societies. A society was to elect a treasurer, and a secretary and was to conduct its business in accordance with a fixed procedure —there were to be minutes of the previous meeting, reports, elections, motions and the chairman, to whom 'every respect and deference' was to be paid, was to be the judge of order. When a barony, or a district within a barony, contained at least three societies they were to elect delegates who would form a baronial committee, and when eight societies were represented on a single baronial committee, another baronial committee was to be constituted. When a county contained at least three baronial committees they were to choose representatives to form a county committee; the county committees were to send representatives to a provincial committee and the provincial committees were to select the members of the national committee.[20] In practice a provincial committee and the national committee appointed some of their members as an executive. The constitution and rules were redolent of legalism and reflect a deep respect for order. This is not surprising since they were largely the handiwork of presbyterians, members of a church which believed in government through a well-planned committee system and in well-established administrative procedures. But the test and constitution show that the United Irishmen felt themselves to be alienated from the existing political order. By its very constitution, the society was a standing defiance of the Convention act, and the test, if it helped to protect members from prosecution under that act, exposed those administering it and those taking it to prosecution under the whiteboy act. The test itself reflects how the members' views had developed. In the 1791 test the word 'representation' was followed by 'in parliament', and the omission of these words in the 1795 test suggests that extensive constitutional changes were in contemplation. In fact a distinguished United Irishman frankly admitted that the omission implied that the members inclined to republicanism.[21] Finally during 1796 the United Irishmen's organization transformed itself from a federation of political clubs into an underground army, or at least developed a military side. Three of the primary societies were to form a company, a considerably

[20] *Commons' Jn. Ire.*, xvii, pp. dcccxxii, xxviii–ix.
[21] W. J. MacNeven, *Pieces of Irish history*, p. 76.

larger number would constitute a battalion, and the units were to elect their officers and N.C.O.s.[22]

From the middle of 1795 the new, popular radical organization spread rapidly, the advance in many areas being accelerated by the absorption of bands of defenders into the United Irishmen. By these mergers the United Irishmen quickly gained large numbers of recruits accustomed to secrecy and ready to take direct action to obtain arms and intimidate opposition; while the defenders, who in the past had formed localized groups, whose co-ordinated activities had rarely spread beyond a barony, now found themselves embodied in a wide organization, with international contacts. This fusion between earnest and informed radicals and agrarian rioters meant that, even amongst farmers and labourers in the movement, different levels of political sophistication were to be found. Arthur O'Connor contrasted 'the people of Ulster . . . perhaps the best educated peasantry in Europe', with the defenders, 'an unthinking, oppressed people entirely without national views'. A pamphlet, circulating amongst Ulster rural radicals contained extracts from Locke, Godwin and Paine, and Ulster countrymen could be seen 'in clusters' reading the *Northern Star*, with 'its paragraphs exquisitely adapted to the taste and understanding of the northerns'.[23] Amongst the defenders political speculation was replaced by religious fervour. One of their tests, for instance, was a promise to support the French army against the protestants. Their aims were agrarian, the regulation of the price of land, labour and provisions, well expressed in the slogan 'half rents and no tithes'. For instance near Youghal men were sworn 'to be true to the old cause and not to pay tithes or rents and to be ready at a moment's notice'. Up in Donegal a farm servant, working in a field, was approached by a brogue-maker, who told him that he had a warrant for making defenders and 'from the good opinion he had of the examinant being a steady, quiet boy he would wish to lead him into the secret'. It was then explained to the informant that he would have brothers and friends and see a great alteration in

---

[22] *Commons' Jn. Ire.*, xvii, p. dccccxxii.
[23] A. O'Connor to C. J. Fox, n.d. (I.S.P.O. 620/15/3/8); pamphlet enclosed in F. Archer to ——, 6 Dec. 1797 (620/33/123); J. Schoales to Fitzwilliam, 7 May 1797 (W.W.M. f. 30).

the world. The informant, who understood they would murder protestants and presbyterians, that the fields would soon be covered with the bodies of dead protestants, took an oath to be true to his fellow defenders and the French.[24] To keen radicals parliamentary reform and catholic emancipation were measures essential to Ireland's future well-being. But Thomas Addis Emmet, whose awareness of popular opinion was based on an acquaintance with the south, frankly said that 'as to catholic emancipation, I don't think the poor think of it. As to parliamentary reform, I don't think the common people ever thought of it until it was put to them that a reform could cause a removal of those grievances which they actually feel.'[25]

Tracing the development of a secret organization presents obvious difficulties.[26] But there is no doubt that by the summer of 1796 the United Irishmen were extremely strong in the east of Ulster and spreading west. As early as August 1795 the post master of Belfast reported that there were rebellious societies linked by a committee of correspondence and that 'some of their members babble out nonsense which they know they have neither the power nor the inclination to put into execution'.[27] By June 1796 there were said to be 6,000 United Irishmen in County Antrim armed with pikes and firelocks; in the following July a strenuous conservative spoke of the Tyrone area as 'teeming with treason, and what is worse, treason methodized',[28] an active magistrate in County Londonderry was convinced that the United Irishmen's system was well established in that county; and by the close of the year the inspector-general of prisons was urging that the County Antrim gaol should be extended (on the lines suggested by 'the benevolent Mr Howard') because 'the horrible association of United Irishmen . . . now infests every village in this opulent county'.[29] By the

---

[24] A paper from Fermanagh (I.S.P.O. 620/33/78); D.E.P., 21 July 1795; G. Holcroft to H. Pelham, 11 May 1797 (620/30/50); General W. Loftus to T. Pelham, 10 Nov. 1797 (620/33/31); information of Thomas Moulheran, 27 July 1795 (Frazer MSS 111A).

[25] W. J. MacNeven, Pieces of Irish history, p. 221.

[26] 'It was part of the system to avoid writing as much as possible' (Commons' Jn. Ire., xvii, p. dccccxix).

[27] R. Johnston to J. Lees, 8 Aug. 1795 (I.S.P.O. 620/22/26); information taken 13 June 1796 (620/23/172).

[28] T. Knox to ——, 6 July 1796 (I.S.P.O. 620/24/12).

[29] G. Hill to E. Cooke, 6 July 1796 (I.S.P.O. 620/23/6); Commons' Jn. Ire., xvii, p. cc.

spring of 1797 returns compiled by the United Irishmen show that in Ulster (together with Louth) the organization could count on 117,000 men (with, according to the returns from only five counties, 7,000 guns). By June the number of men had risen to 121,000 (60 per cent being in three counties, Antrim, Armagh and Down).[30]

In Dublin during 1794–5 there were at least two popular political clubs, the Philanthropic and the Telegraphic, resembling the English corresponding societies. They were founded by John Burke, the son of a Cork schoolmaster, who had been expelled from Trinity for airing heretical and blasphemous opinions (he seems to have been a unitarian). The societies ostensibly met for the purpose of learning reading, writing and French. In fact they seem to have been radical discussion clubs. Some of their members came in touch with a defender society, organized by James Weldon, a breeches-maker, which met in public houses and expected its members to know a set of signs and a catechism which referred to the French national convention. In August 1795 a number of the members of this society were arrested and a dozen, mainly apprentices, were brought to trial. Three were found guilty and two of them, Weldon and Patrick Hart, who had been out at night trying to procure arms, were executed, Hart, who was only sixteen, showing remarkable fortitude. Three of the group were found not guilty and the others were discharged.[31]

Weldon's trial showed that defenderism was seeping into Dublin, and in the summer of 1796 the government was informed that 'meetings are now again holding in Dublin—some defenders—others mere democrats'. Admittedly it was also informed a couple of months later that there were no clubs of an openly political nature in Dublin; but this information came from a man whose circle was largely professional people and successful businessmen.[32] In fact the movement grew at first comparatively slowly in Dublin. According to the United Irishmen's returns in April 1797 there were 2,700 members in Dublin; County Dublin and Kildare had each fewer than 1,000

---

[30] *Commons' Jn. Ire.*, xvii, pp. dccclix, dccclx.

[31] *D.E.P.*, 24, 26, 29 Dec. 1795; information, 3 Aug. 1796 (620/24/77); L. MacNally, 1 Oct. 1796 (I.S.P.O. 620/10).

[32] Information, 3 Aug. 1796 (I.S.P.O. 620/24/77); L. MacNally to ——, 10 Oct. 1796 (I.S.P.O. 620/10).

members, but Meath, where in February arms were being taken from houses by 'the French militia as they now call themselves', had 2,400 members. In the next few months the movement grew rapidly in Leinster. By June 1797 according to the returns Dublin City had 7,000 members and an optimist was able to write to a friend in Belfast, 'you will not meet many people in Dublin that is not up'. The total number of members in the city of Dublin, and the counties of Dublin, Kildare, Louth, Meath and Westmeath was 56,000. This total includes a return from Westmeath of 20,000—a suspiciously high figure, though a Westmeath magistrate declared in the spring of 1797 that 'almost all the lower orders will be in the course of a few days sworn United Irishmen', and by the end of the year it was reported that near Athlone a number of United Irishmen had been sworn, including 'respectable and substantial people'.[33] Moreover there were signs that the organization had spread to King's County by the second half of 1797, and the local magistrates believed it was becoming strongly established in Carlow. At the very beginning of 1797 the system spread to Wexford, and in October the United Irishmen were said to be active in Waterford.[34] Across the Shannon, at the beginning of 1797 it was said the United Irishmen's oath was being taken in Mayo; shortly afterwards the magistrates reported that the spirit of disaffection had spread to Sligo; early in 1798 'the infection' was discerned in County Galway. In May 1797 defenderism, it was said, was spreading in Clare and some months later it was reported that in Ennis, the county town, emigrants from the north had sworn 'a hundred persons . . . mostly young men, shop keepers and servants', not one in twenty, a conservative said, 'knowing what they were about'.[35] In County Cork as early as the autumn of 1795 it was rumoured that the United Irishmen had established their system, with

---

[33] *Commons' Jn. Ire.*, xvii, p. dccclx; J. Hamilton to S. Quil, 2 Apr., 25 May 1797 (I.S.P.O. 620/30/183); information, 13 Dec. 1797 (620/33/149); W. Smith to E. Cooke, 21 May 1797 (620/30/140).

[34] Information, 5 Feb. 1797 (I.S.P.O. 620/28/214); Carrick to ——, 16 Nov. 1797 (620/33/65); C. Colclough to ——, 23 Apr. 1797 (620/29/299); R. Musgrave to ——, 28 Oct. 1797 (620/32/188).

[35] Information, Feb. 1797 (I.S.P.O. 620/28/279); magistrates of County Sligo (620/30/99); information, 18 Mar. 1798 (620/36/25); information (620/30/129); L. Comyn to ——, 21 May 1797 (620/30/129); H. G. Sankey to ——, 5 Oct. 1797 (620/32/152); information (620/33/149).

'sub-societies or committees in most towns throughout the county'. During 1797 there were signs the organization was growing. It was reported that there was oath-taking in east Cork, that large numbers had been sworn in at a funeral at Sunday's Well, that there were many disaffected round Bandon and that near Youghal, men were taking an oath 'to be true to the old cause'. By 1798 it was estimated there were between 75,000 and 90,000 United Irishmen in the city and county of Cork, but it was admitted that the organization was imperfect. In the city there seem to have been four baronial committees, but throughout the county, and indeed Munster, the individual societies, grouped round a man of drive and enthusiasm, were uncoordinated.[36] Outside Ulster and Leinster in fact, the United Irishmen's organization does not seem to have conformed to the pattern laid down by the constitution. It is doubtful if county committees were regularly constituted and as late as February 1798 it was proposed that two delegates should be sent from the north to organize Connaught.[37] As for the national directory, during 1796 with Ulster the only well-organized province, the affairs of the society as a whole were managed by the Ulster provincial executive (Neilson, Robert and William Simms, Tennent and Dr White), and persons in Dublin associated with them—O'Connor supplies the names of these associates or of at least two of them, Lord Edward Fitzgerald and himself. Indeed O'Connor claimed later that it was by his sole exertions that Leinster was organized. About the beginning of 1797 a Leinster provincial committee was formed and from then on the Leinster and Ulster executives in intermittent consultation constituted the national leadership. By the close of 1797 it was reported that there were executive committees in Cork and Galway, but they do not seem to have had close contact with the national executive in Dublin.[38]

[36] 'J.W.', 13 Sept. 1795 (I.S.P.O. 620/10/121); information, May 1797 (620/30/196); R. L. Conner to T. Pelham, 25 Feb. 1797 (620/28/298); E. Coote to T. Pelham, 11 Apr. 1797 (620/28/298); E. Coote to T. Pelham, 11 Apr. 1797 (620/29/221); W. Loftus to T. Pelham, 11 Nov. 1797 (620/33/31); court martial of D. Keefe (620/17/4); D. Keefe's confession (620/40/13); examination of J. McSwiney (620/48/47).

[37] *Commons' Jn. Ire.*, xvii, p. dccclxxi.

[38] R. R. Madden, *United Irishmen*, ii, pp. 232–3; W. J. MacNeven, *Pieces of Irish history*, pp. 181–5; *Commons' Jn. Ire.*, xvii, p. dxxxlxii; A. Marsden, Memorandum of conversation with state prisoners (P.R.O. 30/8/325).

Though two leading radicals of the early nineties, Thomas Addis Emmet and Dr MacNeven, served on the national executive, the most vigorous members seem to have been two recent recruits to radicalism, Arthur O'Connor and Lord Edward Fitzgerald, a younger son of the first duke of Leinster. Fitzgerald, a man of strong affections, cheerful and spontaneous, had been a keen professional soldier. Commissioned at seventeen, he served with distinction in the American war of Independence. Later, stationed in Canada, he boldly snow-shoed through very desolate country, and when the time came to return to Europe, he travelled by canoe down the Mississippi to New Orleans where he embarked for home. In 1783 his brother, the second duke of Leinster, arranged for Lord Edward to be returned as M.P. for Athy, and at the general election of 1790 he was elected for County Kildare. Though he was a strong whig, rather disturbed by his brother's indecisiveness, he seems to have been intent on a professional rather than a political career. But by an ironic turn of fate politics compelled him to leave the army shortly before the outbreak of a major war. In the autumn of 1792 he impulsively decided to pay a visit to Paris. There he lodged with Tom Paine, and fell completely under his intellectual domination. 'There is', Lord Edward wrote, 'a simplicity of manner, a goodness of heart and a strength of mind in him which I never knew a man before to possess.' Lord Edward was swept off his feet by the revolutionary camaraderie of Paris; he subscribed to a fund for assisting the French, raised by the Society for constitutional information, and was promptly deprived of his commission.[39] Before the close of the year he had connected himself with a great aristocratic family, conspicuous or notorious for revolutionary sympathies, by marrying Pamela, the ward of the duke of Orleans, and, returning to Ireland, he expressed his views with that uncompromising vehemence regarded as characteristic of military men who take to politics. In the house of commons, where naturally he supported catholic emancipation and parliamentary reform, he shocked his fellow members by his unparliamentary language, and his 'uncautious-unreserved' comments on politics startled even Drennan. As early as 1793

---

[39] *Star*, 28 Nov. 1792; *Gazetteer*, 2 Dec. 1797. Lord Edward subscribed £2.11s. It was pointed out that a musket cost £1.5s 6d. (*Star*, 1 Dec. 1792).

he was convinced that a parliamentary reform would never satisfy the people of Ulster; by 1796 he was seeking French assistance for a radical insurrection.[40]

The rapid growth of the United Irishmen's membership can be largely explained by the zeal with which the active members went about securing recruits. Enthusiastic United Irishmen were quick to seize opportunities, to swear friends and acquaintances, often in convivial circumstances. Emissaries also went out on recruiting drives. The United Irishmen of Newry, for instance, employed a delegate to form societies in Cavan and Leinster. Samuel Morrow, a schoolmaster of Belfast, was reported to be riding through the countryside, 'swearing people to be United Irishmen'; in County Roscommon a shoemaker who was an emissary of the society was arrested with a copy of its constitution in his pocket; 'a missionary' who called at a house in County Antrim, said he was one of six, and that he had distributed 132 copies of the constitution. Persuasion was sometimes supplemented by coercion. The disaffected, it was said, 'force honest and well disposed people into their associations by threats', an example of which was a letter, signed, 'A friend to Humanity', warning the recipient that if he did not join 'the new society' he would be beheaded and his corn, hay and turf burned. A farmer in County Kildare was half hanged, until he took the oath; a Wexford farmer, who, after being plied with ale and whiskey in a public house, refused to take the oath, was knocked about and cut. A Cork man was more adroit. Pressed by a publican when he was sitting in a porter house to take the oath, he explained that he was emigrating to America, and managed to slip away.[41] A large popular movement was bound to sweep into its ranks the volatile and the opportunist— a leading Ulster United Irishman pointed out that 'many people joined the United Irish supposing them to be the strongest party in the state'.[42] The apologia of one lukewarm member, John Dawson, the employee of a linen-draper in

---

[40] W. Drennan to S. McTier, Feb. 1793 (Drennan papers, 386).

[41] *Commons' Jn. Ire.*, xvii, p. dcccxli; P.R.O.I., 1A 40, 111A; Petition of J. O'Leary (I.S.P.O. 620/8/83); confession of W. Elliott (620/51/113). The emissaries in some instances received 'expenses' (*Commons' Jn. Ire.*, xvii, p. dccccxxiii; 620/28/143; enclosure in G. Hill to ——, 11 Mar. 1797 (620/29/53); C. Asgill to C-in-C, 27 Nov. 1797 (620/33/96); B. Kelly to E. Cooke, 8 Aug. 1797 (620/32/27).

[42] *Commons' Jn. Ire.*, xvii, p. dcccxxvi.

Dublin, survives. Early in February 1796 when he was in a
Fishamble Street public house, he was approached by Dunn,
an employee of a well-known radical, Jackson, the ironmonger,
who asked him if he had heard of the 'new system', which
needed the support of every sensible man, since it was 'framed
for the sole purpose of reconciling all religious disputes'.
Dawson, favourably impressed, took the test, was given a copy
and at once started to make recruits amongst his acquaintances.
He found they all approved of the test but were reluctant to
take it. Some weeks later he attended a meeting of about thirty
persons who had taken the test, and they agreed to form a
society of which Dawson was elected treasurer. Shortly afterwards they met in a public house and spent a pleasant evening
in 'drinking, singing and good humour', (some swearing-in
taking place in another room). But some nights later when
Dawson attended a baronial meeting at the Black Bull in High
Street, he was 'struck with terror at the appearance of those
men it was my duty to associate with', blacksmiths and poor
weavers. However, he did attend two further baronial meetings.
At the first the business was purely financial; at the second the
manufacture of pikes was discussed, designs being drawn on the
floor. Dawson at this stage had had enough. He confessed to his
master, who firmly told him to have nothing more to do with
the business, advice which Dawson promptly accepted. It is not
a heroic story but Dawson was probably not unique in his
reactions.[43]

Another United Irishman whose participation in the society's
activities abruptly ceased was Valentine Lawless, the son and
heir of the first Lord Cloncurry. An exuberant young man and
a fervent liberal, he became a United Irishman and was placed
on the national executive. But his father, a successful businessman, and a recently created peer, was determined to prevent
him getting into trouble, and at the close 1797 he firmly insisted on his leaving Dublin and starting to read law in London.
There, with some other Irish law students he formed a 'United
Irish club', which had 'the character rather of a debating and
convivial club than of a political body'.[44]

Besides spreading rapidly through Ireland, the United

[43] John Dawson's statement, 1799 (I.S.P.O. 620/8/72/1).
[44] Lord Cloncurry, *Personal recollections* (1849), pp. 48, 57.

Irishmen's organization recruited its members from many levels of Irish life. It was of course a mass movement, with small farmers, labourers and artisans composing the bulk of its membership. But radicalism was a political faith powerful enough to impel many middle-class men into a secret society dedicated to realizing the reforms they believed to be just and urgently necessary. Even if the middle-class membership was small in proportion to the number of United Irishmen and the size of the Irish middle class, it provided ideas, administrative ability and officer material. Lord Clare emphasized one of the principal elements of the movement's strength when he spoke of it as a conspiracy of 'a deluded peasantry aided by more intelligent treason'.[45] A rough guide to the higher command and staff of the United Irishmen provided by three statutes enacted after the '98 insurrection shows what a variety of professions and occupations were active in the movement.[46] Nearly 160 names are listed, comprising amongst others 5 army officers, 8 lawyers, 5 barristers, 3 attorneys, 11 medical men (including 2 dentists and 4 apothecaries), 8 clergymen (4 dissenting ministers, a probationer, 2 catholic priests ,and a sometime theological student, William Duckett), a painter, Robert Neilson of Belfast, a 'very young man, genteely and delicately bred'); at least half a dozen persons styled Esq., some of whom could claim to be connected with the landed world, including Deane Swift, an Etonian, who contributed to the *Press*, and Morgan Kavanagh, 'a favoured tenant' of Walter Kavanagh;[47] about 40 businessmen, including 3 booksellers, Jackson, the iron-founder, who called his country house Fort Paine, brewers, millers and shopkeepers; 22 farmers and a grazier; two clerks, a minor civil servant, an apprentice, 2 land surveyors, a land steward, a ship's captain, a huxter, a gardener, 2 brick-layers, and a plasterer. A list of Ulster state prisoners detained in Belfast at the close of 1798 is somewhat similar in composition. It comprises 4 presbyterian ministers, a priest, 3 medical men, 2 schoolmasters, a gentleman, 7 businessmen (merchants and shopkeepers), a butcher, 4 farmers, 2 weavers and a shoemaker.[48]

[45] *D.E.P.*, 21 Mar. 1797.   [46] 38 George III, cc. 77, 78, 80.
[47] I.S.P.O. 620/10/148; L. MacNally ——, 4 Nov. [1797] (620/18).
[48] W. Kavanagh to ——, 23 Sept. 1798 (I.S.P.O. 620/40/90); Robert Neilson, petition (S.P.P.), list of prisoners in Belfast (620/10/116); W. Drennan to Mrs McTier, 8 July 1795, Drennan papers 568).

Within such a large and heterogeneous movement as the United Irishmen, in time tensions, religious, regional, social and economic would probably have developed.[49] But between 1795 and 1798 enthusiastic United Irishmen threw themselves energetically into running the society—electing officers and committee men, obtaining and distributing printed constitutions and broadsheets, collecting subscriptions, helping radicals in gaol and encouraging their members 'to set your face against bank notes and excise business'.[50] The military side of the movement was time-absorbing. Units had to be organized, arms had to be obtained, either by the manufacture of pikes or seizure of firearms, officers were expected to get to know their men and in the north it was suggested they should study Dundas's *Military movements*—stiff going for amateurs. About the beginning of 1796 one large group of United Irishmen even worked out contingency plans for a rising. There was to be an easily improvised system of war taxation—a contribution was to be imposed on the people and rents and tithes were to be 'considered' (presumably a euphemism for either very heavily taxed or confiscated). A national or provincial fund would provide support for wounded insurgents and the widows and orphans of those who fought for their country. 'Proper men' with armed detachments were to assume responsibility for law and order in each district. Revolutionary committees were to fix moderate prices for food, persons 'inimical to the cause' were to be tried and their property confiscated. Clearly revolution was to be a controlled process.

Fund raising and financial management took time and trouble. In 1798 for instance, the Wicklow county committee viewed with concern 'the apathy of their fellow citizens' who refused 'as small a pittance as 1*d*. per man for the relief of prisoners in gaol'. On the other hand members were not always satisfied with the way financial business was managed. In April 1797 the Down county committee felt it necessary to apologize for the sketchy nature of their accounts (the treasurer was away) and assure their critics that every penny of their

---

[49] At a County Down committee meeting in July 1797 'Great fears were expressed of the catholics and the dissenters becoming two separate parties' (*Commons' Jn. Ire.*, xvii, p. dccclxi).

[50] *Commons' Jn. Ire.*, xvii, p. dcccxliii.

money had been properly expended. A year later however in County Down 'great reflections were thrown out against the money committee for some of them not attending to give an account of the business of the last assizes'. At the close of 1797 the Ulster provincial committee, finding their resources seriously depleted by heavy legal expenses, adopted a fund-raising expedient which aroused moral disapproval—a lottery, tickets a guinea each. The Down county committee denounced the scheme as 'an encouragement to the immorality of the people', the tickets sold slowly, and in February it was decided to send 500 tickets to Dublin to be sold there and that the draw should take place early in April. But Oliver Bond's arrest in March disorganized the arrangements and plans for the lottery were still under consideration about a month before the rising. [51] The lottery is a reminder the movement had a social and convivial side. The leaders dined frequently together and their followers often met in public houses. There was interminable political talk, the war and the intentions of the French providing plenty of conversational material.

The cohesion and secrecy which characterized the new society of United Irishmen, together with the superimposition of a military organization on the federation of political clubs which formed the basis of the movement, clearly indicated that many Irish radicals were prepared to use direct action to obtain their objectives. This is scarcely surprising. The right of a people to resist tyrannical rulers was a fundamental tenet of whiggery. By a careful exegesis of the writings of the whig founding fathers, Burke in the early nineties had demonstrated to the satisfaction of conservatives that the resistance sanctioned by the old whigs was purely for the purpose of compelling an arbitrarily minded government to conform to long-established constitutional custom. But Irishmen who had sympathized with the Americans when they challenged the authority of George III, and who were following with admiration the exploits of the French, were not likely to set such narrow limits to popular intervention. The United Irishmen of north Down enunciated what they regarded as political truisms when they asserted that it was 'the invariable opinion of all sound philosophers, statesmen and divines, that all power is radically in the

[51] Ibid., pp. dcccxli, dcccxlix, dccclxii, dccclxiii–xiv.

people', and that when such 'as are delegated by the people degenerate into tyrants' the people ought to reclaim their rights. Volunteering had made politically-minded Irishmen conscious of the power which could be wielded by citizens in arms.[52] The victories of the French roused enthusiasm amongst European liberals, and after the French had in November 1792 promised help to any people who wished to be free, it behoved Irish radicals to consider taking steps to avail themselves of the offer. But amongst Irish radicals military ardour was bound to be diluted by pacifism. Radicalism and economic development were closely associated and many radical leaders were concerned to see Ireland rapidly advancing in the arts and manufactures. The great war, which was being waged against France was regarded by both British and Irish radicals as unnecessary and unjust, a counter-revolutionary crusade, directed by a conspiracy of despots against a people who had been engaged in calmly reshaping their constitution. Naturally then the radicals dwelt on the horrors of war:

> The dire campaign, the reeking plain,
> The widows's shriek, the orphan's cry

The *Northern Star*, seeing thousands bleeding to death, asked bitterly, could not cock-fights be substituted for battles, and it printed a poignant report about a poor woman, 'the wife of a labouring man', found drowned near Sixmiletown. One of her sons had enlisted, another had been press-ganged, and grief at their departure had driven her out of her mind. 'This', the *Star* commented, 'is one of the effects of this *glorious and necessary war*.'[53] It is significant that the first northern radical to be charged with a political offence was Joseph Cuthbert, a Belfast tailor, who at the 1793 spring assizes was found guilty of trying to seduce a soldier from his duty by showing him an extract from the writings of Cooper, the Manchester radical, 'respecting the nature of the military occupation [and of] implicit obedience to the command of superiors'. Cuthbert, who was found guilty, was sentenced to be pilloried and imprisoned. An abhorrence of destruction and violence does not necessarily

52 Ibid., pp. dccclix, dccclxii–dccclxvi, dccclxxii.
53 *N.S.*, 20 Apr. 1793, 25 May 1795, 17 Mar. 1796.

prevent a man bearing arms in a just cause. Nevertheless constant denunciations of the ugly face of war may have made some, who believed in the right of resistance, hesitate before embarking on civil conflict. The Dublin society of United Irishmen was striving to reconcile a reluctance to use force with an acceptance of the fact that direct action might be necessary, when it asserted that 'war, an occasional duty, ought never to be made an occupation. Every man should become a soldier for the defence of his rights, no man ought to continue a soldier for offending the rights of others.'[54]

The mixed feeling with which an Irish radical intellectual regarded armed force is strikingly reflected in one of the most powerful political poems of the period, William Drennan's *The wake of William Orr*. It ends with the stirring lines:

> Conquer fortune—persevere—
> Lo it breaks—the morning clear!
> The cheerful cock awakes the skies
> The day is come—Arise, arise!

But an earlier verse:

> God of mercy, God of peace
> Make the mad confusion cease!
> O'er the mental chaos move,
> Through it speak the light of love.

expresses the author's aversion to violence. In the event, Drennan, who had withdrawn from active politics in the mid-nineties, took no part in the rising. Nor, may it be added, did another Irish poet, a Glasgow graduate, William Hamilton Drummond, who in his poem *A man of age*, published in 1797, implied that revolution might be the remedy for Ireland's ills. Having described how a landlord, 'a ruthless tyrant', ruined and betrayed a tenant's daughter, and sent her brothers to serve in the fleet, he reflects:

> Thus on man's right's oppression's minions tread,
> Toil tills the ground, the sluggard eats the bread.

[54] *B.N.L.*, 5 Apr. 1793; *N.S.*, 6, 10 Apr. 1793.

and ends his poem with the ringing lines:

> But hark I hear a more than mortal voice,
> Irene's gallant sons rejoice rejoice
> Triumph is sure where liberty's the prize.

But the poem was dedicated to a whig county M.P. and Drummond did not take part in the '98 rising. Nevertheless, he had a narrow escape when, a few days after the battle of Antrim, he was strolling in the streets of Larne. An angry yeomanry officer ('in other circumstances a man of great humanity'), exclaiming 'You young villain, it is you and the like of you, that have brought this upon us with your infernal poetry', put a pistol to his head. Fortunately a bystander pushed the pistol aside and Drummond soon afterwards became a tutor in a strongly conservative household where the king's health was 'drunk every day in a bumper'. His next published poem commemorated the battle of Trafalgar and 'in his maturer years he was a consistent liberal in politics but never a violent partisan'.[55]

The morality and expediency of rebellion were dangerous topics to discuss publicly when Great Britain was at war with revolutionary France, and much of what the Irish radicals put into print on these questions was, if very vehement, rather vague. Direct action while hinted at is not definitely recommended. This may reflect understandable caution: it also suggests that radical thinking was influenced by a mixture of exasperation and hesitancy. In the spring of 1796 the *Northern Star*, having declared that the Insurrection act 'unhinges the social compact and dissolves the bonds of civil society', in a frank editorial indicated the circumstances in which insurrection would be justified. Accepting that 'resistance is in certain cases the duty of the people', the *Star* laid down that they should act when 'public oppression has arrived at that height when it comes home to the body of the people—when there is but one general sentiment pervading the mass of the community that they are in a state of slavery—and when all other means of procuring redress have failed'. At the same time (as a correspondent complained) it poured cold water on local insurrectionary action. Early in 1797 the *Star* was telling its

---

[55] W. H. Drummond, *Posthumous sermons*, ed. J. S. Porter (1867), pp. iv–viii.

readers 'your will must prevail—let it then be matured—let it result from reflection, from a cool, determined adherence to your principles'. It also warned them that 'the plan of your enemies is to draw you forth into an untimely conflict'. In almost its last issue it stressed that they hoped to achieve their aims through 'calm discussion and their own unquestionable justice.' Near the close of the year, some months after the *Northern Star* had been compelled to cease publication, the more extreme radical newspaper, the *Press*, having pointed out that the situation might arise when the people would see 'no middle course between absolute and miserable slavery . . . [and] open revolution', concluded 'I should be sorry indeed to think that such was the situation of Ireland'.[56] Irish conservatives might think that by emphasizing the need for restraint the United Irishmen were trying to conceal their real intentions. But much of what they published on the use of force may have reflected the genuine feelings of those who hoped that the threat of direct action might render violence unnecessary.

For some radicals, who were convinced that the Irish situation justified rebellion, expediency was almost a matter of military mathematics. Thomas Addis Emmet, for instance, was ready to join in leading an insurrection if a French force, fifteen to twenty thousand strong, landed in Ireland. 'Yet when so small a force as 800 were sent, he would not recommend to his friends to come forward'.[57] Shortly before the rising of 1798 Lord Edward Fitzgerald had an illuminating conversation with William Murphy, a Dublin businessman, who thought that the United Irishmen should remain a non-military pressure group, but who had continued in contact with the movement. Murphy at first maintained that the aid of a French expeditionary force of 15,000 was essential for a successful rising. Fitzgerald forced him to admit that 5,000 might be sufficient and finally persuaded him there would be a prospect of success if 300 French officers were available to train the insurgents.[58] Murphy did not take part in the rising.

Many men of strongly liberal views would recoil from the

[56] *N.S.*, 30 May 1796, 17 Mar. 1797; *Press*, 3 Oct. 1797.
[57] A. Marsden, memorandum of conversations with state prisoners (P.R.O. 30/8/325).
[58] R. R. Madden, *United Irishmen* (2nd ed.), i, pp. 286–9.

prospect of a long-drawn-out debilitating civil war. A large French expeditionary force, composed of first-class troops commanded by an able revolutionary general and aided by widespread insurrection, might by swiftly inflicting a series of defeats on the government forces soon bring about the total overthrow of the existing order. Then a convention, perhaps meeting at Dungannon, would fill the power vacuum and negotiate a treaty with France. This of course meant postponing action until French co-operation could be secured. Delay, however, was probably not altogether unacceptable to those radicals who were instinctively strongly averse to violence and acutely aware that an armed rising would mean the death of neighbours and devastation. There was, too, always the possibility that the government and the ruling world, overawed by the spectacle of a people in arms, might yield without a struggle; or—a less drastic solution—a turn of the political wheel might bring the whigs to power in Great Britain and Ireland, with the result that a policy of concession would be inaugurated which, if pressure was applied, would soon progress beyond the bounds of whig prudence. Hesitancy over the expediency of revolution was bound to have a dampening effect on martial ardour. It is impossible to measure the currents of opinion at this time but there is no doubt that when at last in May 1798 the leaders of the United Irishmen called on their followers to rise in arms, many who might have been expected to answer the call enthusiastically either joined the insurgents' ranks under pressure or stayed at home.

The formation of the new societies of United Irishmen in Ulster during the winter of 1794–5 coincided with a major change in the strategic balance which encouraged Irish radicals to hope that with the arrival of a French expeditionary force, swift surgical revolution would ensue. When after the failure of Hoche's expedition the prospect of French assistance was temporarily ruled out, the United Irishmen's leadership—or at least a section of it—fell on another method of attaining their objectives, a sudden, widespread rising which would confuse and surprise the government. In January 1797 it was proposed that insurrection should begin by the capture of the lightly-guarded munition depots at Athlone and Mullingar by the local United Irishmen. This would be the signal for a

rising in the belt of country stretching from Athlone to Drogheda, which would sever communications between the forces
stationed in the north and Dublin. Then O'Connor at the head
of 20,000 men from the south would attack Dublin and 'that
once taken the game was their own'. The scheme seems to have
been strongly supported by the Ulster delegates to the national
committee, but the more cautious members of the committee,
the Leinster members, with the exception almost certainly of
Lord Edward and O'Connor, turned it down. The northern
delegates, contemptuous of what they regarded as cowardice,
then toyed for a moment with a bold solution, the capture of the
Castle by the Ulster United Irishmen resident in Dublin. But
feeling they could not rely on the backing of the Dublin mob
they dropped the plan.[59] A few months later a section of the
leadership again had 'some thought of bringing matters to a
crisis'. The United Irishmen were to assemble and take the
field, in Ulster headed by O'Connor and Robert Simms, in
Leinster by Lord Edward. With 'the militia almost to a man
gained over', the United Irishmen, could, in the opinion of an
optimist, have seized the barracks and other public buildings
in Dublin, and 'accomplished the whole revolution by a single
proclamation'. But again caution prevailed. In the opinion of
Lord Edward and O'Connor it was the catholics on the committee who prevented action being taken, Richard McCormick,
the poplin manufacturer, who had been a leading member of
the catholic committee, being a very vigorous opponent of
an immediate rising.[60] The attitude of the catholics is easily
explained. As businessmen and experienced agitators they
were well accustomed to weighing possibilities and they
could reasonably have decided that the odds were heavily
against a rising being successful. It may be added that a leading
protestant radical, Thomas Addis Emmet, was also apparently
averse to a rising at this time, and in May he ceased to be a
member of the national executive.

During the summer and autumn of 1797 with 'the French
having everything ready for a descent' and the Texel expedition ready to sail, the Irish radicals were full of optimistic
expectation—the Ulster provincial committee suggested that

[59] S. Turner, information, Oct. 1797 (H.O. 100/70).
[60] S. Turner to ——, Nov. 1797 (H.O. 100/75); T. W. Tone, *Life*, ii, pp. 428–9.

the people 'should look out for good horses as the French did not mean to bring any'; and it even contemplated the possibility of insurrection in June. Military outposts were to be captured, large concentrations of United Irishmen were to threaten the military camps, cutting off supplies, and it was expected that 'when all the resources were cut off from the camps the greater part of the men would turn over' to the insurgents. But planning was complicated by the failure of the Ulster delegates to attend a meeting in Dublin and though the County Down committee was 'unanimously for rising', the County Antrim United Irishmen were unwilling to move and insurrection was postponed. Then, when at the beginning of October 1797 de Winter sailed from the Texel in the hope of defeating or disabling Duncan's blockading squadron, he was decisively defeated off Camperdown and during the winter of 1797–8 the United Irishmen were still waiting for French help and preparing for insurrection.[61]

[61] *Commons' Jn. Ire.*, xvii, pp. ccclx–xi.

15

Ireland and the great French war

Not only did the French revolution strongly influence Irish political thinking, but Ireland was closely involved in the revolutionary wars and the great struggle against Napoleon. Ireland both added to Great Britain's strategic responsibilities by greatly increasing the area to be defended and made a considerable contribution to the imperial war effort.

At the beginning of the war 5,000 men were added to the army in Ireland by expanding existing units and during the following year 32 new regiments were raised in Ireland of which 20 (totalling 13,000 officers and men) were immediately sent out of the kingdom. These new regiments, composed of raw recruits, were soon broken up, their men being drafted to other units.[1] In 1793 a large force was raised for home defence, the Irish militia. The militia act provided for the formation in Ireland of 'a respectable force under officers possessing landed property'. Each county or city of a county was to raise a regiment, the men being selected by ballot. The lieutenant-colonel commandant of each regiment was to be appointed by the crown, and was to nominate its officers, subject to the lord lieutenant's approval. A lieutenant-colonel or major had to be in possession of, or heir to, a landed property of a specific value. A captain could be the younger son of a landed proprietor. In peacetime a militia regiment would be mobilized annually for four weeks' training; in times of emergency it could be permanently embodied and the officers and men would receive the same pay as regulars and come under the mutiny act. The militia could not 'on any account be carried or ordered out of Ireland.' Very elaborate arrangements were made for conducting the militia ballot, but as substitutes were permitted and as many recruits came forward the militia ranks seem to have been largely filled by volunteers. After all the militia provided for officers and men many of the attractions of

[1] *Commons' Jn. Ire.*, xvi, p. cxxiv.

military life along with a firm guarantee against exposure to the hazards of service abroad.[2]

The militia were, of course, second line troops, and their discipline was bound to be impaired by their officers, Irish gentlemen, serving in their own country, taking liberal leave from regimental duties. The standard of discipline in some units is indicated by the rumour that there were instances of a militia surgeon keeping an apothecary's shop and only joining his regiment for reviews and the report that when militia battalions were supplied with field pieces the limbers were used for market carts.[3] But the *esprit de corps* in some regiments seems to have been good, and the Irish militia, besides being available to assist the regular army in the event of an invasion, provided it, during the Napoleonic wars, with a flow of recruits and helped to maintain internal security.

With the militia embodied, troops were sent from Ireland to Great Britain and overseas. Between the beginning of 1794 and early 1795, 40,000 men in all were dispatched from Ireland, while 16,000 were disembarked to serve there, units at or near full strength being replaced by weak regiments, which presumably were expected to some extent to recruit in Ireland. There was also a tendency to reduce the number of regular infantry serving in Ireland, their place being taken by fencibles, many of whom were unfit. Westmorland was concerned about the situation, and at the beginning of 1794 he pointed out that 'no enterprise however hazardous, however improbable, may not be expected from France', and he emphasized that in the event of an invasion a large force would be required to maintain internal order. Dundas in reply reminded the lord lieutenant that the cabinet was concerned with 'the general defence of His majesty's European dominions', adding that an invasion was unlikely.[4]

But from the close of 1796 the danger of invasion overshadowed the Irish administration's military thinking. The number of regulars and fencibles stationed in Ireland by March 1797 totalled 19,000, and two years later the number

---

[2] H. McAnally, *The Irish militia 1793–1816* (1949).

[3] *D.E.P.*, 4 Apr. 1795; Camden to Portland, 6 Oct. 1797 (H.O. 100/68); R. Duncan, *History of the Royal regiment of artillery*, i, p 18.

[4] Westmorland to H. Dundas, 14 Jan. 1794, H. Dundas to Westmorland, 30 Jan. 1794 (H.O. 100/47).

had risen to 29,500. During the Napoleonic wars a substantial force was maintained in Ireland, and at the beginning of the war a series of defensive works, signal posts and martello towers commanding probable landing places, was constructed. The presence of large military forces in Ireland must have been a stimulus to recruiting and the inspection returns suggest that by the close the Napoleonic wars almost one-third of the rank and file recruited in the British Isles was drawn from Ireland.

Ireland had less contact with the Royal navy than with the army. There were proportionately fewer Irish naval than army officers—it has been estimated that of the officers who joined the navy between 1793 and 1815 about 12 per cent were Irish. The great naval ports and dockyards were all in England, though Cork was important as a victualling station and port of call for East and West Indian fleets. The navy was entirely maintained by Great Britain, but on three occasions the Irish parliament showed its awareness of the importance of 'that element on which Great Britain has long rode triumphant,'[5] by voting substantial sums for raising men for the navy. In 1782, £100,000 was voted of which £52,000 was spent in raising 6,300 men. In 1791 £61,000 out of a vote of £200,000 was expended in securing 1,450 men and in February 1795 a vote of £200,000 was again made, of which £50,000 was expended in raising 1,860 men.[6] Statistical information on naval recruiting in Ireland is scanty. In 1790 there were regulating officers at three Irish ports, by 1797 the number of ports at which regulating officers were stationed had risen to seven. There were two rendezvous stations in Dublin, and it was reported that between May 1793 and March 1795 about 2,400 men were raised there. But for the year beginning May 1797 only 1,200 men were returned as raised by the recruiting service over the whole of Ireland. Many Irishmen however must have entered the navy, voluntarily or involuntarily, at British ports, and, if the muster books of the ships of the line at Trafalgar provide a true sample, about a quarter of the lower deck was

---

[5] M. Lewis, *A social history of the navy 1793–1815* (1960), pp. 67–8, 73–8, Monument to William Dobbs in Lisburn parish church.

[6] *Commons' Jn. Ire.*, x, p. 354; xi, p. xl; xiv, p. lxxxii; xvi, p. ccclxix; xvii, pp. ccv-ccvi.

Irish at the beginning of the nineteenth century. Of the recruits raised in Dublin between 1793 and 1795 a surprisingly low number—52—are returned as pressed. But this figure is not to be relied on, since many men who found themselves in the grip of the press gang decided to volunteer and become eligible for bounties. The press was naturally unpopular in Dublin, and the naval authorities, who claimed they were careful only to press seamen, arranged that the 'gang' should avoid clashing with the mob by operating only at night. In March 1803 however the regulating captain (it was rumoured 'after a night's debauch') ordered the press gang out early in the morning when artisans were going to work. A riot broke out and some the of naval party were badly hurt.[7]

It might have been expected that as disaffection spread in Ireland during the nineties Irish sailors, especially those sent to the fleet by the civil power, might prove a dangerous element. To some extent this was so. A marine who played a leading part in the Spithead mutiny, Robert Lee, was an Irishman. Lee, a man of middle-class background (his brother Edmund Lee was a businessman and a member of the Dublin society of United Irishmen), was a poet and after reading the *Age of reason* he adopted heterodox opinions. At the close of an unhappy love-affair he enlisted as a marine and in the spring of 1797 organised a conspiracy amongst the marines and soldiers stationed at Plymouth. The conspirators, largely recent recruits from Ireland, swore to stand together until they secured higher pay and made England 'like France and America a free country'. The mutiny was easily suppressed and Lee and two other ringleaders, both Irishmen, were court-martialled and shot.[8] In the following year, when insurrection was raging in Ireland, there was some disaffection amongst Irishmen serving in the Channel fleet. United Irishmen in at least four ships of the line, *Captain*, *Caesar*, *Defiance* and *Glory*, planned to seize their ships and carry them to Ireland or France. Seventy men from these ships were court-martialled, 27 being sentenced

[7] Crosby to admiralty, 2 Nov. 1796 (Adm 1/640); Report on the Dublin rendezvous, Mar. 1795, May 1797, May 1798 (Adm. 1/640); Muster rolls (Adm. 36); Journal kept in Dublin, 29 Mar. 1803 (R.I.A. 24 K 14); *D.E.P.*, 29 Mar. 1803.

[8] Camden to Grenville, 4 July 1797 (H.O. 100/70); *Britannia Magazine*, v, p. 228; *The Times*, 1 June 1797; *Star*, 8 June 1797.

to death and 17 executed.[9] About this time inquiry showed that on 20 ships of the line and 13 frigates with the Channel fleet, there were 2,101 Irish seamen and 646 Irish marines. Of these 475 of the seamen and 137 of the marines were thought to be 'evil disposed'.[10] In 1797 and 1798 St Vincent was convinced that the United Irishmen were trying to stir up trouble in his fleet off Cadiz. He gave orders that marines should not be allowed to converse in Irish and several Irish seamen were court-martialled for mutiny.[11]

During the great mutinies the admiralty decided not to accept as recruits from Ireland persons who had been taken into custody by the civil power, and when at this time John Connolly, a poet who had made several songs about the mutiny, and who was reported to be an emissary of the United Irishmen, was sent to the fleet by the civil power, the secretary to the admiralty specially selected the commanding officer under whom he was to serve.[12] Cooke, the under-secretary, tried to persuade the admiralty that the bulk of the men sent from Irish prisons to the fleet were not likely to be mutinous since they were defenders, 'in general deluded and ignorant men'. The Irishmen who might cause mischief, he thought, were of a higher class, 'such as surgeons' mates . . . or those who enlist voluntarily with a view to promote mutiny'.[13] In fact Irishmen were not disproportionately numerous amongst the mutineers. Of the delegates of the fleet at Spithead 4 out of 33 were Irish and of about 450 seamen and marines, who after the mutinies were designated as trouble-makers, only approximately 20 per cent were Irish. The mutineers in general were more concerned with service grievances than politics, and an Irishman, Thomas Jephson, who emphatically expressed radical opinions, does not seem to have been taken very seriously. Jephson, a bandsman on the *Sandwich*, when asked to play 'God save the King', declared 'by Jasus it is an old stale tune, and I care nothing for kings or queens. Bad luck to the whole lot of them.' But he was

[9] Adm. 1/5346–7.
[10] A return . . . 18 Sept. 1798 (Adm. 1/111).
[11] J. S. Tucker, *Life of St Vincent* (1844), i, pp. 333, 379.
[12] E. Nepean to regulating officers in Ireland, 10 June 1797 (Adm. 2/1186); L. Brabazon to R. King, 2 June 1797; R. King to E. Nepean, 7 June 1797 (Adm. 1/812).
[13] E. Cooke to Grenville, 21 June 1797 (Adm. 1/812).

not elected a member of the ship's committee and a court martial let him off comparatively lightly.[14]

The vast majority of Irish seamen and marines seem to have been successfully absorbed into the rough but not necessarily unhappy life of the navy during a great epoch in its history. Collingwood in an irritable humour paid them an equivocal compliment. Complaining that twenty Irishmen on a ship gave as much trouble as five hundred Englishmen, he went on to say that Irishmen were 'only good in battle because it is much like the mischief they delight in'.[15] At home, the Irish parliament passed votes of thanks to Rodney, Hood, Howe, Jervis and Nelson. At the close of 1797 subscriptions were raised in Dublin and Belfast for the widows and orphans of the brave men who fell at Camperdown and immediately after the news of Trafalgar arrived in Ireland steps were taken to erect in the centre of Dublin a tall Doric pillar, carrying a colossal statue of Nelson— a tribute which anticipated London's column by twenty years. A few years earlier, when the *Spitfire*, a sloop which distinguished itself at Copenhagen, was moored by the Custom house, hundreds of ladies and gentlemen boarded it to see every nook and corner, the crush becoming so great that marines had to be ordered to the gangway.[16]

Ireland also apparently made a considerable contribution to the financial cost of the war. In the early nineties the Irish fiscal situation was generally speaking satisfactory. The budget balanced with something over a million on each side, the national debt was comparatively small (about two and a half millions) and if, with the country 'in a progressive state to opulence', expenditure was bound to rise, existing taxes were expected to prove more productive. With the outbreak of the war in 1793 military expenditure began to rise rapidly and by the end of the century had increased sevenfold. At the same time there was a slight rise in civil expenditure and a considerable rise in debt charges. The reaction of the Irish chancellors of the exchequer, Sir John Parnell and his successor, Corry, to this striking, indeed frightening, fiscal phenomenon was simple.

---

[14] G. E. Manwaring and B. Dobrée, *The floating republic* (1935), pp. 262–3; Adm. 2/1162; court martial of Thomas Jephson (Adm. 1/5340).

[15] *The correspondence of Lord Collingwood* (1957), pp. 113–14.

[16] Journal kept in Dublin, 14 Jan. 1803 (R.I.A. 24 K 14); *D.J.*, 14 Oct. 1797.

Loans, Parnell explained, were 'infinitely preferable to taxes, to which it will at all times be disagreeable and painful for me to recur'. Nothing, he said, when presenting his 1795–6 budget, would 'disquiet him more than disquieting the people', and he considered that the expenses of the war should be met by borrowing, so that when 'we increase the strength of the empire we do not add to the sufferings of the people'. Admittedly, during the period 1793 to 1800 an eclectic range of taxes was imposed or increased. They included a small export tax on cattle and hogs (which Grattan believed would ultimately be paid by the English consumer), import duties on carpets, timber, slates and hops and salt, increased duties on cotton, wine and tea (the price of tea had fallen), increased spirit duties (desirable for social reasons), increased hearth taxes on houses with six hearths and upwards, increased stamp duties, a window tax on houses with more than four windows (retrospective from 1 January 'to prevent the evasions of the disaffected') and taxes on paper, cards, carriages, menservants, armorial bearings, hats (worth more than five shillings) and leather. Two of these taxes, the salt tax and the leather tax, were strongly opposed on the ground they would bear oppressively on the poor, Duquery arguing that the latter tax increased the price of a pair of brogues by 3d. to 1s. 3d. In reply Parnell asserted that the salt tax would stimulate home production and that the leather tax would tend to improve the quality of leather which came on the market. 'The great part of the people of Ireland', he remarked, 'do not wear shoes and those who did wore them but seldom'.[17] But both Parnell and Corry wanted to avoid imposing taxation on the poor classes, though they both believed that 'a partial tax [i.e. tax falling only on the higher income groups] was almost always unproductive', and Corry when he imposed a small surcharge on existing import duties exempted sugar, tea, hops and salt, 'articles of habitual if not actual necessity to the poor.' Corry also thought that it was impossible to impose in Ireland 'the great efficient taxes' on land and income which were being levied in Great Britain.[18]

---

[17] *Proceedings of the parliament of Ireland, 1793*, iii, p. 37; *Parl. Reg. Ire.*, xiii, p. 148; xv, p. 87.

[18] *Parl. Reg. Ire.*, xvi, p. 60; *D.E.P.*, 18 Feb. 1794; *D.J.*, 18 Feb. 1794, 10 Feb. 1798, 26 Feb. 1799; *D.E.P.*, 1 Mar. 1800.

One tax, which would have fallen heavily on some individuals in the higher groups, was proposed during the budget debates in 1797 and 1798, an absentee tax (it would not of course have affected M.P.s). The administration successfully opposed the tax as a threat to the connection but on each occasion it was supported by a substantial minority.[19] In February 1798 subscriptions to a voluntary contribution were invited and during the ensuing year £122,000 was subscribed. The list of subscribers commemorates generous loyalty. It also shows that self-taxation leaves considerable taxable capacity untapped. In the spring of 1799 Pitt proposed that an income tax, which in 1798 he had introduced in England, should be imposed in Ireland. The Irish administration thoroughly approved but pointed out that the proposal might strengthen opposition to the union and it was not pressed.[20]

As a result of it being accepted as axiomatic by two successive chancellors of the exchequer, their colleagues and the Irish house of commons, that neither the poor nor the comfortably-off could be heavily taxed, Irish taxation between 1792 and 1800, a period when expenditure quadrupled, rose by only a little over 60 per cent. The gap was met by loans which added about 23 millions to the Irish national debt. This policy had an effect on the British financial situation at a critical time. By 1796 the bank of England was finding its resources severely strained by the government's wartime requirements. Parnell had 'the greatest difficulty' in securing the bank's assistance in raising an Irish loan of £300,000 on the English market, 'the bank being disinclined to let any money go out of England'; and Pitt, when Parnell told him that the Irish government might soon be applying for another loan of £1,500,000, ominously remarked that 'he would not at present enter into what might hereafter happen'. Within a few weeks the arrival of Hoche off the south Irish coast led to a rush for gold in Ireland, and then in Scotland and the north of England, and in addition the British government had to remit £50,000 in specie to meet the immediate needs of the Irish administration. In these circum-

---

[19] Camden to Portland, 1 Mar. 1797 (H.O. 100/69); D.J., 2 Mar. 1797, 24 Feb. 1798.
[20] Castlereagh to W. Pitt, 24 Apr. 1799; Cornwallis to W. Pitt, 4 May 1799 (H.O. 100/86).

stances, at the beginning of February 1797, the bank of England heard with dismay that the Irish administration wanted to raise a loan of £1,500,000 in England. Such a measure, the directors declared, 'would threaten ruin to the house'. But Pitt emphasized that the loan was 'indispensable for the public service', and suggested that it might be included in a large loan he intended to raise for general purposes. But before the matter could be settled the demands on the bank forced it to suspend cash payments—a step immediately imitated by the bank of Ireland.[21] It would be a gross exaggeration to suggest that Ireland's danger and fiscal difficulties were important factors in the great financial crisis of 1797. Other factors, including an enormous imperial loan, were far more influential. But the demands of the Irish exchequer certainly increased the sense of strain at this critical time and contributed to the desperate and what might have been disastrous decision to suspend cash payments. In fact of course the British financial system proved remarkably resilient, the public credit remained good and Great Britain successfully waged war with a paper currency.

After the union Ireland continued to have a separate financial system, Irish expenditure being Ireland's contribution to the running expenses of the United Kingdom (fixed at two-seventeenths of the total) and Ireland's debt charges. War expenditure rose steeply after 1803 and by 1814 Ireland's expenditure amounted to approximately £13,000,000. Four successive post-union Irish chancellors of the exchequer adhered to pre-union fiscal principles. They took for granted that Ireland must support the war effort. They agreed that it was desirable that expenditure should, so far as possible, be met out of taxation, not loans. They were also very conscious that Ireland's taxable capacity was limited. The poor should not be burdened and, because Ireland 'had but small capital', taxation 'by withdrawing capital from the operations of industry might have the effect of repressing that enterprising spirit which led to the improvement and growing progress of manufacture'.[22] This meant of course that it would be highly inadvisable to extend the income tax to Ireland. The Irish

---

[21] H. Parnell to H. Pelham, 14 Dec. 1796 (Official papers, 2 series 509/22); *Third report of the committee on the outstanding demands on the bank of England.*
[22] *Hansard* i, xvii, p. 206.

gentry, Grattan declared, 'would be ready to maintain the British empire with their property and their blood, but the property tax would be infinitely more injurious to the sensations of Irishmen than taxes much more productive to the state'.[23] With an income tax ruled out, Irish chancellors relied on slightly increased import duties (with exceptions for materials used in manufacture), on considerable increases in the malt and spirit duties, on a sugar duty and on increases in the assessed taxes. The poor must have felt the incidence of the leather, malt, tobacco and spirit taxes—though it could be argued that an increase in spirit duties was socially beneficial, and gloomily accepted that much of the whiskey consumed was illegally distilled. The assessed taxes and the house taxes fell on the middle and upper classes. The pressure may be illustrated by taking two instances. An occupant of a two-hearth house with seven windows, which might be assumed to be on the lowest middle- class level, paid twenty-two shillings. The occupant of a large house, who possessed a four-wheeled carriage and three riding horses and employed three male servants, paid about £62 per annum—which did not compare badly with an inhabitant of Great Britain, paying both assessed taxes and a 10 per cent income tax.

By the close of the war, the burden on the Irish tax-payer, the gross yield from Irish taxation, amounted to about £7,755,000, the net yield (after the expenses of collection had been deducted) amounting to approximately £6,750,000). This left a considerable gap between expenditure and income which was met, as in pre-union years, by loans, with the result that by the end of the war the Irish funded debt amounted to £80,000,000. But about half the money loaned was raised in England, so that the creation of debt did not proportionately check Irish consumption. Indeed the loans led to an influx of money into Ireland, which, a parliamentary committee austerely observed, counteracted 'the natural effect' of growing indebtedness 'to force out export and check imports'.[24] It was

---

[23] *Hansard* i, xxx, p. 712.

[24] *Report from the committee on the circulating paper, the specie and the current coin of Ireland*, p. 16, H.C. (28), 1810, iii. To the cost of common services, largely expended out of Ireland, might be added the interest paid on Irish government stock held by English residents; it being said that some of the money raised in Ireland was in fact subscribed by English houses (*Hansard*, vii, p. 42).

fortunate for Ireland that the cost of local services, together with the expenses of the forces stationed in Ireland, nearly equalled the net yield of Irish taxation. So much of what was taken out of the pocket of the Irish tax-payer was spent in Ireland. It could of course be argued that it would have been better if it had remained in his pocket. But that assumes it would have been profitably invested. On 1 July 1814, when the war seemed at last to have ended, William Fitzgerald, the Irish chancellor of the exchequer, reminded the house of commons that not only had Ireland throughout the war contributed in accordance with her means but that a few days earlier parliament had thanked for his services an Irishman, the duke of Wellington. Fitzgerald could have referred to another important, indeed essential, if humdrum, contribution which Ireland had made to the British war effort. Ireland had played a significant part not only in victualling the forces but in provisioning the home front. Nearly one-third of the vital corn and flour supplies imported into Great Britain during these critical years came from Ireland. In one year (1808) Ireland seems to have met four-fifths of Great Britain's imported cereal requirements and in 1812–13, when the great struggle with France was at its height, Ireland supplied over two-thirds of the corn and flour imported into Great Britain.[25]

From the outbreak of war in 1792 until the summer of 1794 France, confronted by a powerful coalition, was essentially on the defensive, even though the French armies made some bold thrusts into enemy territory. But during the campaigning season of 1794 the French definitely went over to the offensive, with dramatic consequences. The Austrians were swept out of the southern Netherlands and the Dutch Netherlands were overrun, the stadtholder arriving as a refugee in England a fortnight after Fitzwilliam assumed office in Dublin. In April

---

[25] *Hansard*, i, xxviii, pp. 497–8; *Corn, grain, meal, flour and rice imported from Ireland and foreign parts*, 1792–1812, H.C. (95), 1812–13, xii; *Corn and grain of all sorts . . . imported into Great Britain from Ireland and foreign countries*, H.C. (159), 1813–14, xii; *Grain, meal and flour imported and exported*, J.C. (86, 87), 1814–15, x; *Grain, meal and flour imported and exported*, H.C. (379), 1816, xiv. A return shows that out of £21,000,000 spent between 1806 and 1815 in obtaining provisions (beef, pork, butter, flour, oatmeal) for the navy, in the British Isles, £7,829,000 was spent on Irish products (An account showing the annual amount spent by the victualling board on provisions, Add. MS 38759, ff. 185–8).

1795 Prussia pulled out of the war and the British army withdrew from the continent. In July Spain made peace with France. At the beginning of the new year, 1796, Napoleon started his spectacular Italian campaign; by May he had reached Milan and Sardinia was out of the war. At home in France, Hoche had almost subdued Brittany, and by his tactics—a blending of severity and conciliation—had won the reputation of being a politically gifted soldier. The time was clearly ripe for striking a decisive blow against France's unsubdued and apparently unshaken rival, Great Britain. Great Britain constituted an exasperating political and strategic problem. The ruling oligarchy should been defied by the English people, but, though the critics of the war were vocal, the national will in the military and naval spheres was not appreciably weakened. Again, it seemed quite clear that British strength was based on unstable supports, commerce and sea power, and if a decisive blow was struck at the heart of the imperial system, Great Britain would be quickly reduced to her proper status that of a second-class power. But, though it was an easy task to muster large forces on the north-west coast of France, in the path of those forces lay the English Channel, twenty-two miles broad. This, Hoche, inspired by revolutionary enthusiasm, declared could be mastered by 'iron, fire and patriotism' and Napoleon dismissed it as a ditch which could be crossed 'lorsque' on aura l'audace de le tenter'.[26] But revolutionary enthusiasm and Napoleonic drive, which achieved so much on land, came up against a baffling obstacle in British sea power. Though a number of Frenchmen, inspired by the speed of technological advance, outlined ingenious schemes for overcoming the Channel, the question which confronted the directory and Napoleon was the same problem which the strategists of the ancien régime had failed to solve, how, by a concentration of naval resources, to obtain the command of the channel required for a successful invasion of southern England. The problem proved to be insoluble, even by Napoleon at the height of his power. In 1796 the only scheme of attack which seemed feasible to the directory was to stir up a *chouannerie* in England by landing small parties of picked men (picked

---

[26] E. Desbrière, *Projets et tentatives de débarquement aux îles Britanniques*, i, (1900), p. 32; *Correspondance de Napoléon I*, ix, p. 116.

largely because France wanted to get rid of them) to conduct a series of guerrilla raids against suitable targets.[27] Though a fitting reprisal for British help to the royalists in the west of France it could scarcely achieve decisive results.

It was during the year 1796, when it was hard to see how a decisive blow could be struck against Great Britain, that Ireland assumed an important place in French strategy. French attention had been turned on Ireland from time to time since the reign of Louis XIV. In 1778 a memorial had been drawn up discussing how Ireland could be detached from Great Britain. Two approaches were suggested. Either the presbyterians of the north could be called on to form a republic, or a kingdom of Ireland could be set up under a prince of the house of Bourbon. The memorial pronounced in favour of the second scheme, went on to suggest that French troops should be landed in the north and at Cork (but definitely not in Kerry because the roads were so bad) and that a proclamation should be issued convoking an assembly and promising toleration. A year later Lafayette suggested to the foreign minister that Edward Bancroft, the American diplomat, should be employed as a French agent in Ireland, pointing out that the presbyterians there were more likely to rebel than the catholics.[28]

During the early years of the revolutionary war there were, as might be expected, contacts between the Irish radicals and France, but they added up to little in the military sphere. In November 1792 some Irish radicals, Lord Edward Fitzgerald, John and Henry Sheares and Caesar Colclough, signed an address of congratulation from the British and Irish residents in Paris to the French, calling for a tight union between the French republic and the people of England, Scotland and Ireland.[29] A month or so later Chauvelin, the French ambassador in London, made 'some démarches' towards the Irish catholic delegates, from which nothing emerged except presumably

[27] E. Desbrière, *Projets et tentatives*, i, pp. 57–69.

[28] General plan of war against England, 1763–5, revised 1778 (A.A.E., Angleterre, Mémoires et correspondance, supp. 19); C. Tower, *The marquis de Lafayette in the American revolution* (Philadelphia, 1895), ii, p. 603. See also A.A.E. Mémoires et documents, Angleterre 53.

[29] Archives nationales, fonds C. Cart. 241 ff. 278–9. At a dinner following the meeting at which the address was voted Lord Edward Fitzgerald seconded the toast, 'The abolition of all hereditary titles' (C. Colclough to John Colclough, 19 Nov. 1792, McPeake typescripts, P.R.O.N.I.).

an exchange of liberal sentiments. [30] After Great Britain entered the war the Brissotins, inspired probably by Paine, who took an interest in the activities of the Dublin society of United Irishmen of which he was an honorary member, sent Eleazer Oswald, an American, to survey the situation in Ireland. Oswald, who met Lord Edward Fitzgerald, came to the conclusion that though there was plenty of discontent in Ireland there was little likelihood of a popular rising in the immediate future. By the time Oswald returned to France and reported, the Girondins had fallen from power and France was fully engaged in a defensive struggle. [31] In the spring of 1794, as has been seen, a French agent, William Jackson, arrived in Ireland, and as a result of his activities Hamilton Rowan was forced to fly to France where he stayed for a year. During his exile from Ireland in France and America, Rowan changed from being a vehement radical into a moderate liberal. His experiences in France must have contributed to this transformation—on landing at Roscoff he was thrown into prison as an English spy. In Paris he was interviewed by Robespierre and the committee of public safety and he seems to have expressed the opinion that a French invasion of Ireland would receive considerable support from catholics and presbyterians. [32] Jackson's mission to Ireland was supervised and probably suggested by Madgett, an Irishman who had worked for many years in the ministry of foreign affairs where he headed a sub-section. [33] Another Irishman, who was at this time in the French official world, or at least hanging on its fringes, was William Duckett. Duckett, a theological student, who became an enthusiastic revolutionary, dabbled in journalism when in Ireland in 1796, and back in France fervently advocated a French invasion of Ireland. But Duckett and Madgett were minor figures and until 1796 Ireland was of little significance in French military and political thinking.

[30] Reinhard to minister for foreign affairs, n.d. (A.A.E., Correspondance politique, Angleterre 589).

[31] Lewins, memoir (A.A.E. iv 1671, ff. 100–5); Thomas Paine to Madgett, 1792 (A.A.E. Correspondance politique, Angleterre, 53).

[32] A. H. Rowan, *Autobiography* (1840), pp. 218–61; Memoir sur l'Irlande (Memoires et documents Angleterre, 19, ff. 378–81).

[33] For Jackson's mission see p. 441 and Madgett to minister for foreign affairs, (Marine GG[11] 67).

Early in 1796, when Carnot was striving to find a means of breaking British resistance, Wolfe Tone arrived in Paris. Before he left Ireland, in the summer of 1795, the leaders of the Ulster United Irishmen had suggested that he should try and interest France in the Irish situation. Tone on arrival in Philadelphia visited the French minister, but meeting with a discouraging reception, reluctantly began planning to farm in New Jersey. However at the end of the year, on receiving letters from friends in Ireland urging him to try and secure French help for the growing Irish republican movement, Tone again visited the French minister. Meeting on this occasion with a favourable reception, he secured a recommendation from the minister, quickly arranged his family affairs and on 1 January sailed for France. On 15 February a few days after he reached Paris, he presented himself at the ministry of foreign affairs where he met the minister, Delacroix, and was put in touch with Madgett, the ministry's Irish expert, who was eager to help and manage an emissary from Ireland. A week later Tone secured a private interview with Carnot by the simple technique of asking for it at a public audience. Carnot having questioned him closely about Ireland, at a second meeting, introduced him to the head of the topographical and historical section of the ministry of war, General Clarke, who had served in the Irish brigade before the revolution and who was to be Napoleon's minister of war. By an adroit mixture of reserve and candour, Tone managed during the next few months to maintain amicable relations with both ministries, though at times his temper was sorely tried.

He found the minister of foreign affairs very ready to discuss military intervention in Ireland but soon discovered that 'his ideas were upon a small scale'. Tone wanted a French expeditionary force of 15,000 to 20,000 strong (though he would, as a minimum, be satisfied with 5,000), headed by a well-known general. Delacroix thought in terms of supplying the Irish insurgents with arms, ammunition and money. Also he and Madgett were enthralled by schemes for enlisting Irish seamen who were prisoners of war and sending them home either to stir up mutiny in the British fleet or spread the news in Ireland that the French were coming. Tone thought these schemes were a waste of time.[34] His relations with Clarke soon were strained.

[34] T. W. Tone, *Life*, ii, pp. 20–1, 33.

Clarke, a first-class staff officer, appeared to Tone to be over-urbane, intellectually arrogant and snobbish. Having visited Ireland, he thought he knew what he was talking about and he wistfully wondered if there was any possibility of securing the co-operation of at least some of the Irish aristocracy, mentioning in his first conversation with Tone that he himself was a relation of Lord Cahir (in later days Clarke's pride in his Plantagenet descent was to amuse the Napoleonic court). Tone also complained in his diary that Clarke would tell him nothing about the French government's plans for a descent on Ireland. In fact for some months Clarke had practically nothing to tell him.[35]

In March Tone dispatched to the ministry of foreign affairs and to Carnot two 'memorials' in which he expounded with forceful lucidity the case for employing 'the indirect approach' when trying to defeat England. Seven-eighths of the population of Ireland, he pointed out, were hostile to the existing regime. The presbyterians and the more vigorous leaders of the catholic middle classes were 'sincere republicans'; the catholic peasantry, the great bulk of whom were 'living in the lowest degree of misery', had joined the defenders and looked 'with the most anxious expectation to France'. Once the French landed the Irish people 'would flock to the republican standard in such numbers as to embarrass the commander-in-chief'. On Ireland becoming independent, England would be deprived of a great source of provisions and man-power. It was with supplies from Ireland that England, Tone wrote, 'victuals and equips her navy, and to a great degree supports her people and garrisons in the West Indies. It is with the poor and hardy natives of Ireland She mans her fleet and army.' France would also gain advantages, obvious to a French strategist, which Tone abstained from pointing out—opportunities to threaten the west coast of Great Britain and to prey on the great trade routes between England and the East and West Indies. In the second of his memorials Tone briskly sketched the steps to be taken to establish a new government in Ireland. The French should on landing issue proclamations promising religious liberty and security of person and property to those who behaved as good citizens. They should also immediately summon a national convention composed of the members of the catholic committee

[35] Ibid., ii, pp. 57–8, 94–8, 104.

and 'delegates from the dissenters'. This body was to assume legislative and executive powers and should, Tone considered, issue proclamations addressed to the Irish militia and Irish sailors in the British navy. Militiamen who joined the Irish cause were to be promised preference in promotion and land grants at the end of the war. The sailors were to be reminded of their hardships and recalled to Ireland, those who managed to bring their ships being promised prize money. The convention was also to issue a proclamation to the people of England and Scotland warning them that it was impossible to conquer a people determined to be free and asking them to contrast their own interests with those of their king and government. The rapid emergence of a strong national government in Ireland would, Tone made clear, facilitate the mobilization of the country's resources. It would also, he was certain, though he naturally did not refer to the matter in his memorials, enable the Irish to adopt an attitude of dignified independence when dealing with their French allies. Having heard that Clarke had remarked that the Irish 'would of course' consult the French government on the shaping of their constitution, Tone wrote in his diary, 'I for one will never be accessory to subjecting my country to the control of France, merely to get rid of that of England. We are able enough to care for ourselves if we were once afloat, or if we were not, we deserve to sink.'[36]

It is impossible to assess with any degree of precision the influence of Tone's memorials, but they certainly seem to have been taken into account by Carnot when he was preparing his plans for an Irish expedition. About the middle of June the directory at last decided to send an expeditionary force to Ireland with the aim of liberating that country and reducing England to the rank of a second-class power. Two detachments were to sail from Brest to Galway bay, the first of 5,000 men from Hoche's army of the west, the second of 6,000 picked men (picked because their units wished to get rid of them), organized in 'free corps'. They were to be joined by a third detachment from Holland, 5,000 strong, recruited from foreign deserters. The quality of the troops suggests the directory was prepared to see the expeditionary force reduced to conducting, in co-operation with Irish insurgents, a *chouannerie* on a large scale.

[36] Ibid., ii .p. 94.

But Hoche was struck by the possibilities inherent in a successful invasion of Ireland. His career had been meteoric. At the beginning of the revolution he had been a young sergeant. By the close of 1793 he was in command of an army. A bold and hard-driving rather than a scientific soldier, he was rough, excitable and overbearing, but quick to learn from experience. He came to Paris in early July and threw himself with *élan* into amending and elaborating the plan for an attack on Ireland. It was settled that a force of about 15,000 under Hoche's command should be landed in Ireland. It was left open for some time at what point the landing should be made. The strength of the United Irishmen's organization in Ulster was a strong argument in favour of landing in the north. But the longer the sea voyage the greater the danger from the British navy, so it was settled the landing place should on the south west coast, Galway bay, the Shannon estuary, or Bantry bay. In October the ministry of marine decided in favour of Bantry bay as having an excellent anchorage. Hoche, who was very conscious of the importance of political factors, read carefully Tone's memorials and went over them with Tone, whom he appointed to his staff. Tone saw in Hoche, handsome, young, full of energy and enthusiasm, his *beau idéal* of a soldier.[37]

As the plans for the invasion were taking shape the planners were encouraged by the arrival of accredited emissaries from the United Irishmen's executive, Lord Edward Fitzgerald and Arthur O'Connor. They arrived at Hamburg in June, travelled to Basle and conveyed their views to Paris through the French minister to Switzerland. There was, they stated, widespread discontent in Ireland, and the arrival of a French expeditionary force, which was essential if an insurrection was to be successful, would be the signal for a general rising. It was decided that Fitzgerald better not come to Paris where he was well known and where his appearance might suggest that an Irish expedition was in the air. So after enjoying a pleasant outdoor holiday with O'Connor in Switzerland, he started for home. O'Connor however had a secret meeting with Hoche near Rennes and was presumably informed that the expedition would sail in the near future. According to O'Connor, during the meeting Hoche

[37] R. W. Phipps, *The armies of the first republic* (1926–39), ii, pp. 78–84, iii, pp. 48–59, iv, pp. 307–10.

expressed the hope that an independent Ireland would give France preferential treatment in commercial matters. O'Connor retorted that 'to transfer the monopoly from Great Britain to France would be to change one master for another', adding for good measure that Hoche 'not having had occasion to study economical science', could not appreciate the advantages Ireland would gain from adopting free trade.[38]

Arriving at Brest in August, Tone found inter-service co-operation was creating a series of difficult and frustrating problems. There was a marked difference of outlook between the French army and navy. The army had by dash, improvisation and unprecedented mobilization of resources won a series of glorious victories and developed a not altogether justifiable contempt for its opponents. The navy had been badly hit by the revolution. It had lost a large number of highly trained officers, its dockyards had been disorganized, its crews had been demolished by long periods in harbour, it had been mauled by the British fleet in a series of engagements so that a French squadron was bound to go into action with the distressing feeling it would probably get the worst of it. There was also in the autumn of 1796 a divergency of opinion between the navy and army as to what was the aim of the coming sally into the Atlantic. The army had a single target, Ireland. The navy had a double objective. Once the fleet reached Ireland, a squadron was to detach itself and make for the East Indies. This, of course, complicated the preparations for the expedition which seemed to army officers to move incredibly slowly—they overlooked the difficulties of getting naval stores to Brest through a discontented countryside. Hoche fretted furiously. In the end he managed to get Villaret Joyeuse, the commander of the Brest fleet, who was unenthusiastic, replaced by Morard de Gall. He secured a ruling that the Irish expedition was to take precedence over the Indies scheme and finally, with the temporary rank of admiral, he was given control over all the preparations. At last towards the middle of December the expedition was ready to sail. By then the directory had decided to abandon the expedition, either because of the danger from winter storms, or because negotiations had begun with England

---

[38] F. MacDermot, 'Arthur O'Connor', in *I.H.S.*, xv, pp. 48–69; A. O'Connor, *Monopoly*, pp. 553–4.

or because the troops were needed in Germany. But before the directory's decision was known in Brest the expedition had sailed.[39]

The expedition numbered 45 ships (including 18 ships of the line, 13 frigates, 7 transports and a number of smaller vessels). The difficult task of getting clear of the waters round Brest was accomplished on the night of 16 December with the loss of a 74 which went aground on the rocks. There was some haze, no British warships were sighted and on 21 December 35 ships were off Cape Clear. But the most important ship in the fleet, the frigate *Fraternité*, carrying Hoche and Morard de Gall, was missing, having, from a combination of bad weather and faulty navigation, run too far south. The ships off Cape Clear began to 'gain the bay by slow degrees', working into Bantry Bay against a head wind by continuous tacking, making in some hours about a hundred yards. On the night of 22–3 December 'a heavy gale' began to blow and the number of ships in company fell to 16. On the 24th a council of war was held on the *Immortalité*, the flagship of Admiral Bruix, the senior naval officer present, with whom was General Grouchy. It was calculated that there were available 6,500 troops and four pieces of artillery and the soldiers at the council were unanimously in favour of making a landing and marching boldly on Cork. The prospect of hazardous action on their own element acted like a tonic on the soldiers and for a few hours they were busy and exhilarated. But on the night of 24–5 December the wind rose, the seas roughened and a landing became impossible. With a strong east wind a British fleet might appear at any moment, catching the French at a disadvantage, so on the evening of the 26th Bruix ordered his ships in the bay to put to sea, he himself setting a prompt example. Some of the squadron disregarded the order and lingered for a couple of days, but when some of them began to drag their anchors they quitted the bay. About nine ships rendezvoused off the Shannon, but on the 29th set sail for France.

During early January the ships of Hoche's expedition

---

[39] A large amount of material relating to the expedition and to the British naval response is to be found in Desbrière, *Projets et tentatives*, i, pp. 135–232, and in *Private papers of George 2nd Earl Spencer . . .*, ed. J. S. Corbett, i, pp. 363–401 and in H.O. 28/22. There is a full and lucid account of the episode in E. H. S. Jones, *An invasion that failed* (1950).

straggled back to France, Hoche himself landing near Rochelle on 13 January. One ship of the line, the *Droits de l'homme*, after a hard-fought engagement with two British frigates, was wrecked on the Brittany coast, and out of 45 ships which sailed, 10 were lost (including two ships of the line), one destroyed in action, 4 wrecked and 5 captured. The British navy lost a frigate, which went ashore after engaging the *Droits de l'homme*. If the French navy had displayed remarkable incompetence when conducting an important amphibious operation, the British navy had not distinguished itself. Towards the close of 1796 a watch on Brest was being maintained by Colpoys's fleet of 15 sail of the line, cruising off Ushant, with a squadron of frigates, keeping as close to the Brest roads as possible. In support of Colpoys was Bridport with 15–17 ships of the line at Plymouth. Both admirals had seen plenty of action, but Colpoys seems to have been unimaginative if courageous, and Bridport was nearly seventy. British intelligence was good, the royalists having plenty of agents in France. The difficulty was to distinguish the hard core of truth from a multitude of rumours. Early in July, Wickham, the British minister in Berne, who was in touch with numerous agents, reported that an invasion of England and Ireland was being planned. Later in the month, however, he heard that the plan had been abandoned and that Hoche had left Paris to command an army on the Rhine. In August Wickham's information was remarkably accurate. Hoche was having long interviews daily with the directory, troops were being massed in Brittany and a descent was going to take place west of Cork. In October he passed on a variety of reports, that the corps under Hoche's immediate command at Brest numbered 15,000; that there were going to be night raids on British and Irish ports; that the project of an invasion had been abandoned, that the main aim of the French was to send an expedition to the East Indies; that they were contemplating an expedition to the West Indies; there would be an invasion on a large scale with 16,000 men from Spain landing in Ireland, a force from Holland striking at the Firth of Forth and 22,000 from Brest landing in Pembrokeshire (Wickham's comment on this report was that while it might be exaggerated it was possibly not wholly incorrect). Finally, on 18 December he was able to report that the plans for an expedition to Ireland

and Lisbon had for the moment been laid aside but that a portion of the Brest fleet might strike at the Windward Islands. In short, intelligence, while keeping the British navy on the *qui vive*, showed what a wide range of possibilities was open to the French.[40]

On 16 December Colpoys learned from Pellew that the French were on the point of leaving Brest. But owing to fog he received no further information: he decided to keep his station until he received information indicating where the French were making for, or was joined by Bridport. After a week of waiting heavy seas forced his ships to take refuge in Torbay, Spithead and Plymouth. On 20 December Bridport was informed the Brest fleet was at sea and ordered to sail for Cape Clear. 'Some accidents and unforeseen delays' prevented him getting under way until the 25th, when a strong south east wind caught him at Saint Helens and held him there until 3 January and he did not arrive off the Irish coast until the 7th. The navy had clearly failed to pay sufficient attention to what Mahan termed 'the supreme strategic factor' in the British watch on Brest, the wind.

In the summer of 1796 the Irish government had been presented with an 'appreciation' of the situation by the commander-in-chief which was not very helpful. General Cunninghame, having emphasized that there were very many places at which the enemy might strike, advised the government to prepare for defence at all points.

The military forces in Ireland in December 1796 amounted to 28,500 effectives of which 5,600 were in the south-west under General Dalrymple, and this force could be rapidly reinforced from the Limerick and Kilkenny areas where there were respectively 4,000 and 3,000 men. Dalrymple was very corpulent and fond of the table—but he was an efficient general, and by 6 January 11,000 men were in the south-west area. This force would have been definitely outnumbered if Hoche had managed to land his whole army, and the sudden emergency revealed serious defects in the Irish military machine. There were deficiencies in the artillery and medical services, and the troops were ill-equipped for campaigning in harsh winter weather. Bernard Shaw of Cork, the collector, on his

---

[40] W. Wickham to Grenville, 12, 23, 30 July, 8, 20, 28 Oct., 2 Nov., 8 Dec. 1796 (F.O. 74/18-19).

own responsibility purchased for the army all the available shoes, and a subscription was started in Dublin to buy flannel waistcoats for the troops—it being reported that Lady Camden was to be seen in the Castle busily stitching waistcoats for the army.[41] Down in Cork, a citizens' committee, under the chairmanship of Sir Patrick O'Connor, a well-known catholic merchant, took steps to assist soldiers' families and to find transport for the army. And at a meeting of the committee on 29 December the Church of Ireland dean of Cork read a pastoral letter from Dr Moylan, the catholic bishop of Cork, whom the committee thanked for his 'timely interference . . . pious care and constitutional attachment'.[42] What was most reassuring was the readiness of the country people to help the troops. 'Nothing', Lord Kenmare wrote, 'can exceed the alacrity of the poor people to assist the military.'[43] In Clare they carried the soldiers' muskets and according to Sir Lawrence Parsons 'when the drifts of snow obstructed the artillery the peasantry had laboured incessantly in clearing the passages, had furnished their carts and horses for the army, and cheerfully shared their provisions with the soldiery'.[44]

The government had to face severe criticism both at Westminster and College Green. The French fleet, Grattan declared, after 'riding triumphant' for seventeen days off the Irish coast had got back to Brest unmolested, and the whigs also dwelt on how insufficient and unprepared was the military force available for the protection of Cork and its immense accumulation of naval stores. Dundas, vigorously defending the admiralty, reminded the house of commons how complex the situation was, with the British fleet being responsible not only for the watch on Brest but also for the protection of large inward and outward convoys. But though the government escaped censure and seems to have convinced parliament and itself that all the decisions taken had been right, the blockade of Brest was tightened and steps taken to increase the Irish militia, and to encourage the formation of yeomanry corps. As a result therefore of Hoche's expedition the forces at the government's

[41] D.E.P., 29 Dec. 1796.
[42] Printed paper, Cork, 29 Dec. 1796 (I.S.P.O. 620/28/38).
[43] Sir Boyle Roche to ——, 3 Jan. 1797 (I.S.P.O. 620/28/26).
[44] E. Burton to ——, 4 Jan. 1797 (I.S.P.O., 620/28/35); Parl. Reg. Ire., xvii, p. 275.

disposal had been appreciably strengthened shortly before the insurrection broke out.

If the British had been taught a salutary lesson, the French had a most discouraging experience. Napoleon, it is said, when he heard the expedition had failed, exclaimed in his usual self-sufficient way, 'why were not those 20,000 men that were confided so recklessly to General Hoche sent to me in Italy'.[45] It was not a generous comment, but a crude enunciation of the principle that military resources should be invested profitably. A careerist in the French army could not have failed to notice that Hoche had gained nothing from his bold gamble, and in fact his expedition was the last time that a large French force under an outstanding general sailed against the British Isles.

This certainly did not mean that all hope was abandoned. The leaders of the United Irishmen still believed that with French co-operation success could be attained. In February the executive appointed a persuasive and pertinacious catholic attorney, Edward Lewins, as their plenipotentiary in France, and Lewins, who arrived in Hamburg in May, had for a short time the backing of a member of the executive, Dr MacNeven. MacNeven, who paid a brief visit to the continent in the summer of 1797, transmitted to the directory a powerful memorial in which he drew attention to the growing strength of the United Irishmen's organization, especially in Ulster, and suggested a landing in Lough Swilly. Hoche remained a strong proponent of an Irish expedition, but after the 1796 failure it was clear that nothing could be done in that direction for some time. Even a comparative optimist in naval circles pronounced that it would be months before another fleet would sail from Brest,[46] and early in February Hoche left Paris to take command of the army of the Sambre and Meuse. In April he was advancing into central Germany when he was halted by the armistice of Leoben. He was engaged in organizing La République Cisrhenane, when the subject of Ireland was brought to his attention by the directory, probably stimulated by the arrival of Lewins. At the beginning of June the directory informed Hoche that an invasion of Ireland was considered to be the best way of inflicting a crippling defeat on England. The

---

[45] *Memoirs of J. Barras*, ed. G. Duruy (1895–6), ii, p. 328.
[46] T. W. Tone, *Life*, ii, p. 345.

dispatch of an expedition might be delayed but arms and ammunitions could be sent to the United Irishmen. The aim would be to establish Irish independence but no guarantees were to be given to the Irish insurgents. France would follow the same policy towards Ireland then as it had pursued with the Italians. 'We have', the directory pointed out, 'protected their liberties but we have not contracted any engagement to maintain the new state.' France was not to be constricted when taking part in peace negotiations and Hoche was advised to preserve a judicious reserve when talking to Lewins.[47]

On 21 June Hoche told Lewins and Tone, who presented themselves to him at Coblentz, that on hearing of Lewins's arrival he had sent a senior staff officer to Paris to press the directory and the ministry of marine to start making plans for an Irish expedition to be launched in the immediate future. He was able to add that he had just received a favourable response, though Tone was perturbed to hear that the ministry of marine was contemplating an expedition on a grand scale which it was thought would take two months to prepare. 'Two months', Tone reminded Hoche, 'in the language of the ministry of marine meant four at least five or six.'[48] Both Tone and Lewins, when discussing the Irish project with Hoche, stressed the importance of time. It would be far better, they declared, to send five thousand men with large supplies of arms and ammunition within weeks than to send a force of 25,000 in a few months' time. Hoche agreed but drew attention to a cheering third choice. It might be possible to send a large force to Ireland almost immediately. He had just been informed that the Dutch government, anxious to raise the prestige of the newly constituted Batavian republic, were ready to employ their fleet and army in an attack on the British Isles. There was available in the Texel a fleet of 15 ships of the line and about 15,000 Dutch troops could be embarked. The French were willing to add 5,000 French troops and to allow Hoche to take command of the expedition. At the end of June Hoche travelled to the Hague and along with Tone and Lewins had discussions with General Daendels and the Dutch committee of foreign affairs. The Dutch were obstinate over one question. They did

---

[47] Executive directory to Hoche, 9 June 1797 (Marine BB⁴ 103 ff. 8–9).
[48] T. W. Tone, *Life*, ii, p. 408.

not want a French general and a French contingent added to their expedition. The Batavian republic was to have undivided credit for what would be achieved. The Irish representatives, who had a high opinion of Hoche as a man and soldier, were dismayed, but realized the importance of not offending the Dutch. Hoche solved the difficulty by gracefully withdrawing. His magnanimity greatly impressed Tone but Hoche seems to have had a plan in view which might greatly strengthen the attack on Ireland and enable Hoche himself to play a leading role in the campaign. He decided to move a force of about 8,000 men from the army of the Sambre and Meuse to Brest, where they could quickly embark on the available ships and under Hoche's command make straight for Ireland, arriving about a fortnight after the Dutch.

Hoche's Irish plans became entangled in French politics. Party strife in France between moderate conservatives and committed republicans, was passing into an acute phase. Carnot belonged to the first group, Hoche was associated with the latter. The appearance of Hoche's troops, moving from the eastern front to Brest, north of Paris, aroused alarm amongst the moderates. Hoche, who for a moment allowed himself to be nominated minister of war, was denounced for preparing a *coup d'état*. Embittered by these attacks and unsure of himself he countermanded the march towards Brest and returned to his headquarters at Wetzlar. He was already in the grip of consumption and on 9 September he died.

By the autumn of 1797 France, at peace with all the continental powers (except Portugal) could concentrate its forces against Great Britain. In October the armée d'Angleterre was formed and Napoleon, already, after his Italian campaigns, the most famous soldier in Europe, was appointed its commander. At the close of 1797 he took up residence in Paris and began to study the problems involved in mounting a successful invasion of Great Britain. It was obviously the time to draw his attention to Ireland, and Lewins and Tone had three interviews with him at his 'small, but neat' house in the rue Chantereine, two in December and one in early January. Napoleon appeared to Tone dry, civil and reserved. He seemed interested, and Lewins tried to 'insense him' on Irish affairs, about which he clearly knew little, and presented him with a good map of

Ireland and copies of Tone's memorials. At the beginning of April Lewins saw Merlin of Douai, the president of the directory, and stressed the importance of sending assistance to Ireland as soon as possible. Merlin assured him that 'the time and place of succor' was 'a state secret', adding that France would make Irish independence a *sine qua non* when negotiating with Great Britain—a promise confirmed a day or so later by his colleague Barras. [49]

By the middle of April, however, Tone, who had been placed on the general staff of the armée d'Angleterre, was perceiving disturbing signs that the great attack on the British Isles might be postponed. [50] At the time he accepted the command of the armée d'Angleterre Napoleon had already a strong bias in favour of an Egyptian expedition which he thought could deliver a devastating blow to the great source of British strength— trade with the east. In February 1798 he presented the directory with a lucid appreciation of the difficulties which would have to be surmounted before an invasion could be attempted with any hope of success—an appreciation which displayed the undis- guised contempt of a brilliant and victorious soldier for a dispirit- ed and disorganized navy. Napoleon was not prepared to gamble when the odds seemed so bad and the stake was not only France's fortunes but his own career. By the beginning of 1798 he had convinced the directory of the advantages to be gained from a thrust into the eastern Mediterranean and by March 1798 preparations for an eastern expedition were under way. From Napoleon's point of view the projected attack on the British Isles was merely a feint, and negotiations between the French government and the United Irishmen was one of the schemes by which he masked his intentions. [51]

A few days after Napoleon sailed from Toulon the outbreak of insurrection in Ireland offered France an opportunity of inflicting a crippling blow on Great Britain. The possibility of a French expeditionary force landing in Ireland heartened the

---

[49] T. W. Tone, *Life*, ii, pp. 454–8, 473–4. During the summer of 1798 Lewins in a memorial to the directory emphasized that the United Irishmen had raised the standard of insurrection on the understanding that the French would honour the promise made by Merlin (Marine BB⁴ 103 ff. 178–179ᵛ).

[50] T. W. Tone, *Life*, p. 477.

[51] *Correspondance de Napoléon I*, iii, pp. 644–8; *Memoirs of Napoleon I*, ed. S. de Chair (1945), p. 272.

insurgents and haunted the government—at the beginning of June the acting chief secretary believed that the Toulon fleet, with Bonaparte on board, was probably making for Ireland. But though the directory expressed its sympathy with the insurgents and readiness to help them, its attention was fixed on France's eastern frontiers, towards which troops were being moved. The ships required for an Irish expedition were not available or not in a state of readiness; the British blockade was well maintained, and all the French achieved at this critical time was a series of commando raids.

During the next two years France was engaged in a series of important continental campaigns and was not until after the rupture of the peace of Amiens that Napoleon began to plan an invasion of the British Isles on a vast scale. Ireland was included in his plans. From a modest 5,000 men, the force destined for an Irish expedition was increased to 18,000, with the possibility that it might be reinforced by a second wave 25,000 strong. Thus at the moment when Great Britain was menaced by a great thrust across the Channel, a French threat would develop on her western flank. But the formation of the Third coalition had already compelled Napoleon to swing the grand army into Germany before Trafalgar spectacularly confirmed Great Britain's naval supremacy. Six years later however the idea of an Irish expedition again attracted Napoleon. He directed that steps should be taken to negotiate a treaty with the Irish exiles and that the fleet collected at the mouth of the Scheldt should be made ready to convey a force of 25,000–30,000 men to Ireland. But at the time Napoleon was considering an Irish expedition relations with Russia had already become strained and soon he was concentrating all his available forces for a great thrust eastwards.[52]

[52] *Correspondance de Napoléon I*, xxi, pp. 500–1, xxii, pp. 331, 350–1, 379, 403.

16

The maintenance of law and order

From the summer of 1795 the Irish administration and the Irish ruling world were challenged by militant political and social discontent, backed by the threat of a French invasion. There were two distinct ways of meeting this challenge. Sweeping concessions might be made which would satisfy the less vehement enemies of the existing regime, and then a broad alliance of those who wanted stability could be formed in defence of the remodelled constitution. The alternative was a defiant and unyielding maintenance of the existing order, inspired by a belief in its virtues and the conviction that a strategic retreat attempted in the face of intransigent foes would quickly degenerate into a rout. The latter, *non possumus* policy, was adopted by the Irish administration, supported by most men of property and by instinctive conservatives in all classes. Camden, on arrival in Ireland, was anxious to improve the quality of Irish life—he welcomed the appointment of assistant barristers, he suggested that justices of the peace should be empowered to fix wages, taking into account the price of provisions, and he wanted to encourage clerical residence (a resident clergy would provide the government with a source of reliable information in every parish). But Portland warned him that schemes of this sort were 'the work of time and the employment of days of peace', and Camden and his advisers were soon immersed in coping with a continuing crisis, in striving to preserve law and order, strengthen the country's defences and make a contribution to the war effort.[1] The forces stationed in Ireland were increased, a local defence force, the yeomanry, raised, the powers of the magistracy extended, the habeas corpus act suspended and determined efforts made to defeat illegally-organized radicalism by prosecutions, arrests and seizures of arms.

[1] Camden to Portland, 25 Sept. 1795 (H.O. 100/58); Portland to Camden, 13 Apr. 1795 (H.O. 100/59).

The Irish administration was not pressed by either the British cabinet or its own Irish supporters to supplement its police and military measures by conciliatory legislation. Camden in 1796 reminded Pitt that when he was leaving for Ireland, 'you candidly acknowledged to me . . . that Ireland occupies little of your thoughts'.[2] In the middle nineties this was scarcely surprising. From the time the war took a decisive turn for the worse in 1795 the British cabinet was conducting a hazardous struggle which might end in catastrophic defeat. At the close of 1796 Hoche's expedition failed by a narrow margin to effect a landing in Ireland and Bonaparte reached the Adige. Early in 1797 Austria, Great Britain's last remaining continental ally, was compelled to sue for peace and soon the two great pillars of British power, finance and the navy, with the suspension of cash payments and the naval mutinies, seemed to be crumbling. In parliament and out-of-doors, opposition to the war and the government was loudly voiced. The British constitution, it was said, 'trembled on the pivot of fortune', and the price of consols fell below the psychologically significant 50 to 48.[3] In such grim circumstances the British cabinet expected the Irish administration simply to try and contain disorder, take steps to repel invasion and, if possible, not to overtax available resources. As for the Irish conservatives, they were not in the mood to seek improvements in a system they had been brought up to venerate and their advice to the government often savoured strongly of sheer exasperation. Sir George Hill suggested that the government should send out some lawyers with 'plenary, summary jurisdiction' and by act of parliament pack off Drennan, O'Connor and 'the *Star* men' to Botany Bay. A neighbouring magistrate, who had a difficult time dealing with disaffection, declared that if 'two or three of your inflammatory orators in the house of commons were hanged and the *Northern Star* suppressed we could return to that happy state we eminently used to enjoy in this part of the kingdom'. Another government supporter wanted 'a tender, a press gang and a troop of horse', a fourth, who 'wished to God something was done to preserve the country from total ruin', suggested that

---

[2] Camden to W. Pitt, 6 May 1796 (P.R.O. 30/8/326).
[3] *Annual Register*, 1797, p. 4.

the army should 'traverse the whole country' disarming everybody.[4]

One section of the governing world however, the whigs, urged that conciliation should be tried. After 1795 the parliamentary party declined rapidly. Many country gentlemen, William Ponsonby bitterly reflected, availed themselves of 'the excuse furnished them by the cry of alarm for the peace of the country', and rallied to the government—a line of action 'their meanness has long induced them to pursue'. One very public-spirited country gentleman, Richard Griffith, gave a different explanation for leaving the whig party at this time. He thought that catholic emancipation and 'the education of the people' should precede parliamentary reform. He added that when a man was defending his house against banditti he was not prepared 'to examine with precision the plans of an ingenious architect'.[5] But if the whigs were reduced in numbers, they had, in Grattan's opinion, an important role, to restore the trust of the people in their natural leaders, the upper classes.[6] By acting in the historic whig revolutionary tradition—the tradition of 1688 not 1789—the whigs hoped they could impose a common-sense compromise, which would both preserve the existing order in essence and conciliate reasonable radicals. Their programme was easily formulated: catholic emancipation, parliamentary reform, an absentee tax, a reduction of British customs duties on Irish imports to the Irish level and in 1797 the repeal of the Insurrection act. Catholic emancipation was simple. All that was required was the admission of catholics to parliament and to senior posts under the crown. Conservatives were divided over this issue, but almost all of them, including Sir Hercules Langrishe, thought that the question should be postponed. The parliamentary reform bill which William Ponsonby introduced in May 1797 was a more sweeping measure than his 1793 bill. It provided that Ireland should be divided into districts containing 5,000 houses, each of which would return two M.P.s. The franchise was to be exercised by forty-shilling freeholders, by persons possessing a house or leasehold of a yearly value to be

[4] G. Hill to E. Cooke, 9 Feb. 1797; D. Browne to Pelham, 10 June 1797; R. Packe to Col Cooper, 22 May 1797; J. Rea to J. Hamilton, 27 Mar. 1797 (I.S.P.O. 620/28/241, 620/31/70, 620/30/144, 620/29/116).

[5] W. Ponsonby to Fitzwilliam, 5 June 1796 (W.W.M. F. 30); *D.J.*, 1 Dec. 1796.

[6] H. Grattan to Fitzwilliam, 19 Apr., 10 Nov. 1796 (W.W.M. F. 30).

fixed by parliament, by freemen of cities and towns and persons resident in urban centres for a certain length of time pursuing a trade. It was a plan, Grattan emphasized, based on 'population mixed with property', and George Ponsonby asserted that it would satisfy many of the United Irishmen. One conservative, who was quick to detect a resemblance between the districts and the French departments, said the scheme would create a pot-walloping commonwealth; another remarked that 'it was bad policy to thatch a house in a hurricane' and the bill was rejected by 117 to 30, the minority including seven county members, the two university representatives, one of the M.P.s for Dublin (Grattan) and (showing that the elderly are not necessarily conservative), Sir Joseph Hoare, aged ninety.[7]

The absentee tax obtained fairly widespread support in the house, a number of 'the servants of the crown' attributing 'the convulsed state of the lower classes . . . to the want of influence which arises from resident landlords', but on a division a proposal to impose a tax of two shillings in the pound on the rents of absentees was defeated by 122 to 49.[8] The other economic plank in the whig programme was expected to have far-reaching consequences. Lowering British duties on Irish manufactures would, it was asserted, encourage Irish industrial expansion. This, by increasing the demand for labour and offering opportunities for industrial investment, would both increase the price of labour and reduce that of land, and these developments would tend to remove two great causes of agrarian discontent, low wages and high rents for potato patches. From the beginning of 1796 the whigs dwelt feelingly on rural distress. Curran (a man of humble origins, a *rara avis* amongst Irish M.P.s) described the Irish peasantry as 'lodged' in hovels, sleeping upon straw, fed (and sometimes half-fed) upon potatoes. Grattan, the last man to deny that Ireland had advanced economically since 1782, seized on the conception that in an affluent society advantages were being distributed unfairly and elaborated it with vivid force. An English visitor, Grattan declared, 'would see the capital enlarged, he would see palaces for the rich, but the habitation of the poor as miserable

---

[7] *D.E.P.*, 18 May 1797.
[8] *D.E.P.*, 28 Feb. 1797; Camden to Portland, 11 Mar. 1797 (H.O. 100/69).

as ever, the old cabin reproaching the vanity of the new palace
and want, misery and dirt in contrast with magnificence. It
would appear to him that in this country the proportion of
things was broken—vain luxury and horrid poverty—the villa
and the hovel, the beggar and the man of fashion.' To O'Beirne,
the bishop of Ossory, who some years before had been a strong
whig, Grattan's speech on the condition of the poor simply
proved how completely he was 'the slave to popularity'.[9]

Both Curran and Grattan stressed the need to encourage
Irish industry. Curran suggested the tithe system should be
modified, Grattan referred with approval to the English poor
law and to a scheme for establishing a minimum wage which
had been under discussion at Westminster and hinted they
might be considered for Ireland. Conservatives felt that the
whig leaders were exaggerating the miseries of the poor. Cuffe
argued that if the Irish cabin had not as good a chimney as the
English cottage, the reason was the Irishman did not like such a
chimney. The peasant in County Mayo at any rate, Cuffe knew,
had plenty of fuel, and sufficient potatoes and milk, which were
shown by 'the athletic person and healthful vigour of the Irishman to be equally wholesome and nutritious'. Robert Stewart,
having pointed out that in every country there must be poor
and that 'the poor must feel calamities for which the legislature
can apply no remedy', rebuked the whigs for calling on the
compassion of the house when compassion could have no effect.
Parliament, he declared, 'always sought to adopt any measure
which appeared likely to benefit the poor', and he instanced a
not very striking example, a bill to promote the formation of
friendly societies, sponsored by Arthur Browne. Browne himself
agreed with his fellow whigs that there was great distress in
some areas, but, he added, 'at a wake, a fair, a funeral, an
assizes' he saw a number of healthy, warmly clothed men. It
was true they might be small farmers rather than labourers,
but then there were thousands of small farmers. Browne was
convinced that many landlords were living beyond their means
and as a result were keeping rents at too high a level. This
unfortunately had long been the usage of the country and 'could
not be corrected by any law but would gradually mend itself

<hr>

[9] *D.E.P.*, 2, 30 Jan., 2 Feb. 1796; L. O'Beirne to Fitzwilliam, 30 Mar. 1796
(W.W.M. F. 30).

by the wisdom of the landlord co-operating with the increasing illumination of the peasant'.

In July 1796 a committee appointed by the Whig club to inquire into the condition of the poor reported that in some counties the price of labour was insufficient for the support of the labourer and his family. Believing that 'there is in general much humanity in the kingdom', the committee suggested that in each barony gentlemen should form a committee to act as 'voluntary overseers of the poor'. These committees could promote domestic industries by making loans for the purchase of materials, encourage cottage gardens and provide sick relief. They might also manage to secure—presumably by persuasion—a rise in wages when there was a rise in the cost of living.[10] The whigs concern for the Irish poor in the late nineties was undoubtedly sincere (if stimulated by apprehension). However for an improvement in conditions they relied largely on goodwill and economic growth rather than on direct legislative intervention, and when endeavouring during 1796–7 to resolve the immediate crisis they attached overwhelming importance to concessions in the political sphere.

In one respect the whigs were badly handicapped. They aimed at being persuasive brokers between frightened conservatives and enthusiastic radicals. But as the latter were unrepresented in parliament, exposition of whig policy in the house of commons inevitably tended to develop into attacks on the British and Irish administrations, attacks accentuated by the debating techniques of the two great whig orators, Grattan and Curran, both of whom had a mastery of flouts and jeers. Convinced that their proposals would satisfy the great majority of the discontented, confronted by conservative intransigence and gripped by a growing sense of urgency, the whigs became deeply discouraged and in May 1797 Grattan ended an angry appeal for concession by announcing that his party intended to withdraw from parliament. He reminded the house of what had happened in America when the British government's response to discontent had been repression, and he painted a grim picture of what might well be the outcome of the Irish administration's policy—insurrection, civil war, a French invasion, separation from Great Britain and possibly the decline

[10] *D.E.P.*, 14 May, 15 June, 5 July 1796.

and fall of the empire. The whigs seceded in varying degrees. Grattan and Curran did not seek re-election at the general election of 1797; Curran never again sat in parliament; Grattan returned to the house in 1800 to oppose the union. But over half the M.P.s who voted for Ponsonby's 1797 reform bill were returned at the ensuing general election, and some of them including Arthur Browne were active in parliament during the session of 1798, and the Ponsonbys were back in 1799.

In addition to waging a parliamentary campaign the whigs also tried to coerce the government into concession by mobilizing public opinion. After the disastrous session of 1795 Grattan, Ponsonby and Curran had meetings not only with the city liberals but with catholic and protestant radicals (Bond, Byrne, Chambers, Bagenal Harvey, Henry Jackson and McCormick), and 'a coalition on the subject of reform' was discussed. In fact whigs and radicals differed on reform. They differed even more sharply on France and on the British connection. The radical leaders were hostile to the connection— at one of the whig–radical meetings Keogh 'spoke very freely against the stand or fall maxim', professed so fervently by Grattan—and some of them were looking forward to a French invasion. On the other hand Grattan was sure that if the French landed they 'would halloo the lower classes against the higher and make the whole country a scene of massacre', and he went out of his way at the beginning of the session of 1796 to stress that 'whatever feelings the country may have of resentment, let them be directed against the ministers only and not against the people of England; with them we have a common constitution and a common empire'.[11] However whigs and radicals were able for a short time to form a united front against the Irish administration as was shown at a Dublin meeting held at the close of 1795 to express loyal sympathy with the king who had been attacked on his way to the opening of parliament. The lord mayor suggested that John Claudius Beresford, a strong conservative, should prepare an address (he seems to have had one ready), but an opposition in which Grattan was prominent succeeded in carrying its address, which

---

[11] E. Cooke to ——, 3 Sept. 1795 (Add. MS 33101); W. Drennan to Mrs McTier, 8 July, 29 Aug. 1795, 4 Jan. 1796 (Drennan papers, 568, 577, 596); D.E.P., 23 Jan. 1796.

though effusively loyal, insisted that measures tending to restrict liberty were unnecessary.[12] During the first half of 1797 the whigs with radical support planned a series of meetings. In Dublin when the sheriffs refused to hold a meeting, the whig leaders and a number of quondam members of the Dublin society of United Irishmen summoned an aggregate (attended according to a conservative by only 600 persons) which declared in favour of catholic emancipation and reform. In the following month the sheriffs agreed to hold a meeting of freeholders and freemen at the Exchange, placing peace officers at the door to ensure that only qualified persons should be admitted. According to a liberal newspaper the Castle exerted itself and M.P.s, revenue officers, paving-board officials, gentlemen from the post office, the chaplain of the house of commons and old Sackville Hamilton, the ex-under-secretary, were persuaded to attend. According to a conservative paper the rabble pushed into the hall and the gentlemen 'who had a majority of legal voices' retired. In the event Grattan was placed in the chair, an address calling for the dismissal of Pitt's administration was carried, and a few days later a protest against the proceedings at the meeting appeared signed by nearly 400 freemen and freeholders.[13] About the same time a bar meeting agreed to a declaration which was signed by 71 barristers in favour of parliamentary reform, but it was reported that a counter-declaration was signed by 135 members of the bar.[14] In Antrim and Armagh county meetings called for the dismissal of the ministers; but in Antrim nearly 1,300 freeholders signed a declaration stating that the address did not represent the opinion of the county and the Armagh meeting, according to conservatives, was simply a collection of the United Irishmen, the gentry of the county having failed to make preparations for meeting the mob.[15] In County Down a group of gentlemen decided not to hold a meeting because the county was pro-claimed but to circulate a petition; at the Monaghan assizes a number of gentlemen considered publicly promising to support

---

[12] *D.E.P.*, and *D.J.*, 19 Dec. 1795.
[13] *D.E.P.*, 4 Mar., 11 Apr. 1797.
[14] *D.E.P.*, 20, 25 May 1797.
[15] *D.E.P.*, 27 May 1797; G. Dawson to ——, 20 Apr. 1797 (I.S.P.O. 620/29/29); C. Warburton to ——, 20 Apr. 1797 (620/29/290); lists of freeholders in H.O. 100/72.

reform if the people remained quiet, 'a mad idea' quashed by Lord Blayney. In King's County a meeting was abandoned, apparently because of the presence of a number of militiamen; in County Kildare and Cork city meetings to petition for the dismissal of ministers were cancelled because the organizers were deterred by the proclamation of 17 May which cautioned the public against meeting in unusual numbers.[16]

The organizers of these two meetings placed themselves in an assailable position by summoning unusual gatherings—the Cork meeting was to be composed of freemen, freeholders and those qualified for jury service, the Kildare meeting of the inhabitants of the county. The Kildare liberals published the declaration calling for the meeting which with its 1,600 signatories headed by the duke of Leinster filled columns of the press. The Kildare conservatives published a petition against holding a meeting with sixty signatories, including eight peers, a bishop and a number of influential freeholders.

Clearly there were men of property and position who strongly opposed the government's policy. But there was certainly not that determined, declared, overwhelming expression of disapproval by the political or middle-class Irish world which might have deflected the Irish administration from the course it was pursuing. Whether the whig policy would have proved successful in averting insurrection and opening the way to reform by general agreement, is impossible to say. Conservatives were convinced that concession, the surrender of defensive outworks in the face of violence, would only prove the prelude to further demands. Alexander Knox, a highly intelligent conservative, thought that 'to hope to tranquillize by anything short of democracy, pure and unqualified, would be just as absurd as to think of appeasing a tiger raging for blood by throwing a sheaf of wheat before him'. 'Those', he wrote, 'whom any reform consistent with the well-being of the constitution would satisfy are sufficiently disposed already to defend the house as it is, till the storm be over and those who under the name of reform are aiming at a democratic revolution are long determined to put up with no compromise.'[17] This

---

[16] *D.E.P.*, 23, 27, 30 May, 8 June 1797; *D.J.*, 10 June 1797; H. Alexander to H. Pelham, 15 Mar. 1797 (I.S.P.O. 620/29/72).
[17] A. Knox to P. Burrowes, 8 Mar. 1797 (I.S.P.O. 620/29/30).

assessment of the situation would not incline a politician to offer a compromise, and Camden, probably re-echoing the views of his Irish advisers, also argued that catholic emancipation, though it might satisfy the catholic peers and gentry, would be regarded by the agitators of the catholic committee as merely a prelude to reform, and reform was a 'shelter' for treason and separation from Great Britain.[18]

With concession as a policy ruled out, the government was committed to meeting discontent head-on with all the forces at its disposal. When bringing these forces to bear it needed to know as much as possible about the strength, organization, and intentions of its opponents, and in making an assessment of the situation the Irish administration had a confusing superabundance of information, of very varying value. The British government supplied it with naval and military intelligence. From the radical newspapers, the *Northern Star* until it was compelled to cease publication in May 1797, and the *Press* between September 1797 and March 1798, it was easy to gather what the advanced reformers were aiming at and what methods they were prepared to use. Then from the middle nineties the Castle was receiving a steady flow, at times mounting to a torrent, of information on the state of the country from officials and magistrates, clergymen, peers and post-masters, army officers and lawyers, many of whom would have agreed with the catholic peer who informed an undersecretary that 'every trifle in this sort of times and in such an irritable country makes one at least suspicious and my conscience is so delicate that the smallest circumstance I cannot but communicate'.[19] Many of these upholders of law and order when corresponding with the government displayed common characteristics, courage, energy, a sense of urgency ('more army is much wanted here', wrote an agitated official in Westmeath),[20] a readiness to employ, if need be, rough measures to preserve the peace and some sense of self-importance when pressing their opinions on the government. Their letters as a whole comprise materials for a graph recording the fluctuations of disorder. The activities of the turbulent (United Irishmen,

---

[18] Camden to Portland, 9 Mar., 3 Apr. 1797 (H.O. 100/69).
[19] Fingal to A. Marsden, 23 July 1804 (I.S.P.O. 620/13/178/25).
[20] Post-master of Mullingar to John Lees, 5 May 1797 (I.S.P.O. 620/30/16).

defenders, whiteboys, Orangemen) are naturally surveyed from without and, often consciously, from above and many of these correspondents based their appreciation of the local situation on gossip, fragments of conversation and trifling incidents. Some however tried to find reliable sources of information. In County Derry, Sir George Hill learned about the workings of the United Irishmen's organization from Charles McFillin, a catholic, who was elected a county and provincial delegate on, he believed, religious grounds, 'to inspire confidence into the Roman catholics.' The Revd William Bristow, the rector of Belfast and a sometime sovereign of the town, a pillar of church and state, was so successful in securing information that the County Down United Irishmen minuted 'Mr Bristow of Belfast... knows our provincial proceedings too well.'[21] In County Waterford Roger Dalton, disturbed by the distribution of seditious pamphlets, 'applied to several of the people to let me know by some means what the devil they were about'. In Westmeath, William Smith of Drumcree, aware that sedition was spreading, was confident that he had found the right man 'to discover the secret springs of this mischief making', a well-educated spendthrift who had dissipated a small fortune and who held 'those republican doctrines which are very fashionable with men in his circumstances'. Sir Edward Newenham, a repentant liberal, anxious to exert himself in defence of order, early in 1796 sent an intelligent fellow into 'the remote parts' of Galway 'frequented by defenders' to obtain information, and in Lisburn, the Revd Snowden Cupples was delighted to be able to secure 'very minute information' about the United Irishmen, from an uncle of Templeton, a clerk in the office of the *Northern Star*—the nephew talked very freely to his uncle, being unaware the latter was prepared to discuss the United Irishmen outside the society.[22] In Dublin Francis Higgins, the robust editor of the strongly conservative *Freeman's Journal*, a journalist of twenty years' experience and a convivial, talkative man with a wide circle of acquaintances, organized an intelligence service which was bound to be of value both to the *Freeman* and the

---

[21] *Commons' Jn. Ire.*, xvii, pp. dcccliv–v.
[22] R. Dalton to ——, 9 Sept. 1797; W. Smyth to ——, 15 Nov. 1795; F. Newenham to ——, 1 Feb. 1796; S. Cupples to F. Archer, 28 Dec. 1797 (I.S.P.O. 620/32/106, 620/22/54, 620/23/30, 620/33/180).

government. At one stage he was employing ten agents to secure information about the United Irishmen's clubs in Dublin and to collect copies of their manifestos; and his lavish hospitality enabled him to obtain over the dinner table a considerable amount of political gossip which he passed on to the government in a series of vigorously written reports.[23] Higgins's greatest scoop was persuading Francis Magan, a young barrister who was a United Irishman, to give him information about the society's activities. The government had another very useful informant in Dublin, Leonard MacNally, a well-known barrister, who frequently appeared for the defence in political trials. MacNally was both an able advocate and a successful man of letters—he was a poet, a playwright and the author of several legal textbooks. But he was clumsily built and lame, at the outset of his career had a struggle with penury, was snubbed by his fellow barristers and, perhaps because of his politics, he failed to attain a very high degree of professional success—after twenty-nine years at the bar he was striving to be appointed a metropolitan stipendary. MacNally was in the early nineties a member of the Dublin society of United Irishmen and was placed on the committee appointed to prepare a plan of reform, but he seems to have become disillusioned with radicalism (he was a strong protestant) and from 1795 he was secretly in touch with the government. He continued to move in radical circles and from confidences, conversational indiscretions and allusions he picked up a considerable amount about the movements of radical opinion and the intentions of the United Irishmen. He was paid intermittently by the government and was finally granted a secret pension of £300 per annum, but in addition to obtaining these financial benefits, he obviously found it very gratifying while living and working in a close-knit, observant and gossipy society, to know that he had a second, secret but perhaps influential, life. His staccato reports, written with verve and acid wit reveal his contempt for his radical associates and at times, for the Irish administration.[24] On a lower level, Thomas

[23] F. Higgins to E. Cooke, 25 Oct. 1801 (I.S.P.O. 620/49/137); F. Higgins to ——, 18 June 1798 (620/12) and a large number of his letters in 620/18.

[24] For MacNally's career and pension see W. J. Fitzpatrick, *Secret service under Pitt* (1892), pp. 174–8.

Boyle, a Drumcondra innkeeper, on his 'country excursions and city perambulations', kept in touch with the views and activities of the middle-grade leadership and the rank and file of the United Irishmen. Boyle seems to have been a member of a baronial committee and to have employed his son, who was also active in the movement, to obtain information. He was brought to the notice of the under-secretary by an alderman, William Worthington, and seems from his reports to have been a humble member of the middle classes, socially overawed by the Dublin shopkeepers whom he met in radical circles. Work for the government, he explained to Cooke, involving 'my keeping a decent appearance, and clean, every day in the week increases much my outlay'. 'As to the people I associate with for information,' he wrote, 'they look upon me as a man of substance and therefore they admit and even court my company, which they have, as I never neglect sitting at all their meetings and paying my expenses with spirit'. But, Boyle emphasized, it was a strain. He had to drink more than he liked and though he received a weekly allowance, his 'zeal for the cause, my constant company keeping, made me spend every half penny I received and more and if it were not for my wife and family's industry and management I could not support it, as my time and the money I got has always been devoted and spent on the cause'. His financial position was so bad that at Christmas 1801 Cooke gave him ten guineas to pay his house rent, and later he was paid through Worthington an allowance of £50 per annum.[25]

In Belfast the authorities had two useful informants, John Smith (whose real name was Bird) and Edward Newell. Bird, a London businessman on the fringe of the Corresponding society, who had met with a financial catastrophe, arrived in Belfast in September 1795 looking for business. A good mixer, if financially suspect, interested in ideas, he was readily received by the local radicals, who talked very freely with him. Early in 1796, resenting the refusal of 'philanthropic politicians' to help him financially, and according to himself because he was

---

[25] Boyle to E. Cooke, July, Aug. 1797 (I.S.P.O. 620/18-. Boyle's letters are unsigned but see W. Worthington to A. Marsden, 1 Feb. 1802 (620/10/125); J. T. Gilbert, *Documents relating to Ireland* (1893), pp. 67, 80. Boyle appeared as a witness before the house of commons secret committee of 1797 (620/34/54).

unjustly accused of being a government spy, he made contact with Charles Skeffington, the collector of Belfast, offering information, but emphasizing he would not give evidence in court, and asking for money, 'to be able to keep appearance with the United Irishmen'. His cover story was that he was engaged in recruiting skilled mechanics for United States employers, but the rumour persisted that he was in the pay of the government. So Bird boldly tackled the 'most ferocious' of the United Irishmen, told them he was deeply hurt by the allegation and obtained a handsome apology. In 1797 he gave evidence before the house of commons secret committee, and at the end of the year was residing in Dublin Castle, waiting to be called as a crown witness. He was highly overwrought, fearing that he might be assassinated when he appeared in court, and early in 1798 he disappeared from the government's ken, and got in touch with some well-known radicals—Dowling, the attorney, Sampson, a barrister, and Stockdale, the printer of the *Press*, and told them he wanted to help the cause. He also said— presumably realizing the saleability of his experiences—that he hoped to make £1,000 by 'a book of his life'. The United Irishmen provided him with lodgings, first in Charlemont Street and later at Harold's Cross and restored his *amour propre* by listening to his views on the political situation and in February a series of letters over his name appeared in the *Press* violently attacking 'the great phalanx of monsters' who supplied the government with information.[26]

Newell detested Smith—'he is a villain by design, I only by accident', he wrote. Undoubtedly Newell's early life was unsettling. Born in 1771, he was unhappy at home and in school, went to sea, studied engraving in Dublin and became a defender. In 1796 he went to Belfast, worked as a miniature painter and teacher of drawing and moved in radical circles. Becoming friendly with Murdoch, a hearth-money collector, he began to supply the authorities with information, assisted in making arrests in Belfast and gave evidence before the 1797 secret committee. Swaggering and officious in Belfast, when in Dublin he lived luxuriously at government expense, and according to himself, contracted 'that worse of maladies, the

---

[26] J. Stoyte to ——, 3 July 1798 (I.S.P.O. 620/51/196); J. Bird to ——, 19 June (620/52/16).

fashionable disorder acquired by improper connections'. By the beginning of 1798 he had quarrelled with Murdoch (having seduced his wife), was making a nuisance of himself while drunk and was awaiting with trepidation the prospect of appearing as a crown witness. Some northern radicals managed to suborn him, he fled to Ulster, leaving a short note for Cooke declaring 'though I can't deny being a villain, I hope clearly to prove I had the honour of being made one by you'. In hiding he published at Belfast a short autobiography, *The apostacy of Newell*, a clever, moralizing amalgam of spicy detail about his own private life and revelations relating to his employment as a government agent.[27]

Newell, when travelling between Dublin and Belfast in April 1797 witnessed at Newry a dramatic incident in the career of another informant, Samuel Turner. Turner, a man of some substance, was engaged in a public fracas with an impetuous soldier, Lord Carhampton. When they met in the hall of the Crown Inn, Carhampton observing that Turner was wearing a green neck-cloth, accused him of being deliberately offensive and told him to take it off. Hot words were exchanged but in the end Carhampton proffered an apology which Turner accepted. Turner had already been involved in a similar incident, when he and a friend had refused to take off their hats during the playing of 'God save the King' in the Newry theatre in spite of angry remarks from the military officers in the audience. Turner, who was obviously vehement and excitable, threw himself enthusiastically into the United Irishmen's organization in Ulster. In May 1797 he arrived at Hamburg *en route* for Paris, and according to himself his political outlook was greatly influenced by what he saw of the areas under French domination. 'Their unhappy situation', he wrote, 'together with that of the French, who found they had changed their good government for a worse', opened his eyes to the dangers facing Ireland. Moreover, according to himself, having become a United Irishman with the aim of securing parliamentary reform, he was deeply disturbed at seeing the movement passing under the control of desperate men, determined to establish a popish tyranny. Quitting France, he travelled via Holland to London, and taking every precaution

[27] For Newell see his *Apostacy of Newell*, 1798.

he could to avoid detection, on a dark evening he called on
Lord Downshire at his London house and from then on steadily
supplied the government with information.[28]

The informants who were members of the United Irishmen's
society were undoubtedly useful, providing the government
with very valuable insights into the workings of the radical
organization. But they had their limitations. They tended to
over-dramatize, much of their information was out of date by
the time it reached the authorities, they were at the best only
indirectly in touch with the United Irishmen's higher command
and they would be of little value as crown witnesses, since, if
they were willing to appear in court, their evidence would be
largely hearsay or uncorroborated.

The picture which emerged when all these sources were
taken together was a thoroughly alarming one. Agrarian
violence was rife over wide areas in the north, midlands and
south, a well-articulated radical organization was preparing to
take drastic action and seeking French assistance, and the
situation in Ulster from early in 1796 posed a grave and novel
threat to the safety of the realm.[29] Discontent was not, as in
other parts of Ireland, largely confined to the humbler levels
of rural society. Ulster radicalism included in its ranks many
able and successful businessmen, professional men and well-
established farmers, whose aim was not the redress of simple
grievances but revolutionary political change. They were
capable of detailed planning, of recruiting and regimenting
large numbers, and of restraining their followers from premature action while keeping up their spirits by meetings and
propaganda. The Ulster radical movement had a double
potency, derived from the secrecy of its organization and the
forceful and sometimes sparkling publicity given to its opinions
through the medium of the *Northern Star*, which maintained a
fusillade of attacks on the government and all its works—
attacks which, whatever might be their implications—stopped
skilfully short of sedition or treason.

In the autumn of 1796 many of the country people in
Counties Antrim, Down and Derry publicly demonstrated

[28] *D.E.P.*, 25 Apr. 1797; *N.S.*, 13 Jan. 1797; S. Turner to ——, 16 June 1803
(I.S.P.O. 620/11/160/4).
[29] T. Knox to ——, 6 July 1796 (I.S.P.O. 620/24/16).

their feelings and the power of disciplined numbers by a series of menacing, if legal, demonstrations.[30] From late September to early November large bodies of men (in some instances, it was said thousands strong) gathered to harvest the crops or dig the potatoes of persons in custody for political reasons or persons known to be keen advocates of parliamentary reform. Assembled, as one group declared when they ordered a whiskey hawker to take his wares elsewhere, on 'a work of friendship, sobriety and virtue', they seemed dangerously disciplined, apparently, as an energetic magistrate wrote, 'accustoming themselves to rise at the shortest notice'. The *Northern Star* commended their activities in swinging verse:

> A digging let us go
> A digging let us go,
> To shew our love for those brave men,
> Who in jail for truth did go.[31]

Lord Castlereagh, when out riding near his father's house met a digging party, and was much impressed by the precision with which they went to work. 'I never', he wrote, 'saw a finer race of young men, full of zeal in a cause they are made to feel a good one. I spoke to several and was answered with good humour.'[32] Lord Moira, a whig peer, visiting his estate near Ballynahinch saw a crowd digging the potatoes of a poor man who was sick on All Hallows, 'a day observed with universal jollity'. Some gentlemen, Moira told the chief secretary, 'have used a tone and manner with the common people which might have answered twenty years ago, although the peasantry in England would not have borne it within this century . . . In my opinion there is no other policy but conciliation. Such a tone would quiet anything.' The chief secretary in a conciliatory reply expressed the sincere hope 'that your lordship's opinion of the disaffected in the north may be more correct than what I have been induced to entertain'.[33] On a few occasions a magistrate dispersed a crowd assembled for potato digging,

---

[30] The *Northern Star* records about 30 instances, largely in Antrim.
[31] *N.S.*, 28 Oct. 1796.
[32] Castlereagh to T. Pelham, n.d. (I.S.P.O. 620/18/7/33).
[33] Moira to H. Pelham, 8 Nov. 1796, H. Pelham to Moira, 11 Nov. 1796 (I.S.P.O. 620/26/31).

but when one such gathering was dispersing, the High sheriff of County Londonderry, to George Hill's intense indignation, pulled out his purse and called out, 'by God you have behaved so well there is a guinea for the woman whose potatoes you came to dig'.[34]

To conservatives it seemed as if the whole province was by 'a system of terror', boycotting, threats and occasional violence, being brought under the complete control of a revolutionary secret society. Both conservatives, sensitive to social unrest, and radicals, impressed by the technical skill with which the United Irishmen's organization was built up and the ease with which recruits were made, almost certainly exaggerated the strength of the movement in Ulster. Once the government launched a counter-offensive the local conservatives recovered their confidence and in the summer of 1798 it was demonstrated that the nominal rolls of the United Irishmen's military organization were inflated by the names of many inactive sympathizers.

The government possessed two well-tried instruments for the preservation of law and order, the unpaid magistracy and the courts. To the challenge of growing disorder and conspiracy a number of justices of the peace responded vigorously, maintaining close touch with the central government and striving to detect and deal with disaffection in their neighbourhood. For these magistrates life could be difficult and dangerous. 'I am environed by enemies', a County Monaghan J.P. wrote, and an active magistrate in adjacent County Tyrone indignantly complained that while he had been compelled by threats to his property to give up a large bleach works, his 'United neighbours from their disloyalty carried on with safety and great emolument'.[35] Several magistrates were fired at and three fell victims to their zeal, the Revd George Knipe, Colonel St George Mansergh, and the Revd William Hamilton. Knipe, a County Meath rector, who as a result of his anti-defender activities in the Clonard area, had become 'the most marked man in the county', was besieged at night in his rectory and, on attempting to escape, shot. Mansergh, who had fought in the

[34] G. Hill to E. Cooke, 18 Nov. 1796 (I.S.P.O. 620/52/13).
[35] J. Wright to T. Pelham, 17 May 1797 (I.S.P.O. 620/30/100); A. Newton to ——, 1 Feb. 1798 (620/35/102).

war of Independence, when visiting his estates in north-east
Cork early in 1798, burned a house in which the United
Irishmen had met and threatened to burn the houses of all he
believed to be disaffected. Shortly after he issued these threats
he was spending the night at the house of his agent William
Uniacke when a gang broke in and murdered them both.[36]
William Hamilton, a sometime fellow of Trinity college, had in
1790 had been presented to the college living of Clondevaddock,
a large parish lying between Mulroy Bay and Lough Swilly,
which included much mountainous country, interspersed with
fertile strips. Hamilton, a man of 'easy volubility flowing from
a fulness of mind', and the author of a survey of the Antrim
coast which displayed a keen interest in geology and sociology,
was by descent and conviction a strong conservative. His
grandfather had been one of the defenders of Derry in 1690 and
Hamilton himself in 1793 published a vigorous attack on French
revolutionary principles. It was said that in 1796 he acquired
considerable unpopularity by his efforts to protect a wreck and
early in 1797 he was scouring the country at the head of a
military detachment, searching for arms, levying fines for those
which were unregistered, administrating the oath of allegiance
to large numbers and trying to track down the roots of conspiracy.
'From common and poor men I have followed up the association
to comfortable farmers, from them to dissenting ministers not
in employment,' he wrote at the beginning of February. His
position was a difficult, and, he must have realized, a dangerous
one. 'I have been unwillingly obliged', he wrote to a Castle
official, 'to raise and guide the tempest of human passion, and
destitute of the regular aid of civil power to suppress a powerful
effort of sedition . . . For in such moments how weak is the
magistrate and his constable.' However, he was happy to say
'the simplicity of my people and the want of low attorney craft
has rendered them extremely open'. At the beginning of
March, returning from a short visit to his bishop, he stopped
for the night midway between Raphoe and home, at the rectory
of the Revd John Waller, also a sometime fellow of Trinity.
About ten o'clock at night, when the Waller family and their
guest were sitting in the drawing room, a large crowd marched
on the house, and thrust their muskets through the windows,

[36] *D.E.P.*, 22 Feb. 1798.

shouting 'Give out Hamilton!'. Mrs Waller, trying to close the
shutters, was mortally wounded, and Hamilton who fled to the
cellars was seized by a few terrified servants and thrust out on
the lawn where he was killed.[37]

More fortunate was another clerical magistrate, Charles
Warburton, who resided in south Armagh. Warburton was
said to be the son of an Irish harper and in 1795 he was the
victim of an 'injurious' rumour that he had been educated a
Roman catholic. In spite of not being a university man he had
a very successful ecclesiastical career. A chaplain to the marquis
of Buckingham, he was in 1791 appointed to the large living of
Loughgilly and early in the nineteenth century he was raised
to the bench. A level-headed man of whiggish opinions, anxious
that Orangemen and over-zealous conservatives should be
restrained, when, early in 1797, the position in his parish was
serious, he acted with courageous decision. Aware that 'the
whole country . . . was sworn and united', about the middle of
March he was conscious of 'an unusual degree of mysterious
bustle' in his parish. A dragoon patrol was attacked by a large
crowd 'with shouts, yells and horn blowing'. On the arrival of
reinforcements from Armagh, requested by Warburton, the
crowd dispersed, shouting 'Murder the magistrates'. The next
day, hearing that 'the united insurgents' were saying the troops
dare not face them, Warburton, who 'thought it absolutely
necessary for our future safety and the honour of the king's
troops that such an idea should be immediately checked',
marched at the head of a small military force, dragoons and
infantry through the countryside. The immediate result in his
opinion was satisfactory. A number of farmers expressed their
regret at the attack on the patrol and Warburton took the
opportunity to advise them to hand over their arms to a
magistrate (who would give a receipt). The situation became
so alarming that Warburton, fearing an attack upon his house,
moved his family to Armagh. He himself soon returned to his
parish, 'determined not to move whilst there is a possibility of
avoiding the guillotine'. By the summer, he found the situation
had so much improved that he was working from 5 a.m. to

[37] W. Hamilton to R. Marshall, 14 Jan. 1797 (I.S.P.O. 620/28/99); W. Hamilton
to G. Knox, 2 Feb. 1797 (620/28/195); W. Hamilton to E. Cooke, 14 Jan., 12 Feb.
1797 (620/28/99, 259); D.J., 7 Mar. 1797; H.J., 25 Sept. 1797.

10 p.m. administrating the oath of allegiance—'I never undertook a more fatiguing job'.[38] According to himself, Warburton was for ten months 'the only resident between Newry and Armagh' and he was very contemptuous of the clergy and gentry who had fled. 'Only look about, My Lord,' he wrote to Grenville, 'and observe the number of Irish bishops now in England.' If a miserable curate was left as the representative of an absent rector, this was 'craftly turned by the republicans into a proof . . . that the whole establishment is burdensome and unnecessary'. The government, Warburton thought, should insist on the Irish clergy of all ranks returning to their posts.

There were energetic and determined magistrates such as Warburton scattered throughout Ireland. But the number of justices of the peace who kept in touch with the government was comparatively small, and active magistrates often implied that they were not getting the local backing they deserved. Many country gentlemen, from timidity, inertia or perhaps, as they might say, disdaining to give way to panic, did not over-exert themselves and the unpaid magistracy provided the country with incomplete coverage in the emergency.

One obvious method of checking disorder and conspiracy, used in the past with some success against the whiteboys, was to prosecute the offenders in the courts, and from 1795 a large number of persons charged with political or agrarian offences appeared before the judges on assize. During 1795 at the Meath lent assizes a number of persons were accused of offences under the whiteboy acts—six were sentenced to death and the rest acquitted. At the Leitrim summer assizes three men convicted of offences under the whiteboy acts were sentenced to death, six others, charged with administering illegal oaths, sentenced to transportation and fourteen in arms bound over to keep the peace. In Roscommon, four men, convicted of seizing arms, were sentenced to death, two, convicted of administering oaths, to transportation and a number charged with whiteboy

---

[38] Archbishop of Tuam to Fitzwilliam, 29 Mar. 1795 (W.W.M. F. 30); C. Warburton to Fitzwilliam, 22 June, 3 Apr. 1797, 8 Mar. 1798 (W.W.M. F. 30); C. Warburton to E. Cooke, 13 Apr., 27 May, 1 June 1797 (I.S.P.O. 620/29/243, 620/30/212, 620/31/100); C. Warburton to ——, 15, 16 Mar. 1797 (620/29/76, 81); C. Warburton to ——, 12 Apr. 1797 (620/29/223); C. Warburton to Grenville, 12 Jan. 1798 (Add. MS 59254A).

offences, though acquitted, bound over. At Longford a man convicted of administering unlawful oaths was sentenced to transportation but many of those brought to trial were acquitted for want of evidence. In Kildare, three men found guilty of shooting at a J.P. were sentenced to death, and Laurence O'Connor and Michael Griffin were sentenced to death for treason.

During the lent assizes of 1796 at Kilmainham three defenders were acquitted; at Naas eight were convicted; at Trim nine were convicted; and many others were acquitted because crown witnesses failed to attend; at Mullingar four were sentenced to transportation and at Longford eight were convicted of being concerned in Harman's murder and executed. At Enniskillen two defenders were found guilty of a riot but Lord Belmore's gardener and his apprentice, who were charged with administrating an illegal oath and drilling men, were found not guilty, being defended by the well-known barrister, Leonard MacNally, 'brought down special'. The crown also sustained a defeat at Armagh, where a man charged with trying to seduce a soldier from his allegiance was acquitted and at Omagh, where Thomas Richardson and Benjamin Brown were charged with administering the United Irishmen's oath. They were clearly men of some substance, indeed the counsel for the crown thought it opportune to emphasize that though 'the lower subordinate system and the lower orders had suffered', their superiors, whose ostensible object was reform, but whose real aims were treasonable, had 'been cautious and escaped punishment'. But the principal crown witness made a poor impression. Having sworn examinations against the prisoners, he made an affidavit in Belfast declaring that he had done so because he had been threatened by a group of Orangemen. At the trial, however, he stated that he had made the affidavit after 'several persons of genteel appearance' in Belfast had given him 'more drink than he could bear'. Understandably the prisoners were acquitted.[39] But before the end of the year they were both again arrested and held for a considerable time. At the summer assizes at Trim, Traynor, 'a most atrocious defender' was convicted and executed; and at Carrickfergus,

[39] *H.J.*, 16, 24, 30 Mar. 1796, 8, 11 Apr. 1796, 16 May 1796; *D.E.P.*, 15, 24, 29 Mar. 1796; *D.J.*, 5 Apr., 7 Aug. 1796; *N.S.*, 4, 6 Apr. 1796.

James Levingston of Bushmills was found guilty of publishing a 'wicked libel', *Liberty and equality*, and sentenced to three years' imprisonment.[40] But at Omagh the crown had to admit that it had decided not to proceed with the prosecution of John Shaw, who, the government had good reason to believe, was a leading active United Irishman (according to Neilson, the editor of the *Northern Star*, Shaw was 'a manly honest man . . . not guilty of any crime . . . save exertions to unite Irishmen and to stop the outrages of Orangemen'). Shaw's wife, while admitting he was a United Irishman, explained to the chief secretary that he was as 'inoffensive as any person of that denomination' and after a year's imprisonment he was released on bail.[41]

During 1797 the government's legal campaign against disaffection seems to have intensified and since, for the first time, information relating to numbers charged and convicted at assizes is available, it is possible to estimate its success. About one in seven of the prosecutions brought at the assizes during the year seem to have been for what might be regarded as political offences. It must be admitted at once that the statistics on which this estimate is based are defective. For one county (Queen's) there is no return of persons charged, and in some counties the official responsible for the return listed charges simply as 'a felony' or 'an offence'. Though it is only fair to say that in other returns the initials 'U.I.' are at times appended to a charge, indicating that in the opinion of the authorities the accused was actuated by political motives. It is of course impossible to draw with any degree of precision a line between political and other offences. Treason, sedition, administering or taking an illegal oath, an attempt to seduce a soldier from his allegiance, the murder of or conspiracy to murder upholders of authority, 'combination', raiding for arms, chalking or 'papering a house', might in the Ireland of 1797 be taken to be essentially political offences, the perpetrators, generally speaking, being actuated by strong hostility to the existing constitutional or agrarian order. But defenders who were 'social rebels' were often charged with burglary (they were probably looking

---

[40] *Hibernian Magazine*, 1796, p. 192; *D.E.P.*, 2 Aug. 1796.
[41] *D.J.*, 19 July, 6, 11 Aug. 1796; T. Knox to ——, 23 Apr. 1796 (I.S.P.O. 620/23/85); S. Neilson to O. Bond, 30 Apr. 1796 (620/23/91); Sally Shaw to T. Pelham, n.d. (620/31/105).

for arms), and it is impossible to list a burglary as a political offence unless some other evidence is available. On the other hand bad neighbour relations or a desire for plunder might be the motive behind a raid for arms.[42]

At the lent assizes about 170 persons were charged with political offences, forty coming from four northern counties (Antrim, Down, Armagh and Monaghan), and seventy-one from a group of midland counties. The conviction rate for political offences was 19 per cent compared with 30 per cent for all offences. At the summer assizes the number of persons accused of political offences rose to 263 (just over two-thirds being from Ulster) and the conviction rate rose to 31 per cent compared to 25·6 per cent for all offences. Taking both assizes and the Dublin county and city commission of oyer and terminer together, the number of persons charged with political offences during the year was 475, and the conviction rate was 25·5 per cent compared to a trifle over 24 per cent for all offences. Of those charged, about 40 per cent were accused of being illegal oath-taking, about 35 per cent were charged with acts of violence—conspiracy to murder, shooting at a magistrate, cutting trees or raiding for arms or defenderism. Others were charged with trying to seduce a soldier, combination, chalking, sedition or treason. Thirty-four persons were sentenced to death for political offences (twenty-three in Ulster), of whom nineteen were reprieved. Amongst those sentenced to death in Ulster was William Orr, 'an industrious and admirable farmer' noted for his hospitality and said to be worth from three to four hundred a year. Orr was charged with administering the United Irishmen's oath to Hugh Wheatly, a private in the Fifeshire fencibles, who was 'to be entrusted with the printed constitutions of the society in order to promote the institution among his fellow soldiers'. Curran tried unsuccessfully to have the indictment quashed on the grounds that Orr should have been charged with high treason. Wheatly as a witness made a

---

[42] Statistics relating to persons charged and convicted or acquitted at the assizes are to be found in the reports of the inspector-general of prisons for 1797, 1798, 1799 (*Commons' Jn. Ire.*, xvii, pp. dlxxiii–dclxxxiii; xviii, pp. ccxxxiii–cccxlvii; xix, pp. dccxxxi–dcccxlix). In a few cases it is surprising to see 'U.I.' appended to a charge, for instance in a case of four men accused of stealing hay. The explanation is that the accused were involved in taking two oaths—one, not to disclose a theft of government property, the other, to assist the French (*Free. Jn.*, 21 Dec. 1797).

good impression on the trial judge, Chief baron Yelverton; the evidence for the defence according to the attorney-general was 'in my judgement supported by subordination only'; and Orr was found guilty and sentenced to death. The jury, who took eleven hours to arrive at a verdict, added a recommendation to mercy and Yelverton, a sensitive man, was greatly moved when delivering sentence. Strenuous efforts were made to obtain a reprieve—it being asserted that some of the jury had drunk a considerable amount of whiskey while deliberating on a verdict and that Wheatly (who may have been unbalanced) was an unreliable witness. Yelverton stated that all but one of the gentlemen of the county whom he had consulted agreed that it was necessary to make an example of Orr, and he was executed in October 1797. At his execution he bore himself well, and in his dying declaration denounced the way in which the trial had been conducted and asserted his innocence—making it clear, however, that he was a United Irishman. The United Irishmen treated his execution as a judicial murder and a mourning card was circulated in Ulster, bearing the words 'sacred to the memory of William Orr . . . an awful sacrifice to Irish freedom on the altar of British tyranny, by the hands of perjury through the influence of corruption and the connivance of partial justice'.[43]

The low conviction rate at both assizes is understandable. The possibility that a severe penalty, death or transportation, might be incurred, probably made juries sometimes reluctant to convict, and the emphasis on a meticulous observance of procedural rules benefited the accused. Curran, an outstanding counsel for the defence, was quick to try and get an indictment quashed on an irregularity. In Weldon's case (1795) he objected to the accused, an ex-soldier, being described as a yeoman; in the Sheares case (1798), he argued that the grand jury, which had returned a true bill, was improperly constituted because it had included a naturalized subject. In both instances he was overruled but his submissions illustrate prevailing standards. It must also be taken into account that in an age which insisted on a strict observance of legal forms, the prosecution had to rely

---

[43] Lady Moira to Napier, 16 Oct. 1797 (Add. MS 49103); A. Wolfe to E. Cooke, 19 Sept. 1797 (I.S.P.O. 620/34/22); Yelverton to ——, 25 Sept. 1797 (620/32/142, 620/36/34).

largely for material on untrained police officers and justices of the peace, who were often careless and whose zeal, when they possessed it, was not always tempered by discretion. The attorney-general's criticism of 'the slowness' with which the justices in Monaghan sent up their cases and 'the little care they take in preparing them', could probably have been repeated in other counties. At the same assizes in Louth, what might have been an important prosecution for treason of an influential group, including Hugh O'Reilly, Esq., a postmaster and a schoolmaster, brought by an active magistrate, completely collapsed owing to the absence of a key crown witness— who, according to the attorney-general, was a man of bad character.[44]

To reduce the number of unsuccessful prosecutions the government, before the summer assizes of 1797, arranged that Robert Day, a K.C. who was soon to be placed on the bench, should visit gaols and make preliminary investigations. At Naas, Day discharged sixteen prisoners who, he thought, could not have been convicted; each of whom, he hoped, instead of being exhilarated by 'the triumph and audacity inspired by impunity', carried home 'impressions of the moderation and mercy of the government'. At Philipstown he held 'a bed of justice', and released on bail about half of 'the wretches cooped up and crammed upon each other like barrelled herrings in this vile gaol'. At Mullingar he suggested that eleven men sentenced to imprisonment for resisting the militia act should be released on account of exemplary conduct, and in dealing with prisoners in that county he had 'no scruples to indulge in mercy, because the lust of plunder was a short lived fever, on which lenient means may satisfactorily be tried'. But, he reflected, 'what is to be done, where a diabolical enthusiasm is the principle of action, where the criminal meets his fate with the intrepidity of a martyr and laughs alike at moderation and death'. At Cork, Day found the gaol crowded, with many of the prisoners likely to escape conviction because the crown witnesses had either bad reputations or were reluctant to come forward. Day himself had one exasperating failure as prosecuting counsel. He had 'set [his] heart' on convicting John Hurley (charged

---

[44] A. Wolfe to E. Cooke, 1, 10 Sept. 1797 (I.S.P.O. 620/32/93, 109); *D.E.P.*, 1 Sept. 1797.

with administering an illegal oath) and his gang, but 'the two principal witnesses betrayed us upon the trial' (he managed to get one of the witnesses sentenced for perjury). However, he secured the conviction of Richard Dry, who had been active in building up the United Irishmen's organization in Cork city. Day considered prosecuting Dry for treason but the prospect of 'inflammatory speeches being made by citizen lawyers', made him substitute the lesser charge of administering an illegal oath. Dry was found guilty and sentenced to transportation. One of the two crown witnesses was 'a reluctant, prevaricating rascal', but the other, a Roscommon militiaman, was excellent.[45]

It was often difficult for the crown in political cases to secure credible witnesses. Needless to say much of the information reaching the government, while useful as indicating trends and dangers, was inadmissible as legal evidence, and some of those who were ready to give information to the government were very reluctant to appear in court. This is understandable. A crown witness could be exposed to bitter hostility and prejudice, especially in a rural community. On occasion a crown witness was murdered; sometimes magistrates were hard put to it to protect witnesses or potential witnesses. Moreover, by getting on the table (the Irish equivalent of entering the box) a crown witness could expose himself to a severe ordeal. Counsel for the accused often decided that attack was the most effective form of defence, and the jury would be asked to take into account much of the witness's past when weighing his credibility. For instance in the Dublin defender trials in 1795, it was suggested that the principal crown witness had denied the existence of God and misappropriated a punch ladle belonging to his employer.[46] When, at the Derry assizes of 1797, a man was accused of administering an illegal oath, a witness for the defence asserted that the principal witness for the crown, a sergeant, had been observed 'admiring himself in the glass [and saying] that he was a very handsome fellow . . . and expected to get a commission'. Since a crown witness had often been an accomplice of the accused and had been rewarded

[45] R. Day to E. Cooke, 2, 4 Aug. 1797 (I.S.P.O. 620/32/68); R. Day to the attorney-general, 19 Aug. 1797 and attorney-general to Day, 16 Aug. 1797 (620/34/14); R. Day to H. Pelham, 12, 22 Sept. 1797 (620/32/130, 136); R. Day to ——, 29 Sept. 1797 (620/32/145).
[46] D.E.P., 29 Dec. 1795.

(or compensated for the risks he ran) by the government, it was easy to suggest mercenary motives for his testimony and to emphasize his duplicity and inconsistency of political purpose. In fact crown witnesses to some extent were bound to be drawn from the confused, impulsive and nervous, many of whom were likely to be recruited into a large and enthusiastic movement. One crown witness, Ferris, an attorney who gave important evidence against a group charged at the close of 1797 with planning the murder of Lord Carhampton, justified himself by explaining that he did not regard the United Irishmen's oath as binding, 'but would have taken it to find out what he wanted . . . it was therefore as a friend to the government that he became a United Irishman'.[47] A violent conservative wanted the counsel for the crown to explain to juries in political trials that it was impossible to procure witnesses among the classes of honest or honourable men for none such would be found to associate with men confederated to murder and plunder. It was a point which the attorney-general, Wolfe, made when he asked, 'but by whom can men that have committed crime in secrecy ever be convicted but by accomplices?' 'If men of purity and innocence only can convict in such cases,' he went on to argue, 'crimes the most dangerous to the public must for ever pass unpunished.'[48]

If the character defects of a prosecution witness could make an unbiased jury hesitant to convict, they provided a juryman biased in favour of the accused with an excuse for finding a verdict of not guilty. During the lent assizes conservatives were convinced that juries in the north were biased or intimidated. According to Marcus Beresford, who appeared for the crown on the north-east circuit, at Armagh, some jurymen, who appeared anxious to serve, manifested their delight when a witness 'prevaricated'. There were no convictions for political offences, and a stout upholder of authority after the assizes decided that 'the game is nearly up . . . no juries, no prosecutors, no evidence against any person under the denomination of a United Irishman, men of property and clergy flying into the

---

[47] *D.E.P.*, 4 May, 23 Oct. 1797. Carhampton secured for Ferris, who, he considered, had displayed 'courage and ability in the matter of the conspiracy', a place in the excise in England. But Ferris, who was idle, would not get up in the morning and was dismissed (Carhampton to E. Cooke, 30 July 1799, H.O. 100/89).

[48] F. Higgins to ——, 29 Jan. 1798 (I.S.P.O. 620/36/226); *D.E.P.*, 31 Dec. 1795.

garrison towns'. In County Down, Beresford was told that 'owing to the misconduct of a bailiff', only six jurymen were summoned from the Hertford estates, and 'those notoriously disaffected'. In fact, in the opinion of an active magistrate, there were only two men on the whole panel that could be 'relied on'. According to the solicitor-general, in Donegal the high sheriff omitted some suitable people from the panel, and in Tyrone, Mr Corry, Lord Belmore's heir, who had been unable to induce his tenants to serve, had himself acted as foreman of a petit jury on which several grand jurors served. In Monaghan, owing to the 'bias of the juries and the terror of the witnesses', together with the failure of the gentry, 'timid to a degree', to back the high sheriff, all the United Irishmen charged were acquitted and the whole county was 'in a flame from bonfires and rejoicing'.[49]

Of course it was also asserted that on occasion the crown or local conservatives attempted by improper means to secure a favourable jury. The *Northern Star* declared that at the London-derry summer assizes in 1796 the panel had been unfairly formed. In reply it was said that what appeared to be a device for putting partisans on the panel was in fact a reasonable administrative practice. Undoubtedly, at the same assizes in the following year Hill, a strong upholder of law and order, was very dissatisfied with 'the complexion' of the juries; and the crown in the case of Robert Moore, an ironmonger, and William McClintock, charged with taking the United Irishmen's oath, decided it was advisable to accept Curran's plea that they had taken an oath 'under the idea that it did not contain any engagement of treasonable nature', and allowed them to be discharged on taking the oath of allegiance. Hill's discomfiture was increased by the behaviour of Mr Justice Downes 'a phlegmatic, cowardly heap', who allowed Grey, a crown witness and 'a very sharp fellow', to be discredited 'for the merest trifle of difference from something he swore'.[50] At the Down assize of 1797 Curran elicited that the Revd John Cleland, Lord Londonderry's agent, had assisted the sheriff in

---

[49] John Maxwell's secret committee, 1797, note-books (I.S.P.O. 620/34/54); A. Ker to T. Pelham, 9 Apr. 1797 (I.S.P.O. 620/29/201); *D.J.*, 28 Feb. 1799.

[50] *D.E.P.*, 8 Sept. 1796, 23 Dec. 1797; G. Hill to E. Cooke, 8 Sept. 1796, 22 July 1797 (I.S.P.O. 620/32/114 and 620/31/262).

forming the panel. Cleland described himself as a very conscientious man being influenced by public opinion in what he
did, and went on to say that he understood United Irishmen to
be robbers, murderers and obstructors of justice. 'What then,'
said Mr Curran, 'was your private opinion in no way biased by
public opinion?' 'Not in the least Sir.' 'Upon your oath Sir,
nothing but a pure regard to abstract justice governed you in
what you did?' 'Upon my oath Sir, nothing else.' 'Very well, as
being a minister of the Gospel of truth you must be believed.'
Both sides seem to have been gratified by this exchange.[51]
Finally in the king's bench early in 1798 it was alleged by
Curran that a County Antrim jury panel had been prepared
not by the high sheriff but by persons 'interested in the prosecution' who marked names as well affected, disaffected, timid
and bad. The only witness he produced in favour of this
allegation was General Barber, who admitted he had questioned
the high sheriff about the panel. But, Barber explained, 'the
high sheriff had answered him harshly and seemed displeased
about any person interfering with his panel but himself'.
In Barber's opinion the panel was, politically speaking,
'chequered'.[52]

The United Irishmen certainly did try and influence juries
by propaganda. At the time of the lent assizes of 1797 printed
papers were distributed addressed to the Antrim, Down and
Armagh jurymen. Jurymen in Antrim and Down were exhorted
not to become agents of coercion nor to proceed 'from vague,
general and indiscriminate condemnation of certain principles'
to the condemnation of human beings. The Armagh jurymen
were reminded that from 1793 the people had been deprived of
their constitutional rights.[53] The United Irishmen in some areas
also spent considerable sums in subsidizing the defence of
persons accused of political offences. By April 1797 the County
Down United Irishmen had spent £500 in legal expenses.
After the lent assizes they paid out £750 to witnesses, attorneys

[51] *D.E.P.*, 4 May 1797.

[52] *D.J.*, 25 Jan. 1798.

[53] Printed papers addressed to Antrim, Armagh and Down juries (I.S.P.O.
620/29/88, 335). The United Irishmen's Antrim county committee in Dec. 1796
declared that 'if there is any United Irishman on the jury that will commit any of
the prisoners that is confined for being a United Irishman [they] ought to lose their
existence' (*Commons' Jn. Ire.*, xvii, p. dcccxliii).

and counsel, including 100 guineas to Curran, whom a Belfast bookseller was directed to get down 'on as cheap terms as he could'. A few months later Curran was paid 300 guineas by the United Irishmen for his work at the Armagh, Antrim and Down summer assizes.[54] At the 1797 summer assizes in Kildare a group of radicals led by Lord Edward Fitzgerald took steps to help a number of the accused and Day indignantly reported that in Cork that 'arch traitor', Roger O'Connor, had provided counsel for prisoners, spirited away witnesses, and, adding insult to injury, had sat amongst the barristers in court, though he never practised.[55]

At the beginning of 1798 the government's legal campaign suffered a series of setbacks in the king's bench. In January Patrick Finney, a tobacco spinner, who had been arrested in 1797, was brought to trial charged with treason. Evidence was given that he had been active in organizing United Irishmen's societies in south-west Dublin, and that he had planned an attack on an ordnance store. Curran conducted the defence with considerable skill. He had some of the prosecution's evidence declared inadmissible on the ground that it related to acts committed in the Coombe, which lay in the county not in the city of Dublin to which the indictment referred; and in cross-examination he forced the principal crown witness to admit that he had probably, when drunk, pretended to be an excise man and extorted a gratuity. Finney was found not guilty; bonfires in the Coombe celebrated his release, and twenty-four persons charged with him were discharged without being brought to trial. When shortly, afterwards, three prisoners from Ulster, Burnside, Barret and Shanahan were brought before the king's bench charged with treason, the first two managed to have their trials postponed and the last-named was discharged, as the principal crown witness, 'Smith' (Bird) had disappeared. At the 1798 lent assizes about 250 persons, approximately 21 per cent of those brought to trial, were charged with political offences, and the conviction ratio for political offences was 35 per cent, compared with 31·7 for all offences. Thirty persons were sentenced to death for

[54] *Commons' Jn. Ire.*, xvii, pp. dccclx, dccccxiv.
[55] J. Pollock to ——, 30 Aug. 1797; R. Day to ——, 29 Sept. 1797 (I.S.P.O. 620/32/89, 145).

political offences (including four Orangemen who had attacked the house of a catholic in county Antrim), of whom thirteen were reprieved.

Taking everything into account it is perhaps not altogether surprising that of those brought to trial in the higher courts for political offences between the beginning of 1797 and the middle of 1798 only about one-third were convicted. It is also scarcely surprising that some upholders of authority were exasperated and resorted to extra-legal methods for enforcing order. During the summer of 1795 the government sent General Lord Carhampton to the disturbed areas in the west. A prominent member of a family whose ambitions and quarrels provided rich material for gossip, Carhampton had been Wilkes's successful opponent in the famous Middlesex election. At Westminster he had defended the slave trade with crude wit; in the Irish house of commons he vigorously attacked the abuses of the tithe system. He had considerable experience of agrarian trouble. During a quarrel with his father he had besieged the family seat at the head of 'a lawless banditti, armed with clubs and bludgeons' (which perhaps explains why his father invited Wilkes to visit Ireland). He had campaigned with success against whiteboys and defenders and his methods, apparently a blend of severity and leniency, won him commendations in the liberal press.[56] In his tour of the west in 1795 he seems to have invigorated the local magistracy, and visiting Roscommon gaol he released some prisoners whom he thought were penitent— possibly there was insufficient evidence against them to secure a conviction. He also captured some 'deluded wretches' taking part in an illegal assembly and sent them off to serve in the fleet—they may possibly have preferred this fate to being tried on a capital charge.[57] His example was followed by magistrates in several districts, who, 'not finding that the regular mode of endeavouring to convict the offenders had the effect which was expected, . . . in cases where they were convicted of the guilt of the person sent them on board the tender' which received recruits for the navy.[58] Two Westmeath justices of the peace,

[56] Lord Mayo, *A history of the Kildare hunt* (1913), pp. 28–9; Carhampton to J. Wilkes, 9 June 1784 (Add. MS 30872); *D.E.P.*, 23 Aug. 1783, 21 May 1795; *H.J.*, 22 Sept. 1790.

[57] *Free. Jn.*, 30 July 1795.

[58] Camden to Portland, 6 Nov. 1795 (H.O. 100/59).

Anthony O'Reilly and William Webb, 'in the dead hour of the night', arrested three men and sent them to the tender. When the matter was brought before the court of common pleas it granted an attachment against the magistrates. They tried to justify their action by explaining that it was impossible to secure sworn informations against their prisoners because of the terror prevailing in the county. 'Whether the times be warm or cold', the chief justice of the common pleas declared, 'this court feels but one climate.' 'God forbid', he added, 'that suspicion should be deemed to be guilt. It is the worst species of tyranny.' Mr Justice Downes reminded the magistrates that their authority was committed to them for the protection not the oppression of the subject. About the same time an attempt by the military authorities to deal in a summary fashion with agrarian disturbances in the north was censured by the courts. Twenty-six men, 'apprehended as defenders' in County Armagh were committed to the Dublin marshalsea as deserters. They were brought before the king's bench by a writ of habeas corpus and discharged, their counsel having argued that the warrant on which they had been committed did not state that they had been enlisted.[59]

Early in 1796 the behaviour of some over-energetic upholders of order received retrospective sanction by an indemnity act. Having stated that magistrates and other persons 'in order to check insurrection and maintain the peace, had since 1 January 1795 committed acts 'not justifiable by law', this measure went on to provide that any proceedings brought against them for such acts should be void. This indemnity act proved to be the first of six almost identical measures passed during the next five years, which, taken together, covered the period 1 January 1795 to July 1801. The protection given was not absolute. In the case of *Wright* v. *Fitzgerald*, heard in March 1799, Mr Justice Chamberlain stated that a defendant who claimed to be protected by the indemnity act was required to show 'in his justification' that he had used every possible means to ascertain the guilt which he had punished and, that above all, no deviation from the common principles of humanity should appear in his conduct. In April 1799 a further indemnity act was introduced

[59] *H.J.*, 29 Jan. 1796; *B.N.L.*, 1 Feb. 1796; *Hibernian Magazine*, 1795, pp. 478–9; *H.J.*, 18 Nov. 1795.

and quickly passed covering the period 1 November 1797 to 6 October 1798. It provided that if a plaintiff was to succeed in any action brought against any person for an act done in suppression of rebellion, the jury must find that the act was done maliciously and not with the purpose of suppressing rebellion. Furthermore, in such an action the judge was empowered to set aside a jury's verdict in favour of the plaintiff, though if he did so the plaintiff would not be subject to double costs.

The indemnity act of 1796 was accompanied by a measure greatly increasing the powers of the justices of the peace, the Insurrection act. It laid down that to administer an unlawful oath was felony punishable by death, and that to take such an oath was a felony punishable by transportation. An unlawful oath was defined as an oath binding the person taking it to be a member of a seditious society, or to obey the orders of a committee not lawfully constituted, or not to give evidence against any associate. It also provided that if a person who had sworn an information was murdered before the trial of the person or persons accused in his information, it could be used in evidence at a trial held subsequent to his murder. Persons having arms in their possession were to notify a justice of the peace and justices of the peace were empowered on 'reasonable grounds' to search for arms. Justices of the peace assembled at a special session could request the lord lieutenant to proclaim their county or a part of it as being in 'a state of disturbance'. In a proclaimed area justices of the peace could search houses for arms, a curfew could be enforced and two justices of the peace could try 'an idle and disorderly person', and sentence him to serve in the fleet—with an appeal to quarter sessions. In a proclaimed area the following were to be regarded as 'idle and disorderly': persons found out of their dwellings during curfew who could not prove they were upon their 'lawful occasions'; persons in a public house between 9 p.m. and 6 a.m.; persons taking unlawful oaths or forming part of a tumultuous assembly, and 'a man or boy' distributing seditious literature (a woman distributing seditious literature could be sent for three months to gaol).

At the end of June 1797, after the great naval mutinies, the navy decided not to accept Irish recruits who had been taken

into custody by the civil power. Perhaps in anticipation of this
move the Irish parliament a few weeks earlier amended the
Insurrection act by empowering justices of the peace to send
disorderly persons to serve in the army as well as the fleet. But
the army was also very reluctant to accept conscripts of this
type though in the end it seems to have agreed that some Irish
political offenders could be sent to the 60th, serving in the West
Indies. The issue might have produced a serious constitutional
crisis in 1798. Portland was extremely annoyed to discover in
the bill of that year, continuing the Insurrection act, a reference
to naval and military service. Only the fear of creating 'a
sensation' overcame his reluctance to return the bill with the
royal assent signified.[60]

The British cabinet seems to have been astonished at the
necessity for a measure on the lines of the Insurrection act 'in a
country enjoying the same form of government as this', but
Pelham despondently explained that if the Insurrection act,
together with the Civil bill act, did not pacify the country they
would be reduced to relying on the sword.[61] When the Insurrection bill was before the house of commons Grattan used the
opportunity to deliver an eloquent denunciation of the
government's failure to cope with the disturbances in Armagh.
Lawrence Parsons however, in a couple of powerful speeches
concentrated on criticizing the bill which he considered to be a
violation of the first principles of the constitution and which
would be regarded by the poor as an example of class legislation.
It was a mistake, he argued, to entrust such extensive powers to
justices of the peace who were 'in a state of inflammation', and
with copious quotations from Blackstone, he pleaded for trial
by jury in prosecutions brought under the act. A blunt conservative, Cuffe, retorted that 'Blackstone's doctrine was
calculated for quiet times', and it was contended that jurymen
living in rural areas could be intimidated and that trial by jury
offered many opportunities to an ingenious advocate to employ

[60] E. Nepean to regulating officers at Dublin, Belfast and Cork, 10 July 1797
(Adm. 2/1186); Portland to Camden, 3 July 1797, 30 Mar. 1798; Camden to
Portland, 25 July 1797 (H.O. 100/72, 75); Portland to Camden, 16 Mar. 1796;
Portland to H. Pelham, 20 Mar. 1796; H. Pelham to Portland, 31 Mar. 1796 (H.O.
100/62).
[61] Portland to Camden, 16 Mar. 1796; Portland to Pelham, 20 Mar. 1796;
Pelham to Portland, 31 Mar. 1796 (H.O. 100/62).

legal technicalities to prevent a conviction. 'Such was the humanity of the law calculated for times of peace when the impunity of the offender did not threaten the subversion of the state', Robert Stewart (the future Lord Castlereagh) explained, 'that the chance was five to one that he would escape though guilty'. Wolfe, the attorney-general, admitted that the bill was 'not altogether founded on the principles of the constitution', but maintained 'it has for its object the preservation of the constitution', and that 'its object is not punishment but prevention'. The country gentlemen were clearly alarmed by the condition of the country and the bill passed without a division, an attempt by Lord Edward Fitzgerald to divide against the second reading being unsuccessful because no other M.P. could be found to act as a teller for the noes. [62] A year later George Ponsonby, arguing that the house had been over-impressed by a few shocking outrages, moved that the Insurrection act should be repealed as a conciliatory gesture to the northern radicals. In the ensuing debate a rising young M.P., Charles Kendal Bushe, declared that only firmness would save Ireland and 'anything like a cowardly, crooked, left-handed policy' would be ruinous; Lawrence Parsons said that while he still thought the act was unconstitutional he opposed its repeal as a concession to men armed against the state and Ponsonby's motion was rejected by 127 to 15.

A year after its enactment Camden confessed that the Insurrection act had failed to achieve the results he had hoped for, largely owing to the passivity of the local magistracy. [63] Some of the most important provisions of the act could be brought into force only if the justices of the peace requested that an area should be proclaimed and by the end of April 1797 only one county (Down) and substantial part of five others (all in Ulster) had been proclaimed. When a group of J.P.s in County Meath, shortly after the act went on the statute book, considered asking for a proclamation an active magistrate (recently the subject of newspaper eulogy) successfully opposed

---

[62] *D.E.P.*, 27 Feb., 3 Mar. 1796.

[63] Camden to Portland, 9 Mar. 1797 (H.O. 100/69). Camden's opinion is borne out by the number of J.P.'s reported as being present at meetings to discuss the proclamation of a county—in Down 30, in Clare 12, in Mayo 8 (*S.N.L.*, 15 Mar. 1797, 21 Apr. 1798, 23 Mar. 1799).

the suggestion. In his private opinion it would have been dangerous to place such 'extensive discretionary powers' in the hands of some of his fellow magistrates.[64] A highly intelligent young M.P., Castlereagh, thought the Insurrection act was in one important respect deficient. The whiteboy act of 1776 empowered a J.P. to examine on oath any person who he suspected might give evidence of an offence. Castlereagh thought that this act (amended to cover political conspiracy) might with advantage be brought into operation in the north.[65] However, between the beginning of May 1797 and the close of the year areas in ten counties in the south and west were proclaimed; and from the beginning of 1798 proclaiming went forward vigorously, six whole counties (Cork, Dublin, Kilkenny, King's, Tipperary and Wexford) being proclaimed by the middle of May.

It is impossible to say to what extent the Insurrection act was enforced within the proclaimed areas. For instance it is hard to know how many persons were sent to serve in the fleet under the powers conferred by the act. Camden in July 1797 asserted that the number of persons sent to the fleet both as a result of Carhampton's 'summary mode' and under the Insurrection act amounted to less than 200. Of the 1,219 men enlisted in the navy in Ireland between May 1797 and May 1798, 185 are said to have been 'sent by the civil power'—of these 97 were enlisted in Dublin, 74 in Belfast and 4 in Londonderry. Of course they may not all have been sent under the Insurrection act and to complicate things further it appears that some United Irishmen and defenders sent to the fleet were allowed by the regulating officers to enlist as volunteers.[66] After the outbreak of the rebellion in May 1798 'disorderly persons' seem to have been largely dealt with by the courts martial, but there are references to men being detained at depots under the Insurrection act in 1799—for instance 51 being held at Belfast and 25 from County Clare, 5 from county Limerick and 99

---

[64] G. Lambart to ——, 23 Apr. 1796 (I.S.P.O. 620/23/72); *D.J.*, 9 Apr. 1796.

[65] Castlereagh to H. Pelham, 12 Nov. 1796 (I.S.P.O. 620/18/8).

[66] Camden to Portland, July 1797 (H.O. 100/72). Return to Irish house of lords (Adm. 1/640); P. Crosby to R. Marshall, 22 June 1797 (I.S.P.O. 620/31/138). Abstract of defenders sent to the fleet (620/31/204).

from counties Cork, Carlow, Tipperary, Wexford and Wicklow.[67]

When striving to enforce the Insurrection act some zealous magistrates came up against legal obstacles. After part of King's County had been proclaimed the justices of the peace sent 'a number of idle and disorderly fellows' to Kilmainham from where they were dispatched to the recruiting tender which received naval recruits. One of them obtained a few guineas from a friend and managed to secure writs of habeas corpus for the recruits from the king's bench. When the prisoners were produced before the court, MacNally argued on their behalf that their committal should be quashed, since the return did not make clear that the requirements of the Insurrection act had been fulfilled, and the court discharged the prisoners. Shortly afterwards the court discharged eleven men from Westmeath and two from County Londonderry, brought before it on writs of habeas corpus from the tender to which they apparently had been sent under the Insurrection act; and early in 1798 MacNally secured writs of habeas corpus on behalf of Carlow men detained in Carlow gaol and on the tender at Duncannon. Some Westmeath J.P.s greatly resented the attitude of the king's bench and a crown council on circuit had to explain to them that it would be 'criminal' for the government to interfere between the courts and a subject.[68] On two occasions when a writ of habeas corpus was resisted it had probably been issued on behalf of persons detained under the Insurrection act. When three men, held in Monaghan gaol, presumably under the Insurrection act, were sent to Duncannon fort to be enlisted in the Glengarry fencibles, the high sheriff of Monaghan was afraid that he might be fined by the assize judge and writs of habeas corpus were served on the general commanding the fort. On his failure to produce the prisoners promptly, MacNally took steps to have an attachment issued against him. It may be added that in the general's opinion the men in dispute were not good military material—they were not young and had families. Shortly afterwards, when Captain Lees, the naval regulating officer at Belfast, refused to accept service of a writ of habeas

[67] Lists, 5 May 1799, 4 June 1799, 20 July 1799 (I.S.P.O. 620/7/79/16, 200, 22).
[68] D.E.P., 22 June, 11 July, 12 Sept. 1796; W. Lambert to ——, 30 July 1797 (I.S.P.O. 620/31/291); R. Day to E. Cooke, 24 Aug. 1797 (620/32/68); D.E.P., 15 Feb. 1798.

corpus, throwing it on the ground and threatening to lodge the server in the guard-house, Sampson secured an attachment against him from the king's bench.[69]

In October 1796, at the beginning of the 1796–7 parliamentary session, the habeas corpus act was partially suspended, it being enacted that any person suspected of treasonable activities could be detained by a warrant signed by the lord lieutenant or the chief secretary. At the same time parliament authorized the formation of a yeomanry force which could assist the army in the event of invasion and perform police duties. Early in the revolutionary war yeomanry corps—cavalry units, officered by the country gentry and recruited from their tenantry—had been raised in England and from the middle nineties volunteer corps were being formed all over the country. There was in Ireland a long tradition of self-help in defence and one of the measures Fitzwilliam had in mind when he came to Ireland was the formation of a yeomanry force, which would both be useful in the event of an invasion and form 'an armed constabulary' to assist the magistracy. Since the more substantial tenants, from whom the rank and file would be recruited, were largely catholics, the creation of the force was closely connected with catholic emancipation.[70] Fitzwilliam's successor Camden was at first against encouraging any section of the Irish public to array themselves in arms, and at the close of 1795 he quietly prompted Lord Mountjoy to oppose a scheme of Carhampton's for organizing armed associations of loyalists in County Dublin. Camden seems to have agreed with Portland that in a country such as Ireland 'where the temper of the public was so liable to irritation . . . and where there are so many parties, religious as well as political', it would be unwise to form yeomanry corps. The success of the Orange societies and the volunteers showed how very easily corps might become sectarian or political associations. But throughout 1796 disorder was spreading, gentlemen were pressing the government to

---

[69] W. Fawcett to ——, 3 Nov. 1797, 12 Feb. 1798 (I.S.P.O. 620/33/10A, 620/35/138); General Wilford to T. Pelham, 15 Aug. 1797 (620/32/50/91A); *D.E.P.*, 15 Feb. 1798.

[70] Grattan at the beginning of 1794 suggested the formation of independent companies with officers commissioned by the crown (S. Douglas to E. Nepean, 12 Feb. 1794, H.O. 100/47); Fitzwilliam to Portland, 10, 15 Jan. 1795 (H.O. 100/56).

encourage the formation of local defence corps, and one active magistrate pointed out that excellent material for such a corps might be found round Moville amongst the marquis of Donegall's tenants, 'hardy, resolute and little acquainted with newspapers and the trash of illuminating absurdity that blaze through them'. Two active Tyrone magistrates, Thomas Knox, M.P., and the Revd William Richardson, a geologist and sometime fellow of Trinity, tried to hustle the government into action by appealing to public opinion. About the middle of June, spending a day *tête à tête*, they agreed civil war was impending. Knox frequently repeated the adage, 'the first up will carry the day', and together they drafted the plan of an association to defend the king and constitution to be joined by loyal men. Having submitted their plan to a number of local magistrates and obtained their approval, they published it. By August, Camden was convinced a yeomanry force was desirable and one of the first measures laid before parliament, when it met in October for a special session, was a bill for encouraging enrolment in voluntary corps under officers commissioned by the crown.[71]

The government was determined to prevent the Irish yeomanry from becoming an independent and possibly politically-inspired force. Not only were its officers appointed by the lord lieutenant, but each corps had a permanent sergeant, a regular, attached and corps were grouped under the supervision of brigade majors, who reported to the general commanding the district. Arms and ammunition issued to a corps had to be strictly accounted for and if part of a corps was placed on permanent duty the men were paid and drilled at regular intervals. The military value of the force was bound to be limited. Yeomen were not given the thorough drilling which it was believed was required if a man was to be an efficient soldier. But they could perform police duties and, having a modicum of discipline and being armed, they could cope with rural rioters. The existence of the force both demonstrated the strength, cohesion, and confidence of Irish conservatives and angered radicals, who regarded it as a symbol of the harsh and arrogant

---

[71] Camden to T. Pelham, 30 Oct. 1796 (Add. MS 33101), 10 Aug. 1796 (Add. MS 33102); Portland to Camden, 24 Aug. 1796 (H.O. 100/62); W. Richardson, *History of the origin of the Irish yeomanry* (1801).

determination of the privileged to maintain their domination. In spite of radical hostility the force grew rapidly. At the beginning of 1797 there were 440 corps with about 24,000 men (rather over half being mounted), and by June 1798 there were 540 corps with about 40,000 men (of whom about one-third were mounted).[72] The force was predominantly protestant but there were numerous catholic yeomen. There were indeed corps whose commanding officers were catholic, for instance those commanded by Lord Kenmare, Lord Fingall and Sir Edward Bellew. In Cork city there were two corps, the protestant Cork volunteers and the Loyal Cork legion, which a number of catholic gentlemen joined. Even in County Down, where the sectarian feeling ran strongly, Lord Downshire was 'happy to say that there are some respectable and loyal papists' in a Newry corps.[73] On the other hand when a yeomanry corps was raised on Lord Downshire's King's County estate, it was only after some hesitation that four catholics were allowed to join (the total strength of the corps was thirty-eight) and Lord Fitzwilliam's agent, who found the Wicklow protestants were against admitting catholics to the yeomanry, managed to get only two catholics into the Newtownmountkennedy corps (about 40 strong). It should also be noted that John Keogh, the catholic and radical leader, boasted that when he heard J. T. O'Brien, the well-known catholic merchant, intended to join the yeomanry, he had cooled O'Brien's volunteer courage by threatening a catholic boycott of his goods.[74]

There was bound to be opposition to the formation of a force which its critics could contend was simply the conservative party in arms. Some liberals, such as Grattan, would almost certainly have preferred a revival of the old volunteers and at the outset William Thomas Smith, sometime colonel of the Independent Dublin volunteers tendered to the government a

---

[72] *Standing orders for the yeomanry corps of Ireland: Dublin Castle, 15 May 1798* (1798); *A list of the counties of Ireland and the respective yeomanry corps, 1 June 1798* (1798). For numbers see returns (I.S.P.O. 620/28/81 and 620/26/175), and Castlereagh to G. Nugent, 24 June 1798 (Army Museum MS 6807/174.)

[73] Downshire to ———, 25 Nov. 1796 (I.S.P.O. 620/26/77).

[74] Downshire to ———, 24 Nov. 1796 (I.S.P.O. 620/26/76); J. N. Everard to Downshire, 17 Oct. 1796 (Downshire typescript); W. Wainwright to Fitzwilliam, 27 Nov., 7 Dec. 1796 (W.W.M. f. 30), F. Higgins to ———, 2 Nov. 1796 (620/18).

unanimous offer of service from his corps. Cooke replied
tactfully, suggesting it would be convenient if gentlemen joined
corps which were already established. When it was proposed
that a corps be raised in Trinity, three of the fellows were said
to have disapproved of the suggestion, as 'tending to idleness
and a relaxation of academical discipline'. A pamphlet was
circulated in the college imploring undergraduates not to lay
aside their gowns 'for the fantastical pageantry of mimic
warfare'. The corps, it was argued, might be used to crush the
people and the news that the government was reduced to
arming undergraduates would arouse the contempt of the
enemy. However, a large number of undergraduates joined the
college corps, which was organized in four companies each
commanded by a fellow, including two well-known liberals,
Stokes and Browne. Browne was so impressed by the complexities of military science that he produced a short manual on
tactics for the corps.[75]

In the north many radicals were strongly opposed to the
formation of the new force. 'No man of honour', a presbyterian
minister declared, 'would wear the coat of a yeoman.' At a
Letterkenny meeting to form a corps a number of men refused
to take the oath of allegiance. At Cookstown it was said that
'the plan of raising a yeomanry corps is so odious to the people'
that Stewart of Killymoon would not be able to form a corps—
but in fact he succeeded. Thomas Knox, while delighted at the
response of the Dungannon area, gloomily prophesied towards
the close of 1796 that not a corps could be raised between there
and 'the northern ocean' except at Stewartstown, Lord
Londonderry's seat.[76] The formation of a yeomanry corps in
Belfast, the headquarters of Ulster radicalism, was bound to be
seen by both conservatives and radicals as a challenge. When
the sovereign, John Brown, broached the subject of a town
meeting to discuss the formation of a corps, he was incensed to
hear that the opportunity would be used to bring forward the

[75] W. Smith to ——, 2 Jan. 1797; E. Cooke to W. Smith, 27 Jan. 1797 (I.S.P.O.
620/28/89); *To the scholars and students of Trinity college Dublin* (1796); F. Higgins to
——, 19 Nov. 1796 (620/36/226); A. Browne, *Some few brief principles of tactics . . . for
the use of the college corps* (1797).

[76] Court martial of the Revd James Thompson, 3 July 1798 (I.S.P.O. 620/2/15/
68); A. J. Walsh to ——, 3 Nov. 1796 (620/26/14); J. Boyd to ——, Oct. 1796
(620/25/148); T. Knox to —— 27 Nov. 1796 (620/26/83).

reform question. The Irish administration, which heard this news at the time when the French fleet was reported to be hovering off the south-west coast, was also highly incensed. For a moment Pelham and Cooke seemed to have considered placing Belfast under military rule. Cooke said that if the citizens refused to join in the national defence effort, 'I would collect some mortars near the town, I would threaten privately to fire it, and I would bring a large corps of yeomanry into it'. Foster, the speaker spoke of detaining in custody any Belfast man 'who should use disaffected or rebellious language not by the civil but the military power'. In a day or so calmer counsels prevailed and it was decided to wait and see whether a Belfast yeomanry corps would be raised.

When a Belfast town meeting was held at the Exchange on 21 December 'the lower orders of the people poured into the meeting under the direction of . . . the set of United Irishmen' and the proceedings were controlled by the radicals. The Revd Mr Bristow who, as vicar of Belfast and a sometime sovereign, symbolized the established order, called on the citizens to support the formation of a yeomanry corps, but Arthur O'Connor, who was a candidate for County Antrim, delivered a violent attack on the government (without, the sovereign had to admit, using 'any treasonable expression'), and the meeting appointed a committee composed of seven radicals, Bristow and the sovereign, to draft resolutions. The two conservatives having resigned, the committee produced a series of resolutions, drafted according to Sampson, with the object of promoting 'a perfect union of sentiment'. These resolutions, which called for reform and emancipation and declared that the Belfast men were willing to embody themselves as volunteers, were passed at a street meeting on 2 January. A few days later an attempt was made to revive the Belfast volunteers. It failed, but only 53 citizens offered to join the yeomanry, which 'caused great exultation in the United body'. However, after 'much intrigue and interest had been employed', 150 recruits were obtained, and ultimately two Belfast yeomanry units were formed, a cavalry corps and an infantry corps which in time amounted to four companies. Though a number of the Belfast yeomanry early in 1797 made it clear that they 'remained firmly attached to the rights and liberties of all the people of Ireland', conservatives could congratulate themselves that Belfast was represented in the yeomanry movement.[77]

In raising a yeomanry force there was the obvious danger that the disaffected might arm themselves by coming forward as recruits. The sovereign of Belfast when he was contemplating forming a corps, considered 'the difficulty was who to take'. Lord O'Neill advised him 'to take all who offered', pointing out that they would have to take the oath of allegiance. In the event the sovereign found it hard to secure yeomanry recruits from a strongly liberal community but it was rumoured that in the north-east of Ulster United Irishmen were only too anxious to join the yeomanry and that in some Ulster towns, including Newry, the yeomanry could not be trusted. About the same time the government were warned (admittedly by a correspondent prone to over-emphasize) that in County Cork many were joining the yeomanry 'who were very far from being friends of king, church or constitution'.[78] In the spring of 1798 two corps near Charleville in north County Cork were found to be disaffected and the commanding officer of the Dunkerrin Cavalry in King's County reported that most of the catholics in his corps were United Irishmen.[79] When, towards the close of 1797, commanding officers in the south Wicklow and north Wexford area asked their men to swear that they were neither Orangemen nor United Irishmen, there was some trouble. Many of the yeomen in Grogan's Castletown cavalry who were catholics resigned; some catholics in Beauman's Colgreney cavalry refused to take the oath and were disarmed; and a number of White's Ballyellis infantry resigned and later acted as instructors to the insurgents. During the insurrection the Waterford merchant infantry expelled 8 yeomen suspected of being United Irishmen. In County Wicklow early in 1798 two corps, the Castle McAdam cavalry and infantry (recruited

[77] J. Brown to H. Pelham, 15, 26 Nov. 1796 (I.S.P.O. 620/26/123, 177); J. Brown to H. Pelham, 4 Jan. 1797 (620/28/31); E. Cooke to H. Pelham, and H. Pelham to J. Foster, 30 Dec. 1796; J. Foster to H. Pelham, 31 Dec. 1796 (620/26/178, 201, 202); N.S. 2, 6 Jan. 1797; D.E.P., 12 Jan. 1797; D.E.P., 16 Mar. 1797; B.N.L., 13 Mar. 1797; J. Brown to H. Pelham, 15 Dec. 1796 (I.S.P.O. 620/26/123).
[78] H. Alexander to ——, 15 Feb. 1797 (I.S.P.O. 620/28/219); J. Dawson to ——, 10 Jan. 1797 (620/28/80); E. Newenham to H. Pelham, 4 Dec. 1796 (620/26/128).
[79] Sir J. Stewart to Castlereagh, 22 Apr. 1798 (I.S.P.O. 620/36/197); J. F. Rolleston to Castlereagh, 19 May 1798 (620/37/106).

largely apparently from miners) were disarmed as unreliable. Later seventeen of Captain Stratford's corps, the Baltinglass cavalry, were reported to have been shot for intriguing with the insurgents. When Dunlavin in west Wicklow was menaced by the insurgents the yeomanry and militia officers of the small garrison decided to clear the gaol in a summary fashion and twenty-eight yeomen (nine of the Narramore cavalry and nineteen of the Ballycrow corps) who were 'notorious traitors' were shot, the other prisoners in the gaol being discharged.[80] During the insurrection three corps in County Kildare, the Athy cavalry, the East Narramore cavalry and the Moon and Talbotstown cavalry, were thought to be unreliable and were disarmed. In County Dublin it was reported that the Rathcoole infantry had agreed to join the rebels 'on first attack' and a sergeant of the corps was said to have become an insurgent colonel.[81]

In Dublin when the insurrection was raging the Merchants corps expelled eight members for being United Irishmen and the Saint Sepulchre's corps, being regarded as disaffected, was paraded and disbanded. A week later the Liberty Rangers expelled Jonathan Gray. As early as May 1797 the Liberty Rangers were rumoured to be disaffected and Gray, a young cotton-manufacturer, tried to build up the United Irishmen's organization in their ranks. He collected together some fellow members of the corps under the guise of planning a dance, told them that a party in the corps was black-balling all catholic and liberal-minded recruits, and proposed they regarded themselves as a baronial. Each member of the baronial was expected to be leader of a group of yeomen and it was said about eighty of the corps were sworn. They do not seem to have been very zealous. One of the baronial, Keane, a member of the Dublin society of United Irishmen, who had acted as Hamilton Rowan's attorney, declared in a long self-justificatory statement addressed to the government that 'I never intended to act and my not calling together my party arose from that motive, but I was afraid to appear so and I believe I said sometimes I did call

---

[80] M. Byrne, *Memoirs*, ed. S. Gwynn (1907), i, pp. 12–15; R. Uniacke to ——, 7 Nov. 1797 (I.S.P.O. 620/33/23); J. Hardy to Fitzwilliam, 15 Mar. 1798 (W.W.M. f. 30); *Oracle*, 14 June 1798; *The Times*, 7 June 1798; R. Musgrave, *Memoir of the rebellions in Ireland* . . . (1801), p. 242.

[81] J. Campbell to R. Dundas, 2 June 1798 (I.S.P.O. 620/38/23); Aldborough to ——, 5 June 1798 (620/38/51); P. O'Shea's petition (S.P.P.) and 620/39/158.

them, for fearing a suspicion and I was led to think three-quarters of Dublin was that way and I would be marked'. Another member of the corps, who had taken the United Irishmen's oath, apparently tried to back out of the conspiracy and did his duty as a yeoman, being up on duty fourteen successive nights before being arrested as a suspect. Gray himself left the country before the rebellion broke out.[82] The Lawyers artillery in June 1798 dissolved and reconstituted itself, a number of members being ejected on a ballot and some gentlemen from the country, who took refuge in Dublin, being admitted. It was reported to the government about this time that over a year earlier a member of the corps, Mr O'Connell, had taken part in a conversation 'in which it was proposed and seemingly agreed to bring out the guns and leave them for the rebels'. Daniel O'Connell, the future catholic leader, was a member of the Lawyers artillery when this conversation was supposed to have taken place, and he seems to have shown his dislike of rough methods employed by some of fellow yeomen when enforcing order. But in the privacy of his diary he had noted, 'of real patriotism moderation is the chief mark', and the report is probably an example of how a keen partisan can confuse moderation with adherence to the opposing side.[83]

Given the prevalence and vigour of Irish radicalism it is not surprising that there was some disaffection in the yeomanry, a widely recruited, part-time force. What was bound to arouse deep intense apprehension in government circles was the possibility that discontent and sedition might spread through the regular army and the militia, weakening the cohesion of the units which were regarded as the mainstay of authority in the event of invasion or rebellion. The great naval mutinies of 1797 showed that discipline could be seriously corroded by bad living conditions—though it was quickly restored by concessions to the seamen on pay and rations. Shortly before trouble broke out in the fleet there were symptoms of discontent amongst the forces in Ireland. At the beginning of 1797 the soldiers' standard of living was seriously affected by rising prices. Fencibles

[82] *D.E.P.*, 12, 21 June 1798; J. Grey's petition, 30 Jan. 1799 (I.S.P.O. 620/46/24); E. C. Keane's petition (620/52/154); memorial of J. Morris (620/52/55).
[83] *D.E.P.*, 14 June 1798; J. Palmer to E. Cooke, 2 June 1798 (I.S.P.O. 620/38/25, 38); A. Houston, *Daniel O'Connell, his early life* (1901), pp. 201-4.

stationed in Belfast were unable to afford three regular meals a day and the commander of the forces, observing that fresh provisions were scarce and dear, advised officers to encourage their men to eat salted and pickled pork, 'the favourite food of the navy'. In the spring a paper was circulated, headed 'Dublin garrison', setting out that the private soldier's three shillings and six pence a week was insufficient to maintain a single man and totally inadequate for a married couple. A soldier's pay, it was pointed out, compared badly with the earnings of a Dublin artisan, and it was suggested that if a shilling a day was not granted, soldiers should stay in their quarters. At least one outlying garrison, detachments of the north Mayo and city of Limerick regiments stationed at Fethard, sympathized with this Dublin protest, adding that prices had risen so high that a soldier could not afford one palatable meal a day.[84]

In Ireland there was another grave threat to discipline— that dissatisfaction with service conditions might render the forces susceptible to political contagion. How easily this could happen was illustrated in 1795 when the 105th and 113th foot stationed at Cork mutinied on being informed that they were going to be drafted into regiments serving in the West Indies. The mutineers issued a manifesto in which they employed language current in radical circles. They were, they declared, 'industrious citizens until a dreadful and atrocious war dried up the channels of our manufacture', then they had been tempted by large sums (in arrears) to enlist. Before discipline was restored the mutineers, to the alarm of Cork conservatives, sallied out of barracks and were joined by a large 'cheering and huzzaring' mob.[85]

In Ireland soldiers and civilians mixed freely together. They frequently met in convivial surroundings, and on innumerable occasions United Irishmen tried to persuade soldiers with whom they were drinking to join their society. The militia, recruited in the Irish countryside, largely catholic and permanently

[84] H. M. Scobie, *An old highland fencible corps* (1914), p. 117; circulars from commander-in-chief, Ireland, and duke of York, W.O. 68/402 (i); protests from soldiers in Dublin and Fethard (I.S.P.O. 620/29/330, Army Museum MS 6807/174).

[85] Manifesto issued by troops in Cork (Army Museum MS 6807/370/42). J. Travers to Lord Lismore, 4 Sept. 1795 (Army Museum MS 6807/370/44). The 104th and 111th stationed in Dublin also mutinied when informed that they were going to be drafted to units in the West Indies (*D.E.P.*, 25 Aug. 1795).

stationed and quartered in Ireland, was dangerously exposed to radical propaganda. In 1796 it was reported that Belfast radicals had been in contact with the soldiers stationed at Blaris (a hutted camp near the town); that about 50 men were defenders and United Irishmen, and that the United Irishmen in the camp had built a hut for themselves into which only those who were 'up and up' were admitted.[86] At the close of the year Bagwell, commanding the Tipperary militia, was 'fretting' because attempts were being made to seduce his men by the United Irishmen of Londonderry where the regiment was billeted. At the 1797 Derry assizes, William Davison was convicted of administering an illegal oath to a Tipperary militiaman in a public house in Bishop Street; by June, 50 men had admitted to Bagwell that they had been sworn and Bagwell believed that there was a plot on foot to supply drink gratis to the regiment, and, when all the men had been sworn, to seize the magazine.[87] A couple of months earlier in April 1797, Colonel Leslie of the Monaghan regiment, stationed at Blaris, after a talk with Newell, the government spy or agent, arrested a corporal, who under interrogation supplied the names of militiamen who were United Irishmen. A number of men in the Monaghan regiment were said to have been sworn and four of them were court-martialled, sentenced to be shot and executed at an impressive military parade, ordered by General Gerard Lake, who was greatly disturbed by the spread of the United Irishmen's movement through the militia. 'Whether', he wrote, 'this proceeds from liquor or a determination to overturn the constitution of the country I am at a loss to guess.' About the same time a conspiracy, or at least a considerable amount of recruiting for the United Irishmen, was discovered in the Cork–Bandon area. Two of the Wexford militia, who it was said had been commissioned by the United Irishmen, were executed at Cork and about ten of the Louth regiment sent to serve abroad. Shortly afterwards two privates of the Kildare regiment, having been court-martialled for inducing soldiers to join the United Irishmen, were shot at a military parade in Phoenix Park. In the following year shortly before the outbreak

[86] E. Cooke to Nugent, 25 July 1796 (Army Museum MS 6807/7/174).
[87] G. Hill to E. Cooke, n.d. (I.S.P.O. 620/52/11); J. Bagwell to ——, 7 Dec. 1796 (620/26/104), to ——, 28 June 1797 (620/31/167).

of the rebellion four Monaghan militia privates were court-martialled in Belfast and sentenced to death for planning to start United Irishmen's societies in the Monaghan, if there were 'scholars good enough in the regiment to carry on the business'.[88]

Efforts were also made to win over regular soldiers to the United Irishmen's cause. In 1797 an attempt was made to induce artillerymen stationed in Clonmel to take the United Irishmen's oath. This was very alarming. The artillery was recognized to be of the greatest importance when it came to defending the country against invasion or overawing the disaffected, and artillerymen, often recruited in the north and better-educated than the average soldier, were, it was feared, especially liable to be influenced by 'the speculative madness of the present day'. It was, Castlereagh pointed out, the artillery which in France was amongst the first to embrace republican principles. In the same year, 1797, Camden was anxious that the 7th Dragoon guards, which had been stationed in Ireland for over thirty years, should be moved to England. It was, he wrote, a fine regiment, but it had 'imbibed the notions which have been so prevalent in this kingdom'. In fact the regiment remained in Ireland, subscribed heavily to the loyalty loan and served throughout the insurrection of 1798. Two other cavalry regiments which helped to suppress the rising, the 5th Dragoon Guards and the 9th Dragoons, were both by 1799 ill-disciplined or semi-mutinous. The 5th was disbanded and disappeared from the army list and at least ten of the 9th were court-martialled. It is impossible to say how far the trouble in these two regiments was politically inspired. The 5th, it was said, had towards the close of 1798, recruited 'many fine looking young fellows' who were 'rebel partizans'. In the 9th the only cause of discontent mentioned was that a married man might not be allowed to remain with his family.[89]

Conservatives were conscious that the fall of the *ancien*

---

[88] Leslie to T. Pelham, 25 Apr. 1797 (Add. MS 33103); *D.J.*, 18 May 1797; G. Lake to T. Pelham, 1 Apr. 1797 (Add. MS 33103); G. Lake to G. Nugent, 27 May 1797 (N.L.I. MS 56); *D.J.*, 3, 8, 27 June 1797; 620/32/130; court-martial records May 1798 (620/2/9/34).

[89] Castlereagh, memorandum on artillery, 10 Nov. 1797 (Add. MS 35105); Camden to Portland, 6 July 1797 (H.O. 100/68); and court-martial records (I.S.P.O. 620/5/58); *British military library*, ii, pp. 231–3; Cornwallis to Portland, 1 Jan. 1799 (H.O. 100/83).

régime in France had been accompanied and partly caused by the collapse of military discipline. In the later nineties the government took steps to ensure that the loyalty and discipline of the army in Ireland would not be undermined. Camden in 1795 was extremely anxious to get the troops lodged in barracks to prevent them being tampered with. In 1797 a measure was passed making an attempt to seduce a soldier from his duty a felony, punishable by death—when the bill was in the lords a group of peers tried unsuccessfully to make it an offence triable by court martial. More important perhaps, in June 1797 a considerable addition was made to the pay of both officers and men, a step which the duke of York hoped would defeat 'those desperate persons who have persisted in methodizing treason'. When the testing time came in 1798, with civil war and invasion, the army, regulars and militia, either conditioned by ingrained habits or mindful of their pledged allegiance, proved reliable. At a number of critical points steadfast courage saved the day and even desertion was comparatively rare.

It was fortunate for the government that the army in Ireland remained on the whole immune from sedition, because it was on the military that it largely relied in the great drive against organized militant disaffection which began in Ulster early in 1796. In April, Thomas Knox arrested John Shaw, a woollen draper and shopkeeper of Dungannon, 'regarded by the disaffected as their principle'[90] and about the same time Clotworthy Soden, a very active clerical magistrate 'bounded' into a house in Maghera and arrested McKeever, a well-known 'insurgent', dragging him 'through a desolate and crestfallen multitude'. In July Sir George Hill, a son-in-law of John Beresford, a popular landlord and a vehement conservative, was raiding for arms in the Derry neighbourhood.[91] Hill had a list of registered holders of arms and if the arms could not be produced he would not accept the story they had been taken by the Orangemen—he knew there were no Orangemen in the area.[92]

---

[90] T. Knox to ——, 23 Apr. 1796 (I.S.P.O. 620/23/85), and see p. 541.

[91] C. Soden to E. Cooke, 23 May 1796 (I.S.P.O. 620/23/120); *D.J.*, 31 May 1796. It was said of Soden, who was archdeacon of Derry 1786–95, that one could trust him with anything but one's purse or bottle (J. B. Leslie, *Derry clergy and parishes* (1937), p. 257).

[92] G. Hill to ——, 6 July 1796 (I.S.P.O. 620/23/6); *D.J.*, 4, 25 Aug. 1796; *N.S.*, 13 Sept. 1796.

Towards the end of the year the government with a display of military power dramatically demonstrated its determination to defeat radicalism. On the morning of 16 September, Lord Downshire and Lord Castlereagh together with Lord Westmeath, who commanded a militia regiment stationed in the neighbourhood, and John Pollock, the crown solicitor, entered Belfast with a force of cavalry and infantry. The artillery paraded, sentinels were posted at a number of key points, seven of the inhabitants arrested, and a number of buildings including the *Northern Star* offices were searched. Amongst these was the house of William Sampson, a barrister who was a legal adviser and contributor to the *Star*. When Lord Westmeath, who conducted a thorough search, insisted on entering Mrs Sampson's bedroom, Sampson jocularly assured him that she was not, as some other ladies, 'in the habit of privately harbouring gentlemen' (a pointed remark which delighted radical Belfast and Tone in exile—Lord Westmeath had recently played the humiliating role of a successful plaintiff in a crim. con. suit).[93] By the afternoon the prisoners had left for Dublin in carriages escorted by dragoons. Four other prisoners were also sent to Dublin—Samuel Musgrave, an apothecary from Lisburn, James Barclay of Ballymacarret, a publican, Charles Teeling, a member of a well-known catholic business family, and James Greer of Newry, a hardware merchant, who was said to be 'a very intelligent person and speaks several of the modern languages'. The *Northern Star*, having praised the restraint shown by the inhabitants of 'this peaceful and prosperous town' during a day of searches and arrests, asked its readers 'how long shall it be thought prudent to submit to this rough-riding of attornies and lordlings'. Two days later a requisition was handed round for a town meeting to express the resentment of the Belfast people at the display of military force and their willingness to arm themselves for the preservation of the peace if a radical reform was granted. Bruce and Joy refused to sign, the former remarking that the word 'radical' seemed to him 'very exceptional' and the latter complaining that nothing was said about loyalty to the crown. The sovereign, Mr Bristow, naturally refused to call a meeting—apparently to the relief of

[93] *N.S.*, 16 Sept. 1796; list of warrants issued (I.S.P.O. 620/25/65).

many of its promoters who were afraid that a meeting might reveal divisions of opinion.[94]

In April 1797 the authorities stepped up their efforts against the Belfast radicals. On 14 April, Fox, the ordnance store keeper, raided a public house. He was 'opposed by the man of the house who he flung down stairs'. Twenty-one men, a United Irishmen's committee, as was made obvious by the very informative documents found in their possession, were arrested and Lake decided they 'should all go to the tender as they are low people'. During the next couple of days a number of other radicals were arrested, Newell, masked, being active in making identifications. At the end of the month and the beginning of May two groups of prisoners, totalling thirty were sent to Dublin. The first batch, which included the Revd Sinclaire Kelburn, Dr Crawford of Lisburn, Thomas Dry, a clothier, who was a link with the Dublin United Irishmen, a dozen businessmen, a painter, weaver and a porter, were dispatched to Dublin in six post-chaises, escorted by dragoons and greatly annoyed the Dublin conservatives by sporting green cockades, 'the emblem of treason'.[95] Towards the close of May Belfast radicalism sustained a crippling blow. The *Northern Star* refused to publish a loyal declaration subscribed to by the N.C.O.s and men of the Monaghan militia unless a sentence referring to Belfast as a town noted for its seditious practices was omitted. The Monaghan men smashed the presses and the paper, whose editor was already under arrest, ceased publication.

In April 1797 the Ancient Britons, a fencible cavalry regiment raised in north Wales, arrived in the north of Ireland and was stationed in Newry. Its commanding officer, Sir Watkin Williams Wynn, 'The Prince of Wales', renowned for his public spirit and munificence, when he heard that one of his main sources of intelligence, 'a spy', had been discovered, moved decisively against the Newry radicals, and arrested Lawson, a bookseller, believed to be the baronial secretary, three merchants (two of whom were 'eminent' by local standards), a grocer, an apothecary, and 'a tin-man'. In Lawson's house

[94] *Hibernian Magazine*, 1796, p. 285. Mrs McTier to W. Drennan, 25 Sept. 1796 (Drennan papers, 632), letter dated 24 Sept. 1796 (620/25/103).

[95] *B.N.L.*, 21 Apr., 3 May 1797; *D.J.*, 25 Apr. 1797; E. Newell to E. Cooke 19 Apr. 1797 (620/29/286).

treasonable papers and pikes were found under the floorboards and he was paraded through the town with pike-heads tied round his neck. A number of other local radicals for whom warrants were issued fled.[96] About the same time, in the spring of 1797, 'a flying column' composed of the 9th Dragoons, the Northamptonshire fencibles and the Longford militia, under the command of Lord Blayney, a keen professional soldier, was operating in south-east Ulster. Blayney, a county Monaghan landlord and a genial, good-natured man, who had been in France at the beginning of the revolution, joined the Whig club in 1796, and strongly supported parliamentary reform, which he believed would enlist the moderates in support of the constitution against 'the Jacobins'.[97] This liberalism rather startled the bishop of Clogher, who detected 'a little disappointment at the bottom of it', but a leading Ulster conservative had to admit in the summer of 1797 that if Blayney 'wavered before he offered his services nothing could be more decisive than his now exertions'.[98] Blayney was determined to discipline his men and check the disturbances in his area. His officers were inexperienced, and 'the militia', he wrote, 'are all politicians and consequently bad soldiers'. Any complaint against a soldier under his command was minutely investigated and the soldier, if found guilty, severely punished. 'A strict severity of discipline', he explained to his men, was necessary on account of 'the variety of snares that were laid with the view of leading you into scrapes'. A magistrate in north-west Meath criticized Blayney for taking 'indiscriminate vengence . . . of the country'. But Blayney's own account of one of his operations suggests that he tried to temper severity with rough justice. About the beginning of June he marched into south Armagh. At Keady he 'got into the pulpit in church' and addressed a large audience on the necessity of disarming the country and on the conduct of the French in the countries they conquered. He then moved into Creggan, an area which he thought was the source of the disturbances in the surrounding countryside. His

---

[96] *B.N.L.*, 10 Apr. 1797; W. W. Wynn to ——, 25 May 1797 (I.S.P.O. 620/30/181); J. Dawson to ——, 10 Jan. 1797 (620/28/80).

[97] Blayney to ——, 26 Apr. 1797 (I.S.P.O. 620/29/314); Blayney to ——, June 1797 (620/34/45); *D.E.P.*, 3 Dec. 1796.

[98] H. Alexander to ——, 22 May 1797 (I.S.P.O. 620/30/149); bishop of Clogher to T. Pelham, 29 July 1797 (620/31/290).

informants, afraid of being murdered, refused to accompany him, but feeling that in the circumstances he 'could not go wrong', he burned several houses, 'the inhabitants of which were not at home', although only one house was completely destroyed. His aims were to prevent witnesses being intimidated and to get in arms. Blayney had decided views on punishment. He refused to accede to Lord Carhampton's request that he should 'transport many' and when a man was discovered trying to induce a soldier to become a United Irishman, Blayney had him flogged, remarking, 'it is useless crowding the gaols'. He also claimed that when he arrested a man he always arranged for some gentlemen of the county to give the prisoner a fair trial. Unfortunately for Blayney in the summer of 1797 he badly mishandled a serious disciplinary problem. On 12 July a parade of Orangemen in Stewartstown, County Tyrone, had a violent clash with a detachment of the Kerry regiment (militia), a number of the Kerry men being injured. The next day a party of dragoons, acting under Blayney's orders, attacked a small group of militiamen and killed three of them. The lord lieutenant appointed a court of inquiry and after it reported removed Blayney, 'so intemperate a man', from his command.[99]

Between September 1796 and the autumn of 1797 numerous arrests were made in Ulster of persons suspected of treason, sedition or being disorderly (as defined by the insurrection act). Of those arrested some were sent to county gaols, a large number were held in the Belfast artillery barracks and many were sent on board the naval recruiting tender. How many were taken into custody is hard to say. The newspapers record the arrest of about 400, often giving names. About 260 persons were brought to trial at the Ulster lent and summer assizes for what might be considered political offences and at the close of the year about 30 were in gaol awaiting trial for such offences. To these should be added persons from Ulster detained in the Dublin prisons, Kilmainham, Newgate or the provost's prison, on a chief secretary's warrant (Newgate at this time was referred to as 'the Belfast hotel').[100] There is of course some

---

[99] Blayney to T. Pelham, *post* 31 Jan. 1798, to ——, 10 June 1797, to ——, 21 July 1797 (I.S.P.O. 620/35/92, 620/31/71, 620/31/254); *D.J.*, 12 Dec. 1797; Camden to Grenville, 3 Nov. 1797 (F.O. 83/4).

[100] *Free. Jn.*, 7 Feb. 1797; *Commons' Jn. Ire.*, xvii, pp. dcxiv., dcxxvii

overlapping, but many of those reported in the press as arrested seem to have been released on bail or were probably dealt with under the Insurrection act. So it would be safe to say that for the twelve months beginning in September 1796, between 500 and 600 persons were arrested in Ulster for political reasons.

The responsibility of deciding what was to be done with many of those arrested devolved on General Lake, who was in command of the Ulster district from the end of 1796. Lake, a hard-fighting soldier and genial man of the world, had an explosive temper, easily ignited by disaffection. According to an admirer, Lake was 'not much of a tactician . . . for manœuvring as such he had always a lofty contempt,' and it was in this spirit he pushed through the jungle of political conundrums into which he had been thrust.[101] At the end of June 1797 Lake was painfully aware that it would be difficult to prosecute with success a number of those by then in custody—the persons who had given information against them were 'very timid' and would not come into court. In the following month the government sent Lake a legal adviser, Joseph Pollock, the assistant-barrister for County Down. After examining carefully the committals, Pollock suggested to Lake, in the latter's words, 'to liberate some of the greatest commanders we took up'. Lake, according to Pollock, politely made it clear that he did not want a lawyer's opinion on a number of the cases because 'the question is not one of law but of policy or of necessity'.[102] However, shortly after Pollock's visit Lake did release on bail some prisoners, who, he sourly commented, were soon more mischievous than ever. At the end of the year Lake sustained an infuriating legal defeat. In May a writ of habeas corpus on behalf of Peter Evans, a United Irishman whom Lake had sent to the tender in Belfast Lough, was served on the regulating captain, who, Lake complained, was 'too much inclined to that sort of man' (litigation over pressing had taught naval officers to be cautious when in home ports). The chief secretary informed Lake that the writ must be obeyed and Evans was sent to Dublin, but he suggested that the tender should keep away from the shore as

---

[101] *Essays and lectures on Indian historical subjects.* By An officer of the Bengal staff corps (1866), p. 38.
[102] G. Lake to T. Pelham, 24 June 1797 (Add. MS 33104), 14 Aug. 1797 (I.S.P.O. 620/32/46), 27 Aug. 1797 (Add. MS 33105); E. Cooke to J. Pollock, 22 July 1797 (620/31/265); J. Pollock to E. Cooke, 24 July 1797 (620/31/272).

much as possible. Shortly afterwards writs of habeas corpus were served on Lake on behalf of thirteen persons detained in the artillery barracks, including three men, John Brown, 'gentleman', Andrew Bryson, a farmer and Thomas Houston, a surgeon, whom Lake had been particularly keen to take into custody. When Houston had been arrested 300 copies of the United Irishmen's constitution had been found under his drawing-room floorboards. On being asked by the officers conducting the search for an explanation, Houston had 'very jocosely' told them 'that his education at college had cost his father a considerable sum' and that he would strongly recommend them 'going for instruction before they assumed the appearance of gentlemen'. When the thirteen were brought before the king's bench Lake in his return stated that they were held on a chief secretary's warrant. Emmet argued that the chief secretary was empowered to detain them only in a prison and that the artillery barracks was not legally a prison. The court accepted his argument and the prisoners were discharged.[103]

Arresting, imprisoning and sometimes bringing to trial United Irishmen was one simple and obvious way of crippling their movement. Another was disarming them. In eighteenth-century Ireland the number of firearms in private hands was very large. There were sporting guns, blunderbusses for the defence of isolated houses, pistols and swords, gentlemanly accoutrements. During the heyday of the volunteers there were many muskets and even cannon in private possession. Plough-shears and other agricultural implements could be beaten into arms, and contemporary France had popularized the pike, an easily improvised weapon, as a revolutionary symbol. The drive in Ulster to get in arms which began about the close of 1796 was intensified in March 1797. At the beginning of the month the chief secretary directed Lake to disarm persons suspected of traitorous activities, assuring him that the lord lieutenant intended 'to give your discretion the greatest latitude' and that he was 'not to suffer the cause of justice to be frustrated by the delicacy which might possibly have actuated the magistracy'.[104]

[103] G. Lake to T. Pelham, 17, 29 May, 15 June 1797; T. Pelham to G. Lake, 20 May 1797 (Add. MS 33104); D.E.P., 25 Nov. 1797.
[104] T. Pelham to G. Lake, 3 Mar. 1797 (Army Museum, MS 6807/174); Camden to Portland, 9 Mar. 1797 (H.O. 100/69); D.E.P., 13 Mar. 1797.

Lake immediately issued a proclamation imploring the people of Ulster to 'reflect on the ruin into which they were rushing' and to surrender any arms in their possession to the military authorities. Considerable quantities of arms were surrendered or seized—by 1 July 1797 6,200 serviceable and 4,400 unserviceable guns had been collected—and though mistakes were made, arms being sometimes taken from wealthy farmers who would have used them against defenders, while the turbulent hid their weapons, a partial disarmament of the Ulster United Irishmen was achieved and, as events in 1798 showed, their military potential seriously weakened.[105]

One method used to obtain arms and generally to check the disaffected was house-burning. About the middle of December 1796, according to the *Northern Star*, the Revd Thomas Torrens, a clerical magistrate, entered Kilkea at the head of a party of militia to make arrests. Not being able to find the men he was looking for, he burned the houses of two or them, which 'stood apart from the town', and the contents of two other dwellings. But, according to a neighbouring clergyman, what happened was that a fifer belonging to a small detachment of the Kerry militia, stationed in Kilkea, found fault with a bed in his billet and that the ensuing dispute escalated into a scuffle. During this time some of the villagers shouted, 'what are you up to Kerrymen, we thought you were all up'. The suggestion that they were disloyal infuriated the soldiers and with Torrens on the scene and condoning their behaviour they burned two houses. Though conservatives highly commended Torrens— the 'burning of insignificant cabins', it was said, had put an end to nocturnal meetings in the neighbourhood—Torrens himself soon found that he might have to pay heavily for his impetuosity. Before the end of the year he heard that 'the enemies of government have already opened a subscription to prosecute me'. To add to his worries his financial circumstances were 'confined', he had a large family and he received only cold comfort from the government. 'You will understand', the chief secretary wrote to one of Torrens's admirers, 'the difficulty there is in holding out any direct support or countenance to a magistrate

---

[105] Return of arms surrendered (I.S.P.O. 620/31/251); A. Stewart to ——, n.d. (620/29/69); Downshire to ——, 29 Mar. 1797 (620/29/114); H. Coddington to H. Pelham, 27 June 1797 (620/31/163).

upon a point that may become the subject of an action or a civil prosecution.'[106]

During 1797 there were a number of instances in Ulster and Westmeath of house-burning being used as a punishment or a warning. In June 1797 George Hill, a quick-tempered magistrate, apparently popular with his tenantry, burned a house in Inishowen in which pike handles were found. A month later another County Derry magistrate, Henry Alexander, levelled two houses in which he found pike shafts (and incidentally ordered a County Tipperary militia officer to flog 'a fellow he found tampering with his men'.[107] About this time the military burned some houses in County Down, including an inn at Newtownards and a Major Mathews of the Downshire militia, a justice of the peace, being asked to report on the burning of a house in the Mourne area, having explained that the owner was the very active secretary of a United Irishmen's society in Newry, added, 'I felt no inclination whatever to restrain the military from executing vengence upon the cabin of the most guilty man in the county.'[108] The Ancient Britons stationed in Newry burned some houses—'the object of emulation between them and the Orangeman', a strong conservative declared with disgust, 'seems to be who shall do most mischief to wretches, who certainly may have seditious minds but are at present quite incapable of resistance.' Some months later however an officer of the Ancient Britons emphasized their restraint. A party which had secured 50 stand of arms near Newry had burned only two houses, in one of which there were seditious papers and a horn for summoning the United; in the other a great quantity of cartridges and a pike were found.[109] In Westmeath, Thomas Rochfort during the summer of 1797 'lost no time in giving the military employment'. They burned, he reported, thirteen

---

[106] N.S., 23 Dec. 1796; T. Torrens to ——, 24 Dec. 1796 (I.S.P.O. 620/26/154); H. Pelham to Knox, 9 Jan. 1797 (620/28/13); R. Babington to ——, 24 Dec. 1796 (620/28/14a); J. Patterson to ——, 25 Dec. 1796 (620/28/14). In 1795 a company of the Leitrim militia ordered out against the County Meath defenders burned 17 houses near Kells of persons said to be defenders (H.J., 14 Sept. 1795).

[107] G. Hill to ——, June 1797, to J. Beresford, 12 June 1797 (I.S.P.O. 620/31/78, 181); N.S., 13 Sept. 1796; H. Alexander to T. Pelham, ante 3 July 1797 (620/31/298).

[108] A view of the present state of Ireland. By An observer (1797), G. Mathews to ——, 3 Oct. 1797 (620/32/161).

[109] John Giffard to ——, 5 June 1797 (I.S.P.O. 620/31/36); extract from a letter to W. W. Wynn, 5 Dec. 1797 (F.O. 83/4).

houses, the dwellings of 'principals in wickedness' and secured information of value.[110]

House-burning did not necessarily mean complete destruction. Blayney, during his sally into south Armagh, in some instances 'burned only the thatch', and a County Cavan magistrate having set fire to two houses, whose owners were suspect, 'to make people discover where arms and papers were', allowed the flames to be extinguished before the houses were consumed. An ensign in the County Wicklow militia, George Bell, whose conduct at Multifarnham, Westmeath, was sharply criticized in the liberal press, explained the procedure he had adopted in detail. Having burned three houses belonging to disaffected persons (two of whom had been heard plotting against the military), he raided the house of William Dodd, a distiller who was said to be a committee man. Dodd was not to be found and, Bell considering 'it necessary to make an immediate example', his offices were consumed, 'but his stock and dwelling house preserved for the sake of his numerous family'. Bell then announced that if the arms which had been taken from the respectable inhabitants were not restored, he would burn the town. This had 'the happiest effect', the arms being returned.[111]

Most references to house-burning suggest that it occurred occasionally and on a limited scale. But in the spring and early summer of 1798 another technique for securing the surrender of arms was applied systematically over fairly wide areas—free-quarters. At the close of March a proclamation was issued directing the military to suppress treasonable activities with 'the utmost vigour and decision', and 12,000 notices were distributed stating that the military had been directed 'to use the most summary methods' to secure arms. A few weeks later the military were directed to live at free-quarters in County Kildare, King's and Queen's Counties, south County Cork and in districts in west Tipperary and on the Tipperary–Limerick border. Free-quarters meant that the troops were billeted on suspected persons and requisitioned provisions until all arms in

[110] T. Rochfort to ——, 18 June 1797 (I.S.P.O. 620/31/115) and (620/31/73).

[111] Blayney to ——, 10 June 1797 (I.S.P.O. 620/31/71); H. Clements to ——, 12 June 1797 (620/31/810); G. Bell to ——, n.d. (620/31/122); *D.E.P.*, 20 June 1797, Dodd's demand for compensation (620/36/160). Later Dodd sued Colonel Radcliffe for £500, the value of the distillery, but the jury found for the defendant (*D.J.*, 25 July 1799).

the area were surrendered and in Queen's County (and perhaps elsewhere) orders were issued directing that a list of persons dwelling in each house was to be placed on the door and imposing a curfew from 9 p.m. to daybreak, the inhabitants being warned that the patrols would make 'domiciliary visits' during the curfew.[112] In County Wicklow, though the military did not take up free-quarters, Major Joseph Hardy commanding a 'flying column' of the Antrim militia, at the close of 1797, imposed a curfew, ordered householders to display lists of occupants on their doors, and, in co-operation with the yeomanry, started a general search for arms. Early in May 1798 he intensified his efforts and after a week or so of vigorous work 600 pikes had been surrendered in the barony of Arklow and 2,000 in the whole county, but 'no muskets of which a great number were known to be concealed'. Large numbers took the oath of allegiance but Hardy observed that in many instances where the head of a family declared his loyalty, the sons were United Irishmen, so that in any event their property was 'covered'. Towards the close of May, Lord Fitzwilliam's Wicklow agent wrote that the drive for arms, 'prepared for the destruction of the protestants', had succeeded 'beyond expectation'. He added, however, that success had not been achieved 'until flogging became general, some have even stood a hundred lashes before they would confess where the offensive weapons were concealed'. John Edwards, a friend of Lord Charlemont, who commanded the Bray infantry, strongly criticized Hardy for displaying excessive severity. Hardy, who was probably aware of Edwards's attitude, treated the Bray infantry as 'an inactive corps', suspending it from permanent duty, 'because', Edwards declared, 'we have not burned houses nor strangled their owners'. But Hardy, who had 'reduced' Captain William West of the Wicklow infantry for cruelty, congratulated himself on having maintained control of a large stretch of mountainous country with only a small force of militia and yeomanry, 'without murder, torture or even free-quarters'.[113]

[112] *D.J.*, 7, 24 Apr. 1798; *D.E.P.*, 3 Apr., *S.N.L.*, 7 Apr. 1798.
[113] Hardy's journal (W.W.M. F. 30), W. Wainwright to Fitzwilliam, 25 May 1798 (W.W.M. F. 89). During the American war Hardy joined the army, obtained a commission at Bunker's Hill and served until the end of the war. He married an Irish woman who possessed a landed estate and in 1793 became a major in the

General John Moore, commanding in south Cork, a very intelligent and clear-headed soldier, bluntly decided 'to excite terror, and by that means obtain our end speedily'. 'I thought', he recorded in his diary, 'this better than to act mildly, and to be obliged to continue for any time the real oppression, and as I was present everywhere myself I had no doubt of being able to prevent any great abuse by the troops.' A few houses were burned, many people fled at the sign of a red coat and large numbers of pikes and guns were handed in. Moore sardonically noted that 'the better sort of people seemed delighted with the operation except when it touched their own tenants, by whose ruin they saw they themselves must suffer, but they were pleased that the people were humbled and would be civil'.[114] Another soldier, who was also to serve with distinction in the Peninsula, Colonel Campbell, commanding at Athy, was quite confident that the harsh measures he adopted were abundantly justified. About the middle of May, he wrote, 'in consequence of burning a few houses in this town and neighbourhood, we have got a number of pikes and some information'. 'We have', he added, 'been more moderate in flogging than report gives us credit for and it has been allowed by the most tender that it has produced a great number of pikes.' Amongst those penalized by Campbell was the Revd Nicholas Ashe, the leader of the duke of Leinster's interest in Athy. Ashe, according to the duke of Leinster, managed to secure the surrender of a large number of pikes and guns. But some 'members of a faction' persuaded Campbell that Ashe's achievement suggested he had suspicious connections, so sixty men were quartered on him and, left without even a pair of shoes, 'he was obliged to do his duty as a magistrate in the street in slippers'.[115]

In Tipperary the drive to secure arms was largely conducted by the civil power in the person of the high sheriff, Thomas Judkin Fitzgerald. Fitzgerald, a landed gentleman and an agricultural improver—he was president of a farming society— had graduated at Trinity college and been called to the Irish

---

Antrim militia (Memorial of Joseph Hardy, H.O. 100/144); J. Edwards to ——, 12 July 1798 (I.S.P.O. 620/39/63); J. Edwards to E. Cooke, 17 May 1798 (620/37/99) and see also 620/37/78, 107, 128, 620/38/163, 620/39/118.

[114] J. Moore, *Diary*, i, p. 290.

[115] J. Campbell to ——, 14, 15 May 1798 (I.S.P.O. 620/37/67, 78); Leinster to Lady S. Napier, 1 Feb. 1799 (Bod. Eng. Letters c 238).

bar. In 1798 he was requested by the gentlemen of his county
to consent to be appointed high sheriff, and once in office he
acted with tremendous and terrifying energy. He believed that
the whole county 'resembled a great volcano, a hidden, subtle
flame pervaded through every part, ready to burst forth on
some unexpected event, and bury all in one indiscriminate heap
of ruin and devastation'. Determined to preserve order, he was
contemptuous of the timid and absentee. He was annoyed when
travelling through three baronies to meet only two beneficed
clergymen and three curates, he was anxious that Lord
Kingston and Lord Lismore, and 'other men of great property'
should be ordered back to their estates, and he directed that
compensation for damage to poor men's property should be
levyed on the absentees. Shortly after becoming high sheriff he
issued a printed notice praising the behaviour of Mrs Bunbury,
who with a couple of menservants had driven a party of rebels
out of her house. He hoped that 'such heroic conduct of a lady
of such high distinction, eminent for beauty and elegance, will
raise the crimson blush of shame on the pallid cheek of those
young heroes who so gracefully surrendered large quantities of
well loaded arms to the rebels . . . without having spirit enough
to fire even a single shot'.

A vigorous if verbose orator, at the beginning of May at
Tipperary he addressed a crowd for three hours—partly in
Irish—explaining what the French would do if they arrived in
Ireland, and promising a free pardon to those who gave up
their arms. When some of his listeners admitted to being
'captains', he shook hands with them, made them kneel down
and pray for the king and forgave them all past offences. His
methods were not always so conciliatory. On 20 May he
marched into Nenagh and flogged some persons, who, he was
informed, were United Irishmen sergeants. This severity,
according to Peter Holmes, the M.P. and penal reformer,
produced 'ample confessions . . . the whole arrangement was
disclosed . . . and showed we stood on the brink of a precipice
. . . the number of pikes which have been given up is truly
astonishing.' About the same time Fitzgerald arrested Fox,
suspected of being a United Irishman leader. After being
flogged Fox admitted he was a rebel general and declared that
a number of the Carrick-on-Suir yeomanry were United

Irishmen. Fitzgerald then marched into Carrick and flogged three of the yeomanry, including David Wells and Francis Doyle. 'My flogging Mr Wells', he wrote, 'had so satisfactory an effect that 60 of the Carrick yeomanry were obliged to confess publicly on their parade that they were United and that eight of them were sworn sergeants . . . I think I showed great mercy in not flogging the whole parcel of them . . . You know it was the cat alone that brought out the truth and 9,500 pikes and 1,500 stand of arms.' While in Carrick Fitzgerald arrested a wealthy merchant, Matthew Scott, on suspicion of having pikes and supplying the rebels with food. A number of local gentlemen remonstrated and on the suggestion of the general commanding the district Scott, finding securities, was released. Another man of means, Michael Burke, described by Fitzgerald as 'a hedge attorney, worth from twenty to thirty thousand pounds', was brought before the justices of the peace at Clonmel on a charge of having concealed arms. Five of the justices were for a conviction and seven for acquittal, and Fitzgerald reluctantly agreed to drop further charges if Burke subscribed £1,000 to the loyalty loan. The money was used by Fitzgerald for public purposes but the government ultimately refunded it to Burke.

Tipperary remained quiet throughout the rising and Fitzgerald noted with pride that when the King's County insurgents sent emissaries into north Tipperary the people 'all answered that they were determined to stand by their engagements with me for them to remain safe and if ever they [the emissaries] returned they would give them up to me—this gave me great joy as it was the most unequivocal proof of their sincerity.' But his methods aroused considerable criticism. He was accused of punishing innocent persons, and, stimulated by a 'brutal and sanguinary passion for flagellation', displaying 'an exuberance in his severities' which could not be justified. Fitzgerald's defenders argued that it was owing to 'the spirited determination of this bold and enterprising man' that cartloads of arms had been discovered and Fitzgerald himself pointed out that other methods of securing information—free-quarters and rewards—had been tried without success. Fitzgerald himself claimed that by whipping only 50 persons he had saved the lives and property of 500,000. After the insurrection, Wright, a Clonmel schoolmaster, whom Fitzgerald had flogged on the suspicion of being a United Irishman, sued Fitzgerald and secured substantial damages, Mr Justice Chamberlain pointing out that the Indemnity act did not 'release' magistrates from 'the feelings of humanity or permit them to act wantonly'. On the other hand Francis Doyle, who sued Fitzgerald in 1801, was unsuccessful and in the same year the ex-high sheriff was created a baronet.[116]

The activities of the disaffected and the determination of the government to crush them led to what the attorney-general termed 'a recrimination of outrage'.[117] Many incidents of ugly violence were reported in the press and ultra-conservatives and vehement radicals, emphasizing exclusively the outrages committed by their opponents, agreed in presenting a highly coloured picture of Irish conditions. Both sides professed to be deeply shocked by the conduct of their opponents. Their humanitarian instincts were genuinely stirred and they clearly appreciated the controversial value of atrocities. (Sampson, the Belfast barrister, at the beginning of 1798 formed an association to collect 'proofs of the enormities lately committed against the rights of the people' by the army.)[118] For the period February 1797 to April 1798 the strongly conservative *Faulkner's Dublin Journal* reported over a hundred outrages which could be presumed to have arisen from political discontent—murders or attempted murders (the victims including justices of the peace or yeomen), raids on houses for arms and attacks on military detachments. The *Press*, representing the extreme radical point of view, dwelling on the outrages committed by 'an army let loose on the country at night, but not satisfied, the sun rising to light the way to new excesses',[119] reported for the period October 1797 to April 1798 about thirty instances of military arrogance or brutality. These ranged from N.C.O.s getting

[116] T. J. Fitzgerald to——, 12 Aug. 1798 (I.S.P.O. 620/39/168); T. J. Fitzgerald; to——, 30 July 1798 (620/39/130); A notice dated 20 April 1798 (620/37/26); T. J. Fitzgerald to——, 24 May 1798 (620/37/151); T. J. Fitzgerald to Castlereagh, 1 June, 1 Sept. 1798 (S.C.P. 1017/68, 620/40/3), 18 Jan. 1799 (S.C.P. 1018/22); J. C. Carden to——, 5 May 1798 (620/37/26); Peter Holmes to——, 21 May 1798 (S.C.P. 1017/68); M. Burke, petitions (620/40/29, 620/46/14a); *True Briton*, 7 May 1799; *Trial of T. J. Fitzgerald . . . with the proceedings in parliament* (1799).
[117] *D.J.* 15 Jan. 1798.
[118] *Press*, 30 Jan. 1798; W. Drennan to Mrs McTier, 22 Feb. 1798 (Drennan papers, 697).
[119] *Press*, 1 Oct. 1797.

drunk in a tavern, officers of the Ancient Britons throwing their weight about in Newry, soldiers smashing windows not illuminated for Camperdown and stopping a Dublin alderman and his family taking a short-cut to church, to much graver incidents—cases of picketing, half-hanging, house-burning and shooting innocent persons (seven cases were cited of countrymen being shot in cold blood, the number of victims being eleven). Moreover the *Press* alleged that in Carlow, Westmeath and Wicklow there was a reign of military terror, marked by 'fire and sword, slaughter and devastation, rapes, massacre and plunder',[120] and it stated that the Wicklow militia when stationed in County Westmeath killed 72 persons. It is difficult to say if this figure is reliable. The tone of the *Press* suggests passionate concern with the political struggle rather than a scientific interest in statistics. Also, during the period the *Press* referred to, County Westmeath and adjacent areas were seriously disturbed, so that some of those who were killed may have lost their lives when resisting in arms the military or yeomanry.

The radical version of some incidents was challenged. For instance the *Press* alleged that the body of an unfortunate countryman who had been wantonly shot by the military had been gibbeted in Derry. A conservative replied that the gibbeted body was that of one of a gang of banditti who had been shot when attacking a farmer's house.[121] When it was asserted that two men had been half-hanged after an attack on a gentleman's house in County Meath, it was retorted that all that happened was that ropes had been put round their necks.[122] Again, when the *Press* reported that in Dublin a member of a yeomanry corps had stabbed a man who refused to give way to him in the street, a conservative newspaper replied that the yeoman had been defending himself against 'a banditti' who was insulting every passer-by in military uniform.[123] General Nugent, after inquiring into allegations of military misconduct in County Down, declared that the complainant was 'a very disaffected and mischievous character and had no authority to speak for

---

[120] *Press*, 23 Nov. 1797.

[121] *Press*, 9 Nov. 1797; *D.J.* 23 Dec. 1797.

[122] *Report of the debate on Lord Moira's motion for an address to the lord lieutenant* (1798), p. 33; *D.J.*, 9 May 1797.

[123] *Press*, 6 Feb. 1798; *D.J.*, 10 Feb. 1798.

the inhabitants'. Nugent assured the adjutant general that 'every means is made use of to quiet the minds of the inhabitants where the place is proclaimed, as far as is consistent with our duty'.[124] When it was asserted that an officer on a curfew patrol had insisted that lights in a cottage where a child was seriously ill must be extinguished, the officer concerned indignantly explained that in fact he found the cottage in darkness and suggested to the mother she should kindle a light.[125]

It should, of course, be taken into account that contemporary newspaper reporting was selective and often partisan and unreliable. For instance the *Dublin Evening Post* in the early months of 1797 was able to contradict three reports which had appeared elsewhere—that the house of Thomas Lynch, Esq., in County Roscommon had been burned by the defenders, that the bishop of Clogher's palace had been sacked by the banditti called the United Irishmen and that Lord Annesley had been shot in the north; and two reports which the *Post* itself published were corrected by correspondents. At the close of 1796 it reported that Seth Jelly, an Orangeman and a linen merchant, had been mortally wounded by Orangemen near Tanderagee, County Armagh when he threatened to inform against them if they committed a robbery. His brother, John Jelly, in a letter published ten days later, declared that the men were not suspected of being Orangemen but that it was widely believed that they were 'people of a different persuasion'. Early in 1797 the *Post* reported that in County Cavan Francis Sheridan, a physician, on his homeward road was accosted by a group of men, who, when he admitted he was a catholic, assaulted him and 'treated him in a most inhuman manner', so that he died soon afterwards. A few weeks later Walter Tweedy, who, according to the *Post*, had played the role of a good Samaritan, wrote a letter to the paper, explaining that he had found poor Dr Sheridan (who had not been attacked) in a ditch 'where he had staggered by mere intoxication'.[126]

It is clear that the army, though often employed during the century to enforce law and order, was by composition, training and tradition, ill-fitted for the task which many military men

---

[124] G. Nugent to G. Hewitt, 30 Mar. 1798 (Army Museum, MS 6708/174).
[125] R. W. W. Steele to Grenville, 5 Dec. 1797 (F.O. 83/4).
[126] *D.E.P.*, 19 Nov. 1796, 10 Jan., 4 Feb., 4 Mar., 17 June 1797.

resented being called on to perform. If Wellington's 'the mere scum of the earth' was too summary a description of the rank and file, it is true that they were, as he also said, drawn 'from the lowest order of society' and as for their officers, they were for the most part easy-going gentlemen, professionally speaking ill-educated or uneducated. Harsh discipline and strict training created out of unpromising material an instrument of proven value in war. Wellington, speaking of the force he led into France in 1814, said 'I could have gone anywhere and done anything with that army'. But a system which welded officers and men into units which could be trusted to respond swiftly and smoothly to orders, was not devised to produce men adept at handling civilian disaffection. There were officers, such as Nugent and Moore, who combined military skill with political acumen but the ordinary soldier, officer or man, had a simple approach to political issues. He abhorred disloyalty, and the Irish radical was not only opposed to the established order but was trying to undermine the loyalty of the forces. When on police duties, the soldier was of course conditioned to a great extent by his own accustomed environment. Officers and men were bound to be influenced by the harsh methods for enforcing discipline which were taken for granted. To quote Wellington again, 'there is no punishment which makes an impression upon anybody except corporal punishment'. Also, according to a Clare man, who after serving with distinction in the Peninsula was commissioned in the field, soldiers did not think it disgraceful to take anything for their own use 'from the inhabitants of the country in which they may be serving, whether foe or friend'.[127]

As for the yeomanry, who were often relied on by active magistrates, they combined a lack of strict discipline with strong political feeling. A County Armagh J.P. admitted that many corps in that county were so anti-catholic that they would certainly condone an attack on a catholic chapel. A J.P. in a neighbouring county, Tyrone, while acknowledging that 'the exertion of the yeomanry, when headed by their officers, had a happy effect in forcing in the arms', told the chief secretary in forceful terms that the country would be ruined if 'a set of armed

---

[127] *Report of the commissioners for inquiry into the system of military punishments in the army*, pp. 256, 324, 327, H.C. [59], 1836, xii.

men, without any gentleman at their head', were permitted 'at their pleasure, day after day, and what is worse, night after night, to scour whole tracts of countryside'. Even General Lake, who appreciated the value of the yeomanry's local knowledge when it came to finding arms illegally held, thought that this knowledge gave them 'an opportunity of gratifying their party spite', and that they had been sometimes 'rather sharp' with their neighbours. However, he did not think that 'they have been guilty of any great act of violence'.[128]

For an officer, aiding the civil power in Ireland was a distasteful and delicate task. The peace-keeping functions of the army were emphasized by proclamations issued by the lord lieutenant in November 1796, and May 1797. The November proclamation, after dwelling on the disaffection in the north, directed the military to aid the civil power. The May proclamation, having stated that there was a widespread, traitorous conspiracy afoot, declared that the officers commanding His Majesty's troops had been ordered to suppress treason. These proclamations acknowledged the role of the soldier in Irish society, but they did not afford him protection if in the execution of his duties he acted illegally. If his zeal carried him beyond the law he would have to trust that his actions would be ultimately covered by an indemnity act. Two officers, Captain Frazer and Captain Keys, were prosecuted at the 1797 summer assizes. Frazer, at the Kildare assizes was charged with killing a suspected person in custody. He asserted the prisoner was trying to escape and was found not guilty. Keys with several of his men was convicted at the Louth assizes of an assault (which he would have probably claimed to have been a rough practical joke on a local radical), and they were sentenced to three months' imprisonment. After the rebellion the colonel of the Wicklow militia was unsuccessfully sued by William Dodd, whose mill had been destroyed during a military raid for arms.[129]

Legal proceedings seem to have been very seldom instituted against members of the armed forces in Ireland for acts committed ostensibly in the maintenance of law and order, because of the indemnity acts and probably from a realization

[128] J. Verner to T. Pelham, 3 June 1797, R. Lowry to T. Pelham, 29 June 1797 (620/31/171, 196); G. Lake to T. Pelham, 17 Mar. 1797 (Add. MS 33103).
[129] *D.E.P.*, 2 Sept. 1797; *D.J.*, 10 Oct. 1797, 25 July 1799.

that the courts, judges and juries, would be strongly biased in favour of men engaged in the suppression of disaffection. Nevertheless, it seemed to Lord Moira, an Irish peer who was an experienced soldier, that an officer stationed in a proclaimed district was 'in a cruel and affecting situation'. Afraid of making a disastrous mistake, with 'his feelings trembling alive to his military reputation', he was liable to overreact to disaffection and thus increase the tension between the army and sections of the population, and, Moira might have added, find himself involved in litigation. Another Irish peer, Lord Cavan, commanding in the Londonderry area, glumly remarked in March 1797, 'the service I am on I now consider as involving more in it than is merely military' (he might have been more glum if he had known that a friendly critic thought that Cavan, though 'good tempered' was 'awkward under discretionary powers'). Some weeks later a fencible colonel, stationed in County Down, gave a depressing account of his activities. Having described how banditti were roving the countryside in large numbers destroying the houses of those who refused to join them and planting trees of liberty on gentlemen's lawns, he went on to say 'I am heartily sick of the whole business, what with the rascally informers, scoundrels of all denominations we are obliged to employ, I begin to tire'.[130]

Efforts were made by those in authority to control the application of military force. In 1797 the chief secretary seems to have been anxious that every military party assisting the civil power should be commanded by an officer. Lake, while agreeing that this was desirable, explained that it would be impossible 'in the wild country where houses were scattered'.[131] Duff, commanding at Limerick, early in 1798 laid down that no military party was to go out in support of the civil power without a magistrate and if there was a yeomanry corps in the neighbourhood, the magistrate who applied for troops should direct that a yeomanry detachment accompanied the party.

---

[130] *D.E.P.*, 20 Feb. 1798; Cavan to T. Pelham, 13 Mar. 1797 (I.S.P.O. 620/29/62); H. Alexander to T. Pelham, *ante* 23 July 1797 (620/31/298); C. Stapleton to ——, 26 May 1798 (W.W.M. F. 30); *Report of the debate on Lord Moira's motion for an address to the lord lieutenant* (1798), p. 7.

[131] G. Lake to T. Pelham, 17 Mar. 1797 (Add. MS 3310). Lake had apparently already laid down that N.C.O.s and privates should not enter a house unless accompanying an officer (General orders, W.O. 68/296).

'The strictest injunctions must be given to patrols', Duff
ordered, 'never to commit acts of severity but where it becomes
unavoidable in cases of resistance to protect the innocent'. Duff's
successor at Limerick, General Morrison, ordered that houses
and buildings of any kind should not be set on fire. 'The
consequences' of house-burning, he declared, 'seldom fall on
the guilty but on the landlord ... and on the wife and children
of the criminals who, however iniquitous the husband or father,
ought always to be spared and protected.' When the military
were directed to take up free-quarters in March 1798 it was laid
down that detachments were to act under the command of an
officer and that 'every possible degree of regularity was to be
maintained and that no unnecessary act of violence be committed' (nevertheless, the lord lieutenant was afraid discipline
was bound to suffer). In 1799 when the situation was less grave,
General Nugent, commanding in the north, ordered that troops
on detached duties were always to be commanded by an officer,
and 'to prevent the possibility of complaints', a house should
only be entered by an officer accompanied by an N.C.O. 'The
person and property of every individual', Nugent declared, 'are
to be considered as sacred.' In no circumstances was property to
be set on fire, if provisions were taken a receipt was to be given,
and persons arrested for malpractices were not to be 'molested'
but were to be lodged in the nearest guard-house. These rules
indicate how military power could be abused.[132]

One Irish lawyer and publicist tackled the problem of what
principles should govern the application of military force in
support of law and order. Joseph Pollock, the radical of the
early eighties, who under the pressure of circumstances had
moved to the right and who had been appointed assistant
barrister for County Down, sent the chief secretary in 1797 a
long memorandum on the employment of the military in support
of the civil power, in which he emphasized that while the
magistracy must always act in accordance with the law, the
government 'as statesmen and politicians' could and should, if
necessary, authorize the army to break the law for the sake of
its ultimate preservation. But, Pollock asked, 'if the soldier is

---

[132] General Duff's order of 28 Mar. 1798 (P.R.O.L., MS 5892); G. Hewett to
R. Dundas, Mar. 1798 (H.O. 100/75); General Nugent's district orders, Belfast,
13 Mar. 1799 (Army Museum, MS 6807/175); D.E.P. 19 June 1798.

obliged *to go beyond* the law in order to preserve it, should not his mode of behaviour show the motive and the measure of any excesses he is obliged to commit'. It should be impressed on military men that while they should be 'on proper occasions feared . . . it may be ruinous that they should be hated'. In the Newry area military force had been applied in the wrong way. Small, ill-disciplined, and sometimes drunken patrols had raided houses, insisted on lights being extinguished, and hustled to the guard-house wayfarers who could not give the counter-sign. In contrast, the form of military control which Lake had established in Belfast—outposts on the roads, written passes and relatively few arrests—was 'mild and inoffensive to the inhabitants'. Pollock not only wrote to Pelham. He raised the subject when dining with the officers of the Ancient Britons, and was answered in 'a high and intolerant manner' by Colonel Puleston, who had 'drunk a little'.[133]

The employment of troops in support of the civil power led to a sharp difference of opinion between the commander-in-chief and the Irish administration only a few months before the outbreak of insurrection in 1798. About a year after his arrival in Ireland Camden came to the conclusion that the commander-in-chief, Cunningham, whose military service except for the battle of Culloden, had been confined to Ireland, was too old for the post, and suggested that he should be replaced by Charles Grey, an experienced soldier. Grey would not accept the Irish command and when at the close of 1796 Cunningham retired with a peerage, he was replaced by Carhampton, an Irish peer who had not been on active service since the close of the Seven Years war. As commander-in-chief he was active and fertile in ideas. But the lord lieutenant soon lost confidence in his strategic judgement and noticed that he had a poor grasp of detail. Some months after Carhampton became commander-in-chief, the question of replacing him by Lord Cornwallis, a keen professional soldier with a wide experience of men and affairs, was under consideration. But Cornwallis was reluctant to accept the Irish command unless concessions were made to the catholics. However, another keen professional soldier, Sir Ralph Abercromby, who, since the outbreak of the war had distinguished himself in the Low Countries, the Mediterranean

[133] J. Pollock to T. Pelham, 17 Dec. 1797 (I.S.P.O. 620/33/156).

and the West Indies, was persuaded to go to Ireland and he replaced Carhampton at the close of 1797.[134]

Abercromby, a Scot, was a man of strong intellect and great intensity of purpose. In his youth he attended the universities of Edinburgh and Leipzig; in later life he went to a course of lectures on church history. Though anxious to succeed in his profession, during the American war of Independence he had deliberately chosen to stay in Ireland performing routine duties rather than fight against the colonists and he was heard to say that 'unless the opinions of a young man of twenty had a tinge of republicanism he would be sure to be a corrupt man of forty'.[135] Clearly Abercromby was bound to be out of sympathy with the Irish ruling world; he must have realized that, professionally speaking, he was considerably superior to either of his immediate predecessors and he obviously saw himself as an invigorating force in Irish military life. Well aware that conflicts of justification could easily arise between lord lieutenant and the officer commanding the forces, he tried in advance to have the position clarified to his own advantage. The army, he emphasized, was 'in time of war to be totally under my command.'[136]

Shortly after he arrived in Ireland he made a tour of his command. Social conditions in Ireland depressed him. 'This is a most wretched country,' he wrote, the 'upper orders have fallen into a lethargy, and are only occupied in eating and drinking'. The Irish gentry, he told Pitt, 'believe or affect to believe that there is a pike in every family and a conspiracy in every parish and they would abandon the country unless the troops were dispersed over it . . . I believe the lower ranks heartily hate the gentlemen because they oppress them and the gentlemen hate the peasants because they know they deserve to be hated.' The lower orders, he thought, were sure 'the moment is at hand when they can glut their revenge and hope for a more equal share of the good things in this life'. Nevertheless he argued, with something of the inconsistency of a very irritated man, that the Irish administration was exaggerating the danger

---

[134] Camden to Pelham, 28 June 1796 (H.O. 100/64), Camden to Portland, 28 Aug., 3, 8 Sept. 1796 (H.O. 100/61/62); 30 Jan., 25 Feb., 24 Apr. 1797 (H.O. 100/67, 69).

[135] Lord Dunfermline, *Lieutenant-general Sir Ralph Abercromby* (1861), pp. 19–38.

[136] R. Abercromby to W. Elliot, 25 Dec. 1797 (H.O. 100/75).

of insurrection.[137] As might be expected he was very critical of the forces in Ireland, insulated from the rigours of active service and demoralized by being scattered on police-keeping duties, and he set briskly to work to bring them up to a satisfactory level of efficiency.

Abercromby was anxious to concentrate his forces, calling troops in from detached service. This would have a threefold advantage—the army would be ready to meet an invasion; discipline would be tightened; and the Irish gentry and yeomanry corps would be forced to accept responsibility for policing the countryside. In his general orders he instructed commanding officers to acquire a knowledge of the terrain and to establish a close liaison with the commanders of yeomanry corps in their districts. Officers were not to employ soldiers as servants in a way which prevented them mounting guard or attending drills, and cavalry officers were cautioned against the practice of charging for the forage of horses which had in fact been turned out to grass. There were to be frequent parades because they promoted 'order, cleanliness, uniformity and sobriety', and officers and men were reminded that when aiding the civil power 'they must not forget they are only called upon to support the law of the land . . . [and that] any outrage or excess on their part is highly culpable'. Finally, on 26 February 1798 Abercromby issued a strongly worded general order deploring the disgraceful frequency of courts martial and the many complaints about 'irregularities'. The army, he declared in a stinging apophthegm, was, 'in a state of licentiousness which must render it formidable to anyone but the enemy'; he ordered officers to attend regularly inspections and roll-calls and positively forbade troops to act in support of the civil power except under the authority of a magistrate.[138]

Abercromby, whose primary aim was to create an effective fighting force, seems to have intended by brutally severe criticism to shock the officers and men under his command into a realization of their faults. The order of the 26 February was, in the opinion of an experienced staff officer, 'calculated to

---

[137] R. Abercromby to W. Pitt, 28 Jan. 1798 (P.R.O. 30/8/325); Lord Dunfermline, *Lieutenant-general Sir Ralph Abercromby*, pp. 125–30.

[138] General orders, 24 Dec. 1797, 13 Feb. 1798 (Army Museum, MS 6807/174), 26 Feb. 1798 (*D.E.P.*, 15 Mar. 1798).

arouse the army into a sense of discipline'.[139] One general officer, Duff, commanding the Limerick district, thought it unfair. He found it hard to express the 'mortification' the six regiments under his command felt when they read the order. 'No men', he wrote, 'could have conducted themselves with greater propriety . . . No complaint has been made of the misconduct of any individual.' As for Lake, after talking with Sir Ralph (whom he thought 'quite in his dotage' and out of touch with the realities of the Irish situation), he came to the conclusion that the general orders would not prevent his acting vigorously against 'the rascals', though he would have to take care that some of his corps were not too' frisky'.[140]

The general order of 26 February, whatever its effects on the army, undoubtedly created a political furore. Conservatives had recently, in two parliamentary debates which attracted immense attention, been defending the troops stationed in Ireland against opposition criticism. Now they felt that their flank had been turned by what Pitt characterized as Sir Ralph's 'indiscriminating and unqualified censure on the whole army' —one sentence of which was almost 'an invitation to invasion'. Moreover, by a slip Abercromby seemed to be deliberately attacking the policy of the Irish administration. When he issued his general order he overlooked the fact that the proclamation of 1797 directing the military to act for the maintenance of law and order, even if a magistrate was not present, was still in force. Nevertheless, Camden and those with whom he was 'in the habit of consulting' were anxious that Abercromby should remain in command in Ireland, and the lord lieutenant tried to explain away the controversial general order as merely a military matter. But Abercromby was thoroughly dissatisfied with the whole Irish situation—the alienation of the people from the government, the supineness of many individuals, and 'the loose texture' of the Irish army, and on the ground that he had lost the confidence of the lord lieutenant's advisers, he insisted on resigning.[141]

---

[139] R. Brownrigg to the duke of York, 11 Mar. 1798 (W.O. 133/1).

[140] J. Duff to Hewett, 10 Mar. 1798 (Army Museum MS 5910/198); G. Lake to ——, 25 Feb., 2, 6 Mar. 1798 (N.L.I. MS 56).

[141] W. Pitt to Camden, 13 Mar. 1798 (P.R.O. 30/8/325); Camden to Portland 15, 26 Mar. 1798 (H.O. 100/75); Camden to W. Pitt, 26 Mar. 1798 (P.R.O. 30/8/326).

The lord lieutenant hoped to secure as Abercromby's successor a soldier of recognized professional attainments. In Camden's opinion, Lake, the senior officer serving in Ireland, though active and good-tempered, was not of the required calibre, 'when great arrangements aie to be considered his capacity does not extend to them'. Camden suggested as possibilities Sir William Fawcett, Grey, or David Dundas, and accepting that 'this government is now become so intermixed with military measures', he even suggested a drastic departure, the appointment of a distinguished soldier as lord lieutenant with a lawyer as his secretary. But Abercromby's short tenure of the Irish command had not been a good advertisement for the post and *faute de mieux*, Lake was appointed commander-in-chief.

17

Insurrection

At the beginning of 1798 politics in both Great Britain and Ireland were dominated by the war. France, with all its continental enemies forced to sue for peace, was now in a position to select the time and place for the decisive blow which would destroy British power. All over the British Isles extreme radicals could look forward to the speedy collapse of the established order. In Ireland the United Irishmen continued to extend their organization, secure arms and propagate their opinions. Though the *Northern Star* had been suppressed, the Irish radicals had two newspapers—in Dublin, the *Press*, started by Arthur O'Connor in September 1797 and in Cork, the *Harp of Erin*, which was managed by a group which included Roger O'Connor and Webb, a barrister who had been a member of the Dublin society of United Irishmen, and which began appearing about the beginning of February 1798. The *Press*, which was exceptionally well produced, not only gave plenty of slanted Irish and foreign news, but also printed poetry and numerous essays, which in high-pitched prose denounced the Irish administration and its instruments and called for radical changes in men and measures.[1]

The *Press* continuously implied that tyranny would soon be vanquished and during the early months of 1798 an Irish radical who was an optimist would have had grounds for believing that his cause would soon triumph. Growing numbers were being enrolled in the United Irishmen's societies, the movement was spreading in Leinster and Munster, the government's repressive measures were arousing widespread indignation (at least amongst liberals and radicals) and with the opening of a new campaign season French help might be expected. In February the Leinster executive was informed that

[1] *Press*, 27 Jan. 1798; N. Murphy to T. Pelham, 30 Jan. 1798 (I.S.P.O. 620/35/85); R. R. Madden, *United Irishmen*, 20 ed., ii, pp. 234–5; papers relating to W. L. Webb (PC1/44/A156).

the directory was engaged in mounting a massive attack to be directed against England and Scotland as well as Ireland and that the British radicals were preparing to co-operate with the invaders; at the end of March it was informed by Bartholomew Teeling, a leading Ulster United Irishman who had fled to France, that the French troops would be embarked and ready to sail by the middle of April.[2]

Time seemed to be on the side of the radicals but postponement of the moment for direct action had its dangers. The government was strengthening its forces and constant harassment was bound to interfere with the efficiency of the United Irishmen's organization. Moreover, there was an argument in favour of immediate action which radicals would be loath to dwell on but which seems to have been mentioned by Lord Edward Fitzgerald. Lord Edward, it was reported, early in 1798 was 'afraid of invasion lest the French should attempt to conquer'. What he wanted from France were arms, munitions and officers, dispatched on a few fast-sailing frigates. Earlier, at the beginning of 1797, Lord Edward, a professional soldier, seems to have thought that the crown forces in Ireland could only be defeated by a large French expeditionary force. Some United Irishmen, he expected, would 'join the French line' and be trained, but the Irish insurgents would be mainly employed in harassing the king's troops and cutting off small detachments.[3] But early in 1798, either because he did not expect the arrival of French forces in the immediate future or because he preferred to act without embarrassing assistance, Lord Edward had come to the conclusion that the United Irishmen, citizens in arms, reinforced probably by mutinous militiamen, could, if they employed the right tactics, defeat the crown forces. Regular troops, he pointed out, were trained to manœuvre on a spacious terrain and fight at musket-shot range. They would soon lose their superiority when pent up in a city or when working through a countryside intersected with numerous ditches and hedges. In Dublin, barricades of hogsheads and carts could be quickly thrown up; and military columns, advancing along narrow streets, 'galled from the housetops by showers of bricks and coping stones' and unable to deploy, would be driven back

[2] *Commons' Jn. Ire.*, xvii, p. dcclxc.
[3] PC1/3118; *Commons' Jn. Ire.*, xvii, p. dccclxviii.

in confusion by a sudden charge of pikemen. While the Dublin garrison was pinned down, the United Irishmen in surrounding counties would rise in arms, block the roads by felling trees and ambushing military detachments unprepared for this form of warfare.[4]

The response of the Irish administration to the growing menace of civil war and invasion was simple—an unflinching and inflexible defence of the established order by every means at its command. In the struggle to 'keep Ireland from being made a Jacobin appendage to the French republic' it had the full support of the British government which realized that the conspiracy which was being carried on in Ireland had 'to be treated in a different manner to an election mob or drunken riot' in England.[5] When parliament met in January 1798 the lord lieutenant, while thankful that 'subordination and industry' had been restored in the north, had to report that disaffection was spreading in the midlands and south, and parliament promptly continued the insurrection act and the suspension of the habeas corpus act, passed an indemnity bill and a bill imposing further liabilities on newspaper proprietors and voted three million for defence. A small band of critics asserted that the administration's approach to the crisis was unimaginative and narrow. They were confident that discontent could be destroyed or significantly diminished by a conciliatory policy. Such a policy, Parsons declared, should comprise catholic emancipation and parliamentary reform. William Smith, Edmund Burke's young disciple, in a powerful and well-publicized plea for conciliation called for catholic emancipation and 'practical reform' (the abolition of cabal, jobbery, extravagances and military oppression) rather than parliamentary reform which he thought inopportune. Lord Moira, attributing discontent to the measures adopted by the government for checking rebellion, asked the lord chancellor 'to show me the rebellion'. On a recent visit to his estates, in what was said to be a discontented area in County Down, he had been greatly impressed by the sincere loyalty of his tenantry (conservatives did not allow Moira to forget this assessment of the Ulster

---

[4] *Commons' Jn. Ire.*, xvii, p. dccccxxviii.
[5] Grenville to Camden, 17 Nov. 1797; Grenville to Clare, 16 Mar. 1798 (Add. MS 59254A).

situation, the *Anti-Jacobin* publishing in the summer of 1798 some light verse on the theme, 'There is no town so loyal as Ballynahinch'.) Conservatives retorted that it was impossible to arrive at a compromise with the partisans of anarchy and democracy; that parliamentary reform would not satisfy men who wished to overturn the constitution and introduce the French system of government, equality and an agrarian law, and that in 'the present temper of the populace' parliamentary reform would mean that 'the specious emissary or the turbulent demagogue' would be returned as M.P.s. Moira's proposal that the lords should consider the causes of discontent was defeated by 44 to 9, and when early in March Parsons moved a similar motion he was defeated by 144 to 19. The parliamentary opposition during the early months of 1798 also strongly criticized the behaviour of the military, Arthur Browne pointing out that 'martial law cannot be exercised in time of peace when the king's courts are open'.[6] On this question liberals and radicals co-operated. When at the end of January the radicals set up a committee to collect proofs of the enormities committed against the rights of the people Grattan visited Sampson, a leading member of the committee, to examine the material it had collected, but by this time the radicals were frankly saying that the whigs should become United Irishmen. An attempt to revive the Whig club at the beginning of 1798 had failed from lack of support, only eight members attending a meeting in February; Grattan was soon to leave for a prolonged visit to England and Arthur Browne, one of the whig remnant in the house of commons, surveying the empty galleries, sadly admitted that the public had lost interest in their proceedings.[7]

Shortly after defeating Moira and Parsons in parliament, the Irish administration was able to inflict a series of crippling blows on the militant radicals. The *Press* having commented in scurrilous terms on one of Moira's opponents in the Lords, its printer Stockdale was summoned to the bar of the house and sentenced to six months' imprisonment. A few days later his presses were seized by a magistrate and the *Press* ceased

[6] *D.E.P.*, 16 Jan. 1798.
[7] William Drennan to Mrs McTier, 8 Feb. 1798 (Drennan papers, 697); 'J.W.' to ——, 7 Feb. 1798 (I.S.P.O. 620/7/74/7); *Press*, 8 Feb. 1798; *D.E.P.*, 13 Feb. 1798.

publication. By the end of March, 'the second edition of the *Press*', the *Harp of Erin* was also suppressed, and the radicals deprived of their newspapers were reduced to circulating broadsheets. The day after Stockdale was committed to prison, the proprietor of the *Press* was arrested.[8] At the beginning of January O'Connor had left for England with the intention of proceeding to France. After his arrival in London he told John Binns, a young Irishman who was an ardent member of the Corresponding society, that he intended to go to France and seek an interview with Bonaparte. They agreed to leave for France together along with two servants and James Coigley, a priest from Dundalk, who was a keen United Irishman. Coigley on his way from Dublin to London had stayed in Manchester where he had met Robert Gray, a warehouseman from Monaghan who, with James Dixon, a Belfast weaver, had been active in trying to build up a working-class radical organization modelled on the United Irishmen, hundreds of 'constitutions' having been secured from Ireland. Coigley, 'a stout, lusty man', told Gray that the United Irishmen would soon overthrow the government of Ireland, 'make Bastilles for the ministerial party to dwell in' and 'revolutionize' England and Scotland.[9]

The efforts of Binns and O'Connor to secure a Channel passage for their party attracted attention and on 28 February they were arrested at Margate by Bow Street runners. All five, charged with high treason, were brought to trial at Maidstone in May. Coigley, who was incautiously carrying compromising documents (a French passport and a highly rhetorical address from the secret committee of England to the directory) was found guilty, sentenced to death and executed. The other prisoners were found not guilty, O'Connor producing as witnesses to character Grattan and some Foxite whigs, all of whom implied that his political opinions were similar to their own. At the conclusion of the trial O'Connor was arrested and sent to Ireland and detained until 1803. Thus he was rendered inactive—except with his pen—during a critical period.

---

[8] *Press*, 20 Feb. 1798; *D.J.*, 8, 29 Mar. 1798; 'J.W.' to ——, 7 Jan. 1798 (I.S.P.O. 620/36/227).
[9] Robert Grey, deposition (P.C. 1/3118); informations of James Dixon, John Grey and Mary Perrins (H.O. 42/45); *Recollections of the life of John Binns* (1854), pp. 83–4. Writing in old age Binns states that O'Connor wanted to get to France to see Bonaparte and Hoche.

A fortnight after the Margate arrests the government was able in one swoop to sweep into detention a number of the Leinster radical leaders. Though from 1796 the government had been receiving a plethora of information relating to radical activities, none of its sources were of the highest rank in the radical organization. For the intentions of the United Irishmen's leadership the administration was reduced to relying on reports from the rank and file or from more or less well-informed outside observers. Nevertheless at the beginning of February 1798 the lord lieutenant's Irish advisers were in favour of arresting the leaders of the United Irishmen even if there was insufficient evidence on which to bring them to trial, the speaker arguing that if the arrests led to insurrection it would be more easily quelled than if it coincided with a French invasion. The British cabinet was against arresting persons who could not be brought to trial but left the question to the Irish executive. However, early in February 1798 the Irish government began to receive information of the greatest value from a member of the Leinster provincial committee, Thomas Reynolds. Reynolds was the only son of a wealthy catholic silk and cotton manufacturer in Dublin who was by descent and marriage related to a number of well-established catholic landed families. He was educated in England and France and on the death of his father in 1788 inherited a substantial amount of property. After enjoying for some years the life of a well-off young man of fashion, Reynolds married the daughter of William Witherington, a Dublin merchant. Then in 1797, having leased Kilkea Castle in County Kildare with 350 acres, he set up as a country gentleman. In 1790 he had succeeded his father as a member of the catholic committee and in 1792 he was elected a member of the catholic convention. A supporter of catholic emancipation and parliamentary reform, early in 1797 he was induced to become a United Irishman. Later he asserted he did not take the United Irishmen's schemes seriously and he certainly was very busy at this time straightening out his involved business affairs and moving into his new home. However, at the close of 1797 a country neighbour, Lord Edward Fitzgerald, pressed Reynolds to take his place for a short time in the United Irishmen's organization in Kildare. Reynolds, according to himself, agreed reluctantly. After all it was a deferential age, and Lord Edward was a brother of the great county magnate who was Reynolds's landlord. Acting for Lord Edward, Reynolds became a colonel, a member of the county committee and county treasurer, a post which gave him a seat on the provincial committee. He soon discovered that preparations for direct action were well advanced and, either because he was scared or because he had a horror of revolutionary violence (he had been in France in July 1789), or from a mixture of motives, he decided to get out of the business, and, if possible, 'neutralize' the United Irishmen. At the close of February he mentioned in the course of conversation to William Cope, a well-known city conservative, that he, Reynolds, knew a man who in return for £500, which would enable him to get out of the country, would supply the government with important information, though he would not appear as a crown witness. Soon afterwards he informed Cope about the next meeting of the Leinster provincial committee.[10]

When the committee met on the morning of 12 March at Oliver Bond's in Bridge Street, Reynolds was not present. But Swan, a senior revenue official and a very active magistrate with a number of sergeants in 'coloured clothes' (i.e. plain clothes), came to the hall door and gave the password. Swan then 'bounced up stairs' and burst into a backroom where the committee was in session and told them to hold up their hands to prevent them destroying the papers with which the table was littered. A dozen men from Dublin and Leinster counties were arrested and brought before the privy council. Some of them offered ingenuous and disingenuous explanations for being there that morning. Thomas Traynor, a merchant and shipper, was in the house 'in the way of business'; Christopher Martin from Meath had called to buy seeds; Cummings from Kildare had been walking along the street when he saw McCann, Bond's clerk, whom he followed into the house; Joseph Thompson, a farmer from Wicklow, on being asked about a list of names, said it was 'very easily explained'—it was for a benefit ball. Bond himself said that he had lent the room to McCann and 'did not really know' who the people sitting in it were. But two delegates admitted that they were United Irishmen, adding

---

[10] Camden to Portland, 8 Feb. 1798; Portland to Camden, 15, 20 Feb. 1798 (H.O. 100/75); T. Reynolds, *Life of Thomas Reynolds*, 2 vols. (1839).

that they were on the point of resigning from the society.[11]

The prisoners taken at Bond's were sent to Kilmainham, where they were joined by Thomas Addis Emmet, Henry Jackson the iron-founder, Dr MacNeven and John Sweetman, the brewer, who were arrested on 12 March; and William Sampson, arrested some days later at Whitehaven, was confined first in Dublin Castle and then in the Bridewell. By the end of March nearly all the prominent United Irishmen and many of the second-rank leaders were in custody or exile. But as Drennan, who had almost dropped out of politics and who was absorbed in an agitating suit for a lady's hand, remarked: 'the chancellor may imagine he has cut off the head of the union but it is a perfect asparagus bed and bears cutting'. A few days after the Bridge Street arrests Lord Edward Fitzgerald, who had evaded capture and was in hiding in Dublin, sent orders to the Kildare United Irishmen to fill the vacancies in their organization, and though Neilson, the sometime editor of the *Northern Star*, acidly remarked that 'the people of Dublin were not like those of the north, who instead of flying about the streets would have quickly proceeded to fill up the places of the arrested delegates', the higher command in Dublin was quickly reconstituted. Two barristers, Henry and John Sheares, who had in the past been fairly prominent members of the Dublin society of United Irishmen, now flung themselves enthusiastically into planning a rising. John Sheares, a man of sensibility—though a fervent supporter of the French revolution he had wept during the king's trial and was moved by the sufferings of Marie Antoinette—was a member of the bar and a vehement writer. Henry, twelve years older than his brother, had substantial private means, was devoted to his wife and children, and allowed his brother, from whom he had borrowed money, to take the lead in politics.[12]

[11] For an account of the arrests see W. Ridgeway, *Report of the trial of John McCann* (1798), pp. 38–49; for examinations before the privy council see I.S.P.O. 620/36/9A. Reynolds, aware that he was suspected by the United Irishmen, and with a destructive military detachment quartered on his Kildare property, soon yielded to government pressure, was an important crown witness in several treason trials, and appeared before the secret committees of the house of lords and house of commons. Shortly afterwards he left Ireland and later became a fervent evangelical.

[12] William Drennan to Mrs McTier, 1, 17 Mar. 1798 (Drennan papers, 701); *Commons' Jn. Ire.*, xvii, p. dccclxx; H. R. Yorke, *France in 1802* (1906), pp. 226–7.

The Sheareses showed themselves to be very energetic, courageous and incompetent conspirators. Realizing that the United Irishmen in the military units stationed near Dublin were bound to play a very important part in the coming rising, they were anxious to find an officer to lead them, and when Byrne, the radical bookseller in Grafton Street, offered to introduce them to a young military man whom he believed to be a radical, they jumped at the opportunity. John Armstrong, a captain in the King's county militia, an avid reader, was in the habit of dropping into Byrne's to look at recent publications, especially political pamphlets. On 10 May Byrne introduced him to John and Henry Sheares, and John quickly plunged into business, according to Armstrong, telling him that he wanted to explain 'how the cause was to be benefitted by my joining the cause in *action*, as he knew I had by *inclination*'. Armstrong, on the advice of his colonel, had a half-dozen meetings with the Sheareses, who discussed freely with him their plans for seducing soldiers from their allegiance and seizing Loughlinstown camp (Lawless, a friend of John Sheares, remarking that 'the trees to the right of the camp would be very convenient for hanging people').[13]

At the time the radical leaders were arrested a number of their subordinates in the Dublin area were taken into custody—one United Irishmen's committee being captured by Swan when meeting on a wherry near the Pigeon house. Steps were also taken to check student radicalism. Two United Irishmen's societies seem to have been meeting in Trinity (in numbers 5 and 26) and enthusiastically toasting radical sentiments. There were political squabbles amongst the undergraduates and on 22 February there was a commotion in the squares, a group led by two undergraduates, who were 'in liquor', singing republican songs. The board promptly expelled three radical under-graduates and rusticated a conservative, and Lord Clare (who was vice-chancellor of the university) decided that a visitation should be held on 19 April by Clare, himself, and Dr Duigenan. Clare, who dominated the proceedings, began by ordering an undergraduate who was wearing boots to appear properly dressed. A number of fellows and undergraduates were in-terrogated and two of the fellows, Browne and Stokes, incurred

[13] W. Ridgeway, *Report of the proceedings in cases of high treason* (1798), p. 71.

Fitzgibbon's wrath for having displayed what he regarded as irresponsible liberalism (Stokes scarcely improved his position by stating he knew of illegal societies in college—Orange societies). Stokes was suspended from tutorship, two recent graduates and seventeen undergraduates were expelled and Clare exhorted the students while in 'a learned seminary' to abstain from politics—'you will be learned men, you will be religious men, you will be great men', he told them. Simultaneously a severe blow was struck at British radicalism.[14] Towards the end of April a number of arrests were made in Manchester, and in London a number of the United Englishmen and the Corresponding society were taken into custody. Though both bodies freely employed revolutionary terminology it is improbable that they had made any serious preparations for direct action. Nevertheless the arrests destroyed any possibility of British co-ordination with the United Irishmen.[15]

By the middle of 1798 it would have been reasonable to conclude that the government had by its vigorous countermeasures forestalled rebellion. But in fact a plan of insurrection had already been prepared and communicated to many of those concerned. The Dublin United Irishmen, supported by military mutineers, who would seize the camps at Loughlinstown (militia) and Chapelizod (artillery) and march on Dublin, were to rise and seize the city; the leading supporters of the government would be imprisoned and 'the mail coaches would be burned as a signal for the whole kingdom to rise'. Admittedly arrangements for the participation of the areas at a distance from Dublin had not been perfected. The Ulster United Irishmen, though greatly impressed by the plan at the beginning of May, at the end of the month were still deliberating on the steps they should take; John Sheares who was to 'go down and organise Cork'[16] was arrested before he left Dublin; and there is evidence that in County Westmeath preparations were far

---

[14] T. Elrington, board diary (T.C.D. MS 4958) and Thomas Prior (T.C.D. MS 3373).

[15] According to Francis Place the aim of the United Englishmen was 'to produce a revolution'. Though the society, whose founder was Thomas Evans, a sometime secretary of the Corresponding society, had a formidable name, it had very few members (*The autobiography of Francis Place*, ed. M. Thale (1971), pp. 177–8).

[16] W. Ridgeway, *A report of the proceedings in cases of high treason* (1798), p. 70. According to F. Higgins, Lidwell and Henry Sheares had been appointed majorgenerals for Meath (F. Higgins to ——, May 1798, I.S.P.O. 620/18).

from completed at the beginning of May. A keen local leader, John McManus of Kilbeggan, informed the Dublin United Irishmen that in his barony they 'could in four hours bring into the field 3,400 men determined to stand or fall in the cause of their country. All they want is a knowledge of the moment.' But when McManus had recently attempted to arrange a county meeting of baronial representatives, 'to my great mortification I was totally disappointed'. 'From the variable dispositions of the lower orders of the people', he charitably wrote, 'I think many of their baronial members excusable, it takes and requires great patience and perseverance to bring them to a proper sense of their duty.'[17] Nevertheless, in the countryside round Dublin, where the organization was strong and the Dublin leaders had been able to exercise considerable influence, insurrection had acquired a momentum which it would have been hard to check and on 23 May the mail coaches which left Dublin that evening for the north and south-west were stopped and burned.

But the rising, which began on 23 May in the wide plain stretching round Dublin and soon spread to south-east Leinster and east Ulster, was not the great revolutionary upheaval which radicals had been looking forward to. They had visualized a national rising in which the popular forces, organized in advance on a military pattern and armed and directed by a recognized higher command, joined by many Irish soldiers in the government ranks and supported by France, would overwhelm the demoralized adherents of a discredited regime. The reality was different. By the time rebellion broke out, the United Irishmen's organization had been severely damaged in the course of a two-year strenuous struggle with authority. Their higher command was shattered and what was intended to be a forcible and formidable expression of the national will turned out to be a number of ill-coordinated localized *émeutes*.

Some idea of the incidence of insurrection may be obtained from the claims for compensation made to the commissioners for the relief of suffering loyalists appointed in October 1798. The claims totalled approximately 6,200, ranging from £5,600

---

[17] *Commons' Jn. Ire.*, xviii, p. dccclxvi; letter from J. McManus to P. Gallagher in proceedings of court martial of J. McManus, 29 June 1798 (I.S.P.O. 620/3/25/1). For Gallagher see (620/3/16/190). McManus was sentenced to death.

for the destruction of a mansion and its contents to £56 for the loss of a mare and a barrel of oats. Of the claims, well over 50 per cent came from two counties, Wexford (36·6) and Wicklow (17·2). Nearly 15 per cent came from two counties in the west, Mayo (11·3) and Sligo (3·4); 10 per cent came from the area round Dublin, Counties Dublin (1·2), Kildare (7·3) and Meath (2·4). Rather more than 4 per cent came from Antrim (2·3) and Down (2·2) and 3·8 per cent from Kilkenny. From seven counties (including five Ulster counties) there were no claims. From two (Cavan and Londonderry) one each, from three (Cork, Kerry and Waterford) two each, from four (Clare, King's, Roscommon and Tipperary) between 3 and 15. These figures, it may be said, indicate the amount of destruction (and the eagerness to claim compensation) rather than the severity of the fighting. But they help to give an approximate indication of the relative intensity of violence throughout the country— reflecting the very short duration of the Ulster rising and the widespread collapse of respect for authority in north Connaught consequent on Humbert's landing and advance to Castlebar.[18]

Not only did the rising fail to develop into a nation-wide upheaval, and the local outbreaks fail to synchronize successfully, but the insurrection lacked the military pattern which the more militant radical leaders had tried to impose on it. Their intention was that if the United Irishmen took the field they should do so well armed and arrayed in organized units— companies and battalions—with N.C.O.s and officers possessing the confidence of the rank and file, and with a higher command and a general staff. But arrests and raids had deprived the United Irishmen's military organization of officers and arms, and when the insurgents at last went into action they had to improvise quickly a division into units (in so far as they bothered about it), men from the same village or parish marching with their neighbours. As for leaders or 'captains', they were men whose experience, physical vigour, personality, status, stature or fighting spirit marked them out as natural leaders. Tactics and strategy were simple. The pike (or a pitchfork) was the insurgents' usual weapon, and with their large numbers they might hope that mass attacks might

[18] *Commons' Jn. Ire.*, xix, pp. clviii–ccccxcviii.

bear down disciplined opposition by sheer weight of numbers. When the insurgents were forced on the defensive they instinctively chose a terrain unfavourable to cavalry or artillery. Strategy, once it was clear that Dublin was well defended, was a question of establishing in each region a local base or bases—only achieved in Wexford and Sligo—and trying to spread insurrection over as wide an area as possible, keeping the flames alive until French help in strength reached Ireland.

It is temptingly easy to employ military terminology freely when discussing the rising, and the hard fighting is to some extent a justification for this. But for all the advanced planning undertaken by radical leaders, when the fighting started the insurgents were in fact badly armed crowds, and their behaviour was in many respects that of a crowd, a crowd animated by strong common loyalties and with common and immediate objectives. Enthusiastic, optimistic, courageous, given the momentum of success, the insurgents could sweep forward with the irresistible and frightening force of a confident, determined crowd. They also had something of the waywardness of a crowd, groups splitting off making for tangible targets, and then rejoining. Cheered by success, the insurgents were badly shaken by a check. Forced to retire, they tended to disperse, and in retreat their forces diminished fast as the less enthusiastic melted away. As is customary with crowds, the hard core of the convinced and determined swept along the more hesitant. After the collapse of the rising, many, especially in Ulster, asserted that they had been forced into the insurgent ranks. For instance in County Down one laggard was told, 'For God's sake, turn out or you will be hung at your door and nailed to that door by the cheek.' In County Antrim when a reluctant recruit asked his fellow insurgents to allow him to go to his master's for breakfast, 'they refused saying they would give him breakfast enough.' Another Antrim insurgent said that he was at work on 7 June when seven or eight men armed with pikes and guns came up to him and told him that 'if he did not go with them he would not be alive in the morning'. Ulster tradition preserved memories of ingenious excuses for avoiding service in the insurgents' ranks—the need to return home for a hat or a conspicuously advertised attack of gout. During the Wexford rising pressure on laggards was officially sanctioned by a proclamation, signed by Bagenal Harvey as commander-in-chief of the insurgent forces, directing that 'guards' should be sent out 'for the purpose of bringing in all men found loitering and delaying at home.' Those who failed to obey the summons might be sentenced to death and 'guards were to be stationed in the rear of the army to prevent desertion'. Even some leaders claimed that they had been swept into the rising at the last moment by popular pressure. Patrick Sutton explained that when, having retreated from Enniscorthy to Wexford with the government forces, he returned to the former town to protect his property, 'the rebels appointed me general, but I told them I would not consider myself in that line'. He used his authority to stop plundering and after the insurgents' defeat he was thrown into Wexford gaol but soon released on finding securities. Another Wexford man, Thomas Cloney, the son of a prosperous farmer, as the county became more disturbed in the rising of 1798 'determined to be peaceable, domestic and unoffending'. Though he decided not to take the oath of allegiance, he was not a United Irishman; but when towards the end of May, three days after the rising began, 'a numerous party' came to his father's house and pressed him to join the insurgents, he agreed to go with them to Enniscorthy; and then his drive and readiness to take the initiative soon made him one of the leaders of the rising.[19]

Again, according to himself, Joseph Holt, an outstanding guerrilla leader in Wicklow, was not a United Irishman before the insurrection and only joined the insurgents when his house was burned by a landlord with whom he had had a dispute over a road presentment. John Moore, the president of the Connaught directory, asserted that for ten days after the French landed at Killala he remained at Moorehall trying to persuade the tenantry to remain quietly at home. Finally, on 31 August he went to Castlebar with the object of securing a protection from the French. Humbert, discovering Moore spoke French, detained him and then induced him to assist in setting up

---

[19] Court martial, Downpatrick, 10 July 1798 (I.S.P.O. 620/15/1); court martial, Glenarm, 20 July 1798 (620/9/12); court martial, Antrim, 5 July 1798 (620/2/9/18); W. S. Smith, 'Memories of '98' in *U.J.A.*, 2nd series, i, pp. 211–12; P. Sutton, petition (S.P.P.); general order, signed B. B. Harvey (620/38/72); T. Cloney, *A personal narrative* (1828), pp. 16–21.

administrative machinery with the object of stopping plundering. Munro, who commanded the County Down insurgents, according to his sister-in-law 'acted more from impulse than reflection' at the time of the outbreak. Shortly before the rising he left his house in Lisburn 'to avoid seeing a man lashed and not with the smallest intention of joining the rebels'—though, she adds, he had been appointed a colonel of the United Irishmen's forces in County Armagh.[20]

Obviously men who found themselves associated with a defeated cause and who in some instances were facing punishment would tend to dwell on their lack of premeditation and to emphasize the part played by popular pressure in filling the insurgents' ranks. As a County Antrim imitator of Burns wrote,

> I'll hae to swear, —— forc'd me out
> Better he swing than I, on some hanging day . . .[21]

It is also obvious that crowds of countrymen, gathered to redress their wrongs, would not hesitate to bring the reluctant into their ranks by rough and ready methods of conscription. That many seem to have been swept into the rising at the last moment evinces the impetus of the movement, and the courage with which the insurgents steadily advanced against disciplined musket fire and artillery shows their spirit.

What animated the insurgent masses? Theoretically the insurgents were fighting for a republic inspired by radicalism, but needless to say only relatively few of them could have fully comprehended the aims and implications of *fin de siècle* enlightened radicalism. Holt, who knew the Wicklow countryside well, thought that the poor 'had little idea of political government. Their minds were more occupied with their own sufferings or enjoyments'. When the radical leaders were being examined by the lords' secret committee, Clare put it to Mac-Neven that the mass of the people 'did not care the value of this pen or the drop of ink it contains' for catholic emancipation

---

[20] Miss Templeton, notes on H. Munro (Madden papers, T.C.D.); J. Holt, *Memoirs*, ed. T. C. Croker (1838), i, pp. 14–30. Major Hardy, commanding in Wicklow, noted in his journal that having heard Holt had seduced some soldiers, 'this irritated me so much that I burned his house' (W.W.M. F. 30); J. Moore, petition (620/513240).

[21] J. Orr, *Poems* (1804), p. 16.

and parliamentary reform. MacNeven agreed with him—
adding however, that the masses realized that they would gain
considerably if they were free from tithe and no longer fleeced
by their landlords. In Wexford in June 1798 'the lower orders
talked of Lord Edward to be their king' and in County Clare
early in 1799 a labourer was charged not only with drinking 'to
the French and to downfall to the English', but for singing a
song which began

> You are welcome home Prince Charles,
> You are the Romans only darling.

The prospect of French intervention aroused widespread
enthusiasm and expectation—a pledge to aid the French was
an important part of many illegal oaths. It was also widely
believed by the insurgents that their victory would inaugurate
an age of economic betterment for the bulk of the population.
Many of them indeed during the rising briefly experienced a
foretaste of such an age. In an insurgent camp which he
stormed, Colonel Gough found sheep, bullocks, a number of
pots on the boil and great quantities of flour, groceries, wine
and spirits. In another camp the insurgents had fat bullocks and
'great quantities of meal, bacon, butter, fine feather beds and
good horses' and 'their tents were formed of fine large Wilton
carpets, bed hangings, window curtains, sheets and table cloths'.
Men who all their lives subsisted on a monotonous diet were,
with the local collapse of the established social order, enjoying
for a short time the pleasures of affluent equality.[22]

Another great bond of union amongst the insurgents was
religion. Radical publicists, men of the enlightenment, were
looking forward to an age of religious equality when denominational issues would no longer obtrude into politics. But in
Antrim and Down many of the insurgents were conscious that
they were presbyterians, protestant dissenters; and the countrymen who in the south and west filled the insurgent ranks were
profoundly aware of being catholics sharing the faith of their
persecuted forefathers. With many of the supporters of authority

[22] W. J. MacNeven, *Pieces of Irish history*, p. 199; *A narrative of the sufferings and
escape of Charles Jackson* (1799), p. 44; court martial, Ennis (620/5/59/10); *D.J.*,
21 July 1798; *D.E.P.*, 2 June 1798.

conscious that they were protestants and members of the established church, the rebellion could be seen as a religious conflict.
This was an aspect of the rising which certainly impressed contemporaries. To John Kearney, a future provost of Trinity, it
seemed as if 'the rage of democracy and the zeal of superstition
. . . Republicanism and bigotry had joined hands in a deadly
league'.[23] The belief that the insurrection was essentially a
catholic rising was expounded with great vigour by Sir Richard
Musgrave, an M.P. and an active magistrate. In 1799 he
pseudonymously published a pamphlet attacking the catholic
clergy of Wexford for their role in the rebellion. He listed a
number of priests who, he said, were prominent insurgent
leaders, and he asserted that the bishop of Ferns and his clergy
had failed during the rising to exert their authority for the
protection of protestants. In the summer of 1798 Musgrave
started to prepare a history of the insurrection. He was able to
see some court martial proceedings and some accounts prepared
by senior army officers and he conscientiously collected accounts
of the same episode from different participants (all of course
loyalists), though many country gentlemen, he complained,
would not 'snatch an hour from swinish gluttony' to help him.
His history contained a considerable amount of valuable
material but is strongly biased by his belief that the fundamental
source of the rebellion which had disgraced Ireland was papal
aggrandizement, and he prefaced his account of '98 with a long
digression on the origins of papal power. Catholic conservatives
and liberal protestants treated Musgrave's theory with contempt, but his work ran rapidly into three editions.[24]

Cornwallis was quick to denounce 'the folly', prevalent in
conservative and government circles, of 'substituting catholic
instead of Jacobin as the foundation of the present rebellion',[25]
and his attitude was reflected in the reports of the secret
committees of the houses of lords and commons, which attributed the rising to the machinations of designing men, inspired
by the French revolution, who had aimed at 'forming a
democratic republic, founded on the destruction of all church

[23] J. Kearney, A sermon (1798), pp. 10–11.
[24] R. Musgrave, Memoirs of the different rebellions in Ireland, 2nd ed., preface;
Prior diary (T.C.D. MS 3365); R. Musgrave to T. Percy, 6 Dec. 1798 (N.L.I. MS
4197).
[25] Cornwallis correspondence, ed. C. Ross (1859), ii, p. 357.

establishments, the abolition of ranks and the confiscation of property'. Such men, a fellow of Trinity declared, had stirred up the working classes, converting 'our contented and happy cottager into a reformer of the state'. Another very intelligent and eloquent conservative, Sir Hercules Langrishe, emphasized that it was not economic distress which had brought about the rising—the country was prospering, the poor were lightly taxed. It was, he declared, 'French politics and French success, it was the jargon of equality, which had been diffused through a deluded multitude by designing men', together with 'the spirit of plunder and popular domination', which had led to the attempt 'to break the bonds of society and set up the capriciousness of the popular will against the stability of settled government'.[26]

The feelings of the higher ranks of the catholic clergy, whose hostility to the revolution was in the early months of 1798 intensified by the French behaviour to the pope, is reflected in a catholic address published during the insurrection, signed by four peers, four baronets, a number of country gentlemen and merchants (including John Keogh), twenty-eight prelates and the president of Maynooth. Though they admitted that they differed on some points of religious concern from the established order, the signatories called on Irish catholics to rally to the defence of 'our constitution, the social order and the Christian religion'.[27] The great bulk of the clergy seem to have followed the lead of their superiors or remained passive. But a movement which included so many catholics naturally swept into its ranks a number of ecclesiastics. In two areas, Sligo–Mayo and Wexford, where masses of catholics rose in revolt, some of the catholic clergy were prominent among the insurgents. In the former area about fourteen were active in the rising; in the latter at least nine.[28] In reply to a conservative who suggested that about twenty priests in Wexford were implicated in the insurrection, Caulfield, bishop of Ferns, pointed out that at least eight had been honourably acquitted, including the parish

[26] 'Eumenes' (J. Walker), *Thoughts on the present rebellion* (1798); *D.J.*, 1 Sept. 1798.
[27] *D.J.*, 31 May 1798.
[28] R.Hayes, 'Priests in the independent movement of '98', in *Ir. Ecc. Rec*, lxvi, pp. 258–70, provides a considerable amount of valuable biographical detail but is uncritical in his use of evidence.

priest of Bannow, a strong loyalist until he was led to believe
the rebels could not be resisted. Caulfield also (privately) made
it clear that in his opinion most of the clergy who were prominent in the Wexford insurrection had in the past failed to
maintain accepted standards of clerical decorum.[29] Taking
Ireland as a whole, at least sixty catholic priests were referred
to as playing a part in the insurrectionary movement, and nine
were killed in action or executed. But it was a time when
political accusations were being freely bandied about and many
of those named (possibly one-third) may in fact have not been
in any way involved in radical politics.

It may be added that some of the clergy of the other great
non-conforming community, the presbyterians, were also
involved in the insurrection, fifteen ministers and nine licen-
tiates or probationers being mentioned as implicated. Of these,
four were court-martialled (two, the Revd James Porter, the
witty political satirist, and Warwick, a probationer, being
executed), and a number of others were imprisoned or thought
it advisable to leave the country.[30] Finally, one church of
Ireland clergyman, Henry Fulton, a curate in Killaloe diocese,
was accused of sedition in 1798. Fulton described by an
indignant magistrate as 'a wolf in sheep's clothing', with a
demeanour 'bordering on Methodism', was sentenced to
transportation by justices of the peace. In New South Wales he
became a chaplain, was active in philanthropic and educational
work and was a vigorous anti-catholic polemicist.[31]

Religion was one element in the compound—denominational
loyalty, systematic radicalism, a vague belief in a better order
of things, a sense of economic injustice, hostility to the landlord
and the tithe owner, resentment of repression, admiration for
France and hope of French assistance, community feeling—
which, influencing different men in widely differing proportions,
gave momentum to insurrection.

To meet insurrection the armed forces which the Irish
government had at its disposal early in 1798 comprised 4,600

[29] J. Caulfield to J. T. Troy, 2, 6 Sept. 1798, 21 May 1799 (Troy papers,
IV/11/7); Veridicus, *A concise account of the material events which occured in the Irish
rebellion* (1799).
[30] *Records of the general synod of Ulster*, iii, pp. 205, 216–17.
[31] For Fulton see Henry Osborn to ——, 28 Oct. 1798 (P.P. 1/77), and *Australian
Dictionary of National biography*.

regular cavalry, 2,600 regular infantry, 2,000 fencible cavalry, 1,800 fencible infantry, 25,000 militia and 40,000 yeomanry (about one-third mounted). The grand total of approximately 76,000 men is impressive. But it must be taken into account that the army in Ireland had a twofold task, the maintenance of internal order and defence against invasion. Moreover, of the grand total well over half was yeomanry, and the yeomanry, sketchily, if at all, trained, was organized in numerous small corps which could not be employed far from home. It was also feared that the loyalty of the militia might have been undermined. In fact when insurrection broke out the militia fought well, and their virtues and weaknesses emerge in an enthusiastic encomium delivered by a militia officer. 'Nothing', he wrote, 'could equal the ardour of our Limerick lads. They would have burned down every house and killed every man they met had I not restrained them. They are the most desperate fellows on earth and I am sure as loyal.' In 1796 the fencibles, it was said, included in their ranks many men who were too young for service or too old. As for the regular cavalry, which was regarded as the most effective instrument for checking disorder, it was discovered during the rising that dragoons could be beaten off by insurgents armed only with pikes and shotguns who positioned themselves sensibly; of the seven regular regiments of foot on the Irish establishment, five, recently returned from that military graveyard, the West Indies, were 'skeleton' units, busy recruiting, and one, the 30th, stationed at Bandon, was not in action during 1798.[32] But in spite of their weaknesses the military—regulars, fencibles and militia—were drilled and disciplined and at many critical points could rely on artillery support. As a result, unless badly handled, they were a match for far superior numbers of insurgents.

At the beginning of May, with many arms being surrendered, it seemed as if the military had the upper hand and General Dundas, commanding in the eastern district, a kindly man full of sympathy for 'the poor deluded people', assured Cooke that 'the head of the Hydra is cut off and the County of Kildare will for a long time enjoy perfect peace and quiet'. But a week later

---

[32] Return of the forces in Ireland, Jan. 1793–Jan. 1804 (I.S.P.O. 620/50/56); Castlereagh to Nugent, 24 June 1798 (Army Museum MS 6807/174); report of Medical board, Apr. 1796 (Army Museum MS 680/7/174); *S.N.L.*, 16 June 1798.

Dundas was undeceived when on the night of 23 May with the burning of the mail coaches, insurrection surged up at numerous points in the wide plain round Dublin.[33]

In Dublin, about the 23rd it was rumoured that the lamplighters were disaffected and intended to leave the city in darkness. They may, of course, simply have been afraid to go through the streets in the dusk. In any event each lamplighter was provided with a yeomanry escort who saw that he performed his duties, and on the evening of the 23rd a County Down landowner on his way to a party at Lord Blayney's in Merrion Square saw a lamplighter being flogged for putting water instead of oil in his lamps. Lord Blayney's party was disturbed by a report that during the night Dublin was going to be attacked by an armed mob. 'A great alarm immediately took place, particularly amongst the women, nor indeed were the male sex quite exempt from trepidation'; the 'casino tables' were deserted and the guests, without waiting for carriages, hurried home.[34] About midnight the drum beat to arms, and the yeomanry moved to defensive positions. Barrington with his eye for the ludicrous, paints a vivid picture of a mass of amateur soldiers, including the Lawyers corps, packed in the dark, amongst the stalls of Smithfield market. The order 'never retreat', he wrote, was superfluous, since nobody could move.[35] The attack from the north, which the force stationed in Smithfield would have had to meet, did not develop, but to the south-west of the city, from Tallaght to Clondalkin, bodies of armed men gathered. The Rathfarnham yeomanry, after a brush with one band, retreated. Reinforced by a party of dragoons, they charged the insurgents and dispersed them. Two of the insurgent leaders, Ledwich and Wade, both yeomen, were captured, tried by court martial, and hanged at Queen's Bridge. From then on Dublin was quiet, 'except for that bustle which necessarily attends the movement of the great bodies of troops'.[36] The commander-in-chief imposed a curfew from 9 p.m. to 5 a.m. on the city, and the lord mayor, who had

---

[33] H. Dundas to E. Cooke, 16 May 1798 (620/37/90); Major-General Sir W. Otway, account of 1798 (Army Museum MS 680/7/414 (1)).

[34] F. Heyland, *The Irish rebellion of 1798* (1913).

[35] J. Barrington, *Historic memoirs of Ireland* (18233), ii, pp. 256–7; La Touche to ——, 24 May 1798 (Army Museum MS 5910/198).

[36] *D.E.P.*, 26 May 1798.

already reminded inhabitants that they must register arms in their possession, ordered every householder to place on the front door of his house a list of its occupants. The lord mayor also suggested that each guild should open a book in which masters could record the names of their employees for the weeks preceding and following the rebellion. This would show which of 'the wretches' had quitted the city. Since there were many disaffected employees, he advised that the names should be checked against the weekly pay books.[37]

The chief police magistrate advised the public, in the event of a riot, to keep off the streets, 'as thereby only the guilty should suffer in case the military should be reduced to the necessity of firing'; he promised that the names of persons giving information about arms should not be revealed, and directed that householders should search their stables and outhouses for concealed arms. The necessity for taking this step was vividly illustrated by an advertisement inserted in the *Dublin Journal* by Thomas Kennedy, a carpenter and undertaker, offering a reward for the apprehension of a clerk and a journeyman who, he believed, were responsible for hiding the pikes which had been found on his premises.[38]

During the next few weeks the atmosphere in Dublin must have been tense. Raids for arms continued. At night fires could seen on the hills near the city. Many arrests were made, prisoners being lodged in the city gaols or sent to tenders in the Liffey. A number of men—it is impossible to say how many— were flogged with the aim of securing information. A Scottish fencible sergeant, after mentioning that the yeomanry brought suspected persons to the barracks where he was stationed to be flogged, remarked, 'I once condemned such practices. I am now convinced of their necessity. Many of them led to the very places where the rebels arms were concealed.' However, on 9 June orders were issued directing that 'no corporal punishment should be inflicted on any person by any of the guards'. Some of the bolder United Irishmen slipped out of the city to join the insurgents. Bacon, the well-known radical tailor and volunteer

---

[37] *D.J.*, 26 May, 7 June 1798.
[38] *D.J.*, 26 May, 29 May 1798. It was rumoured that many servants were bound by an oath to kill their masters and that 7,000 of them had bought poison. Prior diary, T.C.D. MS 3365; T.C.D. MS 2575; *St James's Chronicle* 31 May 1798.

major, was arrested when leaving the city disguised as a woman, in a hackney coach. He was court-martialled and hanged at Carlisle Bridge. Radical Dublin was overawed, while the rising fervour of Dublin conservatism (and possibly some opportunism) was indicated by hundreds coming forward to join the yeomanry and generous subscriptions to a fund for the relief of soldiers' widows and orphans. The Trinity undergraduates raised a fund to supplement the allowances granted to wives of militiamen; the archbishop of Dublin (who was at Clifton near Bristol) sent a circular letter to his clergy 'permitting them in the present exigent state of the times' to assume a military character; and 'the elegant equestrian statue of' George I, which had been removed when Essex Bridge had been rebuilt, was placed in front of the Mansion house, with an inscription declaring it had been re-elevated by the loyal corporation of Dublin, 'at a time when rebellion and disloyalty were the characteristics of the day'.[39]

During the night of 23–4 May, insurrection broke out at a number of points in Counties Dublin, Kildare and Meath. The insurgents made no attempt to assemble for a concentrated drive on Dublin, but armed bands attacked a number of small towns and villages. Dunboyne was burned to the ground. At Dunshaughlin a number of protestants including a clergyman were killed. At Prosperous, a small garrison of the North Cork militia with a few Ancient Britons, quartered in a barracks and billets, was surprised. The barracks was set on fire and when the roof fell in the crowd gave 'many shouts that seemed to rend the sky [and] exclaimed "The day was their own and they would plant the tree of liberty" '. The garrison was almost annihilated and Stamers, a local landowner and a magistrate was dragged from a garden in which he was hiding and shot. A few miles away, Richard Griffith of Millicent, the M.P., was awakened at 3 a.m. He quickly assembled his yeomanry corps, the Clane cavalry, and moved across country burning cabins in which insurgents had taken refuge. The corps caught six insurgents, one of whom was promptly shot (the other five were hanged later at Naas), and dispersed a party of insurgents from Prosperous. It then prudently withdrew to Naas. At Ballymore Eustace, ten miles to the south, Captain Beevor, who commanded a troop of the 9th dragoons billeted in the village, was wakened by the cry that the rebels would have his blood. While he fought with some insurgents, who were already in his quarters, most of his men struggled through the pikemen in the street to the house. For some hours they held it against attacks, pikes being little use against armed men behind walls, and in the morning, sallying out, dispersed the insurgents. The most important engagement took place at Naas, the county town of Kildare, and an important road centre. The garrison, Armagh militia commanded by Lord Gosford, the Ancient Britons, and some yeomanry, had been warned and were standing to arms when at 2 a.m. the town was attacked from several directions. The Armagh regiment had been issued with battalion guns in 1797, 'grape shot did wonders', and cavalry charges completed the insurgents' discomfiture.[40]

During the 24th there was skirmishing in the plain around Dublin. A small party of militia clashed with the insurgents near Lusk, ten miles to the north; near Dunshaughlin two companies of the Reay fencibles, marching towards Dublin were ambushed by the insurgents and though they extricated themselves they lost their baggage. On the same day a party of the Suffolk fencibles, moving from Barretstown to Kildare, had a similar experience. There was also a sharp engagement at Kilcullen. General Dundas, moving up to secure control of the bridge over the Liffey, found that a party of insurgents had posted themselves in Old Kilcullen Churchyard, with a pond on their right flank and a deep ditch on their left. Confident that cavalry could easily disperse a crowd, he ordered a troop of the 9th dragoons, commanded by Captain William Erskine, to charge them. Erskine, remarking that 'neither he nor his men would breakfast until they had breakfasted on the croppies', advanced. But the insurgents had firearms and were behind a wall. Two charges were beaten back, the rebels driving their 12-foot pikes into the horses' noses, and Erskine was killed. Then the insurgents, exhilarated by their success, decided to attack, came

---

[40] *D.J.*, 23, 26 May, 6 Nov. 1798; J. B. Gordon, *A history of the rebellion in Ireland* (1801), p. 89; E. W. Sheppard, *The ninth Queen's Royal lancers* (1939), p. 39.

up against steady musketry fire from a detachment of the Suffolk fencibles, broke and were scattered by the dragoons.[41]

On the morning of the 25th an important county town, Carlow near the Kildare–Carlow border, was attacked by insurgents hoping to surprise the garrison, two companies of militia and a small detachment of dragoons, who were 'in general quartered in cabins'. But the troops had been alerted and the attack was repulsed by heavy musketry fire. Shortly after this, Sir Edward Crosbie, a baronet and country gentleman, who lived a few miles from Carlow, was arrested and brought into the town. Crosbie, a strong liberal, had in the past expressed his views on parliamentary reform and social injustice 'with an ardour and in the presence of those who felt themselves galled', and early in 1798 he had protested against having to register his arms under the insurrection act and informed the high sheriff that he would not serve as a grand juror while the act was on the statute book. He was brought before a court martial and charged with high treason on very flimsy grounds (some of the force which attacked Carlow apparently assembled on his lawn and his steward was implicated in the rising), found guilty, and executed on 2 June. On 27 May the news reached Carlow that Ballitore, a village in south Kildare, was in possession of the insurgents, and Major Dennis of the 9th dragoons dispatched in that direction a party of his men and a detachment of the North Cork militia, the militiamen riding pillion behind the dragoons. At Ballitore there was a Quaker colony and it was there that the Shackletons, a well-known Quaker family, had conducted for over seventy years their famous school. Mary Shackleton kept for many years a journal, a gentle chronicle of the simple life of a small community, living happily in a quiet corner of the countryside. Suddenly the violence and horrors of civil war erupted into her narrative. On 24 May, after a military detachment was withdrawn from the village, it was seized by the insurgents and a young yeomanry officer, who was the son of a local landowner, was taken prisoner and killed. At Narraghmore, a couple of miles away, 'a mob who were armed with guns, swords, pikes and forks', stormed the court house and killed three men who had taken

[41] *D.E.P.*, 26 May 1978; E. W. Sheppard, *The ninth Queen's Royal lancers*, p. 40; W. Otway, account of 1798 (Army Museum MS 680/7/414 (1)).

refuge there. After a day or two many of the people in the district wanted to negotiate a surrender and a deputation was sent to Colonel Campbell in Athy. While negotiations were being conducted with Campbell the detachment from Carlow arrived and took control of Ballitore. Some of the inhabitants suspected of being involved in the rebellion were killed, provisions were seized, houses burned, and when the troops withdrew earthenware and glass littered the streets.[42] The Revd Cadogan Keating, dean of Clogher, and uncle of Maurice Keating, the liberal M.P. for Kildare, seems to have narrowly escaped Crosbie's fate. He lived at Narraghmore and was, according to Campbell, court-martialled by him for 'the atrocities' committed there. However, the dean survived to claim as 'a suffering loyalist' compensation for the loss of two gold watches, plate and cattle.[43]

To the north of Athy, Rathangan, which had been occupied by the insurgents, was on 29 May attacked by a force composed of the Royal Cork regiment, commanded by Colonel Longfield, and a detachment of the 5th dragoons. The insurgents, who had barricaded the streets, repulsed two attacks by the dragoons, but Longfield brought up his battalion guns and after the second discharge the insurgents scattered. To the south-east of Athy there was skirmishing between parties of military and yeomanry round some small towns in Wicklow and east Carlow —Baltinglass, Hacketstown, Roundwood and Newtownmount-kennedy. On 30 May the insurgents, moving in from 'the woods and rocks', managed to secure a foothold in Newtownmount-kennedy, but fencibles and yeomanry 'charging with great impetuosity' drove them out.[44]

To the north on 25 May General Craig marched out from

[42] *S.N.L.*, 1 June 1798; *An accurate and impartial narrative of the apprehension, trial and execution of Sir E. Crosbie* (1802); *D.J.*, 6 Nov. 1798; *S.N.L.*, 2 June 1798; M. Leadbeater, *The Leadbeater papers*, i, pp. 221–50.

[43] J. Campbell to R. Dundas, 2 June 1798 (I.S.P.O. 620/38/2). It was rumoured that a Miss Keating, said to be a sister of the M.P., had led the insurgents near Narraghmore (*The Times* and *St James's Chronicle*, 7 June 1798). According to the Keating pedigree in *Kildare Arch. Soc. Jn.*, vii, p. 410, the M.P. had no sister, but the Miss Keating referred to might be his cousin, the daughter of Dean Keating. According to Musgrave she played the part of a 'mediatrix' (R. Musgrave, *Memoirs of the different rebellions in Ireland*, 2nd. ed., p. viii.

[44] M. Longfield to ——, 29 May 1798; (I.S.P.O. 620/37/208–9); J. Hardy to ——, (620/37/224).

Dublin towards Dunboyne. He was unable to bring the insurgents to action but on its return march his force 'set fire to croppies' houses'.[45] On the following day, Captain Scobie, with five companies of the Reay fencibles, a company of yeomanry infantry and three corps of yeomanry cavalry, attacked a large body of insurgents who had stationed themselves on the Hill of Tara. Scobie's force had a six-pounder which opened fire 'with good effect 'and the fencibles charging uphill attacked the insurgents in the churchyard on the summit. The insurgents made 'a most daring and obstinate resistance' and just as they were dislodged from the churchyard a great crowd attacked the fencibles from the rear and nearly captured the six-pounder. But once the field piece was brought into action on the assailants, they fell back and dispersed over the countryside pursued by the dragoons. The government forces lost forty-one killed and wounded, the insurgents left 350 dead on the field. It was probably the last time that two Gaelic-speaking forces met in conflict.[46]

On 29 May the troops operating in Kildare were unexpectedly reinforced. General Duff, commanding the Limerick district, was a popular and kindly officer who had never been on active service, but faced with an emergency he rose to the occasion. Realizing how important it was to concentrate every available man in the seriously disturbed areas, and confident that his own district would remain quiet, on the morning of the twenty-seventh he started eastwards at the head of a small force composed of 6th dragoons and 350 of the city of Dublin militia, the infantry being carried in carts. Duff's force covered 70 miles in twenty-four hours, and on the 29th arrived at the town of Kildare which had been occupied by the insurgents after its garrison had left on the 24th to join Dundas. Having taken Kildare, where his men found lying on the street the body of Lieutenant Giffard, the son of one of his own officers, who had been taken from the Limerick coach and killed by the insurgents, Duff marched on to the Curragh, where he met a large party of insurgents who were willing to surrender. Unfortunately a shot was fired and 'nothing could stop the rage of the troops'; they

<hr/>

[45] *London Gazette*, 31 May 1798; A. McLaren, *A genuine account* (1799), p. 5.
[46] *D.J.*, 29 May 1798; H. Scobie, *An old highland fencible corps* (1914), pp. 168–94, 391–5.

'fell upon the villains and took ample revenge for their fellow soldiers'. Two hundred of the insurgents were killed.[47]

On 30 May the indefatigable Duff pushed into the Blackmore hills to the east of Kildare, captured an insurgents' camp, and bringing up his guns over difficult country, scattered the insurgents by artillery fire, 'though so nimble were the wretches that not about 14 or 15 were killed'. He then marched into that 'wild barbarous tract of country in which the collieries are situated', in Queen's County. But 'finding the colliers well disposed and peaceable had no occasion to make use of his power'.[48]

The vigour displayed by the government forces soon disheartened many of the insurgents. A London liberal newspaper was dismayed to see in Dundas's letter describing the affair at Kilcullen, 'the terrible word "No prisoners" '. But in fact Dundas seems to have been very willing to accept submissions, and it was reported that Lake on 28 May received the surrender of 7,000 insurgents on the Curragh. The parish priest of Kilcullen, from the outbreak of the insurrection, refused to have anything to do with his parishioners, who, men, women and children, were encamped on Knockaulin Hill (Hill of Allen), 'living on the plunder of gentlemen's houses and demesnes' and shooting persons believed to be Orangemen. But on Sunday, 27 May, on being asked to say mass at the camp, he took the opportunity to exhort them to surrender and having secured the assent of twenty-five leaders he went at once to Generals Lake and Dundas. General Dundas was highly gratified and went unattended to the camp. He told the insurgents they would be pardoned if they laid down their arms, which they did, 'making the air and hills resound with acclamations of joy'.[49] Incidents such as the clash between Duff's men and the insurgents on the Curragh may have discouraged, but did not altogether check, submissions which seem to have gone on steadily in the Dublin

[47] *D.J.*, 31 May 1798; *D.E.P.*, 2 June 1798; J. Duff to (I.S.P.O. 620/37/211). An incident similar to what occurred on the Curragh happened a few days later when a party of insurgents which had made an unsuccessful attack on Monasterevin retreated to Rath on the Curragh and offered to surrender. Their offer was refused and, charged by dragoons and fencible cavalry, 'they were obliged to give way with great slaughter' (*D.J.*, 29 May, *S.N.L.*, 8 June 1798).

[48] *S.N.L.*, 2, 7 June 1798; Crosby to ——, 3 June 1798 (Adm. 1/648).

[49] *Morning Post*, 30 Mar. 1798; *S.N.L.*, 30 May; *D.E.P.*, 9 May 1798; N. Pephoe to Dr J. T. Troy, 8 June 1798 (Troy papers IV/116/7).

plain. The policy of accepting submissions was publicly endorsed by the government at the end of May when in the house of commons a vote of thanks was moved to Duff which was meant to be an implied censure of the general officers who had accepted surrenders. The government opposed it and carried the adjournment by 91 to 10.[50]

By the end of May, after just about a week of disturbance and fighting, it seemed clear that in the flat, fertile zone stretching round Dublin, the government forces had the upper hand. Insurrection had not been completely suppressed but the insurgents had been driven to the hills and boglands and certainly did not constitute a serious threat to the capital. This was just as well for the Irish government, since by the close of May it was clear that a very serious situation had developed in the south-east corner of Leinster. Wexford was considered to be a relatively prosperous county. If the county town, Wexford, with about 10,000 people, appeared to a foreign visitor 'one of the ugliest and dirtiest towns in Ireland', he did grant that a number of the inhabitants seemed to be comfortably off, and the recently built long bridge across the mouth of the Slaney was a striking sign of commercial progress. The farming community in south Wexford was believed to enjoy satisfactory living standards. The poorest farmers, it was said by a knowledgeable observer, ate meat twice a week and the table of the wealthy farmer was 'daily covered with beef, mutton or fowl'. Farmhouses were well built and well thatched and had out-offices for cattle and fowl. Towards the north-west of the county the soil was poorer and the small farmers had a harder struggle. It is probable too that in the later nineties farm labourers were finding it harder to obtain employment. Wexford had been a barley growing county but the abolition of land carriage bounties on grain brought to Dublin and the introduction of a new licensing system which closed many local maltings encouraged farmers to turn from tillage to pasture.[51]

In the middle seventies the whiteboys were active in central

[50] *D.E.P.*, 2 June 1798.

[51] R. Fraser, *A statistical survey of County Wexford* (1807), pp. 4–6, 67–86, 140–2; T. J. Powell, 'The background to the Wexford rebellion 1790–98' in *Irish economic and social history*, ii, pp. 61–3; La Tocnaye, *Rambles through Ireland* (1799), pp. 90–1; A. Young, *A tour of Ireland* (1780), i, p. 119., Luke Cullen papers, f. 21 (Madden papers, T.C.D.).

and north Wexford for a few months 'but were suppressed immediately by the spirited associations of the gentlemen'. In the summer of 1793 towards the north of the county, round Enniscorthy, 'a mob armed with guns and other weapons' was administering unlawful oaths. After the ringleaders had been arrested and lodged in Wexford gaol, a large crowd marched on to the town to secure their release. It was met at Taghore by a detachment of the 56th foot, and in the ensuing rencontre Major Valotton, commanding the military party, was killed by a blow from a scythe, and his men opened fire and killed thirteen insurgents. Wexford was one of the most catholic counties in Leinster, the catholics being to the protestants in a ratio of about nine to one and Wexford catholics, many of them prosperous farmers or small landowners, were very conscious of the misfortunes sustained by their community in the past and laboured under a strong sense of injustice. It is significant that two of the representatives of Wexford at the catholic convention of 1792, Devereux and Sweetman, were prominent amongst the leaders of the forward section, and another Wexford delegate, Edward Hay, eagerly planned a scheme for collecting denominational statistics, to provide an argument for immediate catholic emancipation. The strength of community feeling amongst the Wexford catholics alarmed a number of protestants. It was said that the Wexford volunteer corps never invited catholics to join them, and one of the M.P.s for the county, the very popular George Ogle, was a leading opponent of the catholic claims. 'When any ill-will lurked even from the days of three grand-sires' a Wexford countryman remarked, 'it was paid off with the highest amount of compound interest' during the insurrection.[52]

In 1797 the United Irishmen had begun to build up their organization in the county, and a well-known radical tract, *The appeal of the people of Ulster* was being circulated.[53] At the close of the year some parishes in Wexford were proclaimed and in April 1798 the whole county. Efforts were made by the magistrates and yeomanry to sweep in arms, corporal punishment being used to secure information. It is impossible to say

---

[52] *H.J.*, 18 July 1793; *The correspondence of Edmund Burke*, viii, p. 264; E. Hay, *A history of the insurrection of the county of Wexford* (1803), p. 13.
[53] C. Colclough to ——, 23 Apr. ,18 Aug. 1797 (I.S.P.O. 620/29/229, 620/34/14).

on what scale repressive force was employed. Some indication of this is given by 'The detail book' of a Wexford yeomanry corps, the Camolin cavalry. It records that on 23 May the corps burned the house of 'a retainer of pikes', pulled down a forge at which pikes had been made and dined at free-quarters in the house of a suspected person. On the 26th the corps was ordered to burn a house but refrained from doing so when the owner promised to give up the arms in his possession: on the same day the corps again dined at free-quarters.[54]

About 10 May Caesar Colclough, a very active magistrate, thought the county was quiet, with no trees being cut or meetings held at night. Colclough himself was busy addressing the people at catholic chapels and during the following week other gentlemen encouraged them 'to take advantage of the fine weather . . . and keep up with the season'.[55] Arms were being surrendered and numbers took the oath of allegiance. But the United Irishmen had been active for over a year. They now had the example of other counties to stir them and an edge may have been put on their determination by harsh repression. On 26 May rumours of rebellion reached Gorey, a patrol of the Camolin cavalry sent into the disturbed area was ambushed, and house-burning by both sides began.

On the 27th, there gathered at two points in the county, the Hill of Oulart and Kilmacthomas Hill, a' large, confused crowd of both sexes and all ages'.[56] Oulart is seven miles north of Wexford, and when Colonel Richard Foote, commanding a detachment of the North Cork militia stationed in the town, heard that a number of 'defenders' were assembled at Oulart, he set out for the hill with a hundred of his men (grenadiers) and a small force of yeomanry. After 'a long march on a hot day', the detachment found itself facing a large crowd. Foot apparently was for retreating, but his officers overbore him, and the small force advancing uphill was overwhelmed by an irresistible rush. Only two men and one officer (Foot himself) escaped.[57] The insurgents then surged westwards towards

[54] H. B. F. Wheeler and A. M. Bradley, *The war in Wexford* (1910), pp. 81–4.

[55] C. Colclough to ——, 10 May 1798 (I.S.P.O. 620/37/51); *D.J.*, 26 May 1798; Luke Cullen papers, f. 13 (Madden papers, T.C.D.).

[56] J. B. Gordon, *History of the rebellion in Ireland*, p. 90.

[57] R. Foote to ——, 27 May 1798 (I.S.P.O. 620/37/177); mayor of Waterford to ——, 27 May 1798 (620/31/178).

Enniscorthy, the principal town in north Wexford, about six miles away. Marching through Ferns, where they plundered the newly furnished bishop's palace, they on the 28th advanced on Enniscorthy in two columns. The town was garrisoned by a small detachment of the militia, commanded by Captain Snow, and three yeomanry corps. Snow, uncertain at which point the attack would be delivered, twice moved his detachment (the situation, a kindly critic remarked, 'might have puzzled the brain of even a Bonaparte'),[58] and after a short struggle in the narrow streets, numbers prevailed: the garrison, accompanied by a great crowd of panic-stricken fugitives retreated, unpursued, to Wexford.

In Wexford there was a detachment of North Cork militia, five yeomanry corps, and 150 of the Donegal militia under Colonel Maxwell, who had served in Germany.[59] After the defeat at Oulart, steps were taken to strengthen the garrison. Lord Bective was ordered to march to Wexford with four companies of the Meath militia, and General Fawcett commanding at Duncannon set off for Wexford late on the afternoon of 28 May taking with him the 13th foot (only eighty strong), a small detachment of the Meath, and, most important of all, a couple of howitzers. In the evening Fawcett, 'a good natured man, but not the general we want', stopped at Foulkes Mill for rest and refreshment. Early in the morning of the 29th Captain Adams of the Meath militia, 'with overzeal' pushed on towards Wexford with the howitzers and a small escort of his own men. A large crowd of insurgents had gathered on his route. They unexpectedly swept down from all sides 'with more of irresistible impetuosity than military skill', the militiamen fled and the guns were captured before the artillery men had time to spike them. Fawcett, riding up with his A.D.C. heard the cries of exultation of the rebels, and sending orders to Bective to march to New Ross, fell back himself to Duncannon. His retirement, Fawcett wrote, was accompanied 'with every danger that retreats before a successful enemy are liable to', and he warned General Eustace, that 'the insurgents were no

[58] J. B. Gordon *History of the rebellion*, p. 115; W. Snow, *A fair and candid statement of the transactions at Enniscorthy* (1801).

[59] R. Maxwell to General Eustace, 1 June 1798, (I.S.P.O. 620/38/29); General Eustace to Lake, 2 June 1798 (620/38/39).

longer to be despised as common peasantry; they are organized and have persons of skill and enterprise with them'.[60]

In Wexford at first plans were made for a vigorous defence. The medieval walls were manned and the gates barricaded. On the news arriving of the engagement at Foulkes Mill, Maxwell sallied out with the Donegal militia to try and recover the lost guns, but, finding himself facing large crowds of insurgents with firearms and artillery, he soon retired quickly to the town. The garrison of Wexford was demoralized by a series of defeats. They were conscious that they were surrounded by enormous crowds of insurgents, who undoubtedly had sympathizers within the walls. So it was decided, at an apparently informal conference of magistrates and officers, to negotiate, and two well-known local radicals, John Colclough and Edward Fitzgerald, who had been arrested, were released and asked to persuade the insurgents to disperse. When their efforts, which do not seem to have been very strenuous, were obviously fruitless, two popular country gentlemen were sent out to obtain terms of surrender. These steps set up a wave of panic, and what a conservative writer later termed, a 'most irregularly executed ... retreat', began, in fact something closely resembling a *sauve qui peut*. The North Cork militia and some of the yeomanry abandoned their posts, a number of citizens took ship or fled by road, finally the Donegal militia and three yeomanry corps retired from the town and marched for Duncannon, affording some protection on their march to the fugitives. During the retreat stragglers were cut off by the insurgents and the military fired recklessly at country people whom they suspected of being hostile.[61]

On the 30th the insurgents poured into Wexford. A green flag was hoisted over the barracks and green ribbons generally worn. A few protestants were rabbled in the street and killed, and a number were imprisoned—for some possibly a form of protective custody. A group of responsible citizens speedily formed a committee of twelve to manage the town during the emergency, and placate the insurgents, most of whom soon left

[60] W. Fawcett to ——, 31 May 1798 (I.S.P.O. 620/38/11); W. Fawcett to ——, 6 June 1798 (Army Museum MS 5910/98); mayor of Waterford to ——, 31 May 1798 (620/37/234); T. Cloney, *A personal narrative* (1823), pp. 20–1.

[61] *D.J.*, 24 July 1798; W. H. Maxwell, *History of the Irish rebellion* (1845), pp. 106–8.

the town. The committee was a middle-class body, but to conciliate 'the lower classes', it co-opted a couple of working men, who were soon emphasizing to their fellows the difficulties facing the committee. Anxious to prevent plunder the committee tried to meet the insurgents' demands. These were not onerous, since the insurgents, who could scour the country for food, demanded only tobacco, whiskey, salt and leather. The committee also established a rationing scheme for the town. Each householder was given a ticket, specifying the number of persons in his household and on presenting this at a depot he received his allowance of bread and meat. Strange to say, during the period of insurgent domination there was a deflationary price-fall in Wexford—the insurgents burning bank-notes.[62]

After capturing Wexford, the insurgents gathered at three great encampments, Vinegar Hill, beside Enniscorthy, Carrigrua to the north, and at Taghore, to the west of Wexford. The leadership seems to have been exercised by an informal committee, composed of those whose ability, personality or status brought them to the front. Beauchamp Bagenal Harvey was chosen as commander-in-chief. As the leading country gentleman in the insurgent ranks, he was an instinctive choice; as a protestant, a politic one. A strong radical (he had joined the Dublin society of United Irishmen in 1792) and a man of courage, thin and intense, he seems to have had military talent. The 'chiefs' included a few other protestants, Mathew Keugh, a retired army officer, who acted as governor of Wexford. Anthony Perry, according to an old schoolfellow, 'an eccentric genius';[63] and Cornelius Grogan, an elderly country gentleman, who had served as high sheriff, and who was forced or persuaded by his tenants to accompany them to Wexford. There, he accepted the office of commissary-general and made an effort to find supplies. Amongst the insurgents' leaders were a number of catholics of some substance—Morgan Byrne, who had served in the yeomanry, whose uncle was a brewer on a large scale; Thomas Dixon, a ship-owner; William Barker, a merchant and brewer; John Hay, a member of an old Wexford family;

[62] T. Cloney, *A personal narrative*, p. 24; E. Hay, *A history of the insurrection of the county of Wexford*, pp. 129, 171; I.S.P.O. 620/38/115.
[63] Prior diary (T.C.D. MS 3365).

Edward Fitzgerald, apparently a landed gentleman; Thomas
Cloney, the only son of Denis Cloney, who rented large tracts
of land and had an income of several hundreds a year; Denis
Doyle, a timber merchant and Thomas Neall, who owned a
warehouse. There were also several priests—Father Philip
Roach, who was tall and handsome; Father Kearns, full of
self-confidence, and with some strategic sense; Father Edward
Redmond and Fathers John and Michael Murphy. Most of the
leaders were 'young men, farmers and farmers' sons' who,
'generally speaking were those to whom the people looked with
confidence'.[64] The leaders strove to impose some order on the
vast crowds of country people who gathered at the insurgents'
camps, separating those armed with guns from the pike men, and
dividing the latter into companies by townlands and parishes.

One thing must have been clear to the insurgent leaders. If
the Wexford insurgents remained encamped in their own
county the government forces would be able to concentrate and
crush them. But if Munster could be roused by a thrust westwards, and the north Leinster rising reanimated by a Wexford column bursting into Wicklow, the government might
find the situation passing beyond its control. So during the first
ten days of June they made three attempts to break out beyond
the boundaries of Wexford. On 1 June the column from Vinegar
Hill, led by Father Kearns, marched up the valley of the Slaney
towards Newtownbarry, a small town on the river, which
commanded an important crossing, defended by Colonel
L'Estrange, with a detachment of the King's County militia and
some yeomanry. The insurgents, advancing with 'promptitude
and vigour', broke into the town, and L'Estrange, as he later
reported, 'retired to collect his forces'. In fact his men seem to
have retreated in disorder but while the insurgents scattered
through the town, looking for whiskey or trying to dislodge the
remnants of the garrison, L'Estrange rallied his men, advanced
and retook the town. The next day, being short of ammunition, he was considering falling back to Carlow, but the
insurgents did not return to the attack so he remained in occupation of Newtownbarry and soon afterwards he was reinforced
by the Midlothian fencibles. At Carnew about ten miles north-
east of Newtownbarry a number of men suspected of sedition

[64] M. Byrne, *Memoirs*, ed. S. Gwynn (1907), i, pp. 169–72.

were being detained in custody. Already on 28 May, after the insurgents had burned some houses in the neighbourhood, half a dozen of the prisoners had been shot. And on 2 June, when the situation at Newtownbarry seemed grave, the lieutenant commanding the militia detachment stationed at Carnew ordered thirty-nine of 'the unhappy people' in the guard house to be shot 'to prevent their interference if the town should be attacked'. [65]

A few days later a great attack was mounted against New Ross on the Barrow, the capture of which would open the way into County Kilkenny and mid-Leinster. Realizing the importance of New Ross, General Eustace on 31 May had ordered the Meath and Donegal militia to the town, and a few days later General Johnson, a veteran of the American war of Independence, arrived with a light battalion, two troops of dragoons and four six-pounders. On 5 June the insurgents, in the opinion of one of their captains, 'an undisciplined, badly armed, ungovernable body of country peasants', moved on New Ross. A summons to surrender was sent to the town under a flag of truce, but the bearer was shot by a sentry, deliberately or by accident. The incident helped to incite the fury of the insurgents, and preceded by a herd of cattle as a battering ram, they moved forward on the town. With an ardour and courage which deeply impressed Robert Craufurd, an experienced professional soldier, they overran the enemy artillery and drove the militia back to the river. A small detachment of dragoons attempted by a bold charge to check the insurgents' advance. But the dragoons found themselves pent up in narrow lanes and harassed by pikemen, who had learned to prick the horses in the flank 'and this obtained an easy conquest over the rider who fell embarrassed'. The insurgents pressing through the town, part of which was on fire, reached the bridge, but at this critical moment discipline and character turned the scale. Johnson rode forward and rallied the militia, who reformed their ranks and advanced. The insurgents had suffered severe losses, and during their initial success they had scattered, losing that cohesion which gave drive to their numbers. They retreated

---

[65] Col. L'Estrange to ——, 11 June 1798 (I.S.P.O. 620/30/4, 9); E. Hay, *A history of the insurrection of the county of Wexford*, p. 138; N.L.S. MS 5750; W. Wainwright to Fitzwilliam, 6 Feb. 1800 (W.W.M. F. 30).

leaving behind many dead and several ships' guns which had been brought into action.[66] Towards the close of the engagement an ugly episode occurred. About two hundred protestants, men, women and children, had been rounded up and imprisoned in a house and barn at Scullabogue about seven miles east of New Ross. Insurgents, probably fugitives from the battle, set fire to the barn and put the prisoners to death.

During the first few days of June the north Wexford insurgents, skirmishing with the yeomanry round Gorey, were greatly exhilarated by a small victory over a detachment commanded by Colonel Walpole. On 4 June General Loftus who had about 1,100 men under his control decided to advance south of Gorey. The bulk of his force moved south in three detachments, the column on the left was commanded by Loftus himself; that on the right, composed of small detachments from no fewer than eleven units, dragoons, fencibles, militia and yeomanry, by Colonel Walpole, a viceregal A.D.C. Walpole advanced boldly—after the event his critics said, precipitately —over a terrain which changed abruptly from open fields to an enclosed country with high hedges. At the point where the change occurred the insurgents lay in ambush. The small column, about 500 strong, marching confidently forward was suddenly greeted with 'a wild yell . . . accompanied by a stream of musketry'. One militia officer, who had never been in action before, heard 'a whizzing which I took to be that of balls'; Walpole was killed; his men, trying to deploy, fell into confusion and the whole force 'in the utmost disorder' fell back to Arklow, losing about 50 killed and wounded and abandoning two guns. Loftus, if he had been facing professional adversaries would have been in a very critical position. As it was, surrounded by unknown but formidable numbers in a hostile countryside, his situation was difficult enough. However, he extricated himself successfully, falling back on Carnew, though 'owing to the disorderly conduct of the militia' most of his ammunition was abandoned at Gorey.[67] Cheered by the retreat of the

---

[66] T. Cloney, *A personal narrative*, p. 38; R. Crawford to G. Lake, 5 and 6 June 1798 (I.S.P.O. 620/38/62, 620/38/235); J. Roche, *A statement* (1799), pp. 34–42; *British military library*, ii, pp. 187, 228; 620/38/62.

[67] *S.N.L.*, 8 June 1798; Armstrong diary (T.C.D. MS 6409); W. H. Maxwell, *History of the Irish rebellion* (1845) p. 111; Castlereagh to T. Pelham, 5 June 1798 (Add. MS 33 105); M. Byrne, *Memoirs*, i, pp. 72–9.

government forces the north Wexford insurgents moved on Arklow, which commanded the coast road northwards into Wicklow. The garrison, commanded by General Needham, the heir to an Irish peerage, comprised yeomanry units, the Ancient Britons, the Durham fencibles and the Cavan militia, the Cavan regiment having rushed down from Dublin in a number of requisitioned vehicles, including noddies, jaunting cars and coaches. On the 9th the insurgents, numbering, Needham estimated, 19,000, advanced on Arklow in two great columns. They had four field pieces manned by captured soldiers and a deserter. The prisoners were careful to point their guns too high but the deserter sighted his piece accurately. The insurgents at the outset 'put their hats on pikes and gave a great yell'. Then they pushed home their attacks boldly. 'Their perseverance, Needham wrote, 'was surprising and their efforts to take the guns on our right were most daring, advancing even to the muzzles where they fell in great numbers'. Needham's artillery, firing grape, 'tumbled them by twenties', and his yeomanry and fencible cavalry charged boldly wherever there was an opportunity.[68]

From the beginning of June, Lake had been determined to beat the Wexford insurgents into subjection by concentrating against them all the troops which could be spared from elsewhere. By the beginning of June he had at his disposal about 10,000 men posted between Duncannon and Arklow for a converging movement on Enniscorthy and Vinegar Hill. Lake also intended to employ units from Munster in a thrust at Wexford from the west, but his movements were delayed by General Stewart's reluctance to release men from his southern command. Stewart considered he had been entrusted with discretionary powers, and having dispatched Johnson to New Ross in time to defeat the insurgents' attack, he was claiming credit for 'the most essential advantage that has yet been gained'. On receiving Lake's orders for the second time, he at last ordered the troops to move as directed and at the

---

[68] General Needham's reports (620/38/114/120); *Analecta Hibernica*, xxv, pp. 117–19, *H.J.*, 6 June; *S.N.L.*, 8 June 1798. It was later said that Needham had contemplated retreating but was steadied by a 'noble reply' from Colonel Skerret of the Durham fencibles (*Mr Gordon's vindication of his history of the rebellion* (1802), pp. 31–6). Possibly Needham was merely making contingency plans.

same time intimated that he wished to resign his command.[69]

On the 18th Loftus and Dundas advanced towards Carnew, in south Wicklow. They were confronted by a crowd of insurgents with a few field pieces. Loftus seems to have learned caution from his experience on the 4th and 'a canonade ensued'. In the end the insurgents seem to have fallen back, unpursued. However, by the 21st Lake thought he was ready to make a decisive thrust, and at seven o'clock on the morning of 21 June the forces under Lake's command went into action against the insurgents posted in Enniscorthy and on Vinegar Hill. Apparently, as a result of bad staff work, the force from Arklow under Needham's command which should have formed Lake's left was not in position. By the evening of the 20th Needham was at Oulart, about six miles west of Wexford, almost across the insurgents' line of retreat. But he was directed to march north towards Lake's headquarters and then redirected south. Consequently, owing to the fatigue of his men, he did not arrive at the base of Vinegar Hill until the close of the engagement. At the beginning of the engagement Johnson stormed Enniscorthy where a number of houses, including an insurgents' hospital, were set on fire. The attack on the hill began with a cannonade, which the insurgents found hard to bear—the bombs, they said 'spit at us', and when the government forces advanced after trying to charge, they fell back in disorder towards Wexford, pursued by Lake's cavalry. Lake's casualties, killed, wounded and missing, amounted to only 95. 'The troops', Lake wrote immediately after the battle, 'behaved excessively well in action, but their determination to destroy everyone they think a rebel is beyond description and wants much correction'.[70]

Moore, with the troops detached from Stewart's command had moved from New Ross on the 19th. On the 20th Moore's force, a light battalion, the 5th battalion of the 60th (a unit

[69] G. Lake to G. Nugent, 30 May 1798 (N.L.I. MS 56); Castlereagh to Elliott, 15 June 1798; Castlereagh to Pelham, 8 June 1798 (Add. MS 33 105); Castlereagh to G. Nugent (Army Museum MS 6807/56); Stewart to Lake, 18 June 1798 (Army Museum MS 5910/198).

[70] Needham to Lake, 21 June 1798 (N.L.I. MS 56); A. McLaren, *A genuine account*, pp. 14–15; W. H. Maxwell, p. 143; *Castlereagh Correspondence*, i, p. 223; *An impartial narrative*, p. 72. An active yeomanry officer complained that instead of pressing the pursuit hard, the generals engaged at Vinegar Hill amused themselves in congratulating each other (W. W. Pole to Mornington, 24 Aug. 1798 (Add. MS 37308); *D.J.*, 15 May 1798).

composed largely of Germans) and Hompesch's Mounted Riflemen, met a large insurgent force near Taghmon. One of the insurgent leaders, as Moore approached, drew off with his followers, so as to be able, he asserted, to cut off Moore's retreat. The insurgents who remained facing Moore positioned themselves with some skill, 'the gunmen' being placed in advance amongst the hedges and ditches. There was a confused struggle in dense smoke, and at one stage Moore's men began to fall back in disorder. Moore himself steadied them and Captain Daniel of the 41st, veteran of continental campaigns, rallied the militia. The insurgents broke off the action and fell back towards Wexford, leaving Moore, whose losses were 55 wounded and killed, in possession of the field. On the 21st Moore, 'with his usual energy and activity', marched towards Wexford, sending forward a small advance guard to take control of the town and release the prisoners; and on the 22nd Lake himself entered Wexford.[71]

With the capture of Wexford, the only town held by the insurgents, it was clear the insurrection had failed. But the very incohesiveness of the rising made its complete suppression a difficult task. Though the main insurgent forces had sustained a decisive defeat at Vinegar Hill, there were at the end of June large bands of insurgents in the field. On the evening of the 21st the insurgents poured out of Wexford in two columns, one marching west to Sleedagh, the other after crossing the long bridge, pushing northwards towards the Wicklow mountains. On the 22nd the insurgents, who had encamped at Sleedagh, began marching north-west, along the course of the Barrow, 'greatly encumbered as usual with vast numbers of females who were following their brothers or other relations'. At Goresbridge, overwhelming a small Wexford militia garrison, they crossed the river into County Kilkenny, and on the 24th attacked the colliery town of Castlecomer, garrisoned by militia and yeomanry. The yeomanry cavalry after skirmishing fell back and the insurgents swarmed into the town, but were unable to take a large house from which 'a tremendous fire was kept up'. General Asgill advancing from Kilkenny with a force of 900 strong (including the Wexford and Waterford regiments), 'cleared the town with guns' and then retired to Kilkenny.

[71] J. Moore, *Diary*, i, pp. 295-9; T. Cloney, *A personal narrative*, pp. 54-60.

About the time Asgill was withdrawing, another force arrived to protect Castlecomer, the Downshire militia, commanded by Major Mathews and two yeomanry corps. This force followed the insurgents, who were marching towards Queen's County, and the following morning Mathews suggested to Asgill that they should co-operate in attacking the insurgent force. Asgill refused—his men, he said, were fatigued—and Mathews went on boldly through hilly country. By the evening however Asgill was ready to move and on the following morning (the 26th) he and Mathews attacked the insurgent camp at Kilcomney, near Goresbridge. 'The engagement began with a terrible fire of artillery', the insurgents broke up and abandonded the hill, and their baggage, the Wicklow militia claiming to have captured fourteen small field pieces and fifteen cartloads of provisions.[72]

Some of the more determined insurgents on retreating from Kilcomney, pressed through the hills to join the other force which had left Wexford on 21 June. This force as it moved north suffered 'a great falling off' as men slipped away and went home. On reaching the Wicklow border the insurgents pitched a camp at White Heaps at the foot of the Crogan mountains and for some days they skirmished with the yeomanry around Carnew and Gorey. For a short time they were able to occupy Gorey, where they obtained 'a scanty supply' of ammunition, and on 30 June they were even able to defeat a cavalry force, composed of detachments of the 5th Dragoons, and of the Ancient Britons, under Colonel Puleston. This force, pursuing a body of insurgents, found itself on a stretch of road near Ballyellis, bounded on one side by a wall and on the other by a deep ditch. Behind the wall were the insurgents' 'gunmen', the road was barricaded by carts, and a dense mass of pikemen barred the cavalry's retreat. However, by a determined charge the dragoons and Ancient Britons broke through the pikemen, their losses amounting to almost forty officers and men.[73]

On 25 June the insurgents, striking north, attacked Hacketstown in east Carlow. The garrison, a detachment of the Antrim

[72] M. Byrne, *Memoirs*, i, p. 154; *D.J.*, 28 June, 7 July 1798; W.O. 68/118.

[73] M. Byrne, *Memoirs*, i, pp. 198–200; *S.N.L.*, 4 July 1798; *D.J.*, 7 July 1798; L. E. S. Parry and B. F. M. Freeman, *Historical records of the Denbighshire hussars*, appendix iv, p. xxix.

militia and yeomen, retreated to the barracks and 'a few good
men', under the Revd James McGhee, threw themselves into
a strongly built house which covered part of the barrack wall,
and held it against determined attacks. In the end the 'insurgents retreated slowly and deliberately, carrying off their
dead and wounded'.[74] On 4 July Duff attacked the insurgents
at Wicklow Gap, and after a running fight extending over
twelve miles the insurgents were dispersed.

Until July, north Kildare, east King's County and Westmeath areas where there were large stretches of bog, continued
to be disturbed. On the 7th July a detachment of the City of
Limerick militia, commanded by Colonel Gough, and some
yeomanry attacked a body of two to three thousand insurgents,
encamped in Lord Harberton's demesne, near Timahoe.
Gough ordered 'a general discharge with such effect that they
started running like furies' and escaped into the bog of Allen.
However, Gough found in their abandoned camp twenty cows
and nearly fifty fat sheep, which, he wrote, he was going to
auction among the men', to whom he was also able to give
19 pairs of stockings each. Ten days later an early morning
attack on Kilbeggan in south-east Westmeath, where there was
a small garrison of the Northumberland fencibles, was beaten
off, the inhabitants after the insurgents retired collecting cartloads of pikes from the streets. Two days later there was an
engagement in the Ovidstown area, lying between Kilcock and
Clonard. The insurgents, who lined the hedges, were attacked
and dispersed by a force composed of Inverness fencibles,
dragoons, yeomanry and artillery. About 400 insurgents were
killed and many more, it was reported, died in the bog 'for want
of care'. On the same day Prosperous, about ten miles south of
Kilcock, which the insurgents had occupied, was attacked by a
force of yeomanry and militia from Naas, commanded by
Colonel Charles Stewart. After Prosperous had been shelled,
the insurgents fled into the surrounding bog, and Stewart
'ransacked and burned that receptacle of rebellion'. On 23 June,
a small force from Edenderry attacked a party of insurgents
camped on Fox's hill. The insurgents fled into the bog, about
100 being killed, and one of their leaders, a native of Edenderry,
was captured, brought back into the town, and 'hung up where

[74] *S.N.L.*, 6 July 1798.

he now remains'. On 12 July Gough marched out from Edenderry with fifty of his Limerick militiamen and 20 dragoons against a party of insurgents which had posted themselves on Nockderry hill. Gough's men advanced uphill by a 'steady, well directed fire' and the insurgents were 'dispersed among corn fields and ditches'.[75]

A few days later the last large insurgent concentrations in the Dublin plain were dispersed by a series of converging attacks. On 14 July a government force, the Dumfriesshire fencibles, militia and yeomanry, engaged a body of insurgents, 600 strong, near Garretstown in north County Dublin. Finding the insurgents protected by a ditch, the cavalry hesitated to attack, but the infantry coming up, they scattered 'with considerable slaughter'. A couple of days earlier a force composed of the Buckinghamshire militia and yeomanry had marched through Meath pursuing a body of insurgents, 'a miserable, flying, exhausted banditti', who were largely fugitives from Wexford. Simultaneously fencibles from Drogheda thrust south and symbolically enough the last engagements of any significance in Leinster were fought near the Boyne.[76]

While the Wexford struggle was raging Munster remained quiet, except for a short engagement in south-west Cork when a small force of militia and fencibles with two six-pounders was attacked by a crowd armed with pikes. 'The guns played with great effect' and the crowd dispersed. Then, rather inconsequently, in mid-July a large crowd assembled to attack Cashel. It was easily dispersed and three of its leaders, after being court-martialled, were executed. At the end of the month a party attacked Castleisland barracks in County Kerry and killed a few yeomen.[77]

In Ulster, on 29 May, a provincial meeting at Armagh dismissed the provincial executive which had inertly failed to make preparations for immediate action and settled that the Antrim and Down leaders should meet on the following day, and, if they decided to act, draw up a plan. A few days later the

---

[75] *S.N.L.*, 16, 20 June, 4, 23 July 1798; *D.J.*, 21 June 1798, I.S.P.O. 620/38/171, 620/39/1; R. S. Rait, *Life . . . of Hugh Viscount Gough* (1903), i, p. 8.

[76] *D.J.*, 21 July, 9 Aug. 1798; *S.N.L.*, 16, 20 July 1798; I.S.P.O. 620/39/63, 86; E. Cooke to W. Wickham, 12 July 1798 (H.O. 100/81).

[77] *D.J.*, 21 June 1798; I.S.P.O. 620/38/183, 190; courts martial in 620/23/22/1 620/6/66/2; *H.J.*, 25 July 1798.

majority of the County Down 'colonels' seem to have been averse to action unless there was a French landing or the Leinster insurgents were successful. The Antrim leaders at first took a similar attitude but at a second meeting the more determined decided to take action and on 6 June Henry Joy McCracken issued a short, staccato order of the day, in the French style, to the Antrim army and on 7 June the Antrim insurrection began, large crowds marching towards the county town, singing the Marseillaise and carrying green branches. The small garrison in Antrim, composed of a troop of dragoons and some yeomanry, placed itself behind the wall of Lord Massareene's demesne at the west end of the town and a brisk engagement began, a party of the insurgents, 'the Spartan band', led by James Hope, a weaver, displaying outstanding determination. Nugent, as soon as he heard that 'there was a pretty general insurrection in County Antrim', ordered troops from Belfast and Blaris camp to move on the county town. About the time the insurgents occupied Antrim, the advance guard of the column from Blaris, two troops of the 22nd dragoons, and two curricle guns, commanded by a young lieutenant-colonel, William Lumley, later a distinguished cavalry general, arriving on the outskirts of the town. Lumley promptly tried to clear the streets by a charge, but his guns were badly served, and the insurgents had a cannon, which had belonged to the volunteers, and used it effectively. The dragoons having lost three officers and twenty men, abandoned their guns and fell back in disorder. The consequences were curious. A large part of north Antrim insurgents, advancing towards the town, seeing dragoons riding fast, concluded they were watching a successful cavalry charge and quickly withdrew. The commander of the column from Belfast, Colonel Durham, was cautious. He decided 'from an eminence to cannonade the town', and when he judged the insurgents shaken, he moved his men forward and occupied it without difficulty.[78]

On 7 June there were disturbances throughout County Antrim. Randalstown, a few miles to the north-west of Antrim,

---

[78] *Commons' Jn. Ire.*, xvii, pp. dccclxvi–vii; C. H. Teeling, *A personal narrative of the Irish rebellion* (1828), pp. 231–2, 237; *B.N.L.*, 8 June 1798; J. Durham to G. Nugent, 7 June 1798 (I.S.P.O. 620/38/85); G. Nugent to —— (620/38/97). Nugent seems to have had some days' warning that an outbreak was imminent (620/52/56).

guarded by a small yeomanry garrison, stationed in the market house, was attacked on the morning of the 7th by a force of United Irishmen and defenders. Though the shooting was brisk, it was later remarked that 'from the firing kept up during the conflict never were combatants less disposed to draw blood'. When the market house was set on fire by burning straw the garrison surrendered. The insurgents then divided into two bodies, one marching towards Antrim town, the other thrusting towards Toome, which commanded the crossing of the Bann. This column had a skirmish with a party of mounted yeomanry, and after losing a man, withdrew to Moneymore, where the local yeomanry corps were concentrating. On 8 June, Clavering, commanding the troops sent into County Antrim from Blaris, occupied Randalstown and Toome. At the same time, Knox, commanding in Tyrone, sent detachments to the nearby towns of Lurgan and Portadown. At Maghera in County Londonderry, about ten miles north-west of Toome, a crowd of insurgents gathered on 8 June. They were dispersed by Captain Heyland at the head of his yeomanry corps of the Bovanagh cavalry. A number of prisoners were taken and a few days later fifteen insurgents were convicted and sentenced by drumhead courts martial in Maghera.[79]

At Carrickfergus, on the east coast, where a detachment of the Tay fencibles was stationed, on the morning of the 7th the drum beat to arms and about 150 of the inhabitants hurriedly formed a yeomanry corps in support of the military. That evening a large crowd gathered on the common near the town but it dispersed on hearing the news from Antrim. During the next few days the garrison sallied out, burning houses and making arrests. On the 13th and 14th reinforcements of fencible cavalry from Scotland were landed at Carrickfergus, and it was noticed that many of the country people were wearing red ribbons as a sign of loyalty. Insurgent attacks on Larne, Limavady and Glenarm were beaten off, the officer in command at Larne returning a summons to surrender unopened. In north Antrim a large crowd gathered at Broughshane on the 7th and marched on Ballymena, with at its head (most

[79] S. McSkimnin, *Annals of Ulster* (1849), p. 115; M. Archdale to ——; H. M. Clavering to ——, 8 June 1798, (N.L.I. MS 56); G. Nugent to ——, 9 June 1798 (I.S.P.O. 620/38/98); *B.N.L.*, 3 July 1798.

unwillingly) Captain James White of Whitehall. On the morning of the 7th he had set out for Antrim to attend the magistrates' meeting, but on seeing parties of armed men on the road, he had turned back with the object of persuading his tenants to stay at home. A band of men came to his house and forced him to go on the march to Ballymena telling him 'that he should receive the first fire from any that should oppose them'. The garrison of Ballymena, a handful of yeomen, was stationed in the market house, and when a fire was started underneath their post they surrendered. A green flag was placed on the church steeple and some of the loyal inhabitants killed, the lead being taken by James Dickey, an attorney, who seems to have been unbalanced. After a couple of days a committee negotiated the surrender of the town with Clavering, who had advanced north, and Boyd, the landlord of Ballycastle, who at the outbreak of the rising had retired to Coleraine, returned to his town at the head of two yeomanry corps.[80] At nearby Ballymoney, when the government forces set fire to four houses, 'owing to an unexpected change in the wind' 63 were burned 'by which some loyal persons were sufferers'.[81]

The government was fortunate in the timing of events in Ulster. The Antrim insurrection was, practically speaking, over before serious trouble broke out in County Down. On 3 June the Down leaders learned that Antrim would probably rise in the next few days; on 5 June the Revd William Steel Dickson, the commander-in-chief of the United Irishmen of County Down, a man of force and intellect, who intended to make Ballynahinch his headquarters, was arrested, and this and other arrests were bound to shake the confidence of the Down leaders who were convinced that without its colonel a battalion of United Irishmen, 'would be in no better order than a mere country mob'. Nevertheless, on the 8th crowds of armed men began to gather. One vigorous young leader, the Revd David Warden, an Edinburgh graduate and a licentiate of the Bangor presbytery, planned an attack on Newtownards, the principal market town of the area. But, though he waited in the fields

[80] S. McSkimnin, *Annals of Ulster*, pp. 97–8; *D.J.*, 14, 16 June 1798; *B.N.L.*, 15 June 1798; *S.N.L.*, 19 June 1798, court-martial records in 620/2/9/23/28.
[81] For destruction in Ballymoney see 620/8/83/14 and *Commons' Jn. Ire.*, xix, pp. clviii–xiv.

until the early morning, 'not a single person' assembled.[82] On the 9th the insurgents in the country south of Newtownards inflicted a severe check on the government forces. Colonel Stapleton, with the York fencibles, and a couple of yeomanry corps, was ambushed near Saintfield. At the outset of the engagement his guns were captured, but on deploying he was able to recover them. He then retreated to Comber, from where he marched to Belfast. His losses amounted to about fifty officers and men—including the Revd Robert Mortimer, the chancellor of Down cathedral, 'an active though violent magistrate', killed at the beginning of the engagement.[83] On the 10th a large crowd of insurgents formed an encampment at Ballynahinch under Henry Munro of Lisburn, who issued a proclamation calling on the people 'Not to pay any rents to disaffected landlords as such rent is confiscated to the use of the national liberty war'.[84] Warden managed to bring a contingent to the camp from the north of the county, having organized them by putting them into companies, but he had to use all his persuasive powers to get some of his men to come and they were soon talking about going home and grumbling at the accommodation offered.

On the evening of the 10th great crowds assembled at Drumbo, near Lisburn. At midnight the drum beat to arms in Lisburn, and the garrison, soldiers and yeomanry, who had had little sleep for some nights, 'seemed quite happy at having an opportunity of engaging the croppies'. But the threatened attack on the town did not develop. On the 11th Portaferry, a small port at the mouth of Strangford Lough was attacked, but the yeomanry garrison, aided by the guns of a revenue cruiser, beat off the attack. Another small port, Donaghadee on the north Down coast, was seized by the insurgents, who boarded a ship becalmed off the port and captured John Brown, a sometime sovereign of Belfast, who was hurrying back from Cheltenham to join his yeomanry corps. The respectable inhabitants tried to persuade the insurgents not to oppose the king's troops but a conservative spokesman was opposed by a gardener—

---

[82] *Commons' Jn. Ire.*, xvii, p. dccccxxi; W. S. Dickson, *A narrative*; D. B. Warden's narrative (H.O. 100/86); *D.J.*, 9 June 1879.

[83] *Courier*, 16 June 1798.

[84] *D.E.P.*, 21 June 1798.

rendered, according to his later defence before a court martial—truculent by drink. 'I am a little man,' the gardener declared, 'but I think I could slay two or three, and if I should lose all, I have the use of my hands and can work for more.' However, on the 13th a report that Nugent was victorious arrived, the insurgents fled, and Brown, who was expecting to be sent before 'a mock court martial' at Ballynahinch was released.[85]

On 10 June Nugent was very conscious of the gravity of the situation in east Ulster. He thought that all he could do was to confine the rebellion to Antrim and Down—where the French would find it difficult to make a landing—until reinforcements could be sent to the north, and he planned to hold on to Blaris camp and a string of towns, Belfast Lisburn, Hillsborough and Newry, withdrawing outlying garrisons from Larne, Glenarm and Downpatrick. The plan was an intelligent one, but Nugent soon proved that it was based on an over-pessimistic appreciation of the situation. On the 12th, presumably realizing that the disturbances in Antrim were dying down, he decided to thrust at the County Down insurgents. He himself, advancing from Belfast, and Colonel Stewart and the Argyle fencibles moving north from Downpatrick, converged on the insurgents at Ballynahinch. Those who were encamped east of the town tried to check Nugent's advance by 'planting an ambuscade on his flank', but galled by heavy artillery fire they retreated to a strong position in Moira's demesne south of the town, which, during the battle, was set on fire and burned fiercely all night. At dawn (3 a.m.) Nugent mounted an attack. Colonel Leslie with the Monaghan militia, dragoons and some yeomanry infantry, moved against the insurgents' front and Colonel Stewart with the Argyle fencibles and dragoons moved to a point from which he could enfile their position. Nugent's artillery, two howitzers and six six-pounders, as he himself said 'annoyed them very much'. The insurgents, musketeers, 'supported by a very great number of pikemen', surged forward against Stewart three times but were driven back by the fencibles and yeomanry covered by the artillery firing grape. Repulsed, the insurgents scattered and the government forces, left in possession of the field, captured three or four green flags and six

---

[85] *D.J.*, 14 June 1798; *S.N.L.*, 15, 18 June 1798; S. Millin, *Sidelights on Belfast history*, p. 92; court-martial proceedings (620/2/15/28).

one-pounders, which as they were unmounted, could not have been very effective. Nugent estimated the insurgents' losses at three or four hundred. His own, he was 'sorry to add were great'—totalling about thirty in all killed and wounded.[86]

On 11 June, the day before the battle of Ballynahinch, the leaders of the United Irishmen in central Down met to discuss action. Two plans were suggested—to march north and reinforce Munro at Ballynahinch, or to attack Newry and try and establish communications between the northern men and the Leinster insurgents. There was a warm debate over the relative merits of these two plans and in the end they were referred to a 'military council'. The next day the discussion was terminated by the arrival of fugitives from Ballynahinch.[87]

The Ulster rising, long dreaded by the government, was confined to a comparatively small zone, and lasted only for a brief week. Though Nugent in mid-June and again in December believed that a general rising was still being planned, and though for months the military authorities and the government's supporters were on the alert, Ulster was henceforth quiet.[88] The hard-headed farmers who formed the backbone of Ulster radicalism took to heart the lesson that citizens in arms hurriedly assembled were no match for competently handled military forces, and by the end of June it was being said in the Ards that 'nobody will ever prevail on them to go to catch cannon balls on the points of pikes and pitchforks'.[89] To defeat in the field was added disillusionment with France. French assistance, so often spoken of in the recent past, had not been available, and, more important in its long-term effect, the face of French power was changing. 'The general impression is now against the French', a shrewd observer of Ulster opinion noted. 'Our northern republicans now see very clearly that an independent republic is not to be expected under the auspices of the directory'.[90] Another development, bound to perturb Ulster

[86] G. Nugent to Lake, 10, 13 June 1798 (I.S.P.O. 620/38/121, 129); G. Nugent to Lake, 31 June 1798 (*British military library*, i, pp. 237–9); *S.N.L.*, 15 June 1798.
[87] C. H. Teeling, *A personal narrative of the Irish rebellion*, pp. 32–3.
[88] G. Nugent to —— (N.L.I. MS 56), G. Nugent to ——, 21 Dec. 1798 (I.S.P.O. 620/41/98).
[89] *B.N.L.*, 29 June 1798.
[90] C. Warburton to ——, 29 Aug. 1798 (S.C.P. 1017/4).

protestants, was that the rising in the south and west was clearly a catholic movement, or at least a movement almost entirely catholic in composition. Details of the atrocities committed against Wexford protestants were not disseminated in Ulster until after the rising.[91] But from the end of May Ulster protestants with a rudimentary knowledge of denominational demography must have been acutely aware that an insurgents' victory in the south of Ireland might well be a prelude to catholic political predominance. General Knox noticed that many presbyterians in mid-Ulster, who were United Irishmen, became yeomen 'when the Wexford atrocities were known', about the end of June 1798.[92] At the close of July, when dwelling on the savagery of the southern insurgents, the *Belfast News-Letter* complacently pointed out to its readers that 'the different character maintained by the catholic of the north and the catholic of the south is well understood by everyone acquainted with Ireland. God be praised the former has better information than the latter and has we believe a degree of liberality with which the other is unacquainted.'[93] It was significant that just before the Ulster rising some well-known Belfast liberals signed an address calling for the surrender to the military authorities of cannon which had belonged to the volunteers. It was also significant that shortly after the rising an ecclesiastical body which could claim to represent to a great extent intelligent and liberal ecclesiastical opinion in the province, the synod of Ulster, meeting at the end of August 1798 in Lurgan, voted a loyal address to the king, lamenting that 'the most stable and sacred principles of many of our people, and some of our members have been shaken by the convulsions of this sceptical and revolutionary era'. The most distinguished presbyterian minister in Belfast, William Bruce, in a powerful sermon tried to show that the evils of the day were linked with the decline in paternal authority. 'Do not let any father hope', he said, 'to receive respect or obedience from a rebel or an atheist'. According to Mrs McTier, the sermon was delivered

---

[91] The massacre at Scullabogue reported in *D.J.*, 21 June 1798, and mentioned in Prior's diary for 3 July.

[92] Knox to R. Musgrave, 16 May 1799 (N.L.I. MS 4157).

[93] *B.N.L.*, 24 July 1798. Todd Jones, a leading northern radical of the eighties and early nineties, at the close of 1798 publicly declared that he was glad the government was able to maintain order and punish traitors (*Sun*, 14 Nov. 1798).

with great animation—approved of by some and stabbing others, who hardly prevailed on themselves to remain seated. 'I expressed disappointment that "Croppies lie down" was not sung after it.'[94]

Though some of his congregation may have expressed sullen or tart disapproval of his politics, Bruce, a reformer in the eighties, a moderate liberal in the early nineties and by 1798 'an alarmed whig', prepared to serve as a yeoman along with other liberals, represented an important trend in Belfast opinion. Prosperity does not inevitably produce political placidity, but economic effort is likely to divert thought and energy from direct action and with Ulster entering on a growth era men were increasing their stakes on the continuance of ordered progress. A few weeks after the fighting in Ulster ended the *Belfast News-Letter* supplied its readers with an interpretation of recent events, acceptable to a businessman who considered himself a political moderate. It began by pointing out that the statement published in a London newspaper, 'it is the people of Ireland who acted the late rebellion', was seriously misleading. The insurgents in fact comprised about one per cent of the population of Ireland, their aim was 'the abolition of property and consequent anarchy,' and in their ranks 'not one man of property in the deliberative north'. In August it was thankfully remarked that owing to drought delaying sowing and harvest the crops had not suffered in the June rising. A couple of months later, during the engagement between Bompard and Warren off the Donegal coast, though gun-fire was heard in Letterkenny, 'it being market day, cloth and yarn notwithstanding [were] selling as high as if there were no fight'.[95]

What the government and Irish conservatives dreaded was a French invasion in conjunction with a popular insurrection. But the '98 rising in Ulster and Leinster was over before the French moved. Reports of an insurrection in Ireland did not reach France until the middle of June, and it was on the day of Vinegar Hill (21 June) that Napper Tandy, who reacted promptly, summoned a meeting of the United Irishmen in Paris, which issued addresses to the Irish people and to the

---

[94] *Records of the synod of Ulster*, iii, pp. 208–9; *B.N.L.*, 5 June 1798; Mrs McTier to W. Drennan, 30 Nov. 1799 (Drennan papers, 730).
[95] *B.N.L.*, 6 July 1798, 16 Oct. 1798.

French directory, demanding aid for Ireland.[96] Some weeks later, on the fête of 14 July, Cabanis called on the Council of five hundred to declare that the Irishmen who were fighting for all Europe were worthy of honour. The directory felt that the Irish insurgents should be supported but were very conscious how little effective help could be sent.[97] During the early months of 1798 French strategic thinking had been dominated by Bonaparte's projected expedition to the south-east Mediterranean. Six months before he sailed the congress of Rastadt had opened and by the middle of 1798 negotiations were in full train, which, it was believed, would shape the future of western Germany and determine France's eastern frontier. It was not easy for the directory to switch its attention to the west and when it did the outlook was not promising. The battles of Saint Vincent and Camperdown had confirmed Great Britain's naval predominance. Though there were plenty of troops available in western France, there was a strong possibility that in the near future large numbers of them would have to be moved to the eastern frontiers; no preparations had been made for an Irish expedition, and few ships of the line were fit for sea.[98]

The directory decided to encourage the Irish insurgents by sending munitions and a few thousand troops, a strong enough force, it was hoped, to create a formidable revolutionary army by adding disciplined striking power to numbers and enthusiasm. A squadron commanded by Admiral Bompard composed of the *Hoche* 80 and six frigates, carrying 2,700 men under General Hardy, was to sail from Brest and three frigates carrying just over 1,000 troops, commanded by General Humbert, were to sail from La Rochelle. On 19 July Hardy was placed in command of 'l'armée d'Irlande' and instructed to land if possible in Donegal. He was directed to surround himself with men known for their devotion to liberty and to set up in the towns, under his control, provisional governing bodies with civil and military functions which would in time come under a central authority. His men were to treat the Irish as allies and

[96] *Moniteur*, 3, 5, 28 Messidor, Year 6.
[97] J. Barras, *Memoirs*, iii, pp. 301, 306.
[98] For French expeditions to Ireland in 1798 see E. Desbrière *Projets et tentatives*, ii, pp. 29–190.

respect their religious practices (the instructions implied that an insurrection was raging in Ireland or could easily be revived).[99] After receiving his instructions Hardy had a long, frustrating wait at Brest. The prevailing winds were westerly; the blockading fleet was alert, and when Bompard's ships ventured into the gulf two of them collided. Hardy impatiently suggested to the minister of Marine that he himself with a carefully selected party of officers and a few hundred men should embark for Ireland on a couple of frigates which could slip out of Nantes or Rochefort.[100] Nothing came of this suggestion and by the middle of September his force was still at Brest.

Humbert, however, managed to sail from La Rochelle at the end of July. He reached Killala Bay at the north-east corner of Mayo on 22 August and landing, marched on Killala, a small town with a round tower, a cathedral on the scale of a substantial parish church and a bishop's palace. The bishop of Killala, Joseph Stock, was entertaining some clergymen and army officers to dinner, and the company was preparing to join the ladies between seven and eight o'clock on a fine summer evening, when a terrified messenger entered with the news the French 'had just landed'. After a skirmish with a small party of yeomanry the French entered the town, Humbert taking up his quarters in the bishop's palace, and the anglican establishment in the person of the bishop and a few of his clergy found themselves confronting the armed forces of revolutionary France. Joseph Stock, who had been a fellow of Trinity, was an urbane scholar whose self-assurance, candour and knowledge of French enabled him to establish reasonable relations with his captors. During the three weeks Killala was in the hands of the French the palace was both the French headquarters and a place of refuge for many protestants, and the bishop was kept busy trying by co-operation with the French and his respectable neighbours to maintain a modicum of civilized order in the midst of civil war. An intelligent and successful man, he reluctantly respected the competent professionalism of the French, and finding that one French officer was an inquiring

[99] Instructions to Hardy (Archives de la marine, BB⁴ 122).

[100] Hardy to the minister of marine, 20, 21 Aug. 1798 (Archives de la marine BB⁴ 122).

deist, he lent him a book on Christian apologetics by a Roman catholic divine.[101]

Connaught was the poorest province in Ireland but, according to the Revd James Little, who knew the area well, conditions in north-east Mayo had been improving with rising prices for black cattle and the spread of tillage and the linen manufacture. Little also noticed, however, that absenteeism was on the increase; and, a strong conservative, he did not fail to observe that when men 'grow fat and rich [they] lament the privation of imaginary blessings, and grow out of humour with all government'. The immediate reaction of the country people to the French landing seems to have been bafflement. But after the collapse of the established order in Killala recruits began to flock into the town. Predictably the French, consciously professional and 'progressive', were shocked by the poverty, indolence and 'superstition' they met in Mayo.[102] But so far as they could, they armed, clothed and drilled the Irish insurgents who joined them. Humbert, a rough, ambitious and crafty soldier, after a few days in Killala, marched south, capturing Ballina and thrusting towards the centre of Connaught. The government forces in the province, about 4,000 strong, were commanded by Major-General Hely-Hutchinson, a son of the provost and an expert tactician. Hutchinson immediately prepared to check the French advance by concentrating a force at Castlebar. By 27 August he collected there a composite force of 1,600–700 (1,100 infantry, 500 cavalry), including a regiment of the line (6th), a 'skeleton' formation, two militia regiments, some dragoons, Irish fencibles cavalry and Scots infantry fencibles. After the event Cornwallis criticized Hutchinson for taking up an advance position with a relatively small force composed of raw troops. If things had gone differently Hutchinson presumably would have been commended for his promptitude. On the evening of the 27th Lake arrived at Castlebar, and though tired out with travelling took command. The following morning his force was drawn up in 'true Dundas style'. But though positioned with textbook precision it was facing in

[101] J. Stock, *A narrative of what happened at Killala* (1800), pp. 52–3.

[102] 'Two diaries of the French expedition of 1798', ed. N. Costello, *Analecta Hibernica*, xi, pp. 15, 16, 17, 19, 70; R. Musgrave to T. Percy, 13 Oct. 1798 (N.L.I. MS 4157).

the wrong direction. There were two routes by which the French might advance on Castlebar, the Foxford road or a mountain road. They were expected to use the former but in fact they debouched for their main attack from the mountain path. The French came on with skill and *élan*; Lake's heterogeneous force, attempting to reform its front, fell into confusion, crumbled and retreated in panic-stricken disorder. A few units tried to cover the retreat but about 500 prisoners were taken, including a large number of militiamen, some of whom deserted and enlisted in the insurgent army.[103]

Occupying Castlebar, Humbert set up a civil administration for Connaught. He appointed a council of twelve, with John Moore, a law student, the son of a catholic merchant and landowner, as president. The immediate duty of the council, Humbert made clear, was to raise men and supplies, a *levée en masse* being ordered. The country round Castlebar and Killala was divided into districts or departments, in each of which there was a magistrate, appointed by his neighbours, with a guard of about twenty men, responsible for keeping the peace, making requisitions of money and distributing meat supplies. These magistrates, according to Stock, were always Roman catholics, 'but commonly of the better sort'. Some of them approached the bishop to discover if they would incur the penalties of treason for assisting the king's enemies. Stock assured them that he had 'always found the law of England to be consonant with reason', and that they would not incur punishment for acting, as they were doing, for the preservation of the community.[104]

Auckland, who in the course of a quarter of a century in active politics had received many 'unexpected and unpleasant accounts of military defeats and disgraces', told Cooke that not even Saratoga had affected him so much as 'your Castlebar catastrophe'.[105] Of course from the purely military point of view it was a minor engagement, simply illustrating what first-class troops, properly handled, could achieve against home

---

[103] *Cornwallis correspondence*, ii, p. 412; H. McAnally, 'The government forces engaged at Castlebar in 1798', *I.H.S* iv, pp. 316–31. It was rumoured that Lake had drunk rather too freely the night before the action and was with difficulty roused in the morning (Prior diary, T.C.D. MS 3365); W. Scott to G. Nugent, 16 Oct. 1800 (Army Museum MS 6807/175).

[104] *Analecta Hibernica*, xi, 55; Stock, *A narrative*, pp. 44–6, 71.

[105] Auckland to E. Cooke, Sept. 1798 (I.S.P.O. 620/18).

defence units. But though the French force was small 'their reception from the country people was very kind' and obviously if Humbert could keep in the field until he was reinforced, insurrection might surge up throughout Ireland. Cornwallis, immediately he heard that the French had landed, started moving large bodies of troops to the west. He sent reinforcements to Lake, moved the guards brigade from Birr to Kilbeggan, and sent 3,000 men from Dublin to Tullamore in a day by the Grand canal. He himself took command of 'the principal army' and advanced west, 'with extraordinary, perhaps with excess of caution'.[106]

But it was important that Humbert should not be allowed to inflict another serious defeat on the government's forces. On 1 September Cornwallis was at Tuam and Humbert was in full retreat northwards. On 5 September the French army was engaged at Colooney (a small village south of Sligo) by Colonel Vereker at the head of the City of Limerick militia, a few dragoons and some yeomen. Vereker, who did not realize that he was greatly outnumbered, considered 'it more desirable to attack than wait to be attacked' After 'a very close and severe action', outflanked, he had to retreat, losing a couple of small guns. But as he retired in decent order in the face of a superior enemy, his 'brilliant effort' was regarded with pride by Irish conservatives, and Vereker when granted an augmentation of honour to his arms, took as his motto one word, 'Colooney'.[107] Perhaps deterred by this action, Humbert ignoring 'the loyal, rich and populous' town of Sligo, turned eastwards, and crossing the Shannon at Ballintra marched into County Leitrim. Cornwallis, having swung round, was advancing up the east bank of the Shannon, while Lake pressed hard on Humbert's heels. On 8 September Lake's advance guard, commanded by Craufurd, who was later to lead the light division in the Peninsula, caught up with the French and after a short action near Ballinamuck in County Leitrim, Humbert surrendered at discretion. About the time the French crossed the Shannon insurrection broke out in the Longford–Westmeath area. On 4 September, a crowd, several hundreds strong, armed with

[106] J. Moore to Dr Moore, 2 Sept. 1798 (Add. MS 57321); *An impartial relation of the military operations* (1799), p. 24; J. Moore, *Diary*, i, p. 324.
[107] *D.J.*, 6 Oct.1798.

'pikes, scythes, pitchforks and some guns', attacked Wilson's
Hospital at Multifarnham. They were beaten off; the following
day an attack on Granard was dispersed and on the 6th a body
of insurgents marching on Mullingar was routed by a detachment of yeomanry and fencibles.[108] The Longford–Westmeath
risings were swiftly suppressed but they indicated how easily
insurrection could be stirred up by foreign invasion.

A week after Humbert surrendered Napper Tandy arrived
off the Irish coast, having sailed from Dunkirk in a brig, the
Anacreon, with a small group of Irish exiles, who might have
formed the staff of a revolutionary army. On 16 September
Tandy landed with sixty men on Rutland island off Donegal,
met government authority in the person of the postmaster (who
turned out to be a connection by marriage), issued a couple of
grandiloquent proclamations, calling on Irishmen to fight for
liberty under the leadership of Tandy, who has 'sworn to lead
them to victory or to die', and indulged in some conspicuous
conviviality.[109] Then, having heard of Humbert's surrender, on
the 17th he re-embarked and after a venturesome voyage
reached Bergen.

On the day Tandy left Rutland Bompard's squadron at last
put out to sea. Bridport had been driven off station by a storm
but the departure of the French squadron was observed by a
British ship of the line, the admiralty was immediately informed
and Bompard's ships as they sailed into the Atlantic were
followed by British frigates, one of which noted how the French
'sail very indifferently . . . particularly the ship of the line'. On
the 23rd the commander-in-chief at Plymouth received a
dispatch directing him to send three ships of the line under
Sir John Warren to cruise between Cork and Cape Clear.
Some days later, the admiralty having received further
information about the course the French ships were keeping,
ordered Warren to cruise off Achill. On 11 October Warren
sighted Bompard's squadron to the north-west and made the
signal for a general chase, which continued in 'bad and
boisterous weather' throughout the following day. On the 12th
Warren, who had five frigates in company with his three
ships of the line, brought Bompard to battle off the north

---

[108] *D.J.*, 8 Sept. 1798.
[109] J. E. Urquart to ——, 14 Sept. 1798 (W.O. 1/1101).

coast of Donegal. The *Hoche*, which fought gallantly, and three French frigates were captured in the action, and three other frigates from Bompard's squadron were captured during the next few days in single-ship actions. Though the number of ships involved was small, Warren's victory was a welcome demonstration of the power of the navy to protect the British Isles and he received the thanks of both houses of the British and Irish parliaments. He also received a rebuke from the admiralty, their lordships expressing their disapproval of his sailing for Plymouth when there was still the possibility of another French expedition arriving off the Irish coast.[110]

[110] See dispatches in Adm. 1/111.

18
Aftermath

The '98 insurrection demonstrated vividly and dangerously the intensity and strength of discontent with the existing social and political order in Ireland, and confronted the government with two major problems. The removal of the causes of discontent called for bold and long-term measures. More immediately, there was the question of how were the discontented, who had resorted to direct action, to be handled? By coercion or conciliation or by a blend of both? The Irish administration, which had to cope with these problems, was headed by Cornwallis and Castlereagh, who took office as lord lieutenant and chief secretary during the insurrection. Cornwallis had been driven to devote himself to the service of king and country, by what he himself termed, 'the irresistible impulse . . . to follow the thorny path I have travelled'.[1] Professionally competent, conscientious and kindly, though capable of severity when he thought it necessary, from the outset he was conscious that his standards contrasted sharply with those of the Irish ruling world, which he regarded as being intolerant, violent and prejudiced. He considered Irish politicians tediously talkative and tended to avoid social contacts with them. Fortunately he found Castlereagh, who was acting as chief secretary when he arrived, temperamentally and intellectually congenial. Castlereagh knew Ireland well, he had a swift grasp of essentials and he faced difficulties and setbacks with serene self-assurance. Alexander Knox, the theological thinker, who was Castlereagh's secretary, wrote of him at this time as 'humane . . . and good natured beyond the usual standard of men. In him it is not merely a habit, or a natural quality, but it is a moral duty. And yet when a firm decision is requisite, he can well exert it . . . He has appeared in this political hurricane, not like Addison's angel, merely directing the storm of party vengeance, but rather like the angel who guided the Ark of Noah through the deluge

[1] *Cornwallis correspondence*, ed. C. Ross (1859), ii. p. 53.

—Shedding from the very serenity of his countenance, a ray of hopeful brightness over the dark and troubled waters. In many instances loyalty has become impetuous, and his has been the happy energy to moderate and restrain it.'[2]

Cornwallis and Castlereagh had a common aim, the speedy restoration of 'complete and perfect tranquillity'.[3] Rebellion and widespread guerrilla warfare would both rend the Irish social fabric and dangerously weaken the empire (Cornwallis must have been concerned to see that Ireland was absorbing about 40 per cent of the forces, including about a third of the regulars available for the defence of the whole British Isles).[4] He and Castlereagh agreed on a policy of 'firmness and leniency', which in practice meant that the insurgent leaders should be punished and their followers pardoned. This policy accorded well with the official interpretation of the rising—which was that most of the insurgents had been forced to join the rebel ranks or deluded into rebellion by the machinations of designing men. At the end of June the government issued a proclamation empowering commanding officers to offer pardon to all those rebels who would desert their leaders and surrender their arms. Points were to be specified in each area where a magistrate and a military officer would be present to receive submissions and grant 'protections'. This proclamation was supplemented by another, issued just after Humbert's surrender, promising pardon to any person who had been armed and equipped by the French, provided he delivered up a French firelock and had not served in a higher rank than private.[5]

There were difficulties in administering the June proclamation. As might be expected, conservatives complained that men with protections in their pockets had been found attacking the military and taking part in 'acts of midnight murder, outrage and rebellion'. On the other hand a liberal M.P. complained that men who had been granted protections had been arrested. In King's County a number of men, having been assured by a magistrate that they would be pardoned, were court-martialled and sentenced to death or transportation.

[2] A. Knox, *Remains*, iv, p. 32.
[3] *D.J.*, 2 July 1798.
[4] Forces in Ireland, May 1799 (P.R.O. 30/8/240).
[5] *Dublin Gazette*, 29 June 1798; *D.E.P.*, 30 June 1798; *D.J.*, 21 July, 15 Sept. 1798.

When the magistrate remonstrated, the general in charge of the district replied that the persons court-martialled had been found to be 'leaders' and that they had been offered, as an alternative to their sentences, service abroad, which they had refused because they had been assured by the magistrate that they would be pardoned. On the other hand General John Moore, not realizing that yeomanry deserters were to be regarded as 'leaders', had allowed them to surrender under the proclamation. In any event, Moore considered being 'a leader' meant nothing; 'their captains', he wrote, '(judging of those I have seen) were of exactly the same description as the privates'. Moore indeed, it was reported, had received the repentant insurgents with 'plenty of food, pipers and whiskey punch'. The policy embodied in the proclamation met with a widespread response, large masses surrendered and claimed protection, the insurgents' forces were weakened and enraged conservatives denied an opportunity for exacting retribution on a sweeping scale.[6]

In the summer of 1798 the policy expressed in the June proclamation was embodied in an act, the pardon act. This declared that all acts of rebellion and all acts done in suppression of rebellion, if committed before 20 August 1798 were pardoned. But from this general pardon certain classes were exempt—persons imprisoned since January 1795 on a charge of treason or murder, yeomen who had deserted to the rebels, members of the national executive, and provincial and county committees, and rebel colonels and captains. Together with the pardon act, three other measures dealing with persons involved in revolutionary activities received the royal assent—two acts of attainder and the banishment act. The first act of attainder attainted Lord Edward Fitzgerald, Beauchamp Bagenal Harvey and Cornelius Grogan, three insurrectionary leaders of conspicuous social standing. The other attainder act, usually known as the fugitive act, provided that each of a number of persons named in the act who had been 'notoriously engaged in rebellion' would be attainted if he did not appear

---

[6] *D.J.*, 2 Aug. 1798; *D.E.P.*, 1 Sept. 1798; M. Keating to E. Cooke, 25 July 1798 (I.S.P.O. 620/51/131); J. Percy to L. Parsons, 8 Aug. 1798 (620/39/159); General Dunne to ——, 16 Aug. 1798 (620/39/180); J. Moore to E. Cooke, 17 Aug. 1798 (620/39/87); *D.J.*, 16 Aug. 1798.

in the king's bench prepared to stand his trial before 1 December 1798. Only two persons, James Napper Tandy and Harvey Morris, were in fact brought to trial under this act. Shortly after Tandy reached Hamburg, Grenville, the foreign secretary, presumably basing himself on Grotius, demanded his surrender as a traitor, and on 24 November 1798 Tandy and three other Irish refugees were arrested by the Hamburg authorities, who almost a year later handed them over to the captain of a British warship. They were dispatched to Ireland, where Tandy's arrival must have embarrassed the Irish administration, which does not seem to have been consulted by the foreign office. Tandy had long been the butt of Irish conservative wit, and the execution of an ageing political clown, who had once been a popular figure in Dublin, would have made a bad impression on public opinion. To ultra-tories it seemed as if Tandy's conviction would automatically follow proof of identity, but when he and Morris appeared before the king's bench their counsel produced an ingenious defence. It was proved to be just possible to travel from Hamburg to Dublin within a week, so the accused had been (hypothetically) prevented from surrendering in time by being imprisoned at the request of a secretary of state. The court accepted this argument and the prisoners were discharged. Tandy was held in custody and a year later tried at Lifford assizes for his descent on Rutland, found guilty, sentenced to death, respited and permitted to return to the continent.[7]

The banishment act, a striking illustration of the government's belief in the value of mercy tempered by justice or measured severity, resulted from negotiations between the government and the state prisoners, begun towards the end of July 1798. On 4 July five leading United Irishmen, John and Henry Sheares, John McCann, William Michael Byrne and Oliver Bond, were brought to trial before the commission of oyer and terminer for Dublin. On 24 July, after John and Henry Sheares and McCann had been executed, some of the leading state prisoners in Newgate informed the government that if Byrne and Bond were spared they would be willing to

---

[7] *H.J.*, 6 Nov. 1799; *D.J.*, 19 Oct. 1799, 11, 16 Apr. 1801. By the time of the Lifford trial the government had decided that Tandy's life should be spared (A. Marsden to attorney-general, 9 Apr. 1801, I.S.P.O. 620/10/115).

acknowledge their guilt and accept banishment to any foreign country not at war with the king. When the lord lieutenant discussed this offer with chief justices and the attorney-general they were against acceptance. Its terms were vague and if they were accepted 'it would be impossible to get a jury to convict a man for high treason'. Byrne was executed on 26 July but on the 28th Clare returned to Dublin from the country and pronounced decisively in favour of making an agreement with the state prisoners, and Bond's trial was not proceeded with.[8]

It was for both sides an advantageous bargain. The state prisoners avoided a series of prosecutions, fraught with danger for some of them. The government, which would have found it difficult to produce satisfactory legal evidence against many of the prisoners, was able to deprive Irish revolutionary radicalism of a large number of its proved or potential leaders. Moreover the government was anxious to have irrefutable, publishable evidence that there had been for some years past a great conspiracy against the established order—the existence of such a conspiracy being a justification of its emergency measures. But the 'memoir' on the origins and development of the revolutionary movement, which a few of the state prisoners hurriedly drafted and handed over to the government, 'though it admitted fairly enough the most material parts of the guilt . . . was written on the pretence of its being an apology for their conduct in the style of a controversial pamphlet'. On the lord lieutenant expressing his surprise at being sent such a document, and the state prisoners readily agreed that the best way for the government to obtain the information it wanted would be for some of the prisoners to be examined by a parliamentary committee. In August, Bond, Emmet, MacNeven, Neilson and O'Connor, appeared before a committee of each house. The dialogue between the prisoners and the committees was informative, frank, outspoken and polite, though they naturally differed sharply in their interpretation of the recent past. The witnesses strove to show that the United Irishmen were essentially political moderates, anxious for reform not revolution, inexorably forced by repression into direct action. The committees were convinced that from the outset in 1791 'the real purpose' of the United Irishmen was separation from

[8] Cornwallis, *Correspondence*, ii, pp. 372–92, 404–5.

Great Britain and the subversion of the constitution and that their conspiracy was part of the movement by which 'the government, the religion and the happiness of France has been destroyed, which has extended its influence over some of the most prosperous countries of Europe and has shaken to the foundations the fabric of regular society throughout the civilized world'.

The government considered that it was entitled to settle the time of the prisoners' departure and their destination. Obviously it would not have been very difficult for an Irish exile to pass from any part of the continent to France. The United States might have provided an asylum both well away from Europe and congenial to Irish radicals but the American government was reluctant to allow Irish radical refugees to enter the United States. Rufus King, the American minister in London and a strong federalist, in September requested Portland not to include the United States amongst the countries to which the state prisoners should be permitted to emigrate. They would not be, he thought, a desirable acquisition to any nation, 'but in none would they prove more mischievous than in mine, where from the sameness of language and a similarity of laws and institutions they have great opportunities for propagating their principles.' Writing to his own secretary of state, King remarked, 'I cannot persuade myself that the malcontents of any country will ever become useful citzens of our own.'[9]

The lord lieutenant thereupon decided that about twenty of the state prisoners, 'men of sufficient talent and consequence to render the place of their exile a matter of material importance', should be detained for the duration of the war.[10] This group, which included Emmet, MacNeven, Neilson, O'Connor, Henry Jackson and John Sweetman—two leading businessmen, Chambers the well-known radical publisher, Deane Swift, a country gentleman and a few others who might reasonably have been regarded as of secondary rank in the movement, were sent to Fort George in Scotland, where they remained until about the end of the war. Though their treatment was, as Neilson wrote, 'as liberal as can be expected'—the prisoners had separate apartments, and were allowed exercise,

[9] *Correspondence of Rufus King*, ii, pp. 570, 639–45.
[10] List of prisoners at St George (I.S.P.O. 620/51/269).

newspapers, books, sea-bathing and a pint of wine per man per day—they spent a wearisomely long time in dreary confinement and nerves were severely taxed. Neilson, a good-natured man, admitted that he tried to avoid some of his companions and O'Connor and Emmet had a serious quarrel which nearly led to a duel after their release.[11] Many of the other state prisoners were allowed to go into exile early in 1799—indeed the government tried to speed their departure by informing them at the close of 1798 that if they did not soon leave for a neutral country they would have to meet their own prison expenses. In addition to those named in the banishment act other persons were permitted or encouraged to transport themselves. For instance Nugent, who believed that 'to disorganize the north it will be necessary . . . to transport every committee man, and every leader, including the captains', issued a proclamation offering persons under detention in his district the terms granted by the government to the Dublin state prisoners. But when a group of northern detainees, including Steel Dickson, Robert Simms and William Tennant, were asked would they accept banishment, only nine of them, of whom one, Thomas Cruise, a Belfast merchant, was described as being 'a weak-minded bigot, an enthusiast on what he calls general philanthropy', agreed to go into exile. Twenty-five of the group rejected the general's offer. 'All the principal traitors refused peremptorily,' Pollock irritably reported.[12] Their obduracy may have been strengthened by the feeling that the government would find it very hard to secure their convictions. When, early in July, four alleged members of the Ulster provincial committee were brought to trial before a court martial they were acquitted, though, according to Nugent, 'no persons who attended their trial nor even the members of the court had the slightest doubt of their guilt'.[13] The prosecution failed largely because the principal crown witness was discredited. Pollock, when considering the prosecutions of those still detained, hoped that Nicholas Maginn, a member of the Down committee, who had appeared before the parliamentary secret committees, might be persuaded

[11] R. R. Madden, *United Irishmen* (2nd. ed.), ix, pp. 103–31.

[12] *D.J.*, 25 Aug. 1798; G. Nugent to ——, 14 Aug. 1798 (I.S.P.O. 620/39/172); J. Pollock to ——, 25 Aug. 1798 (I.S.P.O. 620/39/205); list of prisoners (I.S.P.O. 620/10/116); *S.N.L.*, 10 Dec. 1798.

[13] G. Nugent to ——, 14 Aug. 1798 (I.S.P.O. 620/39/172).

to 'come forward like a man' as a crown witness. Maginn
however hesitated either from 'the shame he would feel at
coming to prosecute those with whom he so long apparently
acted', or uncertain as to the reward he should demand, and by
the end of August Pollock ruefully admitted that the loss of
Maginn's testimony made it impossible to convict the principal
traitors.[14]

The banishment act covered relatively few of those who were
alleged to be involved in insurrection. Many others were either
brought before the ordinary courts or dealt with by extraordinary military tribunals. The maxim *silent leges inter arma*
applied only in a very limited sense to Ireland in 1798. True,
over those areas where civil war raged, the law was for brief
periods in abeyance. But throughout the year the normal
routine machinery of the courts continued to function. The
spring assizes were over before the rising began. It ended about
the time the summer circuits commenced—though understandably in the Connaught counties the assizes were postponed
for a fortnight and in two counties, Wicklow and Wexford, they
were not held. At these summer assizes 152 persons (about a
fifth of those brought to trial) were charged with a political
offence. The Trinity law term began on 8 June and in the four
courts the judges sat, though only peremptory motions were
heard and members of the bar (with the exception of the law
officers) and attorneys were expected to appear in yeomanry
uniform.[15] A few weeks earlier, on 22 May, the attorney-
general, determined to keep the civil law operating 'so long as
its dignity and influence could be maintained', had introduced a
bill, which quickly passed, empowering the judges of oyer and
terminer for the county and city of Dublin, to continue their
sessions while the king's bench was sitting, and it was before this
court that at the beginning of July five leading United Irishmen
were brought to trial for high treason.

Shortly after the outbreak of insurrection, the ordinary courts
were supplemented by a number of military tribunals. On 24
May a proclamation was issued by the lord lieutenant in
council, directing all military officers to use their utmost
endeavours to suppress the rebellion, and over wide areas

---

[14] J. Pollock to ——, 2 July, 26 Aug. 1798 (I.S.P.O. 620/39/4, 213).
[15] *D.J.*, 9 June, 18 Sept. 1798.

military force became the principal mainstay of law and order. Martial law (as distinct from military law, embodied in the mutiny acts and the articles of war) was a concept known to lawyers, but it had not been enforced in the British Isles since the middle of the seventeenth century. During the Williamite wars in Ireland and during the '15 and '45 martial law had not been proclaimed, and though during the Gordon riots London had been placed under military control, those arrested had been tried in the civil courts. However, Blackstone reluctantly accepted that when 'the contracts of society are in danger of dissolution', 'eccentrical remedies' might be required, and it was generally held that the crown had a prerogative power to take the necessary steps to meet a grave emergency such as an invasion or rebellion.[16] Martial law might be considered simply as a facet of the force employed to deal with such an emergency, an expression of the will of the commanding officer. Martial law, John Foster, the speaker, explained to the Irish house of commons, 'was a principle founded upon public exigency for the suppression of rebellion . . . under which the king gave power to his generals to punish with immediate death all persons acting in rebellion The general on his own view of the guilt, might of his own authority order such persons to be put to death, but sometimes in order to ascertain more effectually the guilt of the party, the general called for the aid of his own officers on a military tribunal, to enquire into the guilt of the party and examine the evidence'.[17] This explanation was expressed in a more compressed way by a Victorian lord chancellor when he laid down that 'if there is war it is found convenient and decorous from time to time to authorize "courts" to administer punishments and to restrain by acts of repression the violence that is committed in time of war'.[18]

Courts martial held under the proclamation of 24 May or under the rebellion acts passed between 1799 and 1801 were formed of officers belonging to the regular army, fencibles, militia or yeomanry, and had a membership varying from three to thirteen. Five or seven seems to have been the usual

---

[16] W. Blackstone, *Commentaries on the laws of England* (1765), i, pp. 244, 395, 405. F. Maitland writes of martial law as 'an improvised justice executed by soldiers, (F. Maitland, *The constitutional history of England* (1908), p. 267).

[17] *D.J.*, 16 Aug. 1798.

[18] *House of lords reports*, 1907, p. 94.

membership of a court. In 1801, under pressure from the house of commons, the government agreed that the minimum number should be seven and that a death sentence must be assented to by at least two-thirds of the officers constituting the court. The procedure followed was that of a court held under the articles of war. A judge-advocate was appointed, a record of the proceedings kept, evidence being summarized or reported verbatim, and the accused could examine or cross-examine witnesses and address the court. Sentences were subject to confirmation by the convening officer. Cornwallis, who directed that court-martial proceedings should be transmitted to him for confirmation, spent hours carefully studying them and making his own assessment of each case. Sometimes he simply wrote on the proceedings in his neat, firm hand, 'confirmed', but he often mitigated the sentence, frequently ordering a prisoner sentenced to transportation or to serve abroad to be released on finding securities. Occasionally too he sharply criticized a court. In October 1798 when a court martial, presided over by Lord Enniskillen, acquitted Hugh Whollaghan, a yeoman, charged with the murder of a County Wicklow man, whom he shot because he suspected him of being a rebel, Cornwallis publicly expressed his disapproval of the verdict. He directed that Whollaghan be dismissed from the yeomanry and that, after a communication conveying his opinion of the verdict had been read in open court, the court martial should be dissolved.[19]

The officers who sat on courts martial must in the course of their regimental duties have gained some experience of weighing evidence and extricating the truth from a quantity of hard swearing. A few of them were justices of the peace, and a conscientious officer might have read Adye's well-known treatise on courts martial, a neat manual, which included a summary of the rules of evidence. Undoubtedly members of a court martial would have a bias which would probably tell against an accused. A military environment breeds a strong respect for loyalty, obedience and subordination, and persons reputedly of a rebellious spirit were bound to be severely scrutinized by officers sitting on a court martial. Moreover, these military tribunals had two duties—to restore order and

[19] *D.E.P.* 23 Oct. 1798; *Parliamentary history*, xxxv, p. 1233.

to render justice in individual cases. These duties were not necessarily conflicting but their co-existence might confuse a not very acute intellect. However, the records suggest that on the whole the courts martial set about their duties conscientiously. When a Queen's County court martial was criticized by a clergyman for its sentences, the members (apparently yeomanry officers) indignantly replied that they had discharged their duties with 'liberality and firmness'.[20] The number of acquittals and the variations in the penalties imposed indicate that courts martial were striving to be just. After all a sense of fair play was a valuable quality to possess when managing a military unit, and might, in a rough and ready way, replace the accumulated rules and precedents of the common law. Indeed a crown solicitor, smarting under the prospect that a court martial would probably acquit some well-known radicals, complained that 'now every captain is a great judge and most of them fond of making popular speeches'.[21] It may be added that for some officers employing military courts in support of the civil power was a disagreeable duty. Lady Nugent, the wife of the general commanding in Ulster during the insurrection, regretted that her husband was 'not only compelled to meet the poor, infatuated, misguided people in the open field, but after defeating them, had also the distressing task of holding courts martial and signing death warrants for very many which was indeed heart-breaking to us both'. Clanricarde, commanding a district in the west, when asked to set up courts martial to try civil offences in June 1798, 'declared my reluctance to erect them except upon urgent occasions', adding that 'acting as I do upon the principle of conciliation', he wanted to bring as few people as possible before military courts. In the same summer of 1798 Sir James Stewart, commanding in Munster, considered sending a circular to justices of the peace, pointing out that the use of courts martial was not 'a better policy than ordinary trials by jury'. On the other hand a barrister of some standing was quick to point out the value of courts martial in disturbed areas. Their procedure was simple and speedy. There was 'no time

[20] Memorial from members of a court martial, 19 July 1798 (I.S.P.O. 620/29/117 and 620/40/74).

[21] J. Pollock to Castlereagh, 17 Aug. 1798 (I.S.P.O. 620/3/27/4); B.N.L., 10 Aug. 1798.

for murdering or tampering with witnesses', the accused could not avail himself of the 'objections in point of form' by which many who were 'substantially guilty' escaped and punishment followed swiftly on conviction.[22]

As has been said, throughout the insurrection of 1798 the ordinary courts remained open, so it was inevitable that once the insurgents were defeated in the field, the competency of military tribunals to investigate the behaviour of civilians and sentence them to punishment, was bound to be questioned. Towards the close of September, Matthew Tone, who had been captured near Ballinamuck, serving with the French forces, when brought before a court martial in Dublin, 'read a paper' challenging the competency of the court to try him, but his plea was overruled and he was convicted and hanged. Ten days after his execution, his more distinguished brother, Theobald Wolfe Tone, who had been captured on the *Hoche*, arrived a prisoner in Dublin. On the following day, 9 November, it was heard in the city that it was the intention of his friends to move in the king's bench for 'a prohibition against his being tried by court martial'. However, a court martial met the next day, Saturday 10 November, apparently rather earlier than the law courts sat, and Tone was tried, convicted and sentenced to be hanged. He made no attempt to deny the competency of the court but on Monday the 12th, the day chosen for the execution, which was to take place at 12.30, Curran applied for a writ of habeas corpus, arguing that Tone, who was 'not a member of His Majesty's army,' had been tried and sentenced while the courts were sitting. Rumour had it that if the writ were granted and Tone brought before the king's bench, Curran was then going to argue that since Tone had already appeared before a court martial, to bring him to trial in a civil court would place him in double jeopardy. Kilwarden, the chief justice, agreed to grant the writ and while it was being prepared sent a message to the barracks to defer the execution. When the writ was delivered Sandys, the brigade major, declared that he would obey only the orders of the general commanding the Dublin district or of the lord lieutenant. On hearing this Kilwarden

[22] Sir J. Stewart to ——, n.d., enclosing circular (I.S.P.O. 620/39/121), *Lady Nugent's journal*, ed. F. Cundall (3rd ed.) p. 1; Clanricarde to Granard, 17 June 1798 (PROI, 3474); *Second report from the committee of secrecy*, pp. 46–8 (H.C. (71), 1801, iii).

immediately directed the sheriffs to go to the barracks and take into custody Tone and his detainers (apparently the provost marshal and Sandys). At this stage the court was informed that during the previous night Tone had severely injured himself in an attempt to commit suicide and could not be moved.[23] On the following day Sandys was brought before the king's bench in custody, humbly apologized and was released. He also seems apparently—to the fury of an irritated conservative—at the lord lieutenant's direction to have made a return to the writ stating that his reason for not obeying it was 'because Tone could not be moved with safety'.[24]

Tone died on 19 November but his attempt at suicide by delaying his execution had opened the way for the beginning of a dramatic conflict of jurisdictions. The government clearly did not want to have a series of clashes between the civil and military authorities, and as early as 16 November Captain Taylor, Cornwallis's military secretary, wrote 'that in consequence of the circumstances which have occurred in the case of Tone . . . it will probably be thought desirable to put a stop to further proceedings by martial law against prisoners confined on charges of treason and rebellion'. Courts martial at Sligo and Castlebar were immediately suspended (and the officer commanding at Sligo advised to move prisoners under sentence of transportation or general service as quickly as possible to depots); in several instances the lord lieutenant directed that persons in military custody should be handed over to the civil authorities and commanding officers were informed that before a civilian was sent for trial by court martial the lord lieutenant's permission must be obtained.[25]

Early in 1799 a clash of jurisdictions might have occurred in

[23] *H.J.*, 14 Nov. 1798; *Morning Chronicle*, 19 Nov. 1798; *Morning Post*, 14, 17 Nov. 1798. The *Morning Post* had an agent in Dublin, 'who constantly attends court-martials' (F. Higgins to ——, 24 Nov. 1798 (620/10/12)).

[24] *Fortescue MSS H.M.C.*, iv, pp. 373–5. The duke of York's military secretary, Robert Brownrigg, considered that 'notwithstanding Tone having partially cut his throat' it would have been advisable to have executed him 'rather than by delay to have given an opportunity for what had occurred' (Brownrigg to the duke of York, 16 Nov. 1798, W.O. 133/2).

[25] H. Taylor to General Trench, 21 Nov. 1798, to the attorney-general, 26 Nov. 1798 and to St George Daly, 16 Nov. 1798 (H.O. 100/86). For instances see references to David Walsh and Joshua Cooper in I.S.P.O. 620/3/24/3, for Thomas Lyons see H.O. 100/86.

County Wicklow, where, on the eve of the lent assizes, the military authorities were planning to court-martial a number of prisoners. But the judges, on the instructions of the lord lieutenant, abandoned the circuit on the grounds that the county was in a gravely disturbed state.[26] About the same time the attorney-general displayed his determination to uphold the common law by taking up the case of two militia privates who at the Kilkenny spring assizes had been convicted of robbery and rape and sentenced to death. Their commanding officer, General Asgill, prevented the sentence being executed and it was said they fought well during the rebellion. But in November the attorney-general brought them up before the king's bench and moved that the sentence of the assize court be carried out. Kilwarden, stating that he would 'exert my utmost authority in enforcing obedience to the law of the land', directed they should be hanged in a few days' time, but the government quietly commuted the sentence to transportation.[27]

From the close of 1798 persons in custody for political reasons started appeals for writs of habeas corpus. At the spring assizes of 1799 in Mayo an attempt was made to have John Moore, who had acted as president of Connaught, brought to trial or discharged. The sheriff made an ingenuous return to the writ of habeas corpus, stating Moore was not in his custody because he was lodged in an apartment in the section of the prison occupied by the military. Nevertheless, it was thought advisable to strengthen the crown's case by arranging to have Moore detained on a secretary's warrant.[28] In County Cork, according to Lord Longueville, the easiest method of being liberated from a prison ship was by a writ of habeas corpus. 'The judge and the generals', Longueville angrily wrote, 'seem to have made war on each other and martial law was defeated everywhere the judge could come near it'.[29] Longueville may have exaggerated but Brian O'Connor, a doctor, and Florence McCarthy, who had been sentenced to transportation by a court martial at Cork for forming a committee and administering illegal oaths, were discharged by the king's bench on

[26] F. Archer to A. Marsden, 24 Mar. 1799 (I.S.P.O. 620/46/88), *Commons' Jn. Ire.*, xix, p. dcccxlvi; B. Yelverton to ——, 24 Mar. 1799 (I.S.P.O. 620/46/4).
[27] *Morning Post*, 2 Dec. 1798; *The Times*, 28 Nov. 1798; *D.J.*, 2 Mar. 1799.
[28] W. Plunkett to ——, 26 Mar. 1799 (I.S.P.O. 620/46/93) and 620/46/100.
[29] Longueville to ——, 3 May 1799 (I.S.P.O. 620/8/81/18).

the grounds their offence had been committed before the proclamation of martial law.[30] The king's bench also freed Fitzgerald, who had been detained by the military for six months in Mullingar gaol, and when four persons of 'respectable connections and tolerable property' were brought into the king's bench from Newry gaol, to which they had been committed by a military officer, the court discharged two of them. Detention warrants, signed by the chief secretary were immediately issued but the two who had been discharged could not be found.[31] George Barnes even applied for a writ of habeas corpus on behalf of two men apparently detained on a secretary's warrant. He argued that the tender on which they were confined was not a legal prison because 'a gale of wind might drive it out of the jurisdiction of the court'. The question was considered by a meeting of the common law judges attended by eleven members of the bench, which decided by 8 to 3 that the detention was lawful. Kilwarden in delivering judgement emphasized that though the government was constrained 'to restrict some of the privileges of the subject' it had provided that the gaoler who held a prisoner under a secretary's warrant should be answerable to the court for the persons entrusted to his care, and he suggested that the tender should be securely moored.[32]

But though the rising had been suppressed, during the winter of 1798 Ireland remained disturbed. 'Banditti' were active in some areas; there were rumours that the United Irishmen were being reorganized, frequent reports from Antrim and Down of districts being 'up', and widespread agrarian troubles in Munster and the west (there was a belief in government circles that the houghing of cattle in Galway and Mayo was part of a plot to deny provisions to the navy). It was noticed furthermore that the mail coaches ,which were strongly guarded, were usually accompanied by a number of post-chaises and horsemen, travelling in convoy.[33] The government therefore decided that if the peace was to be maintained military tribunals must be authorized. They would, Castlereagh

[30] E. Hutchins to ——, 17 Aug. 1799 (I.S.P.O. 620/47/135), 620/4/27/55, and court martial of Bryan O'Conor and Florence McCarty (620/17/6).
[31] D.E.P., 8 Dec. 1798; Morning Post, 10 Feb. 1799.
[32] Morning Post, 5 Dec. 1798.
[33] The Times, 1 Jan., 28 May 1799.

explained to the house of commons, 'deny to a great part of the country the advantages of the civil law, unless it were incorporated with the martial law'.[34] Tone's case had dramatically illustrated how a clash of jurisdictions could arise, so the government decided to settle the question by legislation and in February 1799 a rebellion bill was introduced, providing that it should be lawful for the lord lieutenant to direct commanding officers to bring to trial and punish persons engaged in rebellion, whether or not the courts of law were sitting. The courts martial set up for this purpose were to be constituted as the lord lieutenant should direct, and the common law courts were not to have cognizance of acts committed by soldiers which were certified by the lord lieutenant as being done in suppression of rebellion. It was also laid down that it would be a sufficient return to a writ of habeas corpus that the prisoner was detained on a warrant of a person authorized by the lord lieutenant to issue such a warrant, the name of such person having been notified to the king's bench by the lord lieutenant. The act was limited to a year, but by legislation passed in 1800 and 1801, it was continued to March 1802. The bill as presented to the Irish house of commons in 1799 was criticized in official circles in England, annoyance being expressed in 'the highest quarters', that a measure of such constitutional importance had not been submitted to the cabinet.[35] When the bill was in the lords amendments suggested in England were inserted in the preamble, including a reference to the king's 'undoubted prerogative of executing martial law' in an emergency, and a statement that the peace in Ireland had been only 'so far restored as to permit the course of the common law partially to take place'—words which implied that martial law had been in continuous existence since May 1798. The Irish judges regarded the bill as 'a measure of lamentable but inevitable necessity'.[36] In the house of commons the attorney-general complained that his 'sober friends of the law' were anxious to attack the principles of the bill before they saw it. One of the leading lawyers in the house, Browne,

[34] *Parliamentary history*, xxxv, pp. 10, 13, 14.
[35] W. Wickham to Castlereagh, 4 Mar. 1799 (H.O. 100/86). For the text of the bill as introduced see *D.J.*, 5 Mar. 1799.
[36] Castlereagh to W. Wickham, 6 Mar. 1798 (H.O. 100/86).

M.P. for the university, arguing vehemently against the bill, contended that the government could have found ample powers in the constitution if it had not been for 'false caution and timidity'. In the house of lords a small group of peers (including Charlemont and Leinster) signed a protest against a measure by which 'the freedom of our civil government is changed to a military despotism'. The government's supporters grounded their defence of the measure on 'imperious necessity'. Over wide areas a system of proscription was being directed against magistrates, witnesses and jurymen—one member quoting effectively what a County Leitrim juryman said to an assize judge—'My lord what can we do? A coal of fire set in our barn or in the thatch of our house, destroys our property, possibly the lives of our wives and children. If you want verdicts of conviction, your juries must be summoned from garrison towns where the individual may look for protection.'[37]

The following year, Castlereagh, when proposing the extension of the rebellion act, explained that its underlying principle was that 'the municipal law should be permitted to act whenever it was possible and that the assistance of the martial law should be resorted to when the circumstances of the case render it absolutely necessary'. Moreover, he emphasized that the lord lieutenant was responsible to parliament for his use of the powers granted by the act, and that it would not afford any protection to an officer who exceeded his instructions. By establishing martial law, he argued in 1801, 'in the long run you will thus do less violence to liberty and be more tender of blood. If you are weak and irresolute many loyal subjects will be murdered and the king's forces must be led out against the murderers'.[38]

At the close of 1798 there were a considerable number of persons accused of insurrectionary activities under detention in Ireland, including those convicted by the ordinary courts, courts martial and by J.P.s acting under the insurrection act, and those arrested on suspicion by zealous supporters of authority. In the city and county gaols there were at least 300 such prisoners (including 78 state prisoners held on a chief secretary's warrant). In Dublin this led to overcrowding, it

[37] D.J., 28 Feb., 15 Mar. 1799.
[38] D.J., 13 Mar. 1800; D.E.P., 19 Mar. 1800.

being pointed out that in Kilmainham apartments intended for respectable debtors were being occupied by traitors and that in Newgate, 'respectable men, who are sometimes imprisoned for assaults' were forced to mix with prisoners confined for high treason. One prisoner in Kilmainham (convicted of rape) so resented having to share a room with three radicals that he moved his bed into the lobby.[39] The state prisoners themselves could give trouble. When the first arrests were made in 1796 Cooke was determined that the state prisoners should have 'no cause of complaint' and their daily allowance seems to have been fixed at 5s. 5d. per head. But a year later the prisoners from the north (generally speaking members of the middle classes) were complaining that their diet was monotonous (beef and mutton almost all the time), that for liquor all they were offered was ordinary porter and that they were expected to make their own beds and clean their cells.[40]

Additional prison accommodation for persons accused of insurrectionary offences was found in Dublin by using the Provost (the military prison), the house of correction and the Royal Exchange together with four tenders in Dublin bay. In Belfast Lough there was a tender on which persons awaiting trial were held, there being about 130 on board in June and in the south there was a depot at New Geneva to which prisoners sentenced to transportation and service abroad were sent, and there were receiving ships at Duncannon and Cove.[41] New Geneva was an 'elegant village', consisting of a number of two-storied houses forming a square with a green in the centre, the whole surrounded by a high wall.[42] Shortly before the insurrection there was a severe fever epidemic on the ship at Duncannon. General Fawcett, commanding the district, established a hospital on shore into which he moved the sick, and arranged for the prisoners to have exercise on deck and two

---

[39] *Report of the commissioners appointed to enquire into . . . state prisons and other gaols in Ireland*, p. 46; *D.E.P.*, 28 Apr. 1791.

[40] E. Cooke to R. Ware, Sept. 1796 (I.S.P.O. 620/4/29/53); R. Ware to ——, n.d. (620/52/64); state prisoners' allowance, Newgate (620/40/38), state of state prisoners from the north (620/32/176).

[41] General P. Craig to ——, 29 May 1798 (I.S.P.O. 620/37/215); list of prisoners in the house of correction, 7 May–7 June 1798 (620/7/79/21); lists of prisoners on tenders (I.S.P.O. 620/7/79/2, 10, 20, 30); *Morning Post*, 26 Dec. 1798; *B.N.L.*, 18, 22 June 1798; Sandys to E. Cooke, 16 July 1798 (Official papers 2nd. series 52/11).

[42] *Hibernian Magazine*, 1794, pp. 556–7.

clean shirts each. When after the rising a hundred prisoners arrived from Waterford, Fawcett commandeered a transport to provide additional accommodation. Though not a very competent general, Fawcett was a man of sensibility, the author of a 'feeling poem' greatly admired by Goldsmith. He had himself spent some years in a debtors' prison and he soon acquired the reputation of being ready 'to let out any man on bail that requires it'.[43]

In July 1798 General Stewart, seriously concerned about conditions in the *Princess*, the prison ship at Cove, persuaded Admiral Kingsmill to appoint a committee to investigate the grounds on which prisoners had been committed to her. The committee—an M.P., the assistant barrister for Cork and three army officers—found that out of 282 prisoners, 142 had not been committed 'under any form of law' and that another 60 had been illegally committed. It went on to condemn severely that 'indiscriminating warmth of conduct which has brought many persons not apparently guilty into situations marked with hardship, injustice and cruelty'. Fawcett, very pleased with this report, suggested to Castlereagh that he might be permitted to release prisoners detained at Duncannon. He was, he said, daily receiving petitions from respectable gentlemen on behalf of wretched people, torn from their families. Castlereagh informed him that he could discharge those who were not properly committed or who were vouched for by respectable persons.[44] Shortly afterwards General Asgill, who was controlling the Kilkenny district with a firm hand, met on the road thirteen convicts, who, he said, had been sentenced to death after a thorough investigation and whom he had reprieved and sent to Duncannon for transportation. They had passes from General Fawcett, 'having received their liberty without any condition'. Asgill managed to rearrest three of them but the others escaped and he heard that twelve more were on the

[43] W. Fawcett to E. Cooke, 25 May 1798 (I.S.P.O. 620/36/65); S. Hulse to ——— 14 July 1798 (620/39/72); W. Fawcett to Castlereagh, 26 July 1798 (620/39/120); *Gent. Mag.*, xcvi, pt. ii, pp. 557–8; Camden to Portland, n.d. (H.O. 100/58); G. Lake to ———, 18 Mar. 1798 (620/36/94).
[44] Stewart to H. Taylor, 7 July 1798 (I.S.P.O. 620/39/33). Report of court of inquiry (620/39/2); W. Fawcett to Castlereagh, 9 July 1798, 12 Aug. 1798 (620/39/44, 620/4/29/20); John Haig to General W. Myers, 10 Sept. 1798 (620/40/48).

point of being released.[45] A few weeks earlier three Waterford
J.P.s had resigned as a protest against the way in which officers
were releasing rebels whom they had sent to the tender, and an
active Cork J.P., when he heard that General Stewart had
pardoned six men, angrily wrote, 'if this conduct is pursued I
will not answer for the consequences'.[46]

At a time of acute civil conflict, when conservatives were
thoroughly alarmed and quick to arrest, mistakes were easily
made. For instance Samuel Watson, a revenue officer and a
yeoman, who during the rebellion was flung into a common
gaol 'with felons and wretches of every description', turned out
to be a victim of mistaken identity. Two men who were being
held as witnesses were by mistake hurried off to New Geneva.
The case of another prisoner at New Geneva was raised by a
clerical magistrate, the Revd James Kenny, who discovered
that the man who had sworn an information against the
prisoner, 'would have shrank from the prosecution had he not
been afraid of me as I took a very active and determined part
against the rebels'. Kenny secured a pardon for the prisoner.
McCann, an Antrim militiaman, asserted that he had been
trying to defeat attempts to corrupt the soldiery, when 'a
cabal of conspirators' hatched a scheme to accuse him of
disloyalty. Edmund Maguire, a currier, imprisoned in the
Provost, explained that he had been arrested on calling at the
home of Ging, a tanner, suspected of being a United Irishman.
His reason for calling simply was that on hearing that Ging,
who owed him money, had been taken into custody, he was
anxious to get his account settled. A Dublin shoemaker,
petitioning for the release of his apprentice, explained that
about the middle of May 1798 the boy 'as is usual with apprentices' was going about 4.30 a.m. to call a journeyman, when he
met a yeomanry patrol and, as the result of some 'stupid and
imprudent expressions' was sent aboard the tender. Another
master, a tailor, pleading on behalf of his apprentice detained
on a tender, pointed out that the boy could not 'write a single
letter and therefore must not be considered as a person deep in

---

[45] C. Asgill to Castlereagh, 1 Sept. 1798 (I.S.P.O. 620/40/4); W. Fawcett to
C. Asgill, 1 Sept. 1798 (620/40/6).

[46] Prior diary, 29 July 1798 (T.C.D. MS 3365); R. Harding to F. Archer, 3 July
1798 (I.S.P.O. 620/39/56).

the business'. A more impressive figure, Ignatius Weldon, a merchant who had been a member of the catholic committee, complained that he had been arrested in June 1798 by a party of the Attorneys corps and thrown into the Provost, though, as he indignantly protested, he had never been a United Irishman. Another Dublin businessman, Miles Duigenan, the grocer, a conspicuous radical, also complained about being arrested. He was, he declared, on his way to the lord mayor to take the oath of allegiance when he was arrested. There were other cases which were certainly pathetic but not very plausible. For instance a Dublin clerk, in custody for possessing pike-heads, declared that he was standing at the door of his lodgings when they were thrust into his hands and that he was about to take them to a justice of the peace or throw them into the Liffey when he was arrested by a patrol. A County Longford farmer, charged with being in arms when Humbert was in the area, said that he was going to the insurgents to persuade them to let his son come home and that 'on leaving his house he took in his hand the first thing he met,' which happened unfortunately to be a pitchfork.[47]

In some areas committees were set up by the general commanding the district to investigate the cases of individual detainees. At the beginning of July Major Charles Sirr, the assistant town major and William Bellingham Swan, a senior revenue official and J.P., were appointed to receive submissions in the city and county of Dublin, a decision which inspired a pamphlet, *Observations on a state paper . . . empowering William Bellingham Swan and Charles Sirr to quell the Irish rebellion*, advertised by a Shakespearian quotation:

> Be these juggling fiends no more believed
> That palter with us in a double sence.[48]

In the north John Pollock, the clerk of the crown for Leinster,

---

[47] Petition of S. Watson (I.S.P.O. 620/48/12); R. Ward to ——, 29 Feb. 1799 (620/46/48A); J. Kenny to ——, 31 July 1799 (620/47/112); H. McCann, petition (620/51/138); E. Maguire, petition (620/51/149), J. Dowlan, petition (S.P.P.); H. Dempsey to E. Cooke, (620/51/74); I. Weldon, petition, 11 June 1798 (S.P.P.), M. Duigenan, petition (620/51/285); S. Madden, petition (S.P.P.) and I.S.P.O. 620/8/82/7; M. Smith, petition (S.P.P.).
[48] *D.J.*, 5, 12 July 1798.

and Charles Rankin, a banker and commander of a yeomanry corps, investigated the cases of a number of persons detained in Belfast.[49] In Dundalk, 'a court of inquiry for examining charges' recommended the release of some prisoners. A committee of inquiry, dealing apparently with a wide area round Dublin, recommended that out of a list of 81 names 69 should be released and 8 court-martialled. What should be done about the other four was left to the government.[50] At Birr a court of inquiry decided which prisoners should be court-martialled.[51] At Wexford a committee was constituted by General Lake to decide which prisoners should be brought to trial. But when Grose took over the Wexford command he was warned by Cornwallis not to accept the committee's decision without further inquiry, 'as its sentiments are in many cases far from impartial'.[52]

Some supporters of the established order were insistent that mercy should be tempered with caution. Thomas Fitzgerald, a Queen's County J.P., was very alarmed when he heard that the decision to court-martial John Murphy, a rebel captain, had been countermanded. Murphy, he stated, had sworn he would murder him, and 'should such a man as I am', Fitzgerald plaintively asked, 'be left to be assassinated in cold blood by a fellow whose life has been one tissue of lies?'. The high sheriff and J.P.s of King's County (including the liberal-minded Sir Lawrence Parsons) were disturbed to hear that convicted rebels were going to be released. If they were let loose 'new plots will be formed particularly against the lives and properties of those justices of the peace and yeomanry officers active in preserving the country from open rebellion'. The dean of Waterford was anxious that his 'confidential servant', who had been a United Irishmen's leader in the city, should be exiled. He was not, the dean emphasized, actuated by 'groundless panic or a sanguinary disposition', but he was concerned to

[49] *B.N.L.*, 13 July 1798; list of prisoners in Belfast, 24 Aug. 1798 (I.S.P.O. 620/10/116); list of those who refused to take the benefit of the proclamation, Belfast (620/39/203).

[50] Report of a court for examining charges against prisoners in Dundalk (620/39/148); report of court of inquiry (I.S.P.O. 620/51/135).

[51] General Dunn to ——, 16 Aug. 1798 (I.S.P.O. 620/39/180).

[52] E. Percival to Cornwallis, 3 July 1798 (I.S.P.O. 620/39/17); H. Taylor to Grose, (H.O. 100/81 f. 42).

establish in Waterford 'that social confidence . . . without which life is of little value'. The dean was supported by nearly eighty of the inhabitants of Waterford (including Sir John Newport, the well-known whig), who, petitioning against the release of half a dozen local insurgent leaders, pointed out that 'no prudence or valour can guard against the poignard of the assassin in the dark or the torch of the incendiary in the hour of sleep'. The loyalists of County Mayo, 'who have been most active in bringing forward evidence against traitors of consequence, will certainly', the lord lieutenant was told, 'conceive they have been throwing away their time unless severe examples are made'.[53]

But there were supporters of authority who, actuated by genuine benevolence and not unreluctant to exercise influence, interceded for persons in custody. Lord Downshire, asking for the release of a young man imprisoned for two years, forcefully remarked, 'the whole of this transaction is shockingly cruel and originated, I fear, in some private spite.'

Lord Blayney, writing on behalf of a man sentenced to transportation for trying by bribery to save his brother from prosecution, emphasized that 'it was a crime you must consider natural from a young man who has a good disposition'. Lord Bective, intervening on behalf of some of his tenants convicted of rebellion, stressed that 'these poor men pay their rents punctually'. Judkin Fitzgerald, the high sheriff of Tipperary, pressing for the release of eight men detained on a tender, remarked, 'the object of punishment I take to be "Ut ponea ad paucos metus ad omnes perveniat" '. Dr Haliday of Belfast asking for the release of a presbyterian minister, described him as a man of 'pleasing temper and good heart', whose political aims were moderate. Lady Louisa Conolly, forwarding to the government a petition from Nicholas Murphy, in whose house her nephew Lord Edward Fitzgerald had been arrested, pointed out that 'the Irish character . . . has so much levity in it that it is easily wrought up to mischief and easily put off'. Thirteen inhabitants of Wexford who had been imprisoned by the insurgents, petitioned in favour of Edward Hay, 'having experienced

---

[53] Thomas Fitzgerald to ——, 4 Aug. 1798 (I.S.P.O. 620/39/147); statement, J.P.s of King's County (620/39/146); Butson to ——, Memorial of the inhabitants of Waterford (620/51/45); St George Day to lord lieutenant, 4 Nov. 1798 (S.P.P.).

every kindness it was in his power to bestow'. A Kerry man, Jeremiah Prendergast, had several influential protectors. In 1797 he went north to visit a sister married to a sergeant in the Tipperary militia, became a United Irishman, was detected and sentenced to transportation. Colonel Bagwell secured a pardon for him on the condition he enlisted in the Tipperary regiment, 'where he immediately renewed his criminal practices'. He was court-martialled and sentenced to death, but Bagwell had the sentence commuted to service abroad and Lady Kenmare, who highly approved of Prendergast's family, 'in their humble line of life exemplary', secured a pardon for him. But Prendergast had 'foolishly' escaped from prison and after lurking for some time in Kerry he was captured in 1801. Then an M.P. for the county, acting for Lady Kenmare, interceded for him.[54]

Good nature, politic leniency and the occasional failure of a prosecution led to the release of many of those taken into custody for disaffection or insurrection. Indeed an optimist, sentenced to serve abroad and detained in New Geneva, told his sister 'to get a character wrote on a sheet of paper and signed by as many gentlemen and farmers as you possibly can get' and he would be released.[55] Nevertheless, a large number of those arrested were convicted and punished. Defective records and the fact that sentences were fairly often commuted make it impossible to say how many. A general impression of the scale on which punishment was administered rather than statistical precision is all that can be obtained. At the 1798 summer assizes approximately 152 persons were charged with what may be termed political offences. Thirty-four were convicted (a conviction rate of 22 per cent). At the spring assizes of 1799 145 were charged with political offences and 23 were convicted (a conviction rate of about 16 per cent). It is impossible to say how many persons were tried by court martial during 1798, the records being incomplete. Castlereagh stated in the house of commons that between approximately 20 June 1798 and

[54] Downshire to E. Cooke, 29 July 1799 (I.S.P.O. 620/47/107); Blayney to ——, 21 Aug. 1798 (P.P. 1/82); Bective to E. Cooke, 24 Nov. 1798 (620/41/57); J. Fitzgerald to ——, 14 Dec. 1798 (620/4/29/51); Dr Haliday to ——, (620/4/29/29); Lady L. Conolly to Castlereagh, 25 July 1798 (620/3/51/12); N. Murphy, petition (620/8/82/17); statement on behalf of E. Hay (S.P.P.); R. I. Herbert to ——, 21 Aug. 1801 (620/49/122).

[55] T. Lindsey to his sister, 20 Sept. 1799 (I.S.P.O. 620/48/1).

February 1799, 418 persons were tried. Of these 131 were sentenced to death, 81 being in fact executed; of the remainder about half were sentenced to transportation for life.[56] From the surviving court-martial proceedings, a summary of Cornwallis's court-martial correspondence, and newspaper reports it seems that between early May and mid-November 1798 about 400 persons were court-martialled in Ulster and about 600 over the rest of Ireland.[57] Of the 600 about 70 were soldiers (either regulars or militia) charged with desertion or mutiny during the insurrection. Of those convicted in Ulster 72 were sentenced to death and about one in seven acquitted. Of those tried in the other three provinces about 260 were sentenced to death and one in three acquitted. About 430 persons in all were sentenced to transportation or service abroad.[58] Finally it is impossible to say how many persons were convicted by magistrates under the insurrection act. Between March 1799 and the close of the year about 660 persons appear to have been tried by court martial for treason, sedition or agrarian crime.[59] Of these about one third were sentenced to death and about one quarter acquitted. At the assizes of 1799 at least 203 persons were charged with political offences, of whom 54 were convicted.

Of course sentences were often mitigated. For instance of those sentenced to death in 1798 at least one fifth and probably at least a quarter had their sentence commuted. It is impossible

[56] Castlereagh's figures may have been based on returns of proceedings of courts martial, made under the banishment act, which reached the chief secretary's office between the end of Nov. 1798 and 18 Feb. 1799 (H.O. 100/86). These give a total of 418.

[57] Material relating to courts martial is to be found in I.S.P.O. 620/2–10 and 620/17. The summary of Cornwallis's court-martial correspondence is in H.O. 100/86.

[58] The figures that have been arrived at are, Ulster—sentenced to death, 72, to imprisonment, 14, to corporal punishment, 67, to transportation or to serve abroad, 186, to find securities or acquitted, 75; for the rest of Ireland—sentenced to death, 264, to imprisonment, 2, to corporal punishment, 15, to transportation or to serve abroad, 241, to find securities or acquitted, 83. It must be emphasized that the material is defective and mistakes may have been made when handling it.

[59] The total number tried, 659, sentenced to death, 231, to imprisonment, 12, to corporal punishment, 22, to the pillory, 2, to transportation or to serve abroad, 240, to find securities or acquitted, 152. In 1800, according to Castlereagh, about 200 persons were tried by courts martial under the act for the suppression of rebellion (*Parliamentary history*, xxx, p. 1015). There are proceedings relating to the above in I.S.P.O. 620/8, 9, 10, 17. See also *Second report of the committee of secrecy*, p. 26, H.C. 1801, iii.

to say what proportion of those sentenced to transportation were in fact transported It has been estimated, however, that of the 1,016 male convicts landed in Australia between 1800 and 1805, approximately 325 were insurgents [60] It is also impossible to say how many of those sentenced to serve were enlisted. However, some information is available about those who were enlisted in the Prussian service. In March 1799 Captain Schouler was allowed to recruit Irish insurgents who were in custody for the Prussian army. The recruits he selected left for Waterford at the end of April 'in the deepest agony'. There were long delays in securing shipping and a convoy and it was not until early in September that three tenders, carrying 310 sailed for Germany. On arrival the recruits sang revolutionary songs and were at once given a taste of Prussian discipline, 12 of the noisiest receiving 50 strokes of the cane. Seven years later, in 1806, a number of these Irishmen in the Prussian army having been captured by the French were drafted into the Irish legion, a unit in the French service. [61]

With so many dubia in the existing material it is impossible to say with anything approaching precision how many persons were convicted and sentenced for insurrectionary activities in the eighteen months following the outbreak of the insurrection in May 1798. The available figures suggest at least 1,450, a number reflecting a policy of measured severity.

[60] G. Rudé, 'Early Irish rebels in Australia', in *Historical Studies* (University of Melbourne), xvi, pp. 17–35.

[61] Balin to ——, 29 Aug. 1799, Balin to J. King, n.d., (H.O. 42/48); Portland to Cornwallis, 20 Mar. 1799 (H.O. 100/38); Castlereagh to J. King, 23 July 1799 (H.O. 100/89); *D.J.*, 14 Sept., 19 Dec. 1799; *Morning Post*, 25 Apr. 1799; M. Byrne, *Memoirs*, i, pp. 279–80.

19
The Union

A policy of pains, penalties, pardons and policing might temporarily restore order in Ireland. But it left the causes of Irish discontent still festering and to some in authority in 1798 it seemed clear that the Irish crisis called for a dynamic approach which would transform Ireland from being a defence liability into a prosperous and contented member of the empire. History suggested an answer to the Irish problem. The attempt which had been made at the beginning of the century to solve the Scottish question by a union had proved a most successful political experiment. After the union Scotland had advanced rapidly economically, Glasgow had become a great port and industrial centre, Edinburgh, at the end of the century was completing a magnificent piece of urban planning and a long list of names, Mansfield, Loughborough, Dundas, Erskine, Abercromby, Heathfield, Hume, Adam Smith, Boswell, were a reminder of the great contribution that Scotland was making to British life and the opportunities afforded to Scotsmen by the union.

From time to time throughout the century the possibility of a union between Great Britain and Ireland had been mooted but no politician had been prepared to embark on a task which would have involved both comprehensive planning and hard parliamentary campaigning on two fronts. But by the close of the century a strong tendency towards union could be discerned. Revolutionary France was annexing, democratic America was federating. In an era marked by a succession of great wars strategic necessity demanded consolidation and centralization. War can often stimulate political thinking, wonderfully concentrating the mind, and the British prime minister in 1798 was a man of creative ability and drive. As early as August Pitt was 'ruminating on some ideas' on the subject of a union with Ireland and he wrote to Cornwallis emphasizing 'the necessity of bringing forward the great work of union which can never be so well accomplished as now'.[1] The Irish parliamentary session of 1798 dragged on until early October but after they were freed from parliamentary duties a number of Irish politicians went over to England to discuss the situation, and by the close of the year the cabinet was agreed on the broad outlines of a union scheme.

The procedure which the government at first had in mind was that each parliament should approve of the union in principle and request the crown to appoint commissioners, British and Irish, to prepare a measure which could be laid before both parliaments for enactment. Cornwallis urged that before the commissioners were appointed all the details of the union scheme should be settled by the government and after the Irish house of commons in January 1799 refused to approve of a union the British government (in practice apparently Pitt and Portland with a small group of advisers, Cornwallis, Castlereagh, Cooke, Corry, Beresford, Auckland), went ahead elaborating a scheme which was perfected by the close of the year and which was, with a few amendments, approved by both parliaments during the session of 1800. Since, therefore, the work of the commissioners would have been, so far as the government was concerned, purely formal, it was not proposed that they should be appointed.[2]

The most important and complex sections of the scheme were those covering representation in the united parliament and the financial and commercial relationships between the two kingdoms. At the outset Portland laid down two principles which should govern Irish representation in the commons— the right of every constituency which returned representatives to the Irish parliament to be directly represented in the house of commons, was to be preserved, presumably to prevent any weakening of the respect for chartered rights; and the number of Irish representatives should on no account exceed one hundred. Portland added that if the Irish agreed to having a smaller number of representatives 'it would certainly be a proof of confidence and forebearance'.[3] But if one hundred was the maximum number of Irish M.P.s that the cabinet was prepared

[1] *Fortescue MSS H.M.C.*, iv, p. 273.
[2] *Castlereagh correspondence*, ii, pp. 59, 117, 339; *Fortescue MSS H.M.C.*, iv, p. 405.
[3] *Cornwallis correspondence*, ii, pp. 452–3.

to accept it was also about the minimum with which Ireland would be content, and these considerations determined the number of Irish M.P.s. At the preliminary stage of planning a union it was suggested that possibly the Irish M.P.s might meet in Dublin and elect 100 of their number to be the Irish representatives at Westminster. The others, sitting in Dublin, could deal with election petitions. But very soon the idea of a subordinate assembly in Dublin 'for the purpose of all Irish business, canals, roads, etc.'[4] was dropped, and it was proposed that all the Irish counties and ten boroughs should each return a member, and that the remaining 108 boroughs should be single-member constituencies divided into two groups, each alternately electing M.P.s. Under this plan the total Irish membership would have been 96. But soon after the struggle for the union began, Castlereagh realized that it was politically inexpedient to reduce the county representation. With a county returning only a single M.P., 'the secondary interest' (or interests) in the county 'would stand absolutely excluded', and the primary interest would have to face harder contests. It was therefore decided that the counties should remain two-member constituencies. With the borough representation inevitably cut down, Castlereagh suggested that while 'open' boroughs might each be allowed to return an M.P. the other boroughs should be grouped in either twos or threes for election purposes; borough patrons receiving compensation for the diminution in value of their property. But this scheme involved an increase above the fixed limit of 100 M.P.s, and Castlereagh wondered if the best course was not to buy out the proprietors of a number of boroughs. It was also obvious that drawing a distinction between 'open' and closed boroughs might encourage 'theoretical notions of reform'. So in the end it was decided that the towns 'most considerable for wealth and population' should be represented and that the other boroughs should be disfranchised, their patrons receiving compensation. Dublin and Cork were each to have two M.P.s, and the university and 31 boroughs, selected as being important urban centres on the basis of the hearth and window taxes, were each to have a

---

[4] 'Heads of a union with Ireland', apparently prepared for the cabinet by Grenville (*Fortescue MSS H.M.C.*, iv, p. 398, Add. MS 59254A); Sheffield to Auckland, 13 Nov. 1798 (Add. MS 34455).

member.[5] The house of commons in committee made a minor change, substituting Carrickfergus, a county of a city, with a fairly large electorate, for Mullingar. The result, it was thought, was that 12 of the boroughs might be considered close boroughs and the remaining 22 'more or less popular'.[6] So the union could have been regarded by parliamentary reformers as a precedent pointing in the right direction.

The Irish peers were to be represented in the united house of lords by twenty-eight temporal and four spiritual peers—the total of thirty-two being double the number of Scottish representative peers. The spiritual peers were to be an archbishop and three bishops, sitting for a session by rotation. It was suggested by Agar, the archbishop of Cashel, that a better arrangement would be for the four archbishops to sit permanently since they were 'from their situations more capable of giving an account of the state of the church than any other prelate'. The bishops did not agree with him, the bishop of Meath pointing out that Agar's plan might result in 'the flagrant neglect of their pastoral functions' by the archbishops, who would become 'eternal absentees'. The archbishop's annoyance at the rejection of his suggestion may have been softened by the viscountcy, seat as a representative peer and the archbishopric of Dublin, all of which he attained in the next few years.[7]

The temporal peers were to be elected by the body of Irish peers for life, unlike the Scottish representative peers who were elected for a single parliament. Election for life, it was argued was 'more congenial to the general spirit and establishment of a peerage'. Moreover the Irish peerage being on the whole composed of comparatively late creations, with inheritance restricted to male heirs, might diminish rapidly, so that an *en bloc* election to a single parliament could be controlled by a small cabal. There was another departure from the Scottish precedent. It was provided that Irish peers could sit in the united house of commons for British constituencies (it being pointed out that to allow them to sit for Irish constituencies

[5] *Fortescue MSS H.M.C.*, iv, pp. 405–6; *Castlereagh correspondence*, ii, pp. 149–53, iii, pp. 425–7; *Cornwallis correspondence*, iii, pp. 6–7.
[6] Castlereagh to J. King, 14 May 1800 (H.O. 100/93).
[7] *Cornwallis correspondence*, iii, p. 89; *Castlereagh correspondence*, iii, p. 255.

'might bear hard on the leading Irish commoners'). This provision was severely criticized in the British house of lords as sanctioning a constitutional anomaly, and encouraging Jacobinism by breaking down the bulwarks between the peerage and the body of the people—they might, Mulgrave pointed out, even see an Irish peer in the dock at the old Bailey. But the anomaly already existed, 'the English-Irish peers' if deprived of the right to sit in the house of commons would have been aggrieved, and by 52 votes to 9 the peers accepted the provision.

A third departure from the Scottish precedent was contemplated. It was at first provided that the crown should retain the power to create Irish peerages. If the crown was deprived of this right, the cabinet felt that 'the pressure of claims for British peerages must in its effects be highly embarrassing whether these claims be satisfied or not'. This proposal dismayed the resident Irish peers. They foresaw that post-union Irish peerages would be granted to 'men of weight and consequence in England', who would always succeed to vacancies amongst the representative peers and that the 'minor peers' of Ireland, debarred by their status from many careers and unable to sit for an Irish constituency would be 'the most insignificant gentry of the kingdom'. Relatively trivial as the issue may seem, it affected an influential group determined 'not to abandon their posterity', and early in 1800 a potentially dangerous rift began amongst the unionist peers. The government yielded, it being agreed that the power of the crown to create Irish peerages should be limited to the creation of one for every three extinctions until the Irish peerage was reduced to 100.[8]

The framers of the union looked forward to the creation of a single, large economic unit, in which Ireland could participate in British progress. Their aim was perfect freedom of trade, or, as Castlereagh expressed it, the difference between Great Britain and Ireland should be no greater than that between two counties in the same kingdom.[9] But with the British national debt about twenty-six times that of Ireland, a fusion of the two

---

[8] *Cornwallis correspondence*, ii, p. 453; *Fortescue MSS H.M.C.*, iv, p. 417; Cornwallis to Pitt, 1, 10 March 1800; Kilwarden to Castlereagh, 26 Feb. 1800 (H.O. 100/93); *Parliamentary register*, xi, pp. 274, 389–97, 531.

[9] *The speech of the Rt. Hon Viscount Castlereagh* (1800). p. 18.

fiscal systems would strike Irishmen as highly inequitable. A unionist could of course argue that the British debt had been incurred in building up an empire, the advantages of which Ireland enjoyed. But this argument would scarcely reconcile Irishmen to having to accept suddenly a share in a burden which had been accumulating steadily for over a century. It was agreed therefore that each country should service its own debt. All the remaining expenditure of the United Kingdom was to be met by Great Britain and Ireland in the proportion of fifteen to two. This ratio was arrived at by taking into account the exports and imports of the two countries and their consumption of a number of articles in general use, malt, tea, sugar. No new duties were to be imposed on the produce of one country imported into the other and all prohibitions and bounties on the exports and imports of either country from or to the other were to be abolished (except the bounties paid on grain exported from Ireland to Great Britain). If a product was subject to an internal duty in one country a countervailing duty could be imposed. Foreign and colonial commodities exported from one country to the other would, on export, receive as a drawback any duty paid and all the products of either country when exported through the other should be subject only to the same charges as on export from the country of origin. Ireland retained its exchequer into which the produce of Irish taxation was to be paid and out of which the Irish debt charge and the Irish contribution to joint expenses would be met. If the debts of the two countries were liquidated or were in the same proportion to one another as the respective national contributions, then the exchequers could be fused and all expenses 'defrayed indiscriminately by equal taxes', subject to such abatements in the cases of Ireland and Scotland as circumstances should dictate. In the event the Irish national debt rose steeply during the first decade or so of the nineteenth century and in 1816 the two exchequers were amalgamated.

The religious issues bound to arise when a scheme of union was being discussed were complex: the position of the established church, the political status of the catholics and relations between the state and the presbyterians. On the catholic question leading unionists were divided. Pitt, Castlereagh and Cooke thought a union would pave the way to catholic emancipation.

Cornwallis, Elliot, the under-secretary for war, and Dundas were strongly in favour of 'coupling' the union with emancipation. It was, Dundas believed, 'the plainest of all political truths' that a country with a free constitution would never agree to three-quarters of the population being sacrificed to the policy, opinions and prejudices of the other quarter.[10] At the other extreme, Clare, a vehement unionist, claimed that during his visit to England in the autumn of 1798 he had made the cabinet give up their 'popish projects' and bring forward the union 'unencumbered' by emancipation. Possibly influenced not so much by Clare's arguments as by his attitude, which could be taken as representative of a powerful section of Irish conservative opinion, Pitt decided to implement his Irish policy in stages, to the disappointment of Cornwallis and Dundas, the latter, it was said threatening at one stage to withdraw from the discussions over the union, if the catholics were excluded. Early in 1799 Cornwallis made a last effort to have concessions to the catholics included in the union scheme. He accepted that complete emancipation before a union would be impolitic, but pointing out that the anti-unionists might be bidding for the support of an influential catholic group, he suggested that the Irish administration should be empowered to inform the catholics that the restrictions on their holding office under the crown would be removed with the union, admission to parliament being left to the united parliament. Portland politely quashed this suggestion by instructing the lord lieutenant to obtain the approval of the protestant supporters of his administration before making an offer to the catholics.[11] As for the protestant dissenters, though Castlereagh (himself of presbyterian stock) was eager that a satisfactory settlement with the presbyterians should accompany the union, it was never suggested it should be included in the scheme submitted to parliament.

With relations between the state and the non-conformist bodies set aside for separate treatment, the ecclesiastical section of the union scheme was short and simple (and simplified further in discussion). It was at first provided that the churches

---

[10] *Fortescue MSS H.M.C.*, iv, p. 322; Dundas to W. Pitt, [May 1798] (P.R.O. 30/8/15).
[11] *Cornwallis correspondence*, iii, pp. 58, 63.

of England and Ireland should be united into one church and that the clergy of the church of Ireland should be summoned to sit in the convocation of the united church. When the article was drafted it seems to have been forgotten that there were two convocations in England, and when it was being considered in committee by the British house of commons, the word convocation was amended to read 'convocations', but as it was not clear what the amended phrase would mean in practice, the whole reference to representation was deleted at the report stage. And though the new church was given a name, 'the United Church of England and Ireland' which survived for seventy-one years without making much imprint on ecclesiastical history, it was not provided with any institutional links.

Supporters and opponents of the union alike thoroughly believed in the righteousness of their cause. They saw the question as one that far transcended ordinary political issues, and their speeches and pamphlets, whatever the level of argument or taste, were inspired by passionate conviction. The advocates of the measure, the first 'unionists', were deeply conscious they were playing a significant role at a momentous time, when Great Britain, 'the champion of the civil liberties of the world', was fighting for 'the protection of the constitution, the religion, the liberties and the social order of the empire'.[12] In the great struggle with France the margin of safety was small, and an error in policy or a weakness in the British power-structure might have catastrophic consequences. Ireland with its bitter divisions was obviously the vulnerable flank of the British Isles, constituting a dangerous weakness at the centre of the empire. 'Where', Canning asked, 'is the country where the state of society is more adapted to receive, cherish and mature the principles of the French revolution—principles which go to array the lower orders of the people against the educated and governing part of the community, to arm poverty against property, labour against privileges and each class of life against its superior, than a country like Ireland?' Lord Minto painted a vivid picture of what would follow if 'an Irish democratic republic or rather anarchy' was established in alliance with France. There would be in Ireland 'universal plunder,

[12] Carleton, *Speech* (1800), p. 17; *D.J.*, 16 Jan. 1800.

confiscation and murder', and the inhabitants of the west coast of Great Britain from Land's End to the Hebrides, 'whose lawns of and gardens' bordered on the Irish sea, would find themselves 'in hail of a powerful savage enemy, which the darkness of a single night can bring to their chamber doors'.[13]

Legislative and administrative consolidation would render Ireland more secure against invasion and would eliminate the ever present danger of administrative and constitutional conflict between the two kingdoms. It might be thought, when the influence exercised by the Irish executive—the instrument of the British cabinet—over the Irish parliament is taken into account, that Great Britain already possessed sufficient control over Irish policy. But Pitt and his colleagues felt that co-operation between Great Britain and Ireland could only be maintained by continuous care and tact, and Grenville, who had been for a brief period chief secretary, pointed out that though in an absolute monarchy the link between two kingdoms provided by the crown, 'the identity of royal power', might ensure unity of action, in a mixed and limited monarchy it might fail to do so. The Irish parliament, he warned the house of lords, could refuse supplies for a war; the army in Ireland was 'at its mercy'; and the debates on the commercial propositions and regency episode had shown that on occasion the Irish parliament might bid defiance to the Irish administration. If catholic emancipation and parliamentary reform were ever carried, the Irish government's parliamentary position would be greatly weakened, and then, if not earlier, a question of 'such peculiar delicacy', that Grenville only made a passing reference to it, might be raised—the practical limitations imposed by parliamentary pressure on the king when he was exercising his right to appoint the ministers of the crown. There was not only the danger of a serious clash between the two parliaments. The very existence of separate administrations and parliaments was bound to create circumlocution and friction. According to Sylvester Douglas, the ex-chief secretary, official relations between the two countries were 'in constant danger of misapprehension and dispute, and subject to the inconveniences which inevitably arise from circuity of communication, and the impediments and embarrassing

[13] *Parliamentary history*, xxiv, pp. 236, 771.

modifications to which jealousy or ignorance on the one side or the other will so often give occasion'.[14]

The union, it was hoped, would make a great contribution to imperial strategy, not only by enabling resources to be mobilized and deployed more effectively, but by transforming Ireland from a dissension-riven, economically retarded country into a prosperous and happy portion of the United Kingdom. If Great Britain and Ireland had the same legislature and government, the Irish social pattern, it might be assumed, would in time approximate to the British, 'a moral assimilation with Britain might be expected',[15] and few, if any, of those active in British politics at the close of the eighteenth century doubted that the English society was developing along the right lines. With property in Ireland 'protected by the faith of the British parliament and the power of the British people', Ireland would become an attractive field for British investment; 'the credit and capital now pent up in Great Britain,' an enthusiastic unionist said, 'would descend like water to a level, and diffuse themselves equally over both kingdoms'. Capital investment combined with up-to-date technology would stimulate economic growth, and rising living standards would, Pitt declared, 'improve the temper and the manners as well as the understanding of the people of Ireland'. Peel, the great industrialist, hoped that the United Kingdom would 'communicate . . . British comforts' to Ireland and Windham was convinced that the only way to remedy the condition of Ireland was 'to meliorate the state of the lower orders and this could only be done by an infusion of British capital and of British manners'.[16]

It was also confidently prophesied by unionists that their policy would eliminate or greatly lessen that major source of Ireland's ills, sectarian animosity. To Pitt and other unionists this seemed capable of mathematical demonstration. In Ireland the catholics were to protestants as three to one; in a United kingdom they would be as three to eleven. In the latter case the catholics would have to accept they were in a decided minority and could not possibly get rid of the protestant

[14] Ibid., xxiv, pp. 657–63, 847.
[15] T. B. Clarke, ed., *Dean Tucker's argument on the propriety of an union* (1799), p. 3.
[16] *Parliamentary history*, xxiv, pp. 248, 481, 379, 727.

ascendancy by force or intimidation. On the other hand protestants, from a position of strength, might be prepared to make concessions. 'Strength and confidence', Castlereagh stressed, 'will produce liberality.' Some unionists, naturally, merely stressed the increased security the Irish protestants would enjoy and said little about their willingness to make concessions.[17]

The case for the union could be compressed into a few simple propositions. The case against it, as expressed by some of the most conspicuous and eloquent of its exponents was equally simple. Ireland was clearly a separate country, entitled to possess its own legislature, 'distinct, national, resident'.[18] The anti-unionists did not suggest that their country had a distinctive culture and a great historic tradition, which had moulded and inspired its people for centuries. They merely stressed that geography had created an Irish community, with its own interests and institutions. 'Our patent to be a state and not a shire', Goold declared in an enthusiastically applauded burst of rhetoric, 'comes direct from Heaven . . . The great creator of the world has given unto our beloved country the gigantic outlines of a kingdom and not the pygmy features of a province. God and Nature, I say, never intended Ireland to be a province, and by God she never shall.'[19] Another eloquent barrister, who listened to Goold, later in a private note remarked, 'let a stranger be told on beholding a country of the size and population of Ireland, that it is radically incompetent to govern itself, he would be surprised'.[20] It should be added that unionists also relied on geography. A glance at the map, Lord Minto said, showed the two islands to be 'not merely contiguous but as it were in the bosom and embraces of each other', and another peer, Lansdowne, pointed out that Saint George's channel, constituted 'a natural navigation', analogous to the canals which were being cut throughout Great Britain.[21]

The opponents of a union were not only convinced that Ireland had a right to possess its own legislature, they were also sure that the Irish parliament had justified itself by its works.

[17] *Speech of the Rt. Hon. Viscount Castlereagh*, p. 36.
[18] *D.E.P.*, 22 Feb. 1800.
[19] *A report of the debate at the Irish bar* (1799), p. 47.
[20] Bushe's MS notes on a copy of Lord Minto's *Speech* in T.C.D. library.
[21] *Parliamentary history*, xxxiv, pp. 747–8, xxv, pp. 166–7.

It was 'a municipal parliament', Bushe told the house of commons, 'which has procured you, within the memory of all, municipal advantages which no foreign parliament can supply'.[22] Under 'the cheering sunshine' of an Irish parliament the country had enjoyed twenty years of growing prosperity.[23] Its face was being changed by the construction of great canals; Ireland had become 'the seat of arts which improve and embellish society'; the Irish metropolis was a great city, with 'splendid piles' springing up every year,[24] and with a theatre which 'mends the public manners, raises the conceptions, impresses the stamp of the patriot upon the soul, and gives the genius of the people elevation of sentiment, not to be derived . . . from any other department in social life'.[25] The hope of acquiring a seat in the house of commons was 'a spur to exertion and industry by which alone commerce and manufactures (the sources of the wealth of nations) were brought to perfection'.[26] It was their own parliament which, during the recent rebellion had emboldened and led the loyalists of Ireland. 'Why', George Knox asked during the union debates, 'was the late rebellion so effectually put down?' Because the property of the country possessed power. Every man of property had an immediate interest and participation in the power.' 'How was the rebellion put down?' Plunket asked, 'By the zeal and loyalty of the gentlemen of Ireland rallying round the laws, the constitution and the independence of their country.'[27] Even a radical pamphleteer—one of the few who joined in the controversy—while deploring the vicious composition of the Irish parliament, was prepared to grant that 'by sitting within the vortex of Irish feelings and resolves, it has occasionally been carried along by the virtues of the people'.[28]

The anti-unionists asserted that while the Irish parliament had promoted Irish prosperity, with a union, whenever the interests of the two kingdoms clashed Ireland would be sacrificed and Ireland would certainly be overtaxed—'tax Ireland

[22] *D.E.P.*, 21 Jan. 1800.
[23] *More thoughts on a union* (1799), p. 9.
[24] M. Weld, *Constitutional considerations* (1799), p. 24.
[25] *Proofs upon proofs* (1799), p. 13.
[26] J. W. Jervis, *A letter* (1790), p. 52.
[27] *D.J.*, 16 Feb. 1799.
[28] *Arguments for independence* (1799), p. 2.

would become the order of the day'.[29] Mr Pitt, Foster told the house of commons, was 'the greatest minister of finance that ever existed in any country' and 'he wanted a union, in order to tax you, to take your money.'[30] To a unionist of course the essence of a union was that separate national economic interests would cease to be of much significance, financially speaking, being seen in a United Kingdom context. 'Under incorporation', an early advocate of union wrote, 'commercial jealousy must subside and each country, forgetting rivalship, enjoy it own natural and artificial advantages.'[31] With a union, absenteeism, its opponents prophesied, would greatly increase as Irish peers and gentlemen made for the centre of power; and Dublin would rapidly decline, since, 'in political economy, the metropolis of a country is to the country at large what in the animal economy of human life the heart is to the rest of the human system'.[32] It was retorted that the presence of an extravagant aristocracy might be a mixed blessing, 'tradesmen copy those whom they serve; that Dublin would suffer no loss except that of hearing parliamentary debates' and would (along with Cork and Belfast) gain considerably from Ireland's commercial expansion. As for absenteeism, a pro-union pamphleteer argued that if the country were quiet 'all the persons of middling fortune, who lead a rambling life among the English watering places, would return to Ireland.'[33]

Opponents of the union, generally speaking, not only emphatically asserted that Ireland must retain its own parliament, they also expressed intense loyalty to the British connection, 'a polar principle in politics'.[34] The two principal articles of their political creed, Ireland's legislative independence and the British connection, were, they believed, embodied in the constitution of 1782, which, Foster declared, 'has not only worked well (to use a modern phrase) to promote the strength and unity of the empire, but to raise this kingdom to prosperity'.[35]

---

[29] J. W. Jervis, *A letter* p. 24.
[30] J. Foster, *Speech* (1799), p. 159.
[31] T. B. Clarke, ed., *Dean Tucker's argument on the propriety of an union . . .* p. 28.
[32] N. P. Leader, *An address* (1800), p. 14.
[33] *Report of the debates of the 5 & 6 Feb. 1800* (1800), p. 201; *Union or not*, p. 31; W. Stevens, *Hints to the Irish people*, p. 15.
[34] *D.E.P.*, 21 Jan. 1800.
[35] J. Foster, *Speech*, p. 159.

Unionists, as have been seen, argued that the 1782 system of Anglo-Irish relations did not guarantee harmonious co-operation between the two kingdoms. Some anti-unionists replied to this argument by suggesting amendments to the settlement—Ireland should agree to accept as regent the person appointed regent in Great Britain; it should be provided that if Great Britain became involved in a war, the Irish parliament would automatically vote the necessary supplies; Ireland should accept a share of the national debt or agree to pay an imperial contribution and all outstanding commercial questions should be settled. Unionists could retort that if these proposals were implemented the constitutional inferiority which Ireland had accepted under the 1782 settlement, would be accentuated. Ireland, Castlereagh pointed out, was very like a colony, and Clare with characteristic vehemence declared that 'hers must be a provincial government of the worst description'—a line of argument which would have had dangerous implications if the union had failed to pass.[36] But during the debates on the measure the anti-unionists accepted as inevitable the existing limitations on Irish sovereignty. Saurin, having referred to 'the imperfect nature of our executive government', went on to say that 'as it is part of the price we pay for our connection I shall not dwell upon it'.[37] Foster approved of the use of the British great seal to authenticate the royal assent to Irish legislation, because 'it secures the union and connection on a secure and lasting basis.'[38]

If the union had been postponed for a generation, its opponents could have based Ireland's right to legislative independence on the by then fashionable contemporary conception of nationality—that a people, recognized as a nationality, was an entity with a personality, expressing itself through a multiplicity of facets, and with a right to control its own political destiny. For an individual, the spirit of nationality was a mystical force, binding him to his fellows and inspiring him to creative action. By these standards, the Irish anti-unionists at the close of the eighteenth century had a cool and austere faith, deficient in doctrinal completeness and lacking in

[36] *D.J.*, 8 Feb. 1800.
[37] W. Saurin, *Speech* (1799), pp. 24–31.
[38] J. Foster, *Speech*, pp. 24–31.

a sympathetic awareness of the many-sided glory of the national being. They simply accepted that Ireland formed a separate community connected by many ties with Great Britain, they revered the Irish constitution (itself an offshoot of the British) and they expressed unbounded pride in the Irish parliament, the theatre in which many of them had gained renown and achieved results. So powerful were these feelings that strong advocates for the union were very anxious to prevent Irishmen, when considering the union, being carried away by 'an erroneous and mistaken sense of national pride'. Dundas, a Scotsman, wanted Irishmen to distinguish between 'manly' and 'childish' ambition. Irish M.P.s, for instance, should realize that 'if their genius be ever so acute, their talents ever so transcendent, their eloquence ever so splendid, all these wonderful powers are confined to one little island'. But, if they entered a United Kingdom parliament, their voices would be heard 'not only in Europe but in Asia, Africa and America'.[39] An Irish unionist, General Hutchinson, who a year later was to succeed Abercromby as commander of the British forces in Egypt, asked the Irish house of commons, 'did they conceive an Irish mind would be narrowed or the Irishman's sphere of ambition limited by a consideration not only of a nation or an empire but of the whole civilized world'.[40] Another Scotsman, Minto, who, as governor of Corsica, had recent experience of a small island struggling for independence, strove to analyse the concept of patriotism (or national pride) and assign it its due place in the union debate. Love of country, 'the expansive love of our fellow creatures . . . compressed into narrow bounds', was, in Minto's opinion, 'the noblest affection of the human breast'; and Ireland, on account of its natural charms and the generous qualities which distinguished its inhabitants, was 'a fit object for that passion'. 'It is no easy abstraction', Minto admitted, 'to love the people of Ireland as distinct from what may be called the love of Ireland', yet the love of our country must be 'rational not fanatical', and a true patriot would place the happiness of those who inhabit a country above everything else. If in the case of Ireland he saw autonomy was contrary to the happiness of its people he would readily embrace a union.

[39] *Parliamentary history*, xxiv, p. 351
[40] *D.E.P.*, 20 Feb. 1800.

To Minto it was plain that 'a species of gravitation . . . an irresistible law of political nature' was drawing the two countries into a union, and he pointed, as a happy precedent, to the heptarchy which had merged in 'the united kingdom of England'.[41] 'The whole argument from the heptarchy', Bushe indignantly wrote, 'is sophistical. Nature points out the folly of the heptarchy but that does not establish a general proposition. Let England now conquer France—is it assumed that a union representing France at Westminster would be a good measure for both countries?' But another eloquent Irish lawyer, Barry Yelverton, the fervent assertor of Ireland's rights in 1782, who by 1800 was a fervent unionist, asserted that 'to a union of states there can be no objection but that the machine can become unwieldy from magnitude, but no empire can be too great, where the arm of the sovereign can reach to every part of it and his will command all its resources'.[42]

There was one move which the opponents of the union might have made which would have greatly strengthened their claim that the constitutional system they were defending best expressed the will of the Irish community. They could have taken up the cause of catholic emancipation. This would have disposed of an important unionist argument and with many grateful catholics enlisted in the anti-unionist ranks it could be said that an enormous segment of Irish opinion was against the union. The Irish whigs had already committed themselves to emancipation but many anti-unionists were upholders of the protestant ascendancy—Foster and Ogle had been outstanding critics of the relief bill of 1793. The anti-unionists seem at first to have put out feelers towards the catholics, and in the debate of 24–5 January 'the vanity of Mr Barrington let out there was a negotiation going on between the opponents of the union and Roman catholics' and he was quickly pulled down by his friends before he revealed more. But at a meeting of the opposition leaders held at the speaker's house on the last day of the month, George Ponsonby, according to an unfriendly source, was 'persuaded to abandon the catholics and support the Orange party', and Foster in his great speech in April swerved away

[41] *Parliamentary history*, xxiv, pp. 759–62, 785–6.
[42] Bushe's MS annotations in copy of Minto's *Speech* in T.C.D. library; Yelverton, *Speech* (1800), p. 30.

from the Irish religious question, as 'too delicate a subject to discuss', simply calling on protestants and catholics 'to join hands and hearts together . . . Forget all difficulties and local partialities . . . and save Ireland, save your country.'[43] In the following year when a Dublin catholic meeting issued a strong declaration against the union, a meeting of the freemen of Dublin hailed the auspicious moment when all sects were co-operating as brothers in a common cause, but stopped short of saying anything about sharing political power.[44]

The reluctance of the anti-unionists to tackle the catholic question was natural enough. Many of the opponents of the union were essentially conservatives, men who wanted to preserve the *status quo*. James Fitzgerald, replying to Lord Castlereagh, put their point of view succinctly. 'The noble lord', he said, 'calls upon us for an alternative—we want no alternative—we call for a sacred adherence to the constitution of 1782.' George Knox, who had resigned a commissionership of the revenue rather than support the union made it quite clear early in 1799 that he intended to limit his opposition to one measure, the union. 'Were party', he said, 'to get aboard the good ship anti-union it must inevitably flounder', and Saurin pathetically suggested that the administration should postpone the union for a few years, and 'in the midst of this arduous war, let the old friends of government be once more of the same mind and act in co-operation'.[45]

About the middle of October 1798 there were rumours in Dublin about a union (rumours which the conservative *Dublin Journal* dismissed as Jacobin-inspired), and at two o'clock on the afternoon of Saturday 1 December, the first shot in the great battle was fired by the appearance in the bookshops of *Arguments for and against the union*.[46] The work of Cooke, the under-secretary, it was a coolly analytical pamphlet in which

---

[43] *Fortescue MSS H.M.C.*, iv, pp. 458–62, 469; J. Beresford, *Correspondence*, ii, pp. 199, 203; J. Foster, *Speech*, p. 111–12.

[44] *D.E.P.*, 18, 25 Jan. 1800.

[45] *D.E.P.*, 25 Jan. 1800; *D.J.*, 16 Feb. 1799; *D.E.P.*, 25 Feb. 1800. It might be added that about this time Drennan, a strong radical, referred to Pitt as 'the minister of innovation' and C. B. Sheridan, in a sparkling attack on the union, argued that the prime minister, 'an arch-Jacobin', had an objective in common with the United Irishmen, the destruction of the existing Irish constitution (W. Drennan, A letter . . . (1799), p. 3; *Parliamentary history*, xxxiv, pp. 292, 323).

[46] *D.E.P.*, 13 Oct. 1798; *D.J.*, 16 Oct., 1 Dec. 1798.

much of the ensuing debates was outlined—the author taking good care not to let the anti-unionists get the best of it. Rather injudiciously perhaps, Cooke explained why the Irish bar would probably be opposed to a union. 'Were a union to take place', he wrote, 'Irish lawyers would be deprived of the parliamentary market for their abilities and ambition since they could not attend the British parliament without renouncing business', though some of them, he broadly hinted, might not have much business to renounce. The Irish bar reacted promptly to the suggestion of a union. Early in December a bar meeting resolved by 162 votes to 32 that it would be dangerous and improper to propose a union at that time.[47] A fortnight later a respectable meeting of attorneys resolved against a union and within the next few weeks resolutions against the union were passed by the city of Dublin, the county of Dublin, the grand jury of County Dublin and the merchants and bankers of Dublin. Duigenan, an early and violent supporter of the union, describing the last-mentioned meeting, said that 'every traitor and democrat in the city of Dublin who could pretend to be the character of a merchant on the score of having bought or sold a roll of tobacco attended.' But he had to admit that some very respectable merchants were present.[48]

That Dublin, so closely and profitably connected with the existing regime, should be perturbed at the prospect of a union might be expected. It is also not surprising that concern at the sudden threat to Ireland's dignity and independence should spread throughout the country—during January a number of county meetings passed resolutions against the union. There was not, during the first few weeks of 1799, a unionist counter-movement expressing itself through the normal, if sometimes misleading, methods for expressing public feeling. Possibly the unionist leaders felt that if they attempted to start such a movement they would meet with humiliating failure. More probably they were so confident in their cause that they did not bother about out-of-doors opinion.

They seem to have been certain that a sound policy, endorsed by both the British government and the Irish administration, ought to succeed and to have been taken aback by the strength

[47] *D.J.*, 11 Dec. 1798.
[48] *Castlereagh correspondence*, ii, p. 52.

and vehemence of the opposition. When the Irish parliament met on 22 January, the lord lieutenant in his speech recommended the houses to consider the most effectual means of maintaining and improving the British connection. In the house of lords two amendments were moved to the address. The first, moved by Lord Powerscourt, implied that the Irish parliament was not competent to enact a union—it could not decree its own extinction. This argument was to be advanced by the opposition with great force during the union debates, but it met with short shrift from Lord Clare, and Powerscourt's amendment was defeated by 46 votes to 19. Another anti-union amendment was defeated by an even larger majority—49 to 16 —and an address echoing the speech was voted. Nevertheless an ominous portent was noticed—Lord Ely, though present did not vote in either division, conspicuously withdrawing behind the throne.[49]

In the commons on 22 January an amendment was moved to the union clause in the address, affirming the right of the people of Ireland to have a free and independent legislature. After a debate which lasted until about 12.30 p.m. on 23 January, it was rejected by one vote—106 to 105. The clause was then voted by 107 to 105. Encouraged by such narrow defeats, the opposition on 24 January moved the deletion of the clause referring to the union and carried their motion by 109 to 104. The debates on the address in the house of commons were hard-fought, many members spoke with much genuine feeling and sometimes with intellectual force and eloquence. On the whole the opposition had the better of it. They carried more debating power. The government leader, Castlereagh, a very able and confident administrator, was to become a great foreign secretary. But though he had a fine presence, he was not an inspiring speaker. 'No man', Brougham later wrote, 'ever attained the station of a regular debater in our parliament with such an entire want of all classical accomplishment, and indeed of all literary provision whatsoever.' His diction, Brougham added, set 'all description at defiance', being distinguished by fragments of 'mixed, incongruous and disjointed images which frequently appear in it'.[50] Castlereagh's speeches do not read as

[49] *Fortescue MSS H.M.C.*, iv, p. 449.
[50] Lord Brougham, *Historical sketches of statesmen*, 2nd series, i, pp. 151–2.

badly as this—perhaps they were revised before appearing in print, and his calm, analytical style—excellent for some parliamentary occasions—set the tone for his side of the house. The unionists spoke as men advocating a rational and hopeful solution for Ireland's problems. The opposition was fighting *pro domo suo*; in an assembly of Irish country gentlemen they were defending the political record of the Irish ruling world, and striving to maintain its right to control the political destinies of the Irish community. Some of the opposition—Parnell and Fitzgerald for instance—must have been conscious of a painful parting with friends; others, notably the Ponsonbys, must have seen the possibility of a whig revival.

On the night of 24 January Dublin was illuminated, Clare's windows, which were defiantly dark, being smashed. But a heavy fall of rain 'prevented much of mobbing'.[51] A week or so later a Dublin aggregate meeting thanked the peers and M.P.s who had defended the constitutional independence of Ireland, a leading businessman, 'without meaning a profane allusion', referring to Foster spending forty days in the wilderness resisting the temptations of a political devil—meaning his visit to England to discuss the union proposals. Later in the month subscriptions were invited for erecting in a conspicuous place a memorial inscribed with the names of those patriots who in the union debates had secured the trade, liberty and constitution of Ireland.[52]

In spite of the decisive check it had sustained the government was undaunted, Pitt's reaction being that the government's defeat in the Irish house of commons 'made it more necessary to open fully and state decidedly our plan'.[53] During the session 1798–9 the British government pressed on at Westminster with the parliamentary preliminaries to a union. On 22 January a royal message recommended the consideration of a union with Ireland to each house. On 31 January the house of commons, by 140 votes to 15, agreed to consider this message in committee. During early February the house in committee passed eight resolutions embodying a scheme of union—there was to be 'one

[51] *Auckland journal and correspondence*, ed. W. Eden, iv, p. 80; *Fortescue MSS H.M.C.*, iv, p. 452.
[52] *S.N.L.*, 4, 14 Feb. 1799.
[53] *Fortescue MSS H.M.C.*, iv, p. 458.

kingdom . . . the United Kingdom, with a single parliament. The Churches of England and Ireland were to be preserved as by law established, there was ultimately to be full trade between Great Britain and Ireland and expenses were to be defrayed by the two countries in fixed proportions. These resolutions were accepted by the house of commons on 14 February and agreed to by the house of lords in April; and on 22 April the two houses presented an address to the king stating their 'firm persuasion . . . that an entire union between Great Britain and Ireland would promote the security and wealth of both kingdoms and augment the stability, power and resources of the empire'. During the debates at Westminster on the union the government had one advantage. Fox and some of his friends had withdrawn from the house of commons in 1797 and Fox, who felt that the British public were apathetic, could not be persuaded to return to attack the union. In his absence the most energetic opponent of the measure was Sheridan, a sparkling speaker, but not as powerful as Fox. On the other hand Pitt's speech of January was a massive and comprehensive exposition of his Irish policy, and this speech, along with those delivered by Dundas, Grenville, Minto and Sylvester Douglas—all reprinted in Ireland—provided valuable propaganda for the unionist cause.

With the government pressing forward at Westminster, the opposition in Ireland had to try and consolidate its victory. In the middle of February they made an attempt to secure from the house of commons a firm declaration against a union. Lord Corry moved the house should go into committee to discuss the state of the nation. The opposition seem to have intended that the committee should produce strong resolutions condemning a union, but Castlereagh opposed Corry's motion, declaring that it would turn the house into a debating society, and after, in Beresford's opinion, 'one of the dullest debates I have ever heard', Corry was defeated by 123 to 103—some of those who voted with the government being members who wanted to remain uncommitted for a time on the subject of a union.[54] What the government feared was that the anti-unionists might put forward a comprehensive programme, catholic emancipation, tithe reform, a commercial agreement with Great

[54] *D.J.*, 16 Feb. 1799; J. Beresford, *Correspondence*, ii, p. 215.

Britain, and measures for strengthening imperial co-operation, as an alternative to the union. Unionists of course held that these proposals taken together would not ultimately be a satisfactory alternative to their policy. But they were afraid of being deprived of useful arguments and the cabinet instructed the Irish administration to pursue delaying tactics if any of these proposals were introduced. However, only one attempt was made to weaken the case for the union by immediate legislation. Towards the end of February James Fitzgerald, the ex-prime serjeant, tried to weaken the unionist case by introducing a bill providing that when the sovereign was incapacitated, the regent of Ireland was to be the person chosen to be regent of Great Britain and was to be subject to the same restrictions as the British regent. Castlereagh, who could not directly oppose the bill, argued that it was badly drafted as the circumstances of the two countries might demand different restrictions, and the bill was dropped at the report stage. However, Foster, the speaker, when the bill was in committee also delivered a speech lasting four and a half hours against the union, an oration which, Charlemont declared, 'if Ireland can be saved, will save it'.[55]

At the close of January 1799 Castlereagh, conducting a post-mortem into the government's defeat at the opening of the session, concluded that the country gentlemen in the house of commons had opposed the union 'more upon points of personal interest than upon a fixed repugnance to the principle of the union'. About the same time Cooke, smarting under disappoint-ment attributed the government's failure to the British government's ignorance of Irish affairs (perhaps an inconsis-tency in an ardent unionist) and to Cornwallis's 'total incapa-city, self-conceit and muleishness.'[56] Cornwallis certainly was deficient in the social graces which appealed to Irish politicians. What was a greater handicap was the reputation his admini-stration had acquired in conservative circles for over-leniency and weakness. Energetic country gentlemen, Orangemen, yeomen and city conservatives, already irritated by the administration's implied criticism of the methods by which they had, in their own opinion, saved the state, learned at the close of 1798 that the government intended to get rid of much

[55] *Charlemont MSS H.M.C.*, ii, p. 350.
[56] *Auckland journals and correspondence*, iv, pp. 82–3.

of the constitution which they had defended and which assured some of them a respected place in the community.

Faced by a large, confident opposition, the Irish administration set to work both to build up a majority in parliament by persuasion and assiduous attention to personal objectives, and to mount what would later be termed an exercise in public relations on a large scale. Though the government handled parliamentary politicians on conventional lines, the situation was in some ways an extraordinary one, characterized by an unusual sense of urgency on the part of the government and a haunting sense of finality amongst Irish politicians. With the disappearance of the framework in which Irish politics had for generations functioned, many public men, accustomed to a system in which public service and personal or family advancement were often inextricably mixed, would lose the opportunity of realizing what they regarded as legitimate private aims, ranging from a British peerage to the reversion of a senior revenue appointment. With peerages, posts in the civil administration and the law, pensions and ecclesiastical preferment lavishly granted to union supporters, it seemed to anti-unionists that the government was making a great take-over bid for political conscience and principle. To the administration, it must have seemed that it was rewarding political fidelity and, in many instances, by conferring a favour, removing a bias against the union which was the product of self-interest. The whole operation might be regarded as the liquidation of the old system by a compounding of claims which would have been met in about a decade. Cornwallis's successor complained, when he arrived in 1801, that he found 'a heavy mortgage on the patronage of the country'.[57]

Besides taking account of personal objectives, the government showed itself to be well aware of the importance of public opinion, which could exercise direct pressure on the M.P.s for open constituencies and influence politicians in general, who could not insulate themselves from the convictions and emotions of the society in which they lived. If the opposition could create the impression that politically minded Ireland was unanimous in rejecting a union, parliamentary resistance would have been incalculably strengthened. Moreover, the government

[57] Hardwicke to ——, 10 Aug. 1801 (Add. MS 35728).

did not want to give the impression that it was forcing a union on a hostile community. Both sides made tremendous efforts to mobilize opinion in the country, the lord lieutenant even going on two tours, to Ulster and the south, to rally the unionists The result was that, according to Ponsonby, the table of the house of commons was covered with petitions against the union from twenty-six counties and cities or towns Castlereagh emphasized that there were seventy-four declarations in favour of the union including nineteen from counties (and Cooke, taking the acreage of these counties, argued that 'we have a fine majority of surface').[58] The value of these declarations and petitions as methods of measuring public opinion is questionable. What is clear is that the country, including the great territorial interests, was divided. There were catholic unionists and anti-unionists. The Orangemen did not officially have an opinion. If Dublin was strongly against the union, Cork, the centre of the provision trade, seems to have been favourable. That a union would guarantee to the linen trade its principal market and expose the cotton industry to the full blast of British competition may have influenced opinion in Ulster. It should be added that there was a section of opinion which it is easy to ignore—the hesitant. A leading borough owner, Lord de Clifford, and a highly intelligent M.P., Edgeworth, found it hard to make up their minds over the measure. In Belfast a number of merchants, who were willing to attend a dinner to Cornwallis at which it was understood only supporters of the union were present, would not sign an address in its favour; and near the close of the exciting session a strong anti-unionist had to confess that the public were not sufficiently alive to the question.[59]

When parliament met in January 1800 the government had a satisfactory majority though not as large or reliable as a keen unionist would have wished. The opposition at once joined battle by moving an amendment to the address, assuring the king that Ireland was inseparably united to Great Britain and conscious of the blessings it enjoyed from possessing an independent legislature. During the debate, Grattan, who had been returned for Wicklow, made a dramatic entry into the house. According to Cooke, 'he feigned illness for some time but being

[58] *D.E.P.*, 6 Mar. 1800; Cooke to Auckland, 6 Dec. 1799 (Add. MS 34455).
[59] *D.E.P.*, 17 May 1800.

allowed to sit speaking gave us a declamation in his old style for two hours'. Cooke was unfair. Grattan was suffering from migraine but like his exemplar Chatham, he did not fail to extract rhetorical advantages from his disabilities. His speeches on the union were splendid and sparkling and characteristically he emphasized that 'the connection between the two countries had not hitherto depended upon a piece of parchment but upon identity of interests—upon similarity of habits and customs and upon constant intercourse'.[60]

On 5 February a viceregal message requested parliament to consider the union resolutions which had been approved by the British parliament. In the lords a motion approving a union was carried by 53 to 19, after a four-hour speech from Clare, a scathing commentary on the workings of the constitution of 1782. In the commons, after two long debates and three divisions, in one of which no fewer than 273 M.P.s voted, 158 for the government, 115 for the opposition—the house agreed to go into committee to consider the message. When the house was in committee a strong protectionist lobby exerted itself, spokesmen for the cotton, calico-printing, muslin and sugar-refining industries, insisting that if they were not encouraged by tariffs they could not sustain British competition. Though unionists asked should not the Irish consumer be permitted to enjoy cheap imports, Castlereagh, who thought all Irish manufacturers were monopolists, agreed that protective duties should be imposed on a number of manufactures imported into Ireland for twenty years after the enactment of the union.[61]

In England also mercantilism raised its head. When the 1800 union resolutions were being debated in the British parliament, representatives of the woollen industry protested strongly against the abolition of the prohibition on the export of English wool to Ireland. After a warm debate the government and free trade triumphed, though the protectionist minority, 58 to 133, was unexpectedly large. Two other important points were raised at Westminster. French Laurence urged unsuccessfully that taxes should be imposed on each country only by its own representatives. Grey, arguing that the addition of 100 M.P.s

[60] *Fortescue MSS H.M.C.*, vi, p. 105; H. Grattan, *Memoirs of the life . . . of the Rt. Hon. Henry Grattan*, iv, p. 439, v, p. 89; *D.E.P.*, 27 May 1800.
[61] Castlereagh to E. Cooke, 11 Apr. 1800 (H.O. 100/93).

from Ireland would increase ministerial influence and create an unwieldy house, proposed that the Irish representatives should be slightly reduced and a number of English 'decayed' boroughs disfranchised. His proposals were rejected but the government introduced an amendment providing that not more than twenty Irish M.P.s should hold an office of profit under the crown. By May the union resolutions had been approved by both parliaments; during the summer the union bills (one British and four Irish) received the royal assent; and on the first day of the nineteenth century the United Kingdom with a new royal style and a new flag came into being.

During an age of rapid change events soon began to vitiate many of the assumptions underlying the great union debate. At the close of the eighteenth century it was generally taken for granted that denominational feeling was withering away and the supporters of the union believed that it would take the theological heat out of Irish politics. Several leading unionists, Pitt, Cornwallis, Castlereagh, and Dundas, hoped that it would be accompanied or immediately followed by a package of ecclesiastical measures—catholic emancipation, subsidization of the catholic clergy, an increase in the *regium donum* and tithe reform—which would conciliate dissent and strengthen the established church. But within six weeks of the union coming into operation, those who thought that religious questions were ceasing to be of decisive importance in British politics received a rude shock when tough toryism presented a formidable barrier against catholic emancipation. Emancipation was delayed for thirty years, and with delay the possibility of a formal alliance between the catholic church and the state vanished. At the same time those unionists who may have hoped that the Irish catholics would resign themselves to being permanently a politically underprivileged minority in the United Kingdom were badly disappointed. Equally disappointed were the liberals who believed that many of the issues which divided Christians were ceasing to be significant and that *odium theologicum* was bound to decline in an enlightened age. In fact during the early decades of the nineteenth century resurgent catholicism and invigorated protestantism were to be very influential forces in Irish life.

During the union debates each side freely employed

economic arguments, while suggesting that its opponents were over-emphasizing material considerations (Castlereagh spoke of Foster as tending 'to measure out the political happiness of a people by the ratios of exports and imports', and Goold declared that 'in a great constitutional question my mind disdained to be governed by the rules of vulgar arithmetic').[62] But during an economic revolution forecasting was bound to be faulty. British industrialists at the close of the eighteenth century still feared that Ireland might become a dangerous competitor, and Irish industrialists asserted that they must have protection if they were to succeed in the face of British competition. But even the most pessimistic Irish manufacturer could scarcely have pictured the strength of British competition in the near future. From early in the nineteenth century much of Irish industry could have only survived behind tariff walls which the Irish consumer, anxious to enjoy the benefits of mass production, would probably have resented and resisted. Again, while during the union debates the possibility of British investment in Ireland was stressed, nothing was said about Irish emigration to Great Britain, which was to have a considerable influence on British and Irish life.

If the supporters of the union failed to foresee the rise of the new nationalism with its impassionate power, anti-unionists were convinced that men of property and intellect in Ireland would cherish an undying antipathy to a union which had been forced on their country. However, in a comparatively short time leading opponents of the union, Foster, Parnell, Plunket and George Ponsonby, had taken office, and George Ponsonby had become the leader of the whig opposition in the house of commons. The ruling world of Ireland, seeing the union as a guarantee of stability and its own position, rapidly came to regard it as politically axiomatic, and the northern liberals, conscious of their ties, economic, intellectual and religious with Great Britain, became within a generation enthusiastic unionists. Even Grattan, when defending the tory corn law of 1815, which he asserted would render Great Britain and Ireland mutually dependent and independent of the rest of the civilized globe, referred to the union as 'firm and lasting'.

[62] *D.E.P.*, 20 Feb. 1800; *A report of the debate at the Irish bar*, p. 42.

Bibliography

MANUSCRIPT SOURCES

LONDON
British Library
Adair papers (Add. MSS 53802–4).
Auckland papers (Add. MSS 34412–61).
Copies of letters from Edward Willes . . . describing the country of Ireland . . .
    (Add. MS 29252).
Dropmore papers (Add. MSS 59251–5).
Grenville papers (Add. MS 57817).
Thomas Grenville papers (Add. MS 41855).
Halsbury papers (Add. MS 56367).
Hardwicke papers (Add. MS 35892).
Holland House papers (Add. MS 51426).
Journals of a visit to England by an Irish clergyman, 1761, 1762 (Add. MS
    27951).
Liverpool papers (Add. MSS 38228, 38231).
Sir John Moore papers (Add. MSS 57320–1).
Napier family papers (Add. MS 49103).
Newcastle papers (Add. MS 32922).
Northington letter book (Add. MS 38716).
Pelham papers (Add. MSS 33100–12, 33117, 33126–130).
Bishop Percy's letters to his wife (Add. MS 32335).
Townshend papers (Add. MS 38497).
Weston papers (Add. MSS 57927–8).
Wilkes papers (Add. MSS 30871–2).
Windham papers (Add. MSS 37873).

Public Record Office
Admiralty records Adm. 1/111 (in-letters, channel fleet); Adm. 1/613–14 (in-
    letters, Cork); Adm. 1/4172–5 (in-letters, secretary); Adm. 2/1186 (letters
    relating to marines); Adm. 2/1186 (letters relating to courts martial);
    Adm. 2/5646–7 (reports of courts martial).
Board of customs and excise CUST 15 (imports and exports Ireland).
Colonial office records C.O. 388–9 (board of trade correspondence and papers).
Home office records S.P. 63 (state papers, Ireland); H.O. 42 (correspondence,
    domestic); H.O. 100 (correspondence, Ireland); H.O. 50 (correspond-
    ence, military).
Treasury records T 14 (out-letters, Ireland).

War office records W.O. 1/611–12 (in-letters, Ireland); W.O. 27 (inspection returns); W.O. 68 (militia records); W.O. 133 (Brownrigg papers).
Chatham papers (P.R.O. 30/8).
Colchester papers (P.R.O. 30/9).
Cornwallis papers (P.R.O. 30/11).
Napier papers (P.R.O. 30/64).

Army Museum
Documents relating to Sir Loftus Otway (6807/414).
Papers of Sir George Nugent (6807/174–5).
Letters relating to the rebellion in Ireland (5910/199).
Letter books of Col. Andrew Ross, 1796–1812 (6406/22).

India Office Library
Writers' petitions, 1749–1805 (J/I/1–30).

London School of Economics
Journal of Sir John Parnell.

PARIS
Archives des Affaires Etrangères
Correspondance politique, Angleterre, 587, 589
Mémoires et documents, Angleterre, 53, supplément 19
Archives de la Marine
Cartons BB IV 102–3, 122–3.

EDINBURGH
National Library of Scotland
Minto papers.

DUBLIN
Public Record Office
Misc. Byrne papers (MS 5892A).
Frazer manuscripts.
Letters between commanding officers and Dublin Castle (MSS 3474–5).

Irish State Paper Office
Official papers, 2nd series.
Prisoners' petitions (P.P.).
Rebellion papers (MSS 620/1–67).
State prisoners' petitions (S.P.P.).
Westmorland correspondence.

National Library
Letters, Lake, Nugent, etc. (MS 56).
Musgrave (MS 4157).

Bolton papers (MSS 15800–978).
Royal Irish Academy
Curran fee book (MS 12 B¹ 10).
O'Conor papers.
Journal kept in Dublin (MS 24 K 14–15).

Trinity College, Dublin
Armstrong papers (MS 6409).
Beaufort papers (MSS 4028–30).
Elrington papers (MS 4958).
Madden papers (MS 873).
Prior diary (MSS 3363, 3365).

BELFAST
Public record office
Abercorn correspondence.
Downshire correspondence.
Drennan papers.
McCance papers.

Linenhall Library
Joy MSS

DERBY
County record office
Wilmot papers.

NORTHAMPTON
Northamptonshire record office
The Fitzwilliam papers from Milton.

NOTTINGHAM
University Library
Portland papers.

SHEFFIELD
Central Library
Wentworth Woodhouse Muniments

OXFORD
Bodleian Library
Napier papers (Eng. letters c 238d 80).

MAIDSTONE
Kent county record office
Pratt manuscripts.

In private ownership
Scrope Bernard papers.

PUBLICATIONS OF THE HISTORICAL MANUSCRIPTS COMMISSION

Eighth report: appendix, part i (*O'Conor MSS* and *Emly MSS*) 1881.

Twelfth report: appendix, part ix (*Donoughmore MSS*), part x (*Charlemont MSS*, i) 1891.

Thirteenth report: appendix, part iii (*Fortescue MSS*, i) 1892 and part viii (*Charlemont MSS*, ii) 1894.

Fourteenth report: appendix, part i (*Rutland MSS*, iii) 1894, part v (*Fortescue MSS*, ii) 1894.

Fifteenth report: appendix, part vi (*Carlisle MSS*) 1897.

Fortescue MSS, iii, 1899.

Report on the MSS of Mrs Stopford-Sackville, i, 1904.

Fortescue iv, 1905.

Report on the MSS of the Marquess of Lothian, 1905.

Fortescue, v, 1908.

Report on MSS in various collections (*Knox MSS*) vi, 1909.

NEWSPAPERS

Belfast News-Letter (*B.N.L.*).
Birmingham Gazette.
Cork Advertizer.
Cork Courier.
Cork Gazette.
Dublin Chronicle.
Dublin Evening Post (*D.E.P.*).
Dublin Gazette.
Faulkner's Dublin Journal (*D.J.*).
Freeman's Journal (*Free. Jn.*).
Gazetteer.
General Advertiser.
Hibernian Journal (*H.J.*).
London Chronicle.
Morning Chronicle.
Morning Herald.
Morning Post.
Moniteur.
Northern Star (*N.S.*).
Press.
Public Advertiser.
Pue's Occurrences.

Saunders News Letter (S.N.L.).
Star.
Volunteer Evening Post (V.E.P.).
Volunteer Journal (V.J.).

PERIODICALS

Anthologia Hibernica.
Bolg an Tsolair or the Gaelic magazine.
Exshaw's Gentleman's and Citizen's Magazine.
Gentleman's Magazine.
Masonic Magazine.
Walker's Hibernian Magazine.

PRINTED COLLECTIONS OF DOCUMENTARY MATERIAL

Barras, J., *Memoirs*, ed. G. Duroy, 4 vols. London 1895–6.

Beresford, J., *Correspondence*, 2 vols. London 1854.

Burke, E., *Correspondence of the Rt. Hon. Edmund Burke*, ed. Lord Fitzwilliam and R. Bourke, 4 vols. London 1844.

——, *Correspondence*, ed. T. Copeland, 10 vols. Cambridge 1958–78.

Calendar of home office papers of the reign of George III, 1760–75, 4 vols. London 1878–99.

Collingwood, Lord. *Private correspondence*, ed. E. Hughes, London 1957.

Cornwallis, C. 1st marquis, *Correspondence*. ed. C. Ross, 3 vols. London 1859.

Costella, N., 'Two diaries of the French expedition, 1798', in *Analecta Hibernica*, xi.

Douglas, S., *Diaries*, ed. F. Bickley, 2 vols. London 1928.

Drennan, W. *The Drennan letters . . . a selection*, ed. D. A. Chart. Belfast 1931.

Eden, W., 1st Baron Auckland, *Journal and correspondence*, 4 vols. London 1861–2.

Edwards, R. D., 'The minute book of the catholic committee', in *Archivium Hibernicum*, ix, pp. 3–172.

Fox, C. J., *Memorials and correspondence*, ed. Lord John Russell, 4 vols. London 1853–7.

George III, *Correspondence*, ed. J. Fortescue, 6 vols. London 1927–8.

George III, *Later correspondence*, ed. A. Aspinall, 5 vols. Cambridge 1962–8.

Grafton, 3rd duke of, *Autobiography and political correspondence*, ed. W. R. Anson. London 1898.

Grattan, H., *The speeches of the Rt. Hon. Henry Grattan*, 4 vols. London 1822.

Additional Grenville papers, ed. J. R. G. Tomlinson, Manchester 1961.

Heffernan, R. J. S., *Edmund Burke, New York agent, with his letters to the New York assembly and intimate correspondence with Charles O'Hara*. Philadelphia 1956.

Horner, F., *Memoirs and correspondence*. London 1843.

Hunt, W., *The Irish parliament, 1775*. London 1907.

Jones, W., *Letters*, ed. G. Cannon, 2 vols. Oxford 1970.

McDowell, R. B., 'The proceedings of the Dublin society of United Irish-men', in *Analecta Hibernica*, No. 17, pp. 1–143.

Manners, John James, 7th duke of Rutland, *Correspondence between the Rt. Hon. W. Pitt and Charles duke of Rutland*. Edinburgh 1890.

Moore, J., *Diary*, ed. J. F. Maurice, 2 vols. London 1904.

Napoleon I, *Correspondance*, 32 vols. Paris 1858–69.

Napoleon I, *Memoirs*, ed. S. de Chair, 2 vols. London 1945.

Nugent, Lady, *Journal*, ed. F. Cundall, 3rd ed. London 1939.

Rundle, T. *Letters with introductory memoir by J. Dallaway*, 2 vols. Gloucester 1789.

Scott, J., *Diary*, n.d.

Spencer, 2nd earl, *Private papers*, ed. G. J. S. Corbett and W. Richmond, 4 vols. London 1913–24.

Stewart, Robert, *Memoirs and correspondence of Viscount Castlereagh*, ed. C. Stewart, 2nd marquis of Londonderry, vols. i–iv. London 1849.

Tone, T. W., *Life . . . with his political writings and fragments of his diary*, ed. W. T. W. Tone, 2 vols. Washington 1826.

Walpole, H., *Correspondence*, ed. W. S. Lewis. London 1937–.

Windham, W., *Windham papers*, 2 vols. London 1913.

Wyvill, C., *Political papers . . .*, 6 vols. York 1794–1802.

PARLIAMENTARY PROCEEDINGS AND PAPERS

Journals of the house of lords, 1634–1800, 8 vols. Dublin 1783–1800.

Journals of the house of commons, 20 vols. Dublin 1796–1800.

The parliamentary history of England from the earliest period to 1803, 36 vols. London 1806–1820.

The parliamentary register, 1774–1803, 66 vols. London 1775–1804.

The parliamentary debates from the year 1803 to the present time, 41 vols. London 1804–20.

The parliamentary register, or histories of the proceedings and debates of the house of commons of Ireland, 17 vols. Dublin 1781–97.

Caldwell, J. *Debates relative to the affairs of Ireland in the years 1763 and 1764 . . .*, 2 vols. London 1766.

A report of the debate in the house of commons of Ireland, on 22 and 23 Jan. 1799. Dublin 1799.

A report of the debate in the house of commons of Ireland, on 15 and 16 Jan. 1800. Dublin 1800.

A report of the debate in the house of commons of Ireland on . . . 5 and 6 Feb. 1800 . . . Dublin 1800.

Proceedings of the parliament of Ireland, 1793, 3 vols. Dublin 1793.

Copies of the claims laid before the commissioners under the act 40 Geo. III c. 34 and of the evidence, H.C. (87), 1805, vii.

Further proceedings of the commissioners under the union compensation act, H.C. (89), 1805, vii.

Second report from the committee of secrecy, H.C. (71), 1801, iii.

Report of the committee appointed to inquire into the tolls on the Grand Canal of Ireland, H.C. (169), 1805, vii.

Papers relating to the established church in Ireland, H.C. (78), 1807, v.

Fourth report . . . on the affairs of the East India company, H.C. (148), 1812, vi.

Report from the select committee on grand jury presentments of Ireland, H.C. (283), 1814–15, vi.

Parochial rates (Ireland) : an account of all sums applotted during the year 1827 by the several vestries in Ireland, H.C. (370), 1828, xii.

Poor (Ireland) : a return of the corporations in the counties and cities and towns in Ireland instituted for the relief of the poor, H.C. (291), 1828, xxii.

Report from the select committee on civil government charges together with the minutes, evidence and appendices, H.C. (337), 1831, iv.

First report of the committee of public instruction in Ireland, H.C. [45] 1835, xxxiii.

First report of the commissioners appointed to inquire into the municipal corporations of Ireland and appendices, H.C. [23, 24, 25, 27, 28], 1835, xxviii (26, 29); 1836, xxiv.

Report of the commissioners for inquiry into the system of military punishments in the army, H.C. [59], 1836, xii.

CONTEMPORARY WORKS AND PAMPHLETS

Place of publication is Dublin unless indicated otherwise.

Account of the proceedings of the governors of the house of industry. 1801.

Aiken, J., *A description of the country for thirty or forty miles round Liverpool*. London 1795.

Anketell, S., *Poems*. 1793.

——, *A Sermon on the distressed curates of the established church*. Drogheda 1787.

Arguments to prove the interposition of the people to be constitutional and strictly legal. 1783.

Baratariana: a selection of political pieces published during the administration of Lord Townshend in Ireland, 1st ed. 1772, 2nd ed. 1773.

Barber, S., *Some remarks on a pamphlet entitled 'The present state of the church of Ireland'*. 1786.

Barrington, J., *Historic memoirs of Ireland*, 2 vols. London 1809–33.

——, *Personal sketches of his own times*, 3 vols. London 1827–32.

Barry, C., *Plan for Rathmines school*. 1790.

Belfast politics, Belfast. 1794.

The benevolent society of St Patrick. London 1822.

Binns, J., *Recollections . . .* Philadelphia 1854.

Boyd, H., *Miscellaneous works*, ed. L. D. Campbell, 2 vols. London 1800.

Boyd, J., *Odes and elegies*. Newry 1797.

Brown, A., *Some brief principles of tactics . . . for the use of the college corps*. 1797.

Browne, A., *Sketches and hints for essays*, 2 vols. London 1798.

Browne, A., *A compendious view of the ecclesiastical law of Ireland*, 2nd ed. 1803.

Burgh, J., *Political disquisitions*, 3 vols. London 1774–5.

Burke, J., *Trial of John Burk of Trinity college for heresy before the board of senior fellows*. 1794.

Burrowes, P., *Plain arguments in the defence of the people's domination over the constitution*. 1784.

Burrowes, R., *Observations on the course of science taught at present in Trinity College*. 1792.

Byrne, M., *Memoirs*, ed. S. Gwynn, 2 vols. 1907.

Campbell, T., *A philosophical survey of the south of Ireland*. 1778.

Campbell, T., *Diary of a visit to England in 1775 by an Irish clergyman*, ed. J. L. Clifford. Cambridge 1947.

Campbell, W., *An examination of the bishop of Cloyne's defence of his principles*. 1787.

A candid and impartial account of the disturbances in the county of Meath in the years 1792, 1793, 1794. By A County Meath freeholder. 1794.

A candid inquiry into the late riots in the province of Munster. [London] 1767.

Carey, W. P., *An appeal to the people of Ireland*. 1794.

A caution to the gentlemen who use Mr Sheridan's dictionary, 3rd ed. London and Cork 1791.

Cloney, T., *A personal narrative*. 1832.

A collection of letters which have been addressed to the volunteers of Ireland on the subject of parliamentary reform. London 1783.

A concise account of the material events which occurred in the Irish rebellion. By Veridicus. 1799.

Cooke, E., *Arguments for and against the union considered*. 1798.

Cooper, G., *Letters on the Irish nation*. London 1800.

Coote, C., *Statistical survey of the county of Armagh*. 1804.

——, *Statistical survey of the county of Monaghan*. 1801.

——, *Statistical survey of the county of Cavan*. 1802.

Day, R., *A charge to the grand jury of the city of Dublin*. 1793, reprinted 1796.

Dermody, T., *The rights of citizens*. 1793.

Dickson, W. S., *Sermons*. Belfast 1776–8.

——, *A narrative . . .* 1812.

Disney, W., *A short history of the establishment of assistant barristers*. 1799.

Dobbs, F., *The true principles of government applied to the Irish constitution, in a code of laws*. 1783.

——, *A history of Irish affairs*. 1787.

Drennan, W., *Letters of Orellena, an Irish helot*. 1785.

——, *A letter to his excellency Lord Fitzwilliam*. 1795.

——, *A letter to the Rt. Hon. William Pitt.* 1799.

——, *A second letter to the Rt. Hon. William Pitt.* 1799.

——, *Fugitive pieces in verse and prose.* Belfast 1815.

Drought, T., *Letters on subjects interesting to Ireland.* 1785.

Drummond, W. H., *The man of age: a poem.* Belfast 1797.

Dubourdiev, J., *Statistical survey of the county of Down.* 1802.

——, *Statistical survey of the county of Antrim.* 1812.

Dutton, H., *Observations on Mr Archer's statistical survey of the county of Dublin.* 1802.

Dwyer, J. J., *The Trinitarian manual.* 1795.

Eden, W., *Letters to the earl of Carlisle.* London and Dublin 1780.

Edgeworth, R. L., *Memoirs . . .*, 2 vols. London 1820.

An essay on the rosary. 1772.

Ferrar, J., *A short history of the city of Limerick.* Limerick 1787.

Fitzpatrick, J., *An essay on gaol abuses.* 1784.

Fitzwilliam, Lord, *A letter from a venerated nobleman to the earl of Carlisle.* 1795.

Fitzwilliam, Lord, *A second letter . . .* 1795.

Foot, J., *Life of Arthur Murphy.* London 1811.

General rules and instructions for all seconds in duels. By A late captain in the army. 1801.

Geoghegan, R., *An utilist to the aggregate body of the Irish nation.* 1784.

Gordon, J. B., *History of the rebellion in Ireland . . .* 1801.

——, *Mr Gordon's vindication of his history of the rebellion.* 1802.

Grattan, H., *Memoirs of the life and times of the Rt. Hon Henry Grattan,* 5 vols. London 1839–46.

Griffith, A., *Six letters addressed to the Rt. Hon. the Countess of* ——, 1780.

Griffith, R., *Thoughts and facts relating to inland navigation,* 2nd ed. 1795.

Hales, W., *Observations on the political influence of the doctrine of the pope's supremacy* 1787.

——, *Observations on the present state of the parochial clergy of the church of Ireland.* 1794.

Hamilton, W. G., *Parliamentary logic,.* ed. E. Malone, London 1808.

Hardy, F., *Memoirs of the political and private life of James Caulfield, earl of Charlemont.* London 1810.

Hay, W., *History of the insurrection of the county of Wexford.* 1803.

Hely-Hutchinson, J., *The commercial restrictions of Ireland considered.* 1779.

Heyland, F., *The Irish rebellion of 1798.* Greenock 1913.

Hickey, W., *Memoirs,* ed. A. Spencer, 4 vols. London 1913.

History of the proceedings and debates of the volunteer delegates of Ireland. 1784.

Hitchcock, R., *An historical view of the Irish stage.* 2 vols. 1788, 1794.

Howard, G. E., *Several special cases on the laws against the further growth of popery in Ireland.* 1775.

Hussey, T., *A pastoral letter to the catholic clergy of the united diocese of Waterford and Lismore.* Dublin and London 1797.

Jackson, W., *Observations in answer to Mr Paine's Age of Reason*. 1795.

Jebb, J. and A. Knox, *Thirty years' correspondence*, ed. C. Forster, 2 vols. London 1834.

Jervis, J. W., *A letter addressed to the gentlemen of England and Ireland upon the inexpediency of a federal union*. 1798.

Jones, W. T., *A letter to the electors of the borough of Lisburn*. 1784.

——, *A letter to the societies of United Irishmen of the town of Belfast*. 1792.

Kearney, J., *A sermon*. 1793.

——, *A sermon . . . preached on 8 July 1798*. 1798.

Kirwan, W. B., *A discourse on religious innovations . . . to which is added his letter . . . giving his reasons for quitting the Roman Catholic religion*. 1787.

Keogh, J., *Thoughts on borough representation*. 1784.

Knox, A., *Essays on the political circumstances of Ireland*. 1798.

——, *Remains*, ed. J. J. Hornly, 4 vols. London 1836-7.

[Knox, W.], *The present state of the nation*. 1768.

Knox, W., *Extra-official state papers*. London 1789.

Leader, N. P., *An address to the merchants, manufacturers and landed proprietors of Ireland . . .* 1800.

Leland, T., *Sermons . . .*, 3 vols. 1788.

Letter from the committee of the Ulster volunteers to the duke of Richmond. 1783.

A letter from Mr Brooke. 1786.

Letters addressed to parliament . . . on various improvements of the metropolis. 1786.

List of the members of the United company of England trading in the Indies . . . who stood qualified as voters on the company's books. London 1753.

A list of the counties of Ireland and their respective yeomanry corps . . . on 1 June 1798. 1798.

A list of the proprietors of licenses on private sedan chairs. [1787].

Lucas, C., *The great charter of the liberties of the city of Dublin*, 1749.

——, *A letter to the free citizens of Dublin*. 1749.

——, *Seasonable advice to the electors . . .* 1760.

Luckombe, P., *A tour through Ireland*. London 1780.

Macartney, G., *An account of Ireland in 1773. By A late chief secretary*. 1773.

McLaren, A., *A genuine account*. Bristol 1799.

Malton, J., *A picturesque and descriptive view of the city of Dublin*. London 1792-9.

MacNeven, W. J., *Pieces of Irish history . . .* New York, 1800.

Madden, S., *Memoirs of the life of . . . Peter Roe*. 1842.

More thoughts on a union . . . 1799.

Newell, E. J., *The apostacy of Newell containing the life and confessions of that celebrated informer . . .* [Belfast] 1798.

Newport, J., *The state of the borough representation of Ireland in 1783 and 1830*. London 1832.

O'Connor, A., *The state of Ireland . . .* London 1798.

——, *Monopoly, the cause of all evil*, 3 vols. London and Paris 1848.

O'Conor, C., *The case of the Roman catholics of Ireland*. 1755.

——, *Dissertations on the history of Ireland.* 1766.

——, *Memoirs of the life and writings of the late Charles O'Conor of Belanagare.* 1796.

O'Halloran, S., *Insula sacra.* Limerick 1770.

O'Keefe, J., *Recollections* . . ., 2 vols. London 1826.

O'Leary, A., *Mr O'Leary's defence, containing a vindication of his conduct and writings.* 1787.

Parsons, L., *Thoughts upon liberty and equality.* 1793.

Place, F., *Autobiography*, ed. M. Thale. Cambridge 1972.

Pollock, J., *Letters of Owen Roe O'Neil.* 1779.

——, *Letters to the inhabitants of the town and lordship of Newry.* 1793.

Pool, R. and J. Cash, *Views of the most remarkable public buildings, monuments and other edifices in Dublin.* 1780.

Porter, J., *Billy Bluff and Squire Firebrand: or a sample of the times*, Belfast, 1796.

The present constitution of the city of Dublin. By A citizen. 1758.

The private correspondence of David Garrick. 2 vols. London 1832.

Proceedings of the catholic meeting of Dublin . . . 31 Oct. 1792 . . . Annexed is the declaration adopted by the general committee, 17 March 1792. . . . Also the letter and plan of the sub-committee for the election of delegates. 1792.

Proofs upon proofs that the union is utterly incompatible with the rights of the . . . independent kingdom of Ireland. 1799.

Rawson, T. J., *Statistical survey of the county of Kildare.* 1807.

Report on the Arigna iron works. 1801.

Report of the debate at the Irish bar. 1799.

Reynolds, T., *Life of Thomas Reynolds*, 2 vols. London 1839.

Rowan, A. H., *Autobiography.* 1840.

Ryan, C., *Oration delivered at a numerous and respectable meeting of the Roman catholics of the city of Dublin.* Cork 1795.

St George, A., *The archdeacon's examination of candidates for holy orders.* 1751.

[Scott, J.], *Parliamentary representation.* By Falkland. 1790.

A serious and affectionate call to the electors of Ireland. 1761.

Sheffield, Lord, *Observations on the manufactures, trade and present state of Ireland.* London 1785.

Sheridan, T., *A short sketch of a plan for the improvement of education.* 1788.

Short structures on the constitution, manufactures and commerce of Ireland. Belfast 1792.

Sketches of Irish political characters. London 1799.

Smith, C., *The ancient and present state of Cork.* 2 vols. 1750.

Smith, R., *Life of the Rev H. Moore.* London 1854.

Smith, W., *The rights of citizens.* 1791.

——, *The patriot or political essays.* 1793.

Smollet, T. G., *The present state of all nations*, 8 vols. London 1768–9.

Society of the United Irishmen of Dublin, addresses, resolutions, etc. 1794.

Spencer, J., *Thoughts on the union.* 1797.

Standing orders for the yeomanry corps of Ireland . . . *15 May 1798.* 1798.

Stevens, W., *Hints to the people.* 1799.

Stewart, J. W., *The gentleman's and citizen's almanack.*

Stokes, W., *A reply to Mr Paine's Age of Reason.* 1795.

A succinct detail of some proceedings at Dundalk. Dundalk 1782.

Taylor, C., *Historical account of the rebellion.* 1800.

Teeling, C. H., *A personal narrative of the Irish rebellion of 1798.* London 1828.

——, *A sequel to a personal narrative* . . . Belfast 1832.

Thompson, R., *Statistical survey of the County of Meath.* 1802.

Tighe, W., *Statistical Observations relative to the County of Kilkenny.* 1802.

A tour through Ireland by two English gentlemen, 2nd edn. 1748.

Townsend, H., *General and statistical survey of County Cork,* 2 vols. 1810.

Trant, D., *Considerations on the present disturbances in the province of Munster.* 1787.

Trial of Francis Graham . . . *for attempting to suborn Joseph Corbally, tailor, to swear that A. H. Rowan and Napper Tandy, Esq., were at the head of the defenders.* 1794.

The trial of Thomas Russell, general in the late insurrection . . . (n.p.) 1803.

Trial of T. J. Fitzgerald . . . *with the proceedings in parliament* (1799).

Twiss, R., *A tour of Ireland.* 1776.

Union or not. 1799.

Valor beneficiorum ecclesiasticorum. 1780.

A view of the rise of incorporate society. 1748.

A view of the present state of Ireland. By An observer. London 1797.

Walker, J., *Historical memorials of the Irish bards.* 1786.

Wallace, J., *A general description of Liverpool.* London 1795.

Wallace, T., *An essay.* 1798.

Walsh, R., J. Warburton, and J. Whitelaw, *History of Dublin,* 2 vols. London 1818.

Weld, M., *Constitutional considerations.* 1800.

Woodward, R., *A scheme for the establishment of county poor houses in Ireland.* 1768.

——, *An argument in support of the right of the poor in the kingdom of Ireland to a national provision.* 1772.

——, *An address to the public on the expediency of a regular plan for the maintenance and government of the poor.* 1775.

——, *The present state of the church of Ireland.* 1786.

Young, A., *A tour in Ireland* . . . London 1780; ed. A. W. Hutton, 2 vols. London 1892.

SECONDARY SOURCES

Addleshaw, G. W. O. and F. Etchells, *The architectural setting of anglican worship.* London 1948.

Ball, F. E., *The judges in Ireland 1221–1921,* 2 vols. London 1926.

Beckett, J. C., *Protestant dissent in Ireland 1687–1780.* London 1948.

Berry, H. F., *History of the Royal Dublin Society.* 1915.

Boyle, P., *The Irish college in Paris 1578–1901*. 1901.

Brown, W., *The king's friends*. Providence (R.I.). 1965.

Bolton, G. C., *The passing of the Irish act of union*. London 1966.

Carrigan, W., *History and antiquities of the diocese of Ossory*, 4 vols. 1905.

Clark, W. S., *The Irish stage in the country towns*. Oxford 1965.

Connell, K. H., *The population of Ireland, 1750–1845*. Oxford 1950.

Corkery, D., *The hidden Ireland: a study of Gaelic Munster in the eighteenth century*. 1925.

Coughlan, R. J., *Napper Tandy*. 1976.

Cullen, L. M., *Anglo-Irish trade 1660–1800*. Manchester 1968.

Derry, J. W., *The regency crisis and the whigs, 1788–9*. Cambridge 1963.

E. Desbrière, *1793–1805: Projets et tentatives de débarquement aux Iles Britanniques*, 4 vols. Paris 1900–1902.

Dickson, C., *The Wexford rising in 1798, its causes and course*. Tralee 1955.

——, *Revolution in the north; Antrim and Down in 1798*. 1960.

Dickson, R. J., *Ulster emigration to colonial America 1717–75*. London 1966.

Dunfermline, Lord, *Life of General Abercromby*. Edinburgh 1861.

Duncan, E., *History of the Royal regiment of artillery*, 3rd ed. 2 vols. London 1879.

Fitzpatrick, W. J., *The secret service under Pitt*. London 1892.

Froude, J. A., *The English in Ireland in the eighteenth century*, 3 vols. London 1872–4.

Harlow, V. T., *The founding of the second British empire, 1763–93*. 2 vols. London 1952–64.

Hayes, R. F., *The last invasion of Ireland: when Connacht rose*. 1937.

Heyland, F., *The Irish rebellion of 1798*. Greenock 1913.

Hodson, V. C. P., *List of the officers of the Bengal army 1758–1834*. 4 vols. London 1927–47.

Inglis, B., *Freedom of the press in Ireland 1784–1841*. London 1954.

Johnston, E. M., *Great Britain and Ireland, 1760–1800*. Edinburgh 1963.

Jones, E. H. S., *An invasion that failed: the French expedition to Ireland, 1796*. Oxford 1950.

Lecky, W. E. H., *A history of Ireland in the eighteenth century*, 5 vols. London 1892.

Lewis, M. A., *A social history of the navy*. London 1960.

McAnally, H., *The Irish militia 1793–1816*. Dublin and London. 1949

McDermott, F., *Theobald Wolfe Tone: a biographical study*. London 1939.

McDowell, R. B., *Irish public opinion 1750–1800*. London 1944.

Madden, R. R., *The United Irishmen*, 2nd ed. 4 vols. 1857–1860.

Manwaring, G. E., and B. Dobrée, *The floating republic*. London 1935.

Maxwell, C. E., *Dublin under the Georges, 1714–1830*. London 1936.

——, *Country and town in Ireland under the Georges*. London 1940.

Mayo, Lord, *A history of the Kildare hunt*. London 1913.

Millin, S. S., *Sidelights on Belfast history*. London 1932.

O'Brien, G., *The economic history of Ireland in the eighteenth century.* 1918.

O'Connell, M. R., *Irish politics and social conflict in the age of the American revolution.* Philadelphia 1965.

O'Conor, C. O., *The O'Conors of Connaught: a historical memoir.* 1891.

Pakenham, T., *The year of liberty: the story of the great Irish rebellion of 1798.* London 1969.

Parry, L. E. S. and B. F. M. Freeman, *Historical records of the Denbighshire hussars.* Wrexham 1909.

Porritt, E., *The unreformed house of commons.* 2 vols. Cambridge 1903.

Reid, J. S., *History of the presbyterian church in Ireland,* 3 vols, new edn. Belfast 1867.

Renehan, F., *Irish ecclesiastical history.* 2 vols. 1861.

Rogers, P., *The Irish volunteers and catholic emancipation.* London 1934.

Scobie, H. M., *An old highland fencible corps.* Edinburgh 1914.

Segrave, C. R., *The Segrave family, 1066–1935.* London 1936.

Senior, H., *Orangeism in Ireland and Great Britain, 1795–1836.* London 1966.

Shaw, A. G. L., *Convicts and the colonies: a study of transportation from Great Britain and Ireland to Australia and other parts of the British empire.* London 1966.

Sheppard, E. W., *The ninth Queen's royal lancers, 1715–1936.* Aldershot 1939.

Stockwell, La T., *Dublin theatres and theatre customs (1637–1820).* Kingsport 1938.

Wall, M., *The penal laws 1691–1760.* 1961.

Wheeler, H. and M. Craig, *The Dublin city churches.* 1948.

Witherow, T., *Historical and literary memorials of presbyterianism in Ireland,* 2 vols. London 1879–80.

Index